# THE IDENTITY OF THE NEW TESTAMENT TEXT IV

**Wilbur N. Pickering, ThM PhD**

ISBN Print: 978-0-9898273-5-5

Cover photo: a rural scene in Goias, Brazil,
courtesy of Dan Jore

# TABLE OF CONTENTS

# 1
# INTRODUCTION[1]

Because this book will be read by people representing a broad spectrum of interest and background, I will begin with a brief review of the textual problem.

That there is a problem concerning the identity of the Greek text of the New Testament is made clear by the existence of a number of competing editions in print. By competing I mean that they do not agree with one another as to the precise wording of the text. Such disagreement is the result of different theories about the transmission of the Text down through the centuries of hand copying and different use of the Greek manuscripts (handwritten copies) that have survived and are known to us (extant). We are dependent upon those copies because the Apostles' Autographs, or original documents, are no longer in existence. (They were probably worn out well before A.D. 200, if not 100.)

In short, we are faced with the challenge of identifying the original wording of the text by consulting the surviving manuscripts, most of which do not entirely agree. In this task we may also appeal to copies of the ancient Versions (translations into Syriac, Latin, Coptic, etc.) and to the surviving writings of the early church Fathers where they quote or refer to New Testament passages.

There are over 5,000 extant (known) Greek manuscripts (hereafter MSS, or MS when singular) of the New Testament, over half of which are continuous text copies, the rest being lectionaries. They range in size from a scrap with parts of two verses to complete New Testaments. They range in date from the second century to the sixteenth.[2] They come from all over the Mediterranean world. They contain several hundred thousand variant readings (differences in the text). The vast majority of these are misspellings or other obvious errors due to carelessness or ignorance on the part of the copyists—such are not proper variant readings and may be ignored. However, many thousands of variants remain which need to be evaluated as we seek to identify the precise

---

[1] A good deal of the research underlying this book was done in connection with the master's thesis I submitted to the Dallas Theological Seminary in 1968 entitled "An Evaluation of the Contribution of John William Burgon to New Testament Textual Criticism". My thesis was subsequently published in edited form in *True or False?*, ed. D. Otis Fuller, (Grand Rapids: Grand Rapids International Publishers, 1972)—the full text of the thesis appears in the 2nd edition, 1975. I have re-used some of the material in the thesis by permission of both entities.

[2] There are over a hundred from the seventeenth and another forty from the eighteenth (and even nineteenth), but since several printed editions of the Greek New Testament appeared during the sixteenth, the manuscripts produced subsequently are usually presumed to be of little interest. But since most of them were clearly copied from non-printed exemplars, that could have been centuries older, they should not be ignored. There may be a few scraps from the 1st century—I am thinking of 7Q5,4,8 and $P^{64,67}$.

original wording of the Text. How best to go about such a project? This book seeks to provide an answer.

Of course, I am not the first to attempt an answer. Numerous answers have been advanced over the years. They tend to form two clusters, or camps, and these camps differ substantially from each other. In very broad and over-simplified terms, one camp generally follows the large majority of the MSS (seldom less than 80 and usually over 95 percent) which are in essential agreement among themselves but which do not date from before the fifth century A.D., while the other generally follows a small handful (often less than ten) of earlier MSS (from the third, fourth and fifth centuries) which not only disagree with the majority, but also disagree among themselves (which obliges the practitioners to be more or less eclectic). The second camp has been in general control of the scholarly world for the last 130 years, at least.

The most visible consequence and proof of that control may be seen in the translations of the New Testament into English done during these 130 years. Virtually every one of them reflects a form of the text based upon the few earlier MSS. In contrast to them, the King James Version (AV) and the New King James Version (NKJV) reflect a form of the text based upon the many later MSS. Thus, the fundamental difference between the New Testament in the American Standard Version, Revised Standard Version, New English Bible, Today's English Version, New American Standard Bible, New International Version, etc., on the one hand, and in the AV and NKJV on the other is that they are based on different forms of the Greek text. There are over 5,500 differences between those two forms.[1] There are also differences between competing editions within each camp, but comparatively far fewer.

To the extent that you may be aware of these matters you may well have accepted as reasonable the statements usually made to the effect that the very considerable improvement in our stock of available materials (Greek manuscripts and other witnesses) and in our understanding of what to do with them (principles of textual criticism) has made possible a closer approximation to the original text in our day than was achieved several hundred years ago. The statements to be found in the prefaces of some versions give the reader the impression that this improvement is reflected in their translations. For example, the preface to the Revised Standard Version, p. ix, says:

> The King James Version of the New Testament was based upon a Greek text that was marred by mistakes, containing the accumulated errors of fourteen centuries of manuscript copying [not true; almost all TR readings are ancient]...We now possess many more ancient manuscripts of the New Testament, and are far better equipped to seek to recover the original wording of the Greek text.

---

[1] F.H.A. Scrivener, ed., *The New Testament in the Original Greek, together with the variations adopted in the Revised Version* (Cambridge: Cambridge University Press, 1880). In spite of the differences between the printed editions of the Greek text in general use, they are all agreed as to the identity of about 90 percent of the Text.

And the preface to the New International Version, p. viii, says:

> The Greek text used in the work of translation was an eclectic one. No other piece of ancient literature has so much manuscript support as does the New Testament. Where existing texts differ, the translators made their choice of readings in accord with sound principles of textual criticism. Footnotes call attention to places where there is uncertainty about what constitutes the original text.

But if you have used a number of the modern versions you may have noticed some things that perhaps intrigued, bewildered, or even distressed you. I am thinking of the degree to which they differ among themselves, the uncertainty as to the identity of the text reflected in the many footnotes regarding textual variants, and the nature and extent of their common divergence from the King James Version.

The bulk of the differences between the modern versions is presumably due to differences in style and translation technique. However, although they are in essential agreement as to the Greek text used, as opposed to that underlying the AV, no two of them are based on an identical Greek text. Nor have the translators been entirely sure as to the precise wording of the text—while some versions have few notes about textual variation, others have many, and even in these cases by no means all the doubts have been recorded.[1] Most people would probably agree with the following statement: no one in the world today really knows the precise original wording of the Greek text of the New Testament.[2]

Such a realization may beget an incipient uneasiness in the recesses of your mind. Why isn't anyone sure, if we have so many materials and so much wisdom? Well, because the present 'wisdom', the 'sound principles of textual criticism' currently in vogue, may be summed up in two maxims: choose the reading that best explains the origin of the competing variants, and choose the variant that the author is more/most likely to have written.

No wonder Bruce Metzger said, "It is understandable that in some cases different scholars will come to different evaluations of the significance of the evidence".[3] A cursory review of the writings of textual scholars suggests that Metzger's "in some cases" is decidedly an understatement. In fact, even the

---

[1] For instance, Tasker said of the NEB translators, "Every member of the Panel was conscious that some of its decisions were in no sense final or certain, but at best tentative conclusions,..." *The Greek New Testament* (being the text translated in the New English Bible) ed. R.V.G. Tasker (Oxford: Oxford University Press, 1964), p. viii. See also B.M. Metzger, *Historical and Literary Studies*, NTTS, VIII (Grand Rapids: Wm. B. Eerdmans, 1968), pp. 160-61.

[2] However, I believe that I do know and am able to demonstrate why; but more about that in Chapter 7.

[3] B.M. Metzger, *The Text of the New Testament* (London: Oxford University Press, 1964), p. 210.

same scholars will vacillate, as demonstrated by the "more than five hundred changes" introduced into the third edition of the Greek text produced by the United Bible Societies as compared with the second edition (the same committee of five editors prepared both).[1] Further, it is evident that the maxims above cannot be applied with certainty. No one living today knows or can know what actually happened in detail. It follows that <u>so long as</u> the textual materials are handled in this way **we will never be sure** about the precise wording of the Greek text.[2] [The purpose of this book is to show that the textual materials are <u>not</u> to be handled in this way.]

It is not surprising that scholars working within such a framework say as much. For example, Robert M. Grant says:

> The primary goal of New Testament textual study remains the recovery of what the New Testament writers wrote. We have already suggested that to achieve this goal is well-nigh impossible. Therefore we must be content with what Reinhold Niebuhr and others have called, in other contexts, an "impossible possibility."[3]

And Kenneth W. Clark, commenting on P[75]:

> ...the papyrus vividly portrays a fluid state of the text at about A.D. 200. Such a scribal freedom suggests that the gospel text was little more stable than the oral tradition, and that we may be pursuing the retreating mirage of the "original text."[4]

Over sixty-five years ago Grant had said, "it is generally recognized that the original text of the Bible cannot be recovered".[5]

---

[1] K. Aland, M. Black, C.M. Martini, B.M. Metzger, and A. Wikgren, eds., *The Greek New Testament*, third edition (New York: United Bible Societies, 1975), p. viii. Although this edition is dated 1975, Metzger's *Commentary* upon it appeared in 1971. The second edition is dated 1968. It thus appears that in the space of three years ('68-'71), with no significant accretion of new evidence, the same group of five scholars changed their mind in over five hundred places. It is hard to resist the suspicion that they were guessing.

[2] Even where there is unanimous testimony for the wording of the text, the canons of internal evidence do not preclude the possibility that that unanimous testimony might be wrong. Once internal evidence is accepted as **the** way to determine the text there is no basis **in principle** for objecting to conjectural emendation. Hence no part of the Text is safe. (Even if it is required that a proposed reading be attested by at least one manuscript, a new Papyrus may come to light tomorrow with new variants to challenge the unanimous witness of the rest, and so on.)

[3] R.M. Grant, *A Historical Introduction to the New Testament* (New York: Harper and Row, 1963), p. 51.

[4] K.W. Clark, "The Theological Relevance of Textual Variation in Current Criticism of the Greek New Testament", *Journal of Biblical Literature*, LXXXV (1966), p. 15.

[5] Grant, "The Bible of Theophilus of Antioch", *Journal of Biblical Literature*, LXVI (1947), 173. For a most pessimistic statement see E.C. Colwell, "Biblical Criticism:

At this point I get uncomfortable. If the original wording is lost and gone forever, whatever are we using? The consequences of such an admission are so far-reaching, to my mind, that a thorough review of the evidence is called for. Do the facts really force an honest mind to the conclusion expressed by Grant? In seeking an answer to this question I will begin with the present situation in New Testament textual criticism and work back. The procedure which dominates the scene today is called "eclecticism".[1]

---

Lower and Higher", *Journal of Biblical Literature*, LXVII (1948), 10-11. See also G. Zuntz, *The Text of the Epistles*, 1953, p. 9; K. and S. Lake, *Family 13 (The Ferrar Group)*, 1941, p. vii; F. C. Conybeare, *History of New Testament Criticism*, 1910, p. 129.

[1] In ordinary usage the term "eclecticism" refers to the practice of selecting from various sources. In textual criticism there is the added implication that the sources are disparate. Just what this means in practice is spelled out in the section "What is it?" in the next chapter.

# 2
# ECLECTICISM

In 1974, Eldon Jay Epp wrote: "The 'eclectic' method is, in fact, **the** 20th century method of NT textual criticism, and anyone who criticizes it immediately becomes a self-critic, for we all use it, some of us with a certain measure of reluctance and restraint, others with complete abandon."[1]

Thus, the RSV (Revised Standard Version), NEB (New English Bible) and NIV (New International Version) are confessedly based upon an eclectic text.

> The two great translation efforts of these years—RSV and NEB— each chose the Greek text to translate on the basis of the internal evidence of readings. F C. Grant's chapter in the expository pamphlet on the RSV made this clear. The translators, he says, followed two rules: (1) Choose the reading that best fits the context; (2) Choose the reading which explains the origin of the other readings. Professor C. H. Dodd informed me that the British translators also used these two principles—Hort's Intrinsic Probability and Transcriptional Probability. One of the RSV translators while lecturing to the New Testament Club at the University of Chicago replied to a question concerning the Greek text he used by saying that it depended on where he was working: he used Souter at the office and Nestle at home. One of the British translators in admitting the unevenness of the textual quality of the NEB translation explained that the quality depended on the ability of the man who made the first draft-translation of a book.

> Whether in early Christian times or today, translators have so often treated the text cavalierly that textual critics should be hardened to it. But much more serious is the prevalence of this same dependence on the internal evidence of readings in learned articles on textual criticism, and in the popularity of manual editions of the Greek New Testament. These latter with their limited citations of variants and witnesses actually reduce the user to reliance upon the internal evidence of readings. The documents which these rigorously abbreviated apparatuses cite cannot lead the user to dependence upon external evidence of documents. These editions use documents (to quote Housman) "as drunkards use lampposts—, not to light them on their way but to dissimulate their instability."[2]

---

[1] E.J. Epp, "The Twentieth Century Interlude in New Testament Textual Criticism", *Journal of Biblical Literature*, XCIII (1974), p. 403.

[2] E.C. Colwell, "Hort Redivivus: A Plea and a Program", *Studies in Methodology in Textual Criticism of the New Testament*, E.C. Colwell (Leiden: E.J. Brill, 1969), pp. 152-53. Tasker records the principles followed by the NEB translators: "The Text to be translated will of necessity be eclectic,..." (p. vii).

The statement in the preface to the NIV has already been noted: "The Greek text used in the work of translation was an eclectic one".

The introduction to the Greek text put out by the United Bible Societies, pp. x-xi (1966), says:

> By means of the letters A, B, C, and D, enclosed within "braces" { } at the beginning of each set of textual variants, the Committee has sought to indicate the relative degree of certainty, arrived at on the basis of internal considerations as well as of external evidence, for the reading adopted as the text. The letter A signifies that the text is virtually certain, while B indicates that there is some degree of doubt. The letter C means that there is a considerable degree of doubt whether the text or the apparatus contains the superior reading, while D shows that there is a very high degree of doubt concerning the reading selected for the text.

A review of their apparatus and its lack of pattern in the correlation between degree of certainty assigned and external evidence makes clear that it is eclectic. In Acts 16:12 they have even incorporated a conjecture! It will be remembered that this text was prepared specifically for the use of Bible translators. The TEV (Today's English Version) is translated directly from it, as is the *Version Popular*, etc. The text-critical conclusions of G.D. Kilpatrick, a thorough-going eclecticist, were finding expression in *A Greek-English Diglot for the Use of Translators*, issued by the British and Foreign Bible Society. And so on. Enough evidence has been given to show that eclecticism is a major, if not controlling, factor on the textual scene today.

## What Is It?

Wherein does 'eclecticism' consist? Metzger explains that an eclectic editor "follows now one and now another set of witnesses in accord with what is deemed to be the author's style or the exigencies of transcriptional hazards."[1]

E. C. Colwell[2] spells it out:

> Today textual criticism turns for its final validation to the appraisal of individual readings, in a way that involves subjective judgment. The trend has been to emphasize fewer and fewer canons of criticism. Many moderns emphasize only two. These are: 1) that reading is to be preferred which best suits the context, and 2) that reading is to be preferred which best explains the origin of all others.

---

[1] Metzger, *The Text*, pp. 175-76.

[2] The late Ernest Cadman Colwell might well have been described as the dean of New Testament textual criticism in North America during the 1950s and 1960s. He was associated with the University of Chicago for many years as Professor and President. Some of his important articles have been collected and reprinted in *Studies in Methodology in Textual Criticism of the New Testament*.

These two rules are nothing less than concentrated formulas of all that the textual critic must know and bring to bear upon the solution of his problem. The first rule about choosing what suits the context exhorts the student to know the document he is working on so thoroughly that its idioms are his idioms, its ideas as well known as a familiar room. The second rule about choosing what could have caused the other readings requires that the student know everything in Christian history which could lead to the creation of a variant reading. This involves knowledge of institutions, doctrines, and events...This is knowledge of complicated and often conflicting forces and movements.[1]

(What living person really possesses these qualifications? And how can such rules be applied when neither the identity nor circumstances of the originator of a given variant is known?)

More recently Colwell seemed to be less enchanted with the method.

The scholars who profess to follow "the Eclectic Method" frequently so define the term as to restrict evidence to the Internal Evidence of Readings. By "eclectic" they mean in fact free choice among readings. This choice in many cases is made solely on the basis of intrinsic probability. The editor chooses that reading which commends itself to him as fitting the context, whether in style, or idea, or contextual reference. Such an editor relegates the manuscripts to the role of supplier of readings. The weight of the manuscript is ignored. Its place in the manuscript tradition is not considered. Thus Kilpatrick argues that certain readings found only in one late Vulgate manuscript should be given the most serious consideration because they are good readings.[2]

J.K. Elliott, a thorough-going eclecticist like Kilpatrick, says of transcriptional probabilities:

By using criteria such as the above the critic may reach a conclusion in discussing textual variants and be able to say which variant is the original reading. However, it is legitimate to ask: can a reading be accepted as genuine if it is supported by only one ms.? There is no reason why an original reading should not have been preserved in only one ms. but obviously a reading can be accepted with greater confidence, when it has stronger support...

Even Aland with his reservation about eclecticism says: "Theoretically the original readings can be hidden in a single ms. thus standing alone against the rest of tradition," and Tasker has a

---

[1] Colwell, "Biblical Criticism", pp. 4-5. For words to the same effect see also K. Lake, *The Text of the New Testament*, sixth edition revised by Silva New (London: Rivingtons, 1959), p. 10 and Metzger, *The Text*, pp. 216-17.

[2] Colwell, "Hort Redivivus", p. 154. Cf. pp. 149-54.

similar comment: "The possibility must be left open that in some cases the true reading may have been preserved in only a few witnesses or even in a single relatively late witness."[1]

Among what Elliott calls "positive advantages of the eclectic method" is the following:

An attempt is made to reach the true or original text. This is, of course, the ultimate aim of any textual critic, but the eclectic method, by using different criteria and by working from a different standpoint, tries to arrive at the true reading, untrammeled by discussion about the weight of ms. Support...[2]

No wonder Epp complains:

This kind of "eclecticism" becomes the great leveller—all variants are equals and equally candidates for the original text, regardless of date, residence, lineage, or textual context. In this case, would it not be appropriate to suggest, further, that a few more conjectural readings be added to the available supply of variants on the assumption that they must have existed but have been lost at some point in the history of the textual transmission?[3]

What shall we say of such a method; is it a good thing?

# What about It?

An eclecticism based solely on internal considerations is unacceptable for several reasons. It is unreasonable. It ignores the over 5,000 Greek MSS now extant, to say nothing of patristic and versional evidence, except to cull variant readings from them. In Elliott's words, it "tries to arrive at the true reading untrammeled by discussion about the weight of ms. support". It follows that it has no principled basis for rejecting conjectural emendations. It has no history of the transmission of the text. Therefore the choice between variants ultimately depends upon guesswork. This has been recognized by Colwell.

In the last generation we have depreciated external evidence of documents and have appreciated the internal evidence of readings; but we have blithely assumed that we were rejecting "conjectural emendation" if our conjectures were supported by some

---

[1] J.K. Elliott, *The Greek Text of the Epistles to Timothy and Titus*, ed., Jacob Geerlings, *Studies and Documents*, XXXVI (Salt Lake City: University of Utah Press, 1968), pp. 10-11. Cf. K. Aland, "The Significance of the Papyri for Progress in New Testament Research", *The Bible in Modern Scholarship*, ed. J.P. Hyatt (New York: Abingdon Press, 1965), p. 340, and Tasker, p. viii.

[2] Elliott, p. 11.

[3] Epp, p. 404.

manuscripts. We need to recognize that the editing of an eclectic text rests upon conjectures.[1]

F.G. Kenyon[2] called conjectural emendation "a process precarious in the extreme and seldom allowing anyone but the guesser to feel confidence in the truth of its results".[3] Although enthusiasts like Elliott think they can restore the original wording of the text in this way, it is clear that the result can have no more authority than that of the scholar(s) involved. Textual criticism ceases to be a science and one is left wondering what is meant by 'sound principles' in the NIV preface.

Clark and Epp are right in calling eclecticism a secondary, tentative, and temporary method.[4] As A.F.J. Klijn says, "This method arrives at such varying results that we wonder whether editors of Greek texts and translations can safely follow this road."[5] This procedure seems so unsatisfactory, in fact, that we may reasonably wonder what gave rise to it.

# What Is Its Source?

Eclecticism grew out of the Westcott and Hort (hereafter W-H) theory of textual criticism. Epp gives a useful summary statement of that theory, for our immediate purpose:

> …the grouping of manuscripts led to the separation of the relatively few early manuscripts from the mass of later ones, and eventually the process reached its climactic point of development and its

---

[1] Colwell, "Scribal Habits in Early Papyri: A Study in the Corruption of the Text", *The Bible in Modern Scholarship*, ed. J.P. Hyatt (New York: Abingdon Press, 1965), pp. 371-72.

[2] Frederick G. Kenyon was an outstanding British scholar during the first half of this century. He was Director and Principal Librarian of the British Museum and his *Handbook to the Textual Criticism of the New Testament* is still a standard textbook.

[3] F.G. Kenyon, Handbook to the Textual Criticism of the New Testament, 2nd ed., 1926, p. 3.

[4] Epp, pp. 403-4. Cf. K.W. Clark, "The Effect of Recent Textual Criticism upon New Testament Studies", *The Background of the New Testament and its Eschatology*, ed. W.D. Davies and D. Daube (Cambridge: The Cambridge University Press, 1956), p. 37. In a paper presented at the forty-sixth annual meeting of the Evangelical Theological Society (Nov., 1994), Maurice A. Robinson reinforces the serious deficiency that "neither 'reasoned' nor 'rigorous' eclecticism offers a consistent history of textual transmission…" (p. 30). The seriousness of this deficiency may be seen from the results. UBS[3], a confessedly eclectic text, repeatedly serves up a patchwork quilt. For example, in Matthew there are at least 34 places where its precise rendering is not to be found, as such, in any single extant Greek MS (cf. R.J. Swanson, *The Horizontal Line Synopsis of the Gospels, Greek Edition, Volume I.The Gospel of Matthew* [Dillsboro, NC: Western North Carolina Press, 1982]).

[5] A.F.J. Klijn, A Survey of the Researches into the Western Text of the Gospels and Acts; part two 1949-1969 (Leiden: E.J. Brill, 1969), p. 65.

11

classical statement in the work of Westcott and Hort (1881-1882), and particularly in their (actually, Hort's) clear and firm view of the early history of the NT text. This clear picture was formed from Hort's isolation of essentially three (though he said four) basic textual groups or text-types. On the basis largely of Greek manuscript evidence from the middle of the 4th century and later and from the early versional and patristic evidence, two of these, the so-called Neutral and Western text-types, were regarded as competing texts from about the middle of the 2nd century, while the third, now designated Byzantine, was a later, conflate and polished ecclesiastical text... This left essentially two basic text-types competing in the earliest traceable period of textual transmission, the Western and the Neutral, but this historical reconstruction could not be carried farther so as to reveal—on historical grounds—which of the two was closer to and therefore more likely to represent the original NT text.[1]

...the question which faced Westcott-Hort remains for us: Is the original text something nearer to the Neutral or to the Western kind of text? ... Hort resolved the issue, not on the basis of the *history of the text*, but in terms of the presumed *inner quality* of the texts and on grounds of largely subjective judgments of that quality.[2]

Hort, following the "ring of genuineness", preferred the readings of the "Neutral" text-type (today's Alexandrian) and especially those of Codex B, while some subsequent scholars have preferred the readings of the "Western" text-type and of Codex D, on the same basis. Although Hort professed to follow external evidence—and he did in fact follow his "Neutral" text-type, by and large—his prior choice of that text-type was based on internal (subjective) considerations.[3] Still, the general impression was given that the W-H theory was based on external (manuscript and historical) evidence.

But various facets of the theory came under attack soon after it appeared in 1881, and with the conflicting voices came confusion. It is this confusion that has given rise to eclecticism. Thus, Elliott frankly states: "In view of the present dilemma and discussion about the relative merits of individual mss., and of ms. tradition, it is reasonable to depart from a documentary study and to examine the N.T. text from a purely eclectic standpoint".[4] In R.V.G. Tasker's words, "The fluid state of textual criticism today makes the adoption of the eclectic

---

[1] Epp, pp. 391-92.

[2] *Ibid.*, pp. 398-99.

[3] Metzger states that "Westcott and Hort's criticism is subjective". *The Text*, p. 138. See also Colwell, *Studies in Methodology in Textual Criticism of the New Testament* (Leiden: E.J. Brill, 1969), pp. 1-2.

[4] Elliott, pp. 5-6.

method not only desirable but all but inevitable".[1] Metzger cites dissatisfaction "with the results achieved by weighing the external evidence for variant readings" as the cause.[2] Epp blames "the lack of a definitive theory and history of the early text" and the resultant "chaotic situation in the evaluation of variant readings in the NT text".[3] Colwell also blames "manuscript study without a history".[4] The practice of pure eclecticism seems to imply either despair that the original wording can be recovered on the basis of external evidence, or an unwillingness to undertake the hard work of reconstructing the history of the text, or both.

But most scholars do not practice **pure** eclecticism—they still work essentially within the W-H framework. Thus, the two most popular manual editions of the Greek text today, Nestle-Aland and UBS (United Bible Societies), really vary little from the W-H text.[5] The recent versions—RSV, NEB, etc.—also vary little from the W-H text.

---

[1] Tasker, p. vii.

[2] Metzger, *The Text*, p. 175.

[3] Epp, p. 403.

[4] Colwell, "Hort Redivivus", p. 149.

[5] See K.W. Clark, "Today's Problems with the Critical Text of the New Testament", *Transitions in Biblical Scholarship*, ed. J.C.R. Rylaarsdam (Chicago: The University of Chicago Press, 1968), pp. 159-60, for facts and figures. Also see Epp, pp. 388-90. G.D. Fee has charged that my treatment of eclecticism is "hopelessly confused" ("A Critique of W. N. Pickering's *The Identity of the New Testament Text*: A Review Article", *The Westminster Theological Journal*, XLI [Spring, 1979], p. 400). He feels that I have not adequately distinguished between "rigorous" (my "pure") and "reasoned" eclecticism and have thereby given a distorted view of the latter. Well, he himself says of the reasoned eclecticism which he espouses, "Such eclecticism recognizes that W-H's view of things was essentially correct,..." (*Ibid.*, p. 402). My statement is, "But most scholars do not practice **pure** eclecticism—they still work essentially within the W-H framework" (p. 28). Are the two statements really that different?
　　The fairness of this assessment may be illustrated from the works of both Fee and Metzger (whom Fee considers to be a practitioner of reasoned eclecticism). In his "Rigorous or Reasoned Eclecticism—Which?" (*Studies in New Testament Language and Text*, ed. J.K. Elliott [Leiden: Brill, 1976]), Fee says: "Rational eclecticism agrees in principle that no MS or group of MSS has a *prima facie* priority to the original text" (p. 179). But on the next page he says of Hort: "if his evaluation of B as 'neutral' was too high a regard for that MS, it does not alter his judgment that compared to all other MSS B **is** a superior witness". Metzger says on the one hand, "the only proper methodology is to examine the evidence for each variant impartially, with no predilections for or against any one type of text" (*Chapters*, p. 39), but on the other hand, "readings which are supported by only Koine, or Byzantine witnesses (Hort's Syrian group) may be set aside as almost certainly secondary" (*The Text*, p. 212).
　　But Fee has more to say. "An even greater error [than my 'distortion' discussed above] is for him to argue that Elliott's method is under 'the psychological grip of W-H' (p. 29)" ("A Critique", p. 401). He goes on to explain that Elliott and W-H are on opposite ends of the internal/external evidence spectrum because "it is well known that W-H gave an extraordinary amount of weight to external evidence, just as do Pickering and

13

Why is this? Epp answers:

> One response to the fact that our popular critical texts are still so close to that of Westcott-Hort might be that the kind of text arrived at by them and supported so widely by subsequent criticism is in fact and without question the best attainable NT text; yet every textual critic knows that this similarity of text indicates, rather, that we have made little progress in textual *theory* since Westcott-Hort; that we simply do not know how to make a definitive determination as to what the best text is; that we do not have a clear picture of the transmission and alteration of the text in the first few centuries; and, accordingly, that the Westcott-Hort kind of text has maintained its dominant position largely by default. Gunther Zuntz enforces the point in a slightly different way when he says that "the agreement between our modern editions does not mean that we have recovered the original text. It is due to the simple fact that their editors...follow one narrow section of the evidence, namely, the non-Western Old Uncials."[1]

Clark agrees with Zuntz: "All are founded on the same Egyptian recension, and generally reflect the same assumptions of transmission".[2] Clark also gives a sharper focus to one aspect of Epp's answer.

---

Hodges" (*Ibid.*). And yet, on another occasion Fee himself wrote: "it must be remembered that Hort did **not** use genealogy in order to discover the original NT text. Whether justified or not, Hort used genealogy solely to dispense with the Syrian (Byzantine) text. Once he has [*sic*] eliminated the Byzantines from serious consideration, his preference for the Neutral (Egyptian) MSS was based **strictly** on intrinsic and transcriptional probability" [emphasis Fee's] ("Rigorous", p. 177). And again: "In fact the very internal considerations for which Kilpatrick and Elliott argue as a basis for the recovery of the original text, Hort used **first** [emphasis Fee's] for the evaluation of the existing witnesses" (*Ibid.*, p. 179).

It seems to me that these latter statements by Fee are clearly correct. Since Hort's preference for B and the "Neutral" text-type was based "strictly" on internal considerations, his subsequent use of that text-type cannot reasonably be called an appeal to external evidence. In sum, I see no essential difference between 'rigorous' and 'reasoned' eclecticism since the preference given to certain MSS and types by the 'reasoned' eclecticists is itself derived from internal evidence, the same considerations employed by the 'rigorous' eclecticists. I deny the validity of 'eclectic method' in whatever guise as a means for determining the identity of the NT Text. (I do agree with Z.C. Hodges, however, that any and all Traditional Text readings can be defended in terms of internal considerations, should one wish to.)

[1] Epp, 390-91. Cf. G. Zuntz, p. 8. Epp reinforces an earlier statement by Aland: "It is clear that the situation with which our present day method of establishing the New Testament text confronts us is most unsatisfactory. It is not at all the case that, as some seem to think, everything has been done in this field and we can for practical purposes rest satisfied with the text in use. On the contrary, the decisive task still lies ahead." "The Present Position of New Testament Textual Criticism", *Studia Evangelica*, ed. F.L. Cross and others (Berlin: Akademie—Verlag, 1959), p. 731.

[2] Clark, "Today's Problems", p. 159.

...the Westcott-Hort text has become today our *textus receptus*. We have been freed from the one only to become captivated by the other... The psychological chains so recently broken from our fathers have again been forged upon us, even more strongly...

Even the textual specialist finds it difficult to break the habit of evaluating every witness by the norm of this current *textus receptus*. His mind may have rejected the Westcott-Hort term "neutral," but his technical procedure still reflects the general acceptance of the text. A basic problem today is the technical and psychological factor that the Westcott-Hort text has become our *textus receptus*...

Psychologically it is now difficult to approach the textual problem with free and independent mind. However great the attainment in the Westcott-Hort text, the further progress we desiderate can be accomplished only when our psychological bonds are broken. Herein lies today's foremost problem with the critical text of the New Testament.[1]

In spite of the prevailing uncertainty and dissatisfaction, when it comes right down to it most textual critics fall back on W-H—when in doubt the safe thing to do is stay with the party line.[2]

Elliott, mentioned earlier, deliberately tried to set the party line aside, and the result is interesting—his reconstruction of the text of the Pastoral Epistles differs from the *Textus Receptus* 160 times, differs from W-H 80 times, and contains 65 readings that have not appeared in any other printed edition. A review of his reasoning suggests that he did not altogether escape the psychological grip of W-H, but the result is still significantly different from anything else that has been done.[3]

Elliott's effort underscores, by contrast, the extent to which UBS, NEB, etc. still hew to the W-H line. To really understand what is going on today we must

---

[1] *Ibid.*, pp. 158-60. Cf. M.M. Parvis, "Text, NT.", *The Interpreter's Dictionary of the Bible* (4 Vols.; New York: Abingdon Press, 1962), IV, 602, and D.W. Riddle, "Fifty Years of New Testament Scholarship", *The Journal of Bible and Religion*, X (1942), 139.

[2] Cf. Clark, "Today's Problems", p. 166, and especially Colwell, "Scribal Habits", pp. 170-71.

[3] Elliott's results are interesting in a further way. He does his reconstruction "untrammeled" by considerations of manuscript support and then traces the performance of the principal manuscripts. Summarizing his statement of the results, considering only those places where there was variation, Codex Aleph was right 38% of the time, A was right 38% of the time, C right 41%, D right 35%, F,G right 31%, and the bulk of the minuscules (Byzantine) was right 35% of the time (pp. 241-43). He claims that doing a reconstruction his way then enables one to trace the behavior of individual MSS and to show their "illogical fluctuations". Such a tracing is based upon his own subjective evaluation of readings but the illogical fluctuations can be seen empirically by comparing the collations of a variety of MSS.

have a clear perception of the W-H critical theory and its implications. Its importance is universally recognized.[1] J.H. Greenlee's statement is representative: "The textual theory of W-H underlies virtually all subsequent work in NT textual criticism".[2]

So, to a discussion of that theory I now turn.

---

[1] See, for example, K. Aland, "The Significance of the Papyri", p. 325; Colwell, "Scribal Habits", p. 370; Metzger, *The Text*, p. 137; V. Taylor, *The Text of the New Testament* (New York: St. Martin's Press Inc., 1961), p. 49; K. Lake, p. 67; F.G. Kenyon, *Handbook to the Textual Criticism of the New Testament* (2nd ed.; Grand Rapids: Wm. B. Eerdmans Publishing Co., 1951), p. 294; Epp, "Interlude", p. 386, and Riddle, Parvis and Clark, noted above.

[2] J.H. Greenlee, *Introduction to New Testament Textual Criticism* (Grand Rapids: Wm. B. Eerdmans Publishing Co., 1964), p. 78.

# 3
# THE WESTCOTT-HORT CRITICAL THEORY

Although Brooke Foss Westcott identified himself fully with the project and the results, it is generally understood that it was mainly Fenton John Anthony Hort[1] who developed the theory and composed the Introduction in their two-volume work.[2] In the following discussion I consider the W-H theory to be Hort's creation.

At the age of 23, in late 1851, Hort wrote to a friend: "I had no idea till the last few weeks of the importance of texts, having read so little Greek Testament, and dragged on with the villainous *Textus Receptus*... Think of that vile *Textus Receptus* leaning entirely on late MSS.; it is a blessing there are such early ones."[3]

Scarcely more than a year later, "the plan of a joint [with B.F. Westcott] revision of the text of the Greek Testament was first definitely agreed upon".[4] And within that year (1853) Hort wrote to a friend that he hoped to have the new text out "in little more than a year".[5] That it actually took twenty-eight years does not obscure the circumstance that though uninformed, by his own admission, Hort conceived a personal animosity for the *Textus Receptus*,[6] and only because it was based entirely, so he thought, on late manuscripts. It appears that Hort did not arrive at his theory through unprejudiced intercourse

---

[1] F.J.A. Hort and B.F. Westcott were highly respected and influential Anglican churchmen of the 19th century—especially during the 70s and 80s. Westcott was Bishop of Durham and Hort a Professor at Cambridge. The Greek text of the N.T. prepared by them was adopted (essentially) by the committee that produced the English Revised Version of 1881. Westcott wrote a number of commentaries on N.T. books which are still considered to be standard works. His prestige and influence were important to the success of their (W-H) undertaking.

[2] B.F. Westcott and F.J.A. Hort, *The New Testament in the Original Greek* (2 Vols.; London: Macmillan and Co., 1881).

[3] A.F. Hort, *Life and Letters of Fenton John Anthony Hort* (2 Vols.; London: Macmillan and Co. Ltd., 1896), I, 211.

[4] *Ibid.*, p. 240.

[5] *Ibid.*, p. 264.

[6] The expression '*Textus Receptus*' properly refers to some one of the printed editions of the Greek text of the N.T. related in character to the text prepared by Erasmus in the sixteenth century. (Of over thirty such editions, few are identical.) It is not identical to the text reflected in the AV (though it is quite close) nor yet to the so-called "Syrian" or "Byzantine" text (these terms will be introduced presently). The critical edition of the "Byzantine" text prepared by Zane C. Hodges, former Professor of New Testament Literature and Exegesis at the Dallas Theological Seminary, Arthur L. Farstad, and others, and published by Thomas Nelson in 1982, differs from the *Textus Receptus* in over 1,500 places.

with the facts. Rather, he deliberately set out to construct a theory that would vindicate his preconceived animosity for the Received Text.

Colwell has made the same observation: "Hort organized his entire argument to depose the Textus Receptus".[1] And again, "Westcott and Hort wrote with two things constantly in mind; the Textus Receptus and the Codex Vaticanus. But they did not hold them in mind with that passive objectivity which romanticists ascribe to the scientific mind."[2]

As the years went by, Hort must have seen that to achieve his end he had to have a convincing history of the text—he had to be able to explain why essentially only one type of text was to be found in the mass of later manuscripts and show how this explanation justified the rejection of this type of text.

## The Basic Approach

Hort started by taking the position that the New Testament is to be treated like any other book.[3] "The principles of criticism explained in the foregoing section hold good for all ancient texts preserved in a plurality of documents. In dealing with the text of the New Testament no new principle whatever is needed or legitimate."[4]

This stance required the declared presupposition that no malice touched the text. "It will not be out of place to add here a distinct expression of our belief that even among the numerous unquestionably spurious readings of the New Testament there are no signs of deliberate falsification of the text for dogmatic purposes."[5]

Such a position allowed him to bring over into the textual criticism of the New Testament the family-tree method, or genealogy, as developed by students of the classics.

## Genealogy

Here is Hort's classic definition of genealogical method:

> The proper method of Genealogy consists … in the more or less complete recovery of the texts of successive ancestors by analysis

---

[1] Colwell, "Hort Redivivus", p. 158.

[2] Colwell, "Genealogical Method: Its Achievements and its Limitations", *Journal of Biblical Literature*, LXVI (1947), 111.

[3] In fact, Hort did not hold to a high view of inspiration. Cf. A.F. Hort, I, 419-21 and Westcott and Hort, II, "Introduction", 280-81.

[4] Westcott and Hort, p. 73.

[5] *Ibid.*, p. 282. In this chapter I am merely presenting Hort's theory in his own words. The next chapter gives my detailed evaluation of each aspect of his theory.

and comparison of the varying texts of their respective descendants, each ancestral text so recovered being in its turn used, in conjunction with other similar texts, for the recovery of the text of a yet earlier common ancestor.[1]

Colwell says of Hort's use of this method:

As the justification of their rejection of the majority, Westcott and Hort found the possibilities of genealogical method invaluable. Suppose that there are only ten copies of a document and that nine are all copied from one; then the majority can be safely rejected. Or suppose that the nine are copied from a lost manuscript and that this lost manuscript and the other one were both copied from the original; then the vote of the majority would not outweigh that of the minority. These are the arguments with which W. and H. opened their discussion of genealogical method... They show clearly that a majority of manuscripts is not **necessarily** to be preferred as correct. It is this *a priori* possibility which Westcott and Hort used to demolish the argument based on the numerical superiority of the adherents of the Textus Receptus.[2]

It is clear that the notion of genealogy is crucial to Hort's theory and purpose. He felt that the genealogical method enabled him to reduce the mass of manuscript testimony to four voices—"Neutral", "Alexandrian", "Western" and "Syrian".

# Text-types and Recensions

To sum up what has been said on the results of genealogical evidence proper, as affecting the text of the New Testament, we regard the following propositions as absolutely certain. (I) The great ancient texts did actually exist as we have described them in Sections II and III...(III) The extant documents contain no readings (unless the peculiar Western non-interpolations noticed above are counted as exceptions), which suggest the existence of important textual events unknown to us, a knowledge of which could materially alter the interpretation of evidence as determined by the above history.[3]

The "great ancient texts" are the four named above. Although Hort's "Neutral" and "Alexandrian" are now generally lumped together and called "Alexandrian", and Hort's "Syrian" is now usually named "Byzantine", and the

---

[1] *Ibid.*, p. 57.

[2] Colwell, "Genealogical Method", p. 111.

[3] Westcott and Hort, pp. 178-9. Note that Hort made use of only a small fraction of the manuscripts extant in his day. Cf. K. Aland, "The Significance of the Papyri", pp. 327-28. A check of W-H's "Notes on Select Readings" in volume 2 of their *The New Testament in the Original Greek* suggests that Aland is probably generous.

literature refers to an added text-type, "Caesarean", the notion of at least three major text-types or recensions dominates the field to this day. Here is another basic tenet of Hort's theory.

Having, ostensibly, justified the handling of the mass of later manuscripts as one witness or text, Hort now moved to demonstrate that this supposed text was an inferior, even inconsequential, witness. The first proof put forward was "conflation".

# Conflation

Once manuscripts are assigned to different text-types on the basis of characteristic variants shared in common, almost any early manuscript that one chances to pick up is observed to exhibit variants thought to be diagnostic or characteristic of alien text-types. Such a situation has been called 'mixture'. 'Conflation' is a special kind of mixture. In Hort's words,

> The clearest evidence for tracing the antecedent factors of mixture in texts is afforded by readings which are themselves mixed or, as they are sometimes called, 'conflate,' that is, not simple substitutions of the reading of one document for that of another, but combinations of the readings of both documents into a composite whole, sometimes by mere addition with or without a conjunction, sometimes with more or less of fusion.[1]

Hort urged the conclusion that a text containing conflate readings must be posterior in date to the texts containing the various components from which the conflations were constructed.[2] Then he produced eight examples[3] where, by his interpretation, the "Syrian" (Byzantine) text had combined "Neutral" and "Western" elements. He went on to say:

> To the best of our belief the relations thus provisionally traced are never inverted. We do not know of any places where the $\alpha$ group of documents supports readings apparently conflate from the readings of the $\beta$ and $\delta$ groups respectively, or where the $\beta$ group of documents supports readings apparently conflate from the readings of the $\alpha$ and $\delta$ groups respectively.[4]

---

[1] Westcott and Hort, p. 49.

[2] *Ibid.*, p. 106. This seems obvious enough, since the materials used to manufacture something must of necessity exist before the resulting product. A clear putative example occurs in Luke 24:53. The "Western" text has "praising God", the "Neutral" text has "blessing God" and the "Syrian" text has "praising and blessing God". According to Hort's hypothesis the longest reading was constructed out of the two shorter ones. Note that the use of the word 'conflation' embodies the rejection of the possibility that the longer reading is original and that the shorter ones are independent simplifications of that original longer reading.

[3] Mark 6:33; 8:26; 9:38; 9:49; Luke 9:10; 11:54; 12:18; 24:53.

[4] Westcott and Hort, p. 106. By "$\alpha$ group" Hort means his "Neutral" text, by "$\beta$

It was essential to Hort's purpose of demonstrating the "Syrian" text to be posterior that he not find any inversion of the relationships between the three "texts". (An "inversion" would be either the "Neutral" or the "Western" text containing a conflation from the other plus the "Syrian".) So he claimed that inversions do not exist.[1]

Hort's statement and interpretation have been generally accepted.[2] Vincent Taylor calls the argument "very cogent indeed".[3] Kirsopp Lake calls it "the keystone of their theory".[4] Here is another tenet crucial to Hort's theory and purpose. For a second and independent proof of the posteriority of the "Syrian" text he turned to the ante-Nicene Fathers.

# "Syrian" Readings Before Chrysostom

After a lengthy discussion, Hort concluded:

> Before the middle of the third century, at the very earliest, we have no historical signs of the existence of readings, conflate or other, that are marked as distinctively Syrian by the want of attestation from groups of documents which have preserved the other ancient forms of text. This is a fact of great significance, ascertained as it is exclusively by external evidence, and therefore supplying an absolutely independent verification and extension of the result already obtained by comparison of the internal character of readings as classified by conflation.[5]

Elsewhere he considered that Chrysostom (who died in 407) was the first Father to characteristically use the "Syrian" text.[6]

The importance of this argument to Hort's theory has been recognized by Kenyon.

> Hort's contention, which was the corner-stone of his theory, was that readings characteristic of the Received Text are never found in the quotations of Christian writers prior to about A.D. 350. Before

---

group" he means his "Western" text, and by "$\delta$ group" he means his "Syrian" text.

[1] In Appendix D the reader will find a refutation of this claim. (Hort himself knew that they do exist.)

[2] Cf. Kenyon, p. 302; E.F. Harrison, *Introduction to the New Testament* (Grand Rapids: Wm. B. Eerdmans Publishing Co., 1964), p. 73; and Metzger, *The Text*, pp. 135-36.

[3] Taylor, p. 53.

[4] Lake, p. 68.

[5] Westcott and Hort, p. 115.

[6] *Ibid.*, p. 91.

that date we find characteristically "Neutral" and "Western" readings, but never "Syrian". This argument is in fact decisive...[1]

Lake, also, considered it to be decisive.[2] (But to have any chance of being 'decisive' it would have to be true.)

Hort's purpose would appear to have been achieved, but for good measure he advanced a third argument against the "Syrian" text, one based on internal evidence.

# Internal Evidence of Readings

Such 'evidence' is based on two kinds of probability, intrinsic and transcriptional. Intrinsic probability is author oriented—what reading makes the best sense, best fits the context, and conforms to the author's style and purpose? Transcriptional probability is scribe or copyist oriented—what reading can be attributed to carelessness or officiousness on the part of the copyist? Aside from inadvertent mistakes, presumed deliberate changes have given rise to two important canons of criticism—*brevior lectio potior*, the shorter reading is to be preferred (on the assumed propensity of scribes to add material to the text), and *proclivi lectioni praestat ardua*, the harder reading is to be preferred (on the assumed propensity of scribes to attempt to simplify the text when confronted with a supposed difficulty).

On the basis of such considerations, Hort declared the "Syrian" text to be characterized by "lucidity and completeness", "apparent simplicity", "harmonistic assimilation", and as being "conspicuously a full text".[3] He said further:

> In themselves Syrian readings hardly ever offend at first. With rare exceptions they run smoothly and easily in form, and yield at once to even a careless reader a passable sense, free from surprises and seemingly transparent. But when distinctively Syrian readings are minutely compared one after the other with the rival variants, their claim to be regarded as the original readings is found gradually to diminish, and at last to disappear.[4]

Hort's characterization of the "Syrian" text has been generally accepted by subsequent scholars.[5]

---

[1] F.G. Kenyon, *Recent Developments in the Textual Criticism of the Greek Bible* (London: Oxford University Press, 1933), pp. 7-8.

[2] Lake, p. 72.

[3] Westcott and Hort, pp. 134-35.

[4] *Ibid.*, pp. 115-16.

[5] See, for example, Kenyon, *Recent Developments*, p. 66, Metzger, *The Text*, p. 131, and Greenlee, p. 91.

Even after demonstrating, so he thought, the "Syrian" text to be eclectic and late, Hort had a major obstacle to hurdle. He had to explain how this "text" came into being, and above all how it came to dominate the field from the fifth century on. An organized revision of the text, executed and imposed upon the churches by ecclesiastical authority, was his solution to the problem.

## The "Lucianic Recension" and the Peshitta

"The Syrian text", Hort said, "must in fact be the result of a 'recension' in the proper sense of the word, a work of attempted criticism, performed deliberately by editors and not merely by scribes."[1]

> An authoritative Revision at Antioch ... was itself subjected to a second authoritative Revision carrying out more completely the purposes of the first. At what date between A.D. 250 and 350 the first process took place, it is impossible to say with confidence. The final process was apparently completed by A.D. 350 or thereabouts.[2]

Hort tentatively suggested Lucian (who died in 311) as perhaps the leader in the movement and some scholars subsequently became dogmatic on the subject.

The matter of the Syriac Peshitta version is often treated in connection with the "Lucianic recension" of the Greek because of a supposed connection between them. Because the Peshitta does witness to the "Byzantine" text Hort had to get it out of the second and third centuries. Accordingly, he posited a late recension to account for it. F.C. Burkitt went further than Hort and specified Rabbula, Bishop of Edessa from A.D. 411-435, as the author of the revision.[3]

Both ideas have had a wide acceptance. H.C. Thiessen's statement is typical, both in content and dogmatism.

> This [Peshitta] was formerly regarded as the oldest of the Syrian versions; but Burkitt has shown that it is in reality a revision of the Old Syriac made by Rabbula, Bishop of Edessa, about the year 425. This view is now held by nearly all Syriac scholars. The text of the Peshitta is now identified as the Byzantine text, which almost certainly goes back to the revision made by Lucian of Antioch about A.D. 300.[4]

---

[1] Westcott and Hort, p. 133.

[2] *Ibid.*, p. 137.

[3] F.C. Burkitt, *Evangelion da-Mepharreshe* (2 vols.; Cambridge: Cambridge University Press, 1904), II, 161.

[4] H.C. Thiessen, *Introduction to the New Testament* (Grand Rapids: Wm. B. Eerdmans Publishing Co., 1955), pp. 54-55.

# Summary and Consequences

And there you have the essence of the W-H critical theory. I have read every word of Hort's "Introduction", all 324 difficult pages of it [I had to read some pages two or three times to be more or less sure that I had understood it], and I believe the description offered above is a reasonable one. Suffice it to say that Hort achieved his purpose, even if it took him twenty-eight years. Although such men as Tischendorf, Tregelles, and Alford had done much to undermine the position of the TR (*Textus Receptus*), Westcott and Hort are generally credited with having furnished the death blow, beginning a new era. Many scholars have written to this effect,[1] but Colwell expresses it as well as anyone.

> The dead hand of Fenton John Anthony Hort lies heavy upon us. In the early years of this century Kirsopp Lake described Hort's work as a failure, though a glorious one. But Hort did **not** fail to reach his major goal. He dethroned the Textus Receptus. After Hort, the late medieval Greek Vulgate was not used by serious students, and the text supported by earlier witnesses became the standard text. This was a sensational achievement, an impressive success. Hort's success in this task and the cogency of his tightly reasoned theory shaped—and still shapes—the thinking of those who approach the textual criticism of the NT through the English language.[2]

And that explains the nature and extent of the common divergence of the modern versions from the AV (King James Version)—they are all based essentially on the W-H theory and text whereas the AV is essentially based on the *Textus Receptus*.

But the question remains: Has the apparent potential for improving the text (arising from increased materials and 'wisdom') been realized? Did the translators of the RSV, for instance, make better use of the manuscripts and employ superior principles of textual criticism than did the translators of the AV? Well, the principles they used led them to adopt the W-H text with very little variation, and that text is based essentially on just two manuscripts, Codices B and Aleph.[3]

---

[1] Cf. Clark, "Today's Problems", pp. 158-60, M.M. Parvis, "Text, NT.", *The Interpreter's Dictionary of the Bible* (4 Vols.; New York: Abingdon Press, 1962), IV, 602, and D.W. Riddle, "Fifty Years of New Testament Scholarship", *The Journal of Bible and Religion*, X (1942), 139.

[2] Colwell, "Scribal Habits", p. 370.

[3] Cf. Colwell, "External Evidence and New Testament Criticism", *Studies in the History and Text of the New Testament*, eds. B.L. Daniels and M.J. Suggs (Salt Lake City: University of Utah Press, 1967), p. 3; Colwell, "Hort Redivivus", p. 162; Clark, "Today's Problems", pp. 159-60; Epp, p. 390.

Hort declared: "It is our belief (1) that the readings of ℵ B should be accepted as the true readings until strong internal evidence is found to the contrary, and (2) that no readings of ℵ B can safely be rejected absolutely..."[1]

Again, Hort said of B and Aleph, "The fullest comparison does but increase the conviction that their preeminent relative purity is likewise approximately absolute, a true approximate reproduction of the text of the autographs."[2] One wonders whether the W-H theory and text would ever have seen the light of day had Codex B not been extant. Hort gave himself away while discussing genealogy.

> In the Apocalypse the difficulty of recognizing the ancient texts is still greater, owing to the great relative paucity of documents, and especially the absence or loss of this book from the Vatican MS (B) which is available for nearly all the rest of the New Testament; and thus the power of using a directly genealogical method is much limited.[3]

The practical effect of the W-H theory was a complete rejection of the "Syrian" text and an almost exclusive preference for the "Neutral" text (equals B and Aleph). Subsequent scholarship has generally rejected the notion of a "Neutral" text but sustained the rejection of the "Syrian" text.

Curiously, there seems to be a determination not to reconsider the status of the "Syrian" text even though each of the arguments Hort used in relegating it to oblivion has been challenged. Thus J.N. Birdsall, after referring to the work of Lake, Lagrange, Colwell and Streeter, as well as his own, declared: "It is evident that all presuppositions concerning the Byzantine text—or texts—except its inferiority to other types, must be doubted and investigated *de novo*".[4] (But doesn't the supposed inferiority depend on those presuppositions?)

Recalling what has already been said above in the discussion of eclecticism, it seems evident that Clark was quite right when he said that "textual theory appears to have reached an impasse in our time".[5]

Since Hort's purpose was to get rid of the "Syrian" text and that is the one point of his theory that subsequent scholars have generally not questioned,

---

[1] Westcott and Hort, p. 225. Cf. pp. 212-13.

[2] *Ibid.*, p. 276. And, "B very far exceeds all other documents in neutrality of text", p. 171.

[3] *Ibid.*, pp. 109-10.

[4] J.N. Birdsall, "The Text of the Gospels in Photius", *Journal of Theological Studies*, VII (1956), p. 43. Some scholars seem even to reflect the emotion of the twenty-three-year-old Hort—not long ago Epp spoke of "the tyrannical *textus receptus*" (p. 386).

[5] Clark, "The Effect of Recent Textual Criticism", p. 50.

perhaps it is time to ask whether that circumstance may not have something to do with the present confusion and impasse, and to wonder whether Hort was really right. I proceed to work through Hort's theory again, point by point, to inquire to what extent it corresponds to the evidence.

# 4
# AN EVALUATION OF THE W-H THEORY

## The Basic Approach

Should the New Testament be treated just like any other book? Will the procedures used on the works of Homer or Aristotle suffice? If both God and Satan had an intense interest in the fate of the New Testament text, presumably not. But how can we test the fact or extent of supernatural intervention? Happily we have eyewitness accounts to provide at least a partial answer. Hort said that "there are no signs of deliberate falsification of the text for dogmatic purposes", but the early Church Fathers disagree. Metzger states:

> Irenaeus, Clement of Alexandria, Tertullian, Eusebius, and many other Church Fathers accused the heretics of corrupting the Scriptures in order to have support for their special views. In the mid-second century, Marcion expunged his copies of the Gospel according to Luke of all references to the Jewish background of Jesus. Tatian's Harmony of the Gospels contains several textual alterations which lent support to ascetic or encratite views.[1]

Gaius, an orthodox Father who wrote between A.D. 175 and 200, names Asclepiades, Theodotus, Hermophilus, and Apollonides as heretics who prepared corrupted copies of the Scriptures and who had disciples who multiplied copies of their fabrications.[2]

Surely Hort knew the words of Origen.

> Nowadays, as is evident, there is a great diversity between the various manuscripts, either through the negligence of certain copyists, or the perverse audacity shown by some in correcting the text, or through the fault of those, who, playing the part of correctors, lengthen or shorten it as they please (*In Matth. tom.* XV, 14; *P. G.* XIII, 1293).[3]

---

[1] Metzger, *The Text*, p. 201. For actual examples from Irenaeus, Clement, Tertullian, and Eusebius, please see Sturz (pp. 116-19), who also has a good discussion of their significance. As he says, "While scribal blunders were recognized by them as one cause of variation, the strongest and most positive statements, by the Fathers, are in connection with the changes introduced by heretics" (p. 120). H.A. Sturz, *The Byzantine Text-Type and New Testament Textual Criticism* (Nashville: Thomas Nelson Publishers, 1984).

[2] J.W. Burgon, *The Revision Revised* (London: John Murray, 1883), p. 323.

[3] Colwell, "The Origin of Textypes of New Testament Manuscripts", *Early Christian Origins*, ed. Allen Wikgren (Chicago: Quadrangle Books, 1961), p. 130.

Even the orthodox were capable of changing a reading for dogmatic reasons. Epiphanius states (ii.3b) that the orthodox deleted "he wept" from Luke 19:41 out of jealousy for the Lord's divinity.[1]

Subsequent scholarship has tended to recognize Hort's mistake. Colwell has done an instructive about-face.

> The majority of the variant readings in the New Testament were created for theological or dogmatic reasons.
>
> Most of the manuals and handbooks now in print (including mine!) will tell you that these variations were the fruit of careless treatment which was possible because the books of the New Testament had not yet attained a strong position as "Bible." The reverse is the case. It was because they were the religious treasure of the church that they were changed.[2]

---

[1] J.W. Burgon, *The Causes of the Corruption of the Traditional Text of the Holy Gospels*, arranged, completed and edited by Edward Miller (London: George Bell and Sons, 1896), pp. 211-12. Cf. Martin Rist, "Pseudepigraphy and the Early Christians", *Studies in New Testament and Early Christian Literature*, ed. D.E. Aune (Leiden: E.J. Brill, 1972), pp. 78-79.

[2] Colwell, *What is the Best New Testament?* (Chicago: The University of Chicago Press, 1952), p. 53. Observe that Colwell flatly contradicts Hort. Hort said there were no theologically motivated variants; Colwell says they are in the majority. But, in the next quote, Colwell uses the term "deliberately", without referring to theology (both quotes come from the same work, five pages apart). What is Colwell's real meaning? We may no longer ask him personally, but I will hazard the following interpretation on my own.

The MSS contain several hundred thousand variant readings. The vast majority of these are misspellings or other obvious errors due to carelessness or ignorance on the part of the copyists. As a sheer guess I would say there are between ten thousand and fifteen thousand that cannot be so easily dismissed—i.e., a maximum of five percent of the variants are 'significant'. It is to this five percent that Colwell (and Kilpatrick, Scrivener, Zuntz, etc.) refers when he speaks of the "creation" of variant readings. A fair number of these are probably the result of accident also, but Colwell affirms, and I agree, that most of them were created deliberately.

But why would anyone bother to make deliberate changes in the text? Colwell answers, "because they were the religious treasure of the church". Some changes would be 'well intentioned'—many harmonizations presumably came about because a zealous copyist felt that a supposed discrepancy was an embarrassment to his high view of Scripture. The same is probably true of many philological changes. For instance, the plain Koine style of the New Testament writings was ridiculed by the pagan Celsus, among others. Although Origen defended the simplicity of the New Testament style, the space that he gave to the question indicates that it was a matter of some concern (*Against Celsus*, Book VI, chapters 1 and 2), so much so that there were probably those who altered the text to 'improve' the style. Again, their motive would be embarrassment, deriving from a high view of Scripture. Surely Colwell is justified in saying that the motivation for such variants was theological even though no obvious doctrinal 'axe' is being ground.

To judge by the emphatic statements of the early Fathers, there were many other changes that were not 'well intentioned'. It seems clear that numerous variants existed in the second century that have not survived in any extant MS. Metzger refers to Gwilliam's

The New Testament copies differ widely in nature of errors from copies of the classics. The percentage of variations due to error in copies of the classics is large. In the manuscripts of the New Testament most variations, I believe, were made deliberately.[1]

Matthew Black stated flatly:

The difference between sacred writings in constant popular and ecclesiastical use and the work of a classical author has never been sufficiently emphasized in the textual criticism of the New Testament. Principles valid for the textual restoration of Plato or Aristotle cannot be applied to sacred texts such as the Gospels (or the Pauline Epistles). We cannot assume that it is possible by a sifting of 'scribal errors' to arrive at the prototype or autograph text of the Biblical writer.[2]

---

detailed study of chapters 1-14 of Matthew in the Syriac Peshitta as reported in "The Place of the Peshitta Version in the Apparatus Criticus of the Greek N.T.", *Studia Biblica et Ecclesiastica V*, 1903, 187-237. From the fact that in thirty-one instances the Peshitta stands alone (in those chapters), Gwilliam concluded that its unknown author "revised an ancient work by Greek MSS which have no representative now extant" (p. 237) (*The Early Versions of the New Testament*, Oxford, 1977, p. 61). In a personal communication, Peter J. Johnston, a member of the IGNT editorial panel working specifically with the Syriac Versions and Fathers, says of the Harklean Version: "Readings confidently referred to in the Harklean margin as in 'well-approved MSS at Alexandria' have sometimes not come down to us at all, or if they have, they are found only in medieval minuscule MSS". In commenting upon the discrepancies between Jerome's statements of MS evidence and that extant today, Metzger concluded by saying, "the disquieting possibility remains that the evidence available to us today may, in certain cases, be totally unrepresentative of the distribution of readings in the early church" ("St. Jerome's explicit references to variant readings in manuscripts of the New Testament", *Text and Interpretation: Studies in the New Testament presented to Matthew Black*, edited by Best and McL. Wilson, Cambridge: University Press, 1979, p. 188).

Some of my critics seem to feel that the extant evidence from the early centuries is representative (cf. Fee, "A Critique", p. 405). However, there is good reason for believing that it is not, and in that event the extant MSS may preserve some random survivors from sets of alterations designed to grind one doctrinal axe or another. The motivation for such a reading in isolation would not necessarily be apparent to us today.

I would go beyond Colwell and say that the disposition to alter the text, even with 'good motives', itself bespeaks a mentality which has theological implications.

(Those who are prepared to take the Sacred Text seriously would do well to ponder the implications of Ephesians 2:2, "the spirit [Satan] presently at work in the sons of the disobedience", not only during the first 200 years of the Church but also during the last 200.)

[1] Colwell, What is the Best New Testament?, p. 58.

[2] M. Black, *An Aramaic Approach to the Gospels and Acts* (Oxford: Oxford University Press, 1946), p. 214.

H.H. Oliver gives a good summary of the shift of recent scholarship away from Hort's position in this matter.[1]

The fact of deliberate, and apparently numerous, alterations in the early years of textual history is a considerable inconvenience to Hort's theory for two reasons: it introduces an unpredictable variable which the canons of internal evidence cannot handle, and it puts the recovery of the Original beyond the reach of the genealogical method.[2]

---

[1] H.H. Oliver, "Present Trends in the Textual Criticism of the New Testament", *The Journal of Bible and Religion*, XXX (1962), 311-12. Cf. C.S.C. Williams, *Alterations to the Text of the Synoptic Gospels and Acts* (Oxford: Basil Blackwell, 1951), pp. 14-17.

[2] The 'inconvenience' referred to is virtually fatal to the W-H theory, at least as formulated in their "Introduction". The W-H theory is much like a multistoried building—each level depends on the one below it. Thus, Hort's simplistic notion of "genealogy" absolutely depends upon the allegation that there was no deliberate alteration of the Text, and his notion of "text-types" absolutely depends upon "genealogy", and his arguments concerning "conflation" and "Syrian" readings before Chrysostom absolutely depend upon those "text-types". The foundation for the whole edifice is Hort's position that the New Testament was an ordinary book that received a troubled transmission. With its foundation removed, the edifice collapses.

Fee seems to miss the point when he says, "if the 'foundation' is found to be secure, then the superstructure may only need some reinforcing, not demolition" ("A Critique", p. 404). The removal of any of the intervening floors as well will 'destroy the building', that is, invalidate Hort's conclusions. It seems to me that the first three floors of Hort's building, at least, are beyond restoration.

Fee claims that I confuse "deliberate" and "dogmatic" changes and in consequence my critique of Hort's foundation fails ("A Critique", pp. 404-8). In his own words, "The vast majority of textual corruptions, though deliberate, are **not** malicious, nor are they theologically motivated. And **since** they are not, Pickering's view of 'normal' transmission (which is the crucial matter in his theory) simply disintegrates" (p. 408).

Fee fastens upon my use of the term 'malicious', which I use only in discussing the **ab**normal transmission. I nowhere say that a majority of variants are malicious. The clear testimony of the early Fathers indicates that some must be, and I continue to insist that Hort's theory cannot handle such variants. (Fee seriously distorts my position by ignoring my discussion of the **ab**normal transmission. It would appear that the distortion was deliberate since he cites my pp. 104-110 for the "normal" transmission, whereas pp. 107-110 contain my treatment of the abnormal transmission.) But what are the implications of Fee's admission that the vast majority of textual corruptions are 'deliberate'? Setting aside the question of theological motivation, can the canons of internal evidence really handle 'deliberate' variants?

Supposed harmonizations may reasonably have other explanations. Fee himself recognizes this possibility ("Modern Text Criticism and the Synoptic Problem", *J.J. Griesbach: Synoptic and Text-Critical Studies 1776-1976*, ed. B. Orchard and T.R.W. Longstaff, Cambridge: University Press, 1976, p. 162). On the next page Fee recognizes another problem.

> It should candidly be admitted that our predilections toward a given solution of the Synoptic Problem will sometimes affect textual decisions. Integrity should cause us also to admit to a certain amount of inevitable circular reasoning at times. A classic example of this point is the well-known 'minor agreement' between Matt. 26:67-8 and Luke 22:64 (//Mark 14:65) of the 'addition' τις εστιν ο παισας σε. B.H. Streeter, G.D.

To illustrate the second point, Hort's view of early textual history may be represented by figure A whereas the view suggested by the Church Fathers may be represented by figure B. The dotted lines in figure B represent the fabrications introduced by different heretics (as the early Fathers called them).

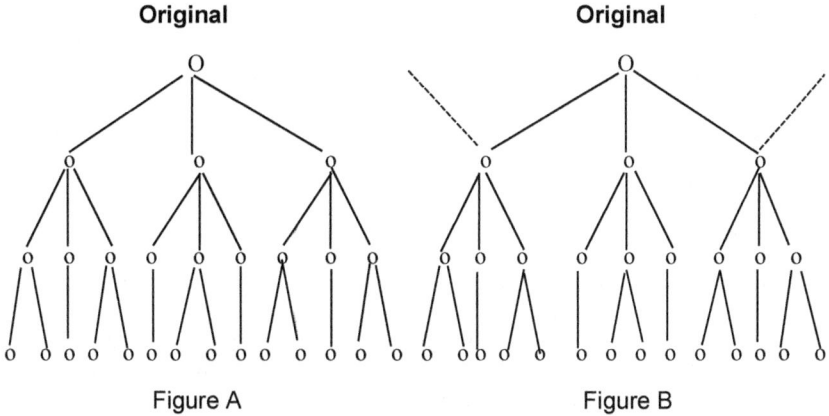

Figure A                                    Figure B

Genealogy cannot arbitrate the conflicting claims posed by the first line of descendants in Figure B.[1] Further, in Colwell's words, this method (genealogy)

> ...rested on identity in *error* as the clue to common ancestry. These errors were unintentional changes which can be identified objectively as error. Agreement in readings of this kind seldom occurs by chance or coincidence. The New Testament copies differ widely from copies of the classics at this point. The percentage of variations due to error in copies of the classics is large. In the manuscripts of the New Testament, on the other hand, scholars now believe that most variations were made deliberately.[2]

---

Kilpatrick, and W.R. Farmer each resolve the textual problem of Mark in a different way. In each case, a given solution of the Synoptic Problem has affected the textual decision. At this point one could offer copious illustrations.

Fee's ("Rigorous") debate with Kilpatrick ("Atticism") demonstrates that possible philological changes are capable of contradictory interpretations on the part of scholars who both use internal evidence. In sum, I reiterate that the canons of internal evidence **cannot** give us dependable interpretations with reference to deliberate variants. Those who use such canons are awash in a sea of speculation.

[1] Further, if a genealogical reconstruction ends up with only two immediate descendants of the Original, as in Hort's own reconstruction, then the genealogical method ceases to be applicable, as Hort himself recognized. Westcott and Hort, p. 42.

[2] Colwell, What is the Best New Testament?, p. 49.

The reconstruction of family trees is seriously complicated by the presence of deliberate alterations. And those are not the only difficulties under which genealogy labors.

## Genealogy

We have already noted Hort's definition and supposed use of genealogy. However, scholars have so far isolated only a few parent-child sets among all 3,000 plus continuous text manuscripts.[1] How then did Hort go about plotting the genealogical descent of the extant MSS? M.M. Parvis answered: "Westcott and Hort never applied the genealogical method to the NT MSS..."[2] Colwell agreed.

> That Westcott and Hort did not apply this method to the manuscripts of the New Testament is obvious. Where are the charts which start with the majority of late manuscripts and climb back through diminishing generations of ancestors to the Neutral and Western texts? The answer is that they are nowhere. Look again at the first diagram, and you will see that a, b, c, etc. are not actual manuscripts of the New Testament, but hypothetical manuscripts. The demonstrations or illustrations of the genealogical method as applied to New Testament manuscripts by the followers of Hort, the "Horticuli" as Lake called them, likewise use hypothetical manuscripts, not actual codices. Note, for example, the diagrams and discussions in Kenyon's most popular work on textual criticism, including the most recent edition. All the manuscripts referred to are imaginary manuscripts, and the later of these charts was printed sixty years after Hort.[3]

How then could Hort speak of only "occasional ambiguities in the evidence for the genealogical relations",[4] or say: "So far as genealogical relations are discovered with perfect certainty, the textual results which follow from them are perfectly certain, too, being directly involved in historical facts; and any apparent presumptions against them suggested by other methods are mere

---

[1] Codex Claromontanus apparently has a 'child' three centuries younger than it (also, minuscule 205 may have been copied from 208). Codices F and G containing Paul's Epistles appear to be almost twin brothers, but we don't have the 'parent'.

[2] Parvis, p. 611. Fee says much the same. "Properly speaking, genealogy must deal with the descent of manuscripts and must reconstruct stemmata for that descent. This Hort never did; rather he applied the method to text-types, and he did so **not** to find the original text, but to eliminate the Byzantine manuscripts from further consideration" ("Modern Text Criticism", pp. 155-56).

[3] Colwell, "Genealogical Method", pp. 111-12.

[4] Westcott and Hort, p. 63.

guesses against knowledge"[1] when he had not demonstrated the existence of **any** such relations, much less with "perfect certainty"?[2]

Another challenge to genealogy is "mixture."

> The second limitation upon the application of the genealogical method to the manuscripts of the New Testament springs from the almost universal presence of mixture in these manuscripts...

> The genealogical diagram printed above (p. 110) from Westcott and Hort shows what happens *when there is no mixture*. When there *is* mixture, and Westcott and Hort state that it is common, in fact almost universal in some degree, then the genealogical method *as applied to manuscripts* is useless.

> *Without* mixture a family tree is an ordinary tree-trunk with its branches—standing on the branches with the single trunk—the original text—at the top. The higher up—or the further back—you go from the mass of late manuscripts, the fewer ancestors you have!

> *With* mixture you reverse this in any series of generations. The number of possible combinations defies computation, let alone the drawing of diagrams.[3]

Other scholars have agreed that the genealogical method has never been applied to the New Testament, and they state further that it *cannot* be applied. Thus, Zuntz says it is "inapplicable",[4] Vaganay that it is "useless",[5] and Aland that it "cannot be applied to the NT".[6] Colwell also declares emphatically "that it *cannot be* so applied".[7] In the light of all this, what are we to think of Hort when he asserts:

> For skepticism as to the possibility of obtaining a trustworthy genealogical interpretation of documentary phenomena in the New

---

[1] Ibid.

[2] Was Hort dishonest, or just deceived? If the latter, by whom?

[3] Colwell, "Genealogical Method", p. 114. The sort of genealogical diagram that one always sees is like a family tree that shows only male parents. Because of mixture the diagrams should be like a family tree that shows **both** parents, at every level—the farther back you go the more hopelessly complicated it gets. Please note that this applies only to any attempt to apply 'genealogy' to manuscripts; the grouping of MSS on the basis of shared **readings** is both possible and necessary.

[4] Zuntz, p. 155.

[5] L. Vaganay, *An Introduction to the Textual Criticism of the New Testament*, translated by B.V. Miller (London: Sands and Company, 1937), p. 71.

[6] Aland, "The Significance of the Papyri", p. 341.

[7] Colwell, "External Evidence", p. 4.

Testament there is, we are persuaded [by whom?], no justification either in antecedent probability or in experience.

...Whatever may be the ambiguity of the whole evidence in particular passages, the general course of future criticism must be shaped by the happy circumstance that the fourth century has bequeathed to us two MSS of which even the less incorrupt must have been of exceptional purity among its own contemporaries.[1]?

After demolishing the genealogical method, Colwell concluded his article by saying, "yet Westcott and Hort's genealogical method slew the Textus Receptus. The *a priori* demonstration is logically irrefutable."[2] However, the *a priori* demonstration cannot stand in the face of an *a posteriori* demonstration to the contrary. Colwell himself, some twelve years prior to this statement, recognized that the "*a priori* demonstration" to which he here refers has been refuted.

The universal and ruthless dominance of the middle ages by one texttype is now recognized as a myth...

The complexities and perplexities of the medieval text have been brought forcibly to our attention by the work of two great scholars: Hermann von Soden and Kirsopp Lake...

This invaluable pioneer work of von Soden greatly weakened the dogma of the dominance of a homogenous Syrian text. But the fallacy received its death blow at the hands of Professor Lake. In an excursus published with his study of the Caesarean text of Mark, he annihilated the theory that the middle ages were ruled by a single recension which attained a high degree of uniformity.[3]

Actually, Hort produced no 'demonstration' at all—just assumptions. Since the genealogical method has not been applied to the MSS of the New Testament it may not honestly be used as an integral part of a theory of NT textual criticism. If it was Hort's genealogical method that "slew the Textus Receptus" then the TR must still be alive and well—the weapon was never used. But Hort claimed to have used it, and the weapon was so fearsome, and he spoke of the "results" with such confidence, that he won the day.

Since Westcott and Hort, the genealogical method has been the canonical method of restoring the original text of the books of the New Testament. It dominates the handbooks. Sir Frederic Kenyon,

---

[1] Westcott and Hort, p. 287. Hort here refers to Codeces B and Aleph, upon which his theory depends. Comparing his 'exceptional purity' with Hoskier's demonstration, the poor 'contemporaries' must have really been terrible.

[2] Colwell, "Genealogical Method", p. 124.

[3] Colwell, "The Complex Character of the Late Byzantine Text of the Gospels", *Journal of Biblical Literature*, LIV (1935), 212-13.

C.R. Gregory, Alexander Souter, and A.T Robertson are a few of the many who declare its excellence.[1]

The situation is essentially the same today, and the warning Colwell gave in 1965 is still valid.

> Many years ago I joined others in pointing out the limitations in Hort's use of genealogy, and the inapplicability of genealogical method—strictly defined—to the textual criticism of the NT. Since then many others have assented to this criticism, and the building of family trees is only rarely attempted. Therefore we might assume that the influence of Hort's emphasis upon genealogical method is no longer a threat. But this assumption is false.
>
> Hort's brilliant work still captivates our minds. So when confronted by a reading whose support is minimal and widely divorced in time and place, we think first and only of genealogical relationships. Hort has put genealogical blinders on our eyes...[2]

Present-day scholars, exegetes, and translators continue to act as though the genealogical method not only can be, but has been, applied to the NT MSS, and to base their work on the supposed results. But what about those "results"?

## Text-types and Recensions

Although Hort claimed absolute certainty for the results of genealogical evidence as described by him, it is clear that the "results" were a fabrication. How could there be results if the method was never applied to the MSS? A contemporary of W-H protested that such claims would only be allowable if the textual critic had first indexed every principal Church Father and reduced MSS to families by a laborious process of induction.[3]

Still, Hort's "results" became accepted as fact by many—George Salmon spoke of "the servility with which his [Hort] history of the text has been accepted, and even his nomenclature adopted, as if now the last word had been said on the subject of New Testament criticism..."[4]

---

[1] Colwell, "Genealogical Method", p. 109.

[2] Colwell, "Scribal Habits", pp. 370-71.

[3] Burgon, *The Revision Revised*, p. 358. Burgon's own index of the Fathers is no doubt still the most extensive in existence—it contains 86,489 quotations.

[4] G. Salmon, Some Thoughts on the Textual Criticism of the New Testament (London, 1897), p. 33.

## Subsequent scholarship

Subsequent scholars have been obliged to reconsider the matter by the discovery of the Papyri and closer looks at MSS previously extant. Parvis complains:

> We have reconstructed text-types and families and sub families and in so doing have created things that never before existed on earth or in heaven. We have assumed that manuscripts reproduced themselves according to the Mendelian law. But when we have found that a particular manuscript would not fit into any of our nicely constructed schemes, we have thrown up our hands and said that it contained a mixed text.[1]

Allen Wikgren shows that sweeping generalizations about text-types in general and the "Byzantine" text and Lectionaries in particular, should not be made.[2] Colwell affirms:

> The major mistake is made in thinking of the "old text-types" as frozen blocks, even after admitting that no one manuscript is a perfect witness to any text-type. *If* no one MS is a perfect witness to any type, then all witnesses are mixed in ancestry (or individually corrupted, and thus parents of mixture).[3]

After careful study of P[46], Zuntz makes certain observations and concludes:

> One would like to think that observations like these must put an end to time-honoured doctrines such as that the text of B is the 'Neutral' text or that the 'Western' text is 'the' text of the second century. If the factors of each of these equations are meant to be anything but synonyms, they are wrong; if they are synonyms, they mean nothing.[4]

Klijn doubts "whether any grouping of manuscripts gives satisfactory results",[5] and goes on to say:

> It is still customary to divide manuscripts into the four well-known families: the Alexandrian, the Caesarean, the Western and the Byzantine.

---

[1] M.M. Parvis, "The Nature and Task of New Testament Textual Criticism", *The Journal of Religion*, XXXII (1952), 173.

[2] A. Wikgren, "Chicago Studies in the Greek Lectionary of the New Testament", *Biblical and Patristic Studies in Memory of Robert Pierce Casey*, ed. J.N. Birdsall and R.W. Thomson (New York: Herder, 1963), pp. 96-121.

[3] Colwell, "The Origin of Texttypes", p. 135.

[4] Zuntz, p. 240.

[5] Klijn, p. 36.

This classical division can no longer be maintained...

> If any progress is to be expected in textual criticism we have to get rid of the division into local texts. New manuscripts must not be allotted to a geographically limited area but to their place in the history of the text.[1]

After a long discussion of the "Caesarean" text, Metzger says by way of summary that "it must be acknowledged that at present the Caesarean text is disintegrating".[2] Two pages later, referring to the impact of $P^{45}$, he asks, "Was there a fundamental flaw in the previous investigation which tolerated so erroneous a grouping?" Evidently there was. Could it be the mentality that insists upon thinking in terms of text-types and recensions as recognized and recognizable entities?[3] Those few men who have done extensive collations of manuscripts, or paid attention to those done by others, as a rule have not accepted such erroneous groupings.[4]

H. C. Hoskier, whose collations of NT MSS are unsurpassed in quality and perhaps in quantity, commented as follows after collating Codex 604 (today's 700) and comparing it with other MSS:

---

[1] *Ibid.*, p. 66.

[2] Metzger, *Chapters in the History of New Testament Textual Criticism* (Grand Rapids: Wm. B. Eerdmans Publishing Co., 1963), p. 67.

[3] Klijn seems to be of this opinion (pp. 33-34). Not so D.A. Carson. He refers to my position here as "a basic flaw in Pickering's overarching argument" (*The King James Version Debate*, Grand Rapids: Baker Book House, 1979, p. 108). After a confused discussion wherein he misrepresents my position (one of at least ten misrepresentations) Carson concludes by saying: "On the face of it, because one manuscript was copied from another or from several others, genealogical relationships **must** exist. The only question is whether or not we have identified such relationships, or can identify them" (p. 109). Exactly. Of course genealogical relationships must exist, or must have existed, but the **whole question** is "whether or not we have identified" them. I take it that Aland, Colwell, Klijn, Parvis, Vaganay, Wikgren, Zuntz, etc. are saying that such relationships have in fact **not** been identified. That is my point! And I insist that until such relationships are empirically demonstrated they may not legitimately be used in the practice of NT textual criticism. (Some of the above named scholars go on to affirm that we **cannot** identify such relationships, at least by direct genealogy—almost all the links are missing.)
The concepts of "text-type" and "recension", **as used by Hort** and his followers, are demonstrably erroneous. It follows that the conclusions based upon them are invalidated. But it remains true that community of reading implies a common origin, and agreement in error convicts the participants of dependence. Carson wishes to retain the term "text-type" to refer to "types of text as indexed by several remarkable extremes" (p. 109). That is fine with me, just so it is made clear to all that the term is not being used in the Hortian sense. For statements of evidence, however, I believe the editors of the UBS editions have set the correct example—no cover symbols for "text-types" are used except for "*Byz*", which refers to the Byzantine manuscript tradition.

[4] Cf. Burgon, *The Revision Revised*, p. 380.

I defy anyone, after having carefully perused the foregoing lists, and after having noted the almost incomprehensible combinations and permutations of both the uncial and cursive manuscripts, to go back to the teaching of Dr. Hort with any degree of confidence. How useless and superfluous to talk of Evan. 604 having a large "Western element," or of its siding in many places with the "neutral text." The whole question of families and recensions is thus brought prominently before the eye, and with space one could largely comment upon the deeply interesting combinations which thus present themselves to the critic. But **do** let us realize that we are in the infancy of this part of the science, and not imagine that we have successfully laid certain immutable foundation stones, and can safely continue to build thereon. It is not so, and much, if not all, of these foundations must be demolished.[1]

## The "text-types" themselves

To take the "text-types" one by one, Kenyon says of the "Western" text:

> What we have called the δ-text, indeed, is not so much a text as a congeries of various readings, not descending from any one archetype, but possessing an infinitely complicated and intricate parentage. No one manuscript can be taken as even approximately representing the δ-text, if by "text" we mean a form of the Gospel which once existed in a single manuscript.[2]

Colwell observes that the Nestle text (25th edition) denies the existence of the "Western" text as an identifiable group, saying it is "a denial with which I agree".[3] Speaking of von Soden's classification of the "Western" text, Metzger says: "so diverse are the textual phenomena that von Soden was compelled to posit seventeen sub-groups of witnesses which are more or less closely related to this text".[4] And Klijn, speaking of "a 'pure' or 'original' Western Text" affirms that "such a text did not exist".[5] K. and B. Aland speak of "the phantom 'Western text'" and replace it with "D text", referring to Codex Bezae.[6] In fact, it

---

[1] H.C. Hoskier, *A Full Account and Collation of the Greek Cursive Codex Evangelium 604* (London: David Nutt, 1890), Introduction, pp. cxv-cxvi.

[2] Kenyon, *Handbook*, p. 356. Whereas Hort used "δ group" to refer to his "Syrian" text, Kenyon uses "δ text" to refer to the "Western" text.

[3] Colwell, "The Greek New Testament with a Limited Critical Apparatus: its Nature and Uses", *Studies in New Testament and Early Christian Literature*, ed. D.E. Aune (Leiden: E.J. Brill, 1972), p. 33.

[4] Metzger, *The Text*, p. 141.

[5] Klijn, p. 64.

[6] K. and B. Aland, *The Text of the New Testament* (Grand Rapids: Eerdmans, 1987), pp. 55, 64.

has been many decades since any critical apparatus used a cover symbol for the so-called "Western" text.

As for today's "Alexandrian" text, which seems essentially to include Hort's "Neutral" and "Alexandrian", Colwell offers the results of an interesting experiment.

> After a careful study of all alleged Beta Text-type witnesses in the first chapter of Mark, six Greek manuscripts emerged as primary witnesses: ℵ B L 33 892 2427. Therefore, the weaker Beta manuscripts C Δ 157 517 579 1241 and 1342 were set aside. Then on the basis of the six primary witnesses an 'average' or mean text was reconstructed including all the readings supported by the majority of the primary witnesses. Even on this restricted basis the amount of variation recorded in the apparatus was dismaying. In this first chapter, each of the six witnesses differed from the 'average' Beta Text-type as follows: L, nineteen times (Westcott and Hort, twenty-one times); Aleph, twenty-six times; 2427, thirty-two times; 33, thirty-three times; B, thirty-four times; and 892, forty-one times. These results show convincingly that any attempt to reconstruct an archetype of the Beta Text-type on a quantitative basis is doomed to failure. The text thus reconstructed is not reconstructed but constructed; it is an artificial entity that never existed.[1] [Hear, hear!]

Hoskier, after filling 450 pages with a detailed and careful discussion of the errors in Codex B and another 400 on the idiosyncrasies of Codex ℵ, affirms that **in the Gospels alone** these two MSS differ well over 3,000 times,[2] which number does not include minor errors such as spelling, nor variants between certain synonyms which might be due to "provincial exchange".[3] In fact, on the basis of Colwell's suggestion that a 70% agreement be required so as to assign two MSS to the same text-type, Aleph and B do not qualify. The UBS and Nestle texts no longer use a cover symbol for the "Alexandrian" text-type.

Of the "Byzantine" text, Zuntz says that "the great bulk of Byzantine manuscripts defies all attempts to group them".[4] Clark says much the same:

---

[1] Colwell, "The Significance of Grouping of New Testament Manuscripts", *New Testament Studies*, IV (1957-1958), 86-87. Cf. also Colwell, "Genealogical Method", pp. 119-123. Colwell follows Kenyon and uses "Beta text-type" to refer to today's "Alexandrian" text, whereas Hort used "$\beta$ group" to refer to his "Western" text.

[2] The demands of logic require that one or the other (perhaps both) must be wrong at those points. More will be said about this in chapter six.

[3] H.C. Hoskier, *Codex B and its Allies* (2 vols.; London: Bernard Quaritch, 1914), II, 1.

[4] Zuntz, "The Byzantine Text in New Testament Criticism", *The Journal of Theological Studies*, XLIII (1942), 25.

The main conclusion regarding the Byzantine text is that it was extremely fluid. Any single manuscript may be expected to show a score of shifting affinities. Yet within the variety and confusion, a few textual types have been distinguished... These types are not closely grouped like the families, but are like the broad Milky Way including many members within a general affinity.[1]

Colwell's emphatic statement to the same effect has been given above. The work of Lake referred to by Colwell was a collation of Mark, chapter eleven, in all the MSS of Mt. Sinai, Patmos, and the Patriarchal Library and collection of St. Saba at Jerusalem. Lake, with R. P. Blake and Silva New, found that the "Byzantine" text was not homogeneous, that there was an absence of close relationship between MSS, but that there was less variation "within the family" than would be found in a similar treatment of "Neutral" or "Caesarean" texts. In their own words:

> This collation covers three of the great ancient collections of MSS; and these are not modern conglomerations, brought together from all directions. Many of the MSS, now at Sinai, Patmos, and Jerusalem, must be copies written in the scriptoria of these monasteries. We expected to find that a collation covering all the MSS in each library would show many cases of direct copying. But there are practically no such cases... Moreover, the amount of direct genealogy which has been detected in extant codices is almost negligible. Nor are many known MSS sister codices. The Ferrar group and family 1 are the only reported cases of the repeated copying of a single archetype, and even for the Ferrar group there were probably two archetypes rather than one...

> There are cognate groups—families of distant cousins—but the manuscripts which we have are almost all orphan children without brothers or sisters.

> Taking this fact into consideration along with the negative result of our collation of MSS at Sinai, Patmos, and Jerusalem, it is hard to resist the conclusion that the scribes usually destroyed their exemplars when they had copied the sacred books.[2]

---

[1] Clark, "The Manuscripts of the Greek New Testament", *New Testament Manuscript Studies*, ed. M.M. Parvis and A.P. Wikgren (Chicago: The University of Chicago Press, 1950), p. 12.

[2] K. Lake, R.P. Blake and Silva New, "The Caesarean Text of the Gospel of Mark", *Harvard Theological Review*, XXI (1928), 348-49. The more recent work of Frederick Wisse furnishes a strong objective demonstration of the diversity within the "Byzantine" textform. *The Profile Method for Classifying and Evaluating Manuscript Evidence* (Grand Rapids: Eerdmans, 1982), is an application of the "Claremont Profile Method" to **1,386** MSS in Luke 1, 10 and 20. He isolated 15 major groupings of MSS (which sub-divide into at least 70 subgroups), plus 22 smaller groups, plus 89 "mavericks" (MSS so mixed that they neither fit into any of the above groupings nor form groupings among themselves). One of the 15 "major" groups is the "Egyptian"

J.W. Burgon,[1] because he had himself collated numerous minuscule MSS, had remarked the same thing years before Lake.

> Now those many MSS were executed demonstrably at different times in different countries. They bear signs in their many hundreds of representing the entire area of the Church, except where versions were used instead of copies in the original Greek.... And yet, of multitudes of them that survive, hardly any have been copied from any of the rest. On the contrary, they are discovered to differ among themselves in countless unimportant particulars; and every here and there single copies exhibit idiosyncrasies which are altogether startling and extraordinary. There has therefore demonstrably been no collusion—no assimilation to an arbitrary standard—no wholesale fraud. It is certain that every one of them represents a MS, or a pedigree of MSS, older than itself; and it is but fair to suppose that it exercises such representation with tolerable accuracy.[2]

Kurt Aland[3] sums it up:

> P[66] confirmed the observations already made in connection with the Chester Beatty papyri. With P[75] new ground has been opened to us. Earlier, we all shared the opinion, in agreement with our professors and in accord with NT scholarship, before and since Westcott and Hort, that, in various places, during the fourth century, recensions of the NT text had been made, from which the main text-types then developed....We spoke of recensions and text-types,

---

("Alexandrian")—it is made up of precisely four (04) uncials and four (04) cursives, plus two more of each that were "Egyptian" in one of the three chapters. If I understand him correctly he considers that virtually all the remaining MSS fall into the broad "Byzantine" stream. In other words, when we talk of examining the "Byzantine" text there are at least 36 strands of transmission that need to be considered!

[1] John William Burgon was Dean of Chichester from 1876 until his death in 1888. His biographer declared him to be "the leading religious teacher of his time" in England (E.M. Goulburn, *Life of Dean Burgon*, 2 Vols.; London: John Murray, 1892, I, vii). Clark lists Burgon along with Tregelles and Scrivener as "great contemporaries" of Tischendorf, whom he calls "the colossus among textual critics" ("The Manuscripts of the Greek New Testament", p. 9). As a contemporary of Westcott and Hort, Burgon strenuously opposed their text and theory and is generally acknowledged to have been the leading voice in the 'opposition' (cf. A.F. Hort, II, 239).

[2] J.W. Burgon, *The Traditional Text of the Holy Gospels Vindicated and Established*, arranged, completed, and edited by Edward Miller (London: George Bell and Sons, 1896), pp. 46-47.

[3] Kurt Aland, former Director of the *Institut fur neutestamentliche Textforschung* at Munster, was perhaps the leading textual critic in Europe until his death (1995). He was a co-editor of both the most popular editions of the Greek N.T.—Nestle and U.B.S. He was the one who cataloged each new MS that was discovered.

and if this was not enough, we referred to pre-Caesarean and other text-types, to mixed texts, and so on.

I, too, have spoken of mixed texts, in connection with the form of the NT text in the second and third centuries, but I have always done so with a guilty conscience. For, according to the rules of linguistic philology it is impossible to speak of mixed texts before recensions have been made (they only can follow them), whereas, the NT manuscripts of the second and third centuries which have a "mixed text" clearly existed before recensions were made....The simple fact that all these papyri, with their various distinctive characteristics, did exist side by side, in the same ecclesiastical province, that is, in Egypt, where they were found, is the best argument against the existence of any text-types, including the Alexandrian and the Antiochian. We still live in the world of Westcott and Hort with our conception of different recensions and text-types, although this conception has lost its *raison d'être*, or, it needs at least to be newly and convincingly demonstrated. For, the increase of the documentary evidence and the entirely new areas of research which were opened to us on the discovery of the papyri, mean the end of Westcott and Hort's conception.[1]

I have quoted men like Zuntz, Clark and Colwell on the "Byzantine" text to show that modern scholars are prepared to reject the notion of a "Byzantine" recension, but the main lesson to be drawn from the variation among "Byzantine" MSS is the one noted by Lake and Burgon—they are orphans, independent witnesses; at least in their generation. The variation between two "Byzantine" MSS will be found to differ both in number and severity from that between two "Western" MSS or two "Alexandrian" MSS—the number and nature of the disagreements between two "Byzantine" MSS throughout the Gospels will seem trivial compared to the number (over 3,000) and nature (many serious) of the disagreements between Aleph and B, the chief "Alexandrian" MSS, in the same space.

## *A recent return*

Both Colwell[2] and Epp[3] take issue with Aland, claiming that the papyri fit right in with Hort's reconstruction of textual history. But the existence of an affinity between B and P[75] does not demonstrate the existence of a text-type or recension. We have just seen Colwell's demonstration and declaration that an "Alexandrian" archetype never existed. Epp himself, after going on to plot the early MSS on three trajectories ("Neutral", "Western" and "midway"), says:

---

[1] Aland, "The Significance of the Papyri", pp. 334-37.

[2] Colwell, "Hort Redivivus", pp. 156-57.

[3] Epp, pp. 396-97.

Naturally, this rough sketch should not be understood to mean that the manuscripts mentioned under each of the three categories above necessarily had any **direct** connections one with another; rather, they stand as randomly surviving members of these three broad streams of textual tradition.[1]

The point is, although different manuscripts exhibit varying affinities, share certain peculiarities, they each differ substantially from all the others (especially the earlier ones) and therefore should not be lumped together. There is no such thing as the testimony of a "Western" or "Alexandrian" text-type (as an entity)—there is only the testimony of individual MSS, Fathers, Versions (or MSS of versions).

In disagreeing with Aland, Epp declared that our extant materials reveal "only two clear textual streams or trajectories" in the first four centuries of textual transmission, namely the "Neutral" and "Western" text-types.[2] He also suggested that $P^{75}$ may be considered as an early ancestor for Hort's "Neutral" text, $P^{66}$ for Hort's "Alexandrian" text, and $P^{45}$ for Hort's "Western" text.

But he himself had just finished furnishing counter evidence. Thus, with reference to 103 variation units in Mark 6-9 (where $P^{45}$ is extant), Epp records that $P^{45}$ shows a 38 percent agreement with Codex D, 40 percent with the *Textus Receptus*, 42 percent with B, 59 percent with $f^{13}$, and 68 percent with W.[3] How can Epp say that $P^{45}$ is a "Western" ancestor when it is closer to chief representatives of every other "text-type" than it is to D? In Mark 5-16, Epp records that Codex W shows a 34 percent agreement with B, 36 percent with D, 38 percent with the *Textus Receptus*, and 40 percent with א.[4] To which "textual stream" should W be assigned?

Both $P^{66}$ and $P^{75}$ have been generally affirmed to belong to the "Alexandrian text-type".[5] Klijn offers the results of a comparison of א, B, $P^{45}$, $P^{66}$ and $P^{75}$ in the passages where they are all extant (John 10:7-25, 10:32-11:10, 11:19-33 and 11:43-56). He considered only those places where א and B disagree *and* where at least one of the papyri joins either א or B. He found eight such places *plus* 43 where all three of the papyri line up with א or B. He stated the result for the 43 places as follows (to which I have added figures for the *Textus Receptus*, BFBS 1946):

---

[1] *Ibid.*, p. 398.

[2] *Ibid.*, p. 397.

[3] *Ibid.*, pp. 394-96.

[4] Ibid.

[5] Cf. Metzger, *A Textual Commentary on the Greek New Testament* (London: United Bible Societies, 1971), p. xviii.

P[45]   agrees  with  ℵ 19 times, with B 24 times, with TR 32 times,
P[66]   agrees  with  ℵ 14 times, with B 29 times, with TR 33 times,
P[75]   agrees  with  ℵ  9 times, with B 33 times, with TR 29 times,
P[45,66,75] agree with  ℵ  4 times, with B 18 times, with TR 20 times,
P[45,66]  agree  with  ℵ  7 times, with B  3 times, with TR  8 times,
P[45,75]  agree  with  ℵ  1 time,  with B  2 times, with TR  2 times,
P[66,75]  agree  with  ℵ  0 times, with B  8 times, with TR  5 times.[1]

As for the eight other places,

P[45] agrees with ℵ 2 times, with B 1 time,  with TR 1 time,
P[66] agrees with ℵ 2 times, with B 3 times, with TR 5 times,
P[75] agrees with ℵ 2 times, with B 3 times, with TR 4 times.[2]

(Each of the three papyri has other readings as well.)

Is the summary assignment of P[66] and P[75] to the "Alexandrian text-type" altogether reasonable?

G.D. Fee goes to considerable lengths to interpret the evidence in such a way as to support his conclusion that "P[66] is basically a member of the Neutral tradition",[3] but the evidence itself as he records it, for John 1-14, is as follows: P[66] agrees with the TR 315 times out of 663 (47.5%), with P[75] 280 out of 547

---

[1] Klijn, pp. 45-48.

[2] *Ibid.* I have used Klijn's study with reference to the existence of texttypes, but his material also furnishes evidence for the antiquity of the "Byzantine" text. Summing up the evidence for the 51 instances Klijn discusses,

P[45] agrees with Aleph 21 times, with B 25 times, with TR 33 times,

P[66] agrees with Aleph 16 times, with B 32 times, with TR 38 times,

P[75] agrees with Aleph 11 times, with B 36 times, with TR 33 times;
or to put it another way,

all three papyri agree  with Aleph  4 times, with B 18 times, with TR 20 times,
any two of them agree   with Aleph  8 times, with B 13 times, with TR 15 times,
just one of them agrees with Aleph 36 times, with B 62 times, with TR 69 times,
for a total of                     48 times,       93 times,        104 times.
In other words, in the area covered by Klijn's study the TR has more early attestation than B and twice as much as Aleph—evidently the TR reflects an earlier text than either B or Aleph! It is clear that P[75] is closer to B than to Aleph, but almost as close to TR as to B. That this is not a 'fluke' is evident from the following: where P[75] and B disagree, one or the other is always with the Byzantine text, about even on both sides, which implies that the Byzantine must be older. The copyist who produced P[75] must have had a Byzantine exemplar in front of him.

[3] G.D. Fee, Papyrus Bodmer II (P[66]): Its Textual Relationships and Scribal Characteristics (Salt Lake City: University of Utah Press, 1968), p. 56.

(51.2%), with B 334 out of 663 (50.4%), with ℵ 295 out of 662 (44.6%), with A 245 out of 537 (45.6%), with C 150 out of 309 (48.5%), with D 235 out of 604 (38.9%), with W 298 out of 662 (45.0%).[1]

Does this evidence really suggest "two clear textual streams"?

> In these third-century manuscripts, whose evidence takes us back into the mid-second century at least, we find no pristine purity, no unsullied ancestors of Vaticanus, but marred and fallen representatives of the original text. Features of all the main texts isolated by Hort or von Soden are here found—very differently 'mingled' in P[66] and P[45].[2]

## The classifying of MSS

A serious part of the problem is the manner in which MSS have been assigned to one "text-type" or another. For example, the editors of P[1] (Oxyrh. 2), Grenfell and Hunt, stated that "the papyrus clearly belongs to the same class as the Sinaitic and Vatican codices, and has no Western or Syrian proclivities". The papyrus contains only Matt.1:1-9a,12b-20 (not all of it legible) but C.H. Turner declared that it agrees closely with the text of B and "may be fairly held to carry back the whole B text of the Gospels into the third century".[3] To this day P[1] is assigned to the "Alexandrian text-type".[4] It evidently agrees with B seven times, against the TR, but four of those variants have some "Western" support; however it **dis**agrees with B ten times, albeit supporting the TR in only two of those.[5] Is it really reasonable to lump P[1] and B together?

For a clear demonstration of the folly of characterizing a manuscript on the basis of just one chapter (or even less!) the reader is referred to the study of P[66] by Fee. He plots the percentage of agreement between P[66] and the TR, P[75], B, ℵ, A, C, D, and W respectively, chapter by chapter, throughout the first 14 chapters of John.[6] For each of the documents the graph bounces up and down from chapter to chapter in an erratic fashion. All of them show a range of variation in excess of 30%—e.g. Codex B goes from 71.1% agreement with P[66] in chapter 5 to 32.3% agreement in chapter 7.

---

[1] *Ibid.*, p. 14.

[2] J.N. Birdsall, *The Bodmer Papyrus of the Gospel of John* (London, 1960), p. 17.

[3] C.H. Turner, "Historical Introduction to the Textual Criticism of the New Testament", *Journal of Theological Studies*, Jan. 1910, p. 185.

[4] Metzger, *The Text*, p. 247; Epp, "Interlude", p. 397.

[5] Hoskier, *Codex B*, p. xi.

[6] Fee, *Bodmer II,* pp. 12-13.

It has already been noted that B and Aleph disagree well over 3,000 times just in the Gospels. (Their agreements are fewer.)[1] Should they be lumped together? It is not enough to notice only the shared peculiarities between two MSS; the extent of disagreement is equally germane to any effort at classification.[2]

Rather than lining up in "clear streams" or "text-types" (as objectively defined entities) the earliest manuscripts are dotted helter-skelter over a wide spectrum of variation. Although varying degrees of affinity exist between and among them, they should be treated as individuals in the practice of textual criticism. Until such time as the relationships among the later manuscripts are empirically plotted, they also should be treated as individuals. To dump them into a "Byzantine" basket is untenable.

Since genealogy has not been (and cannot be?) applied to the MSS, the witnesses must be counted, after all—including many of the later minuscules, which evidently had independent lines of transmission. It will immediately be protested that "witnesses are to be weighed, not counted". Because of the importance of this question I will discuss it in some detail, in its turn.[3] But first, we must continue our evaluation of the W-H theory and for that purpose I will still speak of "text-types" in Hort's terms.

## Conflation

Hort's whole case against the *Textus Receptus*, under this heading was based upon just *eight* examples, taken from two Gospels (Mark and Luke). To characterize a whole text for the whole New Testament on the basis of eight examples is foolish. Colwell states the problem well.

> No text or document is homogeneous enough to justify judgment on the basis of *part* of its readings for the rest of its readings. This was Hort's Achilles' heel. He is saying here that since these eight conflate readings occur in the Syrian text that text as a whole is a mixed text; if a manuscript or text lacks these readings, it is in its other readings a witness to a text antecedent to mixture...

---

[1] A hurried count using Nestle's (24th) critical apparatus (I assume that any agreement of ℵ and B will infallibly be recorded) shows them agreeing 3,007 times, where there is variation. Of these roughly 1,100 are against the "Byzantine" text, with or without other attestation, while the rest are against a small minority of MSS (several hundreds being singular readings of Codex D, one of the papyri, etc.). It appears that B and Aleph do not meet Colwell's requirement of 70 percent agreement in order to be classified in the same text-type.

[2] This is one of the central features in the method proposed by Colwell and E.W. Tune in "The Quantitative Relationships between MS Text-Types", *Biblical and Patristic Studies in Memory of Robert Pierce Casey*, eds. J.N. Birdsall and R.W. Thomson (Frieberg: Herder, 1963).

[3] See the section with that heading in Chapter 6.

Westcott and Hort state this fallacy very clearly in their argument for the importance of the evidence of a document as over against readings:

"Where then one of the documents is found habitually to contain these morally certain or at least strongly preferred readings, and the other habitually to contain their rejected rivals, we can have no doubt, first, that the text of the first has been transmitted in comparative purity, and that the text of the second has suffered comparatively large corruption; and, next, that the *superiority of the first must be as great in the variations in which Internal Evidence of Readings has furnished no decisive criterion as in those which have enabled us to form a comparative appreciation of the two texts.*" [Emphasis his.]

This would be true if we knew that there was no mixture involved and that manuscripts and texts were rigorously homogeneous. Everything we have learned since Hort confirms the opposite position.[1]

It has been generally supposed and stated that there are many other examples. Thus Harrison says, "Another objection was the paucity of

---

[1] Colwell, "Genealogical Method", p. 118. In spite of this demonstrably correct statement by Colwell, Bart Ehrman, in his M.Div. thesis at Princeton, 1981, virtually repeats Hort's words:

> ...two points must constantly be kept in mind. First, if a reading were proved to be a conflation, then the documents containing it—to a greater or lesser extent—would preserve a text that is mixed (by definition). This is true, that is to say, if only one proved instance of conflation should be found in these documents. And since most mixing would have resulted in non-conflated readings, i.e. in the arbitrary or intentional choice by a transcriber of one manuscript's reading over another's, then the solitary proven case of mixture would indicate that more numerous instances exist which cannot be so readily demonstrated. Second, the textual character of groups of documents can be fairly assessed by ascertaining the degree to which they contain conflations. If, for example, there are two groups of documents that never contain conflated readings, and one that sometimes does, then clearly the latter group must represent a mixed text. Whether the other groups do or not is indeterminable by this criterion. But the point is that even isolated instances of mixture do show that a text is mixed, and hence both late and secondary in its witness to the true text. Hort's contention was that the Syrian text, and the Syrian alone, contained conflations. Whether it contained eight or eight hundred would be immaterial on this score. The simple presence of conflations of any number prove the text to be mixed ("New Testament Textual Criticism: Quest for Methodology", pp. 55-56).

It has been demonstrated repeatedly that the textual quality of a MS may change significantly from chapter to chapter, let alone from book to book. A proved conflation does indeed convict its MS of mixture at that point, but only at that point. Ehrman's statement about "eight or eight hundred" is simply stupid. Even the eight examples that Hort adduced have all been challenged, and by scholars with differing presuppositions.

examples of conflation. Hort cited only eight, but he could have given others."[1] Kenyon and Lake made the same claim,[2] but where are the "other" examples? Why does not Harrison, or Kenyon, or Lake produce them? Because there are very few that have the required phenomena. Kenyon does refer in passing to *An Atlas of Textual Criticism* by E. A. Hutton (London: Cambridge University Press, 1911) which he says contains added examples of conflation.

Upon inspection, the central feature of the 125-page work proves to be a purportedly complete list of triple variant readings in the New Testament where the "Alexandrian", "Western" and "Byzantine" texts are pitted against each other. Hutton adduces 821 instances exhibiting the required phenomenon. Out of all that, a few cases of possible "Syrian conflation", aside from Hort's eight, may be culled—such as in Matt. 27:41, John 18:40, Acts 20:28 or Rom. 6:12. Fifty years ago a Hortian might have insisted that John 10:31 also has a "Syrian conflation", but now that P[66] moves the "Syrian" reading back to 200 AD a different interpretation is demanded.

Hutton's list may well be open to considerable question, but if we may take it at face value for the moment it appears that the ratio of "Alexandrian-Western-Byzantine" triple variants to possible "Syrian conflations" is about l00:1. In other words, for every instance where the "Syrian" text is possibly built on the "Neutral" and "Western" texts there are a hundred where it is *not*.

That raises another problem. If the "Syrian" text is eclectic, where did it get the material that is its private property? As Burgon observed at the time: "It is impossible to 'conflate' in places where B, ℵ and their associates furnish no materials for the supposed conflation. Bricks cannot be made without clay. The materials actually existing are those of the Traditional Text itself."[3]

But there is another consideration which is fatal to Hort's purpose. He claimed that inversions do not exist; but they do. He himself cited one of each kind; D conflates in John 5:37 and B conflates in Col. 1:12 and 2 Thess. 3:4.[4] Further,

---

[1] Harrison, p. 73.

[2] Kenyon, *Handbook*, p. 302; Lake, p. 68. Ehrman states that "it is significant that other examples can be found with little difficulty. Hort provided four examples of conflation from Mark and four from Luke; the following examples complement his list, four being from Matthew and four from John" (*Ibid.*, p. 56). He gives examples from Matt. 10:3, 22:13, 27:23, 27:41 and John 5:37, 9:25, 10:31, 17:23. All these may be found in Appendix D except for John 9:25, because the "Western" reading has no Greek attestation and is therefore not valid for the present purpose. Ehrman misstates the evidence for John 5:37, giving a false impression. In Appendix D I speak to all these examples, plus all of Hort's eight.

[3] Burgon, The Traditional Text, p. 229.

[4] Westcott and Hort, p. 94 and pp. 240-41. (Since Hort regarded D and B as adequate to represent the "Western" and "Neutral" texts elsewhere, he should not object here.) But Ehrman favors us with the following:

What is most noteworthy is that the significance of such 'inversions' is rarely explained by advocates of the Majority text. Pickering, for instance, is content to

there are a number of other conflations, not only on the part of D, B, and Aleph, but also the "Western" and "Alexandrian" text-types. Please see Appendix D for examples and evidence. Marcion (2nd century) conflates the "Byzantine" and "Neutral-Western" readings in 1 Corinthians 14:19!

Bodmer II shows some "Syrian" readings to be *anterior* to corresponding "Neutral" readings around 200 A.D.

> The Bodmer John (P[66]) is also a witness to the early existence of many of the readings found in the Alpha text-type (Hort's "Syrian"). Strangely enough to our previous ideas, the contemporary corrections in that papyrus frequently change an Alpha-type reading to a Beta-type reading (Hort's "Neutral"). This indicates that at this early period readings of both kinds were known, and the Beta-type

---

list the inverted conflations, apparently assuming that this alone negates Hort's contention. But there are two considerations that obviate any appeal to these inversions for the purpose of critiquing Hort's basic position on the late and secondary nature of the Syrian text. In the first place, most of the instances that have been granted as genuine inversions occur in isolated members of a text-type, but not throughout the larger grouping itself. [He had finished his thesis before he saw my Appendix D, which was not in the first edition.] In other words, the three cases of conflation in Codex B do not indicate that the Alexandrian text-type is mixed, but only that B is. And the fact that B was transcribed in the 4th century would suggest that in some cases it might be expected to contain evidence of mixture from prior texts. [An interesting admission.] This can hardly vitiate Hort's proof, since he himself acknowledged the presence of conflations in both D and B, in the latter case, especially in the Pauline epistles.[!]

Secondly, by adducing this kind of argument against Westcott and Hort, the advocates of the Majority text have placed themselves on the horns of a dilemma. On the one hand, if they choose to deny the validity of Hort's assertion—that a text containing conflations is secondary, and that the more conflations it contains the less it is a trustworthy witness to the original text—then an appeal to inverted conflations is no argument at all. If conflations do not show that a text is secondary, then why point to them? In such a case, contrary examples would only show Hort's error in assuming that Syrian texts alone contain conflations, but would indicate absolutely nothing about the character of the respective text-types. Thus, clearly, the argument is viable only if Hort's premise is accepted.

But, on the other hand, by accepting this premise, the advocates of the Majority text are faced with a serious problem. If the Alexandrian and Western text-types contain conflations, then all three texts are late and secondary (*Ibid.*, pp. 60-61).

Either Ehrman misses the point or he is being duplicitous. Of course we advocates of the Majority text recognize that a conflation is a secondary reading, of necessity. If all three text-types contain conflations, "then all three texts are late and secondary". Just so! And that invalidates Hort's use of "conflation" to disqualify the "Syrian" text. Since the "Alexandrian" and "Western" texts both contain evident conflations, they are both secondary. If Hort had only admitted that at the outset, a great deal of needless debate would have been spared. However, I have yet to see any putative "Byzantine" conflation that impresses me as really being one—Appendix D gives numerous examples with 2nd or 3rd century attestation; if any is a conflation it is an early one. (Of course, a genuine conflation is by definition secondary even if created in A.D. 100!)

were supplanting the Alpha-type—at least as far as this witness is concerned.[1]

Hoskier, after his thorough (450 pages) study of Codex B, offered this verdict: "the maligned Textus Receptus served in large measure as the base which B tampered with and changed."[2] The evidence from $P^{66}$ is decidedly inconvenient to the Hortian theory. The first hand has Byzantine readings that a corrector changed to Alexandrian ones—the Byzantine text-type existed in 200 A.D.

It is clear that Hort's characterization of the "Syrian" text as eclectic and secondary, as posterior to and building upon the "Western" and "Neutral" texts, does not square with the evidence. But while we are on the subject, what of Hort's eight examples; do they lend themselves to his interpretation? We must ask whether they really qualify as possible conflations and then consider the reverse explanation, namely that the shorter forms are independent simplifications of the original long form.

Burgon examined the eight at length and observed that most of them simply do not exhibit the required phenomena.[3] The reader may see for himself by consulting any reasonably complete *apparatus criticus* (all are included in Appendix D). Whatever explanation may be given of the origin of the "Byzantine" readings in Mark 8:25, Luke 11:54, and Luke 12:18, they are not "conflations" of the "Neutral" and "Western" readings. The same thing may be said, though not so emphatically, about Mark 6:33 and Luke 9:10.

In almost every case the witnesses within the "Neutral" and "Western" camps are divided among themselves, so that a somewhat arbitrary choice has to be made in order to give *the* "Neutral" or "Western" reading. Hort approached his discussion of the eight examples of conflation he adduced "premising that we do not attempt to notice every petty variant in the passages cited, for fear of confusing the substantial evidence".[4]

But in a question of this sort the confusion must be accounted for. If the "Neutral" witnesses disagree among themselves, what credence can we give to the "Neutral" testimony as a whole?

Given an instance, such as Luke 24:53, where the required phenomena for a conflation are present, it must be demonstrated that the two shorter readings did not arise through independent omissions of different parts of the longer reading before it can be asserted that conflation took place. Apart from such demonstration it is not fair to assume a conflation and then build a theory upon

---

[1] Colwell, "The Origin of Texttypes", pp. 130-31.

[2] Hoskier, *Codex B*, I, 465.

[3] Burgon, *The Revision Revised*, pp. 257-65.

[4] Westcott and Hort, p. 95.

it. Hort's total demonstration relative to Luke 24:53 is, "This simple instance needs no explanation".[1]

Burgon (who personally collated D) observed that in the last chapter of Luke the Received Text has 837 words—of these D omits 121, or one word in seven.[2] To someone using Nestle's Text (24th) D omits 66 out of 782, or one in twelve (Nestle has omitted thirty-eight words from the Greek text of Luke 24 on the sole Greek authority of D, and another five on D and ℵ alone).

In the face of such an inveterate propensity for omission, it is not unreasonable to suspect that in verse 53 D has omitted "and blessing" from the original "praising and blessing" rather than that the reading of all but six of the extant Greek MSS is a conflation. Furthermore, the reading of D may easily have arisen from the "Byzantine" by homoioteleuton (*OYNTEC...OYNTEC*). Kilpatrick is among the most recent of a number of scholars who have argued that at least some of Hort's "Syrian conflations" are the original reading.[3]

K. Lake spoke of the problem of deciding which interpretation to take.

> The keystone of their [W-H] theory is in the passages where we get this triple variation, and the point of the argument lies in the assumption that the longer reading is made by uniting the two shorter ones—not the two shorter by different dealings with the longer. This point can be tested only by an appeal to Patristic evidence and general probability.
>
> The latter argument is precarious because subjective, so that the ultimate and decisive criterion is Patristic evidence.[4]

It appears, according to Lake, that patristic evidence is to decide the issue. But neither Lake nor anyone else has produced any Patristic citations of these passages in the first three centuries. The few citations available after that time all support the Byzantine readings.[5]

Actually, the whole matter of "conflation" is a pseudo-issue, a tempest in a teapot. There simply are not enough putative examples to support generalizations. Such evidence as there is, however, is certainly not

---

[1] *Ibid.*, p. 104.

[2] Burgon, The Revision Revised, p. 264.

[3] G.D. Kilpatrick, "The Greek New Testament Text of Today and the *Textus Receptus*", *The New Testament in Historical and Contemporary Perspective*, H. Anderson and W. Barclay, eds. (Oxford: Basil Blackwell, 1965), pp. 190-92. Cf. Bousset, *TU*, vol. 11 (1894), pp. 97-101, who agreed with Hort on only one of the eight.

[4] Lake, p. 68.

[5] Victor of Antioch for Mark 8:26, 9:38 and 9:49; Basil for Mark 9:38 and Luke 12:18; Cyril of Alexandria for Luke 12:18; Augustine for Mark 9:38.

unfavorable to the "Syrian" text. As Zuntz says, the idea that the late text was derived from the two earlier "recensions" combined is erroneous.[1]

# "Syrian" Readings Before Chrysostom

Hort's statements concerning the nature of the ante-Nicene patristic testimony are still widely believed. Thus, Chrysostom is widely affirmed to have used the "Byzantine" text.[2] But, Lake has stated:

> Writers on the text of the New Testament usually copy from one another the statement that Chrysostom used the Byzantine, or Antiochian, text. But directly any investigation is made it appears evident, even from the printed text of his works, that there are many important variations in the text he quotes, which was evidently not identical with that found in the MSS of the Byzantine text.[3]

Metzger calls attention to the work of Geerlings and New.

> It has often been stated by textual scholars that Chrysostom was one of the first Fathers to use the Antiochian text. This opinion was examined by Jacob Geerlings and Silva New in a study based on evidence which, in default of a critical edition; was taken from Migne's edition of Chrysostom's *opera*. Their conclusions are that "Chrysostom's text of Mark is not that of any group of manuscripts so far discovered and classified....His text of Mark, or rather the text which can faintly be perceived through his quotations, is a 'mixed

---

[1] Zuntz, *The Text*, p. 12. Sturz (pp. 70-76) has a chapter entitled, "Byzantine-Western Alignments Go Back Into The Second Century Independently And Originate In The East—Not In The West". He makes heavy use of Zuntz' work and concludes that

> ...his findings deal a devastating blow to WH's basic theory of the history of the text, i.e. they destroy the supposed partial dependence of the K-text on Western sources.

> If this dependence in K-Western alignments must be reversed as Zuntz demonstrates, then one half of the support for Hort's basic theory of conflation collapses immediately! But, not only does the WH theory fail at this point, it is changed into the opposite! This is more than the "general consensus of scholarship" can concede. It is an intolerable thought and too revolutionary to acknowledge that the Antiochian text may have been the source rather than the recipient of the common material in such Byzantine-Western alignments (p. 76).

I have not knowingly misrepresented Zuntz, or Colwell, Metzger, Aland, etc., in quoting from their works. I take it that Colwell does reject Hort's notion of genealogy, that Aland does reject Hort's notion of recensions, that Zuntz does reject Hort's notion of "Syrian" conflation, and so on. However, I do not mean to imply, and it should not be assumed, that any of these scholars would entirely agree with my statement of the situation at any point, and they certainly do not agree (so far as I know) with my total position.

[2] Westcott and Hort, p. 91.

[3] Lake, p. 53.

text' combining some of the elements of each of the types which had flourished before the end of the fourth century."[1]

They say further: "No known manuscript of Mark has the text found in Chrysostom's homilies, or anything approaching it. And probably no text which existed in the fourth century came much nearer to it."[2] They did a collation of Chrysostom's text and observe concerning it: "The number of variants from the Textus Receptus is not appreciably smaller than the number of variants from Westcott and Hort's text. This proves that it is no more a typical representative of the late text (von Soden's **K**) than it is of the Neutral text."[3]

What about Origen; does he really represent the "Neutral" text?

> It is impossible to reproduce or restore the text of Origen. Origen had no settled text. A reference to the innumerable places where he is upon *both* sides of the question, as set forth in detail herein, will show this clearly. Add the places where he is in direct opposition to אand B, and we must reconsider the whole position.[4]

Zuntz agrees.

> The insuperable difficulties opposing the establishment of 'the' New Testament text of Origen and Eusebius are well known to all who have attempted it....Leaving aside the common difficulties imposed by the uncertainties of the transmission, the incompleteness of the material, and the frequent freedom of quotation, there is the incontestable fact that these two Fathers are frequently at variance; that each of them quotes the same passage differently in different writings; and that sometimes they do so even within the compass of one and the same work....Wherever one and the same passage is extant in more than one quotation by Origen or Eusebius, variation between them is the rule rather than the exception.[5]

Metzger affirms: "Origen knows of the existence of variant readings which represent each of the main families of manuscripts that modern scholars have isolated."[6] (That includes the "Byzantine".) Edward Miller, in his exhaustive study of the Fathers, found that Origen sided with the Traditional Text 460

---

[1] Metzger, *Chapters*, p. 21.

[2] J. Geerlings and S. New, "Chrysostom's Text of The Gospel of Mark", *Harvard Theological Review*, XXIV (1931), 135.

[3] *Ibid.*, p. 141.

[4] Hoskier, *Codex B*, I, ii-iii.

[5] Zuntz, *The Text*, p. 152.

[6] Metzger, "Explicit References in the Works of Origen to Variant Readings in N.T. MSS.", *Biblical and Patristic Studies in Memory of Robert Pierce Casey*, ed. J.N. Birdsall and R.W. Thomson (New York: Herder, 1963), p. 94.

times while siding with the "Neologian" text 491 times.[1] (The "Neologian"[2] text, as Miller used the term, includes both "Neutral" and "Western" readings; while "Traditional Text" is his term for Hort's "Syrian" text.) How then could Hort say of Origen, "On the other hand his quotations to the best of our belief exhibit no clear and tangible traces of the Syrian text"?[3]

What about Irenaeus; does he really represent the "Western" text? Miller found that Irenaeus sided with the Traditional Text 63 times and with the "Neologian" text 41 times.[4] He said further:

> Hilary of Poictiers is far from being against the Traditional Text, as has been frequently said: though in his commentaries he did not use so Traditional a text as in his *De Trinitate* and his other works. The texts of Hippolytus, Methodius, Irenaeus, and even of Justin, are not of that exclusively Western character which Dr. Hort ascribes to them. Traditional readings occur almost equally with others in Justin's works, and predominate in the works of the other three.[5]

Hoskier adds a word concerning Hippolytus.

> Let us take another most interesting witness, viz. *Hippolytus*, who, like *Lucifer*, frequently quotes at such length from both Old and New Testaments that it is absolutely beyond question that he was **copying** from his exemplar of the Scriptures.

> Hippolytus cites 1 Thess. iv.13-17, 2 Thess. ii.1-12, in full. In the face of these quotations it is seen how loosely Turner argues when he says "Hort was the last and perhaps the ablest of a long line of editors of the Greek Testament, commencing in the eighteenth century, who very tentatively at first, but quite ruthlessly in the end, *threw over the LATER in favor of the EARLIER Greek MSS*, and that issue will never have to be tried again."

> But permit me to ask what Mr. Turner means by this lighthearted sentence. What does he mean by earlier and later Manuscripts? He cannot mean that Hippolytus' manuscript was later than that of B? Yet, allow me to state that in these long passages, comprising twelve consecutive verses from one epistle and four from the other,

---

[1] Burgon, *The Traditional Text*, pp. 100, 121.

[2] To be precise, the Greek text used by the English Revisers in 1881 is meant here, or rather those places where it differs from the TR.

[3] Westcott and Hort, p. 114.

[4] Burgon, The Traditional Text, p. 99.

[5] *Ibid.*, p. 117.

Hippolytus' early third-century MS is found generally on the side of what Turner would call the "later" MSS.[1]

According to Miller's study, the advantage of the Traditional Text over the "Neologian" before Origen was actually 2:1, setting aside Justin Martyr, Heracleon, Clement of Alexandria and Tertullian. If these four are included, the advantage of the Traditional Text drops to 1.33:1 since the confusion which is most obvious in Origen is already observable in these men. From Origen to Macarius Magnus the advantage of the Traditional Text drops to 1.24:1 while from Macarius to 400 A.D. it is back up to 2:1.[2] Please note that the Traditional Text was always ahead, even in the worst of times.

## Miller vs. Kenyon

Because of the importance of Miller's study, already cited, I will now consider it more in detail along with Kenyon's answer. Miller saw clearly the crucial nature of Hort's proposition.

> It is evident that the turning point of the controversy between ourselves and the Neologian school must lie in the centuries before St. Chrysostom. If, as Dr. Hort maintains, the Traditional Text not only gained supremacy at that era but did not exist in the early ages, then our contention is vain....On the other hand if it is proved to reach back in unbroken line to the time of the Evangelists, or to a period as near to them as surviving testimony can prove, then Dr. Hort's theory of a 'Syrian' text formed by recension or otherwise just as evidently falls to the ground.[3]

Miller, posthumous editor to Burgon, probed the question of ante-Nicene testimony exhaustively, making full use of Burgon's massive index of patristic citations (86,489 of them) from the New Testament. He deserves to be heard, in detail.

> As to the alleged absence of readings of the Traditional Text from the writings of the Ante-Nicene Fathers, Dr. Hort draws largely upon his imagination and his wishes. The persecution of Diocletian is

---

[1] Hoskier, *Codex B*, I, 426-27.

[2] Burgon, *The Traditional Text*, pp. 99-101. Fee calls my use of Miller's figures "absurd" and rejects them in sweeping terms ("A Critique", pp. 419 and 422). However, Peter J. Johnston (personal communication) gives the following report on an independent check of early Fathers, using critical editions. Checking six from the 3rd century (Irenaeus, Clement Alex., Tertullian, Hippolytus, Origen, Cyprian), five from the 4th century (Aphraates, Ephraem Arm., Ephraem Syr., Gregory Naz., Gregory Nys.) and seven from the 5th century (Chrysostom, Pelagius, Niceta, Theodore Mop., Augustine, Cyril Alex., Faustus), in the Gospels, he found them siding with the Majority Text "approximately 60%" of the time, where there is variation. This is very close to the results stated by Miller!

[3] Burgon, The Causes of the Corruption, pp. 2-3.

here also the parent of much want of information. But is there really such a dearth of these readings in the works of the Early Fathers as is supposed?[1]

I made a toilsome examination for myself of the quotations occurring in the writings of the Fathers before St. Chrysostom, or as I defined them in order to draw a self-acting line, of those who died before 400 A.D., with the result that the Traditional Text is found to stand in the general proportion of 3:2 [this is 60%, precisely as Peter Johnston verified—see the second footnote before the last one] against other variations, and in a much higher proportion upon thirty test passages. Afterwards, not being satisfied with resting the basis of my argument upon one scrutiny, I went again through the writings of the seventy-six Fathers concerned (with limitations explained in this book), besides others who yielded no evidence, and I found that although several more instances were consequently entered in my notebook, the general results remained the same. I do not flatter myself that even now I have recorded all the instances that could be adduced:—any one who is really acquainted with this work will know that such a feat is absolutely impossible, because such perfection cannot be obtained except after many repeated efforts. But I claim, not only that my attempts have been honest and fair even to self-abnegation, but that the general results which are much more than is required by my argument, as is explained in the body of this work, abundantly establish the antiquity of the Traditional Text, by proving the superior acceptance of it during the period at stake to that of any other.[2]

Kenyon acknowledged Miller's work and stated the results correctly.

Here is a plain issue. If it can be shown that the readings which Hort calls "Syrian" existed before the end of the fourth century, the keystone would be knocked out of the fabric of his theory; and since he produced no statistics in proof of his assertion,[!] his opponents were perfectly at liberty to challenge it. It must be admitted that Mr. Miller did not shirk the test. A considerable part of his work as editor

---

[1] E. Miller, *A Guide to the Textual Criticism of the New Testament* (London: George Bell and Sons, 1886), p. 53.

[2] Burgon, *The Traditional Text*, pp. ix-x. Miller's experiment pitted the Received Text against the Greek text pieced together by the body of revisers who produced the English Revised Version of 1881, which Miller aptly styles the "Neologian". He used Scrivener's *Cambridge Greek Testament* of 1887 which gives the precise Greek text represented by the E.R.V. but prints in black type the places that differ from the Received Text. Miller limited the investigation to the Gospels. He said that he discarded doubtful quotations and mere matters of spelling, that in doubtful cases he decided against the *Textus Receptus*, and that in the final tabulation he omitted many smaller instances favorable to the *Textus Receptus* (*Ibid.*, pp. 94-122).

of Dean Burgon's papers took the form of a classification of patristic quotations, based upon the great indices which the Dean left behind him, according as they testify for or against the Traditional Text of the Gospels.

The results of his examination are stated by him as follows. Taking the Greek and Latin (not the Syriac) Fathers who died before A.D. 400, their quotations are found to support the Traditional Text in 2,630 instances, the "neologian" in 1753. Nor is this majority due solely to the writers who belong to the end of this period. On the contrary, if only the earliest writers be taken, from Clement of Rome to Irenaeus and Hippolytus, the majority in favour of the Traditional Text is proportionately even greater, 151 to 84. Only in the Western and Alexandrian writers do we find approximate equality of votes on either side. Further, if a select list of thirty important passages be taken for detailed examination, the preponderance of early patristic evidence in favour of the Traditional Text is seen to be no less than 530 to 170, a quite overwhelming majority.

Now it is clear that if these figures were trustworthy, there would be an end to Hort's theory, for its premises would be shown to be thoroughly unsound.[1]

Before proceeding to Kenyon's rebuttal it will be well to pause and review the implications of this exchange. Hort, and the many like Kenyon who have repeated his words after him, have asserted that not a single "strictly Byzantine" reading is to be found in the extant works of any Church Father who dates before Chrysostom (d. 407). To disprove Hort's assertion, it is only necessary to find *some* "strictly Byzantine" readings before the specified time, since the question immediately in focus is the existence of the "Byzantine" readings, not necessarily their dominance. Miller affirms that the Byzantine text not only is to be found in the writings of the early Fathers, but that in fact it *predominates*.

As far as the Fathers who died before 400 A.D. are concerned, the question may now be put and answered. Do they witness to the Traditional Text as existing from the first, or do they not? The results of the evidence, both as regards the quantity and the quality of the testimony, enable us to reply, not only that the Traditional Text was in existence, but that it was predominant, during the period under review. Let any one who disputes this conclusion make out for the Western Text, or the Alexandrian, or for the Text of

---

[1] Kenyon, *Handbook*, pp. 321-22. Both Hort and Kenyon clearly stated that no strictly "Syrian" readings existed before the end of the 4th century. It is encouraging to see that both Carson (p. 111) and Fee ("A Critique", p. 416) have retreated to the weaker statement that it is all such readings together or the whole "text-type" that had no early existence.

B and ℵ, a case from the evidence of the Fathers which can equal or surpass that which has been now placed before the reader.[1]

**No one has ever taken up Miller's challenge.**

As quoted above, Kenyon recognized that if Miller's figures are right then Hort's theory is at an end. But Kenyon continued:

> An examination of them however, shows that they cannot be accepted as representing in any way the true state of the case. In the first place, it is fairly certain that critical editions of the several Fathers, if such existed, would show that in many cases the quotations have been assimilated in later MSS to the Traditional Text, whereas in the earlier they agree rather with the "Neutral" or "Western" witnesses. For this defect, however, Mr. Miller cannot be held responsible. The critical editions of the Greek and Latin Fathers, now in course of production by the Academies of Berlin and Vienna, had covered very little of the ground at the time when his materials were compiled, and meanwhile he might legitimately use the materials accessible to him; and the errors arising from this source would hardly affect the general result to any very serious extent.[2]

After raising the 'quibble' about critical editions he admitted that "the errors arising from this source would hardly affect the general result". However, Kenyon's suggestion that "in many cases the quotations have been assimilated in later MSS to the Traditional Text" gives the essence of a contention (that begs the question) widely used today to parry the thrusts of the mounting evidence in favor of an early "Byzantine" text. To this we must presently return.

Kenyon proceeded:

> The real fallacy in his statistics is different, and is revealed in the detailed examination of the thirty select passages. From these it is clear that he wholly misunderstood Hort's contention. The thirty "traditional" readings, which he shows to be so overwhelmingly vindicated by the Fathers, are not what Hort would call pure "Syrian" readings at all. In nearly every case they have Western or Neutral attestation in addition to that of the later authorities.[3]

He then referred briefly to specific instances in Matt. 17:21, Matt. 18:11, Matt. 19:16, Matt. 23:38, Mark 16:9-20, Luke 24:40, and John 21:25 and continued:

> In short, Mr. Miller evidently reckoned on his side every reading which occurs in the Traditional Text, regardless of whether, on

---

[1] Burgon, The Traditional Text, p. 116.

[2] Kenyon, *Handbook*, pp. 322-23.

[3] *Ibid.*, p. 323.

Hort's principles, they are old readings which kept their place in the Syrian revision, or secondary readings which were then introduced for the first time. According to Hort, the Traditional Text is the result of a revision in which old elements were incorporated; and Mr. Miller merely points to some of these old elements, and argues therefrom that the whole is old. It is clear that by such argumentation Hort's theory is untouched.[1]

It is hard to believe that Kenyon was precisely fair here. He had obviously read Miller's work with care. Why did he not say anything about "to repentance" in Matt. 9:13 and Mark 2:17,[2] or "vinegar" in Matt. 27:34,[1] or "from the door" in

---

[1] Ibid.

[2] Supported by Barnabas (5), Justin M. (*Apol.* i.15), Irenaeus (III. v. 2), Origen (Comment. in Joh. xxviii. 16), Eusebius (Comment. in Ps. cxlvi), Hilary (Comment. in Matt. *ad loc.*), Basil (*De Poenitent.* 3; Hom. in Ps. xlviii. 1; *Epist. Class.* I. xlvi. 6). The evidence cited in this and the next seven footnotes was taken from Burgon, *The Traditional Text*.

Among the numerous dubious affirmations with which Fee favors us, none is more startling than his charge that "Burgon's and Miller's data are simply replete with useless supporting evidence" ("A Critique", p. 417). Anyone who studies their works with care (as I have) will come away convinced that they were unusually thorough, careful and scrupulous in their treatment of Patristic evidence. Not so Fee. Of the reading "vinegar" in Matt. 27:34 he says, "I took the trouble to check over three-quarters of Burgon's seventeen supporting Fathers and **not one of them** [emphasis Fee's] can be shown to be citing Matthew!" (pp. 417-18). (The term οξος, "vinegar," also occurs in the near-parallel passages—Mark 15:36, Luke 23:36 and John 19:29.)

Before checking the Fathers individually, we may register surprise at Fee's vehemence in view of his own affirmation that it is "incontrovertible" that "the Gospel of Matthew was the most cited and used of the Synoptic Gospels" and that "these data simply cannot be ignored in making textual decisions" (*Ibid.*, p. 412). We are grateful to Fee for this information but cannot help but notice that he himself seems to be "ignoring" it. We might reasonably assume that at least nine of Burgon's 17 citations are from Matthew. But we are not reduced to such a weak proceeding.

Even though a Father may not say, "I am here quoting Matthew," by paying close attention to the context we may be virtually as certain as if he had. Thus, although all four Gospels use the word "vinegar," only Matthew uses the word "gall", χολε, in association with the vinegar (and Acts 8:23 is the only other place in the N.T. that "gall" appears). It follows that any Patristic reference to vinegar and gall together can only be a citation based on Matthew (or Psalm 69:21). When Barnabas says, ποτιζειν χολεν μετα οξος (7:5), can there be any doubt as to his source? When the Gospel of Peter says Ποτισατε αυτον χολεν μετα οξους (5:16), must the source not be Matthew? When Gregory of Nyssa says, χολε τε και οξει διαβροχος (*Orat.* x:989:6), can there be any question at all? It may be noted in passing that Alford's Greek N.T., in *loc.*, says plainly that Origen and Tertullian both support the "Byzantine" reading under discussion. (The research reflected in the discussion above was done by Maurice A. Robinson and kindly placed at my disposal.)

Note also that Irenaeus wrote, "He should have vinegar and gall given Him to drink" (*Against Heresies*, XXXIII:12), in a series of O.T. prophecies that he says Christ fulfilled. Presumably he had Psalm 69:21 in mind—"they gave me gall for food, and in my thirst they gave me vinegar to drink"—but he seems to have assimilated to Matthew

Matt, 28:2,[2] or "the prophets" in Mark 1:2,[3] or "good will" in Luke 2:14,[4] or the Lord's prayer for His murderers in Luke 23:34,[5] or "an honeycomb" in Luke 24:42,[6] or "whom" in John 17:24?[7]

These instances are also among "the thirty". They would appear to be "strictly Syrian" readings, if there really is such a thing. Why did Kenyon ignore them? The cases Kenyon cited fell within the scope of Miller's inquiry because they are Traditional readings; whatever other attestation they may also have, and because the English Revisers of 1881 rejected them. (Please note that since Hort et al. rejected the non-Byzantine witnesses that agree with the Byzantine text, in those places, they must be viewed as having departed from the "norm"

---

27:34 (the "Byzantine" reading). The Gospel of Nicodemus has, "and gave him also to drink gall with vinegar" (Part II, 4). The Revelation of Esdras has, "Vinegar and gall did they give me to drink." The Apostolic Constitutions has, "they gave him vinegar to drink, mingled with gall" (V:3:14). Tertullian has, "and gall is mixed with vinegar" (Appendix, reply to Marcion, V:232). In a list of Christ's sufferings where the readers are exhorted to follow His example, Gregory Nazianzus has, "Taste gall for the taste's sake; drink vinegar" (Oratio XXXVIII:18).

Whatever interpretation the reader may wish to give to Fee's statement, noted at the outset, it is clear that the reading "vinegar" in Matthew 27:34 has second century attestation (or perhaps even first century in the case of Barnabas!). Since he affirms that he did check the Fathers himself, the most charitable construction that can be placed on Fee's words is that the check was hasty and careless. With reference to the Patristic evidence for "to repentance" in Matthew 9:13 and Mark 2:17, the concerned reader will be well advised to check the sources for himself.

[1] Supported by Gospel of Peter (5), Acta Philippi (26), Barnabas (7), Irenaeus (pp. 526, 681), Tertullian, Celsus, Origen, Eusebius of Emesa, ps-Tatian, Theodore of Heraclea, Ephraem, Athanasius, Acta Pilati.

[2] Supported by Gospel of Nicodemus, Acta Phillipi, Apocryphal Acts of the Apostles, Eusebius (ad Marinum, ii. 4), Gregory Nyss. (De Christ. Resurr. I. 390, 398), Gospel of Peter.

[3] Supported by Irenaeus (III. xvi. 3), Origen, Porphyry, Eusebius, Titus of Bostra.

[4] Supported by Irenaeus (III. x. 4), Origen (c. Celsum i. 60; Selecta in Ps. xlv.; Comment. in Matt. xvii.; Comment. in Joh. i. 13), Gregory Thaumaturgus (De Fid. Cap. 12), Methodius (Serm de Simeon. et Anna), Apostolic Constitutions (vii. 47; viii. 12), Diatessaron, Eusebius (Dem. Ev. pp. 163, 342), Aphraates (i. 180, 385), Jacob-Nisibis, Titus of Bostra, Cyril of Jerusalem (p. 180), Athanasius, Ephraem (Gr. iii. 434).

[5] Supported by Hegesippus (Eus. H.E. ii. 23), Marcion, Justin, Irenaeus (c. Haer. III. xviii. 5), Archelaus (xliv), Hippolytus (c. Noet. 18), Origen (ii. 188), Apostolic Constitutions (ii. 16; v. 14), Clementine Homilies (Recogn. vi. 5; Hom. xi. 20), ps-Tatian (E. C. 275), Eusebius (canon x), Hilary (De Trin. 1. 32), Acta Pilati (x. 5), Theodore of Heraclea, Athanasius (i. 1120), Titus of Bostra, Ephraem (ii. 321).

[6] Supported by Marcion (ad loc.), Justin M. (ii. 240, 762), Clement Alex. (p. 174), Tertullian (i. 455), Diatessaron, Athanasius (i. 644), Cyril of Jerusalem (iv. 1108), Gregory Nyss. (i. 624).

[7] Supported by Irenaeus (c. Haeres. IV. xiv. 1), Clement Alex. (Paed. i. 8), Cyprian (pp. 235, 321), Diatessaron, Eusebius (De Eccles. Theol. iii. 17--bis; c. Marcell. p. 292), Hilary (pp. 1017, 1033), Basil (Eth. ii, 297), Caelestinus (Concilia iii. 356).

that he chose. If they assimilated to the Byzantine text they may not reasonably be adduced as evidence against that text.) Kenyon asserted that Miller's figures "cannot be accepted as representing in any way the true state of the case", but he has not shown us why. Kenyon said nothing about the alleged "secondary readings" that have early Patristic support.

Miller's figures represent precisely what he claimed that they represent "the true state of the case" is that the Traditional Text ("Byzantine") receives *more support* from the early Church Fathers than does the critical text (essentially W-H) used by the English Revisers. It should be noted that there are doubtless numerous so-called "Western" and "Alexandrian" readings[1] to be found in the early Fathers which are not included in Miller's figures because the Revisers rejected them. If they were all tabulated the "Byzantine" readings would perhaps lose the absolute majority of early patristic attestation but they would still be present and attested, from the very first, and that is the question just now in focus.

## *Pure "Syrian" readings*

Kenyon's statement contains another problem. He referred to "pure 'Syrian' readings" and in effect denied to the "Syrian" text any reading that chances to have any "Western" or "Alexandrian" attestation (which attestation has been arbitrarily pigeon-holed according to the presuppositions of the theory). But just which are those late or "pure Syrian" elements?

E. F. Hills evidently conducted a search for them. He observes:

> The second accusation commonly urged against the Byzantine text is that it contains so many late readings. A text with all these late readings, it is said, must be a late text. But it is remarkable how few actually were the Byzantine readings which Westcott and Hort designated as late. In his *Notes on Select Readings* Hort discussed about 240 instances of variation among the manuscripts of the

---

[1] Again we are faced with the question-begging of Hort and many subsequent writers. Irenaeus, for instance, is arbitrarily declared to be a witness to the "Western text-type" and then any reading he has is thereupon declared to be "Western". Even if we granted the existence of such entities as the "Western" and "Alexandrian" text-types (for the sake of the argument), if the requirement were imposed that only those readings which are supported by a **majority** of the witnesses assigned to a text-type may be claimed for that text-type then the number of "Western", "Alexandrian" and "Caesarean" readings would shrink **drastically**. By contrast, the number of "Byzantine" readings would remain about the same.

There is a further detail that, I think, has not received sufficient attention. Miller pitted the Traditional Text against the "Neologian" (W-H) because it represented the Revisers' judgment as to what was the original text. It follows that any "Western" and, especially, "Alexandrian" witnesses that attested something else were rejected, at each point. So presumably any rejected "Alexandrian" witnesses would no longer be "Alexandrian", at that point—or were there several "Alexandrian" text-types? On what basis can those rejected "Alexandrian" witnesses (rejected by Hort and the Revisers) be used to invalidate "Byzantine" readings?

Gospels, and in only about twenty of these instances was he willing to characterize the Byzantine reading as a late reading. Thus it would seem that even on Hort's own admission only about ten percent of the readings of the Byzantine text are late readings, and since Hort's day the number of these allegedly late Byzantine readings has been gradually dwindling.[1]

(And yet Hort wrote off the whole "Syrian" witness as late.)

It seems clear that the "Byzantine" text cannot win in a court presided over by a judge of Kenyon's bent. Whenever an early witness surfaces it is declared to be "Alexandrian" or "Western" or "Caesarean" and thereupon those "Syrian" readings which it contains cease to be "pure Syrian" and are no longer allowed as evidence. Such a procedure is evidently useful to defenders of Hort's theory, but is it right?

It is commonplace among the many who are determined to despise the "Byzantine" text to dodge the issue, as Kenyon did above. The postulates of Hort's theory are assumed to be true and the evidence is interpreted on the basis of these presuppositions. Apart from the imaginary nature of the "Alexandrian" and "Western" texts, as strictly definable entities, their priority to the "Byzantine" text is the very point to be proved and may not be assumed. Kirsopp Lake's statement is representative. Taking Origen, Irenaeus, and Chrysostom as representatives of the "Neutral", "Western" and "Byzantine" texts respectively, he asserted:

> Though Chrysostom and Origen often unite in differing from
> Irenaeus, and Chrysostom and Irenaeus in differing from Origen,
> yet Chrysostom does not differ from them both at once. And this is
> almost demonstrative proof that his text, characteristically
> representative of the later Fathers, versions and MSS, is an eclectic
> one.[2]

Even if Lake's description of the phenomena were true (but remember what he himself said about scholars copying from each other, regarding Chrysostom), there is another perfectly adequate interpretation of such phenomena. In Hill's words,

> There is surely a much more reasonable way of explaining why
> each non-Byzantine text (including Papyrus Bodmer II) contains

---

[1] E.F. Hills, *The King James Version Defended*! (Des Moines: The Christian Research Press, 1956), p. 73. Carson continues to beg the question (p. 111). If the present trend continues until all "purely Byzantine" readings have early attestation he will not be disturbed since he will continue to arbitrarily declare such readings to be "Western" or "Alexandrian". May I respectfully submit that the generally accepted norms of scholarship do not permit the continued begging of this particular question.

[2] Lake, p. 72. On the contrary: such a situation reflects three independent lines of transmission. If Chrysostom is never alone then his is clearly the best line. Lake had a blind spot here.

Byzantine readings not found in other non-Byzantine texts. If we regard the Byzantine text as the original text, then it is perfectly natural that each non-Byzantine text should agree with the Byzantine text in places in which the other non-Byzantine texts have departed from it.[1]

Also, given the priority of the "Byzantine" text, the places where all the divergent texts happened to abandon the "Byzantine" at the same time would be few. To arbitrarily assign Fathers and manuscripts and versions to the "Alexandrian" and "Western" families and then to deny to the "Byzantine" text readings which one or more of these arbitrarily assigned witnesses happen also to support seems neither honest nor scholarly.

## *A biased expedient*

Before closing this section, it remains to take up the expedient, alluded to earlier, whereby many seek to evade the ante-Nicene patristic evidence for the "Byzantine" text. Vincent Taylor states the expedient as baldly as anyone. "In judging between two alternative readings [of a given Father in a given place] the principle to be adopted is that the one which *diverges* from the later ecclesiastical text (the TR) is more likely to be original."[2]

---

[1] J.W. Burgon, *The Last Twelve Verses of the Gospel According to Saint Mark* (Ann Arbor, Mich.: The Sovereign Grace Book Club, 1959), p. 55. This reprint of Burgon's 1871 work contains an Introduction by E.F. Hills occupying pages 17-72.

[2] Taylor, p. 39. Fee continues to vigorously propound this expedient. "My experience is that in every instance a critical edition of the Father moves his New Testament text in some degree **away from** the Byzantine tradition" ("Modern Text Criticism", p. 160). He has recently observed that "all of Burgon's data...is suspect because of his use of uncritical editions" ("A Critique", p. 417).

But there is reason to ask whether editors with an anti-Byzantine bias can be trusted to report the evidence in an impartial manner. Certainly a critical edition of Irenaeus prepared by Fee could not be trusted. In discussing the evidence for "in the prophets" versus "in Isaiah the prophet" in Mark 1:2 ("A Critique", pp. 410-11) Fee does not mention Irenaeus under the Majority Text reading, where he belongs, but says "except for one citation in Irenaeus" under the other reading. He then offers the following comment in a footnote: "Since this one citation stands alone in all of the early Greek and Latin evidence, and since Irenaeus himself knows clearly the other text, this 'citation' is especially suspect of later corruption". He goes on to conclude his discussion of this passage by affirming that the longer reading is "the only reading known to every church Father who cites the text". By the end of his discussion Fee has completely suppressed the unwelcome testimony from Irenaeus.

But is the testimony of Irenaeus here really suspect? In *Adv. Haer.* III.10.5 we read: "Mark...does thus commence his Gospel narrative: 'The beginning of the Gospel of Jesus Christ, the Son of God, as it is written in the prophets, Behold,... [the quotations follow].' Plainly does the commencement of the Gospel quote the words of the holy prophets, and point out Him...whom they confessed as God and Lord." Note that Irenaeus not only quotes Mark 1:2 but comments upon it, and in both quote and comment he supports the "Byzantine" reading. But the comment is a little ways removed from the quote and it is entirely improbable that a scribe should have molested the comment even if he felt called upon to change the quote. Fair play requires that this

This expedient is extended even to cases where there is no alternative. The allegation is that copyists altered the Fathers' wording to conform to the "Byzantine", which the copyists regarded as "correct".[1] It is obvious that the

---

instance be loyally recorded as 2nd century support for the "Byzantine" reading.

Another, almost as unambiguous, instance occurs in *Adv. Haer.* III.16.3 where we read: "Wherefore Mark also says: 'The beginning of the Gospel of Jesus Christ, the Son of God; as it is written in the prophets.' Knowing one and the same Son of God, Jesus Christ, who was announced by the prophets...." Note that again Irenaeus not only quotes Mark 1:2 but comments upon it, and in both quote and comment he supports the "Byzantine" reading.

There is also a clear allusion to Mark 1:2 in *Adv. Haer.* III.11.4 where we read: "By what God, then, was John, the forerunner...sent? Truly it was by Him...who also had promised by the prophets that He would send His messenger before the face of His Son, who should prepare His way...." May we not reasonably claim this as a **third** citation in support of the "Byzantine" reading? In any case, it is clear that Fee's handling of the evidence from Irenaeus is disappointing at best, if not reprehensible.

While on the subject of Fee's reliability, I offer the evaluation given by W.F. Wisselink after a thorough investigation of some of his work (W.F. Wisselink, *Assimilation as a Criterion for the Establishment of the Text*, 4 vols. [Kampen: Uitgeversmaatschappij J.H. Kok, 1989]).

While studying Fee's account ["P$^{75}$, P$^{66}$, and Origen: The Myth of Early Textual Recension in Alexandria", *New Dimensions in New Testament Study*, ed. R.N. Longenecker and M.C. Tenney (Grand Rapids: Zondervan, 1974), pp. 42-44] it became apparent to me that it is incomplete and indistinct, and that it contains mistakes. Fee gives account of his investigation in a little more than one page. He introduces this account as follows: "The full justification of this conclusion will require a volume of considerable size filled with lists of data. Here we can offer only a sample illustration with the further note that the complete data will vary little from the sampling" (Fee, 1974, 42).

Therefore I called upon Fee for the complete data. I received six partly filled pages containing the rough data about the assimilations in Luke 10 and 11. After studying these rough data I came to the conclusion that the rough data as well are incomplete and indistinct, and contain mistakes. So question marks can be placed at the reliability of the investigation which those rough data and that account have reference to. (P. 69.)

Wisselink then proceeds to document his charges on the next three pages.

I repeat that a critical edition of Irenaeus prepared by Fee could not be trusted, and I begin to wonder if any edition prepared by someone with an anti-Byzantine bias is to be trusted. This quite apart from their fallacious starting point, namely that the "Byzantine" text is late.

The three quotations from Irenaeus are taken from A. Roberts and J. Donaldson, eds. *The Ante-Nicene Fathers*, 1973, Vol. I, pp. 425-26 and 441, and were checked for accuracy against W. W. Harvey's critical edition (*Sancti Irenaei: Episcopi Lugdunensis: Libros Quinque Adversus Haereses*, Cambridge: University Press, 1857). I owe this material on Irenaeus to Maurice A. Robinson.

[1] Of course this principle is also applied to the Greek MSS, with serious consequences. A recent statement by Metzger gives a clear example.

It should be observed that, in accord with the theory that members of f$^1$ and f$^{13}$ were subject to progressive accommodation to the later Byzantine text, scholars have established the text of these families by adopting readings of family witnesses that differ from the Textus Receptus. Therefore the citation of the siglum

effect of such a proceeding is to place the "Byzantine" text at a disadvantage. An investigation based on this principle is 'rigged' against the TR.[1]

Even if there appear to be certain instances where this has demonstrably happened, such instances do not justify a widespread generalization. The generalization is based on the pre-supposition that the "Byzantine" text is late—but this is the very point to be proved and may not be assumed.

If the "Byzantine" text is early there is no reason to suppose that a "Byzantine" reading in an early Father is due to a later copyist unless a clear demonstration to that effect is possible. Miller shows clearly that he was fully aware of this problem and alert to exclude any suspicious instances from his tabulation.

> An objection may perhaps be made, that the texts of the books of the Fathers are sure to have been altered in order to coincide more accurately with the Received Text. This is true of the Ethica, or Moralia, of Basil, and of the Regulae brevius Tractatae, which seem to have been read constantly at meals, or were otherwise in continual use in Religious Houses. The monks of a later age would not be content to hear every day familiar passages of Holy Scripture couched in other terms than those to which they were accustomed and which they regarded as correct. This fact was perfectly evident upon examination, because these treatises were found to give evidence for the Textus Receptus in the proportion of about 6:1, whereas the other books of St. Basil yielded according to a ratio of about 8:3. [But might it possibly be the case that, precisely because of the "continual use in Religious Houses" (the more so if that use began early on), the 6:1 ratio reflects a pure/faithful transmission while "the other books" suffered some adulterations?]
>
> For the same reason I have not included Marcion's edition of St. Luke's Gospel, or Tatian's Diatessaron, in the list of books and authors, because such representations of the Gospels having been

---

$f^1$ and $f^{13}$ may, in any given instance, signify a minority of manuscripts (or even only one) that belong to the family. (A *Textual Commentary on the Greek New Testament* [companion to UBS[3]], p. xii.)

Such a procedure misleads the user of the apparatus, who has every right to expect that the siglum will only be used when all (or nearly all) the members agree. A distorted view of the evidence is created—the divergence of $f^1$ and $f^{13}$ from the "Byzantine" text is made to appear greater then it really is, and the extent of variation among the members is obscured. Greenlee's study of Cyril of Jerusalem (p. 30, see next footnote) affords another example. Among other things, he appeals to "the well-known fact that all the Caesarean witnesses are more or less corrected to the Byzantine standard, but in different places, so that the groups must be considered as a whole, not by its [sic] individual members, to give the true picture". Would not the behavior of the individual MSS make better sense if viewed as departing from the Byzantine standard?

[1] I believe J.H. Greenlee's study of Cyril of Jerusalem is an example. *The Gospel Text of Cyril of Jerusalem* (Copenhagen: Ejnar Munksgaard, 1955).

in public use were sure to have been revised from time to time, in order to accord with the judgment of those who read or heard them. Our readers will observe that these were self-denying ordinances, because by the inclusion of the works mentioned the list on the Traditional side would have been greatly increased. Yet our foundations have been strengthened, and really the position of the Traditional Text rests so firmly upon what is undoubted, that it can afford to dispense with services which may be open to some suspicion. (Yet Marcion and Tatian may fairly be adduced as witnesses upon individual readings.) And the natural inference remains, that the difference between the witness of the Ethica and Regulae brevius Tractatae on the one hand, and that of the other works of Basil on the other, suggests that too much variation, and too much which is evidently characteristic variation, of readings meets us in the works of the several Fathers, for the existence of any doubt that in most cases we have the words, though perhaps not the spelling, as they issued originally from the author's pen. Variant readings of quotations occurring in different editions of the Fathers are found, according to my experience, much less frequently than might have been supposed. Where I saw a difference between MSS noted in the Benedictine or other editions or in copies from the Benedictine or other prints, of course I regarded the passage as doubtful and did not enter it. Acquaintance with this kind of testimony cannot but render its general trustworthiness the more evident.[1]

After this careful screening Miller still came up with 2,630 citations, from 76 Fathers or sources, ranging over a span of 300 years (100-400 A.D.), supporting readings of the "Byzantine" text as opposed to those of the critical text of the English Revisers (which received 1,753 citations). Will anyone seriously propose that all or most of those citations had been altered? What objective grounds are there for doing so?

---

[1] Burgon, *The Traditional Text*, pp. 97-98. I believe that Suggs tends to agree with Miller that the assimilating proclivity of medieval scribes can easily be overestimated ("The Use of Patristic Evidence", p. 140). The Lectionaries give eloquent testimony against the supposed assimilating proclivity. After discussing at some length their lack of textual consistency, Colwell observes: "Figuratively speaking, the Lectionary is a preservative into which from time to time portions of the living text were dropped. Once submerged in the Lectionary, each portion was solidified or fixed" (Colwell and Riddle, *Prolegomena to the Study of the Lectionary Text of the Gospels*, p. 17). Similarly, Riddle cites with favor Gregory's estimate: "He saw that as a product of the liturgical system they were guarded by a strongly conservative force, and he was right in his inference that the conservatism of the liturgy would tend frequently to make them media for the preservation of an early text. His analogy of the Psalter of the Anglican church was a good one" (*Ibid.*, pp. 40-41). Many of the lessons in the Anglican Prayer Book are much older than the AV but have never been assimilated to the AV. In short, we have good reason to doubt that medieval copyists were as addicted to assimilating the text as scholars such as Taylor would have us believe.

Hills discusses the case of Origen as follows:

> In the first fourteen chapters of the Gospel of John (that is, in the area covered by Papyrus Bodmer II) out of 52 instances in which the Byzantine text stands alone Origen agrees with the Byzantine text 20 times and disagrees with it 32 times. Thus the assertion of the critics that Origen knew nothing of the Byzantine text becomes difficult indeed to maintain. On the contrary, these statistics suggest that Origen was familiar with the Byzantine text and frequently adopted its readings in preference to those of the Western and Alexandrian texts.
>
> Naturalistic critics, it is true, have made a determined effort to explain away the "distinctively" Byzantine readings which appear in the New Testament quotations of Origen (and other ante-Nicene Fathers). It is argued that these Byzantine readings are not really Origen's but represent alterations made by scribes who copied Origen's works. These scribes, it is maintained, revised the original quotations of Origen and made them conform to the Byzantine text. The evidence of Papyrus Bodmer II, however, indicates that this is not an adequate explanation of the facts. Certainly it seems a very unsatisfactory way to account for the phenomena which appear in the first fourteen chapters of John. In these chapters, 5 out of the 20 "distinctively" Byzantine readings which occur in Origen occur also in Papyrus Bodmer II. These 5 readings at least must have been Origen's readings, not those of scribes who copied Origen's works, and what is true of these 5 readings is probably true of the other 15, or at least of most of them.[1]

This demonstration makes it clear that the expedient deprecated above is in fact untenable.

## The testimony of the early Fathers

To recapitulate, "Byzantine" readings are recognized (most notably) by the *Didache*, Diognetus, and Justin Martyr in the first half of the second century; by the Gospel of Peter, Athenagorus, Hegesippus, and Irenaeus (heavily) in the second half; by Clement of Alexandria, Tertullian, Clementines, Hippolytus, and Origen (all heavily) in the first half of the third century; by Gregory of Thaumaturgus, Novatian, Cyprian (heavily), Dionysius of Alexandria, and Archelaus in the second half; by Eusebius, Athanasius, Macarius Magnus, Hilary, Didymus, Basil, Titus of Bostra, Cyril of Jerusalem, Gregory of Nyssa,

---

[1] Burgon, *The Last Twelve Verses*, p. 58. Sturz lists a number of further "Byzantine" readings that have had early Patristic support (Clement, Tertullian, Marcion, Methodius) and which now also have early Papyrus support (pp. 55-56). Here again it will no longer do to claim that the Fathers' MSS have been altered to conform to the "Byzantine" text.

Apostolic Canons and Constitutions, Epiphanius, and Ambrose (all heavily) in the fourth century. To which may be added the testimony of the early Papyri.

## The testimony of the early Papyri

In Hort's day and even in Miller's the early Papyri were not extant—had they been the W-H theory could scarcely have appeared in the form that it did. Each of the early Papyri (300 A.D. or earlier) vindicates some "Byzantine" readings. G. Zuntz did a thorough study of $P^{46}$ and concluded:

> To sum up. A number of Byzantine readings, most of them genuine, which previously were discarded as 'late', are anticipated by $P^{46}$....How then—so one is tempted to go on asking—where no Chester Beatty papyrus happens to vouch for the early existence of a Byzantine reading? Are all Byzantine readings ancient? In the cognate case of the Homeric tradition G. Pasquali answers the same question in the affirmative.[1]

Colwell takes note of Zuntz's statement and concurs.[2] He had said of the "Byzantine New Testament" some years previous, "Most of its readings existed in the second century".[3]

Hills claims that the Beatty papyri vindicate 26 "Byzantine" readings in the Gospels, 8 in Acts and 31 in Paul's epistles.[4] He says concerning $P^{66}$:

> To be precise, Papyrus Bodmer II contains thirteen percent of all the alleged late readings of the Byzantine text in the area which it covers (18 out of 138). Thirteen percent of the Byzantine readings which most critics have regarded as late have now been proved by Papyrus Bodmer II to be early readings.[5]

Colwell's statement on $P^{66}$ has already been given.

Many other studies are available, but that of H. A. Sturz sums it up.[6] He surveyed "all the available papyri" to discover how many papyrus-supported "Byzantine" readings exist. In trying to decide which were "distinctively Byzantine" readings he made a conscious effort to "err on the conservative side" so that the list is shorter than it might be (p. 144).

---

[1] Zuntz, The Text, p. 55.

[2] Colwell, "The Origin of Texttypes", p. 132.

[3] Colwell, What is the Best New Testament?, p. 70.

[4] Burgon, The Last Twelve Verses, p. 50. (Hills wrote the Introduction.)

[5] Ibid., p. 54.

[6] H.A. Sturz, The Byzantine Text-Type and New Testament Textual Criticism.

He found, and lists the evidence for, more than 150 "distinctively Byzantine" readings that have early (before 300 A.D.) papyrus support (pp. 145-59). He found 170 "Byzantine-Western" readings with early papyrus support (pp. 160-74). He found 170 "Byzantine-Alexandrian" readings with early papyrus support (pp.175-87). He gives evidence for 175 further "Byzantine" readings but which have scattered "Western" or "Alexandrian" support, with early papyrus support.[1] He refers to still another 195 readings where the "Byzantine" reading has papyrus support, but he doesn't bother to list them (apparently he considered these variants to be of lesser consequence).[2]

The magnitude of this vindication can be more fully appreciated by recalling that only about 30 percent of the New Testament has early papyrus attestation, and much of that 30 percent has only one papyrus. Where more than one covers a stretch of text, each new MS discovered vindicates added Byzantine readings. Extrapolating from the behavior of those in hand, if we had at least 3 papyri covering all parts of the New Testament, almost all the 6000+ Byzantine readings rejected by the critical (eclectic) texts would be vindicated by an early papyrus.

It appears that Hort's statement or treatment of external evidence has no basis in fact. What about his statement of internal evidence?

# Internal Evidence of Readings

We have already noted something of the use Hort made of internal evidence, but he himself recognized its weaknesses. He said: "In dealing with this kind of

---

[1] Pp. 188-208. Sturz remarks that a number of readings (15 from this list) really should be considered as "distinctively Byzantine" but one or another so-called "Western" or "Alexandrian" witness also has them and so...

Sturz draws the following conclusions from the evidence he presents: 1) "Distinctively Byzantine" readings are found in early papyri (p. 55). 2) Such readings are therefore early (p. 62). 3) Such readings cannot be the result of editing in the 4th century (p. 62). 4) The old uncials have not preserved a complete picture of the textual situation in the 2nd century (p. 62). 5) The "Byzantine" texttype has preserved some of the 2nd century tradition **not** found in the others (p. 64). 6) The lateness of other "Byzantine" readings, for which early papyrus attestation has not yet surfaced, is now questionable (p. 64). 7) "Byzantine-Western" alignments go back into the 2nd century; they **must** be old (p. 70).

(Fee speaks of my "misrepresentations of the papyrus evidence" and says with reference to it that I have "grossly misinterpreted the data" ("A Critique", p. 422). I invite the reader to check the evidence presented by Sturz and then to decide for himself whether or not there has been misrepresentation and misinterpretation.)

[2] P. 189. This means that the early Papyri vindicate "Byzantine" readings in 660 (or 885) places where there is significant variation. One might wish that Sturz had also given us the figures for "distinctively Western" and "distinctively Alexandrian" readings, but how are such expressions to be defined? Where is an objective definition for "Western reading", for example?

evidence [Intrinsic Evidence of Readings] equally competent critics often arrive at contradictory conclusions as to the same variations".[1]

And again, four pages later: "Not only are mental impulses unsatisfactory subjects for estimates of comparative force; but a plurality of impulses recognized by ourselves as possible in any given case by no means implies a plurality of impulses as having been actually in operation".[2]

Exactly! No twentieth century person confronting a set of variant readings can know or prove what actually took place to produce the variants.

Again Hort's preaching is better than his practice:

> The summary decisions inspired by an unhesitating instinct as to what an author must needs have written, or dictated by the supposed authority of "canons of criticism" as to what transcribers must needs have introduced, are in reality in a large proportion of cases attempts to dispense with the solution of problems that depend on genealogical data.[3]

If we but change the words 'genealogical data' to 'external evidence' we may agree with him. Unfortunately, however, the fine sentiments quoted above were but a smoke screen. As Fee says:

> The internal evidence of readings was also the predominant factor in the choice of his "Neutral" text over the "Western" and "Alexandrian" texts...and his choice of B...

> The point is that Hort did not come to his conclusion about the Byzantines and B by the genealogical method,...[4]

The precarious and unsatisfactory nature of internal evidence has already received some attention in the discussion of eclecticism. Colwell says specifically of the use of intrinsic and transcriptional probability: "Unfortunately these two criteria frequently clash in a head-on collision, because ancient scribes as well as modern editors often preferred the reading which best fits the context".[5] "If we choose the reading that best explains the origin of the other reading, we are usually choosing the reading that does not fit the

---

[1] Westcott and Hort, p. 21.

[2] *Ibid.*, p. 25. Fee criticizes me rather severely for my "agnosticism" ("A Critique", p. 409), but my statement is scarcely stronger than Hort's.

[3] *Ibid.*, p. 286.

[4] Fee, "Modern Text Criticism and the Synoptic Problem", *J.J. Griesbach: Synoptic and Text-Critical Studies 1776-1976*, ed. B. Orchard and T.R.W. Longstaff (Cambridge: University Press, 1978), p. 156.

[5] Colwell, "The Greek New Testament", p. 37.

context. The two criteria cancel each other out."[1] And that leaves the scholar "free to choose in terms of his own prejudgments".[2]

Burgon said of internal considerations: "Often they are the product of personal bias, or limited observation: and where one scholar approves, another dogmatically condemns. Circumstantial evidence is deservedly rated low in the courts of justice: and lawyers always produce witnesses when they can."[3]

> We venture to declare that inasmuch as one expert's notions of what is 'transcriptionally probable' prove to be the diametrical reverse of another expert's notions, the supposed evidence to be derived from this source may, with advantage, be neglected altogether. Let the study of **Documentary Evidence** be allowed to take its place. Notions of 'Probability' are the very pest of those departments of Science which admit of an appeal to **Fact**.[4]

He also called attention to a danger involved in the use of a system of strict canons. "People are ordinarily so constituted, that when they have once constructed a system of Canons they place no limits to their operation, and become slaves to them."[5] (Gordon Fee's use of *ardua lectio potior* seems to me to be a case in point.)[6]

## The shorter reading

Perhaps the canon most widely used against the "Byzantine" text is *brevior lectio potior*—the shorter reading is to be preferred. As Hort stated the alleged basis for the canon, "In the New Testament, as in almost all prose writings which have been much copied, corruptions by interpolation are many times more numerous than corruptions by omission".[7] Accordingly it has been customary since Hort to tax the Received Text as being full and interpolated and to regard B and Aleph as prime examples of non-interpolated texts.[8]

---

[1] Colwell, "External Evidence", p. 4.

[2] *Ibid.*, p. 3.

[3] Burgon, The Traditional Text, p. 67.

[4] Burgon, *The Revision Revised*, p. 251 [emphasis his].

[5] Burgon, The Traditional Text, p. 66.

[6] Fee, Papyrus Bodmer II.

[7] Westcott and Hort, p. 235.

[8] Actually, a look at a good apparatus or at collations of MSS reveals that the "Byzantine" text-type is frequently shorter than its rivals. Sturz offers charts which show that where the "Byzantine" text with early papyrus support stands against both the "Western" and "Alexandrian" it adds 42 words and omits 36 words in comparison to them. The "Byzantine" comes out somewhat longer but the picture is not lopsided. Among the added words are 9 conjunctions and 5 articles but among the omitted are 11 conjunctions and 6 articles, which would make the "Byzantine" **less** smooth than its

But is it really true that interpolations are "many times more numerous" than omissions in the transmission of the New Testament? B.H. Streeter thought not.

> Hort speaks of "the almost universal tendency of transcribers to make their text as full as possible, and to eschew omissions"; and infers that copyists would tend to prefer an interpolated to an uninterpolated text. This may be true of some of the local texts of the second century; it is the very opposite of the truth where scribes or editors trained in the tradition of Alexandrian textual criticism are concerned. The Alexandrian editors of Homer were as eagle-eyed to detect and obelise "interpolations" in Homer as a modern critic...

> That Christian scholars and scribes were capable of the same critical attitude we have irrefragable evidence....The notion is completely refuted that the regular tendency of scribes was to choose the longer reading, and that therefore the modern editor is quite safe so long as he steadily rejects...

> Now, whoever was responsible for it, the B text has been edited on the Alexandrian principle.[1]

> The whole question of interpolations in ancient MSS has been set in an entirely new light by the researches of Mr. A. C. Clark, Corpus Professor of Latin at Oxford....In *The Descent of Manuscripts*, an investigation of the manuscript tradition of the Greek and Latin Classics, he proves conclusively that the error to which scribes were most prone was not interpolation but accidental omission....Hitherto the maxim *brevior lectio potior* ...has been assumed as a postulate of scientific criticism. Clark has shown that, so far as classical texts are concerned, the facts point entirely the other way.[2]

Burgon had objected long before.

> How indeed can it possibly be more true to the infirmities of copyists, to the verdict of evidence on the several passages and to the origin of the New Testament in the infancy of the Church and amidst associations which were not literary, to suppose that a terse production was first produced and afterwards was amplified in a

---

rivals. (Sturz, p. 229.)

[1] B.H. Streeter, *The Four Gospels: A Study of Origins* (London: Macmillan and Co., 1930), pp. 122-24. For a more recent discussion of critical activity at Alexandria, see W.R. Farmer, *The Last Twelve Verses of Mark* (Cambridge: Cambridge University Press, 1974), pp. 13-22.

[2] *Ibid.*, p. 131. I am aware that Kenyon and others have criticized Clark's treatment of this maxim, but I believe that it has sufficient validity to be worth taking into account. Having myself done collating in over 70 MSS, in those MSS omission was far more common than addition.

later age with a view to 'lucidity and completeness,' rather than that words and clauses and sentences were omitted upon definitely understood principles in a small class of documents by careless or ignorant or prejudiced scribes.[1]

Leo Vaganay also had reservations concerning this canon.

> As a rule the copyist, especially when at the work of revision, is inclined to amplify the text....But the rule suffers many exceptions...Distraction of the copyist,...intentional corrections...And finally,...the fundamental tendency of some recension, of which a good example is the Egyptian recension...And also we must not forget that the writers of the New Testament were Orientals, who are more given to length than to brevity.[2]

Kilpatrick actually suggests that a substitute canon, "the longer reading is preferable", would be no worse. He concludes:

> On reflection we do not seem able to find any reason for thinking that the maxim *lectio brevior potior* really holds good. We can only hope that a fuller acquaintance with the problems concerned will enable us increasingly to discern reasons in each instance why the longer or the shorter reading seems more probable.[3]

Colwell has published a most significant study of scribal habits as illustrated by the three early papyri $P^{45}$, $P^{66}$, and $P^{75}$. It demonstrates that broad generalizations about scribal habits should never have been made and it follows that ideas about variant readings and text-types based on such generalizations should be reconsidered. It will be well to quote Colwell at some length.

> The characterization of these singular readings can go on further until the individual scribes have been characterized. Their peculiar readings are due to their peculiarities. This has been well said by Dain. He reminds us that although all scribes make mistakes and mistakes of the same kind, yet each scribe has a personal coefficient of the frequency of his mistakes. Each has his own pattern of errors. One scribe is liable to dittography, another to the omission of lines of text; one reads well, another remembers poorly; one is a good speller; etc., etc. In these differences must be included the seriousness of intention of the scribe and the peculiarities of his own basic method of copying.[4]

---

[1] Burgon, The Causes of the Corruption, p. 156.

[2] Vaganay, pp. 84-85.

[3] Kilpatrick, p. 196.

[4] Colwell, "Scribal Habits", p. 378.

In general, $P^{75}$ copies letters one by one; $P^{66}$ copies syllables, usually two letters in length. $P^{45}$ copies phrases and clauses.

The accuracy of these assertions can be demonstrated. That $P^{75}$ copied letters one by one is shown in the pattern of the errors. He has more than sixty readings that involve a single letter, *and* not more than ten careless readings that involve a syllable. But $P^{66}$ drops sixty-one syllables (twenty-three of them in "leaps") and omits as well a dozen articles and thirty short words. In $P^{45}$ there is not one omission of a syllable in a "leap" nor is there any list of "careless" omissions of syllables. $P^{45}$ omits words and phrases.[1]

As an editor the scribe of $P^{45}$ wielded a sharp axe. The most striking aspect of his style is its conciseness. The dispensable word is dispensed with. He omits adverbs, adjectives, nouns, participles, verbs, personal pronouns—without any compensating habit of addition. He frequently omits phrases and clauses. He prefers the simple to the compound word. In short, he favors brevity. He shortens the text in at least fifty places in *singular readings alone*. But he does *not* drop syllables or letters. His shortened text is readable.[2]

Enough of these have been cited to make the point that $P^{66}$ editorializes as he does everything else—in a sloppy fashion. He is not guided in his changes by some clearly defined goal which is always kept in view. If he has an inclination toward omission, it is not "according to knowledge," but is whimsical and careless, often leading to nothing but nonsense.[3]

$P^{66}$ has 54 leaps forward, and 22 backward; 18 of the forward leaps are haplography.
$P^{75}$ has 27 leaps forward, and 10 backward.
$P^{45}$ has 16 leaps forward, and 2 backward.
From this it is clear that the scribe looking for his lost place looked ahead three times as often as he looked back. In other words, the loss of position usually resulted in a loss of text, an omission.[4]

The tables have been turned. Here is a clear statistical demonstration that interpolations are **not** "many times more numerous" than omissions. Omission is more common as an unintentional error than addition, and $P^{45}$ shows that with some scribes omissions were *deliberate* and extensive. Is it mere

---

[1] *Ibid.*, p. 380.

[2] *Ibid.*, p. 383.

[3] *Ibid.*, p. 387.

[4] *Ibid.*, pp. 376-77.

coincidence that Aleph and B were probably made in the same area as P[45] and exhibit similar characteristics? In any case, the "fullness" of the Traditional Text, rather than a proof of inferiority, emerges as a point in its favor.

## The harder reading

Another canon used against the "Byzantine" text is *proclivi lectioni praestat ardua*—the harder reading is to be preferred. The basis for this is an alleged propensity of scribes or copyists to simplify or change the text when they found a supposed difficulty or something they didn't understand. But where is the statistical demonstration that warrants such a generalization? Probably, as in the case of the canon just discussed, when such a demonstration is forthcoming it will prove the opposite.

Vaganay said of this canon:

> But the more difficult reading is not always the more probably authentic. The rule does not apply, for instance, in the case of some accidental errors...But, what is worse, we sometimes find difficult or intricate readings that are the outcome of intentional corrections. A copyist, through misunderstanding some passage, or through not taking the context into account, may in all sincerity make something obscure that he means to make plain.[1]

Have we not all heard preachers do this very thing?

Metzger notes Jerome's complaint: "Jerome complained of the copyists who 'write down not what they find but what they think is the meaning: and while they attempt to rectify the errors of others, they merely expose their own'."[2] (Just so, producing what would appear to us to be 'harder readings' but which readings are spurious.)

After recounting an incident at an assembly of Cypriot bishops in 350 A.D. Metzger concludes:

> Despite the vigilance of ecclesiastics of Bishop Spyridon's temperament, it is apparent from even a casual examination of a critical apparatus that scribes, offended by real or imagined errors of spelling, grammar, and historical fact, deliberately introduced changes into what they were transcribing.[3]

Would not many of these changes appear to us to be 'harder readings'?

In any case, the amply documented fact that numerous people in the second century made deliberate changes in the text, whether for doctrinal or other reasons, introduces an unpredictable variable which invalidates this canon.

---

[1] Vaganay, p. 86.

[2] Metzger, *The Text*, p. 195.

[3] *Ibid.*, p. 196.

Once a person arrogates to himself the authority to alter the text there is nothing in principle to keep individual caprice from intruding or taking over—we have no way of knowing what factors influenced the originator of a variant (whoever he was) or whether the result would appear to us to be 'harder' or 'easier'. This canon is simply inapplicable.[1]

Another problem with this canon is its vulnerability to the manipulation of a skillful and determined imagination. With sufficient ingenuity, virtually any reading can be made to look 'convincing'. Hort is a prime example of this sort of imagination and ingenuity. Zuntz has stated:

> Dr. Hort's dealing with this and the other patristic evidence for this passage [1 Cor.13:3] requires a word of comment. No one could feel greater respect, nay reverence, for him than the present writer; but his treatment of this variant, in making every piece of the evidence say the opposite of its true meaning, shows to what distortions even a great scholar may be driven by the urge to square the facts with an erroneous, or at least imperfect theory. Souter, Plummer, and many others show the aftereffect of Dr. Hort's tenacity.[2]

Salmon has noted the same thing: "That which gained Hort so many adherents had some adverse influence with myself—I mean his extreme cleverness as an advocate; for I have felt as if there were no reading so improbable that he could not give good reasons for thinking it to be the only genuine".[3]

Samuel Hemphill wrote of Hort's role in the New Testament Committee that produced the Revised Version of 1881:

> Nor is it difficult to understand that many of their less resolute and decided colleagues must often have been completely carried off their feet by the persuasiveness and resourcefulness, and zeal of Hort,...In fact, it can hardly be doubted that Hort's was the strongest will of the whole Company, and his adroitness in debate was only equaled by his pertinacity.[4]

---

[1] To anyone who feels that we are obligated to explain the origin of any or every peculiar variant reading, even if found in only one or two copies—especially if the copies happen to be B, Aleph or one of the Papyri—Burgon calls attention to the far greater correlative obligation. "It frequently happens that the one remaining plea of many critics for adopting readings of a certain kind, is the inexplicable nature of the phenomena which these readings exhibit. 'How will you possibly account for such a reading as the present,' (say they,) 'if it be not authentic?'...They lose sight of the correlative difficulty:— How comes it to pass that the rest of the copies read the place otherwise?" (*The Causes of the Corruption*, p. 17.)

[2] Zuntz, *The Text*, p. 36.

[3] Salmon, pp. 33-34.

[4] S. Hemphill, *A History of the Revised Version* (London: Elliot Stock, 1906), pp. 49-50.

(It would appear that the composition of the Greek text used by the English Revisers—and consequently for the RSV, NASB, etc.—was determined in large measure by Hort's cleverness and pertinacity, inspired by his devotion to a single Greek manuscript.)

Hort's performance shows the reasonableness of Colwell's warning against "the distortion of judgment which so easily manipulates the criteria of internal evidence".[1]

## *Harmonization*[2]

It has been widely asserted that the "Byzantine" text is characterized by harmonizations, e.g. Metzger: "The framers of this text sought…to harmonize divergent parallel passages".[3] By the choice of this terminology it is assumed that the diverse readings found in the minority of MSS are original and that copyists felt impelled to make parallel accounts agree. Perhaps it is time to ask whether it ever has been or can be proved that such an interpretation is correct. Jakob Van Bruggen says of Metzger's statement, "this judgment has not been proven, and cannot be proven".[4]

---

[1] Colwell, "External Evidence", p. 2. The application is mine; Colwell would perhaps not have agreed with it.

[2] We now have access to W.F. Wisselink's massive four volume evaluation of this question. His work deprives the opponents of the Byzantine text of this their last argument.

[3] Metzger, A Textual Commentary, p. xx.

[4] Jakob Van Bruggen, *The Ancient Text of the New Testament* (Winnipeg: Premier, 1976), p. 30. Cf. W.F. Wisselink, *Assimilation as a Criterion for the Establishment of the Text*, 4 vols. (Kampen: Uitgeversmaatschappij J.H. Kok, 1989). Wisselink concludes: "Assimilations occur in all manuscripts. Even in manuscript B there is a question of assimilation in 31 percent of the 1489 variations that have been investigated. In $P^{75}$ the number of assimilations is: 39 percent of the 165 variations that have been investigated" (p. 87). Maurice A. Robinson contributes the following relevant questions:

1) Why did not the Byzantine Textform develop as it should have [by the Hortian hypothesis], and move more consistently toward harmonization of all passages?
2) Why do we instead find as many or more possible harmonizations among the minority texttypes as is alleged to have occurred in regard to the Byzantine Textform?
3) Further, why did the keepers and guardians of the Byzantine tradition correctly reject the vast bulk of such harmonizations? Most harmonizations never gained more than a slight foothold which could not and did not endure.
4) Why also—if harmonization were so common, as well as a popular tendency within a growing and continuing process—did not the plain and clear "early harmonizations" among representatives of the Alexandrian and Western texttypes endure as the text progressed into the Byzantine era?
5) Why, especially, were pre-existing harmonizations as found in the Western and Alexandrian traditions *de*-harmonized by the scribes of the Byzantine era,

## 1) Van Bruggen

Because Van Bruggen's valuable work may not be available to many readers, I will quote from his treatment of the subject in hand at some length. His reaction to Metzger's statement continues:

> Often illustrative examples are given to support this negative characterization of the Byzantine text. But it would not be difficult to "prove", with the aid of specially chosen examples from other text-types, that those types are also guilty of harmonizing, conflating readings and smoothing the diction.[1]

Kilpatrick, using strictly internal evidence, concludes that, "though the Syrian text has its share of harmonizations, other texts including the Egyptian have suffered in this way. We cannot condemn the Syrian text for harmonization. If we do, we must condemn the other texts too on the same grounds."[2]

Van Bruggen continues:

> Here illustrations do not prove anything. After all, one could without much difficulty give a large number of examples from the Byzantine text to support the proposition that this text does *not* harmonize and does *not* smooth away. In commentaries the exegete is often satisfied with the incidental example without comparing it to the textual data as a whole. Yet a proposition about the Byzantine *type* should not be based on illustrations, but on arguments from the text *as a whole*. Whoever wishes to find such arguments will meet a number of methodical problems and obstacles which obstruct the way to the proof. Here we can mention the following points:
>
> 1. Methodically we must first ask how a "type" is determined. This can not be done on the basis of selected readings, because then the selection will soon be determined by what one is trying to prove. You can only speak of a text-type if the characteristics which must distinguish the type are not incidental but are found all along, and if they do not appear in other types from which the type must be distinguished. The criteria must be distinctive and general. As far as this is concerned, suspicion is roused when Hort remarks that the harmonizing and assimilating interpolations in the Byzantine text are "fortunately capricious and incomplete" (*Introduction*, p. 135). Did Hort then indeed generalize and make characteristics of some

---

since this was precisely the opposite of what should have occurred?
Robinson, "Two Passages in Mark: A Critical Test for the Byzantine-Priority Hypothesis", presented to the forty-sixth annual meeting of the E.T.S., Nov., 1994, p. 25.
The interested reader would do well to read pp. 24-34 of this paper—Robinson makes a number of telling points.

[1] *Ibid.* Cf. E.F. Hills, "Harmonizations in the Caesarean Text of Mark", *Journal of Biblical Literature*, 66 (1947), 135-152.

[2] Kilpatrick, p. 193.

readings into characteristics of the text-type? This suspicion becomes certainty when Metzger in his *Textual Commentary* has to observe more than once that non-Byzantine readings, for example, in the Codex Vaticanus, can be explained from the tendencies of scribes to assimilate and to simplify the text.[1]

In a footnote, Van Bruggen cites Metzger's discussion of Matthew 19:3 and 19:9, John 6:14, James 2:3, 4:14, 5:16, and 5:20, where harmonization and other smoothing efforts are ascribed to Codex B and its fellow-travelers. His discussion proceeds:

> What is typical for the Byzantine text is apparently not so exclusive for this text-type! But if certain phenomena seem to appear in all types of text, then it is not right to condemn a type categorically and regard it as secondary on the ground of such phenomena.
>
> 2. Moreover, it is methodically difficult to speak of harmonizing and assimilating deviations in a text, when the original is not known. Or is it an axiom that the original text in any case was so inharmonious, that every harmonious reading is directly suspect? Hort lets us sense that he personally does not prefer a New Testament "more fitted for cursory perusal or recitation than for repeated and diligent study" (*Introduction*, p. 153). Yet who, without the original at his disposal, can prove that this original had those characteristics which a philologist and a textual critic considers to be most recommendable?[2]

P. Walters comments upon Hort's sense of style as follows:

> Hort's sense of style, his idea of what was correct and preferable in every alternative, was acquired from a close acquaintance with his "neutral" text. It did not occur to him that most of its formal aspects tallied with his standards just because these were taken from his model. So far his decisions are in the nature of a vicious circle: We today who live outside this magic circle, which kept a generation spellbound, are able to see through Hort's illusion.[3]

Van Bruggen continues:

> 4. If editors of the Byzantine text would have been out to harmonize the text and to fit parallel passages of the Gospels into each other, then we must observe that they let nearly all their opportunities go by....In addition, what seems to be harmonization is in a different direction often no harmonization. A reading may seem adjusted to

---

[1] Van Bruggen, pp. 30-31.

[2] *Ibid.*, pp. 31-32.

[3] P. Walters, *The Text of the Septuagint. Its Corruptions and their Emendation*, ed. D.W. Gooding (Cambridge: University Press, 1973), p. 21. (Cited by van Bruggen.)

the parallel passage in another Gospel, but then often deviates again from the reading in the third Gospel. A reading may seem borrowed from the parallel story, yet at the same time fall out of tune in the context of the Gospel itself. Here the examples are innumerable as long as one does not limit himself to a few texts and pays attention to the context and the Gospels as a whole.[1]

With reference to giving due attention to the context, Van Bruggen reports on a study wherein he compared the TR with Nestle[25] in fourteen extended passages to see if either one could be characterized as harmonizing or assimilating.

> The comparison of the edition Stephanus (1550) with Nestle-Aland (25th edition) led to the result that the dilemma "harmonizing/not harmonizing" is unsuited to distinguish both of these text-editions. We examined Matthew 5:1-12; 6:9-13; 13:1-20; 19:1-12; Mark 2:18-3:6; Luke 9:52-62; 24:1-12; John 6:22-71; Acts 18:18-19:7; 22:6-21; 1 Corinthians 7; James 3:1-10; 5:10-20; Revelation 5. In the comparative examination not only the context, but also all the parallel passages were taken into account. Since the Stephanus-text is closely related to the Byzantine text and the edition Nestle-Aland is clearly non-Byzantine, the result of this investigation may also apply to the relation between the Byzantine text and other text-types: the dilemma "harmonizing/not harmonizing" or "assimilating/not assimilating" is unsound to distinguish *types* in the textual tradition of the New Testament.[2]

One is reminded of Burgon's observation that decisions based on internal considerations are often "the product of personal bias, or limited observation".[3] In this connection it will be well to consider some examples.

## 2) Examples

Mark 1:2—shall we read "in Isaiah the prophet" with the "Alexandrian-Western" texts or "in the prophets" with the "Byzantine" text? All critical editions follow the first reading and Fee affirms that it is "a clear example of 'the most difficult reading being preferred as the original'."[4] I would say that Fee's superficial discussion is a "clear example" of personal bias (toward the 'harder reading' canon) and of limited observation. The only other places that Isaiah 40:3 is quoted in the New Testament are Matthew 3:3, Luke 3:4, and John 1:23. The first two are in passages parallel to Mark 1:2 and all three are

---

[1] Van Bruggen, pp. 32-33.

[2] *Ibid.*, p. 33.

[3] Burgon, The Traditional Text, p. 67.

[4] Fee, "A Critique of W.N. Pickering's *The Identity of the New Testament Text*: A Review Article", *The Westminster Theological Journal*, XLI (Spring, 1979), p. 411.

identical to the LXX. The quote in John differs from the LXX in one word and is also used in connection with John the Baptist. The crucial consideration, for our present purpose, is that Matthew, Luke, and John all identify the quote as being from Isaiah (without MS variation). It seems clear that the "Alexandrian-Western" reading in Mark 1:2 is simply an assimilation to the other three Gospels. It should also be noted that the material from Malachi looks more like an allusion than a direct quote. Further, although Malachi is quoted (or alluded to) a number of times in the New Testament, he is never named. Mark's own habits may also be germane to this discussion. Mark quotes Isaiah in 4:12, 11:17, and 12:32 and alludes to him in about ten other places, all without naming his source. The one time he does use Isaiah's name is when quoting Jesus in 7:6.[1] It is the "Byzantine" text that has escaped harmonization and preserves the original reading.

Mark 10:47 -- *Ναζαρηνος* B L W Δ Θ Ψ 1 lat cop
              *Ναζορηνος* D
              *Ναζωραιος* Byz ℵ A C (K) X Π 13 *pl* it[pt] syr

//Luke 18:37 -- *Ναζαρηνος* D 1 *pc*
             *Ναζωραιος* *rell*

Mark 1:24 -- *Ναζαρηνε* all agree
Mark 14:67 -- *Ναζαρηνου* all agree
Mark 16:6 -- *Ναζαρηνον* all agree except that ℵand D omit.

All critical editions follow the first reading in Mark 10:47 and interpret the "Byzantine" reading as an assimilation to Luke 18:37 (where they reject the reading of D). It should be observed, however, that everywhere else that Mark uses the word the -*αρην*- form occurs. Is it not just as possible that Codex B and company have assimilated to the prevailing Markan form?[2]

Mark 8:31 -- *μετα τρεις ημερας* all agree

//Matt 16:21 -- *μετα τρεις ημερας* D *al*
         *τη τριτη ημερα* *rell*

//Luke 9:22 -- *μεθ ημερας τρεις* D it
         *τη τριτη ημερα* *rell*

Mark 9:31 -- *μετα τρεις ημερας* ℵ B C D L Δ
        *τη τριτη ημερα* Byz Θ *pl*

//Matt 17:23 -- *μετα τρεις ημερας* D it
        *τη τριτη ημερα* *rell*

Mark 10:34 -- *μετα τρεις ημερας* ℵ B C D L Δ Ψ it cop
        *τη τριτη ημερα* Byz A[c] K W X Θ Π 1 13 *pl* syr

---

[1] I owe the material in the above discussion to Maurice A. Robinson.

[2] This discussion is adapted from Van Bruggen, pp. 33-34.

//Matt 10:19 -- τη τριτη ημερα    all agree
//Luke 18:33 -- τη ημερα τη τριτη all agree

All critical editions follow the first reading in Mark 9:31 and 10:34 and interpret the "Byzantine" reading as an assimilation to Matthew, in both cases. But why, then, did the "Byzantines" not also assimilate in Mark 8:31 where there was the pressure of both Matthew **and** Luke? Is it not more likely that the "Alexandrians" made Mark consistent (note that Matthew is consistent) by assimilating the latter two instances to the first one? Note that in this example and the preceding one it is Codex D that engages in the most flagrant assimilating activity.[1]

Mark 13:14—shall we read "spoken of through Daniel the prophet" with the "Byzantine" text or follow the "Alexandrian-Western" text wherein this phrase is missing? All critical editions take the second option and Fee assures us that the "Byzantine" text has assimilated to Matthew 24:15 where all witnesses have the phrase in question.[2] But let us consider the actual evidence:

> Matt 24:15 -- το ρηθεν <u>δια</u> Δανιηλ του προφητου
> Mark 13:14 -- το ρηθεν <u>υπο</u> Δανιηλ του προφητου

If the "Byzantines" were intent on copying from Matthew, why did they alter the wording? If their purpose was to harmonize, why did they <u>dis</u>harmonize, to use Fee's expression? Furthermore, if we compare the full pericope in both Gospels, Matthew 24:15-22 and Mark 13:14-20, using the "Byzantine" text, although the two accounts are of virtually equal length, fully one third of the words are different between them. The claim that the "Byzantines" were given to harmonizing becomes silly. Still further, there appear to be three clear assimilations to Mark on the part of the "Alexandrian-Western" witnesses, and one to Matthew—επι to εις in Matthew 24:15, καταβαινετω to καταβατω in Matthew 24:17, τα ιματια to το ιματιον in Matthew 24:18, and the omission of ων in Mark 13:16—plus three other "Western" assimilations—τα to τι in Matthew 24:17, και to ουδ in Mark 13:19, and δε added to Matthew 24:17. But, returning to the first variant, why would the "Alexandrians" have omitted the phrase in question? A comparison of the LXX of Daniel with the immediate context suggests an answer. Mark's phrase, "where he ought not", is not to be found in Daniel. That some people felt Mark's integrity needed protecting is

---

[1] This discussion is adapted from Van Bruggen, p. 34. I suspect that a thorough check will reveal that it is the "Western" text that leads all others in harmonization, not the "Byzantine". Wisselink confirms this, "D especially has been assimilated" (p. 87). Here is his conclusion.

> With rather great certainty we can come to this conclusion: Assimilation is not restricted to a single group of manuscripts, neither to a single gospel; assimilation has not taken place to any one gospel to a strikingly high degree. So if an assimilation is signalized, nothing can be concluded from that regarding the age of any variant or the value of any text-type. (Wisselink, p. 92.)

[2] Fee, "A Critique", pp. 411-12.

clear from the remedial actions attempted by a few Greek and version MSS. The Alexandrian omission may well be such an attempt.[1]

To conclude, it is demonstrable that all "text-types" have many possible harmonizations. It has not been demonstrated that the "Byzantine" text has more possible or actual harmonizations than the others. It follows that "harmonization" may not reasonably or responsibly be used to argue for an inferior "Byzantine" text type.

## Inferiority

Hort did not offer a statistical demonstration in support of his characterization of the "Byzantine" text.[2] Metzger refers to von Soden as supplying adequate evidence for the characterization. Upon inspection of the designated pages,[3] we discover there is no listing of manuscript evidence and no discussion. His limited lists of references purportedly illustrating addition or omission or assimilation, etc., may be viewed differently by a different mind. In fact, Kilpatrick has argued for the originality of a considerable number of Byzantine readings of the sort von Soden listed.[4]

The length of the lists, in any case, is scarcely prepossessing. No one has done for the "Byzantine" text anything even remotely approximating what

---

[1] I owe the material used in the above discussion to Robinson.

[2] Hort's characterization is similar to contemporary descriptions of Koine Greek in New Testament times.
   Non-biblical sources attest that there was such a simple and plain style of Greek writing and speaking stemming from the earliest New Testament times. Such sources as the non-biblical papyri and the Discourses of Epictetus, the Stoic philosopher, attest this style. In addition, there is a formal delineation of what the plain style ought to be, which has been dated at approximately the same time in which the New Testament was being written. *Demetrius, On Style*, names "the plain style"...as one of four which he describes and discusses....parts of his treatment of this subject tend to remind one of descriptions of the Koine of the Hellenistic period and the kind of Greek supposed to characterize the New Testament...
   In spite of the known existence of such a plain style as set forth by Demetrius and found in Epictetus, there were those in the early period of the Church and its writings who scoffed at the plain style and spoke contemptuously of it as it is found in the Scriptures. One of these was the pagan Celsus, who sought to refute the Christian faith in a literary attack penned sometime between 161-180 A.D. Origen indicates that Celsus ridiculed the Scriptures by holding them up to unfavorable comparison with the writings of the philosophers in places where there seemed to be some parallel (Sturz, pp. 112-13).

[3] H.F. von Soden, *Die Schriften des Neuen Testaments* (2 Vols.; Gottingen: Vandenhoeck und Ruprecht, 1911), Vol. 1, part ii, pp. 1456-1459 (cf. 1361-1400), 1784-1878.

[4] Kilpatrick, *Op. Cit.*

Hoskier did for Codex B, filling 450 pages with a careful discussion, one by one, of many of its errors and idiosyncrasies.[1]

As we have already noted, Hort declared the *Textus Receptus* to be "villainous" and "vile" when he was only twenty-three years old—before he had studied the evidence, before he had worked through the text to evaluate variant readings one by one. Do you suppose he brought an open mind to that study and evaluation?

Elliott and Kilpatrick profess to do their evaluating with an open mind, with no predilections as to text-types, yet inescapably use the ambiguous canons of internal evidence. What do they conclude? Elliott decided the "Byzantine" text was right about as often as Aleph and D, the chief representatives of the "Alexandrian" and "Western" texts (in the Pastorals).[2] Kilpatrick affirms:

> Our principal conclusion is that the Syrian text is frequently right. It has avoided at many points mistakes and deliberate changes found in other witnesses. This means that at each variation we must look at the readings of the Byzantine manuscripts with the possibility in mind that they may be right. We cannot dismiss their characteristic variants as being in principle secondary.[3]

The basic deficiency, both fundamental and serious, of any characterization based upon subjective criteria is that the result is only opinion; it is not objectively verifiable. Is there no better way to identify the original wording of the New Testament? I believe there is, but first there is one more tenet of Hort's theory to scrutinize.

# The "Lucianic Recension" and the Peshitta

Burgon gave the sufficient answer to this invention.

> Apart however from the gross intrinsic improbability of the supposed Recension,—the utter absence of one particle of evidence, traditional or otherwise, that it ever did take place, must be held to be fatal to the hypothesis that it *did*. It is simply incredible that an incident of such magnitude and interest would leave no trace of itself in history.[4]

It will not do for someone to say that the argument from silence proves nothing. In a matter of this "magnitude and interest" it is conclusive. Kenyon, also, found this part of Hort's theory to be gratuitous.

---

[1] Hoskier, *Codex B*, Vol. I. I fail to see how anyone can read this work of Hoskier's with attention and still retain a high opinion of Codices B and Aleph.

[2] Elliott, pp. 241-43.

[3] Kilpatrick, p. 205.

[4] Burgon, The Revision Revised, p. 293.

The absence of evidence points the other way; for it would be very strange, if Lucian had really edited both Testaments, that only his work on the Old Testament should be mentioned in after times. The same argument tells against any theory of a deliberate revision at any definite moment. We know the names of several revisers of the Septuagint and the Vulgate, and it would be strange if historians and Church writers had all omitted to record or mention such an event as the deliberate revision of the New Testament in its original Greek.[1]

Colwell is blunt: "The Greek Vulgate—the Byzantine or Alpha text-type—had in its origin no such single focus as the Latin had in Jerome".[2] F.C. Grant is prepared to look into the second century for the origin of the "Byzantine" text-type.[3] Jacob Geerlings, who has done extensive work on certain branches of the "Byzantine" text-type, affirms concerning it: "Its origins as well as those of other so-called text-types probably go back to the autographs".[4]

In an effort to save Hort's conclusions, seemingly, Kenyon sought to attribute the "Byzantine" text to a "tendency".

> It seems probable, therefore, that the Syrian revision was rather the result of a tendency spread over a considerable period of time than of a definite and authoritative revision or revisions, such as produced our English Authorised and Revised Versions. We have only to suppose the principle to be established in Christian circles in and about Antioch that in the case of divergent readings being found in the texts copied, it was better to combine both than to omit either, and that obscurities and roughnesses of diction should be smoothed away as much as possible.[5]

But what if we choose not "to suppose" anything, but rather to insist upon evidence? We have already seen from Hutton's *Atlas* that for every instance that the "Syrian" text possibly combines divergent readings there are a hundred where it does not. What sort of a "tendency" is that? To insist that a variety of scribes separated by time and space and working independently, but all feeling a responsibility to apply their critical faculties to the text, should produce a uniformity of text such as is exhibited within the "Byzantine" text seems to be asking a bit much, both of them and of us. Hodges agrees.

---

[1] Kenyon, *Handbook*, pp. 324-25.

[2] Colwell, "The Origin of the Texttypes", p. 137.

[3] F.C. Grant, "The Citation of Greek Manuscript Evidence in an Apparatus Criticus", *New Testament Manuscript Studies*, ed. M.M. Parvis and A.P. Wikgren (Chicago: The University of Chicago Press, 1950), pp. 90-91.

[4] J. Geerlings, *Family E and Its Allies in Mark* (Salt Lake City: University of Utah Press, 1967), p. 1.

[5] Kenyon, *Handbook*, p. 325.

It will be noted in this discussion that in place of the former idea of a specific revision as the source-point for the Majority text, some critics now wish to posit the idea of a "process" drawn out over a long period of time. It may be confidently predicted, however, that this explanation of the Majority text must likewise eventually collapse. The Majority text, it must be remembered, is relatively uniform in its general character with comparatively low amounts of variation between its major representatives. No one has yet explained how a long, slow process spread out over many centuries as well as over a wide geographical area, and involving a multitude of copyists, who often knew nothing of the state of the text outside of their own monasteries or scriptoria, could achieve this widespread uniformity out of the diversity presented by the earlier forms of text. Even an official edition of the New Testament— promoted with ecclesiastical sanction throughout the known world— would have had great difficulty achieving this result as the history of Jerome's Vulgate amply demonstrates. But an unguided process achieving relative stability and uniformity in the diversified textual, historical, and cultural circumstances in which the New Testament was copied, imposes impossible strains on our imagination.[1]

An ordinary process of textual transmission results in divergence, not convergence. Uniformity of text is usually greatest near the source and diminishes in transmission.

The accumulating evidence seemed not to bother Metzger. He still affirmed in 1968 that the "Byzantine" text is based on a recension prepared by Lucian.[2] There is an added problem with that view.

Lucian was an Arian, a vocal one. Does Metzger seriously invite us to believe that the victorious Athanasians embraced an Arian revision of the Greek New Testament?

As to the Syriac Peshitta, again Burgon protested the complete lack of evidence for Hort's assertions.[3] A. Vööbus says of Burkitt's effort:

Burkitt has tried to picture the lifespan of Bishop Rabbula as a decisive period in the development of the New Testament text in the Syrian church.

---

[1] Hodges, "A Defense of the Majority Text", p. 42. For a further discussion of the problems confronting the "process" view see the section headed **"Objections"** in Appendix C.

[2] Metzger, *The Text*, (2nd ed., 1968), p. 212. In 1972 he wrote "Whether it really was Lucian...", so he may have retreated from that position. "Patristic Evidence and the Textual Criticism of the New Testament", *New Testament Studies*, XVIII (1972), p. 385.

[3] Burgon, *The Revision Revised*, pp. 276-77.

Regardless of the general acceptance of the axiom, established by him, that "the authority of Rabbula secured an instant success for the new revised version..." and that "copies of the Peshitta were rapidly multiplied, it soon became the only text in ecclesiastical use"—this kind of reconstruction of textual history is pure fiction without a shred of evidence to support it.[1]

Vööbus finds that Rabbula himself used the Old Syriac type of text. His researches show clearly that the Peshitta goes back at least to the mid-fourth century and that it was not the result of an authoritative revision.[2]

Here again there is an added historical difficulty.

> The Peshitta is regarded as authoritative Scripture by both the Nestorians and the Monophysites. It is hard to see how this could have come to pass on the hypothesis that Rabbula was the author and chief promoter of the Peshitta. For Rabbula was a decided Monophysite and a determined opponent of the Nestorians. It is almost contrary to reason, therefore, to suppose that the Nestorian Christians would adopt so quickly and so unanimously the handiwork of their greatest adversary.[3]

It is hard to understand how men like F.F. Bruce, E.C. Colwell, F.G. Kenyon, etc. could allow themselves to state dogmatically that Rabbula produced the Peshitta.

# Conclusion

And that completes our review of the W-H critical theory. It is evidently erroneous at every point. Our conclusions concerning the theory of necessity apply also to any Greek text constructed on the basis of it, as well as to those versions based upon such texts (and to commentaries based upon them).

K.W. Clark says of the W-H text: "The textual history postulated for the *textus receptus* which we now trust has been exploded".[4] Epp confesses that "we simply do not have a theory of the text".[5] The point is that "the establishment

---

[1] A. Vööbus, *Early Versions of the New Testament* (Stockholm: Estonian Theological Society in Exile, 1954), p. 100.

[2] *Ibid.*, pp. 100-102. Carson chides me for failing to mention "Matthew Black's decisive critique of Vööbus" (p. 112). Well, Metzger evidently did not regard it to be "decisive". "The question who it was that produced the Peshitta version of the N. T. will perhaps never be answered. That it was not Rabbula has been proved by Vööbus's researches" (*Early Versions of the New Testament* [Oxford: Clarendon Press, 1977], pp. 57-61).

[3] Burgon, *The Last Twelve Verses*, p. 56. Metzger recognizes the force of this circumstance (*Loc. Cit.*).

[4] Clark, "Today's Problems", p. 162.

[5] Epp, p. 403.

of the NT text can be achieved only by a reconstruction of the history of that early text...".[1] Colwell agrees: "Without a knowledge of the history of the text, the original reading cannot be established".[2]

In Aland's words, "Now as in the past, textual criticism without a history of the text is not possible".[3] Or as Hort himself put it, "ALL TRUSTWORTHY RESTORATION OF CORRUPTED TEXTS IS FOUNDED ON THE STUDY OF THEIR HISTORY".[4]

As already noted, one of the fundamental deficiencies of the eclectic method is that it ignores the history of the text. Hort did not ignore it, but what are we to say of his "clear and firm view"[5] of it? What Clark says is:

> The textual history that the Westcott-Hort text represents is no longer tenable in the light of newer discoveries and fuller textual analysis. In the effort to construct a congruent history, our failure suggests that we have lost the way, that we have reached a dead end, and that only a new and different insight will enable us to break through.[6]

The evidence before us indicates that Hort's history never was tenable.

The crucial question remains—*what sort of a history does the evidence reflect*? The identity of the New Testament text, our recognition of it, hinges upon our answer!

---

[1] *Ibid.*, p. 401.

[2] Colwell, "The Greek New Testament with a Limited Apparatus", p. 37. This theme pervades his "Hort Redivivus".

[3] Aland, "The Present Position", p. 731.

[4] Westcott and Hort, p. 40.

[5] Epp, "Interlude", pp. 391-92.

[6] Clark, "Today's Problems", p. 161.

# 5
# THE HISTORY OF THE TEXT

The logical place to start is with the possibility that the process of transmission of the text was normal.

> Under normal circumstances the older a text is than its rivals, the greater are its chances to survive in a plurality or a majority of the texts extant at any subsequent period. But the **oldest** text of all is the autograph. Thus it ought to be taken for granted that, barring some radical dislocation in the history of transmission, a majority of texts will be far more likely to represent correctly the character of the original than a small minority of texts. This is especially true when the ratio is an overwhelming 8:2. Under any reasonably normal transmissional conditions, it would be…quite impossible for a later text-form to secure so one-sided a preponderance of extant witnesses.[1]

But were the transmissional conditions reasonably normal?

## Were the N.T. Writings Recognized?

Naturalistic critics like to assume that the New Testament writings were not recognized as Scripture when they first appeared and thus through the consequent carelessness in transcription the text was confused and the original wording 'lost' (in the sense that no one knew for sure what it was) at the very start. Thus Colwell said: "Most of the manuals and handbooks now in print (including mine!) will tell you that these variations were the fruit of careless treatment which was possible because the books of the New Testament had not yet attained a strong position as 'Bible'."[2] And Hort had said:

> Textual purity, as far as can be judged from the extant literature, attracted hardly any interest. There is no evidence to show that care was generally taken to choose out for transcription the exemplars having the highest claims to be regarded as authentic, if indeed the requisite knowledge and skill were forthcoming.[3]

---

[1] Z.C. Hodges, "A Defense of the Majority Text" (unpublished course notes, Dallas Theological Seminary, 1975), p. 4.

[2] Colwell, *What is the Best New Testament?*, p. 53. [He subsequently changed his mind.]

[3] Westcott and Hort, p. 9. Cf. p. 7. It is clear that Hort regarded the "extant literature" as representative of the textual picture in the early centuries. This gratuitous and misleading idea continues to be an important factor in the thinking of some scholars today.

Rather than take Hort's word for it, prudence calls for a review of the premises. The place to start is at the beginning, when the apostles were still penning the Autographs.

## *The apostolic period*

It is clear that the apostle Paul, at least, considered his writings to be authoritative—see Romans 16:26,[1] 1 Corinthians 2:13 and 14:37, Galatians 1:6-**12**, Ephesians 3:4-6, Colossians 1:25-26, 1 Thessalonians 2:13, 2 Thessalonians 2:15 and 3:6-**14**. And it is reasonable to infer from Colossians 4:16 and 1 Thessalonians 5:27 that he expected his writings to have a wider audience than just the particular church addressed. In fact, in Galatians 1:2 he addresses "the church**es** of Galatia"; not to mention 2 Corinthians 1:1, "all the saints in Achaia", and 1 Corinthians 1:2, "all who in every place"! John also is plain enough—Revelation 1:1-3 and 21:5. And so is Peter—1 Peter 1:12, 22-25 and 2 Peter 3:2. Both Paul (Romans 16:25-6, Ephesians 3:4-5) and Peter (1 Peter 1:12, 25; 2 Peter 3:2) declare that a number of people are writing Scripture in their day, presumably including themselves. I take it that in 1:3 Luke claims divine authority—"having faithfully followed all things from Above".[2]

In I Timothy 5:18 Paul puts the Gospel of Luke (10:7) on the same level as Deuteronomy (25:4), calling them both "Scripture". Taking the traditional and conservative point of view, 1 Timothy is generally thought to have been written some fifteen years after Luke. Luke was recognized and declared by apostolic authority to be Scripture not very long after it came off the press, so to speak. For a man who was once a strict Pharisee to put Luke (still alive) on a level with Moses is astounding; it would have required the direction of the Holy Spirit.

In 2 Peter 3:15-16, Peter puts the Epistles of Paul on the same level as "the other Scriptures". Although some had been out for perhaps fifteen years, the ink was scarcely dry on others, and perhaps 2 Timothy had not yet been penned when Peter wrote. Paul's writings were recognized and declared by apostolic authority to be Scripture as soon as they appeared. In 1 Corinthians 15:4, "the Scriptures" presumably refers to the Gospels. In John 2:22 I would translate, "so they believed the Scripture, even the word that Jesus had spoken"—what Jesus said in John 2:19 was already circulating as 'Scripture' in Matthew 26:61 and 27:40 (when John wrote).

Clement of Rome, whose first letter to the Corinthians is usually dated about A.D. 96, made liberal use of Scripture, appealing to its authority, and used New Testament material right alongside Old Testament material. Clement quoted Psalm 118:18 and Hebrews 12:6 side by side as "the holy word" (56:3-

---

[1] According to 95% of the Greek manuscripts, the correct position for 16:24-26 is 14:24-26, while the wording remains the same.

[2] The normal, basic meaning of $\alpha\nu\omega\theta\epsilon\nu$ is "from up/above"; since that meaning fits here perfectly well I see no reason to appeal to a secondary meaning.

4).[1] He ascribes 1 Corinthians to "the blessed Paul the apostle" and says of it, "with true inspiration he wrote to you" (47:1-3). He clearly quotes from Hebrews, 1 Corinthians and Romans and possibly from Matthew, Acts, Titus, James and 1 Peter. Here is the bishop of Rome, before the close of the first century, writing an official letter to the church at Corinth wherein a selection of New Testament books are recognized and declared by episcopal authority to be Scripture, including Hebrews.

The Epistle of Barnabas, variously dated from A.D. 70 to 135, says in 4:14, "let us be careful lest, as it is written, it should be found with us that 'many are called but few chosen'." The reference seems to be to Matthew 22:14 (or 20:16) and the phrase "as it is written" may fairly be taken as a technical expression referring to Scripture. In 5:9 there is a quote from Matthew 9:13 (or Mark 2:17 or Luke 5:32). In 13:7 there is a loose quote from Romans 4:11-12, which words are put in God's mouth. Similarly, in 15:4 we find: "Note, children, what 'he ended in six days' means. It means this: that the Lord will make an end of everything in six thousand years, for a day with Him means a thousand years. And He Himself is my witness, saying: 'Behold, the day of the Lord shall be as a thousand years'."[2]

The author, whoever he was, is clearly claiming divine authorship for this quote which appears to be from 2 Peter 3:8.[3] In other words, 2 Peter is here regarded to be Scripture, as well as Matthew and Romans. Barnabas also has possible allusions to 1 and 2 Corinthians, Ephesians, Colossians, 1 and 2 Timothy, Titus, Hebrews, and 1 Peter.

---

[1] I am aware that it could be Proverbs 3:12 (LXX) rather than Hebrews 12:6. Clement quotes from both books repeatedly throughout the letter, so they are equal candidates on that score. But, Clement agrees verbatim with Hebrews while Proverbs (LXX) differs in one important word. Further, the main point of Clement's chapter 56 is that correction is to be received graciously and as from the Lord, which is also the point of Hebrews 12:3-11. Since Clement evidently had both books in front of him (in the next chapter he quotes nine consecutive verses, Proverbs 1:23-31) the verbatim agreement with Hebrews is significant. If he deliberately chose the wording of Hebrews over that of Proverbs, what might that imply about their rank?

[2] I have used the translation done by Francis Glimm in *The Apostolic Fathers* (New York: Cima Publishing Co., Inc., 1947), belonging to the set, *The Fathers of the Church*, ed. Ludwig Schopp.

[3] J.V. Bartlet says of the formulae of citation used in Barnabas to introduce quotations from Scripture, "the general result is an absolute doctrine of inspiration", but he is unwilling to consider that 2 Peter is being used. Oxford Society of Historical Research, *The New Testament in the Apostolic Fathers* (Oxford: Clarendon Press, 1905), pp. 2, 15.

## An aside—the implication of intended widespread circulation

By the time that Matthew 'published' his Gospel in AD 38,[1] the production of books in the Roman Empire was wide spread, but there was no 'copyright'. As soon as a book was turned loose it became 'public domain', anyone could use it and change it. Now then, if the Holy Spirit gave thought to protecting the works that He was inspiring, protecting against free editing, what could He do? I suggest that the most obvious way would be to have those works 'published' in the form of multiple copies. Today the first run of a book will be thousands of copies, but in those days each copy had to be handwritten (manuscript).

A book the size of Matthew's Gospel would represent a considerable investment of time and effort, as well as papyrus and ink. I believe the NT writings were prepared in book form from the first (not scroll), and the material used was probably papyrus.[2] However, papyrus cannot stand a lot of handling, and by the year 38 there were many Christian congregations just in Palestine, not to mention elsewhere. If the Holy Spirit intended that the NT writings should have a wide circulation, which would seem to be obvious, it would be necessary to start out with multiple copies. A single copy of Matthew would be falling apart before it got to the twentieth congregation (if on papyrus).

But why do I insist on papyrus instead of parchment? Well, a single copy of Matthew would represent around fifteen sheep or goats; on that basis, who could afford multiple copies? That said, however, the master copy may indeed have been done on parchment, for two reasons: if a master copy was to be kept, for quality control, it should be on durable material; if multiple copies of the master copy were to be made before turning it loose, a master copy on papyrus could not last.

The idea of publishing a book in the form of multiple copies may be inferred from the Epistles. 2 Corinthians was written to "the church of God which is at Corinth, with all the saints who are in all Achaia" (verse 1). How many congregations would there have been "in all Achaia"? Was Paul thinking of multiple copies? 1 Corinthians was addressed to "all those everywhere who call on the name of our Lord Jesus Christ" (verse 2). Now how many copies would **that** take? Galatians was written to "the churches of Galatia" (verse 2). Could a single copy get to all of them?

---

[1] The colophones in 50% of the MSS, including Family 35, say that Matthew was 'published' eight years after the ascension of the Christ. Since Jesus ascended in 30 AD, Matthew was released in 38. The colophones say that Mark was published two years later (40), and Luke another five years later (45), and John in 62.

[2] "Bring the books, especially the parchments" (2 timothy 4:13). We may gather from this that parchment was already in use, but the 'books' were presumably on papyrus; otherwise, why the contrast?

Consider the case of Peter's first letter: it is addressed to believers in "Pontus, Galatia, Cappadocia, Asia and Bithynia" (verse 1). Well now, what basis could Peter (apostle to the circumcised, Galatians 2:8) have for writing to people in those places? Probably a good number of the older leaders had been with Peter at Pentecost, and had sat under his ministry until the persecution under Saul sent them packing back home, presumably (Acts 8:4). Notice that the list of places in Acts 2:9-11 includes the following places in Asia Minor: Asia, Cappadocia, Pamphylia, Phrygia and Pontus. Three of the five are in Peter's list, and we need not assume that his list was exhaustive; for that matter, the list in Acts 2:9-11 is probably not exhaustive.

Have you ever looked at a map to see the location of Peter's five provinces? They basically represent the whole of Asia Minor (today's Turkey)! 'Asia' seems to have been used in different ways. Acts 27:2 has Asia including Cilicia and Pamphylia (verse 5). The glorified Christ put the seven churches in Asia (Revelation 1:4). In Acts 16:6 the term seems to refer to a more limited area, which, however, presumably included Ephesus, to which Paul returned later. Proconsular Asia included Mysia and Phrygia. Now how many congregations would there have been in all of Asia Minor? And how could a single copy get around to all of them? If the letter was written on papyrus (as seems likely—cheaper, more abundant) it would be falling apart by the time it got to the twentieth congregation, if not before (papyrus can't stand all that much handling).

Now let's just suppose, for the sake of the argument, that Peter sent five copies of his letter, one to each province. What would the implications be for the transmission of its Text? It means that you multiply the process and progress of transmission by five! It means that you have the beginnings of a 'majority text' very early on. It means that the basic integrity of the text would be guaranteed (the more so if God was superintending the process). If Peter sent out more than five copies, so much the more. And what about James; how many copies would it take to reach "the twelve tribes that are in the dispersion" (verse 1)? (Doesn't the very term 'dispersion' suggest that they were widely scattered? And what if the 'twelve tribes' is literal?) Peter's second letter doesn't list the five provinces, but 3:1 would appear to indicate that he was targeting the same area.

To see that I didn't pull the idea of multiple copies out of thin air, let's consider 2 Peter 1:12-15. Verses 12 & 13 refer to repeated reminders while he is still in his 'tent', which would be his own ongoing activity; so why the 'moreover' in verse 15? In the NKJV verse 15 reads: "Moreover, I will be careful to ensure that you always have a reminder of these things after my decease". Well, how can you 'ensure' that someone will 'always have a reminder' of something? It seems clear to me that the something has to be written down; a reminder has to be in writing, to be guaranteed. So what is Peter's intention? He specifies "a reminder of these things", so what are the 'these things'? They are evidently the things he will discuss in this letter. But he must be referring to something more than the initial draft of the letter (or the verse becomes meaningless)—hence, multiple copies.[1]

If Peter wrote his second letter under divine inspiration, then 1:15 is inspired, and in that event the idea of multiple copies came from God. It would be an efficient means of preserving the Text and guaranteeing its integrity down through the years of transmission. The churches in Asia Minor could always cross check with one another whenever a doubt arose or need required. If it was God's idea that a small letter be 'published' in the form of multiple copies, then how much more the larger books. Obviously God knew what He was doing, so the practice would have begun with the very first NT book, Matthew.[2]

The idea is so good that it became the norm, the more so if it was a divine order. I believe all the NT books were released in the form of multiple copies, with the exception of the letters addressed to individuals. (Since Luke and Acts are addressed to an individual, they also may have started out as a single copy, unless Theophilus was a 'benefactor' who was financing the multiple copies. Luke and Acts are the two longest books of the NT, and multiple copies of them would represent a significant financial investment.) Again I say, the idea is so good, I wouldn't be surprised if once they got it the churches would set about making multiple copies of other writings they considered to be inspired, such as letters to individuals. A 'majority text' would be well established throughout the Aegean area (Greece and Asia Minor) already in the first century. The 'heartland of the Church' (to use K. Aland's phrase)

---

[1] It was Mike Loehrer, a pastor in California, www.michaelcannonloehrer.com, who called 2 Peter 1:12-15 to my attention and got me started thinking about it. With reference to verse 15 he wrote me the following: "Could choosing to use μνεμε with ποιεο in the middle voice mean to ensure a way of always being able to validate a memory? In those days most people could not afford their own copy of a writing, and the church would no doubt become the repository of an autograph anyway. The usual way of getting the Scripture back then was by committing it to memory when hearing it during the public reading. Having multiple autographs in multiple locations would definitely ensure a way of validating a memory. Even if the leaders of a church or synagogue were imprisoned and their autograph was seized or destroyed, they could rest assured that they could locate another autograph to validate their memory of the way a verse or passage was actually written."

The idea of validating a memory is as interesting as it is suggestive. Peter's use of μνημη, basically reflexive, with ποιεω in the middle voice, makes Mike's suggestion a reasonable one, as it seems to me. It goes along with the multiple copies. Irenaeus puzzled over verse 15 and came up with the suggestion that Peter intended to get copies of Mark's Gospel to those regions. Evidently the idea of multiple copies was not strange to him. And how about other books?

[2] Quite apart from the idea of 'publishing' via multiple copies, consider what would happen when a congregation received a copy of 1 Peter, James, or any of Paul's Epistles, accompanied by the instruction that they had to pass it on. If you were one of the elders of that congregation, what would you do? I would most certainly make a copy for us to keep. Wouldn't you? The point is, as soon as an inspired book began to circulate, the proliferation of copies began at once. And that means that a 'majority text' also began at once!

simply kept on using and copying that form of text—hence the mass of Byzantine MSS that have come down to us.

## *The second century*

The seven letters of Ignatius (c. A.D. 110) contain probable allusions to Matthew, John, Romans, 1 Corinthians and Ephesians (in his own letter to the Ephesians Ignatius says they are mentioned in "all the epistles of Paul"—a bit of hyperbole, but he was clearly aware of a Pauline corpus), and possible allusions to Luke, Acts, Galatians, Philippians, Colossians, 1 Thessalonians, 1 and 2 Timothy, and Titus, but very few are clear quotations and even they are not identified as such.

Polycarp, writing to the Philippian church (c. 115 A.D.?), weaves an almost continuous string of clear quotations and allusions to New Testament writings. His heavy use of Scripture is reminiscent of Clement of Rome; however, Clement used mostly the Old Testament while Polycarp usually used the New. There are perhaps fifty clear quotations taken from Matthew, Luke, Acts, Romans, 1 and 2 Corinthians, Galatians, Ephesians, Philippians, Colossians, 1 and 2 Thessalonians, 1 and 2 Timothy, 1 and 2 Peter, and 1 John, and many allusions including to Mark, Hebrews, James, and 2 and 3 John. (The only NT writer not included is Jude! But remember that the above refers to only one letter—if Polycarp wrote other letters he may well have quoted Jude.) Please note that the idea of NT 'canon' evidently already existed in 115 A.D., and Polycarp's 'canon' was quite similar to ours.

His attitude toward the New Testament writings is clear from 12:1: "I am sure that you are well trained in the sacred Scriptures,…Now, as it is said in these Scriptures: 'Be angry and sin not,' and 'Let not the sun go down upon your wrath.' Blessed is he who remembers this."[1]

Both parts of the quotation could come from Ephesians 4:26 but since Polycarp split it up he may have been referring to Psalm 4:5 (LXX) in the first half. In either case he is declaring Ephesians to be "sacred Scripture". A further insight into his attitude is found in 3:1-2.

> Brethren, I write you this concerning righteousness, not on my own initiative, but because you first invited me. For neither I, nor anyone like me, is able to rival the wisdom of the blessed and glorious Paul, who, when living among you, carefully and steadfastly taught the word of truth face to face with his contemporaries and, when he was absent, wrote you letters. By the careful perusal of his letters you will be able to strengthen yourselves in the faith given to you, "which is the mother of us all",…[2]

---

[1] Francis Glimm, again.

[2] Ibid.

(This from one who was perhaps the most respected bishop in Asia Minor, in his day. He was martyred in A.D. 156.)

The so-called second letter of Clement of Rome is usually dated before A.D. 150 and seems clearly to quote from Matthew, Mark, Luke, Acts, I Corinthians, Ephesians, 1 Timothy, Hebrews, James, and 1 Peter, with possible allusions to 2 Peter, Jude, and Revelation. After quoting and discussing a passage from the Old Testament, the author goes on to say in 2:4, "Another Scripture says: 'I came not to call the just, but sinners'" (Matthew 9:13; Mark 2:17; Luke 5:32). Here is another author who recognized the New Testament writings to be Scripture.

Two other early works, the *Didache* and the letter to Diognetus, employ New Testament writings as being authoritative but without expressly calling them Scripture.

The *Didache* apparently quotes from Matthew, Luke, 1 Corinthians, Hebrews, and 1 Peter and has possible allusions to Acts, Romans, Ephesians, 1 and 2 Thessalonians and Revelation.

The letter to Diognetus quotes from Acts, 1 and 2 Corinthians while alluding to Mark, John, Romans, Ephesians, Philippians, 1 Timothy, Titus, 1 Peter and 1 John.

Another early work—the Shepherd of Hermas—widely used in the second and third centuries, has fairly clear allusions to Matthew, Mark, 1 Corinthians, Ephesians, Hebrews, and especially James.

From around the middle of the second century fairly extensive works by Justin Martyr (martyred in 165) have come down to us. His "Dialogue with Trypho" shows a masterful knowledge of the Old Testament to which he assigns the highest possible authority, evidently holding to a dictation view of inspiration— in *Trypho* 34 he says, "to persuade you that you have not understood anything of the Scriptures, I will remind you of another psalm, dictated to David by the Holy Spirit."[1] The whole point of *Trypho* is to prove that Jesus is Christ and God and therefore what He said and commanded was of highest authority.

In *Apol.* i.66 Justin says, "For the apostles in the memoirs composed by them, which are called Gospels, thus handed down what was commanded them..."[2] And in *Trypho* 119 he says that just as Abraham believed the voice of God, "in like manner we, having believed God's voice spoken by the apostles of Christ..."

It also seems clear from *Trypho* 120 that Justin considered New Testament writings to be Scripture. Of considerable interest is an unequivocal reference

---

[1] I have used the translation in Vol. I of *The Ante-Nicene Fathers*, ed., A. Roberts and J. Donaldson (Grand Rapids: Wm. B. Eerdmans Publishing Co., 1956).

[2] I have used the translation by E.R. Hardy in *Early Christian Fathers*, ed., C.C. Richardson (Philadelphia: The Westminster Press, 1953).

to the book of Revelation in *Trypho* 81. "And further, there was a certain man with us whose name was John, one of the apostles of Christ, who prophesied, by a revelation that was made to him, that those who believe in our Christ would dwell a thousand years in Jerusalem."[1]

Justin goes right on to say, "Just as our Lord also said", and quotes Luke 20:35, so evidently he considered Revelation to be authoritative. (While on the subject of Revelation, in 165 Melito, Bishop of Sardis, wrote a commentary on the book.)

A most instructive passage occurs in *Apol.* i.67.

> And on the day called Sunday there is a meeting in one place of those who live in cities or the country, and the memoirs of the apostles or the writings of the prophets are read as long as time permits. When the reader has finished, the president in a discourse urges and invites us to the imitation of these noble things.[2]

Whether or not the order suggests that the Gospels were preferred to the Prophets, it is clear that they both were considered to be authoritative and equally enjoined upon the hearers. Notice further that each assembly must have had its own copy of the apostles' writings to read from and that such reading took place every week.

Athenagoras, in his "Plea", written in early 177, quotes Matthew 5:28 as Scripture: "...we are not even allowed to indulge in a lustful glance. For, says the Scripture, 'He who looks at a woman lustfully, has already committed adultery in his heart'" (32).[3] He similarly treats Matthew 19:9, or Mark 10:11, in 33.

Theophilus, bishop of Antioch, in his treatise to Autolycus, quotes 1 Timothy 2:1 and Romans 13:7 as "the Divine Word" (iii.l4), quotes from the fourth Gospel, saying that John was "inspired by the Spirit" (ii.22); Isaiah and "the Gospel" are mentioned in one paragraph as Scripture (iii.l4), and he insists in several passages that the writers never contradicted each other: "The statements of the Prophets and of the Gospels are found to be consistent, because all were inspired by the one Spirit of God" (ii.9; ii.35; iii.l7).[4]

---

[1] Roberts and Donaldson, again.

[2] E.R. Hardy, again. His careful study of the early Christian literary papyri has led C.H. Roberts to conclude: "This points to the careful and regular use of the scriptures by the local communities" (*Manuscript, Society and Belief in Early Christian Egypt* [London: Oxford Univ. Press, 1979], p. 25). He also infers from P. Oxy. iii. 405 that a copy of Irenaeus' *Adversus Haereses*, written in Lyons, was brought to Oxyrhynchus within a very few years after it was written (*Ibid.*, pp. 23, 53), eloquent testimony to the extent of the traffic among the early churches.

[3] I have used the translation by C.C. Richardson in *Early Christian Fathers*.

[4] Taken from G.D. Barry, *The Inspiration and Authority of Holy Scripture* (New York: The McMillan Company, 1919), p. 52.

The surviving writings of Irenaeus (died in 202), his major work *Against Heretics* being written about 185, are about equal in volume to those of all the preceding Fathers put together.

> His testimony to the authority and inspiration of Holy Scripture is clear and unequivocal. It pervades the whole of his writings; and this testimony is more than ordinarily valuable because it must be regarded as directly representing three churches at least, those of Lyons, Asia Minor, and Rome. The authoritative use of both Testaments is clearly laid down.[1]

Irenaeus stated that the apostles taught that God is the Author of both Testaments (*Against Heretics* IV. 32.2) and evidently considered the New Testament writings to form a second Canon. He quoted from every chapter of Matthew, 1 Corinthians, Galatians, Ephesians, Colossians and Philippians, from all but one or two chapters of Luke, John, Romans, 2 Thessalonians, 1 and 2 Timothy, and Titus, from most chapters of Mark (including the last twelve verses), Acts, 2 Corinthians, and Revelation, and from every other book except Philemon and 3 John. These two books are so short that Irenaeus may not have had occasion to refer to them in his extant works—it does not necessarily follow that he was ignorant of them or rejected them. Evidently the dimensions of the New Testament Canon recognized by Irenaeus are very close to what we hold today.

From the time of Irenaeus on there can be no doubt concerning the attitude of the Church toward the New Testament writings—they are Scripture. Tertullian (in 208) said of the church at Rome, "the law and the prophets she unites in one volume with the writings of evangelists and apostles" (*Prescription against Heretics*, 36).

# Were Early Christians Careful?

It has been widely affirmed that the early Christians were either unconcerned or unable to watch over the purity of the text. (Recall Hort's words given above.) Again a review of the premises is called for. Many of the first believers had been devout Jews who had an ingrained reverence and care for the Old Testament Scriptures which extended to the very jots and tittles. This reverence and care would naturally be extended to the New Testament Scriptures.

Why should modern critics assume that the early Christians, in particular the spiritual leaders among them, were inferior in integrity or intelligence? A Father's quoting from memory or tailoring a passage to suit his purpose in sermon or letter by no means implies that he would take similar liberties when transcribing a book or corpus. Ordinary honesty would require him to produce a faithful copy. Are we to assume that everyone who made copies of New Testament books in those early years was a knave, or a fool? Paul was certainly as intelligent a man as any of us. If Hebrews was written by someone

---

[1] *Ibid.*, p. 53.

else, here was another man of high spiritual insight and intellectual power. There was Barnabas and Apollos and Clement and Polycarp, etc., etc. The Church has had men of reason and intelligence all down through the years. Starting out with what they **knew** to be the pure text, the earliest Fathers did not need to be textual critics. They had only to be reasonably honest and careful. But is there not good reason to believe they would be **especially** watchful and careful?

## The apostles

Not only did the apostles themselves declare the New Testament writings to be Scripture, which would elicit reverence and care in their treatment, they expressly warned the believers to be on their guard against false teachers—see Acts 20:27-32, Galatians 1:6-12, 2 Timothy 3:1-4:4, 2 Peter 2:1-2, 1 John 2:18-19, 2 John 7-11, Jude 3-4, 16-19. Peter's statement concerning the "twisting" Paul's words were receiving (2 Peter 3:16) suggests there was awareness and concern as to the text and the way it was being handled. I recognize that the Apostles were focusing on the interpretation rather than the copying of the text, and yet, since any alteration of the text may result in a different interpretation we may reasonably infer that their concern for the truth would include the faithful transmission of the text. Indeed, we could scarcely ask for a clearer expression of this concern than that given in Revelation 22:18-19; since it is the glorified Christ who is speaking, would not any true follower of His pay careful attention? Sovereign Jesus clearly expressed this protective concern early in His earthly ministry. In Matthew 5:19 we read: "whoever annuls one of the least of these commandments, and teaches men so…" Note, "one of the least"; the Lord's concern extends down to "the least". 2 Thessalonians 2:2 is evidently concerned with authenticity.

## The early Fathers

The early Fathers furnish a few helpful clues as to the state of affairs in their day. The letters of Ignatius contain several references to a considerable traffic between the churches (of Asia Minor, Greece, Rome) by way of messengers (often official), which seems to indicate a deep sense of solidarity binding them together, and a wide circulation of news and attitudes—a problem with a heretic in one place would soon be known all over, etc. That there was strong feeling about the integrity of the Scriptures is made clear by Polycarp (7:1), "Whoever perverts the sayings of the Lord…that one is the firstborn of Satan". Present-day critics may not like Polycarp's terminology, but for him to use such strong language makes clear that he was not merely aware and concerned; he was <u>exercised</u>.

Similarly, Justin Martyr says (*Apol.* i.58), "the wicked demons have also put forward Marcion of Pontus". Again, such strong language makes clear that he was aware and concerned. And in *Trypho* xxxv he says of heretics teaching doctrines of the spirits of error, that fact "causes us who are disciples of the true and pure doctrine of Jesus Christ to be more faithful and steadfast in the hope announced by Him."

It seems obvious that heretical activity would have precisely the effect of putting the faithful on their guard and forcing them to define in their own minds what they were going to defend. Thus Marcion's truncated canon evidently stirred the faithful to define the true canon. But Marcion also altered the wording of Luke and Paul's Epistles, and by their bitter complaints it is clear that the faithful were both aware and concerned. We may note in passing that the heretical activity also furnishes backhanded evidence that the New Testament writings were regarded as Scripture—why bother falsifying them if they had no authority?

Dionysius, Bishop of Corinth (168-176), complained that his own letters had been tampered with, and worse yet the Holy Scriptures also.

And they insisted that they had received a pure tradition. Thus Irenaeus said that the doctrine of the apostles had been handed down by the succession of bishops, being guarded and preserved, without any forging of the Scriptures, allowing neither addition nor curtailment, involving public reading without falsification (*Against Heretics* IV. 32:8).

Tertullian, also, says of his right to the New Testament Scriptures, "I hold sure title-deeds from the original owners themselves...I am the heir of the apostles. Just as they carefully prepared their will and testament, and committed it to a trust...even so I hold it."[1]

## *Irenaeus*

In order to ensure accuracy in transcription, authors would sometimes add at the close of their literary works an adjuration directed to future copyists. So, for example, Irenaeus attached to the close of his treatise *On the Ogdoad* the following note: "I adjure you who shall copy out this book, by our Lord Jesus Christ and by his glorious advent when he comes to judge the living and the dead, that you compare what you transcribe, and correct it carefully against this manuscript from which you copy; and also that you transcribe this adjuration and insert it in the copy."[2]

If Irenaeus took such extreme precautions for the accurate transmission of his own work, how much more would he be concerned for the accurate copying of the Word of God? In fact, he demonstrates his concern for the accuracy of the text by defending the traditional reading of a **single letter**. The question is whether John the Apostle wrote $\chi\xi\varsigma'$ (666) or $\chi\iota\varsigma'$ (616) in Revelation 13:18. Irenaeus asserts that 666 is found "in all the most approved and ancient copies" and that "those men who saw John face to face" bear witness to it. And he warns those who made the change (of a single letter) that "there shall

---

[1] *Prescription against Heretics*, 37. I have used the translation done by Peter Holmes in Vol. III of *The Ante-Nicene Fathers*.

[2] Metzger, *The Text*, p. 21.

be no light punishment upon him who either adds or subtracts anything from the Scripture" (xxx.1). Presumably Irenaeus is applying Revelation 22:18-19.

Considering Polycarp's intimacy with John, his personal copy of Revelation would most probably have been taken from the Autograph. And considering Irenaeus' veneration for Polycarp his personal copy of Revelation was probably taken from Polycarp's. Although Irenaeus evidently was no longer able to refer to the Autograph (not ninety years after it was written!) he was clearly in a position to identify a faithful copy and to declare with certainty the original reading—this in 186 A.D. Which brings us to Tertullian.

## Tertullian

Around the year 208 he urged the heretics to

> ...run over the apostolic churches, in which the very thrones of the apostles are still pre-eminent in their places, in which their own authentic writings (*authenticae*) are read, uttering the voice and representing the face of each of them severally. Achaia is very near you, (in which) you find Corinth. Since you are not far from Macedonia, you have Philippi; (and there too) you have the Thessalonians. Since you are able to cross to Asia, you get Ephesus. Since, moreover, you are close upon Italy, you have Rome, from which there comes even into our own hands the very authority (of the apostles themselves).[1]

Some have thought that Tertullian was claiming that Paul's Autographs were still being read in his day (208), but at the very least he must mean they were using faithful copies. Was anything else to be expected? For example, when the Ephesian Christians saw the Autograph of Paul's letter to them getting tattered, would they not carefully execute an identical copy for their continued use? Would they let the Autograph perish without making such a copy? (There must have been a constant stream of people coming either to make copies of their letter or to verify the correct reading.) I believe we are obliged to conclude that in the year 200 the Ephesian Church was still in a position to attest the original wording of her letter (and so for the others)—but this is coeval with $P^{46}$, $P^{66}$ and $P^{75}$!

Both Justin Martyr and Irenaeus claimed that the Church was spread throughout the whole earth, in their day—remember that Irenaeus, in 177, became bishop of Lyons, in **Gaul**, and he was not the first bishop in that area. Coupling this information with Justin's statement that the memoirs of the apostles were read each Sunday in the assemblies, it becomes clear that there must have been thousands of copies of the New Testament writings in use by 200 A.D. Each assembly would need at least one copy to read from, and there must have been private copies among those who could afford them.

We have objective historical evidence in support of the following propositions:

---

[1] *Prescription against Heretics*, 36, using Holmes' translation.

• The true text was never 'lost'.

• In A.D. 200 the exact original wording of the several books could still be verified and attested.

• There was therefore no need to practice textual criticism and any such effort would be spurious.

However, presumably some areas would be in a better position to protect and transmit the true text than others.

# Who Was Best Qualified?

What factors would be important for guaranteeing, or at least facilitating, a faithful transmission of the text of the N.T. writings? I submit that there are four controlling factors: access to the Autographs, proficiency in the source language, the strength of the Church and an appropriate attitude toward the Text.

## *Access to the Autographs*

This criterion probably applied for well less than a hundred years (the Autographs were presumably worn to a frazzle in that space of time) but it is highly significant to a proper understanding of the history of the transmission of the Text. Already by the year 100 there must have been many copies of the various books (some more than others) while it was certainly still possible to check a copy against the original, or a guaranteed copy, should a question arise. The point is that there was a swelling stream of faithfully executed copies emanating from the holders of the Autographs to the rest of the Christian world. In those early years the producers of copies would know that the true wording could be verified, which would discourage them from taking liberties with the text.

However, distance would presumably be a factor—for someone in north Africa to consult the Autograph of Ephesians would be an expensive proposition, in both time and money. I believe we may reasonably conclude that in general the quality of copies would be highest in the area surrounding the Autograph and would gradually deteriorate as the distance increased. Important geographical barriers would accentuate the tendency.

So who held the Autographs? Speaking in terms of regions, Asia Minor may be safely said to have had twelve (John, Galatians, Ephesians, Colossians, 1 and 2 Timothy, Philemon, 1 Peter, 1 and 2 and 3 John, and Revelation), Greece may be safely said to have had six (1 and 2 Corinthians, Philippians, 1 and 2 Thessalonians, and Titus in Crete), Rome may be safely said to have had two (Mark and Romans)—as to the rest, Luke, Acts, and 2 Peter were probably held by either Asia Minor or Rome; Matthew and James by either Asia Minor or Palestine; Hebrews by Rome or Palestine; while it is hard to state even a probability for Jude it was quite possibly held by Asia Minor. Taking Asia Minor and Greece together, the Aegean area held the Autographs of at least eighteen (two-thirds of the total) and possibly as many as twenty-four of the twenty-seven New Testament books; Rome held at least two and possibly up to seven; Palestine may have held up to three (but in A.D. 70 they would have been sent away for safe keeping, quite possibly to Antioch); Alexandria (Egypt) held **none**. The Aegean region clearly had the best start, and Alexandria the worst—the text in Egypt could only be second hand, at best. On the face of it, we may reasonably assume that in the earliest period of the transmission of the N.T. Text the most reliable copies would be circulating in the region that held the Autographs. Recalling the discussion of Tertullian above, I believe we may reasonably extend this conclusion to A.D. 200 and beyond. So, in the year 200 someone looking for the best text of the N.T. would presumably go to the Aegean area; certainly not to Egypt. [1]

## *Proficiency in the source language*

As a linguist (PhD) and one who has dabbled in the Bible translation process for some years, I affirm that a 'perfect' translation is impossible. (Indeed, a tolerably reasonable approximation is often difficult enough to achieve—the semantic areas of the words simply do not match, or only in part.) It follows that any divine solicitude for the precise form of the NT Text would have to be mediated through the language of the Autographs—Greek. Evidently ancient Versions (Syriac, Latin, Coptic) may cast a clear vote with reference to major variants, but precision is possible only in Greek (in the case of the N.T.). That by way of background, but our main concern here is with the copyists.

To copy a text by hand in a language you do not understand is a tedious exercise—it is almost impossible to produce a perfect copy (try it and see!). You virtually have to copy letter by letter and constantly check your place. (It is even more difficult if there is no space between words and no punctuation, as was the case with the N.T. Text in the early centuries.) But if you cannot understand the text it is very difficult to remain alert. Consider the case of P[66]. This papyrus manuscript is perhaps the oldest (c. 200) extant N.T. manuscript of any size (it contains most of John). It is one of the worst copies we have. It has an average of roughly two mistakes per verse—many being obvious mistakes, stupid mistakes, nonsensical mistakes. From the pattern of mistakes it is clear that the scribe copied syllable by syllable. I have no qualms in affirming that the person who produced P[66] did not know Greek. Had he understood the text he would not have made the number and sort of mistakes that he did.

---

[1] Aland states: "Egypt was distinguished from other provinces of the Church, so far as we can judge, by the early dominance of gnosticism". He further informs us that "at the close of the 2nd century" the Egyptian church was "dominantly gnostic" and then goes on to say: "The copies existing in the gnostic communities could not be used, because they were under suspicion of being corrupt". Now this is all very instructive— what Aland is telling us, in other words, is that up to A.D. 200 the textual tradition in Egypt **could not be trusted**. (K. and B. Aland, p. 59 and K. Aland, "The Text of the Church?", *Trinity Journal*, 1987, 8NS:138.)

Now consider the problem from God's point of view. To whom should He entrust the primary responsibility for the faithful transmission of the N.T. Text (recall 1 Chronicles 16:15)? If the Holy Spirit was going to take an active part in the process, where should He concentrate His efforts? Presumably fluent speakers of Greek would have the inside track, and areas where Greek would continue in active use would be preferred. For a faithful transmission to occur the copyists had to be proficient in Greek, and over the long haul. So where was Greek predominant? Evidently in Greece and Asia Minor; Greek is the mother tongue of Greece to this day (having changed considerably during the intervening centuries, as any living language must). The dominance of Greek in the Aegean area was guaranteed by the Byzantine Empire for many centuries; in fact, until the invention of printing. Constantinople fell to the Ottoman Turks in 1453; the Gutenberg Bible (Latin) was printed just three years later, while the first printed Greek New Testament appeared in 1516. (For those who believe in Providence, I would suggest that here we have a powerful case in point.)

How about Egypt? The use of Greek in Egypt was already declining by the beginning of the Christian era. Bruce Metzger observes that the Hellenized section of the population in Egypt "was only a fraction in comparison with the number of native inhabitants who used only the Egyptian languages".[1] By the third century the decline was evidently well advanced. I have already argued that the copyist who did P[66] (c. 200) did not know Greek. Now consider the case of P[75] (c. 220). E.C. Colwell analyzed P[75] and found about 145 itacisms plus 257 other singular readings, 25% of which are nonsensical. From the pattern of mistakes it is clear that the copyist who did P[75] copied letter by letter![2] This means that he did not know Greek—when transcribing in a language you know you copy phrase by phrase, or at least word by word. K. Aland argues that before 200 the tide had begun to turn against the use of Greek in the areas that spoke Latin, Syriac or Coptic, and fifty years later the changeover to the local languages was well advanced.[3]

Again the Aegean Area is far and away the best qualified to transmit the Text with confidence and integrity. Note that even if Egypt had started out with a good text, already by the end of the 2nd century its competence to transmit the text was steadily deteriorating. In fact the early papyri (they come from Egypt) are demonstrably inferior in quality, taken individually, as well as exhibiting rather different types of text (they disagree among themselves).

---

[1] Metzger, *Early Versions*, p. 104.

[2] Colwell, "Scribal Habits", pp. 374-76, 380.

[3] K. and B. Aland, *The Text of the New Testament* (Grand Rapids: Eerdmans, 1981), pp. 52-53.

## The strength of the Church

This question is relevant to our discussion for two reasons. First, the law of supply and demand operates in the Church as well as elsewhere. Where there are many congregations and believers there will be an increased demand for copies of the Scriptures. Second, a strong, well established church will normally have a confident, experienced leadership—just the sort that would take an interest in the quality of their Scriptures and also be able to do something about it. So in what areas was the early Church strongest?

Although the Church evidently began in Jerusalem, the early persecutions and apostolic activity caused it to spread. The main line of advance seems to have been north into Asia Minor and west into Europe. If the selection of churches to receive the glorified Christ's "letters" (Revelation 2 and 3) is any guide, the center of gravity of the Church seems to have shifted from Palestine to Asia Minor by the end of the first century. (The destruction of Jerusalem by Rome's armies in A.D. 70 would presumably be a contributing factor.) Kurt Aland agrees with Adolf Harnack that "about 180 the greatest concentration of churches was in Asia Minor and along the Aegean coast of Greece". He continues: "The overall impression is that the concentration of Christianity was in the East....Even around A.D. 325 the scene was still largely unchanged. Asia Minor continued to be the heartland of the Church."[1] "The heartland of the Church"—so who else would be in a better position to certify the correct text of the New Testament?

What about Egypt? C.H. Roberts, in a scholarly treatment of the Christian literary papyri of the first three centuries, seems to favor the conclusion that the Alexandrian church was weak and insignificant to the Greek Christian world in the second century.[2] Aland states: "Egypt was distinguished from other provinces of the Church, so far as we can judge, by the early dominance of gnosticism."[3] He further informs us that "at the close of the 2nd century" the Egyptian church was "dominantly gnostic" and then goes on to say: "The copies existing in the gnostic communities could not be used, because they were under suspicion of being corrupt".[4] Now this is all very instructive—what Aland is telling us, in other words, is that up to A.D. 200 the textual tradition in Egypt **could not be trusted**. Aland's assessment here is most probably correct. Notice what Bruce Metzger says about the early church in Egypt:

> Among the Christian documents which during the second century either originated in Egypt or circulated there among both the orthodox and the Gnostics are numerous apocryphal gospels, acts, epistles, and apocalypses... There are also fragments of exegetical and dogmatic works composed by Alexandrian Christians, chiefly

---

[1] *Ibid.*, p. 53.

[2] Roberts, pp. 42-43, 54-58.

[3] K. and B. Aland, p. 59.

[4] K. Aland, "The Text of the Church?", *Trinity Journal*, 1987, 8NS:138.

Gnostics, during the second century... In fact, to judge by the comments made by Clement of Alexandria, almost every deviant Christian sect was represented in Egypt during the second century; Clement mentions the Valentinians, the Basilidians, the Marcionites, the Peratae, the Encratites, the Docetists, the Haimetites, the Cainites, the Ophites, the Simonians, and the Eutychites. What proportion of Christians in Egypt during the second century were orthodox is not known.[1]

It is almost enough to make one wonder whether Isaiah 30:1-3 might not be a prophecy about N.T. textual criticism!

But we need to pause to reflect on the implications of Aland's statements. He was a champion of the Egyptian ("Alexandrian") text-type, and yet he himself informs us that up to A.D. 200 the textual tradition in Egypt could not be trusted and that by 200 the use of Greek had virtually died out there. So on what basis can he argue that the Egyptian text subsequently became the best? Aland also states that in the 2nd century, 3rd century, and into the 4th century Asia Minor continued to be "the heartland of the Church". This means that the superior qualifications of the Aegean area to protect, transmit and attest the N.T. Text carry over into the 4th century! It happens that Hort, Metzger and Aland (along with many others) have linked the "Byzantine" text-type to Lucian of Antioch, who died in 311. Now really, wouldn't a text produced by a leader in "the heartland of the Church" be better than whatever evolved in Egypt? Of course I ask the above question only to point out their inconsistency. The 'Byzantine' text-type existed long before Lucian.

## Attitude toward the Text

Where careful work is required, the attitude of those to whom the task is entrusted is of the essence. Are they aware? Do they agree? If they do not understand the nature of the task, the quality will probably do down. If they understand but do not agree, they might even resort to sabotage—a damaging eventuality. In the case of the N.T. books we may begin with the question: "Why would copies be made?"

We have seen that the faithful recognized the authority of the N.T. writings from the start, so the making of copies would have begun at once. The authors clearly intended their writings to be circulated, and the quality of the writings was so obvious that the word would get around and each assembly would want a copy. That Clement and Barnabas quote and allude to a variety of N.T. books by the turn of the 1st century makes clear that copies were in circulation. A Pauline corpus was known to Peter before A.D. 70. Polycarp (XIII) c. 115, in answer to a request from the Philippian church, sent a collection of Ignatius' letters to them, possibly within five years after Ignatius wrote them. Evidently it was normal procedure to make copies and collections (of worthy writings) so each assembly could have a set. Ignatius referred to the

---

[1] Metzger, *Early Versions*, p. 101.

free travel and exchange between the churches and Justin to the weekly practice of reading the Scriptures in the assemblies (they had to have copies).

A second question would be: "What was the attitude of the copyists toward their work?" We already have the essence of the answer. Being followers of Christ, and believing that they were dealing with Scripture, to a basic honesty would be added reverence in their handling of the Text, from the start. And to these would be added vigilance, since the Apostles had repeatedly and emphatically warned them against false teachers. As the years went by, assuming that the faithful were persons of at least average integrity and intelligence, they would produce careful copies of the manuscripts they had received from the previous generation, persons whom they trusted, being assured that they were transmitting the true text. There would be accidental copying mistakes in their work, but no deliberate changes. It is important to note that the earliest Christians did not need to be textual critics. Starting out with what they knew to be the pure text, they had only to be reasonably honest and careful. I submit that we have good reason for understanding that they were especially watchful and careful—this especially in the early decades.[1]

As time went on regional attitudes developed, not to mention regional politics. The rise of the so-called "school of Antioch" is a relevant consideration. Beginning with Theophilus, a bishop of Antioch who died around 185, the Antiochians began insisting upon the literal interpretation of Scripture. The point is that a literalist is obliged to be concerned about the precise wording of the text since his interpretation or exegesis hinges upon it.

It is reasonable to assume that this "literalist" mentality would have influenced the churches of Asia Minor and Greece and encouraged them in the careful and faithful transmission of the pure text that they had received. For example, the 1,000 MSS of the Syriac Peshitta are unparalleled for their consistency. (By way of contrast, the 8,000+ MSS of the Latin Vulgate are remarkable for their extensive discrepancies, and in this they follow the example of the Old Latin MSS.) It is not unreasonable to suppose that the Antiochian antipathy toward the Alexandrian allegorical interpretation of Scripture would rather indispose them to view with favor any competing forms of the text coming out of Egypt. Similarly the Quarto-deciman controversy with Rome would scarcely enhance the appeal of any innovations coming from the West.

To the extent that the roots of the allegorical approach that flourished in Alexandria during the third century were already present, they would also be a negative factor. Since Philo of Alexandria was at the height of his influence when the first Christians arrived there, it may be that his allegorical interpretation of the O.T. began to rub off on the young church already in the

---

[1] Having myself collated at least one book in some 70 MSS belonging to the line of transmission that I call Family 35, I have a perfect copy of at least 22 of the 27 NT books, copies made in the 11th, 12th, 13th and 14th centuries. For a copy to be perfect in the 14th century, all of its 'ancestors' had to be perfect, all the way back to the family archetype. I believe that the archetype of Family 35 is the Autograph, but if not, it must date back to the 3rd century, at least.

first century. Since an allegorist is going to impose his own ideas on the text anyway, he would presumably have fewer inhibitions about altering it—precise wording would not be a high priority.

The school of literary criticism that existed at Alexandria would also be a negative factor, if it influenced the Church at all, and W.R. Farmer argues that it did. "But there is ample evidence that by the time of Eusebius the Alexandrian text-critical practices were being followed in at least some of the scriptoria where New Testament manuscripts were being produced. Exactly when Alexandrian text-critical principles were first used…is not known."[1] He goes on to suggest that the Christian school founded in Alexandria by Pantaenus, around 180, was bound to be influenced by the scholars of the great library of that city. The point is, the principles used in attempting to 'restore' the works of Homer would not be appropriate for the NT writings when appeal to the Autographs, or exact copies made from them, was still possible.

## Conclusion

What answer do the "four controlling factors" give to our question? The four speak with united voice: "The Aegean area was the best qualified to protect, transmit and attest the true text of the N.T. writings." This was true in the 2nd century; it was true in the 3rd century; it continued to be true in the 4th century. And now we are ready to answer the question, "Was the transmission normal?", and to attempt to trace the history of the text.

# Was the Transmission Normal?

Was the transmission normal? Yes and no. Assuming the faithful were persons of at least average integrity and intelligence they would produce reasonable copies of the manuscripts they had received from the previous generation, persons whom they trusted, being assured that they were transmitting the true text. There would be accidental copying mistakes in their work, but no deliberate changes. But there were others who expressed an interest in the New Testament writings, persons lacking in integrity, who made their own copies with malicious intent. There would be accidental mistakes in their work too, but also deliberate alteration of the text. I will trace first the normal transmission.

## The normal transmission

We have seen that the faithful recognized the authority of the New Testament writings from the start—had they not they would have been rejecting the authority of the Apostles, and hence not been among the faithful. To a basic honesty would be added reverence in their handling of the text, from the start. And to these would be added vigilance, since the Apostles had repeatedly and emphatically warned them against false teachers.

---

[1] W.R. Farmer, *The Last Twelve Verses of Mark* (Cambridge: University Press, 1974), pp. 14-15. He cites B.H. Streeter, *The Four Gospels*, 1924, pp. 111, 122-23.

With an ever-increasing demand and consequent proliferation of copies throughout the Graeco-Roman world and with the potential for verifying copies by having recourse to the centers still possessing the Autographs, the early textual situation was presumably highly favorable to the wide dissemination of MSS in close agreement with the original text. By the early years of the second century the dissemination of such copies can reasonably be expected to have been very widespread, with the logical consequence that the form of text they embodied would early become entrenched throughout the area of their influence.

The considerations just cited are crucial to an adequate understanding of the history of the transmission of the text because they indicate that a basic trend was established at the very beginning—a trend that would continue inexorably until the advent of a printed N.T. text. I say "inexorably" because, given a normal process of transmission, the science of statistical probability demonstrates that a text form in such circumstances could scarcely be dislodged from its dominant position—the probabilities against a competing text form ever achieving a majority attestation would be prohibitive no matter how many generations of MSS there might be. (The demonstration vindicating my assertion is in Appendix C.) It would take an extraordinary upheaval in the transmissional history to give currency to an aberrant text form. We know of no place in history that will accommodate such an upheaval.

The argument from probability would apply to secular writings as well as the New Testament and does not take into account any unusual concern for purity of text. I have argued, however, that the early Christians did have a special concern for their Scriptures and that this concern accompanied the spread of Christianity. Thus Irenaeus clearly took his concern for textual purity (which extended to a single letter) to Gaul and undoubtedly influenced the Christians in that area. The point is that the text form of the N.T. Autographs had a big advantage over that of any secular literature, so that its commanding position would become even greater than the argument from probability would suggest. The rapid multiplication and spread of good copies would raise to absolutely prohibitive levels the chances against an opportunity for aberrant text forms to gain any kind of widespread acceptance or use.[1]

---

[1] I have avoided introducing any argument based on the providence of God, up to this point, because not all accept such argumentation and because the superiority of the Byzantine Text can be demonstrated without recourse to it. Thus, I believe the argument from statistical probability given above is valid as it stands. However, while I have not argued on the basis of Providence, I wish the reader to understand that I personally do not think that the preservation of the true text was so mechanistic as the discussion above might suggest. From the evidence previously adduced, it seems clear that a great many variant readings (perhaps most of the malicious ones) that existed in the second century simply have not survived—we have no extant witness to them. We may reasonably conclude that the early Christians were concerned and able watchdogs of the true text. I would like to believe that they were aided and abetted by the Holy Spirit. In that event, the security of the text is considerably greater than that suggested by probability alone, including the proposition that none of the original wording has been lost.

It follows that within a relatively few years after the writing of the N.T. books there came rapidly into existence a 'Majority' text whose form was essentially that of the Autographs themselves. This text form would, in the natural course of things, continue to multiply itself and in each succeeding generation of copying would continue to be exhibited in the mass of extant manuscripts. In short, it would have a 'normal' transmission. The law of supply and demand operates within the Church, as well as elsewhere. True believers would be far more interested in obtaining copies of the NT writings than people who were not. Opponents of Christianity, who might attempt to confuse the issue by producing altered copies, would have a much smaller 'market' for their work.

The use of such designations as "Syrian", "Antiochian", and "Byzantine" for the Majority Text reflects its general association with that region. I know of no reason to doubt that the "Byzantine" text is in fact the form of the text that was known and transmitted in the Aegean area from the beginning.

In sum, I believe that the evidence clearly favors that interpretation of the history of the text which sees the normal transmission of the text as centered in the Aegean region, the area that was best qualified, from every point of view, to transmit the text, from the very first. The result of that normal transmission is the "Byzantine" text-type. In every age, including the second and third centuries, it has been the traditional text.[1]

So then, I claim that the N.T. text had a normal transmission, namely the fully predictable spread and reproduction of reliable copies of the Autographs from the earliest period down through the history of transmission until the availability of printed texts brought copying by hand to an end.

## The abnormal transmission[2]

Turning now to the abnormal transmission, it no doubt commenced right along with the normal. The apostolic writings themselves contain strong complaints and warning against heretical and malicious activity. As Christianity spread and began to make an impact on the world, not everyone accepted it as 'good news'. Opposition of various sorts arose. Also, there came to be divisions

---

[1] Within the broad Byzantine stream there are dozens of rivulets (recall that Wisse isolated 36 groups, which included 70 subgroups), but the largest distinct line of transmission is Family 35, the main stream, and it was specifically this family that God used to preserve the precise original wording. For more on this please see chapter 7.

[2] I have been accused of inconsistency in that I criticize W-H for treating the NT like any other book and yet myself claim a "normal transmission" for the Majority Text. Not at all; I am referring to a normal transmission of an inspired Text, which W-H denied. I refer to believers copying a text that **they** believed to be inspired. Further, I also recognize an "abnormal transmission", whereas W-H did not. Fee seriously distorts my position by ignoring my discussion of the abnormal transmission ("A Critique", pp. 404-08) and miss-stating my view of the normal transmission (*Ibid.*, p. 399). I hold that 95% of the variants, the obvious transcriptional errors, belong (for the most part) to the normal transmission, whereas most of the remaining 5%, the 'significant' variants, belong to the abnormal transmission.

within the larger Christian community—in the N.T. itself notice is taken of the beginnings of some of these tangents. In some cases faithfulness to an ideological (theological) position evidently became more important than faithfulness to the N.T. Text. Certain it is that Church Fathers who wrote during the second century complained bitterly about the deliberate alterations to the Text perpetrated by 'heretics'. Large sections of the extant writings of the early Fathers are precisely and exclusively concerned with combating the heretics. It is clear that during the second century, and possibly already in the first, such persons produced many copies of N.T. writings incorporating their alterations.[1] Some apparently were quite widely circulated, for a time. The result was a welter of variant readings, to confuse the uninformed and mislead the unwary. Such a scenario was totally predictable. If the N.T. is in fact God's Word then both God and Satan must have a lively interest in its fortunes. To approach the textual criticism of the N.T. without taking due account of that interest is to act irresponsibly.

## 1) Most damage done by 200 A.D.

It is generally agreed that most significant variants existed by the end of the second century. "The overwhelming majority of readings were created before the year 200", affirmed Colwell.[2] "It is no less true to fact than paradoxical in sound that the worst corruptions to which the New Testament has ever been subjected, originated within a hundred years after it was composed", said Scrivener decades before.[3] Kilpatrick commented on the evidence of the earliest Papyri.

> Let us take our two manuscripts of about this date [A.D. 200] which contain parts of John, the Chester Beatty Papyrus and the Bodmer Papyrus. They are together extant for about seventy verses. Over these seventy verses they differ some seventy-three times apart from mistakes.
>
> Further in the Bodmer Papyrus the original scribe has frequently corrected what he first wrote. At some places he is correcting his own mistakes but at others he substitutes one form of phrasing for another. At about seventy-five of these substitutions both alternatives are known from other manuscripts independently. The scribe is in fact replacing one variant reading by another at some seventy places so that we may conclude that already in his day there was variation at these points.[4]

---

[1] Burgon, The Revision Revised, pp. 323-24.

[2] Colwell, "The Origin of Texttypes", p. 138.

[3] F.H.A. Scrivener, A Plain Introduction to the Criticism of the New Testament, fourth edition edited by E. Miller (2 Vols.; London: George Bell and Sons, 1894), II, 264.

[4] G.D. Kilpatrick, "The Transmission of the New Testament and its Reliability", The Bible Translator, IX (July, 1958), 128-29.

Zuntz also recognized all of this. "Modern criticism stops before the barrier of the second century; the age, so it seems, of unbounded liberties with the text".[1]

Kilpatrick goes on to argue that the creation of new variants ceased by about 200 A.D. because it became impossible to 'sell' them. He discusses some of Origen's attempts at introducing a change into the text, and proceeds:

> Origen's treatment of Matthew 19:19 is significant in two other ways. First he was probably the most influential commentator of the Ancient Church and yet his conjecture at this point seems to have influenced only one manuscript of a local version of the New Testament. The Greek tradition is apparently quite unaffected by it. From the third century onward even an Origen could not effectively alter the text.
>
> This brings us to the second significant point—his date. From the early third century onward the freedom to alter the text which had obtained earlier can no longer be practiced. Tatian is the last author to make deliberate changes in the text of whom we have explicit information. Between Tatian and Origen Christian opinion had so changed that it was no longer possible to make changes in the text whether they were harmless or not.[2]

He feels this attitude was a reaction against the rehandling of the text by the second-century heretics. Certainly there had been a great hue and cry, and whatever the reason it does appear that little further damage was done after A.D. 200.

## 2) The aberrant text forms

The extent of the textual difficulties of the 2nd century can easily be exaggerated. Nevertheless, the evidence cited does prove that aberrant forms of the N.T. text were produced. Naturally, some of those text forms may have acquired a local and temporary currency, but they could scarcely become more than eddies along the edge of the 'majority' river. Recall that the possibility of checking against the Autographs must have served to inhibit the spread of such text forms.

For example, Gaius, an orthodox Father who wrote near the end of the second century, named four heretics who not only altered the text but had disciples who multiplied copies of their efforts. Of special interest here is his charge that they could not deny their guilt because they could not produce the originals from which they made their copies.[3] This would be a hollow accusation from

---

[1] Zuntz, The Text, p. 11.

[2] Kilpatrick, "Atticism and the Text of the Greek New Testament", Neutestamentliche Aufsatze (Regensburg: Verlag Friedrich Pustet, 1963), pp. 129-30.

[3] Cf. Burgon, *The Revision Revised*, p. 323.

Gaius if he could not produce the Originals either. I have already argued that the churches in Asia Minor, for instance, did still have either the Autographs or exact copies that they themselves had made—thus they **knew**, absolutely, what the true wording was and could repel the aberrant forms with confidence. A man like Polycarp would still be able to affirm in 150 A.D., letter by letter if need be, the original wording of the text for most of the New Testament books. And presumably his MSS were not burned when he was.

Not only would there have been pressure from the Autographs, but also the pressure exerted by the already-established momentum of transmission enjoyed by the majority text form. As already discussed, the statistical probabilities militating against any aberrant text forms would be overwhelming. In short, although a bewildering array of variants came into existence, judging from extant witnesses, and they were indeed a perturbing influence in the stream of transmission, they would not succeed in thwarting the progress of the normal transmission.

## The Stream of Transmission

Now then, what sort of a picture may we expect to find in the surviving witnesses on the assumption that the history of the transmission of the New Testament Text was predominantly normal? We may expect a broad spectrum of copies, showing minor differences due to copying mistakes but all reflecting one common tradition. The simultaneous existence of abnormal transmission in the earliest centuries would result in a sprinkling of copies, helter-skelter, outside of that main stream. The picture would look something like *Figure C*.

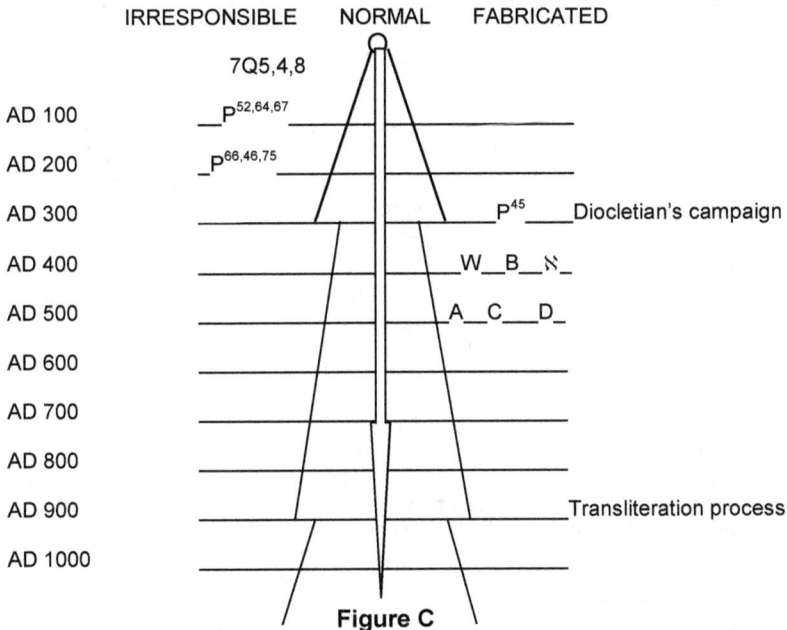

**Figure C**

113

The MSS within the cones represent the "normal" transmission. To the left I have plotted some possible representatives of what we might style the "irresponsible" transmission of the text—the copyists produced poor copies through incompetence or carelessness but did not make deliberate changes. To the right I have plotted some possible representatives of what we might style the "fabricated" transmission of the text—the scribes made deliberate changes in the text (for whatever reasons), producing fabricated copies, not true copies. I am well aware that the MSS plotted on the figure above contain both careless and deliberate errors, in different proportions (7Q5,4,8 and p52,64,67 are too fragmentary to permit the classification of their errors as deliberate rather than careless), so that any classification such as I attempt here must be relative and gives a distorted picture. Still, I venture to insist that ignorance, carelessness, officiousness and malice all left their mark upon the transmission of the New Testament text, and we must take account of them in any attempt to reconstruct the history of that transmission.

As the figure suggests, I argue that Diocletian's campaign had a purifying effect upon the stream of transmission. In order to withstand torture rather than give up your MS(S), you would have to be a truly committed believer, the sort of person who would want good copies of the Scriptures. Thus it was probably the more contaminated MSS that were destroyed, in the main, leaving the purer MSS to replenish the earth (please see the section "Imperial repression of the N.T." in Chapter 6). The arrow within the cones represents Family 35 (see Chapter 7).

Another consideration suggests itself—if, as reported, the Diocletian campaign was most fierce and effective in the Byzantine area, the numerical advantage of the "Byzantine" text-type over the "Western" and "Alexandrian" would have been reduced, giving the latter a chance to forge ahead. But it did not happen. The Church, in the main, refused to propagate those forms of the Greek text.

What we find upon consulting the witnesses is just such a picture. We have the Majority Text (Aland), or the Traditional Text (Burgon), dominating the stream of transmission with a few individual witnesses going their idiosyncratic ways. We have already seen that the notion of "text-types" and recensions, as defined and used by Hort and his followers, is gratuitous. Epp's notion of "streams" fares no better. There is just one stream, with a number of small eddies along the edges.[1] When I say the Majority Text dominates the stream, I mean it is represented in about 95% of the MSS.[2]

---

[1] One might speak of a $P^{45}$,W eddy or a $P^{75}$,B eddy, for example.

[2] Although I have used, of necessity, the term 'text-type' throughout the book, I view the Majority Text as being much broader. It is a textual tradition which might be said to include a number of related 'text-types', such as von Soden's $K^a$, $K^i$, and $K^r$. I wish to emphasize again that it is only agreement in error that determines genealogical relationships. It follows that the concepts of 'genealogy' and 'text-type' are irrelevant with reference to original readings—they are only useful (when employed properly) for identifying spurious readings. Well, if there is a family that very nearly reflects the original its 'profile' or mosaic of readings will distinguish it from other families, but most

Actually, such a statement is not altogether satisfactory because it does not allow for the mixture or shifting affinities encountered within individual MSS. A better, though more cumbersome, way to describe the situation would be something like this: 100% of the MSS agree as to, say, 50% of the Text; 99% agree as to another 40%; over 95% agree as to another 4%; over 90% agree as to another 2%; over 80% agree as to another 2%; only for 2% or so of the Text do less than 80% of the MSS agree, and a disproportionate number of those cases occur in Revelation.[1] And the membership of the dissenting group varies from reading to reading. (I will of course be reminded that witnesses are to be weighed, not counted; I will come to that presently, so please bear with me.) Still, with the above reservation, one may reasonably speak of up to 95% of the extant MSS belonging to the Majority text-type.

I see no way of accounting for a 95% (or 90%) domination unless that text goes back to the Autographs. Hort saw the problem and invented a revision. Sturz seems not to have seen the problem. He demonstrates that the "Byzantine text-type" is early and independent of the "Western" and "Alexandrian text-types", and like von Soden, wishes to treat them as three equal witnesses.[2] But if the three "text-types" were equal, how could the so-called "Byzantine" ever gain a 90-95% preponderance?

The argument from statistical probability enters here with a vengeance. Not only do the extant MSS present us with one text form enjoying a 95% majority, but the remaining 5% do not represent a single competing text form. The minority MSS disagree as much (or more) among themselves as they do with the majority. For any two of them to agree so closely as do $P^{75}$ and B is an oddity. We are not judging, therefore, between two text forms, one representing 95% of the MSS and the other 5%. Rather, we have to judge between 95% and a fraction of 1% (comparing the Majority Text with the $P^{75}$,B text form for example). Or to take a specific case, in 1 Timothy 3:16 some 600 Greek MSS (besides the Lectionaries) read "God" while only nine read something else. Of those nine, three have private readings and six agree in reading "who".[3] So we have to judge between 98.5% and 1%, "God" versus

---

of those readings will not be errors (the competing variants distinctive of other families **will** be errors).

[1] I am not prepared to defend the precise figures used, they are **guesses**, but I believe they represent a reasonable approximation to reality. I heartily agree with Colwell when he insists that we must "rigorously eliminate the singular reading" ("External Evidence", p. 8) on the altogether reasonable assumption (it seems to me) that a solitary witness against the world cannot possibly be right.

[2] Sturz, *Op. Cit.* A text produced by taking two 'text-types' against one would move the UBS text about 80% of the distance toward the Majority text.

[3] The readings, with their supporting MSS, are as follows:

*o* - D
*ω* - 061
*ος Θεος* - one cursive, 256 (and one Lectionary)
*ος* - א,33,365,442,1175,2127 (three Lectionaries)

$\Theta\varepsilon o\varsigma$ - A,C[vid],F/G[vid],K,L,P,Ψ, some 600 cursives (besides Lectionaries) (including four cursives that read o $\Theta\varepsilon o\varsigma$ and one Lectionary that reads $\Theta\varepsilon o\upsilon$).

It will be observed that my statement differs from that of the UBS text, for example. I offer the following explanation.

Young, Huish, Pearson, Fell, and Mill in the seventeenth century, Creyk, Bentley, Wotton, Wetstein, Bengel, Berriman, and Woide in the eighteenth, and Scrivener as late as 1881 all affirmed, upon careful inspection, that Codex A reads "God". For a thorough discussion please see Burgon, who says concerning Woide, "The learned and conscientious editor of the Codex declares that so late as 1765 he had seen traces of the $\Theta$ which twenty years later (viz. in 1785) were visible to him no longer" (*The Revision Revised*, p. 434. Cf. pp. 431-36). It was only after 1765 that scholars started to question the reading of A (through fading and wear the middle line of the *theta* is no longer discernible).

Hoskier devotes Appendix J of *A Full Account* (the appendix being a reprint of part of an article that appeared in the *Clergyman's Magazine* for February 1887) to a careful discussion of the reading of Codex C. He spent three hours examining the passage in question in this MS (the MS itself) and adduces evidence that shows clearly, I believe, that the original reading of C is "God". He examined the surrounding context and observes, "The **contracting-bar** has often vanished completely (I believe, from a cursory examination, more often than not), but at other times it is plain and imposed in the same way as at 1 Timothy iii.16" (Appendix J, p. 2). See also Burgon, *Ibid.*, pp. 437-38.

Codices F/G read OC wherein the contracting-bar is a slanting stroke. It has been argued that the stroke represents the aspirate of $o\varsigma$, but Burgon demonstrates that the stroke in question never represents breathing but is invariably the sign of contraction and affirms that "$o\varsigma$ is **nowhere** else written OC [with a cross-bar] in either codex" (*Ibid.*, p. 442. Cf. pp. 438-42). Presumably the cross-line in the common parent had become too faint to see. As for cursive 365, Burgon conducted an exhaustive search for it. He not only failed to find it but could find no evidence that it had ever existed (*Ibid.*, pp. 444-45) [I have recently been informed that it was later rediscovered by Gregory].

(I took up the case of 1 Timothy 3:16, in the first edition of this book, solely to illustrate the argument from probability, not as an example of "how to do textual criticism" [cf. Fee, "A Critique", p. 423]. Since the question has been raised, I will add a few words on that subject.)

The three significant variants involved are represented in the ancient uncial MSS as follows: O, OC, and $\Theta$C (with a contracting-bar above the two letters), meaning "which", "who", and "God" respectively. In writing "God" a scribe's omitting of the two lines (through haste or momentary distraction) would result in "who". Codices A, C, F, and G have numerous instances where either the cross-line or the contracting-bar is no longer discernible (either the original line has faded to the point of being invisible or the scribe may have failed to write it in the first place). For both lines to fade away, as in Codex A here, is presumably an infrequent event. For a scribe to inadvertently omit both lines would presumably also be an infrequent event, but it must have happened at least once, probably early in the second century and in circumstances that produced a wide ranging effect.

The collocation "the mystery...who" is even more pathologic in Greek than it is in English. It was thus inevitable, once such a reading came into existence and became known, that remedial action would be attempted. Accordingly, the first reading above, "the mystery...which", is generally regarded as an attempt to make the difficult reading intelligible. But it must have been an early development, for it completely dominates the Latin tradition, both version and Fathers, as well as being the probable reading of the Syr[p] and Coptic versions. It is found in only one Greek MS, Codex D, and in no Greek

116

"who". It is hard to imagine any possible set of circumstances in the transmissional history sufficient to produce the cataclysmic overthrow in statistical probability required by the claim that "who" is the original reading.

It really does seem that those scholars who reject the Majority Text are faced with a serious problem. How is it to be explained if it does not reflect the Original? Hort's notion of a Lucianic revision has been abandoned by most scholars because of the total lack of historical evidence. The eclecticists are not even trying. The "process" view has not been articulated in sufficient detail to permit refutation, but on the face of it that view is flatly contradicted by the argument from statistical probability.[1] How could any amount of 'process' bridge the gap between B or Aleph and the TR?

But there is a more basic problem with the process view. Hort saw clearly, and correctly, that the Majority Text must have a common archetype. Recall that Hort's genealogical method was based on community of **error**. On the hypothesis that the Majority Text is a late and inferior text form, the large mass

---

Father before the fifth century.

Most modern scholars regard "God" as a separate therapeutic response to the difficult reading. Although it dominates the Greek MSS (over 98 percent), it is certainly attested by only two versions, the Georgian and Slavonic (both late). But it also dominates the Greek Fathers. Around A.D. 100 there are possible allusions in Barnabas, "*Ιησους . . . ο υιος του Θεου τυπω και εν σαρκι φανερωθεις*" (Cap. xii), and in Ignatius, "*Θεου ανθρωπινως φανερουμενου*" (*Ad Ephes.* c. 19) and "*εν σαρκι γενομενος Θεος*" (*Ibid.*, c. 7). In the third century there seem to be clear references in Hippolytus, "*Θεος εν σωματι εφανερωθη*" (*Contra Haeresim Noeti*, c. xvii), Dionysius, "Θεος γαρ εφανερωθη εν σαρκι" (*Concilia*, i. 853a) and Gregory Thaumaturgus, "*και εστιν Θεος αληθινος ο ασαρκος εν σαρκι φανερωθεις*" (quoted by Photius). In the 4th century there are clear quotes or references in Gregory of Nyssa (22 times), Gregory of Nazianzus, Didymus of Alexandria, Diodorus, the Apostolic Constitutions, and Chrysostom, followed by Cyril of Alexandria, Theodoret, and Euthalius in the fifth century, and so on (Burgon, *Ibid*, pp. 456-76, 486-90).

As for the grammatically aberrant reading, "who", aside from the MSS already cited, the earliest version that clearly supports it is the gothic (fourth century). To get a clear Greek Patristic witness to this reading pretty well requires the sequence *μυστηριον ος εφανερωθη* since after any reference to Christ, Savior, Son of God, etc. in the prior context the use of a relative clause is predictable. Burgon affirmed that he was aware of no such testimony (and his knowledge of the subject has probably never been equaled) (*Ibid.*, p. 483).

It thus appears that the "Western" and "Byzantine" readings have earlier attestation than does the "Alexandrian". Yet if "which" was caused by "who", then the latter must be older. The reading "who" is admittedly the most difficult, so much so that to apply the "harder reading" canon in the face of an easy transcriptional explanation [the accidental omission of the two strokes of the pen] for the difficult reading seems unreasonable. As Burgon so well put it:

I trust we are at least agreed that the maxim "*proclivi lectioni praestat ardua*," does not enunciate so foolish a proposition as that in choosing between two or more conflicting readings, we are to prefer **that** one which has the feeblest external attestation,—provided it be but in itself almost unintelligible? (*Ibid.*, p. 497).

[1] For further discussion see the final pages of Appendix C.

of common readings which distinguish it from the so-called "Western" or "Alexandrian text-types" must be **errors** (which was precisely Hort's contention) and such an agreement in error would have to have a common source. The process view fails completely to account for such an agreement in error (on that hypothesis).

Hort saw the need for a common source and posited a Lucianic revision. Scholars now generally recognize that the "Byzantine text-type" must date back at least into the second century. But what chance would the original "Byzantine" document, the archetype, have of gaining currency when appeal to the Autographs was still possible?

Candidly, there is only one reasonable explanation for the Majority Text that has so far been advanced—it is the result of an essentially normal process of transmission and the common source for its consensus is the Autographs. Down through the centuries of copying, the original text has always been reflected with a high degree of accuracy in the manuscript tradition as a whole. The history of the text presented in this chapter not only accounts nicely for the Majority Text, it also accounts for the inconsistent minority of MSS. They are remnants of the abnormal transmission of the text, reflecting ancient aberrant forms. It is a dependence upon such aberrant forms that distinguishes contemporary critical/eclectic editions of the Greek New Testament, and the modern translations based upon them.

# What Is the Actual Evidence?

## *The Uncials*

In *The Text of the New Testament*[1] K. Aland offers a summary of the results of a "systematic test collation" for the more important uncials from centuries IV-IX. He uses four headings: "Byzantine", "original", "agreements" between the first two, and "independent or distinctive" readings. Since by "original" he seems to mean essentially "Egyptian" (or "Alexandrian") I will use the following headings: Egyptian, Majority ("Byzantine"), both ("agreements") and other ("independent"). I proceed to chart each MS from the IV through IX centuries for which Aland offers a summary:

By way of explanation: "cont." stands for content, **e** = Gospels (but Aland's figures cover only the Synoptics), **a** = Acts, **p** = Pauline Epistles (including Hebrews) and **c** = Catholic Epistles; "Cat." refers to Aland's five categories (*The Text*, pp. 105-6) and "class." stands for a classification devised by me wherein **E** = Egyptian, **M** = Majority and **O** = other. It has the following values, which are illustrated with M:

|          |   |         |   |      |   |            |
|----------|---|---------|---|------|---|------------|
| M+++++   | = | 100%    |   |      |   |            |
| M++++    | = | over 95% | = | 19:1 | = | very strong |
| M+++     | = | over 90% | = | 9:1  | = | strong     |
| M++      | = | over 80% | = | 4:1  | = | good       |

---

[1] K. and B. Aland (Grand Rapids: Eerdmans, 1987), pp. 106-125.

| M+ | = | over 66% | = | 2:1 | = | fair |
|----|---|----------|---|-----|---|------|
| M | = | over 50% | = | 1:1 | = | weak |
| M- | = | plurality | = | | = | marginal |
| M/E | = | a tie | | | | |

I assume that Aland will agree with me that E + M is certainly original, so the "both" column needs to be disregarded as we try to evaluate the tendencies of the several MSS. Accordingly I considered only the "Egyptian", "Majority" and "other" columns in calculating percentages.

| Codex | Date | cont. | Egypt. | both | Major. | other | total | class. | Cat. |
|-------|------|-------|--------|------|--------|-------|-------|--------|------|
| 01 | IV | e | 170 | 80 | 23 | 95 | 368 | E | I |
| | | a | 67 | 24 | 9 | 17 | 117 | E+ | I |
| | | p | 174 | 38 | 76 | 52 | 340 | E | I |
| | | c | 73 | 5 | 21 | 16 | 115 | E | I |
| 03 | IV | e | 196 | 54 | 9 | 72 | 331 | E+ | I |
| | | a | 72 | 22 | 2 | 11 | 107 | E++ | I |
| | | p | 144 | 31 | 8 | 27 | 210 | E++ | I |
| | | c | 80 | 8 | 2 | 9 | 99 | E++ | I |
| 032 | IV | e | 54 | 70 | 118 | 88 | 330 | M- | III |

----------------------------------------------------------------------------400

| Codex | Date | cont. | Egypt. | both | Major. | other | total | class. | Cat. |
|-------|------|-------|--------|------|--------|-------|-------|--------|------|
| 02 | V | e | 18 | 84 | 151 | 15 | 268 | M++ | III |
| | | a | 65 | 22 | 9 | 12 | 108 | E+ | I |
| | | p | 149 | 28 | 31 | 37 | 245 | E+ | I |
| | | c | 62 | 5 | 18 | 12 | 97 | E+ | I |
| 04 | V | e | 66 | 66 | 87 | 50 | 269 | M- | II |
| | | a | 37 | 12 | 12 | 11 | 72 | E | II |
| | | p | 104 | 23 | 31 | 15 | 173 | E+ | II |
| | | c | 41 | 3 | 15 | 12 | 71 | E | II |
| 05 | V | e | 77 | 48 | 65 | 134 | 324 | O- | IV |
| | | a | 16 | 7 | 21 | 33 | 77 | O- | IV |
| 016 | V | p | 15 | 1 | 2 | 6 | 24 | E | II |
| 026 | V | e | 0 | 5 | 5 | 2 | 12 | M+ | V |
| 048 | V | p* | 26 | 7 | 3 | 4 | 40 | E+ | II |
| 0274 | V | e | 19 | 6 | 0 | 2 | 27 | E+++ | II |

----------------------------------------------------------------------------500

| Codex | Date | cont. | Egypt. | both | Major. | other | total | class. | Cat. |
|-------|------|-------|--------|------|--------|-------|-------|--------|------|
| 06 | VI | p | 112 | 29 | 137 | 83 | 361 | M- | II |
| 08 | VI | a | 23 | 21 | 36 | 22 | 102 | M- | II |
| 015 | VI | p | 11 | 0 | 5 | 1 | 17 | E | III |
| 022 | VI | e | 8 | 48 | 89 | 15 | 160 | M+ | V |

| 023 | VI | e | 0 | 4 | 9 | 3 | 16 | M+ | V |
|---|---|---|---|---|---|---|---|---|---|
| 024 | VI | e | 3 | 16 | 24 | 0 | 43 | M++ | V |
| 027 | VI | e | 0 | 4 | 11 | 5 | 20 | M+ | V |
| 035 | VI | e | 11 | 5 | 3 | 2 | 21 | E+ | III |
| 040 | VI | e | 8 | 2 | 2 | 3 | 15 | E | III |
| 042 | VI | e | 15 | 83 | 140 | 25 | 263 | M+ | V |
| 043 | VI | e | 11 | 83 | 131 | 18 | 243 | M++ | V |

----------------------------------------------------------------------------600

| 0211 | VII | e | 10 | 101 | 189 | 23 | 323 | M++ | V |
|---|---|---|---|---|---|---|---|---|---|

----------------------------------------------------------------------------700

| 07 | VIII | e | 1 | 107 | 209 | 9 | 326 | M++++ | V |
|---|---|---|---|---|---|---|---|---|---|
| 019 | VIII | e | 125 | 75 | 52 | 64 | 316 | E | II |
| 044 | VIII | e | 52 | 21 | 40 | 19 | 132 | E- | III |
|  |  | a | 22 | 25 | 43 | 15 | 105 | M | III |
|  |  | p | 38 | 42 | 135 | 33 | 248 | M | III |
|  |  | c | 54 | 8 | 21 | 14 | 97 | E | II |
| 047 | VIII | e | 6 | 96 | 175 | 21 | 298 | M++ | V |
| 0233 | VIII | e | 3 | 23 | 47 | 5 | 78 | M++ | III |

----------------------------------------------------------------------------800

| 09 | IX | e | 0 | 78 | 156 | 11 | 245 | M+++ | V |
|---|---|---|---|---|---|---|---|---|---|
| 010 | IX | p | 91 | 12 | 41 | 69 | 213 | E- | III |
| 011 | IX | e | 4 | 87 | 176 | 21 | 288 | M++ | V |
| 012 | IX | p | 91 | 12 | 43 | 66 | 212 | E- | III |
| 013 | IX | e | 2 | 82 | 174 | 7 | 265 | M++++ | V |
| 014 | IX | a | 2 | 22 | 48 | 1 | 73 | M+++ | V |
| 017 | IX | e | 8 | 107 | 197 | 15 | 327 | M++ | V |
| 018 | IX | p | 8 | 32 | 154 | 8 | 202 | M+++ | V |
|  |  | c | 4 | 9 | 77 | 6 | 96 | M++ | V |
| 020 | IX | a | 1 | 23 | 51 | 3 | 78 | M+++ | V |
|  |  | p | 5 | 44 | 188 | 4 | 241 | M++++ | V |
|  |  | c | 5 | 9 | 78 | 3 | 95 | M+++ | V |
| 021 | IX | e | 7 | 106 | 202 | 12 | 327 | M+++ | V |
| 025 | IX | a | 1 | 29 | 70 | 0 | 100 | M++++ | V |
|  |  | p | 87 | 31 | 87 | 31 | 236 | E/M | III |
|  |  | c | 26 | 6 | 46 | 9 | 87 | M | III |

| | | | | | | | | | |
|---|---|---|---|---|---|---|---|---|---|
| 030 | IX | e | 1 | 38 | 105 | 11 | 155 | M++ | V |
| 031 | IX | e | 8 | 101 | 192 | 17 | 318 | M++ | V |
| 034 | IX | e | 4 | 95 | 192 | 6 | 297 | M++++ | V |
| 037 | IX | e | 69 | 88 | 120 | 47 | 324 | M | III |
| 038 | IX | e | 75 | 59 | 89 | 95 | 318 | O- | II |
| 039 | IX | e | 0 | 10 | 41 | 2 | 53 | M++++ | V |
| 041 | IX | e | 11 | 104 | 190 | 18 | 323 | M++ | V |
| 045 | IX | e | 3 | 104 | 208 | 10 | 325 | M+++ | V |
| 049 | IX | a | 3 | 29 | 69 | 3 | 104 | M+++ | V |
| | | p | 0 | 34 | 113 | 3 | 150 | M++++ | V |
| | | c | 1 | 9 | 82 | 4 | 96 | M+++ | V |
| 063 | IX | p | 0 | 3 | 15 | 0 | 18 | M+++++ | V |
| 0150 | IX | p | 65 | 34 | 101 | 23 | 223 | M | III |
| 0151 | IX | p | 9 | 44 | 174 | 7 | 234 | M+++ | V |
| 33 | IX | e | 57 | 73 | 54 | 44 | 228 | E- | II |
| | | a | 34 | 19 | 21 | 11 | 85 | E | I |
| | | p | 129 | 35 | 47 | 36 | 247 | E | I |
| | | c | 45 | 3 | 21 | 14 | 83 | E | I |
| 461 | 835 | e | 3 | 102 | 219 | 5 | 329 | M++++ | V |

-----------------------------------------------------------------------------------------------900

(*Aland shows **ap**, but gives no figures for **a**.)

So, what can we learn from this chart? Perhaps a good place to begin is with a correlation between "Cat." and "class." in terms of the values we have each given to specific MSS:

| <u>I</u> | <u>II</u> | | | <u>III</u> | | <u>IV</u> | <u>V</u> |
|---|---|---|---|---|---|---|---|
| E++ | E+++ | M- | O- | E+ | M++ | O- | M+++++ |
| E+ | E+ | | | E | M | | M++++ |
| E | E | | | E- | M- | | M+++ |
| | E- | | | E/M | | | M++ |
| | | | | | | | M+ |

Categories I, IV and V are reasonably consistent, but how are we to interpret II and III? This is bothersome because in Aland's book (pp. 156-59) a very great many MSS are listed under III and not a few under II. It might be helpful to see how many MSS, or content segments, fall at the intersections of the two parameters:

| | I | II | III | IV | V | total |
|---|---|---|---|---|---|---|
| E+++ | | 1 | | | | 1 |
| E++ | 3 | | | | | 3 |
| E+ | 5 | 2 | 1 | | | 8 |
| E | 6 | 5 | 2 | | | 13 |
| E- | | 1 | 3 | | | 4 |
| O- | | 1 | | 2 | | 3 |
| E/M | | | 1 | | | 1 |
| M- | | 3 | 1 | | | 4 |
| M | | | 5 | | | 5 |
| M+ | | | | | 5 | 5 |
| M++ | | | 2 | | 10 | 12 |
| M+++ | | | | | 10 | 10 |
| M++++ | | | | | 8 | 8 |
| M+++++ | | | | | 1 | 1 |

0274 and 063 are fragmentary, which presumably accounts for their exceptional scores, E+++ and M+++++ respectively; if they were more complete they would probably each come down a level. Out of 45 M segments 31 score above 80%, while 9 are over 95% 'pure'. It should be possible to reconstruct a "Byzantine" archetype with tolerable confidence. But one has to wonder how Aland arrived at the "Egyptian" norm in the Gospels since the best Egyptian witness (except for the fragmentary 0274, which has less than 10% of the text but scores 90%), Codex B, barely passes 70%. (In *The Text*, p. 95, Aland gives a summary for $P^{75}$ in Luke—it scores 77%.) Further, besides B and 0274, $P^{75}$ and Z (both also fragmentary) are the only Greek MSS that score so much as an E+ in the Gospels. One is reminded of E.C. Colwell's conclusion after attempting to reconstruct an 'average' or mean Alexandrian text for the first chapter of Mark. "These results show convincingly that any attempt to reconstruct an archetype of the Beta [Alexandrian] Text-type on a quantitative basis is doomed to failure. The text thus reconstructed is not reconstructed but constructed; it is an artificial entity that never existed."[1]

For the other content areas the situation is not much better. Only $P^{74}$ (86%), B (85%) and 81 (80%) rate an E++ in **a**; apart from them only A and Aleph manage even an E+. Codex B is the only E++ (80%) in **p**, and only $P^{46}$, A, C, 048 and 1739 manage an E+. Aside from B's 88% in **c**, only $P^{74}$, A and 1739 manage even an E+. How did Aland arrive at his "Egyptian" norm in these areas? Might that "norm" be a fiction, as Colwell affirmed?

Codex $A^e$ is 82% Byzantine and must have been based on a Byzantine exemplar, which presumably would belong to the IV century. Codex W in Matthew is also clearly Byzantine and must have had a Byzantine exemplar.

---

[1] "The Significance of Grouping of New Testament Manuscripts", *New Testament Studies*, IV (1957-1958), 86-87.

The sprinkling of Byzantine readings in B is sufficiently slight that it could be ascribed to chance, I suppose, but that explanation will hardly serve for Aleph. At least in p, if not throughout, Aleph's copyist must have had access to a Byzantine exemplar, which could have belonged to the III century. But Asterius offers much stronger evidence: he died in 341, so presumably did his writing somewhat earlier; it seems likely that his MSS would be from the III century—since he shows a 90% preference for Byzantine readings those MSS must have been **Byzantine**. (Using my classification, Asterius would be M++, the Byzantine preference being 83%. On a percentage basis Asterius is as strongly Byzantine as B is Egyptian.) Adamantius died in 300, so he did his writing earlier. Might his MSS have been from the first half of the III century? Since he shows a 52% preference for Byzantine readings (or 39%, using my classification) at least some of his MSS were presumably Byzantine. For that matter $P^{66}$ has so many Byzantine readings that **its** copyist must have had access to a Byzantine exemplar, which would necessarily belong to the II century! The circumstance that some Byzantine readings in $P^{66*}$ were corrected to Egyptian readings, while some Egyptian readings in $P^{66*}$ were corrected to Byzantine readings, really seems to require that we posit exemplars of the two types—between them the two hands furnish clear evidence that the Byzantine text, as such, existed in their day. (For evidence from the early Fathers, Papyri and Versions please see the section, "But There Is No Evidence of the Byzantine Text in the Early Centuries", in Chapter six.)

Returning to the chart of the uncials above, in the IV century E leads in all four areas, although in Aleph E is weak and M is gaining. If W is IV century,[1] M has gained even more. I remind the reader that I am referring only to the information in the chart given above. In reality, I assume that the IV century, like all others, was dominated by Byzantine MSS. Being good copies they were used and worn out, thereby perishing. Copies like B and Aleph survived because they were 'different', and therefore not used. By "used" I mean for ordinary purposes—I am well aware that Aleph exercised the ingenuity of a number of correctors over the centuries, but it left no descendants. In the V century M takes over the lead in **e** while E retains **apc** (it may come as a surprise to some that $C^e$ is more M than anything else). In the VI century M strengthens its hold on **e** and moves in on **a** (it may come as a surprise to some that $D^p$ is more M than anything else). After the V century, with the sole exception of the fragmentary Z, all the "Egyptian" witnesses are weak—even the "queen of the cursives", 33, does not get up to an E+. Of X century uncials for which Aland offers a summary, all are clearly Byzantine (028, 033, 036, 056, 075 and 0124) except for 0243, which scores an E.[2]

_____

[1] There is reason to believe that it is II century, because of the circumstances surrounding the place where it was discovered.

[2] In February,1990, I debated Daniel Wallace at the Dallas Theological Seminary, where he was teaching. He used a graph purporting to show the distribution of the Greek MSS from the III to the IX centuries according to the three main "text-types" (a graph that he was using in the classroom). He has since used the same graph in a

## The Cursives

When we turn to the cursives, Aland offers summaries for 150, chosen on the basis of their "independence" from the Byzantine norm. He lists 900 MSS only by number because "these minuscules exhibit a purely or predominantly Byzantine text", and therefore he considers that "they are all irrelevant for textual criticism" (*The Text*, p. 155). To do for the 150 "independent" cursives what I did for the uncials would take too much space, so I will summarize Aland's statistics in chart form, using my classification:

| cont. | M+++++ | M++++ | M+++ | M++ | M+ | M | M- | M/E | E- | E | E+ | E++ |
|---|---|---|---|---|---|---|---|---|---|---|---|---|
| e |  | 10 | 23 | 12 | 6 | 16 | 1 |  | 2 | 1 |  |  |
| a |  | 12 | 15 | 23 | 21 | 14 | 12 | 1 | 4 | 2 |  | 1 |
| p | 1 | 25 | 17 | 17 | 28 | 19 | 4 |  | 2 | 3 | 1 |  |
| c | 1 | 9 | 18 | 6 | 30 | 21 | 10 | 1 | 5 | 10 | 1 |  |
| total | 2 | 56 | 73 | 58 | 85 | 70 | 27 | 2 | 13 | 16 | 2 | 1 |

Even among these "independent" cursives there are two content segments that actually score 100% Byzantine! (Just imagine how many more there must be among the 900 that are so Byzantine that Aland ignored them.) The best Egyptian representative is 81 in Acts, with an even 80%. 1739 scores 70% (E+) in **c** and 68% (E+) in **p**. These are the only three segments that I would call "clearly Egyptian". There are sixteen segments that score between 50 and 66% (E). Pitting M through M+++++ against E through E++ we get 344 to 19, and this from the "independent" minuscules. If we add the 900 "predominantly Byzantine" MSS, which will average over two content segments each, the actual ratio is well over 100 to one. I assume that almost all of these 900 will score at least M++, and most will doubtless score M+++ or higher. If we were to compute only segments that score at least 80%, the Byzantine:Egyptian

---

paper presented to the Evangelical Theological Society. The graph is very seriously misleading. I challenge Wallace to identify the MSS that the graph is supposed to represent and to demonstrate that each one belongs to the "text-type" that he alleged. It was stated that the extant MSS do not show the Byzantine text in the majority until the IX century, but according to Aland's statistics the Byzantine text took the lead in the Gospels in the V century, and kept it.

But let us consider the MSS from the IX century. Out of 27 Byzantine MSS or content segments (Gospels, Pauline corpus, etc.), eight are over 95% 'pure', ten are over 90% pure, and another six are over 80% pure. Where did these 24 MSS or segments get their Byzantine content? Since they are all distinct in content they were presumably copied from as many separate exemplars, exemplars of necessity earlier in date and also Byzantine. And what were those exemplars copied from? Evidently from still earlier Byzantine MSS, etc. Hopefully Wallace will not attempt to argue that all those IX century MSS were not copied from anything, but were independently created from nothing by each scribe! It follows that a massive majority in the IX century presupposes a massive majority in the VIII, and so on. Which is why scholars from Hort to Aland have recognized that the Byzantine text dominated the transmission from the IV century on.

Textual scholars of all persuasions, down through the years, have recognized that the extant witnesses from the early centuries are not necessarily representative of the actual state of affairs in their day. To insist that the extant witnesses are the whole story is unreasonable and begs the question.

ratio would be more like **1,000** to one—the MSS that have been classified by Aland's "test collation", as reported in his book, represent perhaps 40% of the total (excluding Lectionaries), but we may reasonably assume that most of the "independent" ones have already been identified and presented. It follows that the remaining MSS, at least 1,500, can only increase the Byzantine side of the ratio. If the Byzantine text is the "worst", then down through the centuries of manuscript copying the Church was massively mistaken!

The MSS discussed in Aland's book (first edition) reflect the collating done at his Institute as of 1981. Many more have doubtless been collated since, but the general proportions will probably not change significantly. Consider the study done by Frederik Wisse. He collated and compared **1,386** MSS in Luke 1, 10 and 20, and found only four uncials (out of 34) and four cursives (out of 1,352) that displayed the Egyptian text-type, plus another two of each that were Egyptian in one of the three chapters.[1]

# Concluding Remarks

In his book Aland's discussion of the transmission of the NT text is permeated with the assumption that the Byzantine text was a secondary development that progressively contaminated the pure Egyptian ("Alexandrian") text.[2] But the chief "Alexandrian" witnesses, B, A (except **e**) and ℵ (*The Text*, p. 107), are in constant and significant disagreement among themselves; so much so that there is no objective way of reconstructing an archetype. 150 years earlier the picture is the same; P[45], P[66] and P[75] are quite dissimilar and do not reflect a single tradition. In A.D. 200 "there was no king in [Egypt]; everyone did what was right in his own eyes", or so it would seem. But what if we were to

---

[1] The Profile Method for the Classification and Evaluation of Manuscript Evidence (Grand Rapids: Eerdmans, 1982).

[2] The progressive 'purification' of the stream of transmission through the centuries, based on the extant MSS (from a Byzantine priority perspective), has been recognized by all and sundry, their attempts at explaining the phenomenon generally reflecting their presuppositions. From my point of view the evident explanation is this: All camps recognize that the heaviest attacks against the purity of the Text took place during the second century. But "the heartland of the Church", the Aegean area, by far the best qualified in every way to watch over the faithful transmission, simply refused to copy the aberrant forms. MSS containing such forms were not used (nor copied), so many survived physically for over a millennium. Less bad forms were used but progressively were not copied. Thus the surviving IX century uncials are fair, over 80% Byzantine, but not good enough to be copied (when the better MSS were put into cursive form). Until the advent of a printed text, MSS were made to be used. Progressively only the best were used, and thus worn out, and copied. This process culminated in the XIV century, when the Ottoman shadow was advancing over Asia Minor, but the Byzantine empire still stood. But by the beginning of the XV century, even though Constantinople didn't actually fall for 45 years, the future was dark and people became preoccupied with survival. It appears to me that the greatest purity is found in the XIV century, and then begins to fall off in the XV, falling more in the XVI and into the XVII. So, in my view special attention should be given to the **XIV** century MSS, for by then only the best tradition was being copied, in the main.

entertain the hypothesis that the Byzantine tradition is the oldest and that the "Western" and "Alexandrian" MSS represent varying perturbations on the fringes of the main transmissional stream? Would this not make better sense of the surviving evidence? Then there would have been no "Western" or "Egyptian" archetypes, just various sources of contamination that acted in such a random fashion that each extant "Western" or "Egyptian" MS has a different 'mosaic'. In contrast, there would indeed be a "Byzantine" archetype, which would reflect the original. The mean text of the extant MSS improves century by century, the XIV being the best, because the worst MSS were not copied or worn out by use; whereas the good ones were used and copied, and when worn out, discarded.

Those who catalog NT MSS inform us that the 12$^{th}$ and 13$^{th}$ centuries lead the pack, in terms of extant MSS, followed by the 14$^{th}$, 11$^{th}$, 15$^{th}$, 16$^{th}$ and 10$^{th}$, in that order. There are over four times as many MSS from the 13$^{th}$ as from the 10$^{th}$, but obviously Koiné Greek would have been more of a living language in the 10$^{th}$ than the 13$^{th}$, and so there would have been more demand and therefore more supply. In other words, many hundreds of really pure MSS from the 10$^{th}$ perished. A higher percentage of the really good MSS produced in the 14$^{th}$ century survived than those produced in the 11$^{th}$; and so on. That is why there is a progressive level of agreement among the Byzantine MSS, there being a higher percentage of agreement in the 14$^{th}$ than in the 10$^{th}$. But had we lived in the 10$^{th}$, and done a wide survey of the MSS, we would have found very nearly the same level of agreement (perhaps 98%). The same obtains if we had lived in the 8$^{th}$, 6$^{th}$, 4$^{th}$ or 2$^{nd}$ century. In other words, THE SURVIVING MSS FROM THE FIRST TEN CENTURIES ARE NOT REPRESENTATIVE OF THE TRUE STATE OF AFFAIRS AT THE TIME.[1]

---

[1] Consider what Maurice Robinson concluded as a result of doing a complete collation of 1,389 MSS that contain the Pericope, John 7:53 – 8:11:

However, contrary to this writer's earlier speculations, the extensive collation of the PA MSS has conclusively demonstrated that cross-comparison and correction of MSS occurred only *rarely* and *sporadically*, with little or no perpetuation of the corrective changes across the diversity of types represented [italics his, also below].

If cross-correction did not occur frequently or extensively in that portion of text which has more variation than any other location in the NT, and if such corrections as were made did not tend to perpetuate, it is not likely that such a process occurred in those portions of the NT which had less textual variety. ...the lack of systematic and thorough correction within the PA as well as the lack of perpetuation of correction patterns appears to demonstrate this clearly. Cross-comparison and correction *should* have been rampant and extensive with this portion of text due to the wide variety of textual patterns and readings existing therein; instead, correction occurred sporadically, and rarely in a thoroughgoing manner.

Since this is the case, the phenomenon of the relatively unified Byzantine Textform *cannot* be explained by a "process" methodology, whether "modified" or not...

Based upon the collated data, the present writer is forced to reverse his previous assumptions regarding the development and restoration/preservation of the Byzantine Textform in this sense: although textual transmission itself is a process, it appears that, for the most part, the lines of transmission remained separate, with relatively little mixture occurring or becoming perpetuated...

Aland seems to grant that down through the centuries of church history the Byzantine text was regarded as "the text of the church", and he traces the beginning of this state of affairs to Lucian.[1] He makes repeated mention of a "school of/at Antioch" and of Asia Minor. All of this is very interesting, because in his book he agrees with Adolf Harnack that "about 180 the greatest concentration of churches was in Asia Minor and along the Aegean coast of Greece".[2] This is the area where Greek was the mother tongue and where Greek continued to be used. It is also the area that started out with most of the Autographs. But Aland continues: "Even around A.D. 325 the scene was still largely unchanged. Asia Minor continued to be the heartland of the Church". "The heartland of the Church"—so who else would be in a better position to identify the correct text of the New Testament? Who could 'sell' a fabricated text in Asia Minor in the early fourth century? I submit that the Byzantine text dominated the transmissional history because the churches in Asia Minor vouched for it. And they did so, from the very beginning, because they knew it was the true text, having received it from the Apostles. The Majority Text is what it is just because it has always been **the Text of the Church**.

---

Certainly, all the types of PA text are distinct, and reflect a long line of transmission and preservation in their separate integrities.

It thus appears that the Byzantine minuscule MSS preserve lines of transmission which are not only independent but which of necessity had their origin at a time well before the 9th century. The extant uncial MSS do not and cannot account for the diversity and stability of PA textual forms found among even the earliest minuscules of the 9th century, let alone the diversity and stability of forms which appear throughout all centuries of the minuscule-era. The lack of extensive cross-comparison and correction demonstrated in the extant MSS containing the PA precludes the easy development of any existing form of the PA text from any other form of the PA text during at least the vellum era. The early uncials which contain the PA demonstrate widely-differing lines of transmission, but not all of the known lines. Nor do the uncials or minuscules show any indication of any known line deriving from a parallel known line. The 10 or so "texttype" lines of transmission remain independent and must necessarily extend back to a point long before their separate stabilizations occurred—a point which seems buried (as Colwell and Scrivener suggested) deep within the second century. ("Preliminary Observations regarding the *Pericope Adulterae* based upon Fresh Collations of nearly all Continuous-Text Manuscripts and over One Hundred Lectionaries", presented to the Evangelical Theological Society, Nov. 1998, pp.   11-13.)

[1] K. Aland, "The Text of the Church?", *Trinity Journal*, 1987, 8NS:131-144 [actually published in 1989], pp. 142-43.

[2] The Text of the New Testament, p. 53.

# 6
# SOME POSSIBLE OBJECTIONS

## Are Not the Oldest MSS the Best?

Burgon recognized the "antecedent probability" with these words:

> The more ancient testimony is probably the better testimony. That it is not by any means always so is a familiar fact... But it remains true, notwithstanding, that until evidence has been produced to the contrary in any particular instance, the more ancient of two witnesses may reasonably be presumed to be the better informed witness.[1]

This **a priori** expectation seems to have been elevated to a virtual certainty in the minds of many textual critics of the past century. The basic ingredient in the work of men like Tregelles, Tischendorf and Hort was a deference to the oldest MSS, and in this they followed Lachmann.

> The 'best' attestation, so Lachmann maintained, is given by the oldest witnesses. Taking his stand rigorously with the oldest, and disregarding the whole of the recent evidence, he drew the consequences of Bengel's observations. The material which Lachmann used could with advantage have been increased; but the principle that the text of the New Testament, like that of every other critical edition, must throughout be based upon the best available evidence, was once and for all established by him.[2]

Note that Zuntz here clearly equates 'oldest' with 'best'. He evidently exemplifies what Oliver has called "the growing belief that the oldest manuscripts contain the most nearly original text". Oliver proceeds:

> Some recent critics have returned to the earlier pattern of Tischendorf and Westcott and Hort: to seek for the original text in the oldest MSS. Critics earlier in the 20th century were highly critical of this 19th century practice. The return has been motivated largely by the discovery of papyri which are separated from the autographs by less than two centuries.[3]

But, the "contrary evidence" is in hand. We have already seen that most significant variants had come into being by the year 200, before the time of the earliest extant MSS, therefore. The **a priori** presumption in favor of age is

---

[1] Burgon, *The Traditional Text*, p. 40. I disagree. Great age in a manuscript should arouse our suspicion: how could it have survived for over 1,500 years? Why wasn't it used and worn out?

[2] Zuntz, *The Text*, pp. 6-7.

[3] Oliver, pp. 312-13.

nullified by the known existence of a variety of deliberately altered texts in the second century. Each witness must be evaluated on its own. As Colwell has so well put it, "the crucial question for early as for late witnesses is still, 'WHERE DO THEY FIT INTO A PLAUSIBLE RECONSTRUCTION OF THE HISTORY OF THE MANUSCRIPT TRADITION?'"[1]

It is generally agreed that all the earliest MSS, the ones upon which our critical/eclectic texts are based, come from Egypt.

> When the textual critic looks more closely at his oldest manuscript materials, the paucity of his resources is more fully realized. All the earliest witnesses, papyrus or parchment, come from Egypt alone. Manuscripts produced in Egypt, ranging between the third and fifth centuries, provide only a half-dozen extensive witnesses (the Beatty Papyri, and the well-known uncials, Vaticanus, Sinaiticus, Alexandrinus, Ephraem Syrus, and Freer Washington).[2] [To these the Bodmer Papyri must now be added.]

But what are Egypt's claims upon our confidence? And how wise is it to follow the witness of only one locale? Anyone who finds the history of the text presented herein to be convincing will place little confidence in the earliest MSS.

## *Their quality judged by themselves*

Quite apart from the history of the transmission of the text, the earliest MSS bear their own condemnation on their faces. $P^{66}$ is widely considered to be the earliest extensive manuscript. What of its quality? Again I borrow from Colwell's study of $P^{45}$, $P^{66}$, and $P^{75}$. Speaking of "the seriousness of intention of the scribe and the peculiarities of his own basic method of copying", he continues:

> On these last and most important matters, our three scribes are widely divided. $P^{75}$ and $P^{45}$ seriously intend to produce a good copy, but it is hard to believe that this was the intention of $P^{66}$. The nearly 200 nonsense readings and 400 itacistic spellings in $P^{66}$ are evidence of something less than disciplined attention to the basic task. To this evidence of carelessness must be added those singular readings whose origin baffles speculation, readings that can be given no more exact label than carelessness leading to assorted variant readings. A hurried count shows $P^{45}$ with 20, $P^{75}$ with 57, and $P^{66}$ with 216 purely careless readings. As we have

---

[1] Colwell, "Hort Redivivus", p. 157.

[2] Clark, "The Manuscripts of the Greek New Testament", p. 3.

seen, P[66] has, in addition, more than twice as many "leaps" from the same to the same as either of the others.[1]

Colwell's study took into account only singular readings—readings with no other MS support. He found P[66] to have 400 itacisms plus 482 other singular readings, 40 percent of which are nonsensical.[2] "P[66] editorializes as he does everything else—in a sloppy fashion."[3] In short, P[66] is a very poor copy and yet it is one of the earliest!

P[75] is placed close to P[66] in date. Though not as bad as P[66], it is scarcely a good copy. Colwell found P[75] to have about 145 itacisms plus 257 other singular readings, 25 percent of which are nonsensical.[4] Although Colwell gives the scribe of P[75] credit for having tried to produce a good copy, P[75] looks good only by comparison with P[66]. (If you were asked to write out the Gospel of John by hand, would you make over 400 mistakes?[5] Try it and see!) It should be kept in mind that the figures offered by Colwell deal only with errors which are the exclusive property of the respective MSS. They doubtless contain many other errors which happen to be found in some other witness(es) as well. In other words, they are actually worse even than Colwell's figures indicate.

P[45], though a little later in date, will be considered next because it is the third member in Colwell's study. He found P[45] to have approximately 90 itacisms plus 275 other singular readings, 10 percent of which are nonsensical.[6] However P[45] is shorter than P[66] (P[75] is longer) and so is not comparatively so much better as the figures might suggest at first glance. Colwell comments upon P[45] as follows:

> Another way of saying this is that when the scribe of P[45] creates a singular reading, it almost always makes sense; when the scribes of P[66] and P[75] create singular readings, they frequently do not

---

[1] Colwell, "Scribal Habits", pp. 378-79.

[2] *Ibid.*, pp. 374-76.

[3] *Ibid.*, p. 387.

[4] *Ibid.*, pp. 374-76.

[5] I am probably being unfair to the scribe who produced P[75]—some or many of those errors may have been in his exemplar. The fact remains that whatever their origin P[75] contains over 400 clear errors and I am trying by the suggested experiment to help the reader visualize how poor these early copies really are. Carson takes a different view. "If P[75], a second-century papyrus [?], is not recensional, then it must be either extremely close to the original or extremely corrupt. The latter possibility appears to be eliminated by the witness of B" (p. 117). How so? If P[75] is "extremely corrupt" and B was copied from it, or something similar, then B must also be extremely corrupt. (Hoskier supplies objective evidence to that effect in *Codex B and its Allies*.)

[6] Colwell, "Scribal Habits", pp. 374-76.

make sense and are obvious errors. Thus P[45] must be given credit for a much greater density of intentional changes than the other two.[1]

As an editor the scribe of P[45] wielded a sharp axe. The most striking aspect of his style is its conciseness. The dispensable word is dispensed with. He omits adverbs, adjectives, nouns, participles, verbs, personal pronouns—without any compensating habit of addition. He frequently omits phrases and clauses. He prefers the simple to the compound word. In short, he favors brevity. He shortens the text in at least fifty places in **singular readings alone**. But he does **not** drop syllables or letters. His shortened text is readable.[2]

Of special significance is the possibility of affirming with certainty that the scribe of P[45] deliberately and extensively shortened the text. Colwell credits him with having tried to produce a good copy. If by 'good' he means 'readable', fine, but if by 'good' we mean a faithful reproduction of the original, then P[45] is bad. Since P[45] contains many <u>deliberate alterations</u> it can only be called a "copy" with certain reservations.

P[46] is thought by some to be as early as P[66]. Zuntz's study of this manuscript is well-known. "In spite of its neat appearance (it was written by a professional scribe and corrected—but very imperfectly—by an expert), P[46] is by no means a good manuscript. The scribe committed very many blunders.... My impression is that he was liable to fits of exhaustion."[3]

It should be remarked in passing that Codex B is noted for its 'neat appearance' also, but it should not be assumed that therefore it must be a good copy. Zuntz says further: "P[46] abounds with scribal blunders, omissions, and also additions".[4]

> …the scribe who wrote the papyrus did his work very badly. Of his innumerable faults, only a fraction (less than one in ten) have been corrected and even that fraction—as often happens in manuscripts—grows smaller and smaller towards the end of the book. Whole pages have been left without any correction, however greatly they were in need of it.[5]

---

[1] *Ibid.*, p. 376.

[2] *Ibid.*, p. 383.

[3] Zuntz, *The Text*, p. 18.

[4] *Ibid.*, p. 212.

[5] *Ibid.*, p. 252.

Hoskier, also, has discussed the "large number of omissions" which disfigure P[46].[1] Again Zuntz says: "We have observed that, for example, the scribe of P[46] was careless and dull and produced a poor representation of an excellent tradition. Nor can we ascribe the basic excellence of this tradition to the manuscript from which P[46] was copied (we shall see that it, too, was faulty)."[2]

It is interesting to note that Zuntz feels able to declare the **parent** of P[46] to be faulty also. But, that P[46] represents an "excellent tradition" is a gratuitous assertion, based on Hort's theory. What is incontrovertible is that P[46] as it stands is a very poor copy—as Zuntz himself has emphatically stated.

Aland says concerning P[47]: "We need not mention the fact that the oldest manuscript does not necessarily have the best text. P[47] is, for example, by far the oldest of the manuscripts containing the full or almost full text of the Apocalypse, but it is certainly not the best."[3]

### *Their quality judged between themselves*

As to B and Aleph, we have already noted Hoskier's statement that these two MSS disagree over 3,000 times in the space of the four Gospels. Simple logic imposes the conclusion that one or the other must be wrong over 3,000 times—that is, they have over 3,000 mistakes between them. (If you were to write out the four Gospels by hand do you suppose you could manage to make 3,000 mistakes, or 1,500?) Aleph and B disagree, on the average, in almost every verse of the Gospels. Such a showing seriously undermines their credibility.

Burgon personally collated what in his day were 'the five old uncials' (ℵ, A, B, C, D). Throughout his works he repeatedly calls attention to the *concordia discors*, the prevailing confusion and disagreement, which the early uncials display between themselves. Luke 11:2-4 offers one example.

> "The five Old Uncials" (ℵABCD) falsify the Lord's Prayer as given by St. Luke in no less than forty-five words. But so little do they agree among themselves, that they throw themselves into six different combinations in their departures from the Traditional Text; and yet they are never able to agree among themselves as to one single various reading: while only once are more than two of them observed to stand together, and their grand point of union is no less than an omission of the article. Such is their eccentric tendency,

---

[1] H.C. Hoskier, "A Study of the Chester-Beatty Codex of the Pauline Epistles", *The Journal of Theological Studies*, XXXVIII (1937), 162.

[2] Zuntz, *The Text*, p. 157.

[3] Aland, "The Significance of the Papyri", p. 333.

that in respect of thirty-two out of the whole forty-five words they bear in turn solitary evidence.[1]

Mark 2:1-12 offers another example.

> In the course of those 12 verses... there will be found to be 60 variations of reading. ...Now, in the present instance, the 'five old uncials' **cannot be** the depositories of a tradition—whether Western or Eastern—because they render inconsistent testimony **in every verse**. It must further be admitted, (for this is really not a question of opinion, but a plain matter of fact,) that it is unreasonable to place confidence in such documents. What would be thought in a Court of Law of five witnesses, called up 47 times for examination, who should be observed to bear contradictory testimony **every time**?[2]

Hort, also, had occasion to notice an instance of this *concordia discors*. Commenting on the four places in Mark's Gospel (14:30, 68, 72a,b) where the cock's crowing is mentioned he said: "The confusion of attestation introduced by these several cross currents of change is so great that of the seven principal MSS אA B C D L Δ no two have the same text in all four places".[3] He might also have said that in these four places the seven uncials present themselves in **twelve** different combinations (and only A and Δ agree together three times out of the four). If we add W and Θ the confusion remains the same except that now there are thirteen combinations. Are such witnesses worthy of credence?

Recalling Colwell's effort to reconstruct an "Alexandrian" archetype for chapter one of Mark, either Codex B is wrong 34 times in that one chapter or else a majority of the remaining primary "Alexandrian" witnesses is wrong (which does nasty things to the pretensions of the "Alexandrian" text), and so for Aleph and L, etc. Further, Kenyon admitted that B is "disfigured by many blunders in transcription".[4] Scrivener said of B:

> One marked feature, characteristic of this copy, is the great number of its omissions... That no small portion of these are mere oversights of the scribe seems evident from the circumstance that this same scribe has repeatedly written words and clauses **twice over**, a class of mistakes which Mai and the collators have seldom thought fit to notice, ...but which by no means enhances our estimate of the care employed in copying this venerable record of primitive Christianity.[5]

---

[1] Burgon, *The Traditional Text*, p. 84.

[2] Burgon, *The Revision Revised*, pp. 30-31.

[3] Westcott and Hort, p. 243.

[4] Kenyon, *Handbook*, p. 308.

[5] Scrivener, A Plain Introduction, I, 120.

Even Hort conceded that the scribe of B "reached by no means a high standard of accuracy".[1] Aleph is acknowledged on every side to be worse than B in every way.

Codex D is in a class by itself. Said Scrivener:

> The internal character of the Codex Bezae is a most difficult and indeed an almost inexhaustible theme. No known manuscript contains so many bold and extensive interpolations (six hundred, it is said, in the Acts alone). ... Mr. Harris from curious internal evidence, such as the existence in the text of a vitiated rendering of a verse of Homer which bears signs of having been retranslated from a Latin translation, infers that the Greek has been made up from the Latin.[2]

Hort spoke of "the prodigious amount of error which D contains".[3] Burgon concluded that D resembles a Targum more than a transcription.[4]

## Their quality judged by the ancient Church

If these are our best MSS we may as well agree with those who insist that the recovery of the original wording is impossible, and turn our minds to other pursuits. But the evidence indicates that the earliest MSS are the worst. It is clear that the Church in general did not propagate the sort of text found in the earliest MSS, which demonstrates that they were not held in high esteem in their day.

Consider the so-called "Western" text-type. In the Gospels it is represented by essentially one Greek MS, Codex Bezae (D, 05), plus the Latin versions (sort of). So much so that for many years no critical text has used a cover symbol for "Western". In fact, K. and B. Aland now refer to it simply as the "D" text (their designation is objective, at least). The Church universal simply refused to copy or otherwise propagate that type of text. Nor can the Latin Vulgate legitimately be claimed for the "Western" text—it is more "Byzantine" than anything else (recall that it was translated in the 4th century).

Consider the so-called "Alexandrian" text-type. In more recent times neither the UBS nor the Nestle texts use a cover symbol for this "text" either (only for the "Byzantine"). F. Wisse collated and analyzed 1,386 MSS for chapters 1, 10 and 20 of Luke.[5] On the basis of shared mosaics of readings he was able to group the MSS into families, 15 "major" groups and 22 lesser ones. One of the

---

[1] Westcott and Hort, p. 233.

[2] Scrivener, *A Plain Introduction*, I, 130. Cf. Rendel Harris, *A Study of the Codex Bezae* (1891).

[3] Westcott and Hort, p. 149.

[4] Burgon, *The Traditional Text*, pp. 185-90.

[5] F. Wisse, The Profile Method for Classifying and Evaluating Manuscript Evidence (Grand Rapids: Eerdmans, 1982).

major ones he calls "Egyptian" ("Alexandrian")—it is made up of precisely four uncials and four cursives, plus another two of each that are "Egyptian" in one of the three chapters. Rounding up to ten, that makes ten out of 1,386—less than 1%!

Again, the Church universal simply refused to copy or otherwise propagate that type of text. Codex B has no 'children'. Codex Aleph has no 'children'—in fact, it is so bad that across the centuries something like 14 different people worked on it, trying to fix it up (but no one copied it). Recall Colwell's study wherein he tried to arrive at the archetype of the "Alexandrian" text in chapter one of Mark on the basis of the 13 MSS presumed to represent that type of text. They were so disparate that he discarded the seven "worst" ones and then tried his experiment using the remaining six. Even then the results were so bad—Codex B diverged from the mean text 34 times (just in one chapter)—that Colwell threw up his hands and declared that such an archetype never existed. If Colwell is correct then the "Alexandrian" text-type _cannot represent the Autograph_. The Autograph is the ultimate archetype, and it did indeed exist.

Consider one more detail. Zuntz says of the scribe of $P^{46}$: "Of his innumerable faults, only a fraction (less than one in ten) have been corrected and even that fraction—as often happens in manuscripts—grows smaller and smaller towards the end of the book. Whole pages have been left without any correction, however greatly they were in need of it."[1]

A similar thing happens in $P^{66}$. Why? Probably because the corrector lost heart, gave up. Perhaps he saw that the transcription was so hopelessly bad that no one would want to use it, even if he could patch it up. It should also be noted that although many collations and discussions of MSS ignore errors of spelling, to a person in the year 250 wishing to **use** a copy, for devotional study or whatever, errors in spelling would be just as annoying and distracting as more serious ones. A copy like $P^{66}$, with roughly two mistakes per verse, would be set aside in disgust.

I recently collated cursive 789 (Athens: National Library) for John, having already done so for Luke. Although the copyist made an occasional mistake, I judge that his exemplar was a very nearly perfect representative of Family 35. However, 789 is presently lacking John 19:12 to the end. A later hand, $789^s$, has 19:26 to the end, but that copyist was a terrible speller, averaging nearly one mistake per verse—reminiscent of $P^{66}$ (although $P^{66}$ is worse, averaging around two mistakes per verse). I found myself becoming angry with the copyist—I was prepared to call down curses on his head! Assuming that the cause of the mistakes was ignorance, rather than perversity, the copyist should not have undertaken a task for which he was so pitifully unqualified. It

---

[1] Zuntz, *The Text*, p. 252.

would be psychologically impossible for me to use 789$^s$ for devotion or study. I would become too angry to continue.[1]

Further, how could the early MSS survive for 1,500 years if they had been used? (I have worn out several Bibles in my short life.) Considering the relative difficulty of acquiring copies in those days (expensive, done by hand) any worthy copy would have been used until it wore out. Which brings us to the next possible objection.

## Why Are There No Early "Byzantine" MSS?

Why would or should there be? To demand that a MS survive for 1,500 years is in effect to require both that it have remained unused and that it have been stored in Egypt (or Qumran). Even an unused MS would require an arid climate to last so long.

But is either requirement reasonable? Unless there were persons so rich as to be able to proliferate copies of the Scriptures for their health or amusement, copies would be made on demand, in order to be **used**. As the use of Greek died out in Egypt the demand for Greek Scriptures would die out too, so we should not expect to find many Greek MSS in Egypt.

It should not be assumed, however, that the "Byzantine" text was not used in Egypt. Although none of the early Papyri can reasonably be called "Byzantine", they each contain "Byzantine" readings. The case of P$^{66}$ is dramatic. The first hand was extensively corrected, and both hands are dated around A.D. 200. The 1st hand is almost half "Byzantine" (a. 47%), but the 2nd hand regularly changed "Byzantine" readings to "Alexandrian" and *vice versa*, i.e. he changed "Alexandrian" to "Byzantine", repeatedly. This means that they must have had two exemplars, one "Alexandrian" and one "Byzantine"— between the two hands the "Byzantine" text receives considerable attestation (in the year 200!!).

Consider the case of Codex B and P$^{75}$; they are said to agree 82% of the time (unprecedented for "Alexandrian" MSS, but rather poor for "Byzantine"). But what about the 18% discrepancy? Most of the time, if not always, when P$^{75}$ and B disagree one or the other agrees with the "Byzantine" reading, and the distribution is about even. If they come from a common source, that source would have been more "Byzantine" than either descendant. Even the Coptic versions agree with the "Byzantine" text as often as not.

---

[1] I continue to insist that most of the early MSS survived because they were intolerably bad; it was psychologically impossible to use them, besides being a criminal waste of good parchment to copy them (is not uncial 06 the only one with an extant copy?).

## "Orphan children"

The study and conclusions of Lake, Blake, and New, already discussed in a prior section, are of special interest here. They looked for evidence of direct genealogy and found virtually none. I repeat their conclusion.

> ...the manuscripts which we have are almost all orphan children without brothers or sisters.

> Taking this fact into consideration along with the negative result of our collation of MSS at Sinai, Patmos, and Jerusalem, it is hard to resist the conclusion that the scribes usually destroyed their exemplars when they had copied the sacred books.[1]

Is it unreasonable to suppose that once an old MS became tattered and almost illegible in spots the faithful would make an exact copy of it and then destroy it, rather than allowing it to suffer the indignity of literally rotting away? What would such a practice do to our chances of finding an early "Byzantine" MS? Anyone who objects to this conclusion must still account for the fact that in three ancient monastic libraries equipped with scriptoria (rooms designed to facilitate the faithful copying of MSS), there are only "orphan children". Why are there no parents?!

---

[1] Lake, Blake and New, p. 349. D.A. Carson offers the following response to this suggestion: "The answers to this ingenious theory are obvious: (1) If only one copy were made before the exemplar was destroyed, there would never be more than one extant copy of the Greek New Testament! (2) If several copies were made from one exemplar, then either (a) they were not all made at the same time, and therefore the destruction of the exemplar was not a common practice after all; or (b) they were all made at the same time. (3) If the latter obtains, then it should be possible to identify their sibling relationship; yet in fact such identification is as difficult and as precarious as the identification of direct exemplar/copy manuscripts. This probably means we have lost a lot of manuscripts; and/or it means that the divergences between copy and exemplar, as between copy and sibling copy, are frequently difficult to detect. (4) Why are there **no** copies of the Byzantine text before about A.D. 350, and **so many** [emphasis Carson's] from there on? This anomaly, it might be argued, demonstrates that the practice of destroying the exemplar died out during the fourth century" (*The King James Version Debate*, Grand Rapids: Baker Book House, 1979, pp. 47-48).

Perhaps it is fortunate that Lake is no longer available for comment upon this extraordinary statement. If I may presume to answer for him, it seems to me apparent that what Lake found was the end of the line, the last generation of copies. Neither Lake nor anyone else has suggested that only one copy would be made of any exemplar, but after a life of use and being copied a worn and tattered MS would be destroyed. Carson's point (4) is hard to believe. Lake, Blake, and New were looking at minuscule MSS, probably none earlier than the tenth century—they had to be copied from something, and it is a fact that Lake and company found no 'parents'. Carson offers no explanation for this *fact*. And what are we to understand from his strange remark about "Byzantine" MSS before and after A.D. 350? There are none from the fourth century, unless W (Matthew) be placed there, two partially so from the fifth, and a slowly expanding stream as one moves up through the succeeding centuries. It is only when we come to the minuscule era that we find "so many". Please see the next section, "the ninth century transliteration process", to find out why.

Van Bruggen addresses the problem from a slightly different direction. He says of the "Byzantine" text:

> The fact that this text-form is known to us via later manuscripts is as such no proof for a late text-type, but it does seem to become a proof when at the same time a different text is found in all older manuscripts. The combination of these two things seems to offer decisive proof for the late origin of the traditional text.[1]

He answers the "seeming proof" in the following way:

> Let us make ourselves aware of **what** we have presupposed with this seemingly convincing argumentation. What conditions must be satisfied if we wish to award the prize to the older majuscules? While asking this question we assumed wittingly or unwittingly that we were capable of making a fair comparison between manuscripts in an earlier period and those in a later period. After all, we can only arrive at positive statements if that is the case. Imagine that someone said: in the Middle Ages mainly cathedrals were built, but in modern times many small and plainer churches are being built. This statement seems completely true when we today look around in the cities and villages. Yet we are mistaken. An understandable mistake: many small churches of the Middle Ages have disappeared, and usually only the cathedrals were restored. Thus, a great historical falsification of perspective with regard to the history of church-building arises. We are not able to make a general assertion about church-building in the Middle Ages on the basis of the surviving materials. If we would still dare to make such an assertion, then we wrongly assumed that the surviving materials enabled us to make a fair comparison. But how is the situation in the field of New Testament manuscripts? Do we have a **representative** number of manuscripts from the first centuries? Only if that is the case, do we have the right to make conclusions and positive statements. Yet it is just at this point that difficulties arise. The situation is even such that we know with certainty that we **do not** possess a representative number of manuscripts from the first centuries.[2]

The conclusion of Lake, Blake, and New reflects another consideration. The age of a manuscript must not be confused with the age of the text it exhibits. Any copy, by definition, contains a text that is older than it is. In Burgon's words, it "represents a MS, or a pedigree of MSS, older than itself; and it is but fair to suppose that it exercises such representation with tolerable accuracy".[3]

---

[1] Van Bruggen, p. 24.

[2] *Ibid.*, p. 25.

[3] Burgon, The Traditional Text, p. 47.

## The ninth century transliteration process

Van Bruggen discusses yet another relevant consideration.

> In the codicology the great value of the transliteration process in the 9th century and thereafter is recognized. At that time the most important New Testament manuscripts written in majuscule script were carefully transcribed into minuscule script. It is assumed that after this transliteration-process the majuscule was taken out of circulation. ... The import of this datum has not been taken into account enough in the present New Testament textual criticism. For it implies, that just the oldest, best and most customary manuscripts come to us in the new uniform of the minuscule script, does it not? This is even more cogent since it appears that various archetypes can be detected in this transliteration-process for the New Testament. Therefore we do not receive one mother-manuscript through the flood-gates of the transliteration, but several. The originals have, however, disappeared! This throws a totally different light on the situation that we are confronted with regarding the manuscripts. Why do the surviving ancient manuscripts show another text-type? Because they are the only survivors of their generation, and because their survival is due to the fact that they were of a different kind. Even though one continues to maintain that the copyists at the time of the transliteration handed down the wrong text-type to the Middle Ages, one can still never prove this codicologically with the remark that older majuscules have a different text. This would be circular reasoning. There certainly were majuscules just as venerable and ancient as the surviving Vaticanus or Sinaiticus, which, like a section of the Alexandrinus, presented a Byzantine text. But they have been renewed into minuscule script and their majuscule appearance has vanished. Historically it **seems** as though the most ancient majuscule manuscripts exclusively contain a non-Byzantine text, but the prespective [sic] is falsified here just like it is regarding church-building in the Middle Ages and at present.[1]

The significance of the transliteration process was explained by A. Dain as follows: "The transliterated copy, carefully written and securely bound, became the reference point for the subsequent tradition. The old papyrus and parchment exemplars that had been copied, doubtless quite worn out, were of no further interest and were usually discarded or destroyed."[2] Apparently there was an organized movement to 'transliterate' uncial MSS into minuscule form or script. Note that Dain agrees with Lake that the "worn out" exemplars were then destroyed (some may have been 'recycled', becoming palimpsests).

---

[1] Van Bruggen, pp. 26-27.

[2] A. Dain, *Les Manuscrits* (Paris, 1949), p. 115.

What if those exemplars were ancient "Byzantine" uncials? Come to think of it, they must have been since the cursives are "Byzantine".

Yes indeed, let's stop and think. To copy a document by hand takes time (and skill) and parchment was hard to come by. If a monastery had only the parchment made from the skins of the animals they ate, the material would always be in short supply. To buy it from others would take money, and where did a monastery get money? So who is going to waste good parchment making a copy of a text considered to be deficient? Yet they might hesitate to destroy it, so it survived, but left no 'children'. Consider the ninth century uncials that we know of: almost all of them are clearly "Byzantine", but not super-good, and none belong to Family 35. I would say that they were not considered to be good enough to deserve putting into minuscule form, and thus survived—had they been 'transliterated' they would have been scraped and turned into a palimpsest.

C.H. Roberts comments upon a practice of early Christians that would have had a similar effect.

> It was a Jewish habit both to preserve manuscripts by placing them in jars ... and also to dispose of defective, worn-out, or heretical scriptures by burying them near a cemetery, not to preserve them but because anything that might contain the name of God might not be destroyed.... It certainly looks as if this institution of a morgue for sacred but unwanted manuscripts was taken over from Judaism by the early Church.[1]

Note that the effect of this practice in any but an arid climate would be the decomposition of the MSS. If "Byzantine" exemplars, worn out through use, were disposed of in this way (as seems likely), they would certainly perish. All of this reduces our chances of finding really ancient "Byzantine" MSS. Nor is that all.

## *Imperial repression of the N.T.*

There is a further consideration. "It is historically certain that the text of the New Testament endured a very hard time in the first centuries. Many good and official editions of the text were confiscated and destroyed by the authorities during the time of the persecutions."[2]

Roberts refers to "the regular requisition and destruction of books by the authorities at times of persecution, so often recorded in the martyr acts".[3] Such official activity seems to have come to a climax in Diocletian's campaign to destroy the New Testament manuscripts around A.D. 300.

---

[1] C.H. Roberts, p. 7.

[2] Van Bruggen, p. 29. Cf. Eusebius, *Historia Ecclesiastica* VIII, II, 1.4 and F.H.A. Scrivener, *A Plain Introduction*, pp. 265-66.

[3] Roberts, p. 8.

If there was any trauma in the history of the normal transmission of the text, this was it; the more so since the campaign evidently centered upon the Aegean area. Many MSS were found, or betrayed, and burned, but others must have escaped. That many Christians would have spared no effort to hide and preserve their copies of the Scriptures is demonstrated by their attitude towards those who gave up their MSS—the Donatist schism that immediately followed Diocletian's campaign partly hinged on the question of punishment for those who had given up MSS. The Christians whose entire devotion to the Scriptures was thus demonstrated would also be just the ones that would be the most careful about the pedigree of their own MSS; just as they took pains to protect their MSS they presumably would have taken pains to ensure that their MSS preserved the true wording.

In fact, the campaign of Diocletian may even have had a purifying effect upon the transmission of the text. If the laxity of attitude toward the text reflected in the willingness of some to give up their MSS also extended to the quality of text they were prepared to use, then it may have been the more contaminated MSS that were destroyed, in the main, leaving the purer MSS to replenish the earth.[1] But these surviving pure MSS would have been in unusually heavy demand for copying (to replace those that had been destroyed) and been worn out faster than normal.

In short, if the history of transmission presented herein is valid we should not necessarily expect to find any early "Byzantine" MSS. They would have been used and worn out. (But the text they contained would be preserved by their descendants.) An analogy is furnished by the fate of the *Biblia Pauperum* in the fifteenth century.

## *The Biblia Pauperum*

Of all the *Xylographic* works, that is, such as are printed from wooden blocks, the *BIBLIA PAUPERUM* is perhaps the rarest, as well as the most ancient; it is a manual, or kind of catechism of the Bible, for the use of young persons, and of the common people, whence it derives its name,—*Biblia Pauperum—the Bible of the Poor*, who were thus enabled to acquire, at a comparatively low price, an imperfect knowledge of some of the events recorded in the Scriptures. Being much in use, the few copies of it which are at present to be found in the libraries of the curious are for the most part either mutilated or in bad condition. The extreme rarity of this book, and the circumstances under which it was produced, concur to impart a high degree of interest to it.[2]

---

[1] Here was an excellent opportunity for the "Alexandrian" and "Western" texts to forge ahead and take 'space' away from the "Byzantine", but it did not happen. The Church rejected those types of text. How can modern critics possibly be in a better position to identify the true text than was the Church universal in the early 4th century?

[2] T.H. Horne, *An Introduction to the Critical Study and Knowledge of the Holy Scriptures*, 4th American edition (4 vols.; Philadelphia: E. Little, 1831), vol. II, p. 217. I

Although it went through five editions, presumably totaling thousands of copies, it was so popular that the copies were worn out by use. I maintain that the same thing happened to the ancient "Byzantine" MSS.

Adding to all this the discussion of the quality of the earliest MSS, in the prior section, early age in a MS might well arouse our suspicions—why did it survive? And that brings us to a third possible objection.

# "But There Is No Evidence of the Byzantine <u>Text</u> in the Early Centuries"

Although Hort and Kenyon stated plainly that no "Syrian <u>readings</u>" existed before, say, A.D. 250, their present day followers have been obliged by the early papyri to retreat to the weaker statement that it is all the readings together, the "Byzantine" ("Syrian") <u>text</u> that had no early existence. Ehrman states the position as baldly as anyone: "No early Greek Father from anywhere in the early Christian world, no Latin nor Syriac Father, and no early version of the New Testament gives evidence of the existence of the Syrian text prior to the fourth century".[1]

## *Evidence from the early Fathers*

This question has already received some attention in Chapter 4, "'Syrian' Readings before Chrysostom", but K. Aland offers us some fascinating new evidence. In "The Text of the Church?" he offers a tabulation of patristic citations of the N.T.[2] The significance of the evidence is somewhat obscured by the presentation, which seems to be a bit tendentious. The turn of phrase is such as to lead the unwary reader to an exaggerated impression of the evidence against the Majority Text. E.g., Origen is said to be: "55% against the Majority text (30% of which show agreement with the 'Egyptian text'), 28% common to both texts, and 17% with the Majority text." 55 + 28 + 17 = 100. The problem lies with the "of which". In normal English the "of which" refers to the 55% (not 100%); so we must calculate 30% of 55%, which gives us 16.5% (of the total). 55 minus 16.5 leaves 38.5% which is neither Egyptian nor Majority, hence "other". I will chart the statistics unambiguously, following this interpretation.

am indebted to Maurice Robinson for calling this material to my attention.

[1] Ehrman, p. 72.

[2] K. Aland, "The Text of the Church?", *Trinity Journal*, 1987, 8NS:131-144 [actually published in 1989], p. 139.

| Father | date | Egyptian alone | both E&M | Majority alone | other (−EM) | # of pass. |
|--------|------|---------|---------|---------|---------|---------|
| Marcion | (160?) | 23% | 10% | 18% | 49% | 94 |
| Irenaeus | (d.202) | 16% | 16.5% | 16.5% | 51% | 181 |
| Clement Alex. | (d.215) | 13.5% | 29% | 15% | 42.5% | 161 |
| Hippolytus | (d.235) | 14.5% | 31% | 19% | 46.5% | 33** |
|  |  | 13.5% | 18% | 21% | 43.5% | 21 |
|  |  | 14.5% | 18% | 21% | 46.5% | 33 |
| Origen | (d.254) | 16.5% | 28% | 17% | 38.5% | 459 |
| Methodius | (280?) | 12.5% | 31% | 19% | 37.5% | 32 |
| Adamantius | (d.300) | 11.5% | 21% | 31% | 36.5% | 29 |
| Asterius | (d.341) | --- | 40% | 50% | 10% | 30 |
| Basil | (d.379) | 2.5% | 39% | 40% | 18.5% | 249 |
| Apost. Const. | (380?) | 3% | 33% | 41% | 23% | 46 |
| Epiphanius | (d.403) | 11% | 33% | 41% | 37% | 114** |
|  |  | 11% | 30% | 22% | 37% | 114 |
| Chrysostom | (d.407) | 2% | 38% | 40.5% | 19.5% | 915 |
| Severian | (d.408) | 3% | 37% | 30% | 30% | 91 |
| Theod. Mops. | (d.428) | 4.5% | 29% | 39% | 27.5% | 28 |
| Marcus Erem. | (d.430) | 5.5% | 35% | 35% | 24.5% | 37 |
| Theodotus | (d.445) | 3% | 37.5% | 37.5% | 22% | 16 |
| Hesychius | (d.450) | 3.5% | 37% | 33% | 26.5% | 84 |
| Theodoret | (d.466) | 1% | 41% | 42% | 16% | 481 |
| John Damascus | (d.749) | 2% | 40% | 40% | 18% | 63 |

**(With reference to Hippolytus and Epiphanius, the first line reflects the statistics as given in Aland's article, but they do not add up to 100%. The second line reflects the statistics as given in a pre-publication draft of the same article distributed by the American Bible Society. For Epiphanius the second line is probably correct, since it adds up to 100%—the 33 and 41 were presumably copied from the line above. For Hippolytus the second line doesn't add up either; so we are obliged to engage in a little textual criticism to see if we can recover the original. The third line gives my guess—the 31 and 19 were probably borrowed from the line below [in his article Methodius is placed before Origen—I put them in chronological order]. Six errors in the pre-publication draft were corrected, but another four were created.)

One thing becomes apparent at a glance. With the sole exception of Marcion, each of the Fathers used the Majority Text **more than** the Egyptian. Even in Clement and Origen (in Egypt, therefore) the Majority text is preferred over the Egyptian, and by the end of the third century the preference is unambiguous. This is startling, because it goes against almost everything that we have been taught for over a century. Perhaps we have misconstrued Aland's statement. Returning to Origen, we are told that he is "55% against the Majority text (30% of which show agreement with the 'Egyptian text'),…" On second thought, the "of which" is probably supposed to refer to the total. In that event a less ambiguous way of presenting the statistics would be to say: "30% with the

Egyptian text, 17% with the Majority text, 28% common to both and 25% differing from both". I will chart his statistics in this way, using "other" for the last category.

| Father | date | Egyptian alone | both E&M | Majority alone | other (-EM) | # of pass. |
|---|---|---|---|---|---|---|
| Marcion | (160?) | 32% | 10% | 18% | 40% | 94 |
| Irenaeus | (d.202) | 24% | 16.5% | 16.5% | 43% | 181 |
| Clement Alex | (d.215) | 24% | 29% | 15% | 32% | 161 |
| Hippolytus | (d.235) | 24% | 18% | 21% | 37% | 33 |
| Origen | (d.254) | 30% | 28% | 17% | 25% | 459 |
| Methodius | (280?) | 25% | 31% | 19% | 25% | 32 |
| Adamantius | (d.300) | 24% | 21% | 31% | 24% | 29 |
| Asterius | (d.341) | --- | 40% | 50% | 10% | 30 |
| Basil | (d.379) | 11% | 39% | 40% | 10% | 249 |
| Apost. Const | (380?) | 11% | 33% | 41% | 15% | 46 |
| Epiphanius | (d.403) | 23% | 30% | 22% | 25% | 114 |
| Chrysostom | (d.407) | 8.5% | 38% | 40.5% | 13% | 915 |
| Severian | (d.408) | 9% | 37% | 30% | 24% | 91 |
| Theod. Mops | (d.428) | 14% | 29% | 39% | 18% | 28 |
| Marcus Erem. | (d.430) | 19% | 35% | 35% | 11% | 37 |
| Theodotus | (d.445) | 12.5% | 37.5% | 37.5% | 12.5% | 16 |
| Hesychius | (d.450) | 12% | 37% | 33% | 18% | 84 |
| Theodoret | (d.466) | 6% | 41% | 42% | 11% | 481 |
| John Damascus | (d.749) | 11% | 40% | 40% | 9% | 63 |

(I will assume that this second display is more probably what Aland intended, so any subsequent discussion of the evidence from these early Fathers will be based upon it.)

Something that Aland does not explain, but that absolutely demands attention, is the extent to which these early Fathers apparently cited neither the Egyptian nor the Majority texts—a plurality for the first four. Should this be interpreted as evidence against the authenticity of both the Majority and Egyptian texts? Probably not, and for the following reason: a careful distinction must be made between citation, quotation and transcription. A responsible person transcribing a copy will have the exemplar before him and will try to reproduce it exactly. A person quoting a verse or two from memory is liable to a variety of tricks of the mind and may create new readings which do not come from any textual tradition. A person citing a text in a sermon will predictably vary the turn of phrase for rhetorical effect. All Patristic citation needs to be evaluated with these distinctions in mind and must not be pushed beyond its limits.

## Evidence from Clement of Alexandria

I wish to explore this question a little further by evaluating a transcription of Mark 10:17-31 done by Clement of Alexandria. Clement's text is taken from *Clement of Alexandria*, ed. G.W. Butterworth (Harvard University Press, 1939 [The Loeb Classical Library]); *Clemens Alexandrinus*, ed. Otto Stahlin (Berlin: Akademie-Verlag, 1970); the Library of Greek Fathers (Athens, 1956, vol. 8). It is compared to UBS$^3$ as a representative of the Egyptian text, to the H-F Majority Text as a representative of the Byzantine text, and to Codex D as a representative of the "Western" text. The Greek text of these four sources has been arranged for ease of comparison. The four lines in each set are always given in the same order: Clement first [where the three editions are not in full agreement, I follow two against one], Majority Text second, UBS$^3$ third and Codex D fourth. The result is interesting and, I think, instructive.

Clem. 17) - - - εκπορευομενω  αυτω  εις οδον προσελθων  τις —— εγονυπετει      - - -   - - -   - - -
MT         και εκπορευομενου αυτου εις οδον προσδραμων εις και γονυπετησας αυτον επηρωτα αυτον
UBS          "       "        "      "    "    "       "   "   "         "      "       "
Bezae        "       "               "   "  "         "    "  γονυπετων     "   ηρωτα      "


λεγων διδασκαλε αγαθε τι αγαθον ποιησω ινα ζωην αιωνιον κληρονομησω 18) ο δε Ιησους λεγει —— τι
- - -   "       "    "   "  _ _ _  "    "    "     "        "         "    "    "  ειπεν αυτω τι
- - -   "       "    "   _ _ _    "    "    "     "         "         "    "    "   "   "    "
λεγων   "       "    "   _ _ _    "    "    "     "         "         "    "    "   "   "    "


με αγαθον λεγεις ουδεις αγαθος ει μη - - - εις ο Θεος 19) τας εντολας οιδας μη μοιχευσας μη φονευσης
με λεγεις αγαθον   "     "    "  "   _ _ _ "  "   "     "    "     "    "    "      "       "    "
 "    "      "     "     "    "  "   _ _ _ "  "   "     "    "     "    "    "      "   φονευσης μη μοιχευσης
 "    "      "     "     "    "  "   μονος " _ _  "     "    "     "    "    "      "   μοιχευσης μη πορνευσης


μη κλεψης μη ψευδομαρτυρησης - -    - - -   τιμα τον πατερα - - και την μητερα 20)ο δε αποκρι-
 "   "    "      "              μη αποστερησης  "   "    "   σου  "   "    "     "   "    _ _ _
 "   "    "  ψευδομαρτυρησεις "  αποστερησεις τειμα "   "    "   - -   "   "     "   "  " αποκρι-


θεις λεγει αυτω    - - -    παντα ταυτα εφυλαξα   - -   - - -   - - 21) ο δε Ιησους εμβλεψας - - -
 "  ειπεν    "   διδασκαλε ταυτα παντα εφυλαξαμην εκ νεωτητος μου  "    "    "    "    "    αυτω
- -  εφη     "     "     "    "     "     "        "     "     "    "    "    "    "    "     "
θεις ειπεν  "      "   παντα ταυτα εφυλαξα        "     "     "    "    "    "    "    "     "


ηγαπησεν αυτον και ειπεν - - -εν σοι υστερει ει θελεις τελειος ειναι - — πωλησον οσα εχεις και διαδος
 "       "    "   "    αυτω "  "    "    "     "    "     "   — - -   - - -υπαγε οσα εχεις πωλησον "  δος
 "       "    "   "    "   σε  "    "    "   - -   "   - - -  - - - - - -   "    "    "     "    "   "
 "       "    "   "    "   σοι "    "    "   — - -  — - - - - - -          "    "    "     "    "   "


- - - πτωχοις και εξεις θησαυρον εν ουρανω και δευρο ακολουθει μοι - - - --   - - - 22) ο δε στυ-
- - -   "     "    "    "        "    "    "    "       "       "  "   "        " αρας τον σταυρον  " " "
(τοις)  "     "    "    "        "    "    "    "       "       "   " _ _ _ _ _  _ _ _          " " "
τοις    "     "    "    "        "    "    "    "       "       "   "  _ _ _ _ _   _ _ _        " " εστυ-


γνασας επι - - -τω λογω - -απηλθεν λυπουμενος ην γαρ πλουσιος εχων κτηματα πολλα και αγρους 23)
  "     "  _ _ _  "   _ _    "        "       "   "    "     "    "       "      _ _ _   _ _ _
  "     "  _ _ _  "   _ _    "        "       "   "    "     "    "      - - -    "  "   _ _  - - -
γνασεν " τουτω "  "  και     "        "       "   "    "   - - -            πολλα χρηματα —  - - -


146

– – περιβλεψαμενος δε ο Ιησους λεγει τοις μαθηταις αυτου πως δυσκολως οι τα χρηματα εχοντες εισε–
και    "  __ "  "  "  "  "   "  "  "  "  "  "   __

    "   "  __ "  "  "  "  "   "  "  "  "  "  "   __
    "   "  __ "  "  "  "  "   "  "  "  "  "  "   __


λευσονται εις την βασιλειαν του Θεου   – – –   24)οι δε μαθηται – – – εθαμβουντο επι τοις λογοις
– – –  "  "  "  "  "  *εισελευσονται*  "  "  "  – – –  "  "  "
– – –  "  "  "  "  "    "  "  "  – – –  "  "  "
– – –  "  "  "  "  *εισελευσοντ*[1] **)[2] "  "  "  *αυτου εθανβουντο* "  "  "


αυτου παλιν δε ο Ιησους αποκριθεις λεγει αυτοις τεκνια πως δυσκολον εστιν τους πεποιθοτας επι – – –
" *ο δε Ιησους παλιν*  "  "  "  *τεκνα* "  "  "  "  "  __ __ ___ __ __
"  "  "  "  "  "  "  "  "  "  "  *τους πεποιθοτας επι τοις*


χρημασιν εις την βασιλειαν του Θεου εισελθειν  25) ευκολωτερον – – – δια της τρυμαλιας της βελονης
"  "  "  "  "  *ευκοπωτερον εστι καμηλον δια της τρυμαλιας της*
– – –  "  "  "  "  "  "  "  "  "  "  "  ("*)  "  ("*)
*χρημασιν* "  "  "  "  "  "  ( fragmented ) *καμηλος* "  — *τρυμαλιδος* —


καμηλος εισελευσεται η πλουσιος εις την βασιλειαν του Θεου  – – –  26)οι δε περισσως εξεπλησσοντο
*ραφιδος  εισελθειν  η πλουσιον* "  "  "  "  *εισελθειν* "  "  "  "
"  *διελθειν* "  "  "  "  "  "  "  "  "  "
"  *διελευσεται  η πλουσιος* "  "  "  "  – – –  "  "  "


και ελεγον – – –   – – –   – – τις ουν δυναται σωθηναι 27) ο δε εμβλεψας — αυτοις- – – – ειπεν οτι
*λεγοντες   προς εαυτους και* "  – –  "   – – –   *δε*  "  *ο Ιησους λεγει* —
"  "  "  "  – –  "  "   – – –  "  "  "  "  —
"  "  "  "  – –  "  "  *— — ενβλεψας  δε* "  "  "  —


παρα ανθρωποις – – – αδυνατον – – – – – παρα —— Θεω – – – — δυνατον εστιν – – – — —
"  "  – – –  "  *— — αλλ ου* "  —— " *παντα γαρ δυνατα* " *παρα τω Θεω*
"  "  – – –  "  — — — "  —— "   — — —   __ — __
"  "  *τουτο* "  *εστιν* – – — " *δε τω* "  – – – — *δυνατον* – – – – – – — —


28)– – ηρξατο ο Πετρος λεγειν αυτω ιδε  ημεις αφηκαμεν παντα και ηκολουθησαμεν σοι 29) αποκριθεις
– –  "  "  "  "  *ιδου*  "  "  "  "  "  "
"  *λεγειν ο Πετρος* "  "  "  "  *ηκολουθηκαμεν* "  *εφη*
*και* " *—Πετρος λεγειν* " *ειδ ου* "  "  "  "  "  *αποκριθεις*


---

[1] D has a lacuna.

[2] D inverts vv. 24 and 25.

147

— ο Ιησους λεγει αμην υμιν λεγω ος αν αγη τα ιδια και γονεις και αδελφους — — — — — — — — —
δε  "    "    ειπεν   "   λεγω υμιν ουδεις εστιν ος αφηκεν οικιαν η      "      η αδελφας η πατερα η
—   "    "    — — —   "    "    "    "    "    "    "    "    — — —   "    "    "    "    "    μητερα "
δε  "    "    — — —   "    "    "    "    "    "    "    — — —   "    "    "    "    "    —


— — — — — — — — — — — και χρηματα ενεκεν εμου και ενεκεν του ευαγγελιου μου 30) απολημψεται
μητερα η γυναικα η τεκνα  η    αγρους      "    "    "    "    "    "    — —    εαν μη λαβη
πατερα— — — —  "    "    "    "    "    "    "    "    "    — —    "  "  "
— — — — — — — — —  "    "    "    "    "    "    η    ενεκα  "    "    — —    ος αν μη λαβη


εκατομπλασιονα    νυν εν τω καιρω τουτω αγρους και χρηματα και οικιας και αδελφους — —   — — —
εκατονταπλασιονα  "    "  "    "    "    — — —  — —  — — —  — —   "    "    "    και αδελφας
                 "              "    "  "    "    — — —  — —  — — —  — —   "    "
                 "    — —  "  "    "    "    ος   δε   αφηκεν οικειαν   "    αδελφας "  αδελφους


— —   — — —  — —  — — — —  — — —  μετα διωγμων εν  δε  τω — — — — — ερχομενω ζωη  εστιν αιωνιος
και μητερας και τεκνα και αγρους   "    "    και εν  "  αιωνι τω     "    ζωην — — — αιωνιον
"    "    "    "    "    "    "    "    "    "    "    "    "    "    "    — — —
"  μητερα  "    "    "    "    "  διωγμου — —  "  "    "    "    "    "    "    — — —  "


— — —  31) πολλοι δε εσονται πρωτοι εσχατοι και οι εσχατοι  πρωτοι.
— — —              "    "    "    "    "    "    "  —  "    "
— — —              "    "    "    "    "    "  " (οι)  "    "
λημψεται           "    "    "    "    "    "    "  —  "    "

The total number of variation units in this passage may vary slightly according
to differing ways of defining such units (e.g., I treated each long omission as a
single variant), but the same basic patterns will emerge. According to my
calculation:

> Clement has a total of  58 'singular' readings (within this comparison),
> Codex D  "   "   "    "  40       "           "       ,
> UBS$^3$    "   "   "    "  10       "           "       ,
> MT         "   "   "    "   4       "           "        .

> Further, Clement and Codex D agree alone together 9 times,
>            "        "   MT        "        "       "  5  "   ,
>            "        "   UBS$^3$   "        "       "  1  "   .

This does not necessarily mean that Clement is more closely related to D than
to the others. Within the variation units:

> the total agreements between Clement and Codex D are 14,
> "    "        "        "        "        "  UBS$^3$  " 26,
> "    "        "        "        "        "  MT       " 33.

It thus appears that of the three most commonly mentioned "text-types"—
Byzantine, Egyptian, and Western—Clement has least relationship to the
"Western" (in this passage), although the 9 singular agreements suggest some
common influence. It has been commonly stated that Clement is one of the
most "Alexandrian" or "Egyptian" of the early Church Fathers, in terms of his

textual preference. In this passage, at least, Clement is closer to the Byzantine than to the Egyptian text-type. 24 of the 26 UBS[3] agreements with Clement are in common with the MT.

Codex D has long been notorious for its 'eccentricity', and this passage provides an eloquent example. But compared to Clement Codex D almost looks tame. I would say that Clement has over 60 mistakes (involving over 120 words) in these 15 verses, or an average of four mistakes per verse! How should we account for such a showing?

Conventional wisdom would argue that with a passage so extensive as this one, 15 verses, the father must have been copying an exemplar that was open in front of him. But it is hard to imagine that an exemplar could have been this bad, or that Clement would have used it if one did exist. I feel driven to conclude that Clement transcribed the passage from memory, but was not well served. I wonder if this doesn't give us a possible explanation for the statistics offered by Aland.

Comparing "other", "Egyptian" and "Majority" the four earliest fathers have "other" leading with a plurality. Among them is Clement, who sides with "other" 32%. However, Aland's statistics are based on a selection of variation units (variant sets) considered to be "significant". If we plot all of Clement's readings within the variation units in Mark 10:17-31 (as given above) on the same chart we get:

$$E = 2(2\%) \quad E\&M = 24(23.5\%) \quad M = 9(9\%) \quad O = 67(65.5\%) \quad \#102$$

The value of "other" rose dramatically. This is because O does not represent a recognizable text-type. In this exercise E and M are discrete entities (UBS[3] and MT) while O is a wastebasket that includes singular readings and obvious errors. Perhaps we could agree that true singular readings should be excluded from such tabulations, but any limitation of variant sets beyond that will presumably be influenced by the bias of whoever conducts the exercise.

So what conclusions should we draw from this study of Clement? I submit that all statements about the testimony of the early Fathers need to be re-evaluated. Most NT citations were presumably from memory—in that case allowance must be made for capricious variation. If they would be likely to make stylistic alterations of the sort that are typical of the Egyptian text (such as moving toward classical Greek) they could happen to make the same 'improvement' independently. Such fortuitous agreements would not signal genealogical relationship. Also, anti-Byzantine bias needs to be set aside. For instance, faced with Clement's preference for Majority readings in Mark 10:17-31 it is predictable that some will try to argue that medieval copyists 'corrected' Clement toward the Byzantine norm. But in that event, why didn't they also correct all the singular readings? Question begging tactics, such as assuming that the Byzantine text was a secondary development, need to be dropped.

Now I wish to return to the chart of the Fathers (the second one) and apply my classification (see Chapter 5) to those statistics. The result looks like this:

| II & III | | | IV | | | V | | |
|---|---|---|---|---|---|---|---|---|
| Marcion | O- | (45%) | Asterius | M++ | (83%) | Theod. Mops. | M | (55%) |
| Irenaeus | O | (51.5%) | Basil | M | (66%) | Marcus Erem. | M | (54%) |
| Clement Al. | O- | (45%) | Apost. Const. | M | (61.5%) | Theodotus | M | (60%) |
| Hippolytus | O- | (44.5%) | Epiphanius | O | (36%) | Hesychius | M | (53%) |
| Origen | E- | (41.5%) | Chrysostom | M | (65%) | Theodoret | M+ | (71%) |
| Methodius | E/O | (36.5%) | Severian | M | (47.5%) | | | |
| Adamantius | M- | (39%) | | | | | | |

(Epiphanius, Chrysostom and Severian presumably did most of their writing in the IV century, and their MSS would date well back into it.)

I imagine that almost everyone who has studied NT textual criticism, as generally taught in our day, will be surprised by this picture. Where is the Egyptian text? The II and III centuries are dominated by **O**—only in Origen does **E** manage a plurality while tying with **O** in Methodius. By the end of the III century (Adamantius), **M** has taken the lead, and is in clear control of the IV and V. The detractors of the Byzantine text have habitually argued that while Byzantine "readings" may be attested in the early centuries the earliest extant attestation for the Byzantine "text", as such, comes from the V. In contrast, say they, the Egyptian "text" is attested in the III and IV. Well, the tabulations of actual readings from the Fathers and uncials that Aland has furnished seem to tell a different story. In the first place, just what is the "Egyptian text"? How did Aland arrive at the 'norm'? Could it be that there is no Egyptian 'text' at all, just 'readings'? Many of the readings that have fallen under "O" have frequently been called "Western". There are Western 'readings', but is there a Western 'text'? Many scholars would say no. If there is no Western 'text', how can there be Western 'readings'? On what basis is a reading to be identified as "Western"? How about the Byzantine "text", can it be objectively defined? Yes. That is why we can tell when we are looking at a Byzantine "reading"—it is characteristic of that objectively defined "text". If the Byzantine "readings" that occur in the II and III century Fathers and papyri do not constitute evidence for the existence of the "text", then neither do the Egyptian and Western "readings" constitute evidence for those "texts".

Does the dishonesty of modern critics have no limits? How can they keep on arguing on the basis of the "Western" and "Alexandrian" text-types when they know good and well that such do not exist? As objectively defined entities those two "text-types" simply do not exist. And until they are objectively defined they may not honestly be used.

## Evidence from the early papyri

On page 140 Aland also appeals to the papyri: "There is not a trace to be found of the Majority text (as defined by Hodges and his colleagues) in any of the forty-plus papyri of the early period (prior to the period of Constantine), or of the fifty more to the end of the 8th century". He is referring to "text", not "readings", but what does he mean by "not a trace"? In normal usage a "trace" is not very much. After his tabulation of the citations in the earliest Fathers, Aland states: "At least one thing is clearly demonstrated: it is impossible to say that the existence outside Egypt in the early period of what Hodges calls the 'Egyptian text' is unproved" (p. 139). He then refers to the first five Fathers by name. Notice that he is claiming that the 24% preference for Egyptian "readings" in Irenaeus, for example, "proves" the **existence** of the Egyptian **text** outside Egypt in the II century. If 24% is enough to prove the existence of a "text", surely 18% would qualify as a "trace"? If Aland's argument here is valid then Marcion's 18% preference for Majority "readings" proves the existence of the Majority "**text**" in the middle of the II century! If Aland is unwilling to grant that the percentage of Byzantine "readings" to be found in these early Fathers constitutes a "trace", then presumably they contain no trace of the Egyptian text either. But what about the papyri?

Unfortunately Aland's book does not contain a summary of the "systematic test collation"[1] for the papyri, as it does for the uncials, so brief mention will be made of Eldon Epp's study of P[45] and Gordon Fee's study of P[66]. With reference to 103 variation units in Mark 6-9 (where P[45] is extant) Epp records that P[45] shows a 38% agreement with D, 40% with the TR, 42% with B, 59% with f[13], and 68% with W.[2] Fee records that in John 1-14 P[66] shows a 38.9% agreement with D, 44.6% with Aleph, 45.0% with W, 45.6% with A, 47.5% with the TR, 48.5% with C, 50.4% with B, and 51.2% with P[75].[3] Does 40% not constitute a "trace"? The picture is similar to that offered by the early Fathers. If we plotted these papyri on a chart with the same headings there would be a significant number of variants in each column—"Egyptian", "Majority" and "other" were all important players on the scene in Egypt at the end of the second century.

Mention should be made of the study done by Harry A. Sturz.[4] He himself collated P[45,46,47,66,72 and 75], but took citations of P[13] and P[37] from apparatuses in Nestle texts (p. 140). He compared these papyri with the Byzantine, Alexandrian and Western texts throughout the NT. He charts the results as follows:

---

[1] Not only that, we are not given the criteria used in choosing the variant sets to be collated. Similarly, we are not given the criteria used in choosing Fathers and citations for his article, "The Text of the Church?". Considering Aland's anti-Byzantine bias, we are probably safe in assuming that no choices were made so as to favor the "Byzantine" text; in that event a wider sampling could well increase the Byzantine percentages.

[2] Eldon Epp, "The Twentieth Century Interlude in New Testament Textual Criticism", *Journal of Biblical Literature*, XCIII (1974), pp. 394-96.

[3] G.D. Fee, Papyrus Bodmer II (P[66]): Its Textual Relationships and Scribal Characteristics (Salt Lake City: U. of Utah Press, 1968), p. 14.

[4] H.A. Sturz, The Byzantine Text-Type and New Testament Textual Criticism (Nashville: Thomas Nelson, 1984).

| Readings<br>Compared | Number of<br>Occurrences | Percentage<br>of Total |
|---|---|---|
| PB/A/W | 31 | 6.3 |
| PB/AW | 121 | 24.7 |
| PBW/A | 169 | 34.4 |
| PBA/W | 170 | 34.6 |
| Total: | 491 | 100.0% |

"PB = papyrus readings supporting the Byzantine text; A = the Alexandrian text; and W = the Western text. Thus PB/A/W means the Papyrus-Byzantine readings are being compared against the Alexandrian where it differs from the Western readings" (p. 228). It thus appears that Sturz identified 152 places where early papyri side with the Byzantine text against both the Alexandrian and Western texts. He gives evidence for 175 further papyrus-supported Byzantine readings but which have scattered Western or Alexandrian support as well, and thus are not "distinctively Byzantine" (pp. 189-212). He refers to still another 195 cases where the Byzantine reading has papyrus support, but he doesn't list them (p. 187). The 169 PBW/A instances remind us of the statement made by Gunther Zuntz. "Byzantine readings which recur in Western witnesses **must** [emphasis his] be ancient. They go back to the time before the Chester Beatty papyrus [P[46]] was written; the time before the emergence of separate Eastern and Western traditions; in short, they reach back deep into the second century."[1] One could wish that Sturz had also given us the PA/BW and PW/AB alignments, but he didn't. In any case, doesn't all that early papyrus attestation of Byzantine readings deserve to be called at least a "trace"?

## Evidence from the early Versions

It has been affirmed that the early versions, Latin, Syriac and Coptic, do not witness to the "Byzantine" text. This is part of the larger question-begging procedure, wherein these versions are assigned to the Alexandrian or Western "text-types" (whose own existence has not been demonstrated) and thus denied to the "Byzantine" text. But what would happen if we looked at the performance of these versions without any such preconceived ideas? I just did a rough check of the statements of evidence in the UBS[3] apparatus for John. 172 variant sets are listed (recall that they included only "significant" ones), but 13 of them are variant sets within disputed verses—these I disregarded since the prior question is whether or not to include the passage. That left 159, some three dozen of which were not very applicable (some differences are ambiguous in a translation). With reference to the Latin, Syriac and Coptic witness, I asked whether it was **with** the Byzantine text, **against** it, or if there was a significant split. Here is the result of that rough count:[2]

---

[1] G. Zuntz, *The Text*, pp. 150-51.

[2] Peter J. Johnston did an independent evaluation of this material and concluded that I was too cautious; especially in the case of the Syriac the attestation for the "Byzantine" text is stronger than my figures indicate (personal communication).

|        | With | Against | Split |
|--------|------|---------|-------|
| Latin  | 60   | 32      | 27    |
| Syriac | 63   | 23      | 35    |
| Coptic | 49   | 45      | 27    |

Even the Coptic sides with the Byzantine more often than not, but the tendency of both the Latin and the Syriac is clearly toward the Byzantine. And there seems to be no predictable correlation between any of these versions and the important early uncials and papyri. The Old Latin frequently disagrees with D, for instance, or divides. I would say that the Old Latin gives clear testimony to the early existence of the Byzantine "text". If the Syriac and Coptic do not witness to the Byzantine "text" then presumably they may not be claimed for any other "text" either.

## *Summary and conclusion*

The distinction between "readings" and "text" is commonly made in a misleading way. For instance, it is not legitimate to speak of "Western" readings until one has defined a "Western" **text**, as such. To define a "text" one should reconstruct the presumed archetype. Having done so, then one can identify the readings that are peculiar to that archetype and therefore characteristic of it. No one has ever reconstructed a "Western" archetype, and there is general agreement among scholars that there never was one. That is why critical editions of the Greek NT do not include a cover symbol for the "Western" text. In their recent textbook the Alands now speak of the "D" text, referring to Codex Bezae. It follows that it is not legitimate to speak of "Western" readings. It is even less legitimate to assign MSS, Fathers or Versions to the phantom "Western" text. It is true that early MSS, Fathers and Versions certainly contain many readings that are neither "Alexandrian" nor "Byzantine", but they appear to be largely random, with a common influence discernible here and there. If the "Western" text has no archetype, **it cannot represent the original**. Let me repeat that: without an archetype the "Western" text **cannot** represent the original; it is impossible.

Similarly, it is not legitimate to speak of "Alexandrian" readings until one has reconstructed the presumed archetype. Colwell tried and gave it up, declaring that it never existed. The UBS editions and N-A[26] no longer use a cover symbol for the "Alexandrian" text. By Aland's figures, the strongest "Alexandrian" witness, Codex B, is only 72% 'pure' in the Synoptics—where shall we go to find the other 28%? P[75] and B are said to have an 82% agreement—where shall we go for the other 18%? The witnesses commonly assigned to the "Alexandrian" text are in constant and significant disagreement between and among themselves. A common influence is indeed discernible, but there is a great deal of seemingly random variation as well. They all show significant agreements with the "Byzantine" text, in different places and in varying amounts. In fact, Codex C is more "Byzantine" than "Alexandrian" in the Synoptics. Since there is no "Alexandrian" archetype in hand, I challenge the legitimacy of speaking of "Alexandrian" readings and of claiming early

MSS, Fathers and Versions for that supposed "text". If the "Alexandrian" text has no archetype, **it cannot represent the original**. Let me repeat that: without an archetype the "Alexandrian" text **cannot** represent the original; it is impossible!

In contrast to the "Alexandrian" and "Western", a "Byzantine" or "Majority" archetype can indeed be reconstructed, with at least 98% certainty. This is why modern critical editions of the Greek NT still use a cover symbol for this type of text. It follows that it is entirely legitimate to speak of "Byzantine" or "Majority" readings—they are defined by the archetype. However, within the broad "Byzantine" river there is a strong central current that I call Family 35, whose precise profile I have identified for the entire NT. So far as I know, it is the only family whose precise profile can be empirically determined with 100% certainty. Since the Autograph is the ultimate archetype, Family 35 is the only viable candidate so far identified.

In any case, the considerations presented demonstrate that if the evidence from the II and III centuries does not attest the presence of the Byzantine "text", then neither does it attest the presence of the Western or Alexandrian "texts". However, I affirm that the evidence is clear to the effect that the Byzantine "text", as such, must have existed in the II century.

# Should Not Witnesses Be Weighed, Rather Than Counted?

The form of the question, which reflects that of the assertion usually made, is tendentious. It infers that weighing and counting are mutually exclusive. But why? In any investigation, legal or otherwise, witnesses should be **both** weighed and counted. First they should be weighed, to be sure, but then they must be counted—or else why bother weighing them, or why bother with witnesses at all? I will discuss the two activities in order, beginning with the weighing.

## *Weighing first*

Just how are MSS to be weighed? And who might be competent to do the weighing? As the reader is by now well aware, Hort and most subsequent scholars have done their 'weighing' on the basis of so-called "internal evidence"—the two standard criteria are, "choose the reading which fits the context" and "choose the reading which explains the origin of the other reading".

One problem with this has been well stated by Colwell. "As a matter of fact these two standard criteria for the appraisal of the internal evidence of readings can easily cancel each other out and leave the scholar free to choose in terms of his own prejudgments."[1] Further, "the more lore the scholar knows, the easier it is for him to produce a reasonable defense of both readings..."[2]

The whole process is so subjective that it makes a mockery of the word 'weigh'. The basic meaning of the term involves an evaluation made by an objective instrument. If we wish our weighing of MSS to have objective validity we must find an objective procedure.

How do we evaluate the credibility of a witness in real life? We watch how he acts, listen to what he says and how he says it, and listen to the opinion of his neighbors and associates. If we can demonstrate that a witness is a habitual liar or that his critical faculties are impaired then we receive his testimony with skepticism. It is quite possible to evaluate MSS in a similar way, to a considerable extent, and it is hard to understand why scholars have generally neglected to do so.

Please refer back to the evidence given in the discussion of the oldest MSS. Can we objectively "weigh" $P^{66}$ as a witness? Well, in the space of John's Gospel it has over 900 clear, indubitable errors—as a witness to the identity of the text of John it has misled us over 900 times. Is $P^{66}$ a credible witness? I would argue that neither of the scribes of $P^{66}$ and $P^{75}$ knew Greek; should we not say that as witnesses they were impaired?[3]

Recall from Colwell's study that the scribe of $P^{45}$ evidently made numerous **deliberate** changes in the text—should we not say that he was morally impaired? In any case, he has repeatedly misinformed us. Shall we still trust him?

Similarly, it has been shown by simple logic/arithmetic that Aleph and B have over 3,000 mistakes between them, just in the Gospels. Aleph is clearly worse than B, but probably not twice as bad—at least 1,000 of those mistakes are B's. Do Aleph and B fit your notion of a good witness?

Even when it is not possible to affirm objectively that a particular witness is misinformed, his credibility suffers if he keeps dubious company. Several references have already been given to the phenomenon Burgon called *concordia discors*. I will add one more. Burgon invites us to turn to Luke 8:35-44 and collate the five old uncials ℵ,A,B,C,D throughout these verses.

---

[1] Colwell, "External Evidence", p. 3.

[2] *Ibid.*, p. 4.

[3] The fact that the transcriber of $P^{75}$ copied letter by letter and that of $P^{66}$ syllable by syllable (Colwell, "Scribal Habits", p. 380) suggests strongly that neither one knew Greek. When transcribing in a language you know you copy phrase by phrase, or at the very least word by word. $P^{66}$ has so many nonsensical readings that the transcriber could not have known the meaning of the text. Anyone who has ever tried to transcribe a text of any length by hand (not typewriter) in a language he does not understand will know that it is a taxing and dreary task. Purity of transmission is not to be expected under such circumstances.

Comparing them to each other against the background of the majority of MSS—A stands alone 2 times; B, 6 times; ℵ, 8 times; C, 15 times; D, 93 times—A and B stand together by themselves once; B and ℵ, 4 times; B and C, once; B and D, once; ℵ and C, once; C and D, once—A, ℵ and C conspire once; B, ℵ and C, once; B, ℵ and D, once; A, B, ℵ and C, once; B, ℵ, C and D, once. Not once do all five agree against the majority. As Burgon observed, they "combine, and again stand apart, with singular impartiality", which led him to conclude:

> Will any one, after a candid survey of the premises, deem us unreasonable, if we avow that such a specimen of the *concordia discors* which everywhere prevails between the oldest uncials, but which especially characterizes ℵ B D, indisposes us greatly to suffer their unsupported authority to determine for us the Text of Scripture?[1]

Must we not agree with him?

We need also to check out the opinion of a witness' contemporaries. Do they testify to his good character, or are there reservations? To judge by the circumstance that Codices like Aleph and B were not copied, to speak of, that the Church by and large rejected their form of the text, it seems they were not respected in their day. What objective evidence do we have to lead us to reverse the judgment of their contemporaries?

Scholars like Zuntz will protest that a MS may represent an excellent tradition in spite of the poor job done by the scribe.[2] Perhaps so, but how can we know? I see only two ways of reaching the conclusion that a certain tradition is excellent—either through the testimony of witnesses that commend themselves as dependable, or through the preference and imagination of the critic. In neither case does the conclusion depend upon the poor copy itself—in the one case it rests upon the authority of independent, dependable witnesses, and in the other it rests upon the authority of the critic. The poor copy itself has no claims on our confidence.

---

[1] Burgon, *The Revision Revised*, pp. 16-18.

[2] Cf. Zuntz, *The Text*, p. 157.

## *Counting next*[1]

Having weighed the witnesses, we must then count them. In the counting, preference must be given to those copies that are not demonstrably poor, or bad. Just as before the law a person is considered innocent until proven guilty, so a witness must be assumed to be truthful until it can be proved a liar. But before counting, we must look for mutual dependence among the witnesses. Any that appear to be mutually dependent should be grouped together. Recall that in this way Wisse reduced over 1,000 MSS to 37 groups in Luke—these then become our 'witnesses'. Then, each witness that appears to be both independent and trustworthy must be allowed to vote; such witnesses must indeed be counted (but only after being assigned a credibility quotient, based on performance). In the footnote below I reproduce some material from *Identity II* (it was no longer in *Identity III*).[2]

---

[1] Carson's representation of my position here calls for some comment. He says that I argue that "we must view most manuscripts as independent authorities that ought to be counted, not weighed" (p. 108). "Should not manuscripts be weighed, not counted? Pickering thinks counting is to be preferred because he has already dispensed with the genealogical principle—at least to his own satisfaction" (p. 107). "The only alternative [to eclecticism] is to resort to a method of counting manuscripts" (p. 105). Does not the reader of Carson's critique have the right to assume that he read my book with reasonable care? If Carson did so read my book he has deliberately misrepresented my position, as the reader can easily verify.

[2] A reading, to be a serious candidate for the original, should be attested by a majority of the *independent* witnesses. Please recall the discussion of weighing and counting given above. A reading attested by only a few witnesses is unlikely to be genuine—the fewer the witnesses the smaller the likelihood. Conversely, the greater the majority the more nearly certain is the originality of the reading so attested. Wherever the text has unanimous attestation the only reasonable conclusion is that it is certainly original. Anyone who offers a conjectural emendation in the face of such attestation is claiming that his authority is greater than that of all the witnesses combined—but since such a person is not a witness at all, does not and cannot know what was written (having rejected 100% attestation), his authority is nil.

Even Hort acknowledged the presumption inherent in superior number. "A theoretical presumption indeed remains that a majority of extant documents is more likely to represent a majority of ancestral documents at each stage of transmission than *vice versa*" (Westcott and Hort, p. 45). The work of those who have done extensive collating of MSS has tended to confirm this presumption. Thus Lake, Blake, and New found only orphan children among the MSS they collated, and declared further that there were almost no siblings—each MS is an "only child" (Lake, Blake and New, pp. 348-49). This means they are independent witnesses, in their own generation. In Burgon's words:

> …hardly any have been copied from any of the rest. On the contrary, they are discovered to differ among themselves in countless unimportant particulars; and every here and there single copies exhibit idiosyncrasies which are altogether startling and extraordinary. There has therefore demonstrably been no collusion—no assimilation to an arbitrary standard,—no wholesale fraud. It is certain that every one of them represents a MS., or a pedigree of MSS., older than itself; and it is but fair to suppose that it exercises such representation with tolerable accuracy. (Burgon, *The Traditional Text*, pp. 46-47.)

Should anyone still care to raise the objection that "Byzantine readings repeatedly prove to be inferior", I reply: "Prove it!" Since all such characterizations have been based upon the demonstrably fallacious canons of "internal evidence" they have no validity. I consider the allegation to be vacuous. I would also require that he openly state his presuppositions. Differing presuppositions normally lead to differing conclusions.

I have demonstrated that the W-H critical theory and history of the text are erroneous. I have outlined the history of the transmission of the text which I believe best accords with the available evidence. It remains to give a coherent statement of the procedure by which we may assure ourselves of the precise identity of the original wording of the New Testament text.

---

In accordance with good legal practice, it is unfair to arbitrarily declare that the ancestors were **not** independent; some sort of evidence must be produced. It has already been shown that Hort's "genealogical evidence", with reference to MSS, is fictitious. But it remains true that community of reading implies a common origin, unless it is the type of mistake that several scribes might have made independently. What is in view here is the common origin of individual readings, not of MSS, but where several MSS share a large number of readings peculiar to themselves their claim to independence is evidently compromised throughout. (The "Claremont Profile Method" gives promise of being an effective instrument for plotting the relationship between MSS.)

However, there is one situation where community of reading does not compromise independence. If the common origin of a reading is the original, then the MSS that have it may not be disqualified; their claim to independence remains unsullied. Of course, we do not know, at this stage in the inquiry, which is the original reading, but some negative help is immediately available. If one or more of the competing variants is an obvious mistake, then those MSS which attest such variants are disqualified, at that one point (recall that genealogy was supposed to be based upon community in **error**).

# 7
# IDENTIFYING THE ORIGINAL WORDING
# OF THE TEXT

In prior editions of this book (except *Identity III*) I began Chapter 7 with Burgon's "Notes of Truth". Burgon was a product of his time, as we all are. He defended the Traditional Text against challenges based on a few early MSS. Then the work of H. von Soden, H.C. Hoskier, and more recently F. Wisse, showed that it is possible to group the MSS empirically, on the basis of a shared mosaic of readings. In the Apocalypse Hoskier identified nine groups or families. Wisse's study in Luke reduced 1,386 MSS to 37 groups (plus 89 "mavericks"). Such groups must be evaluated for independence and credibility.

I am sure that if Burgon were alive today he would agree that the discoveries and research of the last hundred and some years make possible, even necessary, some refinements on his theory. I proceed to outline what I used as a stepping-stone to my present approach to N.T. textual criticism. (I ventured to call it Original Text Theory.)[1]

1) First, OTT is concerned to identify the precise original wording of the N.T. writings.[2]

2) Second, the criteria must be biblical, objective and reasonable.[3]

3) Third, a 90% attestation will be considered unassailable, and 80% virtually so.[4]

4) Fourth, Burgon's "notes of truth" will come into play, especially where the attestation falls below 80%.[5]

5) Fifth, where collations exist, making possible an empirical grouping of the MSS on the basis of shared mosaics of readings, this must be done.

---

[1] I had thought of resurrecting the term 'traditional', but since Burgon and Miller were not here to protest, I hesitated; besides, that term is no longer descriptive. Terms like 'antiochian' or 'byzantine' carry an extraneous burden of antipathy, or have been preempted (besides not being precisely descriptive). So here's our **Original Text Theory**. Since I really do believe that God has preserved the original wording to our day, and that we can know what it is on the basis of a defensible procedure, I do not fear the charge of arrogance, or presumption, or whatever because I use the term 'original'. All textual criticism worthy the name is in search of original wording.

[2] Here I reject the allegation that the original wording is lost and gone.

[3] Here I reject the dependence on subjective criteria and a purely rationalistic approach.

[4] This is now superseded by advances in point 5, although a 90% attestation remains difficult to assail.

[5] This is also basically superseded by point 5, although his 'notes' remain valid, in general.

Such groups must be evaluated on the basis of their performance and be assigned a credibility quotient. A putative history of the transmission of the Text needs to be developed on the basis of the interrelationships of such groups. **Demonstrated groupings and relationships supersede the counting of MSS.**[1]

6) Sixth, it presupposes that the Creator exists and that He has spoken to our race. It accepts the implied divine purpose to preserve His revelation for the use of subsequent generations, including ours. It understands that both God and Satan have an ongoing active interest in the fate of the N.T. Text—to approach N.T. textual criticism without taking due account of that interest is to act irresponsibly.[2]

7) Seventh, it insists that presuppositions and motives must always be addressed and evaluated.[3]

I use the term 'stepping-stone' because I was still thinking in terms of a large majority, and that was because Family 35 had not yet come to my attention (I was still limited to generalities). However, the fifth point above shows the direction in which I was heading; note especially the last sentence, that has always been in bold type, and most especially the term 'demonstrated'.[4] For example, my critical apparatus for Revelation gives the evidence in terms of Hoskier's nine groups, rather than percentages of MSS.

It was the H-F Majority Text's representation of the evidence for the *Pericope Adulterae* that caught my attention, being based on von Soden's supposed collation of over 900 MSS.[5] As stated in their apparatus, there were three main streams: $M^5$, $M^6$ and $M^7$. 7 was always in the majority [except for one five-way split where there is no majority] because it was always accompanied by either **5** or **6** [5 + 6 never go against 7]. This looked to me like three independent streams, where seldom would more than one go astray at any

---

[1] Please note that I am not referring to any attempt at reconstructing a genealogy of MSS—I agree with those scholars who have declared such an enterprise to be virtually impossible (there are altogether too many missing links). I am indeed referring to the reconstruction of a genealogy of **readings**, and thus of the history of the transmission of the Text. The last sentence has always been emphasized. Once all MSS have been collated and empirically grouped, we can dispense with counting them.

[2] Those who exclude the supernatural from their model are condemning themselves to never arrive at the Truth—God and Satan exist, and both have been involved in the transmission of the NT Text.

[3] In any scientific inquiry a rigorous distinction must be made between evidence, presupposition and interpretation. Since one's presuppositions heavily influence, even control, his interpretation of the evidence (that should be the same for everyone), any honest scholar needs to state his presuppositions openly. It is doubtless too much to expect sinners to expose their motives to the light of day (John 3:20).

[4] Hort did the discipline a considerable disservice by positing theoretical text-types, devoid of evidence, and then treating them as established fact.

[5] Robinson's collations show that Soden 'regularized' the data.

given point. Being the common denominator, **7** was clearly the best of the three.

Then I went to Revelation (in H-F) and noticed three main streams again: $M^{a-b}$, $M^c$ and $M^{d-e}$. The picture was analogous to that of the *PA*. Revelation represents a very much larger corpus than does the *PA*, but even so, there are only 8 cases where **a-b** and **d-e** join against **c** (+ 6 others where one of the four is split), compared to over 100 each for **a-b** and **c** against **d-e** and for **c** and **d-e** against **a-b**. Again, being the common denominator, **c** was clearly the best of the three (see the apparatus of my Greek Text of the Apocalypse).

Now then, it so happens that $M^7$ in the *PA* and $M^c$ in Revelation equal Soden's $K^r$, so I began to smell a rat.[1] Then the *Text und Textwert* series proved that $K^r$ is independent of $K^x$ throughout the NT. It follows that $K^r$ <u>cannot</u> be a revision of $K^x$. Then there are hundreds of places where $K^r$ has overt early attestation, against $K^x$, but there is no pattern to that early attestation. There being no pattern then $K^r$ must be early, as the picture in the *PA* and in Revelation has already implied. <u>If $K^r$ is early and independent, then it must be rehabilitated in the practice of NT textual criticism</u>. **If it is the best line of transmission in the *PA* and Revelation, it just might be the best elsewhere as well**.

But there is an ingrained disdain/antipathy toward the symbol $K^r$, so I have proposed a new name for the text-type. We should substitute $f^{35}$ for $K^r$—it is more objective and will get away from the prejudice that attaches to the latter. Minuscule 35 contains the whole NT and reflects $K^r$ throughout, and it is the MS with the smallest number that meets those qualifications[2] (just as cursives 1 and 13 are the smallest number in their families; and like them, 35 is not always the best representative [it is generally excellent]—but it is 11th century [and it is a copy of an older exemplar, not a new creation], so the text-type could not have been created in the 12th, Q.E.D.).

Please note: the evidence already adduced shows that $f^{35}$/ $K^r$ is early and independent. However, the antipathy/disdain toward this text-type is so ingrained, and such evidence is so contrary to the ruling paradigm, or 'party line', that I will continue with further evidence.

# The Dating of $K^r$ (alias $f^{35}$, nee $f^{18}$) Revisited

When Hermann von Soden identified $K^r$ and proclaimed it to be a revision of $K^x$ made in the **XII** century, he rendered a considerable disservice to the Truth and to those with an interest in identifying the original wording of the NT Text. This section argues that if von Soden had really paid attention to the evidence available in his day, he could not have perpetrated such an injustice.

---

[1] Why 'smelled a rat'? Because $M^7$ is clearly older than $M^5$ and $M^6$ in the *PA*, and $M^c$ than $M^{a-b}$ and $M^{d-e}$ in Revelation, but von Soden claimed $K^r$ was a revision of $K^x$ (how could it be a revision if it was older?).

[2] Minuscule 18 has a smaller number and also contains the whole NT, but it defects from the text-type in Revelation.

Those familiar with my work know that I began by using $f^{18}$ instead of $K^r$, because minuscule 18 is the family member with the smallest number. I then switched to $f^{35}$ for the following reasons:

1) although 18 is sometimes a purer representative of the texttype than is minuscule 35, in the Apocalypse 18 defects to another type, while 35 remains true [both MSS contain the whole NT];

2) while 18 is dated to the XIV century, 35 is dated to the XI, thus giving the lie, all by itself, to von Soden's dictum that $K^r$ was created in the XII century. Further, if 35 is a copy, not a new creation, then its exemplar had to be older, and so on.

After doing a complete collation of 1,389 MSS that contain the whole *Pericope Adulterae* (there were a few others that certainly contain the pericope but could not be collated because the microfilm was illegible), Maurice Robinson concluded:

> Based upon the collated data, the present writer is forced to reverse his previous assumptions regarding the development and restoration/preservation of the Byzantine Textform in this sense: although textual transmission itself is a process, it appears that, for the most part, the lines of transmission remained separate, with relatively little mixture occurring or becoming perpetuated…
>
> Certainly, all the types of PA text are distinct, and reflect a long line of transmission and preservation in their separate integrities…
>
> It thus appears that the Byzantine minuscule MSS preserve lines of transmission which are not only independent but which of necessity had their origin at a time well before the 9th century.[1]

Fair enough. If $K^r$ ($M^7$) was preserved in its 'separate integrity' during 'a long line of transmission' then it would have to have its origin 'at a time well before the 9th century'. Besides the witness of 35, Robinson's collations demonstrate that minuscule 1166 and lectionary 139, both of the X century, reflect $K^r$. If they are copies, not new creations, then their exemplars had to be older, and

---

[1] "Preliminary Observations regarding the *Pericope Adulterae* based upon Fresh Collations of nearly all Continuous-Text Manuscripts and over One Hundred Lectionaries", presented to the Evangelical Theological Society, Nov., 1998, pp. 12-13. However, I have received the following clarification from Maurice Robinson: "I would request that if my name gets cited in regard to your various $K^r$ or $M^7$ articles that you make it clear that I do not concur with your assessment of $K^r$ or $M^7$. This is particularly the case with the "Preliminary Considerations regarding the Pericope Adulterae" article; it should not be used to suggest that I consider the $M^7$ line or $K^r$ text to be early. This would be quite erroneous, since I hold with virtually all others that $K^r/M^7$ are indeed late texts that reflect recensional activity beginning generally in the 12th century (perhaps with 11th century base exemplars, but nothing earlier)." [Assuming that he was sincere when he wrote that article, I wonder what new evidence came his way that caused him to change his mind—his language there is certainly plain enough. Further, I had a copy of his collations in my hand for two months, spending much of that time poring over them, and saw no reason to question his conclusions in the Nov., 1998 article.]

so on. Without adducing any further evidence, it seems fair to say that **K$^r$** must have existed already in the **IX** century, if not the **VIII**.

For years, based on the *Text und Textwert* series, I have insisted that **K$^r$** is both ancient and independent. Robinson would seem to agree. "The lack of extensive cross-comparison and correction demonstrated in the extant MSS containing the PA precludes the easy development of any existing form of the PA text from any other form of the PA text during at least the vellum era."[1] "The vellum era"—doesn't that take us back to the **IV** century, at least? As a matter of fact, yes. Consider:

Acts 4:34—τις ην **K$^r$** ℵA (~21 B) [**K$^r$** is independent, and both **K$^r$** and **K$^x$** are **IV** century]
τις υπηρχεν **K$^x$** P$^8$D

Acts 15:7—εν υμιν **K$^r$** ℵABC,it$^{pt}$ [**K$^r$** is independent, and both **K$^r$** and **K$^x$** are ancient]
εν ημιν **K$^x$** (D)lat

Acts 19:3—ειπεν τε **K$^r$** B(D)
[**K$^r$** is independent, and both **K$^r$** and **K$^x$** are ancient]
ο δε ειπεν ℵA(P$^{38}$)bo
ειπεν τε προς αυτους **K$^x$** sy$^p$,sa

Acts 21:8—ηλθομεν **K$^r$** ℵAC(B)lat,syr,cop
[**K$^r$** is older than **K$^x$**, very ancient]
οι περι τον παυλον ηλθον **K$^x$**

Acts 23:20—μελλοντες (33.1%) **K$^r$** lat,syr,sa [**K$^r$** is independent and very ancient;
μελλοντα (27.2%) {HF,RP} there is no **K$^x$**]
μελλοντων (17.4%)
μελλων (9.2%) AB,bo
μελλον (7.5%) {NU} ℵ
μελλοντας (5.4%)

Rom. 5:1—εχωμεν (43%) **K$^r$** **K$^{x(1/3)}$** ℵABCD,lat,bo [did part of **K$^x$** assimilate to **K$^r$**?]
εχομεν (57%) **K$^{x(2/3)}$**

Rom. 16:6—εις υμας **K$^r$** P$^{46}$ℵABC [**K$^r$** is independent and very ancient, **II/III** century]
εις ημας **K$^x$**
εν υμιν D

2 Cor. 1:15—προς υμας ελθειν το προτερον **K$^r$** [**K$^r$** is independent!]
προς υμας ελθειν ℵ
προτερον προς υμας ελθειν ABC
προτερον ελθειν προς υμας D,lat
ελθειν προς υμας το προτερον **K$^x$**

2 Cor. 2:17—λοιποι **K$^r$**K$^{x(pt)}$ P$^{46}$D,syr [**K$^r$** is very ancient, **II/III** century]
πολλοι **K$^{x(pt)}$** ℵABC,lat,cop

---

[1] *Ibid.*, p. 13.

James 1:23—νομου  **K**<sup>r</sup>  [**K**<sup>r</sup> is independent][1]
     λογου  **K**<sup>x</sup> אABC

James 2:3—την λαμπραν εσθητα  **K**<sup>r</sup>  [**K**<sup>r</sup> is independent]
     την εσθητα την λαμπραν  **K**<sup>x</sup> אABC

James 2:4— — ου  **K**<sup>r</sup> אABC  [**K**<sup>r</sup> is independent and ancient]
     και ου  **K**<sup>x</sup>

James 2:8—σεαυτον  **K**<sup>r</sup> אABC  [**K**<sup>r</sup> is independent and ancient]
     εαυτον  **K**<sup>x</sup>

James 2:14—εχει  **K**<sup>r</sup>  [**K**<sup>r</sup> is independent]
     εχη  **K**<sup>x</sup> אABC

James 3:2—δυναμενος  **K**<sup>r</sup> א  [**K**<sup>r</sup> is independent and ancient]
     δυνατος  **K**<sup>x</sup> AB

James 3:4—ιθυνοντος  **K**<sup>r</sup>  [**K**<sup>r</sup> is independent; a rare classical spelling]
     ευθυνοντος  **K**<sup>x</sup> אABC

James 4:11—ο γαρ  **K**<sup>r</sup>  [**K**<sup>r</sup> is independent]
     ο --  **K**<sup>x</sup> אAB

James 4:14—ημων  **K**<sup>r</sup>  [**K**<sup>r</sup> is independent]
     υμων  **K**<sup>x</sup> אA(P<sup>100</sup>B)

James 4:14—επειτα  **K**<sup>r</sup>  [**K**<sup>r</sup> is independent]
     επειτα και  אAB
     επειτα δε και  **K**<sup>x</sup>

1 Pet. 3:16—καταλαλουσιν  **K**<sup>r</sup> אAC,sy<sup>p</sup>,bo  [**K**<sup>r</sup> is independent and ancient]
     καταλαλωσιν  **K**<sup>x</sup>
     καταλαλεισθε  P<sup>72</sup>B,sa

1 Pet. 4:3—υμιν  **K**<sup>r</sup> אbo  [**K**<sup>r</sup> is independent and ancient]
     ημιν  **K**<sup>x</sup> C
     (omit)  P<sup>72</sup>AB,lat,syr,sa

2 Pet. 2:17—εις αιωνας  **K**<sup>r</sup>  [**K**<sup>r</sup> is independent]
     εις αιωνα  **K**<sup>x</sup> AC
     (omit)  P<sup>72</sup>אB,lat,syr,cop

3 John 12—οιδαμεν  **K**<sup>r</sup>  [**K**<sup>r</sup> is independent]
     οιδατε  **K**<sup>x</sup>
     οιδας  אABC

---

[1] For the examples from James I also consulted *Editio Critica Maior*.

So what conclusions may we draw from this evidence? **K$^r$** is independent of **K$^x$** and both are ancient, dating at least to the **IV** century.[1] A few of the examples could be interpreted to mean that **K$^r$** is older than **K$^x$**, dating to the **III** and even the **II** century, but I will leave that possibility on the back burner and look at some further evidence. The following examples are based on *Text und Textwert* and the IGNTP *Luke*.

Luke 1:55—εως αιωνος    **K$^r$** C    [**K$^r$** is independent and **V** century]
εις τον αιωνα    **K$^x$** ℵAB

Luke 1:63—εσται    **K$^r$** C    [**K$^r$** is independent and **V** century]
εστιν    **K$^x$** ℵAB

Luke 3:12—υπ αυτου και    **K$^r$** C    [**K$^r$** is independent and **V** century]
—— —— και    **K$^x$** ℵABD

Luke 4:7—σοι    **K$^r$**    [**K$^r$** is independent]
σου    **K$^x$** ℵAB

Luke 4:42—εζητουν    **K$^r$**    [**K$^r$** is independent]
επεζητουν    **K$^x$** ℵABCD

Luke 5:1—περι    **K$^r$**    [**K$^r$** is independent]
παρα    **K$^x$** P$^{75}$ℵABC

Luke 5:19—ευροντες δια    **K$^r$**    [**K$^r$** is independent]
ευροντες ——    **K$^x$** ℵABCD

Luke 5:19—πως    **K$^r$**    [**K$^r$** is independent]
ποιας    **K$^x$** ℵABC

Luke 6:7—— τω    **K$^r$** D    [**K$^r$** is independent and **V** century]
εν τω    **K$^x$** ℵAB

Luke 6:10—ουτως και    **K$^r$**    [**K$^r$** is independent]
—— και    **K$^x$** ℵABD

Luke 6:26—καλως ειπωσιν υμας    **K$^r$** ℵA    [**K$^r$** is independent and **IV** century]
καλως υμας ειπωσιν    **K$^x$** D
υμας καλως ειπωσιν    P$^{75}$B

---

[1] Someone may object that it is the readings that are ancient, not the text-types; but if a text-type is clearly independent, with constantly shifting alignments among the early witnesses, then it has ancient readings because it itself is ancient. And in the case of **K$^r$** there are many hundreds, if not thousands (I haven't counted them, yet), of variant sets where its reading has overt early attestation. (Recall that Aland's **M** and Soden's **K** include **K$^r$**—the poor text-type itself should not be held responsible for the way modern scholars treat it.) If it can be demonstrated objectively that a text-type has thousands of early readings, but it cannot be demonstrated objectively to have any late ones, on what basis can it be declared to be late?

Luke 6:26—παντες οι   **K<sup>r</sup> P<sup>75</sup>AB(ℵ)**   [**K<sup>r</sup>** is independent and early III century]
—— οι   **K<sup>x</sup> D,syr**

Luke 6:49—την οικιαν   **K<sup>r</sup> P<sup>75</sup>**   [**K<sup>r</sup>** is independent and early III century]
— οικιαν   **K<sup>x</sup> ℵABC**

Luke 8:15—ταυτα λεγων εφωνει ο εχων ωτα ακουειν ακουετω   **K<sup>r</sup>**   [**K<sup>r</sup>** is independent]
(omit)   **K<sup>x</sup> ℵABD**

Luke 8:24—και προσελθοντες   **K<sup>r</sup>**   [**K<sup>r</sup>** is independent]
προσελθοντες και   **K<sup>x</sup> ℵABD**

Luke 9:27—εστηκοτων   **K<sup>r</sup> ℵB**   [**K<sup>r</sup>** is independent and IV century]
εστωτων   **K<sup>x</sup> ACD**

Luke 9:56—(have verse)   **K<sup>r</sup> K<sup>x</sup>** lat,syr,Diat,Marcion   [**K<sup>r</sup>** and **K<sup>x</sup>** are II century]
(omit verse)   P<sup>45,75</sup>ℵABCDW,cop

Luke 10:4—πηραν μη   **K<sup>r</sup> P<sup>75</sup>ℵBD**   [**K<sup>r</sup>** is independent and early III century]
πηραν μηδε   **K<sup>x</sup> AC**

Luke 10:6—εαν μεν   **K<sup>r</sup>**   [**K<sup>r</sup>** is independent]
εαν ——   **K<sup>x</sup> P<sup>75</sup>ℵABCD**

Luke 10:39—των λογων   **K<sup>r</sup>**   [**K<sup>r</sup>** is independent]
τον λογον   **K<sup>x</sup> P<sup>45,75</sup>ℵABC**

Luke 10:41—ο Ιησους ειπεν αυτη   **K<sup>r</sup>D**   [**K<sup>r</sup>** is independent and V century]
ο Κυριος ειπεν αυτη   P<sup>45</sup>   [the word order is III century]
ειπεν αυτη ο Ιησους   **K<sup>x</sup> ACW,syr,bo**
ειπεν αυτη ο Κυριος   P<sup>75</sup>ℵB,lat,sa

Luke 11:34—— — ολον   **K<sup>r</sup>CD**   [**K<sup>r</sup>** is independent and V century]
και ολον   **K<sup>x</sup> P<sup>45,75</sup>ℵAB**

Luke 11:53—συνεχειν   **K<sup>r</sup>**   [**K<sup>r</sup>** is independent!]
ενεχειν   **K<sup>x</sup> P<sup>75</sup>ℵAB**
εχειν   P<sup>45</sup>D
επεχειν   C

Luke 12:22—λεγω υμιν   **K<sup>r</sup> P<sup>75</sup>ℵBD,lat**   [**K<sup>r</sup>** is independent and II century]
υμιν λεγω   **K<sup>x</sup> AW**

Luke 12:56—του ουρανου και της γης   **K<sup>r</sup> P<sup>45,75</sup>D** [**K<sup>r</sup>** is independent and early III century]
της γης και του ουρανου   **K<sup>x</sup> ℵAB**

Luke 12:58—βαλη σε   **K<sup>r</sup>(D)**   [**K<sup>r</sup>** is independent]
σε βαλη   **K<sup>x</sup> A(P<sup>75</sup>ℵB)**

Luke 13:28—οψεσθε   **K<sup>r</sup>BD**   [**K<sup>r</sup>** is independent and IV century]
οψησθε   **K<sup>x</sup> P<sup>75</sup>AW**
ιδητε   ℵ

Luke 19:23—επι την **K<sup>r</sup>**   [**K<sup>r</sup>** is independent]
       επι —   **K<sup>x</sup>** אABD

Luke 21:6—επι λιθον **K<sup>r</sup>**   [**K<sup>r</sup>** is independent]
       επι λιθω **K<sup>x</sup>** אAB

Luke 21:15—αντειπειν η αντιστηναι   **K<sup>r</sup>A**   [**K<sup>r</sup>** is independent and **V** century]
       αντειπειν ουδε αντιστηναι **K<sup>x</sup>W**
       ——   — αντιστηναι   D,it,syr
       αντιστηναι η αντειπειν   אB,cop

Luke 22:12—αναγαιον **K<sup>r</sup>** אABD   [**K<sup>r</sup>** is independent and **IV** century]
       αναγεον   CW
       ανωγεον   **K<sup>x</sup>**

Luke 22:66—απηγαγον **K<sup>r</sup>** P<sup>75</sup>אBD   [**K<sup>r</sup>** is independent and early **III** century]
       ανηγαγον **K<sup>x</sup>AW**

Luke 23:51—ος — **K<sup>r</sup>** P<sup>75</sup>אBCD,lat   [**K<sup>r</sup>** is independent and **II** century]
       ος και **K<sup>x</sup>AW**

There are a number of further examples where **K<sup>r</sup>** is alone against the world, showing its independence, but I 'grew weary in well doing', deciding I had included enough to make the point. Note that N-A[27] mentions only a third of these examples from Luke—to be despised is to be ignored. This added evidence confirms that **K<sup>r</sup>** is independent of **K<sup>x</sup>** and both are ancient, only now they both must date to the **III** century, at least.

It will be observed that I have furnished examples from the Gospels (Luke, John), Acts, Paul (Romans, 2 Corinthians), and the General Epistles (James, 1 Peter, 2 Peter, 3 John), with emphasis on Luke, Acts and James.[1] Throughout the New Testament **K<sup>r</sup>** is independent and ancient. Dating to the **III** century, it is just as old as any other text-type. Therefore, **it should be treated with the respect that it deserves!!**

I have cited Maurice Robinson twice and shown that the evidence vindicates his claims. Both **K<sup>r</sup>** and **K<sup>x</sup>** date to the beginning of the velum era. But he makes a further claim that is even bolder:

> Nor do the uncials or minuscules show any indication of any known line deriving from a parallel known line. The 10 or so "texttype" lines of transmission remain independent and must necessarily extend back to a point long before their separate stabilizations occurred—a point which seems buried (as Colwell and Scrivener suggested) deep within the second century.[2]

---

[1] I also have a page or more of examples from Revelation that confirm that **K<sup>r</sup>** (**M<sup>c</sup>**) is independent and **III** century in that book as well.

[2] Ibid.

Well, well, well, we're getting pretty close to the Autographs! Objective evidence from the II century is a little hard to come by. For all that, the examples above taken from Acts 21:8, Acts 23:20, Romans 5:1, Luke 9:56, Luke 12:22 and Luke 23:51 might place $K^r$ (and $K^x$) in the II century. However, it is not the purpose of this section to defend that thesis. For the moment I content myself with insisting that $K^r$ must date to the III century and therefore must be rehabilitated in the practice of NT textual criticism.

In conclusion, I claim to have demonstrated that $K^r$ is independent and ancient, dating to the III century (at least). But there is an ingrained disdain/antipathy toward that symbol, so I have proposed a new name for the texttype. We should substitute $f^{35}$ for $K^r$—it is more objective and will get away from the prejudice that attaches to the latter.

Having criticized von Soden's dating of $K^r$, I now ask: what led him to that conclusion and why has his conclusion been almost universally accepted by the scholarly community? I answer: the number of $K^r$ type MSS first becomes noticeable precisely in the 12th century, although there are a number from the 11th. That number grows in the 13th and grows some more in the 14th, calling attention to itself.[1]

Those who catalog NT MSS inform us that the 12th and 13th centuries lead the pack, in terms of extant MSS, followed by the 14th, 11th, 15th, 16th and 10th, in that order. There are over four times as many MSS from the 13th as from the 10th, but obviously Koine Greek would have been more of a living language in the 10th than the 13th, and so there would have been more demand and therefore more supply. In other words, many hundreds of really pure MSS from the 10th perished. A higher percentage of the really good MSS produced in the 14th century survived than those produced in the 11th; and so on. That is why there is a progressive level of agreement among the Byzantine MSS, there being a higher percentage of agreement in the 14th than in the 10th. But had we lived in the 10th, and done a wide survey of the MSS, we would have found very nearly the same level of agreement (perhaps 98%). The same obtains if we had lived in the 8th, 6th, 4th or 2nd century. In other words, THE SURVIVING MSS FROM THE FIRST TEN CENTURIES ARE NOT REPRESENTATIVE OF THE TRUE STATE OF AFFAIRS AT THE TIME.

# Early Uncial Support for $f^{35}$ in the General Epistles

I take it that Klaus Wachtel, in his *Der Byzantinische Text der Katholischen Briefe*, recognizes that the Byzantine **text** is early (though often deciding against it on internal grounds), thereby bidding adieu to the prevailing canard. I believe that the evidence presented below demonstrates the same for the **text** of $f^{35}$.

---

[1] Those who had already bought into Hort's doctrine of a late 'Syrian' text would see no reason to question von Soden's statement, and would have no inclination or motivation to 'waste' time checking it out.

I proceed to tabulate the performance of the early uncials (5th century and earlier) as they appear in the apparatus of my Greek text of the seven General Epistles. I do not include any variant set where *rell* appears. I use $\mathbf{f}^{35}$ as the point of reference, but only tabulate variant sets where at least one of the extant early uncials (extant at that point) goes against $\mathbf{f}^{35}$ (since most words have unanimous attestation).

Thirteen early uncials appear in my apparatus: $P^{20,23,72,78,81,100}$,ℵ,A,B,C,048,0173,0232. Only $P^{72}$,ℵ,A,B,C are not fragments (048 is a variety of pieces, here and there). Codex C is missing basically chapters 4 and 5 of James, 1 Peter and 1 John [curiously, the same two chapters for all three books], as well as all of 2 John. Of course, $P^{72}$ has only 1 & 2 Peter and Jude. Four of them never side with $\mathbf{f}^{35}$: $P^{78}$ appears once, $P^{23}$ twice, 0173 thrice and 0232 five times. Of the other fragments, $P^{20}$ shows 1 for, 3 against [25%]; $P^{81}$ shows 3 for, 11 against [21.4%]; $P^{100}$ shows 7 for, 10 against [41%]; 048 shows 10 for, 25 against [28.6%]. Not allowing for lacunae, $P^{72}$ would come in with 23.9%, ℵ with 28.7%, A with 27.7%, B with 21.1%. If we divide C's 117 by 473 (the total of variant sets involved) we get 24.7%, but of course C is missing seven chapters (out of 21), so if we divide 117 by, say, 320, we get 36%—of the four main codices, C is clearly the closest to $\mathbf{f}^{35}$. Out of the total of 473 variant sets, $\mathbf{f}^{35}$ receives overt early attestation 60% of the time (284 ÷ 473).

Before drawing conclusions I present the evidence (only combinations with at least one instance are tabulated).[1]

| | James | 1 Peter | 2 Peter | 1 John | 2&3 John | Jude | TOTAL |
|---|---|---|---|---|---|---|---|
| $\mathbf{f}^{35}$ alone | 56 | 49 | 18 | 32 | 19 | 15 | 189 |
| $\mathbf{f}^{35}\,P^{72}$ | | 7 | | | | 1 | 8 |
| $\mathbf{f}^{35}\,P^{100}$ | 2 | | | | | | 2 |
| $\mathbf{f}^{35}$ ℵ | 7 | 9 | 7 | 9 | 5 | | 37 |
| $\mathbf{f}^{35}$ A | 9 | 8 | 3 | 9 | 2 | 1 | 32 |
| $\mathbf{f}^{35}$ B | 1 | 2 | 1 | 4 | 2 | | 10 |
| $\mathbf{f}^{35}$ C | 5 | 8 | 3 | 4 | 1 | 2 | 23 |
| $\mathbf{f}^{35}$ 048 | 1 | | | | | | 1 |
| $\mathbf{f}^{35}\,P^{20}$ℵ | 1 | | | | | | 1 |
| $\mathbf{f}^{35}\,P^{72}$A | | 2 | | | | | 2 |
| $\mathbf{f}^{35}\,P^{72}$B | | 2 | 1 | | | | 3 |
| $\mathbf{f}^{35}\,P^{72}$C | | 3 | 1 | | | | 4 |
| $\mathbf{f}^{35}\,P^{100}$A | 1 | | | | | | 1 |
| $\mathbf{f}^{35}$ ℵA | 7 | 2 | 7 | 5 | | | 21 |
| $\mathbf{f}^{35}$ ℵB | 2 | 3 | | 8 | | 1 | 14 |
| $\mathbf{f}^{35}$ ℵC | | 1 | 2 | 5 | | 2 | 10 |

---

[1] Having neither secretary nor proof-reader, I do not guarantee complete accuracy, but a slip here or there will not alter the big picture, nor invalidate our conclusions.

| | | | | | | | |
|---|---|---|---|---|---|---|---|
| $f^{35}$ ℵ048 | | | 1 | | | | **1** |
| $f^{35}$ AB | 2 | 1 | 1 | 6 | 2 | 1 | **13** |
| $f^{35}$ AC | 6 | 4 | 2 | 1 | | | **13** |
| $f^{35}$ BC | | | 2 | | | | **2** |
| | | | | | | | |
| $f^{35}$ $P^{72}$ℵA | | 4 | | | | | **4** |
| $f^{35}$ $P^{72}$ℵB | | 3 | | | | | **3** |
| $f^{35}$ $P^{72}$ℵC | | 2 | | | | | **2** |
| $f^{35}$ $P^{72}$AB | | 3 | | | | | **3** |
| $f^{35}$ $P^{72}$AC | | 3 | | | | 1 | **4** |
| $f^{35}$ $P^{72}$BC | | 1 | 9 | | | 1 | **11** |
| $f^{35}$ $P^{81}$BC | | 1 | | | | | **1** |
| $f^{35}$ $P^{100}$ℵA | 1 | | | | | | **1** |
| $f^{35}$ $P^{100}$AB | 1 | | | | | | **1** |
| $f^{35}$ $P^{100}$AC | 1 | | | | | | **1** |
| $f^{35}$ ℵAB | | | 1 | 2 | | | **3** |
| $f^{35}$ ℵAC | 2 | 4 | 1 | 2 | | 1 | **10** |
| $f^{35}$ ℵA048 | | | 1 | | | | **1** |
| $f^{35}$ ℵBC | 2 | | 1 | 6 | | | **9** |
| $f^{35}$ ABC | 2 | 1 | | 2 | | 1 | **6** |
| $f^{35}$ AB048 | 1 | | | | | | **1** |
| $f^{35}$ AC048 | | | 2 | | | | **2** |
| $f^{35}$ BC048 | | | 1 | | | | **1** |
| | | | | | | | |
| $f^{35}$ $P^{72}$ℵAB | | 1 | 1 | | | | **2** |
| $f^{35}$ $P^{72}$ℵAC | | 2 | 1 | | | | **3** |
| $f^{35}$ $P^{72}$ℵBC | | 1 | 3 | | | | **4** |
| $f^{35}$ $P^{72}$ABC | | 1 | | | | | **1** |
| $f^{35}$ $P^{81}$ℵAB | | 1 | | | | | **1** |
| $f^{35}$ $P^{100}$ℵBC | 1 | | | | | | **1** |
| $f^{35}$ ℵABC | | 4 | 1 | | | 1 | **6** |
| | | | | | | | |
| $f^{35}$ $P^{72}$ℵAB048 | | | 1 | | | | **1** |
| $f^{35}$ $P^{72}$ABC048 | | | 1 | | | | **1** |
| $f^{35}$ $P^{81}$ℵABC | | 1 | | | | | **1** |
| $f^{35}$ ℵABC048 | | | 1 | | | | **1** |
| | | | | | | | |
| Total w/ uncial | 55 | 85 | 54 | 65 | 12 | 13 | **284** |

% of variants with
uncial support | 49.5% | 63.7% | 75% | 67% | 38.7% | 46.4% | **60%**[1]

| | involving $P^{20}$ | -- | **1** |
|---|---|---|---|
| | involving $P^{72}$ | -- | **56** |
| | involving $P^{81}$ | -- | **3** |
| | involving $P^{100}$ | -- | **7** |
| | involving ℵ | -- | **136** |

---

[1] 2 & 3 John have the lowest percentage (if C had 2 John it would likely come up a bit) and 2 Peter the highest—a whopping 75%! Given all the 'bad press' 2 Peter has received, I find this datum to be interesting.

| | |
|---|---|
| involving A | -- **131** |
| involving B | -- **100** |
| involving C | -- **117** |
| involving 048 | -- **10** |

Each of these nine uncials is plainly independent of all the others. The total lack of pattern in the attestation that these early uncials give to $f^{35}$ shows just as plainly that $f^{35}$ is independent of them all as well, quite apart from the 40% without them. But that 60% of the units receive early uncial support, without pattern or dependency, shows that the $f^{35}$ **text** is early.

I invite special attention to the first block, where a single uncial sides with $f^{35}$; each of the seven uncials is independent of the rest (and of $f^{35}$) at this point, of necessity, yet together they attest 23.9% of the total (113 ÷ 473). Since there is no pattern or dependency for this 24%, how shall we account for these 113 early readings in $f^{35}$?[1] Will anyone argue that whoever 'concocted' the first $f^{35}$ MS had all these uncials in front of him, arbitrarily taking 8 readings from $P^{72}$, 2 from $P^{100}$, 37 from ℵ, etc., etc., etc.? Really now, how shall we account for these 113 early readings in $f^{35}$?

Going on to the next block, we have another 85 readings where there is no pattern or dependency; 113 + 85 = 198 = 41.9%. Really now, how shall we account for these 198 early readings in $f^{35}$? Going on to the next block, we have another 63 readings where there is no pattern or dependency; 198 + 63 = 261 = 55.2%. Really now, how shall we account for these 261 early readings in $f^{35}$? And so on.

To allege a dependency in the face of this EVIDENCE I consider to be dishonest. $f^{35}$ is clearly independent of all these lines of transmission, themselves independent. If $f^{35}$ is independent then it is early, of necessity. $f^{35}$ has all those early readings for the sufficient reason that its **text** is early, dating to the 3$^{rd}$ century, at least. But if $f^{35}$ is independent of all other lines of transmission (it is demonstrably independent of $K^x$, etc.) then it must hark back to the Autographs. What other reasonable explanation is there?[2]

# Is $f^{35}$ Ancient?

I have received feedback that goes something like this: "ok, the evidence you have presented indicates that $f^{35}$ is independent, but it doesn't prove that it's ancient" [I affirm both]. I consider that the point deserves a bit of 'chewing'. For instance: minuscules 35, 2587 and 2723 are generally dated to the 11$^{th}$ century; although minuscule 1897 is generally dated to the 12$^{th}$, I have collated

---

[1] Should anyone demure that the 5$^{th}$ century MSS included really aren't all that early, I inquire: are they copies, or original creations? If they are copies their exemplars were obviously earlier—all of these 113 readings doubtless existed in the 3$^{rd}$ century.

[2] Should anyone wish to claim that $f^{35}$ is a recension, I request (and insist) that he specify who did it, when and where, and furnish evidence in support of the claim. Without evidence any such claim is frivolous and irresponsible.

it and must say that it looks older to me, just as old as the other three, so I claim it for the 11$^{th}$ as well. What about their provenance? 35 is presently in Paris, but was acquired in the Aegean area [18, also in Paris, was done in Constantinople]; 1897 is in Jerusalem and presumably was produced there; 2587 is in the Vatican and may well have been produced there; 2723 is in Trikala and was doubtless produced there.

I now consider their performance in the seven General Epistles (a corpus of sufficient size and diversity to preclude reasonable challenge—I have done a complete collation of all four MSS throughout that corpus). As best I can tell, the exemplars of 35 and 2723 were perfect representatives of the presumed family archetype—not one variant in all seven books. The exemplar of 1897 participates in a splinter group (within the family) at three points, with no further variants. The exemplar of 2587 participates in a splinter group at six points, with no further variants. So the four monks who produced our four 11$^{th}$ century copies were each looking at a perfect (virtually) representative of the family's ($f^{35}$) archetypal text. But how old were the exemplars?

If a MS was not in constant or regular use it would easily last for a century or more, even several. Would Greek MSS in Rome be likely to be much in use at that time? Probably not, so the exemplar of 2587 could easily have been an uncial. How about Jerusalem? The chances of greater use there were probably little better than in Rome. In Constantinople (35?) and Trikala Greek was certainly still in use. But do we know to what extent Christians were actually reading Scripture in those years? I think we may reasonably assume that the exemplars were at least a century older than their copies. But 1897 and 2587 join splinter groups, so we are looking at some transmissional history—there must be the parent of the splinter between our exemplar and the archetype.

So, the exemplars were presumably no later than 10$^{th}$ century. If we allow one generation for the creation of splinters, that generation would be no later than the 9$^{th}$ and the archetype no later than the 8$^{th}$. (I have given an absolute minimum, but obviously there could have been any number of further intervening generations, which would place the archetype much earlier.) But what are the implications of perfect representatives of a family in the tenth century in four diverse locations? How could there be **perfect** copies of *anything* in the 10$^{th}$ century?? That there were four perfect (virtually) representatives of the $f^{35}$ archetype in diverse locations in the 10$^{th}$ century is a fact. That they were separated from that archetype by at least one intervening generation is also a fact. So how can we explain them?

Did someone concoct the $f^{35}$ archetype in the 8$^{th}$ century? Who? Why? And how could it spread around the Mediterranean world? There are $f^{35}$ MSS all over the place—Jerusalem, Sinai, Athens, Constantinople, Trikala, Kalavryta, Ochrida, Patmos, Karditsa, Rome, Sparta, Meteora, Venedig, Lesbos, and most monasteries on Mt. Athos (that represented different 'denominations'), etc. [If there were six monasteries on Cyprus—one Anglican, one Assembly of God, one Baptist, one Church of Christ, one Methodist and one Presbyterian—to what extent would they compare notes? Has human nature changed?] But the Byzantine bulk ($K^x$) controlled at least 60% of the transmissional stream ($f^{35}$ = a. 18%); how could something concocted in the 8$^{th}$ century spread so far, so fast, and in such purity? How did it inspire such loyalty? Everything that we know about the history of the transmission of the Text answers that it couldn't and didn't. It is simply impossible that $f^{35}$ could have been 'concocted' at any point subsequent to the 4th century. The loyalty with which $f^{35}$ was copied, the level of loyalty for $f^{35}$ being much higher than that for any other line of transmission, indicates that it was never 'concocted'—it goes back to the Original.

However, although $f^{35}$ has been demonstrated to be independent of $K^x$ (Byzantine bulk), they are really very close and must have a common source. (I would say that $K^x$ represents a departure from $f^{35}$, that $f^{35}$ is therefore older.) In the General Epistles $f^{35}$ does not differ from the H-F Majority Text all that much. For instance, in James $f^{35}$ differs from H-F nineteen times, only two of which affect the meaning (not seriously). If $f^{35}$ and $K^x$ have a common source, but $f^{35}$ is independent of $K^x$, then $f^{35}$ must be at least as old as $K^x$—Q.E.D. [*quod erat demonstrandum*, for those who read Latin; "which was to be proved", for the rest of us; and in yet plainer English, "the point to be proved has been proved"].

Further, if $f^{35}$ is independent of all other known lines of transmission, then it must hark back to the Autographs. If it was created out of existing materials at some point down the line, then it is dependent on those materials and it should be possible to demonstrate that dependence. So far as I know, no such dependence has been demonstrated, and to the extent that I have analyzed the evidence, it cannot be demonstrated.

# When is a 'Recension'?

"The Syrian text must in fact be the result of a 'recension' in the proper sense of the word, a work of attempted criticism, performed deliberately by editors and not merely by scribes."[1] It is not my wont to appeal to Fenton John Anthony Hort, but his understanding of 'recension' is presumably correct. A recension is produced by a certain somebody (or group) at a certain time in a certain place. If someone wishes to posit or allege a recension, and do so responsibly, he needs to indicate the source and supply some evidence.[2]

Are there any recensions among the MSS that contain the Catholic Epistles? I will base my response on the collations presented in *Text und Textwert* (*TuT*).[3] They collated about 555 MSS, some 30 of which are fragmentary; this

---

[1] B.F. Westcott and F.J.A. Hort, *The New Testament in the Original Greek* (2 vols.; London: Macmillan and Co., 1881), *Introduction*, p. 133.

[2] Hort did suggest Lucian of Antioch as the prime mover—a suggestion both gratuitous and frivolous, since he had not really looked at the evidence available at that time. (Were he to repeat the suggestion today, it would be patently ridiculous.)

[3] *Text und Textwert der Griechischen Handschriften des Neuen Testaments* (Ed. Kurt Aland, Berlin: Walter de Gruyter, 1987), volumes 9 and 11.

represents around 85% of the total of extant MSS. I will use Colwell's requirement of 70% agreement in order for MSS to be classified in the same text-type (although for myself I require at least 80%). Since *TuT* presents 98 variant sets, spread over the seven epistles, we have a corpus that presumably is reasonably representative. Although the *Institut* has never divulged the criteria by which they chose the sets, so far as I know, the chosen sets are significant (not trivial).

## *An Alexandrian Recension?*

Is there an Egyptian or Alexandrian recension, or text-type? *TuT* follows the 'standard' text, which it calls LESART 2. No single MS has this profile. The closest is Codex B, that diverges from it 13 times out of 98, three being sub-variants and four being singulars (including two of the sub-variants)—the agreement is 86.7% [ignoring the sub-variants it is 89.8%]. Next is cursive 1739 that diverges 29 times out of 98, four being sub-variants and no singulars—the agreement is 70.4% [ignoring the sub-variants it is 74.5%]. Next is $P^{74}$ [7th century] that diverges 3 times out of 10, one being a sub-variant and one being a singular—the agreement is 70% [ignoring the sub-variant it is 80%]. Next is Codex A that diverges 34 times out of 98, four being sub-variants and no singulars—the agreement is 65.3% [ignoring the sub-variants it is 69.4%]. Next is Codex C that diverges 24 times out of 66, one being a sub-variant and four being singulars—the agreement is 63.6% [ignoring the sub-variant it is 65.2%]. Next is cursive 1852 that diverges 36 times out of 95, two being sub-variants and no singulars—the agreement is 62.1% [ignoring the sub-variants it is 64.2%]. Next is Codex ℵ that diverges 40 times out of 98, seven being sub-variants and nine being singulars (including four of the sub-variants)—the agreement is 59.2% [ignoring the sub-variants it is 66.3%]. Next is Codex 044 [a. 800] that diverges 40 times out of 97, four being sub-variants and seven being singulars (including three of the sub-variants)—the agreement is 59% [ignoring the sub-variants it is 62.9%]. Next is Codex 048 [5th century] that diverges 8 times out of 18, one being a sub-variant and no singulars—the agreement is 55.6% [ignoring the sub-variant it is 61.1%]. Not next is $P^{72}$ that diverges 18 times out of 38, six being sub-variants and nine being singulars (including three of the sub-variants)—the agreement is 52.6% [ignoring the sub-variants it is 68.4%]. Codex B is clearly the most important MS in Aland's scheme of things; and the 'standard' text is a composite.

But is there an Egyptian text-type here? Well, **B** and ℵ disagree in 44 out of 98 sets, so their agreement is 55.1%. **B** and **A** disagree in 43 out of 98 sets, so their agreement is 56.1%. **B** and $P^{72}$ disagree in 19 out of 38 sets, so their agreement is 50%. **B** and **C** disagree in 27 out of 66 sets, so their agreement is 59.1%. **B** and $P^{74}$ disagree in 5 out of 10 sets, so their agreement is 50%. **B** and **1739** disagree in 37 out of 98 sets, so their agreement is 62.2%. **A** and ℵ disagree in 35 out of 98 sets, so their agreement is 64.3%. **A** and $P^{72}$ disagree in 24 out of 38 sets, so their agreement is 36.8%. **A** and **C** disagree in 26 out of 66 sets, so their agreement is 60.6%. **A** and $P^{74}$ disagree in 4 out of 10 sets, so their agreement is 60%. **A** and **1739** disagree in 36 out of 98 sets, so their agreement is 63.3%. ℵ and $P^{72}$ disagree in 26 out of 38 sets, so their agreement is 31.6%. ℵ and **C** disagree in 30 out of 66 sets, so their agreement is 54.5%. ℵ and **P**[74] disagree in 5 out of 10 sets, so their agreement is 50%. ℵ and **1739** disagree in 46 out of 98 sets, so their agreement is 53.1%. **C** and **P**[72] disagree in 18 out of 31 sets, so their agreement is 41.9%. **C** and **P**[74] disagree in 3 out of 7 sets, so their agreement is 57.1%. **C** and **1739** disagree in 23 out of 66 sets, so their agreement is 65.2%. **1739** and **P**[72] disagree in 22 out of 38 sets, so their agreement is 42.1%. **1739** and **P**[74] disagree in 3 out of 7 sets, so their agreement is 57.1%. Based on this evidence Colwell would not allow us to claim a text-type. The early MSS evidently suffered a common influence, but each wandered off on a private path. No two sets have the same roster of disagreements. They each are certainly independent in their own generation. The common influence observable in the early MSS must have had a source, but that source is really too shadowy to qualify as a recension.

## A Byzantine Recension?

LESART 1 is a majority text in the strictest sense. Aland followed the majority reading in every case, except for two variant sets where there is no majority variant and there he followed the plurality (set 32, 1 Peter 3:16—καταλαλωσιν has 49.8%, against καταλαλουσιν with 44.6%) (set 34, 1 Peter 4:3—ημιν has 47.1%, against υμιν with 41.7%). As a byproduct of that procedure no single MS has that precise profile—I found four MSS that come within two variants (607, 639, 1730, 2423) and five that miss by three. The basic **f**[35] profile diverges by five.

Having analyzed the profiles for the ± 555 MSS, apart from **f**[35] I found precisely one cluster of four MSS (82, 699, 1668, 2484), with a few hangers-on, and one cluster of three MSS (390, 912, 1594), also with a few hangers-on, and nine pairs—<u>all</u> the rest have private profiles (including the 'hangers-on').

Within **f**[35] 31 MSS have the basic profile; there is a sub-group of 6 MSS, another of 4, another of 3, plus two pairs—these 17 MSS, plus another 10, differ from the basic profile in only one variant. There are 15 MSS that differ by two and 7 by three, making a total of 80 MSS (32 of which have private profiles), plus a few others on the fringes.

Setting aside all the MSS with a shared profile, plus about 30 that have less than 11% of the total, we are left with around 450 MSS that have a private profile (based on the 98 variant sets), the heavy majority of which are Byzantine. We are looking at a normal transmission; no mass production of a single exemplar.

Setting aside the fragmentary MSS, there are about 40 that fall below Colwell's 70% threshold; all the rest (± 485) would qualify as members of one text-type, which we may call Byzantine. Using my 80% threshold we lose another 17 MSS, leaving ± 470. But I would really rather have 90%, and with that threshold we lose another 46—call it ± 420 MSS. Setting aside the 30 fragmentaries, dividing 420 by 525 we have 80% of the MSS that are strongly

Byzantine[1] (using the 80% threshold gives almost 90%) [using the 70% threshold gives 92%]. 345 of the 420 have private profiles—with the possible exception of $f^{35}$ there was no 'stuffing the ballot box'.

Although $f^{35}$ obviously falls within the Byzantine stream, I will factor it out and treat it separately. 420 less 80 equals 340 strongly Byzantine MSS, only 25 of which share a profile. We obviously have a text-type, but is it a recension? To posit a recension we need a source—who did it, when and where? And using what? Did he merely edit existing materials or did he invent some of the variants? If he invented, is there an observable pattern to explain his attitude?

We have 315 strongly Byzantine MSS (without $f^{35}$) with private profiles—they are independent in their own generation, presumably representing as many exemplars, also presumably independent in their own generation, etc. Which is at least partly why scholars from Hort to Aland have recognized that any Byzantine 'recension' could not have been created later than the 4th century.

As a preliminary to taking up the question of $f^{35}$ ($K^r$) as possibly a recension, I wish to consider other aspects of the general evidence presented in *TuT*. Of the MSS that were collated, 78 are dated. There are nine pairs of MSS with the same date (but no more than two MSS to a year—so 60 have a private year); in eight of them the two MSS are quite different in profile; in the ninth pair both MSS are $f^{35}$ but differ in one variant. Both are at Mt. Athos, but in different monasteries—it is highly improbable that they had the same exemplar. There is no evidence here of mass production. But why would a monk on Mt. Athos produce a copy in 1280 AD? If the copy is still there, it was not to fill an order from the city. So why did he do it, as a religious exercise or duty? But what would he copy? It seems to me most likely that he would copy an aged exemplar that was showing signs of wear, to preserve its text. I will demonstrate below that the MSS produced in a single monastery were based on distinct exemplars (as Lake, Blake and New indicated some 85 years ago).[2]

## Mt. Athos

I have heard it said that the MSS at Mt. Athos are under suspicion of having been mass produced, and of being made to conform to an arbitrary standard. I suspect that the speaker was not aware that there are a number of distinct monasteries in that area. *TuT* lists a mere twenty. Recall that these monasteries represented different patriarchates, orders, countries and even languages. An average small city in the U.S. will likely have an Assembly of God, a Baptist church, a Bible church, a Congregational church, an Episcopal church, a Methodist church, a Presbyterian church, some kind of neo-pentecostal church, among others. How do they relate to each other? To what

---

[1] For a 95% threshold we lose another 35 MSS; $385 \div 525$ gives 73%. 75% of the MSS reflect a very strong consensus, and yet most have private profiles.

[2] K. Lake, R.P. Blake and Silva New, "The Caesarean Text of the Gospel of Mark", *Harvard Theological Review*, XXI (1928), 348-49.

extent do they join forces? Even a city-wide evangelistic campaign will not get them all together. Were monks in the Byzantine empire any different than pastors in the U.S.? Has human nature changed? The point I am making is that there was probably very little comparing of notes between monasteries on a subject like copying MSS.

Consider: Grigoriu, Pavlu and Protatu are listed with one MS each (for the Catholic Epistles),[1] none of which are $f^{35}$. Karakallu and Kavsokalyvion are listed with one each that is $f^{35}$. Konstamonitu, Philotheu and Stavronikita are listed with two MSS, one $f^{35}$ and one not. Xiropotamu has two MSS, neither being $f^{35}$. Pantokratoros has three, one of which is $f^{35}$. Dochiariu has five MSS, none being $f^{35}$. Esphigmenu also has five, one being $f^{35}$. Panteleimonos is listed with seven MSS, two being $f^{35}$. Dionysiu is listed with nine MSS, three being $f^{35}$. Kutlumusiu is listed with ten MSS, two being $f^{35}$. Iviron is listed with twelve MSS, five being $f^{35}$. Vatopediu is listed with 28 MSS, five being $f^{35}$. M Lavras is listed with 52 MSS, 22 being $f^{35}$. With the possible exception of M Lavras, there was evidently no $f^{35}$ 'steamroller' at work.

But what about within a single monastery? Although MSS presently located at places like London or Paris were presumably produced elsewhere, those located at places like Mt. Athos, Patmos, Jerusalem and Sinai were probably produced right there. The monastery at Mt. Sinai is sufficiently isolated that we might expect that a good deal of 'inbreeding' took place. So let's take a look at the Sinai MSS listed by *TuT*.

## Mt. Sinai

I will list the MSS in a descending order of 'Alexandrishness',[2] with the proviso that such an ordering is only relevant for the first seven or eight:[3]
1. א,01[4]– IV, eapr  (2 = 57 [2 subs],[5] 1/2 = 5 [1 sub], 1 = 19 [3 subs], sing = 9, odd = 8) = 98  variants;
2. 1243 – XI, eap  (2 = 51, 1/2 = 6, 1 = 22 [5 subs], sing = 2, odd = 16) = 97;
3. 1241 – XII, eap  (2 = 47 [5 subs], 1/2 = 4, 1 = 17 [2 subs], sing = 5, odd = 18) = 91;
4. 1881 – XIV, ap  (2 = 42 [3 subs], 1/2 = 3 [1 sub], 1 = 16 [1 sub], sing = 1, odd = 11) = 73;
5. 2495 – XIV, eapr  (2 = 37 [2 subs], 1/2 = 4, 1 = 37 [4 subs], sing = 2, odd = 17) = 97;
6. 2492 – XIII, eap  (2 = 17 [2 subs], 1/2 = 8, 1 = 58 [2 subs], sing = 1, odd = 9) = 93;
7. 2494 – 1316, eapr  (2 = 11, 1/2 = 4, 1 = 73 [2 subs], odd = 10) = 98;

---

[1] TuT lists a MS each for Andreas and Dimitriu, but did not collate them. Esphigmenu has an added three MSS that were not collated.

[2] I consider a high 'erraticity' quotient to be a defining feature of 'Alexandrishness'.

[3] TuT includes two 6th century uncial fragments: 0285 has one reading (of the 98) and 0296 has two. Such a scant basis only allows us to guess that they are not Byzantine.

[4] Of course Aleph is presently located in London, but it became extant in Sinai; to this day the monks at St. Catharine's refer to Tischendorf as 'the thief'.

[5] 'subs' stands for sub-variants, which are included in the larger number. Where a 'sub' is also a singular I list it only as a singular—each variant is counted only once.

From here on down all the MSS fall within the Byzantine stream.

8.  1874 – X, ap  (2 = 4, 1/2 = 9, 1 = 78 [2 subs], sing = 1, odd = 6) = 98;
9.  1877 – XIV, ap  (2 = 2, 1/2 = 9, 1 = 81 [5 subs], sing = 2, odd = 4) = 98;
10. 2086 – XIV, ap  (2 = 2, 1/2 = 8, 1 = 82 [2 subs], sing = 1, odd = 5) = 98;
11. 1251 – XIII, eap  (2 = 2, 1/2 = 9, 1 = 82 [3 subs], odd = 4) = 97;
12. 1245 – XII, ap  (2 = 3, 1/2 = 10 [1 sub], 1 = 83 [6 subs], odd = 2) = 98;
13. 1240 – XII, eap  (2 = 1, 1/2 = 7, 1 = 82 [7 subs], odd = 4) = 94;
14. 2356 – XIV, eap  (2 = 1, 1/2 = 9, 1 = 76 [2 subs], odd = 4) = 90;
15. 1880 – X, ap  (2 = 2, 1/2 = 10, 1 = 84 [5 subs], odd = 2) = 98;
16. 2502 – 1242, eap  (2 = 1, 1/2 = 9, 1 = 73 [6 subs], odd = 2) = 85;
17. 1242 – XIII, eap  (2 = 1, 1/2 = 9, 1 = 86 [4 subs], odd = 2) = 98;
18. 1250 – XV, eap  (2 = 1, 1/2 = 10, 1 = 77 [3 subs], odd = 3) = 91;       [$f^{35}$ ± 2]
19. 1247 – XV, eap  (2 = 1, 1/2 = 10, 1 = 81 [3 subs], odd = 3) = 95;       [$f^{35}$ ± 2]
20. 1876 – XV, apr  (2 = 1, 1/2 = 11, 1 = 83 [3 subs], odd = 3) = 98;       [$f^{35}$ ± 2]
21. 1249 – 1324, ap  (2 = 1, 1/2 = 10, 1 = 84 [3 subs], odd = 2) = 97;      [$f^{35}$ ± 1]
22. 1248 – XIV, eap  (2 = 1, 1/2 = 11, 1 = 84 [3 subs], sing = 1, odd = 1) = 98;  [$f^{35}$ ± 1]
23. 2501 – XVI, ap  (2 = 1, 1/2 = 11, 1 = 83 [5 subs], odd = 1) = 96;       [$f^{35}$ ± 4]
24. 2085 – 1308, ap  (2 = 0, 1/2 = 11, 1 = 84 [3 subs], sing = 1, odd = 2) = 98;
25. 1244 – XI, ap  (2 = 0, 1/2 = 10, 1 = 85 [3 subs], odd = 2) = 97;
26. 2799 – XIV, ap  (2 = 0, 1/2 = 3, 1 = 28 [2 subs], sing = 1, odd = 1) = 33.[1]

Absolutely no two MSS are identical; even the six $f^{35}$ MSS all differ by at least one variant. The rest of the Byzantine MSS are all distinct, some really so,[2] yet all clearly fall within the Byzantine tradition.[3] These 26 MSS represent as many exemplars; there was no 'inbreeding', no stuffing the ballot box; each copyist tried to reproduce what was in front of him, regardless of the type of text. Since the MSS were still there in 1800, they were not made to fill an order from elsewhere. Given its isolation, some of the ancestors of the 26 extant MSS may well have been brought to the monastery before the Islamic conquest.

---

[1] The last three MSS have very different profiles.

[2] Notice that no MS scores a perfect 87 for LESART 1, and only four score a perfect 11 for LESART 1/2.

[3] Remember that we are only looking at 98 variant sets—if we had complete collations for the seven books it is almost certain that no two MSS would be identical (from all sources); perhaps for a single book, the smaller the better, a few might be found. [I wrote the above in 2004, when I was just beginning to really pay attention to $f^{35}$—in fact, within that family, considering only the MSS that I myself have collated, we can say the following: I have in my possession copies of thirty identical MSS for both 2 and 3 John (not identical lists), twenty-nine for Philemon, twenty-two for Jude, fifteen for 2 Thessalonians, nine for Titus, six each for Galatians, Colossians and 1 Thessalonians, five each for Philippians and 2 Peter, four each for Ephesians, James and 1 John, three each for 2 Timothy and 1 Peter, and two each for Romans and 1 Timothy. It is not the same selection of MSS in each case, and they come from all over.] Apart from $f^{35}$ I would still be surprised to find identical copies of any book with over 3 chapters.

The profiles of the first five MSS in the above list are **very** different, distinct from each other; none is a copy of ℵ, which I find to be curious. Evidently ℵ was not copied—why?[1]

## Megistis Lavras

Well, ok, but what about M Lavras? Isn't the disproportionate percentage of $f^{35}$ MSS suspicious? To find out we must do for M Lavras what we did for Sinai, which will be twice as much work (52 X 26). Again, I will list the MSS in a descending order of 'Alexandrishness', with the proviso that such an ordering is only relevant for the first nine or ten:

1. 1739 – X, ap  (2 = 66 [4 subs], 1/2 = 7, 1 = 12 [2 subs], odd = 13) = 98;
2. 044 – VIII, ap  (2 = 52 [1 sub], 1/2 = 7, 1 = 20, sing = 7, odd = 11) = 97;
3. 1735 – XI, ap  (2 = 43 [2 subs], 1/2 = 7 [1 sub], 1 = 35 [2 subs], sing = 1, odd = 12) = 98;
4. 1505 – XII, eap  (2 = 41 [3 subs], 1/2 = 4, 1 = 35 [3 subs], odd = 18) = 98;
5. 1448 – XI, eap  (2 = 23, 1/2 = 7 [1 sub], 1 = 58 [2 subs], sing = 1, odd = 8) = 97;
6. 1490 – XII, eap  (2 = 13, 1/2 = 7 [1 sub], 1 = 69 [4 subs], odd = 9) = 98;
7. 1751 – 1479, ap  (2 = 7 [1 sub], 1/2 = 11 [1 sub], 1 = 69 [3 subs], sing = 5, odd = 6) = 98;
8. 1501 – XIII, eap  (2 = 8 [1 sub], 1/2 = 8, 1 = 73 [1 sub], sing = 1, odd = 8) = 98;
9. 1661 – XV, eap  (2 = 6, 1/2 = 9 [1 sub], 1 = 73 [5 subs], sing = 3, odd = 7) = 98;

From here on down all the MSS fall within the Byzantine stream.

10. 1609 – XIV, eap  (2 = 9 [1 sub], 1/2 = 9, 1 = 76 [4 subs], odd = 3) = 97;
11. 1646 – 1172, eap  (2 = 3, 1/2 = 10, 1 = 77 [6 subs], sing = 5, odd = 3) = 98;
12. 1509 – XIII, eap  (2 = 3, 1/2 = 9, 1 = 77 [5 subs], sing = 3, odd = 5) = 97;
13. 1744 – XIV, ap  (2 = 2, 1/2 = 8, 1 = 81 [2 subs], sing = 2, odd = 5) = 98;
14. 1643 – XIV, eap  (2 = 3, 1/2 = 7, 1 = 82 [3 subs], odd = 6) = 98;
15. 1626 – XV, eapr  (2 = 2, 1/2 = 9, 1 = 81 [6 subs], sing = 1, odd = 5) = 98;
16. 1743 – XII, ap  (2 = 1, 1/2 = 7 [1 sub], 1 = 83 [2 subs], odd = 7) = 98;
17. 1622 – XIV, eap  (2 = 4, 1/2 = 10, 1 = 81 [4 subs], odd = 3) = 98;
18. 2194 – 1118, ap  (2 = 2, 1/2 = 8, 1 = 83 [2 subs], odd = 5) = 98;
19. 1495 – XIV, eap  (2 = 4, 1/2 = 10, 1 = 82 [5 subs], odd = 2) = 98;
20. 1642 – 1278, eap  (2 = 1, 1/2 = 10, 1 = 82 [6 subs], sing = 1, odd = 3) = 97;
21. 1738 – XI, ap  (2 = 2, 1/2 = 10, 1 = 82 [8 subs], odd = 3) = 97;
22. 1649– XV, eap  (2 = 2, 1/2 = 9, 1 = 84 [5 subs], odd = 3) = 98;
23. 1734– 1015, apr  (2 = 1, 1/2 = 9, 1 = 82 [1 sub], odd = 4) = 96;
24. 049– IX, ap  (2 = 1 [1 sub], 1/2 = 9, 1 = 84 [4 subs], odd = 3) = 97;
25. 1741 – XIV, ap  (2 = 0, 1/2 = 7 [1 sub], 1 = 87 [4 subs], odd = 4) = 98;
26. 1456– XIII, eap  (2 = 0, 1/2 = 8 [1 sub], 1 = 69 [2 subs], odd = 4) = 81;
27. 1747– XIV, ap  (2 = 1, 1/2 = 9, 1 = 84 [6 subs], odd = 2) = 96;
28. 1736– XIII, ap  (2 = 1, 1/2 = 10, 1 = 83 [4 subs], odd = 2) = 96;
29. 2511 – XIV, eap  (2 = 1, 1/2 = 10 [1 sub], 1 = 76 [I sub], odd = 2) = 89;
30. 1750– XV, ap  (2 = 0, 1/2 = 9, 1 = 87 [3 subs], odd = 2) = 98;

---

[1] But over ten people did try to correct it, down through the centuries, so they knew it was there. 1243 and 1241 are almost as bad, and they were produced in the 11th and 12th centuries, respectively.

31. 1733 – XIV, apr  (2 = 1, 1/2 = 11, 1 = 83 [3 subs], odd = 3) = 98;   [$f^{35} \pm 2$]
    (16, 91)
32. 1732 – 1384, apr (2 = 2, 1/2 = 11 [1 sub],1 = 83 [3 subs], odd = 1) = 97; [$f^{35} \pm 2$]
    (1, 72)
33. 1508 – XV, eap  (2 = 1, 1/2 = 10, 1 = 85 [4 subs], odd = 2) = 98;   [$f^{35} \pm 2$]
    (21, 65)
34. 1482 – 1304, eap  (2 = 1, 1/2 = 10, 1 = 85 [2 subs], odd = 2) = 98;   [$f^{35} \pm 2$]
    (45, 65)
35. 1656 – XV, eap  (2 = 1, 1/2 = 11, 1 = 84 [2 subs], odd = 2) = 98;   [$f^{35} \pm 2$]
    (8, 45)
36. 1748 – 1662, ap  (2 = 1, 1/2 = 11, 1 = 85 [4 subs], odd = 1) = 98;   [$f^{35} \pm 2$]
    (32, 62)
37. 1737 – XII, ap  (2 = 1, 1/2 = 11, 1 = 85 [3 subs], odd = 1) = 98;   [$f^{35} \pm 2$]
    (32, 77)
38. 1749 – XVI, ap  (2 = 2, 1/2 = 11, 1 = 78 [3 subs], odd = 1) = 92;   [$f^{35} \pm 1$]   (29)
39. 1637 – 1328, eapr  (2 = 2, 1/2 = 11, 1 = 84 [3 subs], odd = 1) = 98; [$f^{35} \pm 1$]   (17)
40. 1740 – XIII, apr  (2 = 1, 1/2 = 11, 1 = 85 [4 subs], odd = 1) = 98;   [$f^{35} \pm 1$]   (39)
41. 1617 – XV, eapr  (2 = 1, 1/2 = 11, 1 = 85 [4 subs], odd = 1) = 98;   [$f^{35} \pm 1$]   (21)
42. 1618 – 1568, eap  (2 = 1, 1/2 = 11, 1 = 85 [2 subs], odd = 1) = 98;   [$f^{35} \pm 1$]   (32)
43. 1072 – XIII, eapr  (2 = 1, 1/2 = 11, 1= 85 [3 subs], odd = 1) = 98;   [$f^{35} \pm 0$]
44. 1075 – XIV, eapr  (2 = 1, 1/2 = 11, 1= 85 [3 subs], odd = 1) = 98;   [$f^{35} \pm 0$]
45. 1503 – 1317, eapr  (2 = 1, 1/2 = 11, 1= 85 [3 subs], odd = 1) = 98;   [$f^{35} \pm 0$]
46. 1619 – XIV, ea(p)  (2 = 1, 1/2 = 11, 1= 85 [3 subs], odd = 1) = 98;   [$f^{35} \pm 0$]
47. 1628 – 1400, eap  (2 = 1, 1/2 = 11, 1= 85 [3 subs], odd = 1) = 98;   [$f^{35} \pm 0$]
48. 1636 – XV, eap  (2 = 1, 1/2 = 11, 1= 85 [3 subs], odd = 1) = 98;   [$f^{35} \pm 0$]
49. 1745 – XV, apr  (2 = 1, 1/2 = 11, 1= 85 [3 subs], odd = 1) = 98;   [$f^{35} \pm 0$]
50. 1746 – XIV, apr  (2 = 1, 1/2 = 11, 1= 85 [3 subs], odd = 1) = 98;   [$f^{35} \pm 0$]
51. 1652 – XVI, eap  (2 = 1, 1/2 = 3, 1= 21) = 25;   [$f^{35}$ frag]
52. 1742 – XIII, ap  (2 = 1, 1/2 = 11, 1= 85 [3 subs]) = 97;   [$f^{35} \pm 5$]

Again, setting aside the $f^{35}$ MSS for the moment, absolutely no two MSS are identical. The rest of the Byzantine MSS are all distinct, some really so, yet all clearly fall within the Byzantine tradition. These 30 MSS represent as many exemplars; there was no 'inbreeding', no stuffing the ballot box; each copyist tried to reproduce what was in front of him, regardless of the quality of text. Since the MSS were still there in 1800, they were not made to fill an order from elsewhere.

Also, where did the monasteries get the parchment for their ongoing production of MSS? Did they have money to go out and buy from tanneries? It seems to me more probable that they made their own from the skins of the sheep and goats that they ate. In such an event it could easily take several years to get enough for a single New Testament. The problem of finding enough parchment mitigates against the mass production of copies at any time in the vellum era. Three of the dated MSS at Sinai are eight years apart (1308, 1316, 1324)—might it have taken that long to gather enough vellum?

Now let's consider the $f^{35}$ group. Seven are $f^{35} \pm 2$, but no two of them have an identical profile—I have put the deviant variants within ( ) at the end of the line, so the reader can check that at a glance. Five are $f^{35} \pm 1$, but no two of them have an identical profile either, as the reader can see at a glance. So these twelve MSS must also have been copied from as many exemplars—we now have 44 MSS that were copied from distinct exemplars. Ah, but there are eight MSS with a perfect $f^{35}$ profile; what of them? Well, let's start with the contents: three contain **eapr**, three contain **eap**, two contain **apr**—at the very least, these three groups must represent distinct exemplars. So now we are down to a maximum of five MSS that might not represent a distinct exemplar. Setting aside preconceived ideas, what objective basis could anyone have for affirming that these five were not copied on the same principle as the rest, namely to preserve the text of the exemplar? It seems to me only fair to understand that the 52 extant MSS at M Lavras represent as many distinct exemplars.[1]

## *An f$^{35}$ (K$^r$) Recension?*

Since $f^{35}$ is the only group of consequence, with a significant number of MSS, with an empirically defined profile, we can determine its archetypal text with certainty—we have the most cohesive of all text-types. But is it a 'recension'? Von Soden claimed that it was, assigning it to the 12th century; I am not aware that he named a source, but if he did he was wrong. Minuscule 35, along with other 11th century MSS, belongs to this group—their exemplars were presumably 10th century or earlier. I have demonstrated elsewhere[2] that $f^{35}$ (K$^r$) is independent of K$^x$, throughout the NT—if it is independent it cannot have been based upon K$^x$. Repeatedly $f^{35}$ has overt early attestation, against K$^x$, but there is no pattern to the alignments, they are hap-hazard. It is supported (against K$^x$) by P$^{45,46,47,66,75}$,אA,B,C,D,W,lat,syr,cop—sometimes just by one, sometimes by two, three, four or more of them, but in constantly shifting patterns. If there is no pattern then there is no dependency; $f^{35}$ has ancient readings because it itself is ancient.

Returning to *TuT* and the Catholic Epistles, I will list the present location of $f^{35}$ MSS by century:

XI— Paris, Trikala, Vatican;
XII—Athos (Kutlumusiu, M Lavras, Panteleimonos, Stavronikita, Vatopediu), Jerusalem;
XIII—Athens, Athos (Iviron, Konstamonitu, M Lavras, Pantokratoros, Philotheu), Bologna, Kalavryta, Leiden, Vatican;
XIV—Athens, Athos (Dionysiu, Esphigmenu, Iviron, Karakally, Kavsokalyvion, M Lavras, Vatopediu), Grottaferrata, Jerusalem, Karditsa, London, Ochrida, Paris, Patmos, Rome, Sinai, Vatican;

---

[1] I remind the reader again that we are only looking at 98 variant sets—if we had complete collations for the seven books it is almost certain that no two MSS would be identical (for the seven books; I have identical copies for a single book). With full collations these five will doubtless prove to be distinct as well. [Having now collated 43 Family 35 MSS for the seven general epistles, I have two that are perfect for all seven books, and four of the exemplars may have been so—they come from different locales.]

[2] See "The Dating of K$^r$ (alias $f^{35}$, nee $f^{18}$) Revisited", above. (See also "Concerning the Text of the *Pericope Adulterae*", below.)

XV—Athens, Athos (Iviron, M Lavras), Bucharest, London, Meteora, Sinai, Sparta, Vatican, Venedig, Zittau;
XVI—Athens, Athos (Iviron, Kuthumusiu, M Lavras), Lesbos, Sinai;
XVII—Athos (Dionysiu, M Lavras).

Manuscripts at Vatican, Grottaferrata, Jerusalem, Patmos, Sinai, Athos, Trikala, Meteora, Lesbos, at least, are most probably based on a line of ancestors held locally; any importing of exemplars probably took place in the early centuries. If there are $f^{35}$ MSS in those places today, it is presumably because there have been $f^{35}$ MSS there from the beginning.

I reject as totally unfounded the allegation that $f^{35}$ is a recension. If anyone wishes to claim that it is, I request that they state who did it, when and where, and that they furnish evidence in support of the claim. Without evidence any such claim is frivolous and irresponsible.

# Archetype in the General Epistles—$f^{35}$ yes, $K^x$ no

If you want to be a candidate for the best plumber in town, you need to be a plumber; the best lawyer, you need to be a lawyer; the best oncologist, you need to be an oncologist; and so on. Similarly, if you want to be a candidate for Autograph archetype, you need to be an archetype; a real, honest to goodness, objectively verifiable archetype. This section addresses the following question: are there any objectively identifiable archetypes in the General Epistles?

I invite attention to the following evidence taken from my critical apparatus of those books. I will take the books one at a time. The reading of $f^{35}$ will always be the first one, and the complete roster defines that family's archetype.[1]

## *James*
1:05 ουκ f35 (70.3%) || μη אA,B,C (29.7%);                                ?[no $K^x$]2
1:23 νομου $f^{35}$ [30%] || λογου אA,B,C [69%] || λογων [1%];
1:26 αλλ $f^{35}$ [35%] || αλλα אA,B,C,0173 [65%];
2:03 λαμπραν εσθητα $f^{35}$ [30%] || εσθητα την λαμπραν אA,B,C [70%];
2:04 ου $f^{35}$ אA,C (26.8%) || και ου (72.2%) || και (0.6%) || --- B (0.4%);
2:08 σεαυτον $f^{35}$ אA(B)C [50%] || εαυτον [50%];                    [no $K^x$]
2:13 ανηλεος $f^{35}$ [20%] || ανελεος אA,B,C [30%] || ανιλεως [50%];           [no $K^x$]
2:14 λεγη τις $f^{35}$ אB [70%] || ~ 21 A,C [1%] || λεγει τις [28%];        ?[no $K^x$]
2:14 εχει $f^{35}$ [46%] || εχη אA,B,C [47%] || εχειν [4.5%] || σχη [2.5%];    [no $K^x$]
3:02 δυναμενος $f^{35}$ א [23%] || δυνατος A,B [76.5%];

---

[1] Setting aside singular readings, over 50% of the words in the Text will have 100% attestation; 80% of the words will have over 95% attestation; 90% of the words will have over 90% attestation; only for some 2% of the words will the attestation fall below 80%. I regard $f^{35}$ as the base from which all other streams of transmission departed, to one extent or another, so in general the Byzantine bulk will have stayed with $f^{35}$. It follows that the roster only includes cases where there is a serious split in the Byzantine bulk, or where $f^{35}$ is alone (or almost so) against that bulk.

[2] For the purposes of this section I use $K^x$ to represent the Byzantine bulk.

3:03 ιδε **f³⁵** [60%] || ει δε [38.5%] || ιδου [0.5%];[1]                                    [no **Kˣ**]
3:04 ανεμων σκληρων **f³⁵** ℵB,C [44%] || ~ 21  A [56%];                          ?[no **Kˣ**]
3:04 ιθυνοντος **f³⁵** [21%] || ευθυνοντος ℵA,B,C [79%];
3:18 δε **f³⁵** A,B,C [56.6%] || δε της [42%] || δε ο ℵ [0.4%] || --- [1%];    [no **Kˣ**]
4:02 ουκ εχετε **f³⁵** P¹⁰⁰A,B [64%] || και 12 ℵ [35%] || 12 δε [1%];          [no **Kˣ**]
4:04 ουν **f³⁵** ℵA,B [58%] || --- [42%];                                                   [no **Kˣ**]
4:07 αντιστητε **f³⁵** [47.5%] || 1 δε ℵA,B [50%] || 1 ουν [2.5%];              [no **Kˣ**]
4:11 γαρ **f³⁵** [26%] || --- ℵA,B [74%];
4:12 και κριτης **f³⁵** ℵA,B [62%] || --- [38%];                                       [no **Kˣ**]
4:14 ημων **f³⁵** [26%] || υμων (P¹⁰⁰)ℵA(B) [74%];
4:14 εστιν **f³⁵** [52%] || εσται (A) [41%] || εστε B [7%] || --- ℵ;             [no **Kˣ**]
4:14 επειτα **f³⁵** [29.5%] || 1 δε και [46%] || 1 δε [15%] || 1 και ℵA,B [9.5%];
                                                                                                            [no **Kˣ**]
5:07 αν **f³⁵** ℵ [53%] || --- A,B,048 [45.5%] || ου [1.5%];                     [no **Kˣ**]
5:10 αδελφοι **f³⁵** (A)B [35%] || αδελφοι μου (ℵ) [62%] || --- [3%];
5:10 εν τω **f³⁵** B [40%] || τω A [58%] || εν ℵ [0.6%] || επι τω [1.4%];
5:11 ειδετε **f³⁵** ℵB [53%] || ιδετε A [45%];                                        [no **Kˣ**]
5:11 πολυσπλαγχνος **f³⁵** ℵA,B [65%] || πολυευσπλαγχνος [35%];          [no **Kˣ**]
5:19 αδελφοι **f³⁵** [72%] || αδελφοι μου ℵA,B,048 [28%].                      ?[no **Kˣ**]

The archetypal profile of **f³⁵** in James is defined by the 28 readings above. It is clear and unambiguous, so we have at least one objectively defined archetype in James. In contrast, there are 14 + ?4 variant sets where **Kˣ** is seriously divided, placing an objectively defined archetype beyond our present reach.[2] (I did not include a number of lesser splits—25%, 20%, 15%—that conceivably could complicate any attempt to come up with an archetype for **Kˣ**.) As Colwell observed for Mark's Gospel, there is no objectively definable 'Alexandrian' archetype;[3] the same applies to any 'Western' archetype, unless we follow the Alands and take a single MS as such, their "D text" (which only includes the Gospels and Acts, however, so there would be no 'D text' for Romans - Revelation).[4] Let's go on to 1 Peter.

---

[1] Since **f³⁵** (**Kʳ**) is distinct from **Kˣ**, its 20% must be subtracted from the 60%, leaving an even split in **Kˣ**.

[2] If all the MSS are ever collated, some smaller groups (in the 5% - 10% range) with an objectively defined archetype may emerge, but I very much doubt that there will be a majority of the MSS with a single archetype; as in the Apocalypse, where there simply is no **Kˣ** (but there is indeed an objectively defined **f³⁵** [**Kʳ**]).

[3] E.C. Colwell, "The Significance of Grouping of New testament Manuscripts", *New Testament studies*, IV (1957-1958), 86-87. What he actually said was: "These results show convincingly that any attempt to reconstruct an archetype of the Beta Text-type [Alexandrian] on a quantitative basis is doomed to failure. The text thus reconstructed is not reconstructed but constructed; it is an artificial entity that never existed." [Amen!]

[4] K. and B. Aland, *The Text of the New Testament* (Grand Rapids: Eerdmans, 1967), pp. 55, 64. They speak of "the phantom 'Western text'".

# 1 Peter

1:03 ελεος αυτου **f³⁵** P⁷² [38%] ‖ ~ 21 אA,B,C [60%] ‖ 1 [2%];　　　　　　[no **Kˣ**]

1:07 δοξαν και τιμην **f³⁵** P⁷²אA,B,C [35%] ‖ ~ 321 [28%] ‖ ~ 32 εις 1 [37%];
　　　　　　　　　　　　　　　　　　　　　　　　　　　　　　　　　[no **Kˣ**]

1:16 γινεσθε **f³⁵** [52%] ‖ γενεσθε [36%] ‖ εσεσθε P⁷²אA,B,C [12%];　　[no **Kˣ**]

1:23 αλλ **f³⁵** C [40%] ‖ αλλα P⁷²אA,B [60%];

2:02 εις σωτηριαν **f³⁵** (P⁷²)אA,B,C [65%] ‖ --- [35%];　　　　　　　[no **Kˣ**]

2:03 χρηστος **f³⁵** אA,B,C [48%] ‖ χριστος P⁷² [52%];　　　　　　　[no **Kˣ**]

2:06 η **f³⁵** C [35%] ‖ εν τη [59%] ‖ εν P⁷²אA,B [6%];　　　　　　?[no **Kˣ**]

2:11 απεχεσθαι **f³⁵** אB [65%] ‖ απεχεσθε P⁷²A,C [35%];　　　　　[no **Kˣ**]

2:12 καταλαλουσιν **f³⁵** P⁷²אA,B,C [52%] ‖ καταλαλωσιν [48%];　　[no **Kˣ**]

2:14 μεν **f³⁵** C [52%] ‖ --- P⁷²אA,B [48%];　　　　　　　　　　　[no **Kˣ**]

2:17 αγαπησατε **f³⁵** [71%] ‖ αγαπατε P⁷²אA,B,C [24%] ‖ --- [5%];　?[no **Kˣ**]

2:20 τω **f³⁵** A [47%] ‖ --- P⁷²,⁸¹ᵛאB,C [53%];　　　　　　　　　　[no **Kˣ**]

2:21 και **f³⁵** P⁷² [23%] ‖ --- אA,B,C [77%];

2:24 αυτου **f³⁵** א [71%] ‖ --- P⁷²,⁸¹ᵛA,B,C [29%];　　　　　　　[no **Kˣ**]

2:25 ημων **f³⁵** [50%] ‖ υμων P⁷²אA,B,C [50%];　　　　　　　　　[no **Kˣ**]

3:06 εγενηθητε **f³⁵** P⁸¹ᵛאA,B,C [63%] ‖ εγεννηθητε P⁷² [35%] ‖ εγεννηθη [2%];
　　　　　　　　　　　　　　　　　　　　　　　　　　　　　　　　　[no **Kˣ**]

3:07 χαριτος ζωης **f³⁵** P⁸¹ᵛB,C [58%] ‖ 1 ζωης [35%]
　　　　　‖ ποικιλης 12 אA [7%] ‖ 12 αιωνιου P⁷²;　　　　　　　[no **Kˣ**]

3:07 εγκοπτεσθαι **f³⁵** P⁸¹(א)A,B [70%] ‖ εκκοπτεσθαι P⁷²C [30%];　?[no **Kˣ**]

3:10 ημερας ιδειν **f³⁵** C [26%] ‖ ~ 21 P⁷²,⁸¹ᵛאA,B [74%];

3:16 καταλαλουσιν **f³⁵** אA,C (44.4%) ‖ καταλαλωσιν (50%)
　　　　　‖ καταλαλεισθε P⁷²B (5%);　　　　　　　　　　　　　[no **Kˣ**]

3:16 τη αγαθη εν χριστω αναστροφη **f³⁵** [20%]
　　　　　‖ την αγαθην 34 αναστροφην (א)A,B [50%]
　　　　　‖ την 34 αγαθην αναστροφην P⁷² [24%]
　　　　　‖ την 34 αγινην αναστροφην C [1%]
　　　　　‖ την καλην 34 αναστροφην [4%] ‖ --- [1%];　　　　　[no **Kˣ**]

3:18 ημας **f³⁵** A,C [64%] ‖ υμας P⁷²B [36%] ‖ --- א;　　　　　[no **Kˣ**]

4:02 του **f³⁵** [22%] ‖ --- P⁷²אA,B,C [78%];

4:03 υμιν **f³⁵** א (41.7%) ‖ ημιν C (47.1%) ‖ --- P⁷²A,B (11.2%);　[no **Kˣ**]

4:03 χρονος **f³⁵** P⁷²אA,B,C [26%] ‖ χρονος του βιου [74%];

4:03 ειδωλολατριαις **f³⁵** אA,C [70%] ‖ ειδωλολατρειαις B [30%];　?[no **Kˣ**]

4:07 τας **f³⁵** [70%] ‖ --- P⁷²אA,B [30%];　　　　　　　　　　?[no **Kˣ**]

4:08 η **f³⁵** [49%] ‖ --- P⁷²אA,B [51%];　　　　　　　　　　　[no **Kˣ**]

4:08 καλυπτει **f³⁵** A,B [60%] ‖ καλυψει P⁷²א [40%];　　　　　[no **Kˣ**]

4:11 ως **f³⁵** [69%] ‖ ης P⁷²אA,B,201 [28%] ‖ --- [3%];　　　　[no **Kˣ**]

4:11 δοξαζηται Θεος **f³⁵** [20%] ‖ 1 ο 2 P⁷²אA,B [73%] ‖ ~ο 21 [6%];

4:11 αιωνας **f³⁵** P⁷² [27%] ‖ αιωνας των αιωνων אA,B [73%];

4:14 αναπεπαυται **f³⁵** [39%] ‖ επαναπαυεται A [6%] ‖ επαναπεπαυται P⁷² [2%]
　　　　　‖ αναπαυεται אB [52%] ‖ αναπεμπεται [1%];　　　　?[no **Kˣ**]

5:03 μηδε **f³⁵** P⁷² [49%] ‖ μηδ אA [50%];　　　　　　　　　　[no **Kˣ**]

5:07 υπερ **f³⁵** [35%] ‖ περι P⁷²אA,B [65%];

5:08 οτι **f³⁵** P⁷² [50%] ‖ --- אA,B [50%];　　　　　　　　　　[no **Kˣ**]

5:08 περιερχεται **f³⁵** [24%] ‖ περιπατει P⁷²אA,B [76%];

5:08 καταπιειν **f³⁵** (א)B [53%] ‖ καταπιει [25%] ‖ καταπιη P⁷²A [22%];　[no **Kˣ**]

5:10 στηριξαι **f³⁵** [33%] ‖ στηριξει P⁷²אA,B [66%] ‖ στηριξοι [1%];

5:10 σθενωσαι **f³⁵** [30%] || σθενωσει ℵA,B [66%]
|| σθενωσοι [1%] || --- P⁷² [3%];
5:10 θεμελιωσαι **f³⁵** [30%] || θεμελιωσει P⁷²ℵ [66%]
|| θεμελιωσοι [1%] || --- A,B [3%];
5:11 η δοξα και το κρατος **f³⁵** ℵ (59.6%) || 125 (31.3%)
|| ~ 45312 (7%) || 4 (-το P⁷²) 5 P⁷²A,B (0.8%). [no **Kˣ**]

The archetypal profile of **f³⁵** in 1 Peter is defined by the 42 readings above. It is clear and unambiguous, so we have at least one objectively defined archetype in 1 Peter. In contrast, there are 24 + ?6 variant sets where **Kˣ** is seriously divided, placing an objectively defined archetype beyond our present reach. (I did not include a number of lesser splits—25%, 20%, 15%—that conceivably could complicate any attempt to come up with an archetype for **Kˣ**. Please go back to James for other comments.) Let's go on to 2 Peter.

## 2 Peter

1:02 ιησου του κυριου ημων **f³⁵** (P⁷²)B,C [68%] [234 1.4%]
|| 1 χριστου 234 ℵA [15%] || χριστου 1234 [8%]
|| σωτηρος 1 χριστου 234 [1.2%] || ~ 2341 χριστου [6%];
[no **Kˣ**]
1:05 δε τουτο **f³⁵** ℵ [66%] || ~ 21 P⁷²B,C [32%] || 1 A [1%] || 2 [0.8%];
[no **Kˣ**]
2:02 ας **f³⁵** [20%] || ους P⁷²ℵA,B,C [80%];
2:09 πειρασμων **f³⁵** ℵ [33%] || πειρασμου (P⁷²)A,B,C [67%];
2:12 γεγενημενα φυσικα **f³⁵** ℵ [26%] || ~ 21 [54%]
|| γεγεννημενα 2 A,B,C [3%] || ~ 2 γεγεννημενα [12%]
|| 1 [4.2%] || 2 P⁷² [0.4%]; ?[no **Kˣ**]
2:17 εις αιωνας **f³⁵** (25.1%) || 1 αιωνα A,C (70.3%)
|| 1 τον αιωνα (2.4%) || --- P⁷²ℵB (2.2%);
2:18 ασελγειας **f³⁵** [40%] || ασελγειαις P⁷²ℵA,B,C [60%];
3:02 υμων **f³⁵** P⁷²ℵA,B,C [70%] || ημων [28.8%] || --- [1.2%]; ?[no **Kˣ**]
3:05 συνεστωτα **f³⁵** ℵ [23%] || συνεστωσα P⁷²A,C(048) [76%];
3:10 η **f³⁵** ℵ,048 [67%] || η οι P⁷²A,B,C [33%]; [no **Kˣ**]
3:15 αυτω δοθεισαν **f³⁵** [60%] || ~ 21 P⁷²(ℵ)A,B,C,048 [40%]; [no **Kˣ**]
3:16 εισιν **f³⁵** A [33%] || εστιν P⁷²ℵB,C [67%];
3:18 αυξανητε **f³⁵** [27%] || αυξανετε ℵA,B [60%] || αυξανεσθε P⁷²C [5%]
|| αυξανησθε [3%] || αυξανοιτε [5%].

The archetypal profile of **f³⁵** in 2 Peter is defined by the 13 readings above. It is clear and unambiguous, so we have at least one objectively defined archetype in 2 Peter. **Kˣ** is in unusually good shape here, so the diagnostic readings are comparatively fewer. The 4 + ?2 variant sets where **Kˣ** is seriously divided are sufficiently few in number that it might be possible to posit an archetype. (I did not include a number of lesser splits—25%, 20%, 15%—that conceivably could complicate any such attempt. Please go back to James for other comments.) Let's go on to 1 John.

## 1 John

1:04 ημων **f³⁵** ℵB [59%] || υμων A,C [41%]; [no **Kˣ**]
1:06 περιπατουμεν **f³⁵** [29%] || περιπατωμεν **f³⁵¹/⁴** ℵA,B,C [71%];

2:16 αλαζονεια **f³⁵** C [72%] || αλαζονια אA,B [28%];                    ?[no **Kˣ**]
2:24 πατρι και εν τω υιω **f³⁵** א [35%] || ~ 52341 A(B)C [65%]
2:27 διδασκη **f³⁵** אA,B [71%] || διδασκει C [28%];                    ?[no **Kˣ**]
2:29 ειδητε **f³⁵** אB,C [37%] || ιδητε A [59%] || οιδατε [4%];
2:29 γεγεννηται **f³⁵** אA,B,C [70%] || γεγενηται [30%];                    [no **Kˣ**]
3:01 ημας **f³⁵** A,B [36%] || υμας אC [63.5%] || --- [0.5%];
3:06 και **f³⁵** [20%] || --- אA,B,C [80%];
3:15 εαυτω **f³⁵** אA,C [70%] || αυτω B [30%];                    [no **Kˣ**]
3:17 θεωρη **f³⁵** אA,B,C [47%] || θεωρει [53%];                    ?[no **Kˣ**]
3:18 εν **f³⁵** אA,B,C [65%] || --- [35%];                    [no **Kˣ**]
3:19 πεισωμεν **f³⁵** [43%] || πεισομεν אA,B,C [56%]
3:21 καταγινωσκη **f³⁵** אB,C [71%] || καταγινωσκει A [29%];                    ?[no **Kˣ**]
3:23 πιστευσωμεν **f³⁵** B (66.9%) || πιστευωμεν אA,C (26.5%)
              || πιστευομεν (5.4%) || πιστευσομεν (1.2%);                    [no **Kˣ**]
3:24 εν **f³⁵** א [30%] || και εν A,B,Cᵛ [70%];
4:02 γινωσκεται **f³⁵** [67%] || γινωσκετε A,B,C [25%] || γινωσκομεν א [8%];
                    [no **Kˣ**]
4:03 ομολογει **f³⁵** א (73.5%) || ομολογει τον A,B (24.2%);                    ?[no **Kˣ**]
4:03 εκ **f³⁵** אA,B [70%] || --- [30%];                    [no **Kˣ**]
4:16 αυτω **f³⁵** A [37%] || αυτω μενει אB [63%];
5:04 ημων **f³⁵** א,A,B (56.4%) || υμων (43.2%) || --- (0.4%);                    [no **Kˣ**]
5:06 και **f³⁵** א [70%] || και εν (A)B [30%];                    [no **Kˣ**]
5:10 εαυτω **f³⁵** א [48%] || αυτω A,B [52%];                    ?[no **Kˣ**]
5:11 ο θεος ημιν **f³⁵** B [24%] || ~ 312 אA [76%];
5:20 γινωσκωμεν **f³⁵** [66%] || γινωσκομεν אA,B [34%];                    [no **Kˣ**]
5:20 η ζωη η **f³⁵** [60%] || 2 אA,B [26%] || 12 [6%]
              || 23 [4%] || --- [4%].                    [no **Kˣ**]

The archetypal profile of **f³⁵** in 1 John is defined by the 26 readings above. It is clear and unambiguous, so we have at least one objectively defined archetype in 1 John. In contrast, there are 11 + ?6 variant sets where **Kˣ** is seriously divided, placing an objectively defined archetype beyond our present reach. (I did not include a number of lesser splits—25%, 20%, 15%—that conceivably could complicate any attempt to come up with an archetype for **Kˣ**. Please go back to James for other comments.) Let's go on to 2 & 3 John.

## 2 John

02 εσται μεθ υμων **f³⁵** [58%] || εσται μεθ ημων אB,0232 [40%] || --- A [2%];
                    [no **Kˣ**]
05 αλλ **f³⁵** A [35%] || αλλα אB [65%];
05 εχομεν **f³⁵** [30%] || ειχομεν אA,B [70%];
09 δε **f³⁵** [20%] || --- אA,B [80%];
12 αλλ **f³⁵** [30%] || αλλα אA,B [70%].

## 3 John

11 δε **f³⁵** [25%] || --- אA,B,C [75%];
12 οιδαμεν **f³⁵** (23%) || οιδατε (61.5%) || οιδας אA,B,C,048 (15.1%) || οιδα (0.4%).

The archetypal profile of **f³⁵** in 2 & 3 John is defined by the 7 readings above. It is clear and unambiguous, so we have at least one objectively defined archetype in these books. $K^x$ is in unusually good shape here, so the diagnostic readings are comparatively fewer. With only one variant set where $K^x$ is seriously divided it may be possible to posit an archetype. Let's go on to Jude.

### Jude

06 αλλ $f^{35}$ C [30%] || αλλα $P^{72}$אA,B [70%];
16 εαυτων $f^{35}$ C [35%] || αυτων אA,B [65%];
24 αυτους $f^{35}$ (68.8%) || υμας אB,C (29.2%) || ημας A (1%).                    ?[no $K^x$]

The archetypal profile of $f^{35}$ in Jude is defined by the 3 readings above. It is clear and unambiguous, so we have at least one objectively defined archetype in this book. $K^x$ is in unusually good shape here, so the diagnostic readings are comparatively fewer. With only one variant set where $K^x$ is seriously divided it may be possible to posit an archetype.

**Conclusion:** Taking the seven epistles as a block or group, the evidence presented furnishes an answer to the opening question: there is only one objectively identifiable archetype in the General Epistles—precisely $f^{35}$. Its distinctive profile is defined by the 119 readings listed above. In contrast, there are 54 + ?18 variant sets where $K^x$ is seriously divided, making it highly doubtful that a single $K^x$ archetype exists for these books. (I did not include a number of lesser splits—28 around 25%, 53 around 20%, 57 around 15%—that conceivably could complicate any attempt to establish an archetype for $K^x$, especially if the membership in the splits is not constant or predictable.) I am not aware of any other possible contenders. Granting the present state of our ignorance, in the General Epistles there is only one qualified candidate for Autograph archetype: $f^{35}$. (If there is only one candidate for mayor in your town, who gets elected?)

# Concerning the Text of the *Pericope Adulterae*

The information offered below is based on Maurice A. Robinson's complete collation of 1,389 MSS that contain the Pericope, John 7:53 - 8:11.[1] I attempted to establish a profile of readings for each of the three main groups of MSS, $M^{5,6,7}$ (as in the apparatus of the H-F Majority Text). I take it that the smaller groups are all mixtures based on the big three. This section presents the results, along with my interpretation of their significance.

---

[1] 240 MSS omit the PA, 64 of which are based on Theophylact's commentary. Fourteen others have lacunae, but are not witnesses for total omission. A few others certainly contain the passage but the microfilm is illegible. So, 1389 + 240 + 14 + 7(?) = about 1650 MSS checked by Robinson. (These are microfilms held by the *Institut* in Münster. We now know that there are many more extant MSS, and probably even more that are not yet 'extant'.)

# $M^7$ Profile

| 7:53 | 01 | απηλθεν |
|------|-----|---------|
| 8:1 | 02 | Ιησους δε |
| 8:2 | 03 | (βαθεως) = omit |
| 8:2 | 04 | παρεγενετο |
| 8:2 | 05 | προς αυτον |
| 8:3 | 06 | προς αυτον |
| 8:3 | 07 | επι |
| 8:3 | 08 | κατειλημμενην |
| 8:3 | 09 | εν μεσω |
| 8:4 | 10 | λεγουσιν |
| 8:4 | 11 | (πειραζοντες) |
| 8:4 | 12 | ταυτην ευρομεν |
| 8:4 | 13 | επαυτοφωρω |
| 8:4 | 14 | μοιχευομενην |
| 8:5 | 15 | ημων Μωσης |
| 8:5 | 16 | λιθοβολεισθαι |
| 8:5 | 17 | (περι αυτης) |
| 8:6 | 18 | κατηγοριαν κατ |
| 8:6 | 19 | μη προσποιουμενος |
| 8:7 | 20 | ερωτωντες |
| 8:7 | 21 | ανακυψας |
| 8:7 | 22 | προς αυτους |
| 8:7 | 23 | τον λιθον επ αυτη βαλετω |
| 8:9 | 24 | και υπο της συνειδησεως ελεγχομενοι |
| 8:9 | 25 | εως των εσχατων |
| 8:9 | 26 | μονος ο Ιησους |
| 8:10 | 27 | και μηδενα θεασαμενος πλην της γυναικος |
| 8:10 | 28 | αυτη |
| 8:10 | 29 | εκεινοι οι κατηγοροι σου |
| 8:11 | 30 | ειπεν δε αυτη ο Ιησους |
| 8:11 | 31 | κατακρινω |
| 8:11 | 32 | και απο του νυν |

**Comment**: This is a single, clear-cut, unambiguous profile/mosaic, as defined by 127 MSS—there is no internal variation among them. This contrasts dramatically with $M^6$ and $M^5$, and I suppose with the lesser groups (though I haven't checked them). As given below, it is possible to come up with a profile for both **5** and **6**, for purposes of distinguishing them from each other and from **7**, but they have so much internal variation that I see no way to come up with an archetype that is objectively defined; both will have to be subdivided. The profile above defines the archetypal text of $M^7$.

## M⁶ Profile

| | | |
|---|---|---|
| 7:53 | 01 | απηλθεν / απηλθον |
| 8:1 | 02 | \*\*και ο Ιησους δε / και ο Ιησους |
| 8:2 | 03 | \*\*βαθεως / βαθεος |
| 8:2 | 04 | \*\*ηλθεν ο Ιησους |
| 8:2 | 05 | προς αυτον |
| 8:3 | 06 | (προς αυτον) / προς αυτον |
| 8:3 | 07 | επι |
| 8:3 | 08 | κατειλημμενην |
| 8:3 | 09 | εν τω μεσω / εν μεσω |
| 8:4 | 10 | \*\*ειπον |
| 8:4 | 11 | (πειραζοντες) = omit |
| 8:4 | 12 | ταυτην ευρομεν |
| 8:4 | 13 | επαυτοφωρω / –φορω / –φορως |
| 8:4 | 14 | μοιχευομενην / –νη |
| 8:5 | 15 | ημων Μωσης / υμων Μωσης / Μ. ενετ. ημιν / Μωσης |
| 8:5 | 16 | \*\*λιθαζειν |
| 8:5 | 17 | (περι αυτης) / περι αυτης |
| 8:6 | 18 | κατηγοριαν κατ |
| 8:6 | 19 | (μη προσποιουμενος) / μη προσποιουμενος |
| 8:7 | 20 | ερωτωντες / επερωτωντες |
| 8:7 | 21 | αναβλεψας / ανακυψας |
| 8:7 | 22 | \*\*αυτοις |
| 8:7 | 23 | \*\*λιθον βαλετω επ αυτην |
| 8:9 | 24 | (και υπο της συνειδησεως ελεγχομενοι) /και υπο της συνειδησεως ελεγχομενοι |
| 8:9 | 25 | εως των εσχατων |
| 8:9 | 26 | ο Ιησους μονος / μονος |
| 8:10 | 27 | \*\*(και μηδενα θεασαμενος πλην της γυναικος) |
| 8:10 | 28 | \*\*ειδεν αυτην και ειπεν |
| 8:10 | 29 | \*\*(αυτη) γυναι |
| 8:10 | 30 | (εκεινοι) / (εκεινοι οι κατηγοροι σου) / (που εκεινοι οι κατηγοροι σου) |
| 8:11 | 31 | ειπεν δε αυτη ο Ιησους |
| 8:11 | 32 | κατακρινω |
| 8:11 | 33 | πορευου και απο του νυν / πορευου απο του νυν και |

**Comment**: I checked the M⁶ MSS from the **XI** century (over 80) and to my surprise no two of them had an identical mosaic of variants. No matter what contrastive set one uses as a basis (e.g. βαθεως X βαθεος), as soon as you look down the roster of other variants the MSS wander back and forth, producing a bewildering array of variation, shifting alliances, or whatever. If all the centuries are checked, there will presumably be a few small groups wherein the member MSS share identical mosaics, but no single definitive profile for **M⁶** will emerge (in contrast to **M⁷**). If there is no single profile, then there is no objective way to define / establish / reconstruct an archetype for **M⁶**. Without a definable

189

archetype, **M**[6] is not a viable candidate for the original form of the Text. However, the ten variants marked by ** do distinguish **M**[6] from both **M**[5] and **M**[7], forming its 'backbone'. But two of the ten, plus another fourteen, have internal variation (besides a variety of further variation not recorded in this list). The individual MSS meander around the plethora of internal (within the group) variation in a bewildering manner, all of which diminishes the credibility of the group. I take it that **M**[6] reflects Alexandrian influence.

## *M*[5] *Profile*

| 7:53 | 01 | **εnoρευθη / εnoρευθησαν |
|------|----|------|
| 8:1  | 02 | Ιησους δε |
| 8:2  | 03 | (βαθεως) = omit |
| 8:2  | 04 | παρεγενετο |
| 8:2  | 05 | **(προς αυτον) |
| 8:3  | 06 | προς αυτον |
| 8:3  | 07 | **εν |
| 8:3  | 08 | **καταληφθεισαν |
| 8:3  | 09 | εν μεσω |
| 8:4  | 10 | λεγουσιν |
| 8:4  | 11 | **πειραζοντες |
| 8:4  | 12 | **αυτη η γυνη |
| 8:4  | 13 | **κατεληφθη / ειληπται / κατειληπται |
| 8:4  | 14 | επαυτοφωρω / –φορω |
| 8:4  | 15 | **μοιχευομενη |
| 8:5  | 16 | **Μωσης ημιν |
| 8:5  | 17 | λιθοβολεισθαι |
| 8:5  | 18 | (περι αυτης) |
| 8:6  | 19 | **κατηγορειν |
| 8:6  | 20 | μη προσποιουμενος |
| 8:7  | 21 | ερωτωντες |
| 8:7  | 22 | ανακυψας |
| 8:7  | 23 | προς αυτους |
| 8:7  | 24 | **επ αυτην τον λιθον βαλετω |
| 8:9  | 25 | και υπο της συνειδησεως ελεγχομενοι |
| 8:9  | 26 | **(εως των εσχατων) |
| 8:9  | 27 | μονος ο Ιησους |
| 8:10 | 28 | και μηδενα θεασαμενος πλην της γυναικος |
| 8:10 | 29 | αυτη / αυτη γυναι |
| 8:10 | 30 | εκεινοι οι κατηγοροι σου |
| 8:11 | 31 | **ειπεν δε ο Ιησους |
| 8:11 | 32 | **κρινω / κατακρινω |
| 8:11 | 33 | και |

**Comment**: Setting aside the splits in #1,13,14,29,32 there is a group of MSS with this profile. There is an equally large group that changes εγραφεν to κατεγραφεν in verse 6 and changes πρωτος to πρωτον in verse 7. Both of these groups have a core of MSS that have a 'perfect' profile, except that both groups split on -φωρω/-φορω. Both groups have 'fuzzy' edges with numerous MSS showing various degrees of variation. There is a large number of mixed MSS, clustering around several roughly defined mosaics. Also there is a three-way split in variant #24, plus a fourth lesser variant (205 MSS x 191 x 104 x 21). However, the variants with ** do distinguish $M^5$ from both $M^6$ and $M^7$, forming its 'backbone', although there is internal variation in three of them, besides #24. There is further internal variation not recorded in this list. $M^5$ is not as 'squishy' as $M^6$, but not as solid as $M^7$. I take it that $M^5$ reflects Latin influence. In any event, it looks to be scarcely possible to establish a single archetype for $M^5$, which it must have to be a viable candidate for the original form of the Text. Evidently the original form is the ultimate archetype.

## Unambiguous $M^7$ ($f^{35}$) representatives = 245 MSS

a) Perfect match (core representatives)—**XI**: 35, 83, 547, 1435; **XII**: 510, 768,1046,1323,1329,1489, 1490,2296,2367,2382; **XIII**: 128, 141, 147, 154, 167, 170, 204, 361, 553, 676, 685, 696, 757, 825, 897, 1072, 1251, 1339, 1400, 1461, 1496, 1499, 1550, 1551, 1576, 1694, 2284, 2479, 2510; **XIV**: 18, 55, 66, 201, 246, 363, 386, 402, 415, 480, 586, 645, 758, 763, 769, 781, 789, 797, 824, 845, 867, 928, 932, 938, 960, 986, 1023, 1075, 1092, 1111, 1117, 1119, 1133, 1146, 1189, 1236, 1328, 1390, 1482, 1488, 1492, 1493, 1548, 1560, 1572, 1584, 1600, 1619, 1620, 1628, 1633, 1637, 1650, 1659, 1667, 1688, 1698, 1703, 2261, 2355, 2407, 2454, 2503, 2765, 2767; **XV**: 955, 958, 962, 1003, 1180, 1250, 1508, 1625, 1636, 1648, 1686, 1713, 2131, 2554; **XVI**: 1596, 1652, 2496, 2636, 2806 = 127 MSS

b) Major subgroup: in 8:4 it has επαυτοφορω (only change)—**XII**: 660, 1145, 1224; **XIII**: 479, 689, 691, 940, 1334, 1487, 1501, 1601, 2584, 2598; **XIV**: 189, 290, 394, 521, 890, 959, 1025, 1165, 1234, 1445, 1462, 1476, 1543, 1559, 1614, 1618, 1622, 1634, 1657, 1658, 2309, 2399, 2466, 2621, 2689; **XV**: 285, 961, 1017, 1059, 1132, 1158, 1247, 1649, 1656, 2204, 2221, 2352, 2692; **XVI**: 1680, 1702, 2255; **XVII**: 1700 = 55 MSS

c) Minor subgroup: in 8:9 it has κατελημφθη (only change)—**XIII**: 155, 2520; **XIV**: 588, 1185; **XV**: 1617; **XVI**: 1088 = 6 MSS

d) Minor subgroup: in 8:7 it has τον λιθον βαλετω επ αυτην (only change)—**XII**: 1199; **XIV**: 953, 1020, 1147; **XV**: 1389 = 5 MSS

e) Other MSS with a single change—**XII**: 520, 1401, 2122, 2322; **XIII**: 2647; **XIV**: 1095, 1503, 2273, 2508; **XV**: 575, 2673; **XVI**: 1030; **XVII**: 2136, 2137, 2497 = 15 MSS

+2) MSS with two changes
    b) + c)—**XII**: 1453, 2559; **XV**: 1131; **XVIII**: 1325
    b) + d)—**XII**: 387, 1813; **XIII**: 1552
    b) + e)—**XII**: 2260; **XIV**: 1599, 1638, 1544
    b) + odd—<u>X: 1166</u>; **XIV**: 952, 978,1062; **XVI**: 1591,2714 $\Big\}$ = 27 MSS
    d) + e)—**XIII**: 1477,1497; **XIV**: 1181,1248; **XVI**: 2635
    2 odd—**XI**: 1314,1384; **XIV**: 2265; **XV**: 1116,1348

+3) MSS with three changes:
    b) + c) + odd—**XII**: 105; **XVI**: 2715
    b) + d) + e)—**XIV**: 806
    b) + d) + odd—**XII**: 353; **XIII**: 966 $\Big\}$ = 10 MSS
    b) + e) + odd—**XV**: 664
    b) + 2 odd—**XII**: 2632; **XV**: 56; **XVI**: 61
    + 3 odd—**XV**: 58

**Comment**: b) and c) differ from a) only in a similar sounding vowel, while variants 8 and 14 involve a single letter. There is a small sub-group (with fuzzy edges) based on variants 17,20,29. There is a larger, fuzzier group that has variants 1,16,17,28,29 as sort of a basis, with 9,19 on the fringes, and then further variation. There are 40-50 MSS with varying amounts of mixture added to an $M^7$ base (adding these to the unambiguous ones and dividing by 1650 we come out with about 18%). Actually, I believe that $M^7$ was the base from which the creators of $M^5$ and $M^6$ (and all other groups) departed.

**Interpretative comment**: The progressive 'purification' of the stream of transmission through the centuries (from a Byzantine priority perspective) has been recognized by all and sundry, their attempts at explaining the phenomenon generally reflecting their presuppositions. From my point of view the evident explanation is this: All camps recognize that the heaviest attacks against the purity of the Text took place during the second century. But 'the heartland of the Church', the Aegean area, by far the best qualified in every way to watch over the faithful transmission, simply refused to copy the aberrant forms. MSS containing such forms were not used (nor copied), so many survived physically for over a millennium. Less bad forms were used (copies were hard to come by) but progressively were not copied. Thus the surviving IX century uncials are fair, over 80% Byzantine, but not good enough to be copied (when the better MSS were put into minuscule form). Until the advent of a printed text, MSS were made to be used. Progressively only the best were used, and thus worn out, and copied. This process culminated in the XIV century, when the Ottoman shadow was advancing over Asia Minor, but the Byzantine empire still stood. But by the beginning of the XV century, even though Constantinople didn't actually fall for 45 years, the future was dark and people became preoccupied with survival.

Please note the 'from a Byzantine priority perspective'. **Family 35 was copied faithfully from beginning to end**. For a number of books I myself have a perfect copy done in the 14th century (also the 13th, 12th, 11th). For a copy done in the 14th to be perfect, <u>all of its 'ancestors' had to be perfect as well</u>. Please note that a perfect copy makes all the 'canons' of textual criticism irrelevant to any point subsequent to the creation of the archetype. But how can we know that a given copy is 'perfect'? The archetypal profile can be empirically established by comparing all the extant family representatives (I am referring to $f^{35}$ only). A copy that matches the archetype perfectly is a perfect copy, of necessity. But perfect copies tell us something important about the attitude of the copyists. That they should do their work with such care presumably indicates at least respect, if not reverence toward what they were copying—they believed they were copying God's Word. Since MSS from all other lines of transmission were copied with less care, presumably the copyists made a distinction in their minds, evidently considering $f^{35}$ to be the best line.

# Incredibly Careful Transmission

This section focuses on the Thessalonian epistles, generally thought to have been the first of the apostle Paul's canonical writings (at least in conservative circles). If so, his prestige and authority as an apostle would not yet have reached its full stature, and in consequence such early writings might not have been accorded as much respect as later ones. As I continue collating more and more $f^{35}$ MSS I have been surprised by a different picture. I have collated the following thirty-four representatives of the family and invite attention to the results.

## *Performance of $f^{35}$ MSS in the Thessalonian Epistles*

| MS | 1 Thess. | 2 Thess | Location | Date[1] | Exemplar |
|---|---|---|---|---|---|
| 18 | --- | --- | Constantinople[2] | 1364 | --- |
| 35 | 2c | --- | Aegean[3] | XI | --- |
| 201 | 2y,2*l* | 2x | London | 1357 | 2x,2y,2*l* |
| 204 | 1*l* | --- | Bologna | XIII | 1*l* |
| 328 | 1*l*,1s | 2s | Leiden | XIII | 1*l* |
| 386 | 1y,1*l*,1s | 1s | Vatican | XIV | 1y,1*l* |
| 394 | 1s | --- | Rome | 1330 | --- |
| 444 | 1s | 2s | London | XV | --- |
| 604 | 1x,1y | 1s | Paris | XIV | 1x,1y |
| 757 | 1s | 1y,1c | Athens | XIII | 1y |
| 824 | --- | 1i | Grottaferrata | XIV | --- |
| 928 | --- | --- | Dionysiu (Athos) | 1304 | --- |
| 986 | 1s | 1s | Esphigmenu (Athos) | XIV | --- |
| 1072 | 1i | --- | M. Lavras (Athos) | XIII | --- |
| 1075 | 1x,1*l* | --- | M. Lavras | XIV | 1x,1*l* |
| 1100 | 1y,1s | 1y | Dionysiu | 1376 | 2y |
| 1248 | 3x,1*l*,4s | 2s,2i | Sinai | XIV | 3x,1*l* |
| 1249 | 1y | --- | Sinai | 1324 | 1y |

---

[1] I give the location and date as in the *Kurzgefasste Liste* (1994), although I must admit to an occasional doubt as to the accuracy of the dating.

[2] Although presently in Paris, 18 was produced in Constantinople.

[3] Although presently in Paris, 35 was acquired in the Aegean area.

| 1503 | 2s | --- | M. Lavras | 1317 | --- |
|------|------|------|-----------|------|------|
| 1548 | 2x,1s | 1s | Vatopediu (Athos) | 1359 | 2x |
| 1637 | 1/ | --- | M. Lavras | 1328 | 1/ |
| 1725 | 2/ | 1/ | Vatopediu | 1367 | 3/ |
| 1732 | 1y,2s | 1/ | M. Lavras | 1384 | 1y,1/ |
| 1761 | 2x,2y,1s | 1s,1i | Athens | XIV | 2x,2y |
| 1855 | --- | 1s | Iviron (Athos) | XIII | --- |
| 1864 | --- | --- | Stavronikita (Athos) | XIII | --- |
| 1865 | 1c | --- | Philotheu (Athens) | XIII | --- |
| 1876 | 4y,1/ | 1y,1/ | Sinai | XV | 5y,2/ |
| 1892 | 10s | 3s | Jerusalem | XIV | --- |
| 1897 | 1/,1c | 3s,1h | Jerusalem | XII | 1/ |
| 2466 | 1x,2y,1s | 1s | Patmos | 1329 | 1x,2y |
| 2554 | 1c | --- | Bucharest | 1434 | --- |
| 2587 | 1s | 1s | Vatican | XI | --- |
| 2723 | --- | --- | Trikala | XI | --- |

Key:

x = an uncorrected variant that it is attested by MSS outside the family;

y = a split that is not limited to the family;

/ = a split within the family (no outside attestation);

c = a variant of any kind that has been corrected to the presumed archetype;

s = singular reading / private variant (until all MSS have been collated, this is just an assumption);

h = an obvious case of homoioteleuton (or –arcton), often involving a line or more, but can be just three or four words;

i = sheer inattention.

**Implications**

I begin with the last column in the chart, 'Exemplar'. Except for 18, 928, 1864 and 2723 that are themselves perfect, most of the others have a different rating. All singular readings should be discounted (including homoioteleuton and inattention); if not introduced by the copyist it was done by the 'father' or 'grandfather'—an ancestor was free of all 'singulars', so they contribute nothing to the history of the transmission, are not relevant to the tracing of that transmission. All variants that were corrected to the presumed family profile should also be discounted—whoever did the correcting, it was done on the basis of a correct exemplar (correct at that point). So I only attribute 'x', 'y' and '/' to the exemplar—of course some of these could be the work of the copyist as well, which would make the exemplar even better, but I have no way of knowing when that occurred.

Notice that of thirty-four MSS, sixteen of their exemplars (almost half) were 'perfect', and another six were off by only one variant (the worst was only off by seven, for two books). If there were no splinters, we could be looking at thirty-four independent lines of transmission, within the family, which to me is simply fantastic.[1] But what about the splinters? There are a few very minor ones in 1 Thessalonians, and only a few pairs in 2 Thessalonians.

I conclude that all thirty-four MSS were independent in their generation, and I see no evidence to indicate a different conclusion for their exemplars. Please note that I am not claiming that all thirty-four lines remain distinct all the way back to the archetype. I cheerfully grant that there would be a number of convergences before getting back to the source. However all that may be, we are looking at very careful transmission.

I now invite attention to location. The MSS come from all over the Mediterranean world. The thirteen Mt. Athos MSS were certainly produced in their respective monasteries (seven). Ecclesiastical politics tending to be what it tends to be, there is little likelihood that there would be collusion between the monasteries on the transmission of the NT writings—I regard the thirteen as representing as many exemplars. MSS from Trikala, Patmos, Jerusalem and Sinai were presumably produced there; cursive 18 was certainly produced in Constantinople; cursive 35 was acquired in the Aegean area. The MSS at the Vatican and Grottaferrata may very well have been produced there.

I now invite special attention to minuscule 18, produced in Constantinople in **1364**! As it stands it is a perfect representative of the presumed family profile for the Thessalonian epistles (I say 'presumed' only out of deference to all the family representatives that I haven't collated yet, but given the geographical distribution of the thirty-four above, I have no doubt that the profile as given in my Text is correct).[2] How many generations of copies would there have been between MS 18 and the family archetype? Might there have been fifteen, or more? I would imagine that there were at least ten. However many there actually were, please note that every last one of them was perfect! *The implications of finding a perfect representative of any archetypal text are rather powerful. All the 'canons' of textual criticism become irrelevant to any point subsequent to the creation of that text* (they could still come into play when studying the creation of the text, in the event). For MS 18 to be perfect, all the generations in between had to be perfect as well. Now I call this **incredibly careful transmission**. Nothing that I was taught in Seminary about New Testament textual criticism prepared me for this discovery! Nor anything that I had read, for that matter. But MS 18 is not an isolated case; all the thirty-four MSS in the chart above reflect an **incredibly careful transmission**—even the worst of the lot, minuscules 1761 and 1874, with their seven variants [the 'singulars' in 1893 and 1248 are careless mistakes {unhappy monks}], are really quite good, considering all the intervening generations.

---

[1] 18, 928, 1864 and 2723 were produced in Constantinople, Dionysiu, Stavronikita and Trikala, respectively—I consider it to be virtually impossible that they should have a common exemplar (of course they could join somewhere back down the line).

[2] Actually I have now collated 39 family representatives for 1 Thessalonians and 38 for 2 Thessalonians. They probably represent at least 40% of the total extant membership, so there can really be no doubt that they correctly represent the family archetype.

This point deserves some elaboration. A typical 'Alexandrian' MS will have over a dozen variants per page of printed Greek text. A typical 'Byzantine' MS will have 3-5 variants per page. MSS 1761 and 1876 have about one per page, and one of the better $f^{35}$ MSS will go for pages without a variant. There is an obvious difference in the mentality that the monks brought to their task. A monk copying an 'Alexandrian' MS evidently did not consider that he was handling Scripture, in stark contrast to one copying an $f^{35}$ MS. For those who do not exclude the supernatural from their model, I submit that the information above is highly significant: obviously God was not protecting any 'Alexandrian' type of MS, probably because it contained 'tares' (Matthew 13:28). A monk copying a 'Byzantine' bulk type MS did far better work than the Alexandrian, but still wasn't being sufficiently careful—he was probably just doing a religious duty, but without personal commitment to the Text. Since God respects our choices (John 4:23-24), the result was a typical 'Byzantine' MS. It is also true that not all $f^{35}$ MSS were carefully done, but I conclude that the core representatives were done by copyists who believed they were handling God's Word and wanted their work to be pleasing to Him[1]—just the kind that the Holy Spirit would delight to aid and protect.

## Performance of $f^{35}$ MSS in 2 & 3 John and Jude

This section focuses on 2 & 3 John and Jude. I have collated forty-six representatives of Family 35, so far (for these three books), and invite attention to the results. I have so far identified 84 MSS as belonging to $f^{35}$ in the General Epistles (plus another 10 or 12 on the fringes), so this sample is certainly representative, considering also the geographic distribution.

| MS | 2 John | 3 John | Jude | Location | Date | Exemplar |
|----|--------|--------|------|----------|------|----------|
| 18 | --- | 1s | --- | Constantinople | 1364 | --- |
| 35 | --- | --- | 2c | Aegean | XI | --- |
| 141 | --- | --- | --- | Vatican | XIII | --- |
| 149 | --- | 1/ | 1/,1c | Vatican | XV | 2/ |
| 201 | --- | 1/ | 1/ | London | 1357 | 2/ |
| 204 | --- | --- | --- | Bologna | XIII | --- |
| 328 | --- | --- | 1x,1s | Leiden | XIII | 1x |
| 386 | --- | --- | --- | Vatican | XIV | --- |
| 394 | --- | 1i | --- | Rome | 1330 | --- |
| 432 | 2s | 1/ | 3s | Vatican | XV | 1/ |
| 444[2] | --- | --- | 1s | London | XV | --- |
| 604 | 1x | 1/ | --- | Paris | XIV | 1x,1/ |
| 664 | 1x,1s | 3s | 3s | Zittau | XV | 1x |
| 757 | 2s | --- | --- | Athens | XIII | --- |
| 824 | --- | --- | --- | Grottaferrata | XIV | --- |

---

[1] It is not at all uncommon to find a colophon at the end of a MS where the copyist calls on God for His mercy, and even for His recognition and blessing.

[2] 444 is a mixed MS. In James, 1&2 Peter it is not at all $f^{35}$, while in 1 John it is a very marginal member of the family.

| 928 | --- | --- | --- | Dionysiu (Athos) | 1304 | --- |
|---|---|---|---|---|---|---|
| 986 | 1s | --- | 1s,1i | Esphigmenu (Athos) | XIV | --- |
| 1072 | --- | --- | --- | M Lavras (Athos) | XIII | --- |
| 1075 | --- | --- | --- | M Lavras | XIV | --- |
| 1100 | --- | --- | --- | Dionysiu | 1376 | --- |
| 1247 | 1x,1/,1s | 1/,1s | 1x,1/,6s | Sinai | XV | 2x,3/ |
| 1248 | 2/ | 1/,3s | 4s | Sinai | XIV | 3/ |
| 1249 | 1/,1c | --- | 1/ | Sinai | 1324 | 2/ |
| 1503 | 1s | --- | --- | M. Lavras | 1317 | --- |
| 1548 | --- | --- | 1s | Vatopediu (Athos) | 1359 | --- |
| 1628 | --- | --- | 1s | M. Lavras | 1400 | --- |
| 1637 | --- | --- | --- | M. Lavras | 1328 | --- |
| 1725 | --- | --- | 1s | Vatopediu | 1367 | --- |
| 1732 | 1/ | --- | 1x,1s | M. Lavras | 1384 | 1x,1/ |
| 1754 | 1s | 1/,1s | 2s | Panteleimonos (Athos) | XII | 1/ |
| 1761 | 1s | 2s | --- | Athens | XIV | --- |
| 1768 | --- | 1y | 1s | Iviron (Athos) | 1516 | 1y |
| 1855 | --- | --- | --- | Iviron | XIII | --- |
| 1864 | --- | --- | --- | Stavronikita (Athos) | XIII | --- |
| 1865 | --- | 1/ | --- | Philotheu (Athos) | XIII | 1/ |
| 1876 | 2/,1s | 1/ | 1/,2s | Sinai | XV | 4/ |
| 1892 | 1x | --- | --- | Jerusalem | XIV | 1x |
| 1897 | --- | --- | 1s | Jerusalem | XII | --- |
| 2221 | --- | --- | --- | Sparta | 1432 | --- |
| 2352 | 1c,1i | --- | --- | Meteora | XIV | --- |
| 2431 | --- | --- | 1i | Kavsokalyvia (Athos) | 1332 | --- |
| 2466 | --- | 1/ | 2s | Patmos | 1329 | 1/ |
| 2554 | --- | --- | --- | Bucharest | 1434 | --- |
| 2587 | --- | --- | 1c | Vatican | XI | --- |
| 2626 | 1/ | 1/,1s | 2/ | Ochrida | XIV | 4/ |
| 2723 | --- | --- | --- | Trikala | XI | --- |

## Implications

In 2 John, 2/3 (thirty) of the MSS are perfect representatives of the family as they stand; in 3 John the percentage is also 2/3 (thirty, but a different selection); in Jude just under ½ (twenty-two); and for all three under 1/3 (fourteen). Over half (twenty-nine) of the exemplars were presumably perfect. Since I have the figures for all seven books of the General Epistles, I can assure the reader that all thirty-seven MSS are independent in their generation, as were their exemplars. Cursives 149 and 201 are clearly related, as are 432 and 604, and all four probably come from a common source short of the archetype. I see no evidence of collusion, of 'stuffing the ballot box'— there was no organized effort to standardize the Text. We are looking at a normal transmission, except that it was **incredibly careful.** The fourteen MSS that are perfect in all three books had perfect ancestors all the way back to the archetype, and so for the twenty-nine perfect exemplars. I refer the reader to the prior section for the explanation of how I arrive at the classification of the exemplars.

As I keep on collating MSS I have observed a predictable pattern. For the first 2 or 3, even 4, pages the MSS tend to have few mistakes, or none. If the scribe is going to make mistakes, it tends to be after he has been at it long enough to start getting tired, or bored. Quite often most of the mistakes are on a single page, or in a single chapter; then the scribe took a break (I suppose) and returning to his task refreshed did better work. I would say that the high percentage of 'perfect' copies is largely due to the small size of our three books—the copyists didn't have a chance to get tired. For all that, this observation does not change the fact that there was **incredibly careful transmission** down through the centuries.[1] Considering the size of my sample and the geographic distribution of the MSS, I am cheerfully certain that we have the precise original wording, to the letter, of the $f^{35}$ archetype for 2 and 3 John and Jude. It is reproduced in my Greek Text.

Given my presuppositions, I consider that I have good reason for declaring the divine preservation of the precise original wording of the complete New Testament Text, to this day. That wording is reproduced in my edition of the Greek NT, available from www.walkinhiscommandments.com. BUT PLEASE NOTE: whether or not the archetype of $f^{35}$ is the Autograph (as I claim), the fact remains that the MSS collated for this study reflect an incredibly careful transmission of their source, and this throughout the middle ages. My presuppositions include: God exists; He inspired the Biblical Text; He promised to preserve it for a thousand generations (1 Chronicles 16:15); so He must have an active, ongoing interest in that preservation [there have been fewer than 300 generations since Adam, so He has a ways to go!]. **If He was preserving the original wording in some line of transmission other than $f^{35}$, would that transmission be any less careful than what I have demonstrated for $f^{35}$?** I think not. So any line of transmission characterized by internal confusion is disqualified—this includes **all** the other lines of transmission that I have seen so far![2]

## Putting it all together

On the basis of the evidence so far available I affirm the following:

1) The original wording was never 'lost', and its transmission down through the years was basically normal, being recognized as inspired material from the beginning.

2) That normal process resulted in lines of transmission.

3) To delineate such lines, MSS must be grouped empirically on the basis of a shared mosaic of readings.

---

[1] I have already demonstrated this for the Thessalonian epistles, above, and am in a position to do the same for all the books of the NT. Of course, the longer the book the greater the likelihood that a copyist would make an inadvertent mistake or two. Even so, I have a perfect copy of Romans (fair size and complexity) and one of Matthew (a Gospel, no less!).

[2] Things like **M⁶** and **M⁵** in John 7:53-8:11 come to mind.

4) Such groups or families must be evaluated for independence and credibility.

5) The largest clearly defined group is Family 35.

6) Family 35 is demonstrably independent of all other lines of transmission throughout the NT.

7) Family 35 is demonstrably ancient, dating to the $3^{rd}$ century, at least.

8) Family 35 representatives come from all over the Mediterranean area; the geographical distribution is all but total.

9) Family 35 is not a recension, was not created at some point subsequent to the Autographs.

10) Family 35 is an objectively/empirically defined entity throughout the NT; it has a demonstrable, diagnostic profile from Matthew 1:1 to Revelation 22:21.

11) The archetypal form of Family 35 is demonstrable—it has been demonstrated (see Appendix B).

12) The Original Text is the ultimate archetype; any candidate must also be an archetype—a real, honest to goodness, objectively verifiable archetype; there is only one—Family 35.

13) God's concern for the preservation of the Biblical Text is evident: I take it that passages such as 1 Chronicles 16:15, Psalm 119:89, Isaiah 40:8, Matthew 5:18, Luke 16:17 and 21:33, John 10:35 and 16:12-13, 1 Peter 1:23-25 and Luke 4:4 may reasonably be taken to imply a promise that the Scriptures (to the tittle) will be preserved for man's use (we are to live "by *every* word of God"), and to the end of the world ("for a thousand generations"), but no intimation is given as to just how God proposed to do it. We must deduce the answer from what He has indeed done—we discover that He **did**!

14) This concern is reflected in Family 35; it is characterized by incredibly careful transmission (in contrast to other lines). [I have a perfect copy of the Family 35 archetypal text for most NT books (22); I have copies made from a perfect exemplar (presumed) for another four (4); as I continue to collate MSS I hope to add the last one (Acts), but even for it the archetypal form is demonstrable.]

15) If God was preserving the original wording in some line of transmission other than Family 35, would that line be any less careful? I think not. So any line of transmission characterized by internal confusion is disqualified—this includes **all** the other lines of transmission that I have seen so far.

16) I affirm that God used Family 35 to preserve the precise original wording of the New Testament Text; it is reproduced in my edition of the Greek Text. (And God used mainly the Eastern Orthodox Churches to preserve the NT Text down through the centuries—they have always used a Text

that was an adequate representation of the Original, for all practical purposes.)

**I claim to have demonstrated the superiority of Family 35 based on <u>size</u>, <u>independence</u>, <u>age</u>, <u>distribution</u>, <u>profile</u> and <u>care</u>. I challenge any and all to do the same for any other line of transmission!**

To conclude, I submit that the title of this book, *The Identity of the New Testament Text*, is not misleading; I have covered the bases. Not only have I refuted false 'answers' but I have presented a credible alternative. I affirm that God has preserved the precise original wording of the New Testament, and that we can, and do, know what it is. It is reproduced precisely in my edition of *The Greek New Testament*, which may be downloaded free from <u>www.walkinhiscommandments.com</u>, but is also available in book form from Amazon.com. I have done a translation of this Text into English (the whole NT, with some 4,400 footnotes), also available from the same site, as well as in book form and Kindle from Amazon.com.[1] All glory and praise to Sovereign Jesus!

---

[1] The title of the translation is, THE SOVEREIGN CREATOR HAS SPOKEN; Objective Authority for Living. The title of the Greek Text is, THE GREEK NEW TESTAMENT, According to Family 35.

# APPENDIX A
## The Objective Authority of the Sacred Text

## Introduction

If the Sovereign Creator exists, and if He has addressed a written revelation to our race, then nothing is more important for us than to know what He said (with a view to obeying it, if we are smart). This because such a revelation will have objective authority over us (although the Creator gives us the option of rejecting that authority [but due regard should be given to the consequences]). The enemy has always understood this better than most of us, and began his attacks early on—"Yea, hath God said, ...?" (Genesis 3:1). Of course many books have been written, pro and con, and I will here content myself with declaring these as presuppositions that I bring to my task: the Sovereign Creator exists, and He has addressed a written revelation to our race.

The discipline of textual criticism (of whatever text) is predicated on the assumption/allegation/ declaration that there is a legitimate doubt about the precise original wording of a text. No one does textual criticism on the 1611 King James Bible since copies of the original printing still exist. With reference to New Testament textual criticism, the crucial point at issue is the preservation of its Text. For any text to have objective authority, we have to know what it is.

> It is often assumed by the ignorant and uninformed—even on a university campus—that textual criticism of the New Testament is supported by a superstitious faith in the Bible as a book dictated in miraculous fashion by God. That is not true. Textual criticism has never existed for those whose New Testament is one of miracle, mystery, and authority. A New Testament created under those auspices would have been handed down under them and would have no need of textual criticism.[1]

Thus wrote Colwell in 1952. In 1948 he was even more antagonistic.[2] In simple terms his argument went like this: If God had inspired the New Testament text, He would have preserved it; He did not preserve it, so therefore He did not inspire it. I tend to agree with his logical inference [if his facts were correct], only I propose to turn the tables: It is demonstrable that God preserved the New Testament Text, so therefore He must have inspired it! I consider that the preservation of the N.T. Text is a strong argument for its inspiration, and since it is inspiration that gives it its authority, the two doctrines

---

[1] E.C. Colwell, *What is the Best New Testament?* (Chicago: The University of Chicago Press, 1952), p. 8.

[2] Colwell, "Biblical Criticism: Lower and Higher", *Journal of Biblical Literature*, LXVII (1948), 10-11.

go hand in hand.[1] Of course my use of the term 'demonstrable' is the red flag here; anyone who has not read my recent work could argue that I am begging the question.

Objective authority depends on verifiable meaning; if a reader/hearer can give any meaning he chooses to a message, any authority it ends up having for him will be relative and subjective (the 'neo-orthodox' approach). As a linguist (PhD) I affirm that the fundamental principle of communication is this: both the speaker/writer and the hearer/reader must respect the norms of language, in particular those of the specific code being used. If the encoder violates the rules, he will be deceiving the decoder (deliberately, if he knows what he's doing). If the decoder violates the rules, he will misrepresent the encoder (deliberately, if he knows what he's doing). In either event communication is damaged; the extent of the damage will depend on the circumstances.

Several times the Lord Jesus referred to the Holy Spirit as "the Spirit of the Truth", and Titus 1:2 affirms that God cannot lie—it is one thing He can't do, being contrary to His essence; "He cannot deny Himself" (2 Timothy 2:13). It should be obvious to one and all that the Sovereign will not take kindly to being called a liar. To interpret the Sacred Text in a way that is not faithful to the rules of Hebrew and Greek, respectively, is to ascribe to the Author the intention of deceiving us, is to call Him a liar—not smart. But to interpret the Text, we must have it, so I return to the subject of preservation. I invite attention to the following evidence, in relief of the term 'demonstrable'.

# The Divine Preservation of the Original Wording of the General Epistles

As a point of departure for this discussion I will use a definition of 'preservation' written by Bart D. Ehrman:

> Any claim that God preserved the text of the New Testament intact, giving His church actual, not theoretical, possession of it, must [emphasis added] mean one of three things—either 1) God preserved it in all the extant manuscripts so that none of them contain any textual corruptions, or 2) He preserved it in a group of manuscripts, none of which contain any corruptions, or 3) He preserved it in a solitary manuscript which alone contains no corruptions.[2]

He limits the concept of preservation in a way that verges on the creation of a straw man, but his definition serves my present purpose very nicely. It is obvious that option 1) cannot stand, but what of 2) and 3)? As the title

---

[1] I consider also that the preservation of the NT Text is a strong argument for its canonicity. Why did God preserve only the 27 books that form that canon, no more, no less, no others?

[2] "New Testament Textual Criticism: Search for Method", M.Div. thesis, Princeton Theological Seminary, 1981, p. 40—from a copy he sent to me personally.

indicates, this section is limited to the General Epistles; this group of seven books is one of the sections into which scribes divided the New Testament for the purpose of making copies.[1] Since of Ehrman's three options the third would appear to be the easiest to meet, if we can, I will begin with it.[2]

We must first define the scope—are we looking for a manuscript that is perfect for a whole book,[3] a whole section, or the whole New Testament? I think it is reasonably clear that the correct answer is a whole book; after all, that is how the New Testament was written; it follows that the very first copies were made book by book (and all subsequent copies are dependent upon them). So far as I know, no one claims divine inspiration for the division into sections—over the centuries of copying this became an accepted response to the constraints of materials and time. However, since most of the extant copies reflect that division, it will be interesting to see if we can find a manuscript that is perfect for a whole section. The formal recognition of the complete canon of the New Testament did not take place until the end of the fourth century, although informally it was known in the second (and many hundreds, if not thousands, of copies were in existence by that time—in fact, the main lines of transmission had been established long since), but the question there was the precise roster of books to be included, not the precise wording of the several books. Although many of us believe that God certainly superintended that choice of books, the wording was not at issue. So, we are looking for manuscripts that are perfect for a whole book.

We must next define the text—precisely what profile are we looking for; how can we know if a MS is 'perfect'? This question lands us squarely in the snake pit of NT textual criticism [and most of the snakes are poisonous]. What I think on that subject began to appear in print in 1977[4] and I will not repeat here what is available elsewhere. As a tactical withdrawal I will retreat to an easier question (but I will return to the main one): How can we know if a MS is a perfect representative of its text-type, that is, of its family archetype? To gain time I will illustrate the theory with a concrete example. I invite attention to the chart that follows:

---

[1] There are comparatively few MSS (about 60) of the complete New Testament (and about 150 more that have all but Revelation); because of the bulk (and the physical and financial difficulty of gathering enough leather) the four Gospels were copied as a unit, and so for the letters of Paul (including Hebrews) and the General Epistles. Acts was usually joined to the Generals, but not always, and there are many MSS (over 300) that join Acts, Paul and the Generals. Revelation was added here and there.

[2] At first glance, but when properly redefined the second may be easier.

[3] Since the Autographs did not contain chapter or verse divisions, or even division between words, anything less than a whole book will not be convincing.

[4] *The Identity of the New Testament Text* (Nashville: Thomas Nelson Inc., Publishers, 1977)—but now please see the present edition, of which this appendix is a part.

# *Performance of f*$^{35}$ *MSS in Individual Books for the General Epistles*[1]

---

[1] I collated all the manuscripts myself.

| MS | James | 1 Peter | 2 Peter | 1 John | 2 John | 3 John | Jude | DATE | LOCATION | Corpus exemplar |
|---|---|---|---|---|---|---|---|---|---|---|
| 18 | --- | 1x,2/ | 1s | 1x,2/ | --- | 1s | --- | 1364 | Constantinople | 2x,4/ |
| 35 | 2c | 2c | --- | 2c | --- | --- | 2c | XI | Aegean | --- |
| 141 | 1/,2s | 1x,4/,2s | 1c,1s | 1/,3s,2h | --- | --- | --- | XIII | Vatican | 1x,6/ |
| 149 | 1x,5/,1c,7s | 1x,8/,3s | 5/,2s | 4/,1c,3s | --- | 1/ | 1/,1c | XV | Vatican | 2x,24/ |
| 201 | 5/,1s | 7/ | 3/ | 2/ | --- | 1/ | 1/ | 1357 | London | 19/ |
| 204 | 1x | 1/ | 2/,2s | --- | --- | --- | --- | XIII | Bologna | 1x,3/ |
| 328 | 1x,5/,2s | 5/,4s | 1x,2/,1s | 2x,4/,1c,1s | --- | --- | 1x,1s | XIII | Leiden | 5x,16/ |
| 386 | 2/ | 1/,1s | 1/,2s | 3/,3s,1h | --- | --- | --- | XIV | Vatican | 7/ |
| 394 | 2/ | 4/,1c,1i | 4/ | 4/,1s | --- | 1i | --- | 1330 | Rome | 14/ |
| 432 | 5/,3s,1h | 10/,6s | 1x,2/,1c,1s | 1x5/1c1s1h | 2s | 1/ | 3s | XV | Vatican | 2x,23/ |
| 604 | 6/,1s | 1x,11/,1s | 4/,1c,1s | 7/,1s | 1x | 1/ | 3s | XIV | Paris | 2x,29/ |
| 664[1] | 4x,5/,21s | 5x9/1c25s | 4/,1c,14s | 6x6/14s1h | 1x,1s | 3s | 3s | XV | Zittau | 16x,24/ |
| 757 | 1x | 3/,1c,1s | 1x,1s | 1/ | 2s | --- | --- | XIII | Athens | 2x,4/ |
| 824 | 1x,2s | 1s | 1s | --- | --- | --- | --- | XIV | Grottaferrata | 1x |
| 928 | 2/ | 3/ | 3/ | 1/,1c | --- | --- | --- | 1304 | Dionysiu | 9/ |
| 986[2] | 4/,2s,1i | 6/,4s | 1/,1s | 3/,3s | 1s | --- | 1s,1i | XIV | Esphigmenu | 14/ |
| 1072 | 2/,1h,1i | 3/,2c,1s | 1s | 1/,1c | --- | --- | --- | XIII | M Lavras | 6/ |
| 1075 | 1/,1s | 7/,2s | 1s | 1/ | --- | --- | --- | XIV | M Lavras | 9/ |
| 1100 | 2x,1s | 1/,1i | 1/ | --- | --- | --- | --- | 1376 | Dionysiu | 2x,2/ |
| 1248 | 1x2/2c2s2h | 1x5/2c3s1h | 2x,1/,7s | 4s,2h | 2/ | 1/,2s,1h | 2s,2h | XIV | Sinai | 4x,11/ |

[1] For all its wildness, 664 has all the diagnostic f³⁵ readings, and thus is clearly a family member (albeit sloppy and promiscuous).

[2] 986 is lacking 1 Peter 1:23 - 2:15.

| MS | | | | | | | | | Location | |
|---|---|---|---|---|---|---|---|---|---|---|
| 1249 | 3/ | 1x,5/,2s | 4/ | 1x,3/ | 1/,1c | --- | 1/ | 1324 | Sinai | 2x,17/ |
| 1503 | 1s | 3/,1c | 1s | 1s | 1s | --- | --- | 1317 | M Lavras | 3/ |
| 1548 | 2/,2s | 1x,6/,1c,2s | 1/,2s | 1/,1s | --- | --- | 1s | 1359 | Vatopediu | 1x,10/ |
| 1637 | 1/,1s | 4/,1c,1s | 1/ | 1c | --- | --- | --- | 1328 | M Lavras | 6/ |
| 1725 | 2/ | 1/,1c | --- | 1s,1i | --- | --- | 1s | 1367 | Vatopediu | 3/ |
| 1732 | 2s | 1/,2s | 1/,1i | 2s | 1h | --- | 1s,1i | 1384 | M Lavras | 2/ |
| 1754[1] | 2,16s | 3/,8s | 2/,9s | 2x1/13s3h | 1s | 1/,1s | 2s | XII | Panteleimonos | 2x,9/ |
| 1761 | 2x,2s | 2x,4/,3s | 1/ | 1/,1s,1h | 1s | 2s | --- | XIV | Athens | 4x,6/ |
| 1768 | 7/,2c,1s | 12/,1i | 6/,2i | 2c | --- | 1/ | 1s | 1516 | Iviron | 26/ |
| 1855 | 1/,1s | 1x,2/ | 2/ | 1/,1c | --- | --- | --- | XIII | Iviron | 1x,6/ |
| 1864 | --- | 3/,2c | --- | 1c,2s | --- | --- | --- | XIII | Stavronikita | 3/ |
| 1865 | 1s | --- | 2s | 1c | --- | 1/ | --- | XIII | Philotheu | 1/ |
| 1876 | 1x,4/,3s | 2x,4/,3s,1h | 4/,1s | 1x,3/,1c,2s | 2/,1s | 1/ | 1/,2s | XV | Sinai | 4x,19/ |
| 1892 | 1x,4/,2c,1s | 3x,4/,4s | 1x,2/,1c | 1/,1c,2s | 1x | --- | 1c,1s | XIV | Jerusalem | 6x,11/ |
| 1897 | 2/,3s | 1/,3s | 2s | 2s | --- | --- | 1/ | XII | Jerusalem | 4/ |
| 2221 | 1s | 2x | 1x,3/,1s | 1x,1/ | --- | --- | --- | 1432 | Sparta | 4x,4/ |
| 2352 | 1/,1c,1i | 6/,1c,1s,1i | 3/,1c | 2/,1c | 1c,1i | --- | --- | XIV | Meteora | 12/ |
| 2431 | 4/,4s,1i | 11/,2s,2i | 2/,1c,2s,2i | 2/,2s,2i | --- | --- | 1i | 1332 | Kavsokalyvia | 19/ |
| 2466 | 1/,1s | 1x,1/,1c,4s | 1x,2s | 3/,1s | --- | 1/ | 2s | 1329 | Patmos | 2x,6/ |
| 2554 | --- | --- | --- | --- | --- | --- | --- | 1434 | Bucharest | --- |
| 2587 | 2/ | 3/ | 3/ | 1/ | --- | --- | 1c | XI | Vatican | 9/ |
| 2626 | 1/,1s | 1x,5/ | 1/,1s | 2/ | 1/ | 1/,1s | 2/ | XIV | Ochrida | 1x,13/ |
| 2723 | --- | --- | --- | 1h | --- | --- | --- | XI | Trikala | --- |

[1] MS 1754 is second only to 664 in sloppiness, but is clearly a family member.

## Interpretation

Now then, the text-type that I call Family 35 ($f^{35}$) is represented by some 84 MSS (extant) in the General Epistles. This sample of forty-three family members is certainly representative of the whole text-type, being fully half of its representatives, and taking into consideration the geographic distribution as well. The question immediately before us is: How can we know if a MS is a perfect representative of its text-type? The answer must obtain for a whole book.

The first book in the section is James. Looking at the chart we observe that cursives 18, 1864, 2554 and 2723 are presumed to be perfect representatives, as they stand—they have no deviations from the presumed archetypal profile.[1] Since 35 has been systematically corrected, its exemplar was also perfect. If we ascribe singular readings to the copyist, then the exemplars of 1503, 1732, 1865 and 2221 were perfect as well. If 18, 1864, 2554 and 2723 are copies, not original creations, then their exemplars were also perfect; and the exemplars of the exemplars were also perfect, and so on. The implications of finding a perfect representative of any archetypal text are rather powerful. All the 'canons' of textual criticism become irrelevant to any point subsequent to the creation of that text (they could still come into play when studying the creation of the text, in the event). Of the other MSS, 204 and 757 have only one deviation; 386, 394, 928, 1075, 1637, 1725, 1732, 1855, 2466 and 2587 have only two; and so on. (MS 664 has thirty, most of them being careless mistakes; 664 attests the basic profile [the diagnostic variants that distinguish it from all other profiles] and is thus clearly a member of the family, albeit sloppy.)

I have referred to 'the presumed archetypal profile'. So how did I identify it? I did so on the basis of a fundamental principle. If we have a family made up of 50 MSS, wherever they are all in agreement there can be no question as to the family reading. Where a single MS goes astray against all the rest, there still can be no question—which is what I argue for James above. Wherever so many as two agree (against the rest) then we have a splinter group—off hand I would say that anything up to 20% of the family total would remain a splinter group, with virtually no chance of representing the archetypal reading (if the other 80% are unanimous). Where the attestation falls below 80%, the more so if there are several competing variants, other considerations must come into play.

---

[1] Before I collated cursive 18 for myself, I was limited to the collation reflected in *TuT* (*Text und Textwert der Griechischen Handschriften des Neuen Testaments* [Ed. Kurt Aland, Berlin: Walter de Gruyter, 1987], volumes 9 and 11), which evidently assigns two errors to the copyist; I am satisfied that there are none.

Returning to James, I claim that we have reasonable certainty as to the precise family profile for that book.[1] That being so, we can now evaluate the individual MSS. That is why I affirm that the exemplars of 18, 35, 1503, 1732, 1864, 1865, 2221, 2554 and 2723 are perfect representatives of the family. To have nine perfect exemplars out of forty-three is probably more than most of us would expect! So in James we have several MSS that meet Ehrman's option 3), with reference to the archetypal text.

But what about Ehrman's second option? When he speaks of a 'group' of MSS, as distinct from a 'solitary' MS (option 3), he presumably is thinking of a family, since they would all have the same profile, of necessity. But if he is thinking of a family, then I submit that option 2) needs to be restated. I suggest: "He preserved it in a family of manuscripts whose archetypal text contains no corruptions —provided that its precise profile can be affirmed beyond reasonable doubt." (Recall that we are speaking of <u>actual</u> possession of the profile.) The obvious mistakes in individual representatives can cheerfully be factored out, leaving the witness of the family unscathed. As restated, Ehrman's second option is met by $\mathbf{f}^{35}$ in James, with reference to the archetypal text. Let's move on to 1 Peter.

Looking at the chart, cursives 1865, 2554 and 2723 are perfect representatives of the presumed archetypal profile, but since 35 has been systematically corrected, its exemplar was also perfect.[2] If we ascribe singular readings to the copyist, then the exemplar of 824 was perfect as well. Of the other MSS, 204 has only one deviation; 386, 1100, 1725 and 2221 have only two; and so on. Arguing as I did for James, in 1 Peter we have five exemplars that meet Ehrman's option 3) and again $\mathbf{f}^{35}$ meets his option 2), with reference to the archetypal text. Let's move on to 2 Peter.

Looking at the chart, cursives 35, 1725, 1864, 2554 and 2723 are perfect representatives of the presumed archetypal profile.[3] If we ascribe singular readings to the copyist, then the exemplars of 18, 824, 1072, 1075, 1503, 1865 and 1897 were perfect as well. Of the other MSS, 1100, 1637 and 1761 have only one deviation; 141, 757, 986, 1732, 1855 and 2626 have only two; and so on. Arguing as I did for James, in 2 Peter we have twelve exemplars that meet Ehrman's option 3) and again $\mathbf{f}^{35}$ meets his option 2), with reference to the archetypal text. Let's move on to 1 John.

Looking at the chart, cursives 204, 824, 1100 and 2554 are perfect representatives of the presumed archetypal profile, but since 35, 1637, 1768 and 1865 have been systematically corrected, their exemplars were also

---

[1] There are only two significant family splits in James, that I discuss in my paper, "$\mathbf{f}^{35}$ sub-groups in the General Epistles".

[2] There are eight significant family splits in 1 Peter, that I discuss in my paper, "$\mathbf{f}^{35}$ sub-groups in the General Epistles".

[3] There are two significant family splits in 2 Peter, that I discuss in my paper, "$\mathbf{f}^{35}$ sub-groups in the General Epistles".

perfect.[1] The single variation in 2723 is the omission of a whole line in an obvious case of homoioteleuton, which to my mind does not constitute a proper variant reading. In any case its exemplar would be perfect. If we ascribe singular readings to the copyist, then the exemplars of 1503, 1725, 1732 and 1897 were perfect as well. Of the other MSS, 757, 1075 and 2587 have only one deviation; 201, 928, 1072, 1548, 1855, 2221 and 2626 have only two; and so on. Arguing as I did for James, in 1 John we have thirteen exemplars that meet Ehrman's option 3) and again $f^{35}$ meets his option 2), with reference to the archetypal text. Let's move on to 2 John.

Looking at the chart, most of the cursives are perfect representatives of the presumed archetypal profile. Arguing as I did for James, in 2 John we have thirty-six exemplars that meet Ehrman's option 3) and again $f^{35}$ meets his option 2), with reference to the archetypal text. Let's move on to 3 John.

Looking at the chart, most of the cursives are perfect representatives of the presumed archetypal profile. Arguing as I did for James, in 3 John we have thirty-two exemplars that meet Ehrman's option 3) and again $f^{35}$ meets his option 2), with reference to the archetypal text. Let's move on to Jude.

Looking at the chart, half of the cursives are perfect representatives of the presumed archetypal profile. Arguing as I did for James, in Jude we have thirty-six exemplars that meet Ehrman's option 3) and again $f^{35}$ meets his option 2), with reference to the archetypal text.

# But is the archetypal text of $f^{35}$ the Autograph?

As they used to say in another world, long departed, "That's the $64 question". In Chapter 7 I presented objective evidence in support of the claim that the text of $f^{35}$ is ancient and independent of all other lines of transmission. If $f^{35}$ is independent of all other lines of transmission then it must hark back to the Autographs. What other reasonable explanation is there? If anyone has a different explanation that accounts for the evidence better than (or as well as) mine does, I would like to see it.[2]

I claim to have demonstrated the superiority of Family 35 based on size, independence, age, distribution, profile and care. I challenge any and all to do the same for any other line of transmission!

---

[1] There are two significant family splits in 1 John, that I discuss in my paper, "$f^{35}$ sub-groups in the General Epistles".

[2] Should anyone wish to claim that $f^{35}$ is a recension, I request (and insist) that he specify who did it, when and where, and furnish evidence in support of the claim. Without evidence any such claim is frivolous and irresponsible—Hort's claim that his 'Syrian' text was the result of a 'Lucianic' recension is a classic example (Burgon protested at the complete lack of evidence, at the time, and no one has come up with any since). I remind the reader that evidence must be rigorously distinguished from presupposition and interpretation.

So then, if the archetypal text of **f³⁵** is the Autograph then we have met two of Ehrman's three options for each of the seven General Epistles. I maintain that in this year of our Lord we have actual (not theoretical) possession of the precise original wording of James, 1 Peter, 2 Peter, 1 John, 2 John, 3 John and Jude!! Furthermore, I am prepared to offer the same sort of demonstration for each of the 27 books that make up our NT. In consequence thereof, I maintain that in this year of our Lord we have actual (not theoretical) possession of the precise original wording of the whole New Testament!!!

I have argued above that preservation is to be demonstrated book by book, but wouldn't it be interesting if we could do the same for a whole section? But of course we have—Ehrman's option 2), as restated, obtains for the whole section of seven books. Not just interesting but astonishing it would be to find a single MS that is perfect throughout a section of seven books![1] And again we have!! 2554 fills the bill, as do the exemplars of 35 and 2723, and as does 2723 itself, virtually. So recently as ten years ago I would not have dreamed of such a thing.

If God demonstrably preserved the precise wording of a text throughout two millennia, this implies rather strongly that He inspired it in the first place— otherwise, why bother with it? And if He went to such pains, I rather suspect that He expects us to pay strict attention to it. When we stand before the Just Judge—who is also Creator, Savior and Inspirer—He will require an accounting based on the objective authority of that Text.

# Some Possible Discrepancies

Not only does the objective authority of Scripture depend upon verifiable meaning, it depends in the first place on divine inspiration. Anything inspired by God should not contain errors, so enemies of an inspired Bible are quick to point out any errors of fact or internal contradictions that they can. Unfortunately, the Hortian theory made it easy for them, since it foists such errors and contradictions upon the NT Text. In Appendix F I discuss some of them in detail (which please see), but I will here include a bare list of the obvious ones I have noticed so far.

### 'Poison' inserted in the 'Bread of Life' by the Hortian theory

When the percentages do not add up to 100, there are other variants that are not mentioned. Numbers within ( ) are more or less exact; those within [ ] are approximations—the percentages refer to the total of extant MSS. For a full statement of the evidence, please see my Greek Text.

John 6:47—  *ο πιστευων* the one believing (0,5%) X *ο πιστευων εις εμε* the one believing into me  (99,5%)

John 7:8—  *ουκ* not [3%] X *ουπω* not yet [96,5%]

---

[1] This would be true for the archetypal text of any group of 70-80 MSS, or even fewer. If the archetype is the Autograph, all the more so.

Luke 4:44 (Mark 1:39, Matthew 4:23)—*Ιουδαιας* of Judea  (4,1%) X
*Γαλιλαιας* of Galilee  (94,7%)

John 1:18— *μονογενης θεος* an only begotten god  (0,3%) || *ο μονογενης
θεος* the only begotten god  (0,1%) X *ο μονογενης υιος* the
only begotten son  (99,6%)

1 Timothy 3:16—*ος* who  (1%) X *Θεος* God  (98,5%)

Mark 16:9-20—absent (0,2%) X present (99,8%)

John 7:53-8:11—absent (15%) X present (85%)

Luke 3:33— *του Αδμιν του Αρνι* of Admin, of Arni  [0.00%] (it is a
'patchwork quilt' put together on the basis of at least ten
variants) X *του Αραμ* of Aram  [95%]

Matthew 19:17 (X Mark 10:18, Luke 18:19)—*τι με ερωτας περι του αγαθου*
Why do you ask me concerning the good?  (0,9%) X *τι με
λεγεις αγαθον* Why do you call me good?  (99%)

Luke 23:45— *εκλιποντος* being eclipsed  (0,8%) X *εσκοτισθη* was
darkened  (97,5%)

Mark 6:22 (Matthew 14:6)—*αυτου ... Ηρωδιαδος* his [daughter] Herodias
(1,3%) X *αυτης της Ηρωδιαδος* Herodias' own [daughter]
(97,2%)

John 6:11 (Matthew 14:19, Mark 6:41, Luke 9:16)—omission [3%] X *τοις
μαθηταις οι δε μαθηται* to the disciples and the disciples
[97%]

Acts 19:16— *αμφοτερων* both [5%] X *αυτων* them [90%]

Matthew 1:7,10—*Ασαφ, Αμος* Asaph, Amos  [2%] X *Ασα, Αμον* Asa,
Amon  [98%]

Matthew 5:22 (see Ephesians 4:26, Psalm 4:4)—omission (1,9%) X *εικη*
without cause  (96,2%)

1 Corinthians 5:1—*ουδε εν τοις εθνεσιν* does not exist even among the
Gentiles  (3,2%) X *ουδε εν τοις εθνεσιν ονομαζεται* is not
named even among the Gentiles  (96,8%)

John 18:24— *απεστειλεν ουν* then he sent  [9%] X *απεστειλεν* he had
sent  [90%]

Matthew 10:10 (Mark 6:8)—*μηδε ραβδον* neither a staff  [5%] X *μηδε
ραβδους* neither staves  [95%]

Mark 1:2 (see Malachi 3:1, Isaiah 40:3)—$\tau\omega$ $I\sigma\alpha\iota\alpha$ $\tau\omega$ $\pi\rho o\phi\eta\tau\eta$ in Isaiah the prophet (3,1%) X $\tau o\iota\varsigma$ $\pi\rho o\phi\eta\tau\alpha\iota\varsigma$ in the prophets (96,7%)

Acts 28:13— $\pi\epsilon\rho\iota\epsilon\lambda o\nu\tau\epsilon\varsigma$ removing [something] [5%] X $\pi\epsilon\rho\iota\epsilon\lambda\theta o\nu\tau\epsilon\varsigma$ tacking back and forth [95%]

2 Peter 3:10—$\epsilon\upsilon\rho\epsilon\theta\eta\sigma\epsilon\tau\alpha\iota$ will be found (3,2%) X $\kappa\alpha\tau\alpha\kappa\alpha\eta\sigma\epsilon\tau\alpha\iota$ will be burned up (93,6%)

Jude 15— $\pi\alpha\sigma\alpha\nu$ $\psi\upsilon\chi\eta\nu$ every soul (0,5%) X $\pi\alpha\nu\tau\alpha\varsigma$ $\tau o\upsilon\varsigma$ $\alpha\sigma\epsilon\beta\epsilon\iota\varsigma$ all the wicked (97,8%)

Luke 9:10(12)—$\pi o\lambda\iota\nu$ $\kappa\alpha\lambda o\upsilon\mu\epsilon\nu\eta\nu$ $B\eta\theta\sigma\alpha\iota\delta\alpha$ a town named Bethsaida [0,5%] X $\tau o\pi o\nu$ $\epsilon\rho\eta\mu o\nu$ $\pi o\lambda\epsilon\omega\varsigma$ $\kappa\alpha\lambda o\upsilon\mu\epsilon\nu\eta\varsigma$ $B\eta\theta\sigma\alpha\iota\delta\alpha$ a deserted place belonging to a town named Bethsaida [98%]

Matthew 21:5—$\kappa\alpha\iota$ $\epsilon\pi\iota$ $\pi\omega\lambda o\nu$ and on a colt (2%) X $\kappa\alpha\iota$ $\pi\omega\lambda o\nu$ that is, a colt (98%)

Mark 10:24— $\pi\omega\varsigma$ $\delta\upsilon\sigma\kappa o\lambda o\nu$ $\epsilon\sigma\tau\iota\nu$ $\epsilon\iota\varsigma$ $\tau\eta\nu$ $\beta\alpha\sigma\iota\lambda\epsilon\iota\alpha\nu$ $\tau o\upsilon$ $\theta\epsilon o\upsilon$ $\epsilon\iota\sigma\epsilon\lambda\theta\epsilon\iota\nu$ how hard it is to enter the kingdom of God (0,4%) X $\pi\omega\varsigma$ $\delta\upsilon\sigma\kappa o\lambda o\nu$ $\epsilon\sigma\tau\iota\nu$ $\tau o\upsilon\varsigma$ $\pi\epsilon\pi o\iota\theta o\tau\alpha\varsigma$ $\epsilon\pi\iota$ $\chi\rho\eta\mu\alpha\sigma\iota\nu$ $\epsilon\iota\varsigma$ $\tau\eta\nu$ $\beta\alpha\sigma\iota\lambda\epsilon\iota\alpha\nu$ $\tau o\upsilon$ $\theta\epsilon o\upsilon$ $\epsilon\iota\sigma\epsilon\lambda\theta\epsilon\iota\nu$ how hard it is for those who trust in riches to enter the kingdom of God (99,5%)

Matthew 1:25—$\upsilon\iota o\nu$ a son (0,5%) X $\tau o\nu$ $\upsilon\iota o\nu$ $\alpha\upsilon\tau\eta\varsigma$ $\tau o\nu$ $\pi\rho\omega\tau o\tau o\kappa o\nu$ her son, the firstborn (99,5%)

Matthew 6:13—omission (1,3%) X $o\tau\iota$ $\sigma o\upsilon$ $\epsilon\sigma\tau\iota\nu$ $\eta$ $\beta\alpha\sigma\iota\lambda\epsilon\iota\alpha$ $\kappa\alpha\iota$ $\eta$ $\delta\upsilon\nu\alpha\mu\iota\varsigma$ $\kappa\alpha\iota$ $\eta$ $\delta o\xi\alpha$ $\epsilon\iota\varsigma$ $\tau o\upsilon\varsigma$ $\alpha\iota\omega\nu\alpha\varsigma$ because yours is the kingdom and the power and the glory forever (98,7%)

John 5:3[b]-4— omission (0,8%) X "—waiting for the moving of the water; because an angel would go down from time to time into the pool and stir up the water—then the first one to get in after the stirring of the water became well of whatever disease was holding him" (99,2%) [NIV has an insulting footnote that adds the injury of making the angel "of the Lord" (following some 2% of the manuscripts).]

Luke 2:14— $\epsilon\nu$ $\alpha\nu\theta\rho\omega\pi o\iota\varsigma$ $\epsilon\upsilon\delta o\kappa\iota\alpha\varsigma$ toward men of goodwill (0,4%) X $\epsilon\nu$ $\alpha\nu\theta\rho\omega\pi o\iota\varsigma$ $\epsilon\upsilon\delta o\kappa\iota\alpha$ goodwill toward men (99,4%) [1627 MSS X 6 MSS]

Luke 2:33— $o$ $\pi\alpha\tau\eta\rho$ $\alpha\upsilon\tau o\upsilon$ his father (0,9%) X $\iota\omega\sigma\eta\phi$ Joseph (98,8%)

Luke 22:43-44—omission (1,3%) X the two verses (98,7%) This is important information that is only recorded here; it is a perversity to challenge it on the basis of such weak evidence.

Mark15:39— omission (0,4%) X *κραξας* shouting (98,6%) (The picture is severely changed.)

Comment: there are many hundreds of other errors (in the 'critical' text) that damage the Text, even though it may not be possible to describe them as errors of fact or obvious contradictions. But they have a cumulative effect that is certainly negative.

Aside from such fabricated 'problems', the actual Text itself presents us with some seeming difficulties that have been used by the Bible's enemies. I will here discuss a few of them.

## *Seeming difficulties actually in the Text*

The difficulty of harmonizing the four Gospel accounts surrounding Peter's denials is notorious. Since my discussion occupies a number of pages, I have dedicated a separate appendix to it (H).

*Harmonizing the accounts of the Resurrection*

*A rough sequence within the parallel accounts*

Matthew 27:62-28:1;
Mark 16:1-3 // Luke 24:1;
Matthew 28:2-4;
John 20:1-10;
Matthew 28:5-8 // Mark 16:4-8 // Luke 24:2-8;
Mark 16:9 // John 20:11-18;
Matthew 28:9-15;
Luke 24:13-35;
Luke 24:36-43 // John 20:19-31.

*The presumed sequence of events*

0. [Saturday—guards seal the stone and set up a watch (Matthew 27:62-66).]
1. Jesus rises from the dead.[1]
2. Early Sunday morning the women set out for the tomb—Magdalene (John 20:1); Magdalene and Mary (Matthew 28:1); Magdalene, Mary and Salome (Mark 16:1-2); Magdalene, Mary, Joanna and others (Luke 23:55-24:1, 10).[2]

---

[1] None of the Evangelists mentions the moment of the resurrection; probably because that information was never revealed. The fact is taken for granted (the "firstborn from the dead"—Col. 1:18, Rev. 1:5; the "firstfruits"—1 Cor. 15:20, 23).

[2] The several accounts say it was very early, as the day began to dawn, while it was still dark, but by the time they got to the tomb the sun had risen. There is no discrepancy: recall that the garden is on the west side of a mountain, so even after the sun had risen the tomb would be in shadow, besides the shade of the trees. It was still darkish when they started out, but away from the mountain it was already day by the time they arrived—the tomb area would still be gloomy.

3. On the way they worry about the stone (Mark 16:3).
4. Before they arrive an angel rolls back the stone, complete with earthquake, etc. (Matthew 28:2-4).[1]
5. They arrive and see that the stone has been rolled back, but the angel was no longer visible outside (Mark 16:4, Luke 24:2, John 20:1).[2]
6. Magdalene takes off immediately to tell Peter—Peter and John run to the tomb to see (John 20:2-3).[3]
7. Before Peter and John get there the other women enter the tomb, and see and hear the angels (Luke 24:3-8, Mark 16:5-7, Matthew 28:5-7).[4]
8. They leave the tomb in fear, saying nothing to the guards or anyone they chance to meet (Mark 16:8, Matthew 28:8a).
9. Probably right after the women leave, and before Peter and John arrive, the guards take off (Matthew 28:11-15).
10. Peter and John come and go [to their own homes] (John 20:4-10; cf. Luke 24:12 that is an historical aside).[5] No mention is made of either

---

[1] The removal of the stone was not to let Jesus out; it was to let witnesses in! If we only had Matthew's record, we could assume that the women saw the shining angel outside the sepulcher, but a comparison of the other accounts leads to a different understanding. So how do we know those details? Matthew 28:11 says that "some" of the guard reported to the priests and accepted big money to spread a false report, but what happened to the other guards? I have no doubt that some of those guards were soundly converted and gave an eyewitness account to the Christian community.

[2] If the angel had been visible, Magdalene would not have taken off, because she would not have thought that the body had been stolen. The hypothesis that she came once alone, before the others, is highly improbable (see next note).

[3] Her use of the plural "we", verse 2, indicates that she was not alone at the tomb.

[4] I take Matthew and Mark to be parallel, describing the same event: the angel who rolled away the stone is now inside the sepulcher, sitting on the right side; he has turned off his neon and appears to be a young man clothed in white; each account furnishes a few distinct details in the angel's speech—Mark includes "and Peter" [was Peter looking over his shoulder?]. The women were not sure they were happy with the situation, and the 'young man' may well have said more than Matthew and Mark record. I take it that Luke records a second inning: the women are having trouble assimilating the missing body (they were loaded with spices to put on that body—was their effort to be wasted?); so the angel calls in a colleague and they both turn on their neon—a little shock treatment; then they appeal to Jesus' own words, which the women remember, and with that they are convinced and go their way.

[5] Verse 8 says that John (the author) "saw and believed". What did John 'see' that made him 'believe'? He saw the linen strips 'lying', that is, in the form of the body, only there was no body inside them! If someone had stolen the body, as Magdalene supposed, they would have taken the wrapped package (much easier to carry) and there would have been no linen strips. If someone had unwrapped the body, for whatever reason, there would have been a sizable mound of linen strips and spices piled up (how much cloth would it take to wrap up a hundred pounds of spices?). No, Jesus simply passed through the cloth, as He would later pass through the wall of the upper room, leaving the package like a mummy case or empty cocoon. When John saw that he understood that the only possible explanation was resurrection.

angels or guards, so presumably Peter and John saw no one—the place appeared to be abandoned.

11. Magdalene returns to the sepulcher but doesn't get there until everyone is gone (that's why she thought Jesus was the gardener); Jesus appears to her <u>first</u> (Mark 16:9, John 20:11-17).[1]

12. Then Jesus appears to the other women and they go on their way to tell the disciples (Matthew 28:9-10, Luke 24:9-11).[2]

13. Magdalene goes and tells the disciples (Mark 16:10-11, John 20:18).

14. Later in the day Jesus appears to Peter (cf. Luke 24:34).[3]

15. The Emmaus road episode (Luke 24:13-35, Mark 16:12-13).[4]

---

[1] When the disciples took off running, of course Magdalene followed them back to the tomb. But she was winded, and could not keep up with them (actually, in that culture women probably seldom ran, so she would really be out of breath, but she was not about to be left out of the action, either). She may have arrived as they were leaving; if not they would pass her on the road. In verse 12 John says that she saw two 'angels'. How did John know they were angels? He had just been there and knew there were no human beings around (the guards were presumably gone before the two got there). The angels were in white, but probably not shining, or Magdalene would have been shaken out of her despair. She was so locked in to her sorrow that not even seeing the wrappings collapsed without the body sank in.

[2] The question may reasonably be asked: How could Magdalene have time to go and come and Jesus appear to her <u>first</u> and still have time to appear to the women before they got to the disciples, the more so since Matthew 28:8 says the women "hurried and ran"? I offer the following considerations in relief of the perceived difficulty: 1) The Jerusalem of that day was small and distances were short ("nearby", John 19:42)—it was probably less than a mile, or even half a mile, between the tomb and Peter's house, as well as where the other disciples were staying; 2) the women were probably slow in entering the tomb—the guards making like dead men, dark, spooky (it's a cemetery), all very strange, Magdalene the impulsive one wasn't there; they would be leery—Magdalene may have been almost to Peter's house before they worked up the courage to enter the tomb; 3) Magdalene, Peter and John were excited and had extra adrenalin—it didn't take that long; 4) the women ran out of the tomb and the garden, but not necessarily all the way to the disciples—once they got away from the garden and on 'safe' ground they may well have slowed down, or even stopped, to get a grip on themselves and discuss what had happened (Mary, the mother of James, was no longer young, and none of the women was used to running, not to mention the type of clothing they wore). Putting it all together, I see no reason to doubt that it all happened just like the Text says.

[3] I see no way of determining the correct sequence of items 14 and 15, it could have been the other way around. Also, during resurrection Sunday (we don't know just when) many resurrected saints "went into the holy city and appeared to many" (Matthew 27:53), which would have been **dramatic** confirmatory evidence to those who were visited.

[4] Some have alleged a discrepancy between the two accounts—their mistake is to tie both accounts to the eleven, which was not the case. There were other people in the upper room, besides the eleven. The eleven were reclining at a table, the 'others' would be nearer the door. The two from Emmaus come bursting in, all excited and probably feeling just a little important; it is the 'others', probably to 'prick their balloon', who say, "Oh, we already know that; He has appeared to Simon". (Human nature hasn't changed, and they didn't have the Holy Spirit yet.) While the two from Emmaus are talking with the

16. Jesus appears to the eleven, Thomas being absent (Luke 24:36-48, Mark 16:14-18, John 20:19-23).
17. After Jesus leaves, Thomas comes in and they tell him (John 20:24-25).

### Post resurrection day events

1. The next Sunday Jesus appears to them again and deals with Thomas (John 20:26-29).
2. Jesus appears to the seven beside the Sea of Galilee (John 21:1-22).
3. On a mountain in Galilee (Matthew 28:16-20).
4. Jesus appears to over 500, also to James (1 Corinthians 15:6-7).[1]
5. The ascension from Olivet (Mark 16:19-20, Luke 24:49-51, Acts 1:3-12).

### Conclusion

In sum, I see no reason for doubt: it all happened just as the Text describes it. There are no discrepancies, in spite of the variety of details supplied by various eyewitnesses (including converted guards) and written down by four different Evangelists. It is just what we should expect from an inspired Text—inspired and preserved, to this day.

### Abiathar is not Ahimelech (Mark 2:26 X 1 Samuel 21:1)

Some of my readers may be aware that this verse has destroyed the faith of at least one scholar in our day, although he was reared in an evangelical home. He understood Jesus to be saying that Abiathar was the priest with whom David dealt, when in fact it was his father, Ahimelech. If Jesus stated an historical error as fact, then he could not be God. So he turned his back on Jesus. I consider that his decision was lamentable and unnecessary, and in the interest of helping others who may be troubled by this verse, I offer the following explanation:

"How he entered the house of God (making Abiathar high priest) and ate the consecrated bread, which only priests are permitted to eat, and shared it with those who were with him."

My rendering is rather different than the 'in the days of Abiathar the high priest' of the AV, NKJV and NIV. We are translating three Greek words that very literally would be 'upon Abiathar high-priest' (but the preposition here, *epi*, is the most versatile of the Greek prepositions, and one of its many meanings/uses is 'toward'—the standard lexicon, BDAG, lists fully eighteen

---

'others', not the eleven, Jesus Himself appears and interacts with the eleven (and they think He's a ghost!). Mark, writing for a Roman audience, is emphasizing that the disciples were not gullible, did not 'believe' because they wanted to—in verse 11 they didn't believe Magdalene, in verse 13 nor the two, in verse 14 Jesus rebukes their unbelief. There is nothing here to impugn the genuineness of these verses—they were certainly written by Mark at the same time that he wrote the rest. According to Matthew 28:17 many days later some were still doubting. In any group of people there are always differing levels of belief and unbelief. People's heads work differently, and at different speeds.

[1] I see no way of determining the correct sequence of the events in items 3 and 4.

<u>areas</u> of meaning, quite apart from sub-divisions). When we go back to the Old Testament account, we discover that David actually conversed with Ahimelech, Abiathar's father, who was the high priest at that moment (1 Samuel 21:1-9). Within a few days Saul massacred Ahimelech and 84 other priests (1 Samuel 22:16-18), but his son Abiathar escaped and went to David, <u>taking the ephod with him</u> (1Samuel 22:20-23; 23:6). That David could use it to inquire of the LORD rather suggests that it had to be the ephod that only the high priest wore, since only that ephod had the Urim and Thummim (1 Samuel 23:9-12; cf. Numbers 27:21, Ezra 2:63).

That ephod was to a high priest like the crown was to a king; so how could Abiathar have it? The Text states that David's visit filled Ahimelech with fear, presumably because he too saw Doeg the Edomite and figured what would happen. Now why wasn't Abiathar taken with the others? I suggest that Ahimelech foresaw what would happen (Doeg probably took off immediately, and Ahimelech figured he wouldn't have much time), so he deliberately consecrated Abiathar, gave him the ephod, and told him to hide—he probably did it that very day (once the soldiers arrived to arrest Ahimelech and the other 84, it would be too late). Abiathar escaped, but carried the news of the massacre with him; only now he was the high priest.

Putting it all together, it was David's visit that resulted in Abiathar's becoming high priest prematurely, as David himself recognized, and to which Jesus alluded in passing (which is why I used parentheses). But why would Jesus allude to that? I suppose because the Bible is straightforward about the consequences of sin, and David lied to Ahimelech. Although Jesus was using David's eating that bread as an example, He did not wish to gloss over the sin, and its consequences.

Recall that Jesus was addressing Pharisees, who were steeped in the OT Scriptures. A notorious case like Saul's massacre of 85 priests would be very well known. And of course, none of the NT had yet been written, so any understanding of what Jesus said had to be based on 1 Samuel ("Have you never read...?"). If we today wish to understand this passage, we need to place ourselves in the context recorded in Mark 2:23-28. The Pharisees would understand that if Abiathar was in possession of the ephod with the Urim and Thummim, then he was the high priest. And how did he get that way? He got that way because of David's visit. It was an immediate consequence of that visit.

Some may object that 'making' is a verb, not a preposition. Well, the 'in the days of' of the AV, etc., though not a verb, is a phrase. Both a pronoun and an adverb may stand for a phrase, and a preposition may as well. TEV and Phillips actually use a verb: 'when...was'; NLT has 'during the days when...was'. Where the others used from two to five words, I used only one.

*Mary's genealogy—Luke 3:23*

Και αυτος ἦν ὁ Ιησους, ὡσει ετων τριακοντα αρχομενος, ων ὡς ενομιζετο υἱος Ιωσηφ, του Ηλει, του Ματθαν, του Λευι, του Μελχι, .
. .

There are four words here that invite special attention: καί, αυτος, ἦν and ὡς. Since verse 22 ends with a statement from the Father at Jesus' baptism, it is clear that verse 23 begins another section. But the conjunction that signals the transition is καί and not δε, as one would expect—this means that 'Jesus' continues as the topic. But in that event, how does one explain the personal pronoun αυτος, the more so in such an emphatic position? If the author's purpose was simply to register Jesus as a son of Joseph, as many suppose, why didn't he just write καί ὁ Ιησους ἦν υίος Ιωσηφ, etc.?

But then, why write ὡς ενομιζετο? It seems to me that the normal meaning of "as was supposed" is to affirm that Jesus was in fact Joseph's son; but that is precisely what Jesus **was not**. Luke has already made clear that Jesus' real Father was the Holy Spirit—1:34-35, 43, 45; 2:49. So what Luke is really saying is that although the people supposed Jesus to be Joseph's son, He actually had a different lineage—we should translate "so it was supposed". (Recall that a faithful and loyal translation seeks to transmit correctly the meaning intended by the <u>author</u>.)

The verb ἦν is the only independent one in the whole paragraph, verses 23-38. Is it working with the participle αρχομενος in a periphrastic construction? That appears to be the tendency of the eclectic text that places the participle right after Jesus (following less than 2% of the Greek MSS), which makes Jesus out to be in fact Joseph's son. It seems to me to be far more natural to take the participial clauses as being circumstantial: "beginning at about thirty years of age" and "being (so it was supposed) a son of Joseph". Setting those two clauses aside, the independent clause that remains is ἦν ὁ Ιησους του Ηλει, "Jesus was of Eli".

The participle 'beginning' requires an object, that the Text leaves implicit; from the context it seems clear that we may supply 'His ministry', or some such thing, which is why most versions do so.

I suggest the following rendering: "Beginning *His ministry* at about thirty years of age, being (so it was supposed) a son of Joseph, Jesus was actually of Eli, of Mathan, of Levi..." I take it that the emphatic pronoun αυτος heightens the contrast between what the people imagined and the reality. Jesus was a grandson of Eli, Mary's father—Luke gives the genealogy of Jesus through His mother, while Matthew gives it through His stepfather. Jesus received some of David's genes through Mary and Nathan; the glorified body now at the Father's right hand, and that will one day occupy David's throne, has some of his genes.

The eclectic text gives our verse a different wording: καί αυτος ἦν Ιησους αρχομενος ὡσει ετων τριακοντα, ων υίος, ὡς ενομιζετο, Ιωσηφ του Ηλι του Μαθθατ του Λευι του Μελχι,... The RSV translates it like this: "Jesus, when he began his ministry, was about thirty years of age, being the son (as was supposed) of Joseph, the son of Heli, the son of Matthat..." Is not the normal meaning of this rendering that Jesus was in fact the son of Joseph? However, every version that I recall seeing has "Joseph, the son of Heli", which directly contradicts Matthew, "Jacob begot Joseph". The word 'son' (without the article) occurs only with Joseph, although most versions supply it on down the genealogy. But Luke is precisely correct in not using it, because it would not hold for the first and last names in the list—Eli did not beget Jesus (nor Joseph) and God did not beget Adam.

So then, properly understood Luke does not contradict Matthew (with reference to Joseph's father), nor does he affirm an error of fact (with reference to Jesus' father).

*Some related anomalies in Matthew's genealogy of the Christ*

Matthew's purpose is to demonstrate that Jesus, the Messiah, has a legal right to sit on David's throne (perhaps answering the Lord's own question in Matthew 22:42). Although there are many kings in the genealogy, David is the only one who is described as 'the king', twice. Since David's throne has to do with the covenant people, and that covenant began with Abraham, the genealogy does as well. It ends with Joseph, Jesus' 'father' by adoption, since Jesus had none of Joseph's genes.[1] It was sufficient to Matthew's purpose to show that Joseph was a linear, and legal, descendant of David, the number of intervening generations was beside the point. Matthew's Gospel was directed primarily to a Jewish audience, to whom legal rights were important.

Matthew divides his genealogy of the Christ into three groups of fourteen 'generations'. A comparison of his genealogy with the OT record indicates that it is not a 'normal', straightforward genealogy—there are some anomalies.[2] In an effort to understand the purpose behind the anomalies, I will begin with the second group, which may be said to be made up of sovereign kings of Judah. Going back to the OT we discover that there were seventeen such kings, not fourteen. But, Matthew says 'generations', not reigns, and since Ahaziah reigned only one year, Amon only two, and Abijah only three, they can be assimilated into the fourteen generations. That said, however, we next observe that Abijah and Amon are duly included in the list, while Ahaziah is not, followed by Joash and Amaziah. The three excluded names form a group between Jehoram and Uzziah.

Verse eight says that "Joram begot Uzziah", the verb 'begot' being the same one used throughout, but in fact Uzziah was Joram's (Jehoram's) great-great-grandson. So we see that 'begot' refers to a linear descendant, not necessarily a son. We also see that the number 'fourteen' is not being used in a strictly literal sense (whatever the author's purpose may have been). It also appears

---

[1] Indeed He could not, because of the prophesies in Jeremiah 22:30 and 36:30, wherein Jeconiah and Jehoiakim are cursed. However, Jesus received some of David's genes through Mary (please see the note that accompanies Luke 3:23 in my translation).

[2] I believe that Matthew composed his Gospel under divine guidance, which leads me to the conclusion that the anomalies were deliberate, on God's part. Therefore, my attempt to unravel the anomalies tries to understand the Holy Spirit's purpose in introducing them into the record.

that 'generation' is not being used in a strictly literal sense. It follows that we are looking at an edited genealogy, edited in accord with the author's purpose.

In an effort to understand why the group of three was excluded, I ask: What might they have in common? They had in common genes from Ahab and Jezebel, as also a direct spiritual and moral influence from them. Ahaziah's mother was Athaliah, daughter of Ahab and Jezebel, so 50% of his genes were from Ahab. 2 Kings 8:27 says that Ahaziah was a son-in-law of the house of Ahab, referring to the mother of Joash, so 75% of his genes were from Ahab. Since Joash married Jehoaddan of Jerusalem, the contamination in Amaziah was down to 37%, and then in Uzziah it was below 20%.[1] This is my best guess as to why that group was excluded; a rebuke after the fact. (Matthew is giving an edited genealogy of the Christ, and Ahab's genes were definitely undesirable.)

We come now to another anomaly: 14 x 3 = 42, but only 41 names are given; what to do? We begin by noticing that both David and Jeconiah are mentioned on both sides of a 'boundary'. I will consider the second boundary first. Verse eleven says that "Josiah begot Jeconiah", passing over Jehoiakim, Jeconiah's father. Since Josiah was the last sovereign king of Judah, and since we need Jeconiah in the third group to make fourteen names, I place Jeconiah in the third group—counting both Jeconiah and Christ we get fourteen names.[2] Please notice that once again 'begot' does not refer to a son. But why was Jehoiakim omitted? So far as I know, he was the only king who had the perversity to actually cut up a scroll with God's Word and then throw it in the fire, Jeremiah 36:23, and the curse that follows in verse 30 is stated to be a consequence of that act. If we count David in the second group, Jehoiakim would make fifteen (but he wasn't a sovereign king). But without Jehoiakim we need David in the second group to make fourteen. But that raises another difficulty: we also need David in the first group, to make fourteen.

If the second group is made up of sovereign kings, the first group is made up of patriarchs. Acts 2:29 calls David a 'patriarch', so we may not disqualify him on that basis, but of course he is better known as a king—indeed he is expressly called that in the genealogy (the only one who is). Although David may be both patriarch and king, he may not be two people, nor two generations. In consequence, I am decidedly uncomfortable with the proposal that David must be placed in both groups—we should neither split him in two, not double him. To my mind, he belongs in the second group, but that leaves only thirteen for the first one. Enter Rahab and Ruth (and if four people were omitted from the second group, why could not some also be omitted from the first?).

---

[1] It was Dr. Floyd N. Jones who started me thinking along this line (*Chronology of the Old Testament: A Return to the Basics*, KingsWord Press, 1999, pp. 38-42).

[2] Of course, if four people were omitted from the second group, some may also have been omitted from the third, but we have no way of knowing, and it would make no difference to the purpose of this genealogy.

There were 340 years between the death of Joshua and the birth of David, and Salmon married Rahab while Joshua was still alive, presumably. That sort of obliges Boaz, Obed and Jesse to do their begetting at age 100, or thereabouts (perhaps not impossible, but certainly improbable). But what if 'begot' is being used for a grandson, as we have already seen? (Josiah begot Jeconiah, with no mention of Jehoiakim.) If Athaliah's genes were enough to disqualify Ahaziah, what about Rahab's genes? She was not even an Israelite, and worse, she was a prostitute. Now the Law says some rather severe things about prostitutes.[1] "You shall not bring the wages of a harlot or the price of a dog [catamite] to the house of the LORD your God,...for both of these are an abomination to the LORD your God" (Deuteronomy 23:18). For a priest to marry a harlot would profane his posterity (Leviticus 21:13-15), so how about an ancestor of the Messiah? Of course it is possible for a prostitute to be saved, but why was she even mentioned? And why were Tamar, Ruth, and Uriah's wife mentioned? Women were not normally included in genealogies.[2]

Now let's think about Ruth. She was a Moabitess, and according to Deuteronomy 23:3 a Moabite could not enter the assembly of the LORD to the tenth generation. [To me it is an astonishing example of the grace of God that she was included in the Messiah's line.] She embraced Naomi's God, but what about her genes? 'Ten generations' has to do with genes, not spiritual conversion. Moab was a son of Lot, and the first 'Moabite' would be his son; probably a contemporary of Jacob. From Jacob to Salmon we have seven generations, certainly fewer than ten, so Ruth could not enter. Could it be possible that Rahab and Ruth each represent a missing generation? Could that be why they are mentioned?[3] If we divide 300 years by five, then the average begetting age would be 60, certainly within the bounds of reason (and if more than two generations were skipped, the number would be further reduced). But even if that possibility is accepted, how can we justify using David in the first group (having already used him in the second)? Well, I would have to suppose that his name is used as a 'stand-in' for the missing generation(s) in the first group.[4] I repeat that this is not a 'normal' genealogy. Why did Matthew want three 'equal' groups, and why did he choose 'fourteen'? Perhaps for stylistic (symmetry, balance) and mnemonic reasons. However,

---

[1] However, "the law was given through Moses, but grace and truth came through Jesus Christ" (John 1:17). This being an edited genealogy of the Messiah, perhaps Rahab, and the other women, were included to emphasize the grace of the Messiah.

[2] None of the decent, honest, honorable, responsible mothers are mentioned, only 'exceptions'!

[3] Tamar had suffered a severe injustice, and David's sin with Bathsheba was unusually perverse (cowardly murder), but Rahab was probably a victim of circumstances, and Ruth was certainly not to blame for having been born a Moabitess.

[4] A 'stand-in', as the name suggests, is a temporary replacement; it refers to someone who occupies the position of a missing actor during a play rehearsal, for instance. So I am not calling David a generation in the first group; I am using his name to represent the missing generation(s)—rather, I am suggesting that Matthew used it in this way.

my concern has been to address any perceived errors of fact, which an inspired Text should not have.

To conclude: Matthew gives us an edited genealogy of the Messiah. If on the one hand it emphasizes the Messiah's grace, on the other it reflects the Messiah's holiness—He cannot overlook sin and its consequences (the four excluded names in the second group are due to that holiness). If the four women were included as a reflection of the Messiah's grace, it is also true that the consequences of sin are not hidden—the fourth is called simply 'Uriah's wife' (not 'widow', even though Solomon was conceived after the murder of Uriah—David did not marry a widow, he stole someone else's wife).

*Where is Mt. Sinai?*

I invite attention to Galatians 4:25, that declares that Mt. Sinai is in Arabia: I don't know Paul's definition of 'Arabia', but what the maps call 'Mt. Sinai' probably is not the real one;[1] consider: When Moses fled from Pharaoh he stopped in Midian (Exodus 2:15). Midian lies on the east side of the eastern 'rabbit-ear' of the Red Sea (the Gulf of Aqaba), in present day Saudi Arabia. It has never been part of the so-called 'Sinai Peninsula'. It was at "Horeb, the mountain of God" that Moses saw the 'burning bush' (Exodus 3:1), and in verse 12 God tells Moses: "when you have brought the people out of Egypt, you shall serve God on this mountain". Mt. Horeb has always been in Midian. (Present day Saudi Arabia calls it 'el Lowz', and has it fenced off.) As God continues with Moses' commission, He specifies "three days' journey into the wilderness" (verse 18). According to Exodus 4:27 Aaron met Moses at "the mountain of God" (Horeb, in Midian), and they went together to Egypt.

When the people left Egypt, God led them on a forced march; notice the "so as to go by day and night" (Exodus 13:21). Three days of forced march (Exodus 3:18) would have gotten them close to Ezion Geber (present day Elath), and just another two days would have put them well into Midian. But then God told them to "turn back" and "encamp by the sea, directly opposite Baal Zephon" (Exodus 14:2). To do this they had to leave the established route from Egypt to Arabia, and head south into the wilderness, and this led Pharaoh to conclude that they had lost their way (obviously he would have spies following them, mounted on good horses, to keep him informed). It would have been simply impossible for them to lose their way between Goshen and the western arm of the Red Sea (the Gulf of Suez), but this is what those who place Mt. Sinai in today's 'Sinai Peninsula' are obliged to say—an evident stupidity. The Israelites would have hunted and explored all over that area, down through the years. (And why the chariots? Pharaoh could have surrounded them with foot soldiers.)

---

[1] The difficulty here is not in the Text itself, but in the circumstance that almost all modern maps, whether in Bibles or elsewhere, place Mt. Sinai in the peninsula between the two gulfs, Suez and Aqaba; so much so that the peninsula itself is even so named. But such a location for the mount makes the Biblical account out to be ridiculous, as I explain below, and an inspired Text should not be ridiculous.

God led them down a ravine called 'Wadi Watir' which comes out on a surprisingly large beach called 'Nuweiba' (it is the only beach on that gulf large enough to accommodate that crowd of people and animals). Most of the Gulf of Aqaba is many hundreds of feet deep, with sheer sides, but precisely at Nuweiba there is a land bridge not far below the surface that goes from shore to shore, the width of the gulf at that point being close to 10 miles—the width of the land bridge is several hundred yards, so there was an ample 'causeway' for the crossing. The ravine that opens out on Nuweiba is narrow, with steep sides, so when God moved the pillar of cloud to the mouth of the ravine, Pharaoh and his chariots were blocked. They could not pass the pillar, they could not climb the sides of the ravine with chariots, and with over six hundred chariots in a narrow ravine they would have a proper 'gridlock' (lots of unhappy horses!). I suppose that God removed the pillar of cloud while part of the crowd was still on the land bridge, which encouraged Pharaoh to chase after them; and we know the rest of the story. If God let them get out to the middle, they would be five miles from either shore, too far for most people to swim.1 I take it that God's purpose was to destroy the Egyptian army so it could not be a threat to Israel in the early years.

*Cainan[2]—Luke 3:36 X Genesis 11:12*

"35 of Serug, of Reu, of Peleg, of Eber, of Shela, 36 of Cainan, of Arphaxad, of Shem, of Noah, of Lamech,"

There are several spelling variations that together are attested by almost 1% of the MSS; 99% have Καιναν. Apparently only two omit, $P^{75v}$ and D, but no printed text follows their lead. So there is no reasonable doubt that Luke in fact wrote that Shelah was fathered by Cainan, not Arphaxad. This Cainan has been widely used to justify treating the genealogies in Genesis like accordions—if one name was demonstrably left out in the Genesis account, then who knows how many others were also left out. This Cainan is also used to deny the validity of constructing a strict chronology based on the time spans given in the genealogies.

But where did Luke get this information? The LXX contains Cainan in Genesis 11:12, but is so different from the Massoretic text here that it looks like fiction. Recall that the LXX we know is based on codices Vaticanus, Sinaiticus and Alexandrinus, produced centuries after Luke. It is more likely that our LXX is based on Luke than vice versa. Where then did Luke get it? I understand that Luke obtained the information about this Cainan from records existing in his day, and being correct information was led by the Holy Spirit to include it in his Gospel. Just like Jude, who quoted Enoch—Enoch's prophecy must have been in existence in Jude's day, but we have no copy in Hebrew today (though Jews are reported to have used one so recently as the 13th century A.D.); similarly we have no copy of Luke's source.[2]

---

[1] In our day chariot pieces have been discovered along that land bridge.

[2] Let's recall Luke's stated purpose in writing: "It seemed good to me also, most excellent Theophilus, having taken careful note of everything from Above, to write to you

This brief note was inspired by the discussion of the subject given by Dr. Floyd N. Jones in *Chronology of the Old Testament*[1] (which book comes close to solving all the alleged numerical discrepancies in the OT, at least as I see it). However, the explanation that follows is original with me (if anyone else has proposed it, I am unaware). Let's recall the exact wording of Genesis 11:12-13. "Arphaxad lived thirty-five years and begot Salah; after he begot Salah, Arphaxad lived four hundred and three years, and begot sons and daughters."

The verb 'begot' requires that Salah be a blood descendent of Arphaxad, not adopted. He could be a grandson, the son of a son of Arphaxad, or even a great-grandson, etc., except that in this case the time frame only has room for one intervening generation. The plain meaning of the formula in the Text, 'W lived X years and begot Y; after W begot Y he lived Z years,' is that W was X years old when Y was born, is it not?[2] I take the clear meaning of the Hebrew Text to be that Arphaxad was 35 years old when Salah was born, whatever we may decide to do about 'Cainan'.

Let's try to imagine the situation in the years immediately following the Flood. After the Flood the 'name of the game' was to replenish the earth. Indeed, the divine command was: "Be fruitful and multiply" (Gen. 9:1). So, whom could Noah's grandsons marry? Obviously their cousins, Noah's granddaughters. There would be an urgency to reproduce—thus, the girls would be married off at puberty, and the boys wouldn't be wasting around either. The women would be giving birth as often as they possibly could. Really, the absolute top priority would be to increase the number of people.

Arphaxad was born two years after the flood, but his wife could have been born a year or two earlier. (The Sacred Text is clear to the effect that only eight souls entered the ark, but some of the women could have conceived during the Flood.) Thus, Arphaxad could have fathered "Cainan" when he was 17/18.

---

with precision and in sequence, so that you may know the certainty of the things in which you were instructed" (Luke 1:**3-4**). Given his stated purpose in writing, Luke's account needs to be historically accurate (cf. 2:2 and 3:1). So then, I take it that the Holy Spirit guided Luke to include Cainan[2]; I will argue the same for Joram below. While I'm on this tack, my solution to the 'Jeremiah' problem in Matthew 27:9-10 is similar. Daniel (9:2) refers to "the books" (plural) in connection with Jeremiah the prophet. So I assume that Matthew had access to other writings of Jeremiah, of which no copy survives.

[1] *Chronology of the Old Testament: A Return to the Basics* (Floyd Nolen Jones, The Woodlands, TX: Kings Word Press, 1999, pp. 29-36). (This is the 14th edition, revised and enlarged—the 1st came out in 1993.) I imagine that many readers may feel uncomfortable with the author's very dogmatic way of expressing himself, but I would urge them to filter out the rhetorical style and concentrate on the substantial arguments, that are of extraordinary value. For example, his solution to the conundrum of the reigns of the kings on the two sides of the divided monarchy is simply brilliant, and to my mind obviously correct, leaving no loose ends. (In this connection, he debunks the claims of Edwin R. Thiele and William F. Albright.)

[2] It follows that this formula destroys the 'accordion' gambit. There were precisely 130 years between Adam and Seth, 105 between Seth and Enosh, 90 between Enosh and Cainan[1], etc., etc.

Similarly, Cainan could have fathered Salah when he was 17/18. In this way Arphaxad could be said to have "begotten" Salah when he was 35. Cainan could have died early or been passed over in Genesis because the time span did not constitute a 'generation', or both. Or, as things got back to normal, culturally speaking, the haste with which Arphaxad and Cainan procreated might have been viewed as unseemly. The expedient of omitting Cainan would make the account more 'normal' while preserving precision as to the elapsed time.

But Luke would be correct in saying that Salah was "of" Cainan who was "of" Arphaxad. Salah was Arphaxad's grandson. In any case, the Messianic line was passed on by Salah. Without Luke's record I, for one, would never have stopped to consider what must have happened immediately following the Flood—the absolute priority must have been to increase the number of people.

*'Prophets' in Matthew 3:23*

"And upon arriving he settled in a town called Natsareth [Branch-town], so that what was spoken through the prophets should be fulfilled, that He would be called a Natsorean [Branch-man]."

We know from Luke that Natsareth was Joseph's home—his house and business were waiting for him (although he had been gone for quite a while). The name of the town in Hebrew is based on the consonants נצר (*resh, tsadde, nun*), but since Hebrew is read from right to left, for us the order is reversed = n, ts, r. This word root means 'branch'. Greek has the equivalent for 'ps' and 'ks', but not for 'ts', so the transliteration used a 'dz' (*zeta*), which is the voiced counterpart of 'ts'. But when the Greek was transliterated into English it came out as 'z'! But Hebrew has a 'z', ז (*zayin*), so in transliterating back into Hebrew people assumed the consonants נזר, replacing the correct *tsadde* with *zayin*. This technical information is necessary as background for what follows.

Neither 'Nazareth' nor 'Nazarene', spelled with a *zayin*, is to be found in the Old Testament, but there is a prophetic reference to Messiah as the Branch, *netser*—Isaiah 11:1—and several to the related word, *tsemach*—Isaiah 4:2, Jeremiah 23:5, 33:15; Zechariah 3:8, 6:12. So Matthew is quite right—the prophets (plural, being at least three) referred to Christ as the Branch. Since Jesus was a man, He would be the 'Branch-man', from 'Branch-town'. Which brings us to the word 'natsorean'. The familiar 'Nazarene' (Ναζαρηνος) [Natsarene] occurs in Mark 1:24, 14:67, 16:6 and Luke 4:34, but here in Matthew 2:23 and in fourteen other places, including Acts 22:8 where the glorified Jesus calls Himself that, the word is 'Natsorean' (Ναζωραιος), which is quite different. (Actually, in Acts 22:8 Jesus introduced Himself to Saul as 'the Natsorean', which strict Pharisee Saul would understand as a reference to the Messiah.) I have been given to understand that the Natsareth of Jesus' day had been founded some 100 years before by a Branch family who called it Branch town; they were very much aware of the prophecies about the Branch and fully expected the Messiah to be born from among them—they called themselves Branch-people (Natsoreans). Of course everyone else thought it was a big joke and tended to look down on them. "Can anything good...?"

The difficulty in this case is caused by differing phonologies; the sounds of Hebrew do not match those of Greek, or of English. Since proper names are often just transliterated, as in this case, and a translator will normally follow the phonology of the target language, what happened here was straightforward, without malice. We would have felt no inconvenience had Matthew not appealed to "the prophets". It is the false transliteration going back to Hebrew, from either Greek or English, that creates the seeming difficulty.

*Who bought what from whom?—Stephen X Genesis*

Acts 7:15-16—"So Jacob went down to Egypt; and he died, he and our fathers; and they were transferred to Shechem and placed in the tomb that Abraham bought for a sum of money from the sons of Hamor of Shechem."

When we compare this text with the relevant passages in Genesis, we appear to be confronted with some discrepancies. Who bought what from whom, and where? Genesis 33:19 informs us that <u>Jacob</u> bought a plot from Hamor, in Shechem. On the other hand, Genesis 23:16-20 explains that Abraham bought an area that included the cave of Machpelah from Ephron, in Hebron. That cave became the sepulcher of Abraham and Sarah, of Isaac and Rebecca, and of Jacob and Lea, because Jacob insisted upon being buried there, as indeed he was (Genesis 49:29-30, 50:13). Looking again at Acts 7, it was 'our fathers' that were buried in Shechem, not Jacob. Indeed, Joshua 24:32 states explicitly that Joseph's bones were buried in Shechem.

Yes but, whenever did Abraham buy anything in Shechem? I believe Genesis 12:6-7 gives us the clue. Abraham stopped in Shechem and built an altar. Now then, to build on someone else's property, with that someone looking on, probably won't work very well. I believe we may reasonably deduce that Abraham bought a plot "from the sons of Hamor of Shechem". The 'Hamor' of Jacob's day would be a descendant of the 'Hamor' in Abraham's (sons were often named after their fathers). In Genesis 14:14 we read that Abraham "armed his three hundred and eighteen trained servants who were born in his own house". If we add women and children, the total number of people under Abraham's command was probably over a thousand. Well now, with such a crowd it is not at all unlikely that someone died while they were stopped at Shechem. (People older than Abraham would not have been 'born in his own house', but there were doubtless older persons in that crowd.) In that event Abraham would need space for a cemetery, if the plot he had already bought for the altar wasn't big enough, or appropriate. That sort of information may have been available to Stephen from an extra-biblical document, or he may have figured it out as I have done (in his case guided by the Holy Spirit—Acts 7:55).

Going back to Genesis 33:19, it is possible that Jacob increased the area that Abraham had bought, by purchase. But why were all of Jacob's sons buried in Shechem? I believe the answer lies in Genesis 34:27-29. We read that Jacob's sons killed all the men of Shechem, looted everything, but <u>kept the</u>

<u>women and children</u>. And what do you suppose they did with the women? So where did you think they found wives for so many men? They got them from Shechem. Since Shechem was the source of their wives and material possessions, it would be a natural place for them to be buried.

To conclude: there is no discrepancy. Both Abraham and Jacob bought land in Shechem. It was Jacob's sons who were buried there, not Jacob himself.

*Bethsaida or Tiberias?*

The question is: just where did the feeding of the 5,000 men take place? Matthew 14:13 and Mark 6:32 merely say that it was in a deserted spot, without identification. But Luke 9:10 says it was in "a deserted place belonging to a town named Bethsaida",[1] while John 6:23 informs us that the spot was near the town of Tiberias. Well now, Tiberias was located on the west side of the Sea, a mile or two above the place where the Jordan River leaves the Sea. But Bethsaida was at the top of the Sea, a little to the east of where the Jordan enters the Sea. What to do?

We may deduce from Mark 6:31 and John 6:17 and 24 that Jesus and His disciples started out from Capernaum, where Jesus had His base of operations. It happens that Capernaum, like Bethsaida, was situated at the top of the Sea, but a little to the west of the entrance of the Jordan. To go from Capernaum to Bethsaida by boat one would not get far from the shore. But John 6:1 says that Jesus "went over the Sea of Galilee", and that agrees better with Tiberias, since there is a large bay between Capernaum and Tiberias, although they are both on the west side of the Sea—they crossed close to ten miles of water. Further, after the feast, Matthew 14:22 says they went by boat "to the other side", and verse 24 has them "in the middle of the Sea"; while Mark 6:45 says that they went by boat "to the other side, to Bethsaida", and verse 47 has them "in the middle of the Sea"; and John 6:17 says that they "started to cross the Sea toward Capernaum", and verse 19 that "they had rowed some three or four miles".

Well now, to stay close to the shore is one thing, to go over the Sea is another. Further, if they were already in or near Bethsaida, how could they cross the Sea in order to get there (Mark 6:45)? It becomes clear that the miracle in fact took place near Tiberias, as John affirms. But that raises another difficulty: how could a property near Tiberias 'belong' to Bethsaida (Luke 9:10)? Either it had been deeded to the town somehow, or, more likely, it belonged to a family that lived in Bethsaida. My reason for saying this is based on the Text.

---

[1] Lamentably, the eclectic Greek text currently in vogue, following a mere half of one percent of the Greek manuscripts (and that half made up of objectively inferior ones), says that they went "to a town named Bethsaida". This is an obvious perversity because two verses later the same text has them in a deserted place. So the editors of that text make Luke contradict himself, as well as contradicting the other three Gospels, since all agree that the place was deserted. Unfortunately, this perversity is duly reproduced by NIV, NASB, TEV, etc.

John 6:17 says that they "started toward Capernaum", while Mark 6:45 says that they went "to Bethsaida". Since the two towns were a short distance apart, at the beginning of the crossing the direction would be virtually the same. I understand that they did indeed go to Bethsaida, but spent very little time there, going from there directly to Genesaret. Indeed, the day after the miracle Jesus was already back in Capernaum (John 6:24-25). But just why did they make that side trip to Bethsaida (Genesaret lies just south of Capernaum)? I imagine the following: a property near Tiberias, but belonging to someone in Bethsaida, would likely be deserted, a great place for a picnic. I suppose that Jesus had permission to use the place, when He wanted to get away, but no one had foreseen a crowd of perhaps 15,000 (5,000 men plus women and children). Please pardon the unpleasant consideration, but what effect would a crowd that size have on the hygiene and appearance of the place? I conclude that Jesus felt obligated to give a report to the owner, in Bethsaida.

While we are here, allow me to call attention to another miracle Jesus performed, that you will not find in the usual lists. As already noted, Matthew 14:24 and Mark 6:46 say that they were in the middle of the Sea, but John 6:19 is more precise, saying that they had gone perhaps four miles. It happens that a crossing from Tiberias to Bethsaida would involve about eight miles. And now, attention please to John 6:21, "Then they wanted to receive Him into the boat, and immediately the boat was at the land to which they were going". If the total distance was eight miles, and they had only managed half of it, then Jesus transported the boat four miles instantly. Now that was a fair sized miracle, to transport a boat four miles in an instant! You won't find this miracle in most lists, because few people take the time to give a detailed examination to the Sacred Text.

*The 'Legion' and the pigs; where was it?*

We need to start with the evidence supplied by the Greek manuscripts. We encounter the episode in three of the Gospels.

Matthew 8:28: γεργεσηνων 98% (Gergesenes) AV, NKJV
　　　　　　　γαδαρηνων　2% (Gadarenes) NIV, NASB, LB, TEV, etc.
　　　NIV footnote: "Some manuscripts *Gergesenes*; others *Gerasenes*".

Mark 5:1: γαδαρηνων 95,5% (Gadarenes) AV, NKJV
　　　　γεργεσηνων　4,1% (Gergesenes)
　　　　γερασηνων　0,3% (Gerasenes) NIV, NASB, LB, TEV, etc.
　　　NIV footnote: "Some manuscripts *Gadarenes*; other manuscripts
*Gergesenes*".

Luke 8:26: γαδαρηνων　97% (Gadarenes) AV, NKJV
　　　　　γεργεσηνων　2% (Gergesenes) TEV
　　　　　γερασηνων　0,3% (Gerasenes) NIV, NASB, LB, etc.
　　　NIV footnote: "Some manuscripts *Gadarenes;* other manuscripts
*Gergesenes;* also in verse 37".

Luke 8:37: γαδαρηνων   96%  (Gadarenes) AV, NKJV
γεργεσηνων 3,5% (Gergesenes) TEV
γερασηνων  0,3% (Gerasenes) NIV, NASB, LB, etc.

I will begin with Mark. Jesus arrived at "the region [not 'province'] of the Gadarenes". Gadara was the capital city of the Roman province of Perara, located some six miles from the Sea of Galilee. Since Mark was writing for a Roman audience,[1] "the region of the Gadarenes" was a perfectly reasonable description of the site. Lamentably, the eclectic Greek text currently in vogue follows about five Greek manuscripts of objectively inferior quality (against at least 1,700 better ones) in reading 'Gerasenes' (to be followed by NIV, NASB, LB, TEV, etc.). The NIV footnote is dishonest: to use 'some' to describe over 1,600 manuscripts against five is a dishonest use of the Queen's English (to use 'others' to refer to some 60 is acceptable).

Luke also has Jesus arriving at "the region of the Gadarenes". Since he was writing for a Greek audience, he follows Mark's example. Again NIV has a dishonest footnote. It is most likely that 'Gerasa' is a fiction, a 'place' that never existed. On the other hand, 'Gergesa' certainly did exist, although we no longer know the exact location. As I will explain while discussing Matthew, below, I have no doubt that it was a village near the spot where Jesus landed.

Matthew clearly wrote 'Gergesenes' rather than 'Gadarenes'. Since he was writing for a Jewish audience, and many Galileans would be quite familiar with the Sea of Galilee, he provided a more localized description. Further, try to picture the events in your mind. Do you suppose that the swineherds ran six miles to Gadara? The populace would certainly not run the six miles back. All of that would have taken entirely too long. To me it is obvious that there was a village close by, probably within half a mile, called 'Gergesa'. It was to that village that the swineherds ran, told their story, and brought the residents back. Galileans familiar with the Sea of Galilee would certainly recognize 'Gergesa'.

Not only does Matthew name a different place, he affirms that there were really two demonized men, whereas Mark and Luke mention only one. As a former tax collector, numerical precision was important to Matthew. Neither Mark nor Luke use the number 'one'; they merely commented on the more prominent of the two, the one who wanted to go with Jesus. I understand that indeed there were two of them.

*Gall, or myrrh? Matthew 27:34 X Mark 15:23*

In the NKJV, Matthew 27:34[a] reads like this: "they gave Him sour wine mingled with gall to drink." And Mark 15:23[a] reads like this: "Then they gave Him wine mingled with myrrh to drink." That Mark used a generic term, 'wine', for the

---

[1] Although, as explained elsewhere, I understand that Matthew was published first, and Mark probably had a copy open before him as he wrote, yet he deliberately changed Matthew's 'Gergesenes' to 'Gadarenes'—to his intended Roman audience 'Gergesa' would be unknown, while some would indeed know about 'Gadara'.

more precise 'sour wine' (or 'wine vinegar'), need not detain us. But what was the mixture? 'Gall' is one thing, an animal substance, and 'myrrh' is another, a vegetable substance; it was either one or the other, but which? Was Matthew influenced by Psalm 69:21? "They also gave me gall for my food, and for my thirst they gave me vinegar to drink." (Matthew wrote for a Jewish audience, and seems to have mentioned fulfilled prophecy whenever he could.) More to the point, perhaps, is Acts 8:23, where Peter says to Simon (the ex-sorcerer), "for I see that you are in a gall of bitterness" (so the Greek Text). Evidently 'gall' was used as a generic term for any bitter substance. I take it that Matthew, perhaps influenced by Psalm 69:21, used the generic term. I conclude that the precise substance used was myrrh, as Mark indicates.

*Jeremiah?—Matthew 27:9-10*

In the NKJV, Matthew 27:9-10 reads like this: "Then was fulfilled what was spoken by Jeremiah the prophet, saying, *And they took the thirty pieces of silver, the value of Him who was priced*, whom they of the children of Israel priced, *and gave them for the potter's field, as the LORD directed me*." The difficulty comes when we try to find this material in our canonical Jeremiah. Cross-references send us to Jeremiah 32:6-9, or 18:1-4, or 19:1-3, but upon inspection they must don't match. In Zechariah 11:12-13 we find a general approximation, but it is not precise—and of course Zechariah is not Jeremiah. Evidently there are Hebrew manuscripts that begin the scroll containing the prophets (major and minor) with Jeremiah, and it has been argued that Matthew used 'Jeremiah' to refer to the contents of the entire scroll. I suppose that could be a possibility, but I prefer to appeal to Daniel 9:2. "In the first year of his reign [Darius] I, Daniel, understood by the books the number of the years *specified* by the word of the LORD through Jeremiah the prophet,…" Note that 'books' is plural. Why should any of us assume that men like Jeremiah, or Isaiah, wrote only what is in our canon? (I myself have written a great deal that has never been published.) Daniel clearly wrote 'book<u>s</u>', presumably referring to Jeremiah. I conclude that such extra-canonical books were still known in Matthew's day, and that he refers to one of them. I am aware that the distinction cannot be insisted upon, but Matthew did use 'spoken' rather than 'written'.

*Who said what? Matthew 27:48-49 X Mark 15:36 X John 19:29-30 (Luke 23:36)*

I take it that the action in John 19:29, as well as Luke 23:36, was carried out by soldiers, and should not be confused with that recorded in Matthew and Mark, although all four refer to offering Jesus sour wine to drink (since Jesus was on the cross for some six hours, there was time for several drinks). The seeming discrepancy I wish to address is in Matthew and Mark. In the NKJV, Matthew 27:48-49 reads like this: "Immediately one of them ran and took a sponge, filled it with sour wine and put it on a reed, and offered it to Him to drink. The rest said, 'Let Him alone; let us see if Elijah will come to save Him'." A single man offers the drink, but the rest say, "Let Him alone,…" And Mark 15:36 reads like this: "Then someone ran and filled a sponge full of sour wine, put it on a reed, and offered it to Him to drink, saying, 'Let Him alone,…'" A single man offers the drink, and **he** says, "Let Him alone,…" I would not be surprised if the man involved here was John Mark himself. But whoever he was, if he knew Hebrew he knew perfectly well that Jesus was not calling Elijah, so he sarcastically repeats their statement, in disgust. I deny any discrepancy.

*Entering or leaving Jericho? Luke 18:35 & 19:1 X Mark 10:46 X Matthew 20:29-30*

In the NKJV, Luke 18:35 and 19:1 read like this: "Then it happened, as He was coming near Jericho, that a certain blind man sat by the road begging….Then Jesus entered and passed through Jericho." Luke plainly states that Jesus healed a blind man before entering Jericho (he mentions only one, but does not say that there was only one). And Mark 10:46 reads like this: "Now they came to Jericho. As He went out of Jericho with his disciples and a great multitude, blind Bartimaeus, the son of Timaeus, sat by the road begging." Mark plainly states that Jesus healed a blind man upon leaving Jericho (he names the blind man, referring only to him, but does not say that there was only one). And Matthew 20:29-30 reads like this: "Now as they went out of Jericho, a great multitude followed Him. And behold, two blind men sitting by the road,…" Matthew plainly states that Jesus healed two blind men upon leaving Jericho. Well now, entering is one thing, and leaving is another, so which was it? Strange to relate, it was both! The Jericho that Joshua destroyed had been rebuilt (at least partially), and was inhabited. But in Jesus' day Herod had built a new Jericho, perhaps a kilometer away from the old one, also inhabited. So where would an intelligent beggar place himself? Presumably between the two towns. I take it that all three of the accounts before us transpired between the two Jerichos, so Jesus was leaving one and entering the other. There is no discrepancy. Luke and Mark probably give us the same incident, but what about Mathew? Besides stating that the men were two, he says that Jesus "touched their eyes", whereas according to Luke and Mark He only spoke. It is entirely probable that there was more than one beggar along that stretch of road, and any shouting could be heard for quite a ways. I take it that Matthew records a different incident. I suppose that Bartimaeus was healed first, and he shouted so loud that the two heard it all and knew what to do when their turn came.

*"This is", or "You are"? Matthew 3:17 X Mark 1:11, Luke 3:22*

In the NKJV, Matthew 3:17 reads like this: "And suddenly a voice came from heaven, saying, 'This is My beloved Son, in whom I am well pleased'." And Mark 1:11 reads like this: "Then a voice came from heaven, 'You are My beloved Son, in whom I am well pleased'." Luke also has "You are". So what did the Voice actually say? In a manner similar to what happened on the Day of Pentecost, I conclude that each hearer received his own interpretation, or message. Matthew records the event from John's perspective: he heard, "This is…" Mark and Luke record the event from Jesus' perspective: He heard, "You are…" At Pentecost, with over a dozen languages being spoken at once, even if one of them was yours, it would require a personal miracle in your ear to enable you to extract your message from the welter of sound.

## Seeming difficulties resulting from faulty translation

I recognize that the line between this type of 'problem' and the former can be 'fuzzy', and in consequence I am not concerned to defend the placement of each case. I further understand that my use of the term 'faulty' transmits an implied criticism of such translations, but since my overriding concern is to defend the Text, that criticism is unavoidable. I use the NKJV because it is my Bible, but any other version, of the way too many that are out there, would also serve the purpose. (It is also true that any particular version may have created 'problems' that are its private property, but chasing down such problems is beyond the scope of this exercise.)

*Before or after? 2 Thessalonians 2:2 X 2:7-8*

In Matthew 24:44 we read, "Therefore you also be ready, because the Son of the Man is coming at an hour that you do not suppose." I take it that for there to be the element of surprise the Rapture of the Church must occur before the "abomination of desolation". When the Antichrist takes his place in the Holy of Holies and declares himself to be god there will be precisely 1,290 days until the return of Christ to the earth. "An hour that you do not suppose" presumably requires a pre-'abomination' rapture—if the rapture is pre-wrath but post-abomination, only a fool will be taken by surprise, unless the Rapture happens immediately after the 'abomination' (2 Thessalonians 2:3-4).

Let's begin with 2 Thessalonians 2:2. Some 15% of the Greek manuscripts have 'day of the Lord' (as in NIV, NASB, LB, TEV, etc.); the 85% that have 'day of Christ' (including the best line of transmission) are doubtless correct. I remember one day in a Greek exegesis class, the professor stated that one reason he preferred the 'critical' text (that reads 'Lord' here) is that it fit better with his view of eschatology—the 'Day of Christ' is usually associated with the Rapture and blessing of the saints, while the 'Day of the Lord' is usually associated with heavy judgment upon the world and unrepentant Israel, including the outpouring of wrath just before and after the Second Coming of Christ, when He returns in glory to establish His Millennial Reign. The perceived difficulty here would appear to be that while verses 1, 6 and 7 evidently relate to the Rapture, verses 3-4 and 8-10 evidently relate to the Great Tribulation and the Second Coming. What to do? Look carefully at the Text. In verse 2, why would the Thessalonian believers be "disturbed"? Someone was teaching that the Rapture had already happened and they had been left behind—I would be disturbed too! So 'day of Christ' is precisely correct with reference to the content of verses 1 and 2. The trouble comes in verse 3 because a clause is elided; as an aid to the reader translations usually supply a clause, preferably in italics, to show that it is an addition, as in NKJV—"*that Day will not come*". But that would put the Rapture after the revelation of the man of sin and the 'abomination of desolation'—definitely not congenial to certain eschatological systems. An easy 'solution' would be to change 'Christ' to 'Lord' in verse 2, but that would put the Rapture within the 'day of the Lord'—also not congenial. I submit that fine-tuning our view of eschatology is preferable to tampering with the Text.

232

If the 'Restrainer' in verses 6-8 is the Holy Spirit, then the Rapture happens before the 'abomination', and may be viewed as its 'trigger'. I translate verse 7 as follows: "For the mystery of the lawlessness is already at work; only He who now restrains *will do so* until He removes Himself." Perhaps more literally, 'gets Himself out of the middle' (the verb γινομαι is inherently middle in voice). I would say that the Holy Spirit is the only one who satisfies the description. But if the 'Day of Christ' includes the Rapture, then verse 3 would appear to place the Rapture <u>after</u> the 'abomination'. So where does that leave us? Although my own training was strongly 'pre-trib', I have moved to a 'meso-trib' position. If the Rapture follows immediately upon the 'abomination', then the 'surprise' factor remains untouched. If the 'abomination' and the Rapture happen within minutes of each other, then from God's point of view they form a single 'package', and the actual sequence is not important—for all practical purposes they happen at the same time.

### Did they hear the Voice, or not? Acts 9:7 X Acts 22:9

In the NKJV, Acts 9:7 reads like this: "And the men who journeyed with him stood speechless, hearing a voice but seeing no one." And Acts 22:9 reads like this: "And those who were with me indeed saw the light and were afraid, but they did not hear the voice of him who spoke to me." Comparing the two accounts, we seem to have a discrepancy: did they hear the Voice, or didn't they? Comparing the verses in the Greek Text, we discover that the verb, 'hear', and the noun, 'voice', are the same in both. Looking more closely, however, we notice that in 9:7 the noun is in the Genitive case, while in 22:9 it is in the Accusative. We have here a subtlety of Greek grammar: in the Genitive 'voice' refers to sound, while in the Accusative it refers to meaning, to the words. Saul's companions heard the Voice, but were not allowed to understand the words—only Saul understood the words. A similar thing happened in John 12:28-29; the people hear the sound (sufficiently impressive that they called it thunder), but only Jesus understood the words.

### "Saved in childbearing"—1 Timothy 2:15

In the NKJV, 1 Timothy 2:14-15 reads like this: "And Adam was not deceived, but the woman being deceived, fell into transgression. Nevertheless she will be saved in childbearing if they continue in faith, love, and holiness, with self-control." We begin with "she will be saved"; 'she' is a pronoun, that stands for a noun, and in the context the reference is clearly to Eve. So how is Eve to be saved? (To render 'preserved' is basically meaningless.) Neither Eve nor any other woman is saved by bearing a child. In the Greek Text we find 'childbirth', a noun, not a verb. Further, there is a definite article with the noun, so it is '<u>the</u> childbirth'. There is only one childbirth that could result in salvation for Eve, and the rest of us, the birth of the Messiah. Of course Eve bore Seth, thus beginning the line that culminated in the Messiah (Genesis 3:15). In the middle of verse 15, and of the sentence, Paul breaks the rules of grammar and switches from 'she' to 'they'—what is true of Eve is applied to all women. Well, strictly speaking, since 'they' has no antecedent I suppose it could include men as well, everybody (unless someone wants to argue that women are saved on a different basis than men [which I think would run afoul of other passages]).

Still, the paragraph is about women. Any sisters in Christ who have been troubled by this verse, thinking that they must bear a child, may relax on that score.

*How many animals? Matthew 21:1-7 X Mark 11:1-10, Luke 19:29-36, John 12:12-15*

Mark, Luke and John are agreed in mentioning a single animal, a donkey colt. It was loosed, brought to Jesus, garments placed upon it, and then Jesus rode on it. Matthew insists on telling us that there were really two animals, the colt and its mother. The AV (KJV) has a most unfortunate translation of both Matthew 21:5 and Zechariah 9:9 (that has been corrected in the NKJV, fortunately). In Zechariah the AV has, "riding upon an ass, and upon a colt the foal of an ass." In Matthew the AV has, "sitting upon an ass, and a colt the foal of an ass." The obvious difficulty is that the AV makes Jesus ride two animals, when in fact He only rode one. For the correct rendering of both Zechariah and Matthew, at this point, please see the NKJV. That said, however, the fact remains that Matthew clearly has the disciples fetching two animals and placing garments on both. Why do you suppose the Holy Spirit had Matthew supply the added information? I wasn't there, of course, but I offer my understanding of the event. Mark and Luke specify that no one had ever sat on the colt; they say that the colt was tied, but Matthew says it was really the mother that was tied. Evidently the colt was so young that it was still staying close to 'mother', so if she was tied, he was too, in effect (they were out in the street, and that may have been a new experience for the colt). Jesus was going to subject the colt to a strange and even frightening situation. From the peace and quiet of his little village, he would be surrounded by a shouting crowd. Strange things would be put on his back, and then someone who was probably bigger and heavier than he was would sit on him! I believe that Jesus had the mother brought along as moral support for her son. Clothes were put on her too (and of course she was surrounded by the shouting crowd as well), and seeing that she was calm would encourage the colt. Just by the way, Jesus probably had to lift His feet to keep them from dragging; it must have been a comical sight. It gives me a warm feeling to see that the Lord Jesus was concerned for the well-being of the colt.

*"Jesus" or "Joshua"? Hebrews 4:8*

Beyond question, the Greek Text has 'Jesus', as in the AV, but most modern versions put 'Joshua'. I suppose that 'Jesus' was judged to be an anachronism, and so 'Joshua' was elected to relieve the situation. To be sure, the Septuagint we know uniformly spells 'Joshua' as $Ιησους$ (Jesus) [as a linguist I wonder why the translators transliterated '*Iehoshua*' as '*Iesus*'], and probably in consequence, in Acts 7:45 Luke refers to Joshua as '*Iesus*' [it was not his purpose to correct the LXX]. However, looking carefully at the context in Psalm 95:7-11, Joshua just does not fit. Consider: it is presumably Jehovah the Son who is speaking ("Jehovah our Maker", verse 6), and since the reference is to those who fell in the wilderness during the forty years, Joshua cannot be in view. Not only that, I invite attention to Joshua 21:43-45 and 23:1, where the Text says that Joshua did in fact give them rest. So whom are you going to believe? Of course the Text is referring to physical rest, not spiritual, since neither Joshua nor anyone else could be responsible for a people's spiritual rest. Ezekiel chapter 18 is very clear to the effect that each individual is responsible for his own eternal destiny. God has no grandchildren, only sons and daughters. In Mathew 23:8-10 Sovereign Jesus forbids any attempt to dominate someone else's faith or conscience. This is consistent with His statement in John 4:23-24. The worship that the Father wants cannot be forced, imposed, controlled or faked.

In relief of the notion of 'anachronism' I offer the following: 1) in John 12:41 John affirms that Isaiah saw Jesus (it was Jehovah the Son on the throne); 2) in 1 Corinthians 10:4 Paul affirms that the Rock that provided water was Christ; 3) in Hebrews 11:26 the same author [as I believe] has Moses choosing "the reproach of Christ"; 4) in 1 Peter 1:19-20 Peter affirms that the shed blood of God's Lamb, Jesus, was foreknown before Creation—but blood requires a body, and the Lamb's body was that of Jesus; so Jesus, as Jesus, was known before Creation. Returning to Hebrews 4:8, it was precisely Jesus, Jehovah the Son, who did not allow that generation to enter the 'rest'.

*"Censer", or "altar of incense"? Hebrews 9:4*

What concerns us here is the Greek word, θυμιατηριον, that occurs only here in the NT. In the LXX the meaning of the word is 'censer', and that is plainly the intended meaning here. But unfortunately modern versions like NIV, TEV, LB, NASB, etc. render 'altar of incense', thus setting up a contradiction with the Old Testament. [What could have motivated such a perverse proceeding?] According to Exodus 30:6 the altar of incense was placed in front of the curtain leading into the Holy of Holies, and so it was in the Holy Place, not the Holy of Holies. The only reference to this particular censer appears to be in Leviticus 16:12, where it was to be used behind the second curtain to hide the Ark with smoke. Since that censer would only be used once a year (on the day of atonement), it may well have been stored just behind a corner of the second curtain (where the high priest could retrieve it without looking in) and thus the author of Hebrews would be correct in saying that the censer was behind the second curtain, whereas the altar was in front of it. In any event, evidently that censer was **used** only within the Holy of Holies, and so it would be appropriate to say that the area 'had' a golden censer.

*Do we command God? Matthew 18:18*

In the NKJV, Matthew 18:18 reads like this: "Assuredly, I say to you, whatever you bind on earth will be bound in heaven, and whatever you loose on earth will be loosed in heaven." The normal meaning of this translation is that Heaven has to follow our lead (is it not?), and there is no lack of religious communities that teach this. But really now, what possible competence might human beings have to tell God what to do? We may ask, but not command. The difficulty arises from an inaccurate translation. The tense of the Greek verb phrase here is a periphrastic future perfect, passive voice (so also in 16:18). Thus, "will have been bound/loosed" not "will be bound/loosed". We are not telling God what to do; we are to apply down here that which He has

235

already done in heaven. (What had been just for Peter is now given to all the disciples.)

In John 5:19 the Lord Jesus stated that He could only do what He saw the Father doing. Our inability to see what the Father is doing is probably one of our worst spiritual problems—it condemns us to waste a lot of time and energy trying to do things that we shouldn't. In practical terms, when I 'bind' something and nothing happens, I conclude that it had not been 'bound' in Heaven. I tried to do something that the Father wasn't doing.

### Buy cleansing? Luke 11:41

In the NKJV, Luke 11:41 reads like this: "But rather give alms of such things as you have; then indeed all things are clean to you." My translation reads like this: "Nevertheless, give what is possible as alms; then indeed all things are clean to you." At first glance this statement seems difficult, but because they were filled with greed, for them to give away as much as possible would represent a major change in their values. Zacchaeus offers a case in point: the Lord Himself declared that he was saved (Luke 19:8-9).

### Are we to handle snakes? Mark 16:18

In the NKJV, Mark 16:18 reads like this: "they will take up serpents; and if they drink anything deadly, it will by no means hurt them; they will lay hands on the sick, and they will recover."[1]

The NIV renders 'they will pick up snakes with their hands', the 'with their hands' being based on just over 2% of the Greek manuscripts. As we know, there are those who take this translation literally, and believe that they must handle poisonous snakes in obedience to God. I respect their sincerity, but believe they have been misled by a faulty translation.

I would say that this particular statement of the Lord's has been generally misunderstood. The verb in question covers a wide semantic area, one of the uses being to pick up the way a garbage man picks up a bag of trash—he does so to get rid of it (hence 'remove'). I believe Luke 10:19 sheds light on this question. In Luke 10:19 the Lord Jesus said: "Behold, I give [so 98% of the Greek manuscripts] you the authority to trample on snakes and scorpions, and over all the power of the enemy, and nothing shall by any means hurt you." The Lord is addressing the Seventy, not the Twelve, and others were doubtless present; further, this was said perhaps four months before His death and resurrection. It follows that this authority is not limited to the apostles, and there is no indication of a time limit. The Lord Jesus affirms that He gives us the authority over all the power of the enemy. In Matthew 28:18 He declares that He holds "all authority …in heaven and earth", and so He has the right and the competence to delegate a portion of that authority to us. We may have

---

[1] Since only three Greek MSS (really only two) omit Mark 16:9-20, against at least 1,700 that contain them, there can be no reasonable question as to the genuineness of those verses. For more on this subject please see the respective appendix in any recent edition of my book, The Identity of the New Testament Text.

any number of enemies, but the enemy is Satan. The phrase, "all the power", presumably includes his works, followed by their consequences.

Returning to Luke 10:19, the Lord gives us the authority to "trample snakes and scorpions". Well now, to smash the literal insect, a scorpion, you don't need power from on High, just a slipper (if you're fast you can do it barefoot). To trample a snake I prefer a boot, but we can kill literal snakes without supernatural help. It becomes obvious that Jesus was referring to something other than reptiles and insects. I understand Mark 16:18 to be referring to the same reality—Jesus declares that certain signs will accompany the believers (the turn of phrase virtually has the effect of commands): they will expel demons, they will speak strange languages, they will remove 'snakes', they will place hands on the sick. ("If they drink…" is not a command; it refers to an eventuality.) But what did the Lord Jesus mean by 'snakes'?

In a list of distinct activities Jesus has already referred to demons, so the 'snakes' must be something else. In Matthew 12:34 Jesus called the Pharisees a 'brood of vipers', and in 23:33, 'snakes, brood of vipers'. In John 8:44, after they claimed God as their father, Jesus said, "You are of your father the devil". And 1 John 3:10 makes clear that Satan has many other 'sons'. In Revelation 20:2 we read: "He seized the dragon, the ancient serpent, who is a slanderer, even Satan, who deceives the whole inhabited earth, and bound him for a thousand years." If Satan is a snake, then his children are also snakes. So then, I take it that our 'snakes' are human beings who chose to serve Satan, who sold themselves to evil. I conclude that the 'snakes' in Luke 10:19 are the same as those in Mark 16:18, but what of the 'scorpions'? Since they also are of the enemy, they may be demons, in which case the term may well include their offspring, the humanoids [see my paper, "In the Days of Noah"]. I am still working on the question of just how the removal is to be done.

*Did Jesus hide? John 8:59*

In the NKJV, John 8:59 reads like this: "Then they took up stones to throw at Him; but Jesus hid Himself and went out of the temple, going through the midst of them, and so passed by." My translation reads like this: "Then they picked up stones to throw at Him;[1] but Jesus was concealed and went out of the temple, going through the middle of them; yes, that's how He got away!" The familiar "hid Himself" is not the best rendering here. Jesus did not try to hide behind a pillar, or whatever. He was surrounded by angry Jews with stones in their hands. Obviously they would have seen Him and started stoning. He became invisible and simply walked out, passing right through the middle of them. About half a percent of the Greek manuscripts, of objectively inferior quality (demonstrably so), omit "going through the middle of them; yes, that's how He got away" (as in NIV, NASB, LB, TEV, etc.). The 99.5% are doubtless correct, and supply an important detail.

*"Valley", or "ravine"? Luke 3:5*

---

[1] Since certain situations demanded a stoning, there were doubtless piles of ammunition placed strategically around the temple premises.

In the NKJV, Luke 3:4-5 reads like this: "The voice of one crying in the wilderness: 'Prepare the way of the Lord; make His paths straight. Every valley shall be filled and every mountain and hill brought low; the crooked places shall be made straight and the rough ways smooth; ...'" Does this mean that the surface of the earth will be flattened out? My translation reads like this: "A voice calling out: 'Prepare the way of the Lord in the wilderness, make His paths straight. 5 Every ravine will be filled up, and every mountain and hill will be leveled; the crooked parts of the roads will be straightened out, and the rough parts will be smoothed out; ...'" The reference is to Isaiah 40:3. Hebrew poetry, and prose, makes heavy use of parallel or synonymous statements. From the context in Isaiah it seems clear that "in the wilderness" goes with the verb "make straight", not "call out". But why a straight road in the wilderness? Any road facilitates the movement of people and goods, but a straight road through accidented terrain is a major asset, and Jerusalem is surrounded by accidented terrain. I render 'ravine' according to the normal meaning of the Greek word here; 'ravine' is also one of the normal meanings of the corresponding Hebrew word in Isaiah. Actually, Isaiah 40:3-4 describes the construction of a modern super highway. Verse 5 describes what happens where the highway passes, not all over the place.

## Lack of attention to details in the Text

I recognize that the line between this type of 'problem' and the former can be 'fuzzy', and in consequence I am not concerned to defend the placement of each case. And there is very little difference in the consequences.

*Did the cross kill Jesus? John 10:18 X Mark 15:39, John 19:30, Matthew 27:50, Luke 23:46*

In the NKJV, John 10:17-18 reads like this: "Therefore My Father loves Me, because I lay down My life that I may take it again. No one takes it from me, but I lay it down of Myself. I have power to lay it down, and I have power to take it again. This command I have received from My Father." Please notice: "**No one takes it from me**". That includes Pilate, etc. In Matthew 27:50 and John 19:30 the Text states that Jesus "dismissed His spirit". Now consider Mark 15:39. "So when the centurion, who stood opposite Him, saw that He cried out like this and breathed His last, he said, 'Truly this Man was the Son of God!'" Now what could convince a hardened Roman centurion? He had doubtless witnessed no end of crucifixions; he knew that the victim died of asphyxiation. Hanging from one's hands, the diaphragm is pressed against the lungs, and the victim can't breathe. Nailing the feet was a sadistic procedure, to prolong the agony—in spite of the pain, the victim would push up so he could get a breath, until finally too worn out to do so. (That is why the Pharisees requested Pilate to have the legs broken; then they died within minutes.) Now then, someone who is dying asphyxiated does not give a tremendous shout; but ordinary people cannot just tell their spirit to leave. So when that centurion observed that Jesus gave a tremendous shout and then immediately died, he drew the obvious conclusion: he was looking at a supernatural being. The cross did not kill Jesus; He gave His life voluntarily, for you and me. Thank you, Lord!

*Did the centurion leave his house? Luke 7:1-10 X Matthew 8:5-13*

It has often been supposed that these are parallel accounts of the same incident. To be sure, both involve a centurion, in Capernaum, a sick servant, and the statement of the centurion along with the Lord's reaction are very similar. But other details simply do not match. Evidently the Romans had an army base in Capernaum, with a centurion as commanding officer, who could be rotated. [Where do you suppose Peter sold most of his fish? And what language did he use?] Looking at the sequence of events in both Matthew and Luke, I would say that the incident recorded by Matthew happened first, and a number of months before the one recorded by Luke. Of course an incident like that would become part of the 'folklore' of the base. I assume that the centurions were different, but they certainly knew each other, so the second one knew every detail of the first incident. When his turn came, he used a different strategy to make his appeal (he was asking for a second favor), but then repeated the statement that had impressed Jesus so favorably. So, the first centurion left his house, but the second did not.

*"Staff", or "bed"? Hebrews 11:21 X Genesis 47:31*

In the NKJV, Hebrews 11:21 reads like this: "By faith Jacob, when he was dying, blessed each of the sons of Joseph, and worshipped, *leaning* on the top of his staff." It has been alleged that this statement disagrees with Genesis 47:31, that has Jacob leaning on the head of the bed (following the Massoretic Text), rather than the top of his staff. However, close attention to the contexts indicates that Hebrews 11:21 and Genesis 47:31 refer to different occasions, so there is no need to imagine a discrepancy. That said, it may be of interest to note the following. The Hebrew words for 'bed' and 'staff' are spelled with the same three consonants, the difference being in the vowels, that were not written. Thus the Original Hebrew Text was ambiguous here. When the Massoretes added vowel pointing to the Hebrew Text, many centuries after Christ, they chose 'bed'. Long before, the Septuagint had chosen 'staff'.

*How did Judas die? Matthew 27:5-8 X Acts 1:18-19*

In the NKJV, according to Matthew, he "went and hanged himself", while according to Acts, "falling headlong he burst open in the middle and all his entrails gushed out". From the context it is clear that this happened at the field that he purchased, posthumously. For a successful hanging, there must be enough altitude so that when the end of the rope is reached the victim is still in the air.

But to fall headlong there has to be a cliff, and you would have to dive off. Putting the two accounts together we may understand that there must have been a tree near the edge of the cliff, with a branch reaching out beyond the edge; Judas tied a cord around that branch and his neck and jumped—either the cord or the branch broke, and the impact was sufficient to split him open. Matthew states that it was actually the chief priests who bought the field, using the money that Judas had thrown on the temple floor; so Judas made the purchase posthumously.

*Buy a ticket to Heaven? Luke 16:9*

In the NKJV, Luke 16:9 reads like this: "And I say to you, make friends for yourselves by unrighteous mammon, that when you fail, they may receive you into an everlasting home [literally, 'the eternal dwellings']." Within the context the Lord is clearly using irony, or sarcasm. In the immediately preceding verse the owner's 'commendation' of the stupid steward is obviously sarcastic, since the steward was sacked. And verse 14 below indicates that what Jesus said was for the benefit of the Pharisees, who were greedy. The use of sarcasm is not rare in the Bible. Getting into the eternal dwellings does not depend on 'buying' friends down here; it depends on pleasing the Owner up there. And who says someone who can be bought with 'unrighteous mammon' is going to Heaven? He would have to get there first in order to 'receive' the buyer. The whole 'scene' is patently ridiculous. Just by the way, verse 13 declares a terribly important truth. To embrace the world's value system (humanism, relativism, materialism) is to reject God. Materialistic 'Christians' are really serving mammon ('mammon' includes more than just money).

*The 'smallest' seed? Mark 4:31-32, Matthew 13:32*

In the NKJV, Mark 4:31-32 reads like this: "It is like a mustard seed which, when it is sown on the ground, is smaller than all the seeds on earth; but when it is sown, it grows up and becomes greater than all herbs, and shoots out large branches, so that the birds of the air may nest under its shade."

The rendering 'the smallest seed in the world/earth' is unfortunate and misleading. The Text has 'of those on the ground', repeating the phrase above it, only eliding the verb. The Lord was not making a global botanical statement, as the next verse makes clear—He was referring to vegetables planted in a garden in His day and in that area, and of such herbs mustard had the smallest seed. To object that tobacco and orchid seeds are smaller is beside the point. My translation reads like this: "It is like a mustard seed, that when it is sown on the ground is the smallest of all such seeds, yet when it is sown, it grows up and becomes larger than all the garden herbs and produces big branches, so that the birds of the air are able to rest in its shade." The verb I have rendered 'to rest' is a compound form. The noun root refers to a temporary shelter, like a tent or a hut. The verbal form means to make use of such a shelter. Here the preposition *kata* is prefixed to the verb, emphasizing, as I suppose, the temporariness. The Text says that the birds can use the <u>shade</u>, not the branches. But shade moves with the sun, and with the wind— how can you build a nest in something that keeps moving around (the Text actually says 'under its shade')? My comments also serve for Matthew 13:32, except that there the birds are nesting in the 'branches', rather than the shade. The verb is the same, and I handle it the same way, 'rest' rather than 'nest', although 'nest' is possible.

*'Size' of faith? Luke 17:6, Matthew 17:20*

In the NKJV, Luke 17:6 reads like this: "If you have faith as a mustard seed, you can say to this mulberry tree, 'Be pulled up by the roots and be planted in the sea,' and it would obey you." Perhaps because of the parables just discussed, I don't remember ever hearing any other interpretation for this than the size of the faith. (The same holds for Matthew 17:20.) But that usually left me disgruntled: surely my faith was bigger than a seed, but I was never able to make a tree or hill obey me! But looking at the Text again, might the intended meaning of 'as a mustard seed' be different? Isn't the phrase ambiguous? Could the verb 'has' be implied? Well then, what kind of 'faith' might a mustard seed have? Albeit so small, it reacts without question to the climactic circumstances, and grows to remarkable proportions. If we reacted similarly, without question, to the Holy Spirit's promptings, our spiritual 'climactic circumstances', we should indeed move mountains, literally. Or to put it another way, a seed has the faith to die, like the Lord Jesus said in John 12:24: "unless a grain of wheat falls into the ground and dies, it remains alone". In 1 Corinthians 15:31 Paul said that he died daily. How so? Obviously he didn't die physically; he died to himself, his own ideas and ambitions, so as to embrace God's will. Dying to self is a prerequisite for moving mountains, because then we will only attempt to do what we see the Father doing (John 5:19).

*How many? Acts 7:14 X Genesis 46:26 X Genesis 46:27*

Again, we need only pay close attention to each context, and the precise wording of the text. The three verses give us three different numbers: 75, 66 and 70, respectively. I will begin with the smallest number, which is in Genesis 46:26: "All the persons who went with Jacob to Egypt, who came from his body, besides Jacob's sons' wives, were sixty-six persons in all." The crucial datum is 'from his body', so who were they? Reuben + four sons = 5, Simeon + six sons = 7, Levi + three sons = 4, Judah + five sons + 6, Issachar + four sons = 5, Zebulun + three sons = 4, that add up to 31, but we must include Dinah to get the total of 32 from Leah. Gad + seven sons = 8, Asher + six sons + 7, but we must add a daughter (mentioned in the record) to get the total of 16 from Zilpah. Joseph + two sons = 3, Benjamin + ten sons = 11, that add up to 14 from Rachel. Dan + one son = 2, Naphtali + four sons = 5, that add up to 7 from Bilhah. The grand total 'from his body' is 69. But of course Joseph and his two sons were already in Egypt, so that leaves 66 who 'went with Jacob to Egypt'. Genesis 46:27 says, "All the persons of the house of Jacob who went to Egypt were seventy." This includes Joseph and Jacob himself, so there is no discrepancy. But what about Acts 7:14? "Then Joseph sent and called his father Jacob and all his relatives to him, seventy-five people." The 75 presumably refers to 'all his relatives', which excludes Jacob and of course Joseph. I take it that nine wives came to Egypt (the wives are mentioned in Genesis 46:26), the other two having died before the migration. (If we include Jacob, there would be eight wives.)

## *Fiction*

I pause to register a fictitious 'problem' that has been used by some to poke fun at the Text. It occurs in 1 Corinthians 13:3. In order to understand what happened, I must use Greek and give the evidence:

καυθησομαι **f**[35] (50.6%) OC
καυθησωμαι C (44.7%) HF,RP,TR,CP
καυχησωμαι P[46]אA,B (1.5%) NU
seven further variants (3.2%)

Before the *Text und Textwert* series came out, it was generally assumed that the second variant enjoyed a clear, if not heavy, majority of manuscript attestation (it is so listed in HF, NU and von Soden, for example). The difficulty is that such a form would be a future Subjunctive, and Greek grammar does not have a future Subjunctive! So there were those who poked fun at the Majority Text and the TR for printing a non-existent word. We now know that the true majority reading is the first one, being future Indicative, which does indeed exist. I suppose that it was another grammatical feature that led to the main minority variant: the conjunction *hina* most often works with the Subjunctive mode (but the Indicative is not infrequent), and scribes may have made the change without thinking, the more so since the two vowels received the same pronunciation. Here we have a stellar example of what may happen when people take a stance based on an inadequate and incomplete knowledge of the evidence.

## Conclusion

The purpose of this appendix is to defend the objective authority of the Sacred Text, with emphasis on the New Testament. For any text to have objective authority in practice we have to know what it is. This means that God had to preserve His revelation down through the centuries. I have presented evidence to the effect that the original wording of the NT has indeed been preserved to this day. Since the objective authority of Scripture not only depends upon verifiable meaning, but in the first place on divine inspiration, and since a text inspired by God should not contain errors, I took up the question of alleged errors. I denounced the 'poison' foisted on the NT Text by the Hortian theory, but I also discussed seeming difficulties that are actually in the Text, as well as pseudo-difficulties created by faulty translation and/or arising from lack of attention to details in the Text. I am not aware of any seeming difficulty in the NT for which I do not have a solution. With an entirely clear conscience I maintain the objective authority of the entire New Testament Text!!

# APPENDIX B
# Family 35 profile for the whole New Testament[1]

**Key:**

| | |
|---|---|
| +++ | around 20% = f³⁵ virtually alone = diagnostic |
| ++-- | around 25% = quite good |
| ++ | around 30% = not bad |
| +-- | around 35% |
| + | around 40% |

I have arbitrarily set the cutoff point at 40%, being sufficient for my present purpose, but of course higher percentages can also contribute to the family mosaic/profile. (Were I to include 45% and 50% the numbers would go up visibly, especially for some books.)

## Matthew

| | | |
|---|---|---|
| ++-- | 1:10 | μανασσην [25%] ‖ μανασση [73%] |
| ++ | 5:31 | ερρεθη [30%] ‖ 1 δε [70%] |
| ++ | 6:6 | ταμειον [30%] ‖ ταμιειον [70%] |
| +++ | 6:25ᵃ | ενδυσεσθε [20%] ‖ ενδυσησθε [80%] |
| +++ | 6:25ᵇ | πλειων [20%] ‖ πλειον [80%] |
| ++-- | 7:19 | ουν [25%] ‖ --- [75%] |
| ++-- | 8:4 | προσενεγκαι [25%] ‖ προσενεγκε [75%] |
| ++ | 8:13 | εκατονταρχω [30%] ‖ εκατονταρχη [70%] |
| +++ | 8:20 | λεγει [20%] ‖ και 1 [80%] |
| +++ | 8:21 | μαθητων [20%] ‖ 1 αυτου [80%] |
| +-- | 9:4 | ειδως (33.3%) ‖ ιδων (65.7%) |
| ++ | 9:11 | και πινει [30%] ‖ --- [70%] |
| +++ | 9:15 | χρονον [20%] ‖ --- [80%] |
| ++ | 9:18 | τις [30%] ‖ εις [62%] |
| +++ | 9:28 | αυτοις [20%] ‖ 1 ο ιησους [80%] |
| ++-- | 9:33 | οτι [25%] ‖ --- [75%] |
| ++ | 10:2 | εισιν [30%] ‖ εστιν [70%] |
| ++ | 10:19 | λαλησετε (1ˢᵗ) [30%] ‖ λαλησητε [70%] |
| ++ | 10:25 | απεκαλεσαν [30%] ‖ εκαλεσαν [49%] ‖ επεκαλεσαν [20%] |
| +++ | 10:31 | πολλω [20%] ‖ πολλων [80%] |
| +-- | 11:20 | ο ιησους [35%] ‖ --- [65%] |
| +++ | 11:21 | χωραζιν [20%] ‖ χοραζιν [65%] |
| +-- | 11:23ᵃ | ἠ [35%] ‖ ἡ [64%] |
| +-- | 11:23ᵇ | υψωθης [35%] ‖ υψωθεισα [63%] |
| +++ | 12:15 | απαντας [20%] ‖ παντας [80%] |
| ++-- | 12:22 | κωφον [25%] ‖ 1 και [75%] |

---

[1] This information was taken from my Greek Text and apparatus.

| | | | |
|---|---|---|---|
| +++ | 12:23 | ο χριστος [20%] \|\| --- [80%] | |
| ++-- | 12:24 | εν [25%] \|\| 1 τω [75%] | |
| ++ | 12:28 | εγω εν πνευματι θεου [28%] \|\| ~ 2341 [70%] | |
| + | 12:29 | διαρπαση [40%] \|\| διαρπασει [60%] | |
| ++ | 13:2 | εις [30%] \|\| 1 το [70%] | |
| ++-- | 13:3 | εν παραβολαις πολλα [25%] \|\| ~ 312 [75%] | |
| ++ | 13:24 | σπειραντι [30%] \|\| σπειροντι [70%] | |
| ++ | 13:32 | παντων [30%] \|\| --- [70%] | |
| ++ | 13:44 | εν αγρω [30%] \|\| 1 τω 2 [70%] | |
| +++ | 14:5 | εφοβειτο [20%] \|\| εφοβηθη [80%] | |
| ++ | 14:22 | αυτου [30%] \|\| --- [70%] | |
| ++-- | 14:28 | δε [25%] \|\| 1 αυτω [73%] | |
| +++ | 14:31 | και ευθεως [20%] \|\| ~ 2 δε [80%] | |
| ++ | 14:34 | γενησαρετ [30%] \|\| γεννησαρετ [55%] | |
| +-- | 14:36 | καν [35%] \|\| --- [65%] | |
| ++-- | 15:6 | μητερα [25%] \|\| 1 αυτου [75%] | |
| ++ | 15:14 | εμπεσουνται [30%] \|\| πεσουνται [70%] | |
| ++ | 15:31 | εδοξαζον [30%] \|\| εδοξασαν [70%] | |
| ++ | 15:32$^a$ | ημερας [30%] \|\| ημεραι [70%] | |
| ++-- | 15:32$^b$ | νηστις [25%] \|\| νηστεις [75%] | |
| ++ | 15:39 | ενεβη [30%] \|\| ανεβη [70%] | |
| +-- | 16:20 | εστιν [35%] \|\| 1 ιησους [65%] | |
| + | 17:2 | εγενετο [40%] \|\| εγενοντο [60%] | |
| +++ | 17:18 | ιαθη [20%] \|\| εθεραπευθη [80%] | |
| ++-- | 17:25 | εισηλθον [25%] \|\| εισηλθεν [72%] | |
| + | 17:27 | αναβαντα [40%] \|\| αναβαινοντο [60%] | |
| ++-- | 18:15$^a$ | αμαρτη [25%] \|\| αμαρτηση [74%] | |
| ++ | 18:15$^b$ | υπαγε [30%] \|\| 1 και [70%] | |
| +++ | 19:5 | προς την γυναικα [20%] \|\| τη γυναικι [80%] | |
| ++-- | 19:16 | τις [25%] \|\| --- [75%] | |
| +++ | 20:26 | εσται [20%] \|\| 1 εν [80%] | |
| +-- | 20:27 | εσται [35%] \|\| εστω [65%] | |
| ++ | 21:8 | αυτων [30%] \|\| εαυτων [70%] | |
| ++-- | 21:35 | εδηραν [25%] \|\| εδειραν [75%] | |
| + | 22:37 | τη [40%] \|\| --- [60%] | |
| ++ | 22:46 | αποκριθηναι αυτω [30%] \|\| ~ 21 [69%] | |
| ++ | 23:8 | διδασκαλος [30%] \|\| καθηγητης [70%] | |
| ++ | 23:10 | εστιν υμων [30%] \|\| ~ 21 [65%] | |
| ++-- | 23:11 | εστω [25%] \|\| εσται [75%] | |
| ++-- | 24:1 | αυτω [25%] \|\| --- [75%] | |
| ++-- | 24:6 | μελησετε [25%] \|\| μελλησετε [72%] | |
| ++ | 24:18 | το ιματιον [30%] \|\| τα ιματια [70%] | |
| ++-- | 24:32 | γινωσκεται [25%] \|\| γινωσκετε [75%] | |
| ++ | 24:49 | τε [30%] \|\| δε [70%] | |
| ++ | 25:29 | δοκει εχειν [30%] \|\| εχει [70%] | |
| ++-- | 25:32 | συναχθησονται [25%] \|\| συναχθησεται [75%] | |

++-- 26:1 ιησους [25%] || 1 παντας [75%]
+ 26:9 τοις [40%] || --- [60%]
+ 26:11 παντοτε γαρ τους πτωχους [40%] || ~ 3421 [60%]
+ 26:15 και εγω [40%] || καγω [60%]
++ 26:26 ευλογησας [30%] || ευχαριστησας [70%]
++ 26:29 γενηματος [30%] || γεννηματος [70%]
++ 26:33ª και [30%] || --- [70%]
+ 26:33ᵇ εγω [40%] || 1 δε [60%]
+-- 26:39 προελθων [35%] || προσελθων [65%]
++ 26:43 ευρεν [30%] || ευρισκει [66%]
+++ 26:46 ιδου [20%] || 1 ηγγικεν [80%]
+ 26:48 εαν [40%] || αν [60%]
++ 26:55 εν τω ιερω διδασκων [30%] || ~ 4123 [69%]
+-- 26:75 ρηματος [35%] || 1 του [65%]
+++ 27:1 πρεσβυτεροι [20%] || 1 του λαου [80%]
++ 27:12 και [30%] || 1 των [70%]
++ 27:33 λεγομενον [30%] || λεγομενος [67%]
++-- 27:35 βαλοντες [25%] || βαλλοντες [75%]
+-- 27:55 και [35%] || --- [65%]
++-- 27:64 οτι [25%] || --- [75%]

**Key:**
+++ around 20% = f³⁵ virtually alone = diagnostic (17)
++-- around 25% = quite good (22)
++ around 30% = not bad (34)
+-- around 35% (10)
+ around 40% (9)

Total: 92

A single diagnostic reading could be happenstance, but several presumably indicate that the MS is at least a fringe member of the family. Probably no two scholars would prepare identical lists—changing rank, adding or subtracting—but there is sufficient evidence here to establish that f³⁵ is a distinct family. The statements here apply to the remaining books as well.

# Mark

+ 1:12 ευθεως [40%] || ευθυς [60%]
++ 1:30 του [30%] || --- [70%]
++ 1:34 χριστον ειναι (28%) || --- (58.9%) || τον 12 (11.6%)
+ 1:38 εληλυθα [40%] || εξεληλυθα [59%]
++-- 1:44 προσενεγκαι [25%] || προσενεγκε [75%]
+ 2:9 τον κραββατον σου [40%] || ~ 312 [59%]
++ 3:20 μηδε [30%] || μητε [70%]
+-- 3:35 μου [35%] || --- [65%]
++ 4:24 αντιμετρηθησεται [30%] || μετρηθησεται [69%]

++  5:3a  οικησιν [30%] || κατοικησιν [70%]
+  5:3b  ηδυνατο [40%] || εδυνατο [60%]
++--  5:4  ισχυσεν [26%] || ισχυεν [74%]
+  5:5  μνημασιν και εν τοις ορεσιν [40%] || ~ 52341 [57%]
+++  6:20  ακουων [20%] || ακουσας [80%]
+  6:45  απολυσει [40%] || απολυση [59%]
++  6:53  γενησαρετ [30%] || γεννησαρετ [53%]
++  7:4  χαλκειων [30%] || χαλκιων [70%]
++  8:3  νηστις [30%] || νηστεις [70%]
+  8:6  και [40%] || --- [60%]
+--  8:14  οι μαθηται αυτου [35%] || --- [64%]
+  8:21  ουπω [41%] || ου [59%]
++--  9:3  κναφευς [25%] || γναφευς [75%]
++  9:20  ιδον [30%] || ιδων [70%]
++  9:48  σκωληξ [30%] || 1 αυτων [70%]
+--  10:8  σαρξ μια [35%] || ~ 21 [65%]
+++  10:17  τις [20%] || εις [70%] || --- [10%]
+++  10:25  γαρ [20%] || --- [80%]
+  10:30  πατερα και μητερα [40%] || μητερας [55%]
+  10:33  τοις [40%] || --- [60%]
+--  10:40  μου [35%] || --- [65%]
+--  10:51  ραβουνι [35%] || ραββουνι [59%]
++  10:52  ηκολουθησεν [30%] || ηκολουθει [69%]
++  11:5  εστωτων [30%] || εστηκοτων [70%]
+--  11:14  φαγη [35%] || φαγοι [65%]
+--  11:18  απολεσουσιν [35%] || απολεσωσιν [65%]
+++  11:30  ανθρωπων [20%] || 1 αποκριθητε μοι [80%]
++  12:3  εδηραν [30%] || εδειραν [70%]
++  12:5  δαιροντες [30%] || δεροντες [70%]
+++  12:26  μωυσεος [20%] || μωσεως [50%] || μωυσεως [30%]
++--  12:28  πασων [25%] || παντων [72%]
++--  12:29a  πασων [25%] || παντων [72%]
++--  12:29b  υμων [25%] || ημων [74%]
+--  12:41  εβαλον [35%] || εβαλλον [65%]
++  13:2a  αποκριθεις ο ιησους [30%] || ~ 231 [68%]
+++  13:2b  ωδε (21.1%) || --- (78.9%)
++  13:9  αχθησεσθε [30%] || σταθησεσθε [70%]
+--  13:11a  αγωσιν [35%] || αγαγωσιν [65%]
+--  13:11b  λαλησετε [35%] || λαλησητε [65%]
++  13:21a  τοτε [30%] || και 1 [70%]
+  13:21b  χριστος [40%] || 1 η [60%]
++  13:28a  ηδη ο κλαδος αυτης (29%) || ~ 4123 (50.2%)
++--  13:28b  γινωσκεται [25%] || γινωσκετε [75%]
+++  13:33  προσευχεσθε [20%] || και 1 [77%]
+  14:11  αγυρια [40%] || αγρυριον [60%]
++  14:15  ανωγεων [30%] || ανωγεον [39%] || ανωγαιον [25%]

246

++-- 14:22    και [25%] || --- [75%]
+++ 14:28    μετα δε [20%] || αλλα 1 [79%]
+-- 14:32    προσευξομαι [35%] || προσευξωμαι [65%]
++ 14:36    παρενεγκαι [30%] || παρενεγκε [70%]
+-- 14:40    καταβαρυνομενοι [35%] || βεβαρημενοι [64%]
++ 15:18    και λεγειν [30%] || --- [68%]
++-- 15:42    παρασκευη ην [25%] || ~ 21 [75%]
+-- 15:43    ελθων [35%] || ηλθεν [65%]
++ 16:1    τον ιησουν [30%] || αυτον [70%]
++ 16:9    ο ιησους [30%] || --- [70%]

**Key:**
+++      around 20% = f$^{35}$ virtually alone = diagnostic (8)
++--     around 25% = quite good (9)
++       around 30% = not bad (23)
+--      around 35% (13)
+        around 40% (12)

Total: 65

# Luke

+-- 1:55    εως αιωνος [35%] || εις τον αιωνα [64%]
++-- 1:63    εσται [26%] || εστιν [74%]
+ 2:40    αυτω [41%] || αυτο [58%]
+ 3:12    υπ αυτου [40%] || --- [60%]
++++ 3:18    τω λαω [15%] || τον λαον [85%]
++-- 3:30    ιωναμ [25%] || ιωναν [48%]
+ 3:34    θαρρα [40%] || θαρα [60%]
++-- 3:35    ραγαβ [25%] || ραγαυ [70%]
++-- 4:7    σοι [25%] || σου [75%]
+ 4:42    εζητουν [40%] || επεζητουν [60%]
++++ 5:1$^a$    περι [18%] || παρα [82%]
++ 5:1$^b$    γενησαρετ [29%] || γεννησαρετ [60%]
++ 5:14    προσενεγκαι [30%] || προσενεγκε [70%]
+-- 5:19    πως [35%] || ποιας [57%]
++-- 5:35    ημεραι [25%] || 1 και [75%]
++-- 6:7    ει [25%] || 1 εν [75%]
+ 6:10    ουτως [42%] || --- [54.5%]
+++ 6:26$^a$    καλως ειπωσιν υμας (22%) || ~ 132 (76.1%)
+ 6:26$^b$    παντες (38.9%) || --- (60.5%)
++ 6:49    την [30%] || --- [70%]
+-- 8:3    σωσαννα [35%] || σουσαννα [65%]
++ 8:24    και προσελθοντες [32%] || ~ 2 δε [68%]
+-- 8:26    αντιπεραν [33%] || αντιπερα [60%]
++++ 9:4    ην [15%] || 1 αν [85%]
++ 9:13    αγορασομεν [30%] || αγορασωμεν [70%]
+ 9:33    ο [40%] || --- [60%]

+++ 9:48 υμων [20%] || υμιν [79%]
+ 9:52 εαυτου [40%] || αυτου [60%]
++-- 10:4 μη [26%] || μηδε [74%]
++-- 10:6 μεν [25%] || --- [75%]
+-- 10:13 χωραζιν [35%] || χοραζιν [29%] || χοραζειν [20%]
+-- 10:39 των λογων [37%] || τον λογον [63%]
+ 10:41 ο ιησους ειπεν αυτη [40%] || ~ 3412 [59%]
++++11:19 αυτοι υμων [18%] || ~ 21 [52%] ||
++ 11:32 νινευι [32%] || νινευιται [35%] || ||
+-- 11:34 η [35%] || 1 και [65%]
++-- 11:53 συνεχειν [26%] || ενεχειν [70%]
++++12:7 πολλω [15%] || πολλων [85%]
+-- 12:11 απλογησεσθε [35%] || απλογησησθε [63%]
++ 12:22ᵃ λεγω υμιν [28%] || ~ 21 [72%]
++-- 12:22ᵇ ενδυσεσθε [25%] || ενδυσησθε [74%]
++-- 12:23 πλειων [23%] || πλειον [77]
+++ 12:27 λεγω [20%] || 1 δε [80%]
+ 12:56 του ουρανου και της γης [40%] || ~ 45312 [60%]
++-- 12:58 βαλη σε [24%] || ~ 21 [76%]
++-- 13:28 οψεσθε [27%] || οψησθε [73%]
+++ 14:9 συ [20%] || σοι [80%]
+ 14:21 τυφλους και χωλους [42%] || ~ 321 [57%]
+-- 14:26 μου ειναι μαθητης [36%] || ~ 132 [60%]
+ 15:20 εαυτου [42%] || αυτου [58%]
++-- 16:22 του [26%] || --- [74%]
++ 16:25 οδε [30%] || ωδε [70%]
++ 17:37 και [29%] || --- [68%]
+-- 19:15 βασιλειαν [37%] || 1 και [63%]
++-- 19:23 την [23%] || --- [77%]
+++ 20:10 δηραντες [20%] || δειραντες [80%]
+++ 20:11 δηραντες [20%] || δειραντες [80%]
++-- 20:15 εκβαλοντες [24%] || 1 αυτον [76%]
+++ 20:28 ο αδελφος αυτου λαβη [20%] || ~ 4123 [80%]
++ 21:6 λιθον (32.2%) || λιθω (65.1%)
+-- 21:12 απαντων [34%] || παντων [66%]
++ 21:15 η [30%] || ουδε [68%]
++ 21:30 προβαλλωσιν [28%] || προβαλωσιν [66%]
++ 21:33 παρελευσεται [32%] || παρελευσονται [68%]
+-- 22:27 ουχ [33%] || ουχι [67%]
+-- 22:52 προς [33%] || επ [67%]
+-- 22:54 εισηγαγον [37%] || 1 αυτον [55%]
+-- 22:63 δαιροντες [35%] || δεροντες [65%]
++-- 22:66 απηγαγον [24%] || ανηγαγον [75%]
++ 23:51 ος [32%] || 1 και [67%]
++ 24:19 ως [32%] || ος [68%]

++  24:36  και [32%] || --- [68%]
++  24:42  μελισσειου [30%] || μελισσιου [70%]

**Key:**
+++     around 20% = $f^{35}$ virtually alone = diagnostic  (12)
++--    around 25% = quite good  (17)
++      around 30% = not bad  (17)
+--     around 35%  (15)
+       around 40%  (12)

Total: 73

# John

++--  1:28   βιθαβαρα [25%] || βηθανια [65%] ||
+     1:45   υιον [40%] || 1 του [60%]
+     3:4    αυτον [40%] || 1 ο [60%]
+++   4:1    ιησους (21.7%) || κυριος (76.9%)
+     4:5    ου [40%] || ο [60%]
+--   4:35   οτι [35%] || 1 ετι [65%]
+++   5:44   ανθρωπων (22.6%) || αλληλων (77.2%)
++--  5:46   εμου γαρ [25%] || ~ 21 [75%]
++--  6:12   των κλασματων [25%] || κλασματα [75%]
++    6:58   μου [30%] || --- [70%]
++    7:3    εργα [30%] || 1 σου [63.5%] ||
+     7:31   σημεια [40%] || 1 τουτων [55%]
++    7:39   ο [30%] || ου [70%]
++++  8:7    τον λιθον επ αυτη βαλετω [18%] || || || || || (5-way split)
+     8:14   η [40%] || και [50%] ||
++    8:33   και ειπον [30%] || --- [70%]
++    9:17   ουν [30%] || --- [70%]
++    9:26   ανεωξεν [30%] || ηνοιξεν [63%]
++--  9:34   ολως [25%] || ολος [75%]
++++  10:39  ουν παλιν πιασαι αυτον (18.9%) || ~ 1243 (32.8%) ||
              ~ 243 (30.3%) || ||
+     11:2   εαυτης [40%] || αυτης [60%]
++    11:46  οσα [29%] || α [70%]
+--   11:51  ο [35%] || --- [65%]
+++   11:56  υμιν δοκει [20%] || ~ 21 [80%]
+     12:6   εμελεν [40%] || εμελλεν [60%]
+     12:12  ο [40%] || --- [60%]
+     12:13  απαντησιν [38%] || υπαντησιν [60%]
++    12:14  αυτω [30%] || αυτο [70%]
+--   13:15ᵃ δεδωκα [35%] || εδωκα [65%]
++--  13:15ᵇ καθως [25%] || 1 εγω [75%]
+++   13:22ᵃ δε [20%] || ουν [79.5%]
++--  13:22ᵇ προς [25%] || εις [75%]
+     18:11  μαχαιραν [40%] || 1 σου [60%]

249

++    18:23    δαιρεις [30%] || δερεις [70%]
++    18:28    πρωι [30%] || πρωια [70%]
+++   18:39    ημιν [20%] || υμιν [80%]
+     18:40    ουν [40%] || 1 παλιν [60%]
+     19:14    ην [40%] || δε [60%]
+     19:23    αρραφος [40%] || αραφος [60%]
++    19:28    ηδη παντα [30%] || ~ 21 [60%] ||
++    19:35    η μαρτυρια αυτου [30%] || ~ 312 [65%]
+++   21:1ᵃ    εαυτον [20%] || 1 παλιν [80%]
+     21:1ᵇ    αυτου [40%] || --- [60%]
++--  21:1ᶜ    εγερθεις εκ νεκρων [25%] || --- [75%]

**Key:**
+++    around 20% = f³⁵ virtually alone = diagnostic  (8)
++--   around 25% = quite good  (7)
++     around 30% = not bad  (12)
+--    around 35%  (3)
+      around 40%  (14)

Total: 44

# Acts

++--  1:8      και [25%] || 1 εν [75%]
++    1:11     ουτος [30%] || 1 ο [70%]
++--  1:13     ιακωβος [25%] || 1 και [73%]
+     1:18     ελακισεν [40%] || ελακησεν [60%]
++--  2:13     διαχλευαζοντες [25%] || χλευαζοντες [75%]
++--  2:14     επεφθεγξατο [25%] || απεφθεγξατο [75%]
+++   2:38     ειπεν δε πετρος [20%] || ~ 32 εφη [72%] ||
+--   3:23     αν [35%] || εαν [65%]
++--  3:24     προκατηγγειλαν [25%] || κατηγγειλαν [75%]
++    4:5      εν [30%] || εις [70%]
++    4:12ᵃ    ουδε [30%] || ουτε [70%]
+++   4:12ᵇ    ετερον εστιν [20%] || ~ 21 [80%]
+     4:12ᶜ    υπο του ουρανου [40%] || --- [60%]
+++   4:14     εστωτα [20%] || 1 τον [80%]
+--   4:17     ανθρωπω [35%] || ανθρωπων [65%]
+++   4:20     α [20%] || --- [80%]
++--  4:23     ανηγγειλαν [25%] || απηγγειλαν [75%]
+++   4:33ᵃ    δυναμει μεγαλη [20%] || ~ 21 [80%]
++    4:33ᵇ    οι αποστολοι το μαρτυριον [30%] || ~ 3412 [70%]
++--  4:34     ην (24.5%) || υπηρχεν (74.8%)
+     5:1      σαπφειρα [40%] || σαπφειρη [56%] ||
++    5:15     του [30%] || --- [70%]
+++   5:16     και [20%] || οιτινες [80%]
+++   5:22     παραγενομενοι υπηρεται [20%] || ~ 21 [80%]
++    5:33     ακουοντες [32%] || ακουσαντες [68%]

| | | |
|---|---|---|
| ++ | 5:36[a] | προσεκλιθη [30%] \|\| προσεκληθη [54%] \|\| |
| +++ | 5:36[b] | ως [20%] \|\| ωσει [80%] |
| ++ | 5:39 | δυνησεσθε [30%] \|\| δυνασθε [58%] \|\| |
| + | 5:40 | δηραντες [40%] \|\| δειραντες [60%] |
| +++ | 5:41 | κατηξιωθησαν υπερ του ονοματος του χριστου [20%] \|\| |
| | | ~ 234561 [15%] \|\| ~ 234 αυτου 1 [15%] \|\| \|\| \|\| \|\| |
| ++-- | 5:42 | τον χριστον ιησουν [25%] \|\| ~ 312 [67%] \|\| |
| + | 6:5 | πληρη [40%] \|\| πληρης [45%] \|\| |
| ++-- | 7:5 | δουναι αυτην εις κατασχεσιν αυτω [25%] \|\| ~ 15342 [65%] \|\| |
| +++ | 7:14[a] | ιακωβ τον πατερα αυτου [20%] \|\| ~ 2341 [80%] |
| ++ | 7:14[b] | αυτου [30%] \|\| --- [70%] |
| ++ | 7:14[c] | εβδομηκοντα πεντε ψυχαις [30%] \|\| ~ 312 [63%] \|\| |
| +-- | 7:16 | εμμωρ [33%] \|\| εμμορ [60%] \|\| |
| ++-- | 7:21 | ανειλετο [25%] \|\| 1 αυτον [60%] \|\| |
| +++ | 7:27 | τουτον [20%] \|\| αυτον [80%] |
| + | 7:31[a] | μωσης [38%] \|\| μωυσης [62%] |
| ++-- | 7:31[b] | εθαυμασεν [25%] \|\| εθαυμαζεν [75%] |
| ++-- | 7:35 | αρχηγον [23%] \|\| αρχοντα [77%] |
| + | 7:37 | ημων [40%] \|\| υμων [55%] \|\| |
| +++ | 7:42 | εν τη ερημω ετη τεσσαρακοντα [20%] \|\| ~ 45123 [80%] |
| ++ | 8:6 | δε [30%] \|\| τε [70%] |
| +++ | 8:21 | εναντιον [20%] \|\| ενωπιον [78%] |
| + | 8:28 | και [40%] \|\| --- [60%] |
| +++ | 9:12 | ανανιαν ονοματι [20%] \|\| ~ 21 [80%] |
| ++ | 9:18 | παραχρημα [30%] \|\| --- [70%] |
| +-- | 9:19 | των [35%] \|\| 1 οντων [65%] |
| +++ | 9:20 | ιησουν [20%] \|\| χριστον [80%] |
| +++ | 9:28[a] | και εκπορευομενος [20%] \|\| --- [80%] |
| ++ | 9:28[b] | εν [30%] \|\| εις [70%] |
| ++-- | 9:29[a] | ιησου [24%] \|\| κυριου 1 [67%] \|\| |
| +++ | 9:29[b] | ανελειν αυτον [20%] \|\| ~ 21 [80%] |
| +++ | 9:30 | εξαπεστειλαν [20%] \|\| 1 αυτον [80%] |
| +++ | 9:37 | τω [20%] \|\| --- [80%] |
| +++ | 9:43 | αυτον ημερας ικανας μειναι [20%] \|\| ~ 2341 [79%] |
| +++ | 10:5 | ος επικαλειται πετρος [20%], τον επικαλουμενον πετρον [80%] |
| ++ | 10:17 | υπο [30%] \|\| απο [70%] |
| +++ | 10:22 | αγγελου [20%] \|\| 1 αγιου [80%] |
| ++-- | 10:26 | ηγειρεν αυτον [25%] \|\| ~ 21 [75%] |
| ++-- | 10:47 | ως [25%] \|\| καθως [75%] |
| +-- | 10:48 | ιησου [35%] \|\| --- [57%] \|\| |
| +++ | 11:3 | εισηλθεις προς ανδρας ακροβυστιαν εχοντας και συνεφαγες [20%] \|\| ~ 2345167 [71%] \|\| |
| +++ | 11:9 | εκ δευτερου φωνη [20%] \|\| ~ 312 [80%] |
| ++ | 11:13[a] | δε [30%] \|\| τε [70%] |
| +++ | 11:13[b] | ιοππην [20%] \|\| 1 ανδρας [80%] |

| | | |
|---|---|---|
| + | 11:16ᵃ | του [40%] \|\| --- [60%] |
| ++-- | 11:16ᵇ | οτι [25%] \|\| --- [75%] |
| ++-- | 11:17ᵃ | ιησουν [25%] \|\| 1 χριστον [75%] |
| +++ | 11:17ᵇ | εγω [20%] \|\| 1 δε [80%] |
| ++-- | 11:26ᵃ | ευρων [25%] \|\| 1 αυτον [75%] |
| + | 11:26ᵇ | ηγαγεν [40%] \|\| 1 αυτον [60%] |
| ++-- | 12:6 | προαγειν αυτον [25%] \|\| ~ 21 [58%] \|\| |
| +++ | 12:20 | τε [20%] \|\| δε [70%] \|\| |
| +++ | 12:22 | θεου φωνη [20%] \|\| ~ 21 [78%] |
| +++++ | 12:25 | εις αντιοχειαν (5.1%)+{19.5%} \|\| 1 ιερουσαλημ [60%] \|\| |
| | | \|\| \|\| \|\| |
| +++ | 13:4ᵃ | μεν [20%] \|\| 1 ουν [80%] |
| ++-- | 13:4ᵇ | τε [27%] \|\| δε [72%] |
| +-- | 13:12 | εκπληττομενος [35%] \|\| εκπλησσομενος [65%] |
| +++ | 13:15 | προς αυτους οι αρχισυναγωγοι [20%] \|\| ~ 3412 [80%] |
| ++ | 13:26 | εξαπεσταλη [30%] \|\| απεσταλη [70%] |
| ++ | 13:27 | κατοικουντες [30%] \|\| 1 εν [70%] |
| +++ | 13:39ᵃ | εν [20%] \|\| 1 τω [80%] |
| ++-- | 13:39ᵇ | μωυσεος [25%] \|\| μωυσεως [35%] \|\| μωσεως [40%] |
| ++-- | 13:41 | ω [25%] \|\| ο [75%] |
| +++ | 13:43 | επιμενειν αυτους [20%] \|\| ~ 21 [64%] \|\| |
| ++ | 14:10 | ηλλατο [30%] \|\| ηλλετο [35%] \|\| \|\| |
| +++ | 14:15 | υμιν εσμεν [20%] \|\| ~ 21 [60%] \|\| |
| +++ | 14:20 | των μαθητων αυτον [22%] \|\| ~ 312 [55%] \|\| |
| +++ | 14:21 | εις [20%] \|\| 1 την [80%] |
| ++ | 15:1 | μωυσεος [28%] \|\| μωυσεως [55%] \|\| |
| +-- | 15:5 | μωσεως [35%] \|\| μωυσεως [60%] \|\| |
| ++ | 15:7 | υμιν [30%] \|\| ημιν [55%] \|\| \|\| |
| + | 15:9 | ουδεν [40%] \|\| ουθεν [60%] |
| +-- | 15:21 | μωσης [35%] \|\| μωυσης [65%] |
| +++ | 15:24 | κατα [20%] \|\| 1 την [80%] |
| +-- | 15:25 | εκλεξαμενοις [35%] \|\| εκλεξαμενους [65%] |
| + | 15:37 | και [39%] \|\| τον [50%] \|\| |
| +++ | 15:39 | χωρισθηναι [20%] \|\| αποχωρισθηναι [75%] \|\| |
| +++ | 16:3 | ηδεσαν [22%] \|\| ηδεισαν [65%] \|\| |
| +++ | 16:9 | την [20%] \|\| --- [80%] |
| +++ | 16:11 | την [20%] \|\| --- [80%] |
| +++ | 16:15 | αυτη [20%] \|\| --- [80%] |
| + | 16:17 | τω σιλα [40%] \|\| ημιν [60%] |
| ++ | 16:26 | δε [30%] \|\| τε [70%] |
| ++ | 16:37 | δηραντες [32%] \|\| δειραντες [67%] |
| +++ | 16:38 | δε [20%] \|\| και [80%] |
| +++ | 16:40 | απο [20%] \|\| εκ [80%] |
| +++ | 17:3 | ιησους ο χριστος [20%] \|\| ~ 231 [75%] \|\| |
| +++ | 17:4 | πληθος πολυ [20%] \|\| ~ 21 [80%] |
| +++ | 17:5 | ανδρας τινας [20%] \|\| ~ 21 [75%] \|\| |

++    17:7    ετερον λεγοντες [30%] || ~ 21 [70%]

++    17:10    βερροιαν [30%] || βεροιαν [70%]

++--    17:11    προθυμιας [25%] || 1 το [75%]

++    17:13    βερροια [30%] || βεροια [70%]

+++    18:6    τας κεφαλας [20%] || την κεφαλην [80%]

++--    18:13    αναπειθει ουτος [25%] || ~ 21 [65%] ||

++    18:19    κακεινους [29%] || και εκεινους [70%]

+--    18:25    ιησου [35%] || κυριου [65%]

+++    19:3    τε (18.3%)+{6.2%} || 1 προς αυτους (61.6%)+{6.2%} || ||

+++    19:11    δε [22%] || τε [78%]

+--    19:13    ο [35%] || --- [65%]

+++    19:17    εγενετο πασιν γνωστον [20%] || ~ 132 [75%] ||

+++    19:19    συνεψηφισαντο [20%] || συνεψηφισαν [67%] ||

++--    19:27[a]    αρτεμιδος ιερον [25%] || ~ 21 [75%]

+    19:27[b]    ουδεν [40%] || ουθεν [60%]

+++    19:40    αποδουναι [20%] || δουναι [80%]

+++    20:3    επιβουλης αυτω [20%] || ~ 21 [80%]

++--    20:4    βερροιαιος [25%] || βεροιαιος [35%] || ||

+++    20:15    τρωγυλιω [20%] || τρωγυλλιω [30%] || || || ||

+++    20:18    ημερας [20%] || 1 αφ [80%]

+++    20:35    του λογου [22%] || τον λογον [55%] || των λογων [23%]

+++    20:36    κλαυθμος εγενετο [20%] || ~ 21 [80%]

+    21:8    ηλθομεν (38.8%) || οι περι τον παυλον ηλθον (46.4%) || ||

++--    21:21    μωυσεος [25%] || μωυσεως [45%] || μωσεως [30%]

+--    21:27    ημελλον [33%] || εμελλον [60%] ||

++    21:31    σπειρας [30%] || σπειρης [70%]

+    21:37[a]    δε [40%] || τε [58%]

+++    21:37[b]    εις την παρεμβολην εισαγεσθαι [20%] || ~ 4123 [80%]

+    21:40    προσεφωνει [40%] || προσεφωνησεν [60%]

++--    22:19[a]    δαιρων [25%] || δερων [75%]

+++    22:19[b]    εις [20%] || επι [80%]

++--    22:20    και [25%] || --- [75%]

+++    22:24    ο χιλιαρχος αγεσθαι αυτον [20%] || ~ 4123 [74%] ||

++    22:25    προετειναν [30%] || προετεινεν [30%] || ||

+++    22:26    τω χιλιαρχω απηγγειλεν [20%] || ~ 312 [73%] ||

++    22:30[a]    υπο [30%] || παρα [70%]

+++    22:30[b]    παν [20%] || ολον [80%]

+++    23:6    φαρισαιων το δε ετερον σαδδουκαιων [20%] || ~ 52341 [80%]

++--    23:8    μητε [25%] || μηδε [75%]

++--    23:12[a]    εαυτους [25%] || 1 λεγοντες [75%]

+++    23:12[b]    ανελωσιν [20%] || αποκτεινωσιν [80%]

+--    23:15    καταγαγη αυτον [35%] || ~ 21 [65%]

+--    23:20    μελλοντες (33.1%) || μελλοντα (27.2%) || || || ||

+--    23:24    φηλικα [35%] || φιληκα [25%] || φιλικα [40%]

+    23:26    φηλικι [40%] || φιληκι [30%] || φιλικι [17%] ||

+++    23:35    του [20%] || --- [79%]

+++ 24:4   πλεον [20%] || πλειον [79%]
++-- 24:10  δικαιον [25%] || --- [75%]
+   24:13  παραστησαι [40%] || 1 με νυν [60%]
++  24:19  εδει [30%] || δει [70%]
+++ 24:26  πυκνοτερον [20%] || 1 αυτον [75%] ||
+   25:2   οι αρχιερεις [40%] || ο αρχιερευς [55%]
+--  25:9   υπ [35%] || επ [63%]
+   25:13  ασπασομενοι [40%] || ασπασαμενοι [60%]
+++ 25:20ᵃ περι την [22%] || ~ 21 [76%]
+--  25:20ᵇ τουτων [35%] || τουτου [65%]
++  26:12  εις [32%] || 1 την [68%]
++  26:18  επιστρεψαι [30%] || υποστρεψαι [35%] || αποστρεψαι [35%]
+--  27:1   σπειρας [35%] || σπειρης [65%]
+++ 27:2   ατραμυτινω [21%] || αδραμυττηνω [25%] || || || || ||
++-- 27:5   κατηχθημεν [23%] || κατηλθομεν [71%] ||
++  27:6   εις [30%] || 1 την [70%]
++  27:10  φορτου [30%] || φορτιου [70%]
+++ 27:31  εν τω πλοιω μεινωσιν [20%] || ~ 4123 [75%] ||
++  27:34  μεταλαβειν [30%] || προσλαβειν [70%]
++  27:38  δε [30%] || 1 της [70%]
++-- 27:41  εμενεν [25%] || εμεινεν [75%]
+--  28:3ᵃ  εξελθουσα [35%] || διεξελθουσα [65%]
++-- 28:3ᵇ  καθηψατο [25%] || καθηψεν [72%]
+++ 28:21  πονηρον περι σου [20%] || ~ 231 [80%]
++-- 28:23  μωυσεος [25%] || μωσεως [35%] || μωυσεως [40%]
+   28:27  ιασωμαι [40%] || ιασομαι [60%]

**Key:**
+++    around 20% = f³⁵ virtually alone = diagnostic  (72)
++--   around 25% = quite good  (36)
++     around 30% = not bad  (36)
+--    around 35%  (19)
+      around 40%  (22)

Total: 185

Of all the books, **f³⁵** has the most distinct profile in Acts, with far and away the most diagnostic variants.

# Pauline Corpus

++-- Rom. 1:23  ηλλαξαντο [26%] || ηλλαξαν [74%]
++-- Rom. 1:27ᵃ  ομοιως [23%] || 1 τε [70%] ||
+++ Rom. 1:27ᵇ  εξεκαυθησαν [20%] || 1 εν [80%]
+++ Rom. 4:16  εκ [20%] || 1 του [80%]
+   Rom. 5:1   εχωμεν (43%) || εχομεν (57%)
+   Rom. 5:11  καυχωμεθα [38%] || καυχωμενοι [52%] ||
++  Rom. 5:14  μωυσεος [30%] || μωυσεως [50%] || μωσεως [20%]

254

| | | | |
|---|---|---|---|
| ++-- | Rom. 9:13 | ησαυ [25%] \|\| ησαυ [75%] | |
| ++ | Rom. 10:5 | μωσης [30%] \|\| μωυσης [70%] | |
| +++ | Rom. 10:19 | μωσης [20%] \|\| μωυσης [80%] | |
| ++ | Rom. 11:7 | τουτου [32%] \|\| τουτο [68%] | |
| ++-- | Rom. 15:9 | κυριε [27%] \|\| --- [73%] | |
| +++ | Rom. 16:6 | υμας (22.8%) \|\| ημας (76.4%) | |
| ++++ | Rom. 16:24 | ημων [18%] \|\| υμων [82%] | |

| | | |
|---|---|---|
| ++-- | 1Cor. 1:2 | υμων [25%] \|\| ημων [75%] |
| + | 1Cor. 4:11 | γυμνιτευομεν [40%] \|\| γυμνητευομεν [60%] |
| +++ | 1Cor. 5:8 | ειλικρινειας [20%] \|\| ειλικρινειας [55%] \|\| |
| +-- | 1Cor. 6:8 | αλλ [35%] \|\| αλλα [65%] |
| +-- | 1Cor. 6:11 | αλλ [35%] \|\| αλλα [65%] |
| ++ | 1Cor. 9:9 | ἀλοωντα [30%] \|\| ἀλοωντα [70%] |
| ++ | 1Cor. 9:10 | ἀλοων [30%] \|\| ἀλοων [70%] |
| +-- | 1Cor. 9:26 | δαιρων [35%] \|\| δερων [65%] |
| ++ | 1Cor. 10:13 | δυνατος [30%] \|\| πιστος [70%] |
| ++ | 1Cor. 11:6 | κειρεσθαι [32%] \|\| κειρασθαι [64%] |
| + | 1Cor. 12:26[a] | συμπασχη [40%] \|\| συμπασχει [60%] |
| + | 1Cor. 12:26[b] | συγχαιρη [40%] \|\| συγχαιρει [60%] |
| ++-- | 1Cor. 14:26 | οντως ο θεος εν υμιν εστιν [23%] \|\| ~ 231456 [75%] |
| ++ | 1Cor. 16:2 | ευοδουται [30%] \|\| ευοδωται [61%] \|\| |

| | | |
|---|---|---|
| ++-- | 2Cor. 1:12 | ειλικρινεια [25%] \|\| ειλικρινεια [60%] \|\| \|\| (also at 2:17) |
| +++ | 2Cor. 1:15 | προς υμας ελθειν το προτερον (21.6%) \|\| ~ 31245 (61.1%) \|\| \|\| |
| +-- | 2Cor. 3:7 | μωυσεος [35%] \|\| μωυσεως [55%] \|\| |
| + | 2Cor. 3:15 | μωσης [40%] \|\| μωυσης [60%] |
| +-- | 2Cor. 5:15 | παντων [35%] \|\| αυτων [55%] \|\| |
| ++-- | 2Cor. 7:11 | αλλ [27%] \|\| αλλα [73%] |
| ++ | 2Cor. 8:4 | δεξασθαι ημας [30%] \|\| --- [70%] |
| + | 2Cor. 8:9 | ημας [40%] \|\| υμας [60%] |
| ++ | 2Cor. 8:12 | καθὸ εαν [30%] \|\| καθ ὃ εαν [58%] \|\| |
| +++ | 2Cor. 11:7 | εαυτον [22%] \|\| εμαυτον [78%] |
| + | 2Cor. 11:20 | δαιρει [40%] \|\| δερει [60%] |
| ++ | 2Cor. 13:11 | της [30%] \|\| --- [70%] |
| + | 2Cor. 13:13 | ημων [40%] \|\| --- [60%] |

| | | |
|---|---|---|
| ++ | Gal. 1:12 | αποκαλυψεως [30%] \|\| 1 ιησου [70%] |
| + | Gal. 3:6,etc. | ἀβρααμ [40%] \|\| ἀβρααμ [60%] |
| + | Gal. 3:16 | ερρεθησαν [40%] \|\| ερρηθησαν [55%] \|\| |
| + | Gal. 4:2 | αλλ [40%] \|\| αλλα [60%] |

++ Eph. 1:12    της [30%] || --- [70%]
+  Eph. 2:17    ημιν [40%] || υμιν [60%]
+-- Eph. 4:32   υμιν [35%] || ημιν [65%]
++ Eph. 5:5     ιστε [30%] || εστε [70%]
+  Eph. 6:6     οφθαλμοδουλιαν [40%] || οφθαλμοδουλειαν [60%]


++ Phip. 1:10    εἰλικρινεις [30%] || εἰλικρινεις [70%]
++-- Phip. 1:19  καραδοκιαν [25%] || αποκαραδοκιαν [74%]
+-- Phip. 2:1    τι [35%] || τις [60%] ||
+  Phip. 2:4     το [40%] || τα [45%] || των [15%]
+  Phip. 2:30    πληρωση [40%] || αναπληρωση [55%] ||
+  Phip. 3:1     το [40%] || --- [60%]
+  Phip. 3:13    ουπω [40%] || ου [60%]


+  Col. 1:22     αυτου [40%] || --- [60%]
+  Col. 1:27     τις ο [40%] || τι το [60%]
+  Col. 1:28     χριστω [40%] || 1 ιησου [60%]
+  Col. 3:22     οφθαλμοδουλιαις [40%] || οφθαλμοδουλειαις [43%] || ||


+  1Th. 1:7      και [40%] || 1 τη [30%] || 1 εν τη [30%]
+  1Th. 1:9      υμων [40%] || ημων [60%]
+  1Th. 3:8      στηκητε [40%] || στηκετε [60%]
++ 1Th. 4:9      γαρ [30%] || 1 υμεις [70%]


**None for 2 Thessalonians. (f³⁵ is always accompanied by at least 40% of the Byzantine bulk.)**


+  1Tm. 3:2      νηφαλιον [40%] || νηφαλεον [50%] ||
+  1Tm. 3:11     νηφαλιους [40%] || νηφαλεους [50%] ||
++ 1Tm. 5:18     ἀλοωντα [30%] || ἀλοωντα [70%]
++-- 1Tm. 5:21   προσκλισιν [25%] || προσκλησιν [75%]
+  1Tm. 6:12     και [40%] || --- [60%]


+++ 2Tm. 3:6     ενδυοντες [20%] || ενδυνοντες [77%]
+++ 2Tm. 3:14    οις [20%] || --- [80%]

+   Titus 2:1   νηφαλιους [40%] || νηφαλεους [40%] || νηφαλαιους [20%]
+++ Titus 3:9   ερις [20%] || ερεις [75%] ||


+   Phin. 1   ιησου χριστου [40%] || ~ 21 [60%]
+++ Phin. 25   ιησου [20%] || 1 χριστου [80%]


+--  Heb. 2:4   σημειοις [35%] || 1 τε [65%]
+   Heb. 2:16,etc. ἀβρααμ [40%] || ἀβρααμ [60%]
+   Heb. 3:16   μωυσεος [40%] || μωυσεως [45%] || μωσεως [15%]
+   Heb. 3:19   δια [40%] || δι [60%]
+   Heb. 6:3   ποιησομεν [40%] || ποιησωμεν [59%]
+++ Heb. 8:3   προσενεγκοι [20%] || προσενεγκη [80%]
+   Heb. 8:6   τετευχεν [40%] || τετυχεν [50%] ||
+--  Heb. 8:11   πλησιον [35%] || πολιτην [65%]
+++ Heb. 9:12   ευρομενος [20%] || ευραμενος [80%]
++  Heb. 9:14   αγιου [29%] || αιωνιου [70%]
+--  Heb. 9:19   μωυσεος [35%] || μωυσεως [45%] || μωσεως [20%]
+   Heb. 10:1   δυναται [40%] || δυνανται [59%]
++  Heb. 10:28   μωυσεος [30%] || μωυσεως [55%] || μωσεως [15%]
++  Heb. 11:20   ἠσαυ [30%] || ἠσαυ [70%]   (also 12:16)
+--  Heb. 12:7   ει [35%] || εις [65%]
++  Heb. 12:24   το [30%] || τον [70%]
+   Heb. 12:25   ουρανου [40%] || ουρανων [60%]

**Key:**
+++    around 20% = f³⁵ virtually alone = diagnostic  (14)
++--    around 25% = quite good  (10)
++    around 30% = not bad  (21)
+--    around 35% = (11)
+   around 40% = (37)

Total: 93

# General Epistles

++   James 1:23   νομου [30%] || λογου [69%]
+--   James 1:26   αλλ [35%] || αλλα [65%]
++   James 2:3   λαμπραν εσθητα [30%] || ~ 2 την 1 [70%]
++-- James 2:4   ου (26.8%) || και 1 (72.2%)
+++  James 2:13   ανηλεος [20%] || ανελεος [30%] || ανιλεως [50%]
++-- James 3:2   δυναμενος [23%] || δυνατος [76.5%]
+++  James 3:4   ιθυνοντος [21%] || ευθυνοντος [79%]
++-- James 4:11   γαρ [26%] || --- [74%]
++-- James 4:14ᵃ   ημων [26%] || υμων [74%]
++   James 4:14ᵇ   επειτα [29.5%] || 1 δε και [46%] || 1 δε [15%] || 1 και [9.5%]

257

+-- James 5:10<sup>a</sup> αδελφοι [35%] || 1 μου [62%] ||
+ James 5:10<sup>b</sup> εν τω [40%] || 2 [58%]


+ 1Peter 1:3 ελεος αυτου [38%] || ~ 21 [60%]
+-- 1Peter 1:7 δοξαν και τιμην [35%] || ~ 321 [28%] || ~ 32 εις 1 [37%]
+ 1Peter 1:23 αλλ [40%] || αλλα [60%]
+-- 1Peter 2:6 ή [35%] || εν τη [59%] ||
++-- 1Peter 2:21 και [23%] || --- [77%]
++-- 1Peter 3:10 ημερας ιδειν [26%] || ~ 21 [74%]
+++ 1Peter 3:16 τη αγαθη εν χριστω αναστροφη [20%] || την αγαθην 34
αναστροφην [50%] || ~ την 34 αγαθην αναστροφην [24%]

|| ||
+++ 1Peter 4:2 του [22%] || --- [78%]
+ 1Peter 4:3<sup>a</sup> υμιν (41.7%) || ημιν (47.1%) || --- (11.2%)
++-- 1Peter 4:3<sup>b</sup> χρονος [26%] || 1 του βιου [74%]
+++ 1Peter 4:11<sup>a</sup> δοξαζηται θεος [20%] || 1 ο 2 [73%] ||
++-- 1Peter 4:11<sup>b</sup> αιωνας [27%] || 1 των αιωνων [73%]
+ 1Peter 4:14 αναπεπαυται [39%] || αναπαυεται [52%] || ||
+-- 1Peter 5:7 υπερ [35%] || περι [65%]
++-- 1Peter 5:8 περιερχεται [24%] || περιπατει [76%]
++ 1Peter 5:10 στηριξαι...σθενωσαι...θεμελιωσαι [30%] ||
στηριξει...σθενωσει... θεμελιωσει [66%] ||


+++ 2Peter 2:2 ας [20%] || ους [80%]
+-- 2Peter 2:9 πειρασμων [33%] || πειρασμου [67%]
++-- 2Peter 2:12 γεγενημενα φυσικα [26%] || ~ 21 [54%] || ||
++-- 2Peter 2:17 εις αιωνας (25.1%) || 1 αιωνα (70.3%) || ||
+ 2Peter 2:18 ασελγειας [40%] || ασελγειαις [60%]
+++ 2Peter 3:1 είλικρινη [20%] || ειλικρινη [80%]
++-- 2Peter 3:5 συνεστωτα [23%] || συνεστωσα [76%]
+-- 2Peter 3:16 εισιν [33%] || εστιν [67%]
++-- 2Peter 3:18 αυξανητε [27%] || αυξανετε [60%] || || ||


++ 1John 1:6 περιπατουμεν [29%] || περιπατωμεν [71%]
+-- 1John 2:24 πατρι και εν τω υιω [35%] || ~ 52341 [65%]
+-- 1John 2:29 ειδητε [37%] || ιδητε [59%] ||
+-- 1John 3:1 ημας [36%] || υμας [63.5%]
+++ 1John 3:6 και [20%] || --- [80%]
++ 1John 3:24 εν [30%] || και 1 [70%]
+-- 1John 4:16 αυτω [37%] || 1 μενει [63%]
++-- 1John 5:11 ο θεος ημιν [24%] || ~ 312 [76%]


258

| | | |
|---|---|---|
| ++ | 2John 5 | εχομεν [32%] ‖ ειχομεν [68%] |
| +++ | 2John 9 | δε [20%] ‖ --- [80%] |

| | | |
|---|---|---|
| ++-- | 3John 11 | δε [25%] ‖ --- [75%] |
| ++-- | 3John 12 | οιδαμεν (23%) ‖ οιδατε (61.5%) ‖ οιδας (15.1%) |

**None for Jude. (f³⁵** is always accompanied by at least 40% of the Byzantine bulk.)

**Key:**

| | |
|---|---|
| +++ | around 20% = **f³⁵** virtually alone = diagnostic (9) |
| ++-- | around 25% = quite good (16) |
| ++ | around 30% = not bad (9) |
| +-- | around 35% (11) |
| + | around 40% (6) |

Total: 51

# Apocalypse

Due to Hoskier's collations, it is possible (and better) to state the evidence in terms of families, instead of percentages, as I have done in my apparatus—please consult it for the evidence.

| | | |
|---|---|---|
| ᵀᵀᵀ | 1″2 | ἅ ‖ ἅτινα ‖ --- |
| + | 1:5 | εκ ‖ --- |
| ++ | 1:13 | μαζοις ‖ μαστοις ‖ μασθοις |
| +-- | 2:2 | κοπον ‖ 1 σου |
| ++-- | 2:7 | δωσω ‖ 1 αυτω |
| ++-- | 2:24 | βαλω ‖ βαλλω |
| +++ | 3:2 | εμελλες αποβαλειν ‖ 1 αποβαλλειν ‖ ημελλες αποβαλλειν ‖ etc. |
| +-- | 3:5 | ουτως ‖ ουτος |
| ++ | 3:18ᵃ | κολλουριον ‖ κουλουριον ‖ κολλυριον |
| +++ | 3:18ᵇ | εγχρισον επι ‖ 1 . ινα εγχριση ‖ ινα εγχρισαι ‖ εγχρισαι ‖ etc. |
| + | 4:3 | ομοια ‖ ομοιος ‖ ομοιως |
| +++ | 4:4 | ειδον ‖ --- |
| + | 4:6 | κρυσταλω ‖ κρυσταλλω |
| +++ | 4:8 | λεγοντα ‖ λεγοντες |
| + | 5:2 | αξιος ‖ 1 εστιν |
| ++-- | 6:8 | θανατος ‖ ὁ 1 ‖ ὁ αθανατος |
| + | 6:9 | των ανθρωπων ‖ --- |
| + | 6:12 | και ‖ --- |
| + | 8:9 | διεφθαρησαν ‖ διεφθαρη |
| + | 8:13 | τρις ‖ --- |
| +++ | 9:4 | μονους ‖ --- |

+++ 9:5    *πληξη* || *παιση* || *πεση*

+-- 9:6    *ζητουσιν* || *ζητησουσιν*

+++ 9:11    *αββαδδων* || *αββαδων* || *αββααδων* || *αββααδδων* || *αβαδδων*

+-- 9:15    *και την ημεραν* || 1 *εις* 23 || 13 || ---

++ 10:7ᵃ    *τελεσθη* || *και* 1 || *και ετελεσθη*

+ 10:7ᵇ    *ὄ* || *ως*

++ 10:7ᶜ    *ευηγγελισατο* || *ευηγγελισεν* || *ευηγγελησε*

++ 11:1    *και ειστηκει ο αγγελος λεγων* || 1 *φωνη λεγουσα* || 5 || *λεγει*

+ 11:11    *επ αυτου*j || *εις* 2 || *εν αυτοις* || *αυτοις*

+ 11:17    *και ο ερχομενος* || ---

+-- 12:3    *μεγας πυρρος* || 1 *πυρος* || ~ 21 || ~ *πυρος* 1

+++ 12:4    *τικτειν* || *τεκειν*

++-- 12:5    *ηρπαγη* || *ηρπασθη*

++-- 12:7    *του πολεμησαι* || 2 || *επολεμησαν*

+ 13:7    *φυλην* || 1 *και λαον*

+ 13:15    *ινα* || ---

+ 14:6    *αλλον αγγελον* || 2 || ~ 21

+++ 14:12    *του ιησου* || 2 || 2 *χριστου*

+ 15:3    *μωυσεος* || *μωυσεως* || *μωσεως*

++-- 15:4    *αγιος ει* || 1 || 2 || *οσιος*

+++ 15:6    *εκ του ουρανου* || 12 *ναου* || ---

+ 16:9    *την* || ---

+ 17:8    *βλεποντες* || *βλεποντων*

+-- 18:2    *εν ισχυρα φωνη* || 123 *μεγαλη* || 123 *και μεγαλη* || 23 || 23 *μεγαλη* || etc.

+ 18:3    *πεπωκεν* || *πεπωκασιν* || *πεπωτικεν* || *πεπτωκασιν* || *πεπτωκαν* || *πεπωκαν*

+ 18:7    *βασανισμον* || 1 *και πενθος*

+ 18:14ᵃ    *απωλοντο* || *απωλετο* || *απηλθεν*

+ 18:14ᵇ    *ου μη ευρησεις αυτα* || 12 *ευρησης* 4 || 12 *ευρης* 4 || 12 *ευρησουσιν* 4 || etc.

++-- 18:17    *ο επι των πλοιων πλεων* || 2345 || 234 *ομιλος* || 234 *ο ομιλος* || etc.

+++ 18:21    *λεγων* || 1 *ουτως*

+++ 19:1    *φωνην οχλου πολλου μεγαλην* || ~ 1423 || 123 || *φωνης* 23

+ 20:4    *το μετωπον αυτου* || 12 || *των μετωπων* 3 ||

++-- 20:11    *ο ουρανος και η γη* || ~ 45312

+++ 20:12ᵃ    *ανεωχθησαν* || *ηνεωχθησαν* || *ηνοιχθησαν* || *ηνοιξαν*

++-- 20:12ᵇ    *ανεωχθη* || *ηνεωχθη* || *ηνοιχθη*

+++ 20:14    *εστιν ο θανατος ο δευτερος* || ~ 1453 || ~ 23451 || ~ 2351 || --- || ~ 4531

+ 21:5    *καινα ποιω παντα* || ~ 312 || ||

+ 21:6    *αρχη και τελος* || *η* 12 *το* 3 || *και η* 12 *το* 3

++-- 21:10    *την μεγαλην την αγιαν* || 12 *και* 4 || 34

+ 21:24    *την δοξαν και την τιμην αυτων εις αυτην* || 12678 || *αυτω* 235 *των εθνων*     78 ||

+-- 22:2 εκαστον αποδιδους || 1 αποδιδον || 1 αποδιδουν || ~ 21 || ~ 2
εκαστος

**Key:**
+++ $f^{35}$ is alone, or virtually so (15)
++-- $f^{35}$ is joined by part of another family (small) (10)
++ $f^{35}$ is joined by a whole small family (not **a** or **e**) (5)
+-- $f^{35}$ is joined by a whole small family (not **a** or **e**) plus (7)
+ $f^{35}$ is joined by less than either of the other two main lines
of transmission (25)

Total: 62

**Here are the totals for the whole New Testament.**

**Key:**
+++ around 20% = $f^{35}$ virtually alone = diagnostic (155)
++-- around 25% = quite good (127)
++ around 30% = not bad (157)
+-- around 35% (89)
+ around 40% (137)

**Total: 665**

The evidence is clear. **Family 35** is an objectively/empirically defined entity throughout the New Testament. It remains to be seen if the same can be said for any other family or line of transmission.

# APPENDIX C
# The Implications of Statistical Probability for
# the History of the Text[1]

Today, the whole question of the derivation of "text-types" through definite, historical recensions is open to debate. Indeed, E.C. Colwell, one of the leading contemporary [1975] critics, affirms dogmatically that the so-called "Syrian" recension (as Hort would have conceived it) never took place.[2] Instead he insists that all text-types are the result of "process" rather than definitive editorial activity.[3] Not all scholars, perhaps, would agree with this position, but it is probably fair to say that few would be prepared to deny it categorically. At least Colwell's position, as far as it goes, would have greatly pleased Hort's great antagonist, Dean Burgon. Burgon, who defended the *Textus Receptus* with somewhat more vehemence than scholars generally like, had heaped scorn on the idea of the "Syrian" revision, which was the keystone to Westcott and Hort's theory. For that matter, the idea was criticized by others as well, and so well-known a textual scholar as Sir Frederic Kenyon formally abandoned it.[4] But the dissent tended to die away, and the form in which it exists today is quite independent of the question of the value of the TR. In a word, the modern skepticism of the classical concept of recensions thrives in a new context (largely created by the papyri). But this context is by no means discouraging to those who feel that the *Textus Receptus* was too hastily abandoned.

The very existence of the modern-day discussion about the origin of text-types serves to set in bold relief what defenders of the Received Text have always maintained. Their contention was this: Westcott and Hort failed, by their theory of recensions, to adequately explain the actual state of the Greek manuscript tradition; and in particular, they failed to explain the relative uniformity of this tradition. This contention now finds support by reason of the questions which modern study has been forced to raise. The suspicion is well advanced that the Majority text (as Aland designates the so-called Byzantine family[5]) cannot

---

[1] This appendix is an edited abstract from "A Defense of the Majority-Text" by Zane C. Hodges and David M. Hodges (unpublished course notes, Dallas Theological Seminary, 1975) used by permission of the authors.

[2] His statement is: "The Greek Vulgate—The Byzantine or Alpha texttype—had its origin in no such single focus as the Latin had in Jerome" (italics in the original). E.C.Colwell, "The Origin of Texttypes of New Testament Manuscripts", Early Christian Origins, p.137.

[3] *Ibid.*, p. 136. Cf. our discussion of this view under "Objections".

[4] Cf. F.G. Kenyon, Handbook to the Textual Criticism of the New Testament, pp. 324ff.

[5] Kurt Aland, "The Significance of the Papyri for Progress in New Testament Research", *The Bible in Modern Scholarship*, p. 342. This is the most scientifically

be successfully traced to a single even in textual history. But, if not, how can we explain it?

Here lies the crucial question upon which all textual theory logically hinges. Studies undertaken at the *Institut für neutestamentliche Textforschung* in Münster (where already photos or microfilms of over 4,500 [now over 5,000] manuscripts have been collected) tend to support the general view that as high as 90 [95] percent of the Greek cursive (minuscule) manuscripts extant exhibit substantially the same form of text.[1] If papyrus and uncial (majuscule) manuscripts are considered along with cursives, the percentage of extant texts reflecting the majority form can hardly be less than 80 [90] percent. But this is a fantastically high figure and it absolutely demands explanation. In fact, apart from a rational explanation of a text form which pervades all but 20 [10] percent of the tradition, no one ought to seriously claim to know how to handle our textual materials. If the claim is made that great progress toward the original is possible, while the origin of 80 percent of the Greek evidence is wrapped in obscurity, such a claim must be viewed as monstrously unscientific, if not dangerously obscurantist. No amount of appeal to subjective preferences for this reading or that reading, this text or that text, can conceal this fact. The Majority text must be explained **as a whole**, before its claims **as a whole** can be scientifically rejected.

It is the peculiar characteristic of New Testament textual criticism that, along with a constantly accumulating knowledge of our manuscript resources, there has been a corresponding diminution in the confidence with which the history of these sources is described. The carefully constructed scheme of Westcott and Hort is now regarded by all reputable scholars as quite inadequate. Hort's confident assertion that "it would be an illusion to anticipate important changes of text from any acquisition of new evidence" is rightly regarded today as extremely naive.[2]

The formation of the *Institut für neutestamentliche Textforschung* is virtually an effort to start all over again by doing the thing that should have been done in the first place—namely, collect the evidence! It is in this context of re-evaluation that it is entirely possible for the basic question of the origin of the Majority text to push itself to the fore. Indeed, it may be confidently anticipated that if modern criticism continues its trend toward more genuinely scientific procedures, this question will once again become a central consideration. For it still remains the most determinative issue, logically, in the whole field.

Do the proponents of the *Textus Receptus* have an explanation to offer for the Majority text? The answer is yes. More than that, the position they maintain is so uncomplicated as to be free from difficulties encountered by more complex hypotheses. Long ago, in the process of attacking the authority of numbers in textual criticism, Hort was constrained to confess: "A theoretical presumption

---

unobjectionable name yet given to this text form.

[1] *Ibid.*, p. 344.

[2] *Ibid.*, pp. 330ff.

indeed remains that a majority of extant documents is more likely to represent a majority of ancestral documents at each stage of transmission than *vice versa*."[1] In conceding this, he was merely affirming a truism of manuscript transmission. It was this: under normal circumstances the older a text is than its rivals, the greater are its chances to survive in a plurality or a majority of the texts extant at any subsequent period. But the **oldest** text of all is the autograph. Thus it ought to be taken for granted that, barring some radical dislocation in the history of transmission, a majority of texts will be far more likely to represent correctly the character of the original than a small minority of texts. This is especially true when the ratio is an overwhelming 8:2 [9:1]. Under any reasonably normal transmissional conditions, it would be for all practical purposes quite impossible for a later text-form to secure so one-sided a preponderance of extant witnesses. Even if we push the origination of the so-called Byzantine text back to a date coeval with $P^{75}$ and $P^{66}$ (c. 200)—a time when already there must have been hundreds of manuscripts in existence— such mathematical proportions as the surviving tradition reveals could not be accounted for apart from some prodigious upheaval in textual history.

## Statistical probability

This argument is not simply pulled out of thin air. What is involved can be variously stated in terms of mathematical probabilities. For this, however, I have had to seek the help of my brother, David M. Hodges, who received his B.S. from Wheaton College in 1957, with a major in mathematics. His subsequent experience in the statistical field includes service at Letterkenny Army Depot (Penna.) as a Statistical Officer for the U.S. Army Major Item Data Agency and as a Supervisory Survey Statistician for the Army Materiel Command Equipment Manuals Field Office (1963-67), and from 1967-70 as a Statistician at the Headquarters of U.S. Army Materiel Command, Washington, D.C. In 1972 he received an M.S. in Operations Research from George Washington University.

Below is shown a diagram of a transmissional situation in which one of three copies of the autograph contains an error, while two retain the correct reading. Subsequently the textual phenomenon known as "mixture" comes into play with the result that erroneous readings are introduced into good manuscripts, as well as the reverse process in which good readings are introduced into bad ones. My brother's statement about the probabilities of the situation follows the diagram in his own words. [The diagram is on the next page.]

> Provided that good manuscripts and bad manuscripts will be copied an equal number of times, and that the probability of introducing a bad reading into a copy made from a good manuscript is equal to the probability or reinserting a good reading into a copy made from a bad manuscript, the correct reading would predominate in any generation of manuscripts. The degree to which the good reading

---

[1] B. F. Westcott and F.J.A. Hort, *The New Testament in the Original Greek*, II, 45.

would predominate depends on the probability of introducing the error.

For purposes of demonstration, we shall call the autograph the first generation. The copies of the autograph will be called the second generation. The copies of the second generation manuscripts will be called the third generation and so on. The generation number will be identified as "n". Hence, in the second generation, n=2.

**Generation**

| | Numbers | | |
|---|---|---|---|
| | **Good** | **Bad** | **Diff.** |

| Generation | Good | Bad | Diff. |
|---|---|---|---|
| 1 | 1 | 0 | 1 |
| 2 | 2 | 1 | 1 |
| 3 | 5 | 4 | 1 |
| 4 | 14 | 13 | 1 |
| 5 | 41 | 40 | 1 |

Assuming that each manuscript is copied an equal number of times, the number of manuscripts produced in any generation is $k^{n-1}$, where "k" is the number of copies made from each manuscript.

The probability that we shall reproduce a good reading from a good manuscript is expressed as "p" and the probability that we shall introduce an erroneous reading into a good manuscript is "q". The sum of p and q is 1. Based on our original provisions, the probability of reinserting a good reading from a bad manuscript is q and the probability of perpetuating a bad reading is p.

The expected number of good manuscripts in any generation is the quantity $pkG_{n-1} + qkB_{n-1}$ and the expected number of bad manuscripts is the quantity $pkB_{n-1} + qkG_{n-1}$, where $G_{n-1}$ is the number of good manuscripts from which we are copying and $B_{n-1}$ is the number of bad manuscripts from which we are copying. The number of good manuscripts produced in a generation is $G_n$ and the number of bad produced is $B_n$. We have, therefore, the formulas:

---

[1] [N.B.—the fifth generation is represented by all three lines; in other words, each MS of the fourth generation was copied three times, just as in the other generations.]

(1) $G_n = pkG_{n-1} + qkB_{n-1}$ and
(2) $B_n = pkB_{n-1} + qkG_{n-1}$ and
(3) $k^{n-1} = G_n + B_n = pkG_{n-1} + qkB_{n-1} + pkB_{n-1} + qkG_{n-1}$.

If $G_n = B_n$, then $pkG_{n-1} = qkB_{n-1} = pkB_{n-1} + qkG_{n-1}$ and $pkG_{n-1} + qkB_{n-1} - pkB_{n-1} - qkG_{n-1} = 0$.

Collecting like terms, we have $pkG_{n-1} - qkG_{n-1} + qkB_{n-1} - pkB_{n-1} = 0$ and since k can be factored out, we have $(p-q)G_{n-1} + (q-p)B_{n-1} = 0$ and $(p-q)G_{n-1} - (p-q)B_{n-1} = 0$ and $(p-q)(G_{n-1} - B_{n-1}) = 0$. Since the expression on the left equals zero, either $(p-q)$ or $(G_{n-1} - B_{n-1})$ must equal zero. But $(G_{n-1} - B_{n-1})$ cannot equal zero, since the autograph was good. This means that $(p-q)$ must equal zero. In other words, the expected number of bad copies can equal the expected number of good copies only if the probability of making a bad copy is equal to the probability of making a good copy.

If $B_n$ is greater than $G_n$, then $pkB_{n-1} + qkG_{n-1} > pkG_{n-1} + qkB_{n-1}$. We can subtract a like amount from both sides of the inequality without changing the inequality. Thus, we have $pkB_{n-1} + qkG_{n-1} - pkG_{n-1} - qkB_{n-1} > 0$ and we can also divide k into both sides obtaining $pB_{n-1} + qG_{n-1} - pG_{n-1} - qB_{n-1} > 0$. Then, $(p-q)B_{n-1} + (q-p)G_{n-1} > 0$. Also, $(p-q)B_{n-1} - (p-q)G_{n-1} > 0$. Also $(p-q)(B_{n-1} - G_{n-1}) > 0$. However, $G_{n-1}$ is greater than $B_{n-1}$ since the autograph was good. Consequently, $(B_{n-1} - G_{n-1}) < 0$. Therefore, $(p-q)$ must also be less than zero. This means that q must be greater than p in order for the expected number of bad manuscripts to be greater than the expected number of good manuscripts. This also means that the probability of error must be greater than the probability of a correct copy.

The expected number is actually the mean of the binomial distribution. In the binomial distribution, one of two outcomes occurs; either a success, i.e., an accurate copy, or a failure, i.e., an inaccurate copy.

In the situation discussed, equilibrium sets in when an error is introduced. That is, the numerical difference between the number of good copies and bad copies is maintained, once an error has been introduced. In other words, bad copies are made good at the same rate as good copies are made bad. The critical element is how early a bad copy appears. For example, let us suppose that two copies are made from each manuscript and that q is 25% or ¼. From the autograph two copies are made. The probability of copy number 1 being good is ¾ as is the case for the second copy. The probability that both are good is 9/16 or 56%. The probability that both are bad is ¼ x ¼ or 1/16 or 6%. The probability that one is bad is ¾ x ¼ + ¼ x ¾ or 6/16 or 38%. The expected number of good copies is $pkG_{n-1} + qkB_{n-1}$ which is ¾ x 2 x 1 + ¼ x 2 x 0 or 1.5. The expected number of bad copies is $2 - 1.5$ or .5. Now, if an error is introduced into the second generation, the number of good and bad copies would, thereafter, be equal. But the probability of this happening is

44%. If the probability of an accurate copy were greater than ¾, the probability of an error in the second generation would decrease. The same holds true regardless of the number of copies and the number of generations so long as the number of copies made from bad manuscripts and the number from good manuscripts are equal. Obviously, if one type of manuscript is copied more frequently than the other, the type of manuscript copied most frequently will perpetuate its reading more frequently.

Another observation is that if the probability of introducing an incorrect reading differs from the probability of reintroducing a correct reading, the discussion does not apply.

This discussion, however, is by no means weighted in favor of the view we are presenting. The reverse is the case. A further statement from my brother will clarify this point.

Since the correct reading is the reading appearing in the majority of the texts in each generation, it is apparent that, if a scribe consults other texts at random, the majority reading will predominate in the sources consulted at random. The ratio of good texts consulted to bad will approximate the ratio of good texts to bad in the preceding generations. If a small number of texts are consulted, of course, a non-representative ratio may occur. But, in a large number of consultations of existing texts, the approximation will be representative of the ratio existing in all extant texts.

In practice, however, random comparisons probably did not occur. The scribe would consult those texts most readily available to him. As a result, there would be branches of texts which would be corrupt because the majority of texts available to the scribe would contain the error. On the other hand, when an error first occurs, if the scribe checked more than one manuscript he would find all readings correct except for the copy that introduced the error. Thus, when a scribe used more than one manuscript, the probability of reproducing an error would be less than the probability of introducing an error. This would apply to the generation immediately following the introduction of an error.

In short, therefore, our theoretical problem sets up conditions for reproducing an error which are somewhat too favorable to the error. Yet even so, in this idealized situation, the original majority for the correct reading is more likely to be retained than lost. But the majority in the fifth generation is a slender 41:40. What shall we say, then, when we meet the actual extant situation where (out of any given 100 manuscripts) we may expect to find a ratio of, say, 80:20? It at once appears that the probability that the 20 represent the original reading in any kind of normal transmissional situation is poor indeed.

Hence, approaching the matter from this end (i.e., **beginning** with extant manuscripts) we may hypothesize a problem involving (for mathematical convenience) 500 extant manuscripts in which we have proportions of 75% to 25%. My brother's statement about this problem is as follows:

> Given about 500 manuscripts of which 75% show one reading and 25% another, given a one-third probability of introducing an error, given the same probability of correcting an error, and given that each manuscript is copied twice, the probability that the majority reading originated from an error is less than one in ten. If the probability of introducing an error is less than one-third, the probability that the erroneous reading occurs 75% of the time is even less. The same applies if three, rather than two copies are made from each manuscript. Consequently, the conclusion is that, given the conditions described, it is highly unlikely that the erroneous reading would predominate to the extent that the majority text predominates.

> This discussion applies to an individual reading and should not be construed as a statement of probability that copied manuscripts will be error free. It should also be noted that a one-third probability of error is rather high, if careful workmanship is involved.

It will not suffice to argue in rebuttal to this demonstration that, of course, an error might easily be copied more often than the original reading in any particular instance. Naturally this is true, and freely conceded. But the problem is more acute than this. If, for example, in a certain book of the New Testament we find (let us say) 100 readings where the manuscripts divide 80 percent to 20 percent, are we to suppose that in every one of these cases, or even in most of them, that this reversal of probabilities has occurred? Yet this is what, **in effect**, contemporary textual criticism is saying. For the Majority text is repeatedly rejected in favor of minority readings. It is evident, therefore, that what modern textual critics are **really** affirming—either implicitly or explicitly—constitutes nothing less than a wholesale rejection of probabilities on a sweeping scale!

Surely, therefore, it is plain that those who repeatedly and consistently prefer minority readings to majority readings—especially when the majorities rejected are very large—are confronted with a problem. How can this preference be justified against the probabilities latent in any reasonable view of the transmissional history of the New Testament? Why should we reject these probabilities? What kind of textual phenomenon would be required to produce a Majority text diffused throughout 80 percent of the tradition, which nonetheless is more often wrong than the 20 percent which oppose it? And if we could conceptualize such a textual phenomenon, what proof is there that it ever occurred? Can anyone, logically, proceed to do textual criticism without furnishing a convincing answer to these questions?

I have been insisting for quite some time that the real crux of the textual problem is how we explain the overwhelming preponderance of the Majority text in the extant tradition. Current explanations of its origin are seriously inadequate (see below under "Objections"). On the other hand, the proposition that the Majority text is the natural outcome of the normal processes of manuscript transmission gives a perfectly natural explanation for it. The minority text-forms are thereby explained, *mutatis mutandis*, as existing in their minority form due to their comparative remoteness from the original text. The theory is simple but, I believe, wholly adequate on every level. Its adequacy can be exhibited also by the simplicity of the answers it offers to objections lodged against it. Some of these objections follow.

## Objections

1. Since all manuscripts are not copied an even number of times, mathematical demonstrations like those above are invalid.

But this is to misunderstand the purpose of such demonstrations. Of course the diagram given above is an "idealized" situation which does not represent what actually took place. Instead, it simply shows that all things being equal **statistical probability** favors the perpetuation in every generation of the original majority status of the authentic reading. And it must then be kept in mind that the larger the original majority, the more compelling this argument from probabilities becomes. Let us elaborate this point.

If we imagine a stem as follows:

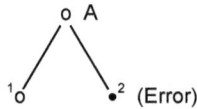

o A

1 o      2 • (Error)

in which A = autograph and (1) and (2) are copies made from it, it is apparent that, **in the abstract**, the error in (2) has an even chance of perpetuation in equal numbers with the authentic reading in (1). But, of course, **in actuality** (2) **may** be copied more frequently than (1) and thus the error be perpetuated in a larger number of later manuscripts than the true reading in (1).

So far, so good. But suppose:

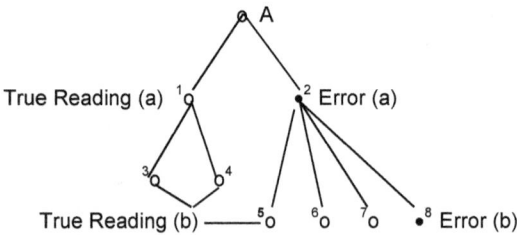

A

True Reading (a) 1 o      2 • Error (a)

3 o      4 o

True Reading (b) —— 5 o    6 o    7 o    8 • Error (b)

Now we have conceded that the error designated (a) is being perpetuated in larger numbers than the true reading (a), so that "error (a)" is found in copies 5-6-7-8, while "true reading (a)" is found only in copies 3 and 4. But when "error (b)" is introduced in copy 8, its rival ("true reading (b)") is found in copies

270

3-4-5-6-7.[1] Will anyone suppose that at this point it is at all likely that "error (b)" will have the same good fortune as "error (a)" and that manuscript 8 will be copied more often than 3-4-5-6-7 combined?

But even conceding this **far** less probable situation, suppose again:

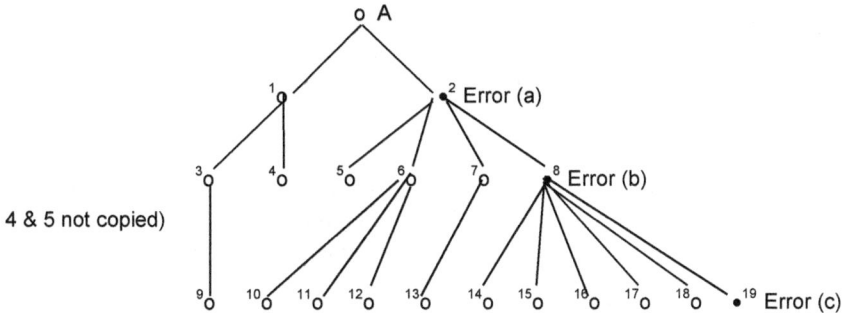

o A

1
2 Error (a)
3   4   5   6   7   8 Error (b)

4 & 5 not copied)

9  10  11  12  13  14  15  16  17  18  •19 Error (c)

Will anybody believe that probabilities favor a repetition of the same situation for "error (c)" in copy 19?

Is it not transparent that as manuscripts multiply, and errors are introduced farther down in the stream of transmission, that the probability is drastically reduced that the error will be copied more frequently than the increasingly large number of rival texts?

Thus to admit that **some** errors might be copied more frequently than the rival, authentic reading in no way touches the core of our argument. The reason is simple: modern criticism repeatedly and systematically rejects majority readings on a very large scale. But, with every such rejection, the probability that this rejection is valid is dramatically reduced. **To overturn statistical probabilities a few times is one thing. To overturn them repeatedly and persistently is quite another!**

Hence, we continue to insist that to reject Majority text readings in large numbers without furnishing a credible overall rationale for this procedure is to fly blindly into the face of all reasonable probability.

**2**. The Majority text can be explained as the outcome of a "process" which resulted in the gradual formation of a numerically preponderant text-type.

The "process" view of the Majority text seems to be gaining in favor today among New Testament textual scholars. Yet, to my knowledge, no one has offered a detailed explanation of what exactly the process was, when it began, or how—once begun—it achieved the result claimed for it. Indeed, the proponents of the "process" view are probably wise to remain vague about it

---

[1] By "error (b)" we mean, of course, an error made in another place in the text being transmitted from the autograph. We do **not** mean that "error (b)" has been substituted for "error (a)." Hence, while copies 5-6-7 contain "error (a)," they also contain the original autograph reading which is the rival to "error (b)."

because, on the face of the matter, it seems impossible to conceive of **any kind** of process which will be both historically credible and adequate to account for all the facts. The Majority text, it must be remembered, is relatively uniform in its general character with comparatively low amounts of variation between its major representatives.[1]

No one has yet explained how a long, slow process spread out over many centuries as well as over a wide geographical area, and involving a multitude of copyists, who often knew nothing of the state of the text outside of their own monasteries or scriptoria, could achieve this widespread uniformity out of the diversity presented by the earlier forms of text. Even an official edition of the New Testament—promoted with ecclesiastical sanction throughout the known world—would have had great difficulty achieving this result as the history of Jerome's Vulgate amply demonstrates.[2] But an unguided process achieving relative stability and uniformity in the diversified textual, historical, and cultural circumstances in which the New Testament was copied, imposes impossible strains on our imagination.

Thus it appears that the more clearly and specifically the "process" view may come to be articulated, the more vulnerable it is likely to be to all of the potential objections just referred to. Further, when articulation **is** given to such a view, it will have to locate itself definitely somewhere in history—with many additional inconveniences accruing to its defenders. For, be it remembered, just as history is silent about any "Syrian recension" (such as the one Hort imagined), so also history is silent about any kind of "process" which was somehow influencing or guiding the scribes as manuscripts were transmitted.

---

[1] The key words here are "relatively" and "comparatively." Naturally, individual members of the Majority text show varying amounts of conformity to it. Nevertheless, the nearness of its representatives to the general standard is not hard to demonstrate in most cases. For example, in a study of one hundred places of variation in John 11, the representatives of the Majority text used in the study showed a range of agreement from around 70 percent to 93 percent. Cf. Ernest C. Colwell and Ernest W. Tune, pp. 28,31. The uncial codex Omega's 93 percent agreement with the *Textus Receptus* compares well with the 92 percent agreement found between $P^{75}$ and B. Omega's affinity with the TR is more nearly typical of the pattern one would find in the great mass of minuscule texts. High levels of agreement of this kind are (as in the case of $P^{75}$ and B) the result of a shared ancestral base. It is the divergencies that are the result of a "process" and not the reverse.

A more general, summary statement of the matter is made by Epp, "...the Byzantine manuscripts together form, after all, a rather closely-knit group, and the variations in question within this entire large group are relatively minor in character." (Eldon Jay Epp, "The Claremont Profile Method for Grouping New Testament Minuscule Manuscripts", p. 33.)

[2] After describing the vicissitudes which afflicted the transmission of the Vulgate, Metzger concludes: "As a result, the more than 8,000 Vulgate manuscripts which are extant today exhibit the greatest amount of cross-contamination of textual types." (*Text of the New Testament*, p. 76.) Uniformity of text is always greatest at the source and diminishes—rather than increases—as the tradition expands and multiplies. This caveat is ignored by the "process" view of the Majority text.

Modern critics are the first to discover such a "process", but before accepting it we shall have to have more than vague, undocumented assertions about it.

It seems not unfair to say that the attempt to explain the Majority text by some obscure and nebulous "process" is an implicit confession of weakness on the part of contemporary criticism. The erosion of Westcott and Hort's view, which traced this text to an official, definitive recension of the New Testament, has created a vacuum very hard indeed to fill. More than ever, it appears, critics cannot reject the Majority text and at the same time also explain it. **And this is our point!** Rejection of the Majority text and credible explanation of that text are quite incompatible with each other. But acceptance of the Majority text immediately furnishes an explanation of this text and the rival texts as well! **And it is the essence of the scientific process to prefer hypotheses which explain the available facts to those which do not!**

# APPENDIX D
# Conflation or Confusion?[1]

Conflation is the theory that when a scribe or editor had before him two or more manuscripts that at a given point had different readings that might "properly" be combined to produce a more "full" reading, he might do so. The result would be called "conflation" according to Hort.

When evaluating a putative example of conflation, due consideration should be given to the possibility that the differences may have come about because of the accidental (or intentional) omission of different parts of a "complete" original reading.

The list that follows comprises possible examples of conflation found to date from all sources. (There may be quite a few more discoverable by a sharp eye.) These are presented to the reader for his own evaluation and decision. They range from cases of obvious conflation and obvious omission to cases of sheer confusion where it is highly doubtful that the mechanism "conflation" was at work. Accordingly, the examples are classified into two sets of two groups each:

1. True, or simple "conflation":
   a) Simple addition or telescoping of readings, or omission;
   b) Addition plus simple coupling links, or omission.
2. Marginal "conflation" or confusion:
   a) Complicated by substitution, transposition or moderate internal changes, or omissions;
   b) Substantial differences—"conflation" dubious.

The full extent of the confusion that exists will not be apparent to the reader since for most of the examples there are one or more further variations not included here because they are not relevant to the possible instances of conflation.

The symbols in the critical apparatus are essentially those in general use. The abbreviations *pc, al, pm* and *rell* have the same meanings as in the Nestle editions. I have represented f[1] and f[13] by the numbers only. Only one text-type symbol is used, *Byz*, which stands for the "Byzantine" manuscript tradition. I have used parentheses in two ways—enclosing a papyrus they mean there is doubt as to what reading is exhibited, enclosing any other kinds of witnesses they mean the witness(es) has a slight variation from the reading of the witness(es) not so enclosed. The reader cannot fail to note that the

---

[1] The title and basic format for this appendix I owe to William G. Pierpont and use with his permission. I have, however, almost tripled the number of examples and the editorial comments are mine. The principal sources for the added examples are H.A. Sturz (*The Byzantine Text-Type*) and Maurice A. Robinson (unpublished paper). Peter J. Johnston has contributed significantly to the statements of evidence.

completeness of the apparatus varies considerably from example to example—this is a reflection of the sources that were available to me.

## Group 1. a) Simple addition or telescoping of readings, or omission.

1. Matt. 3:12 αυτου εις την αποθηκην     Byz ℵ C K Δ 0233 1 pm lat cop
       εις την αποθηκην αυτου     L 892 al b ff¹ g¹ sy$^{p,h}$
    αυτου εις την αποθηκην αυτου     B W pc

(This would appear to be a conflation on the part of B and W. Since Hort did not follow B here, he must have been of a similar opinion.)

2. Matt. 16:11 προσεχειν     Byz D$^c$ W X pm sy$^{c,s,h}$
       προσεχετε     D Θ 13 124 pc lat sy$^p$
       προσεχετε δε     ℵ B C L 1 pc cop
   προσεχειν προσεχετε δε     C$^c$ 33 237 al q

(An evident conflation on the part of some later MSS, building on the "Byzantine" and "Alexandrian/ Western" readings.)

Matt. 17:25 οτε εισηλθεν     Byz E F G K L W Y Π
       ελθοντα     B 1
       εισελθοντα     ℵ
       εισελθοντων     Θ 13
       εισελθοντι     D

(Might this be a conflation on the part of ℵ, with "Caesarean" and "Western" embellishments?)

4. Matt. 20:21 δεξιων σου . . . ευωνυμων     D Θ 1 pc lat
       δεξιων    . . . ευωνυμων σου     ℵ B
       δεξιων σου . . . ευωνυμων σου     Byz C L N W Z 085 13 pm sy$^{p,h}$

(Is this a "Byzantine" conflation of the "Western" and "Alexandrian" readings, or are the latter independent simplifications of the former? It should be noted that ℵ and B are alone in omitting the first σου.)

5. Matt. 23:25 ακρασιας     ℵ B D L Δ Θ Π 1 13 33 al it sy$^h$
       αδικιας     Byz C K Γ pm f sy$^p$
   ακρασιας αδικιας     W

(It seems clear that Codex W here conflates the "Alexandrian" and "Byzantine" readings.)

6. Matt. 24:38 εκειναις    προ     D 253 pc it$^{pt}$ sy$^{h,pal}$
       ταις προ     Byz ℵ L W Θ 067 0133 1 13 pl it$^{pt}$ vg bo
   εκειναις ταις προ     B

(This would appear to be a conflation on the part of B. Since Hort used brackets here, he must have tended to a similar opinion.)

7. Matt. 26:22 εις εκαστος     ℵ B C L Z 0281 33 pc sa
       εκαστος αυτων     Byz P$^{37,64}$(P$^{45}$) A W Γ Δ Π Σ Ψ 074 1 13 pl sy$^p$
       εις εκαστος αυτων     (P$^{45}$) D M Θ 69 pc bo

(This would appear to be a "Western" conflation of "Byzantine" and "Alexandrian" elements. A recent meeting of papyrologists dated P[64] in the first century [!] and confirmed that it supports the Byzantine reading.)

8. Matt. 26:36 ου     *Byz* B E F G 067 *pm*
         αν     D K L W Δ Θ 074 1 69 *al*
      ου αν     P[53] A *pc*

(Before the advent of P[53] presumably all would agree that A has here conflated the "Byzantine" and "Western" readings. Although the papyrus antedates any extant witness to these two "text-types", I suggest that the proper conclusion is that the conflation is a very early one.)

9. Matt. 26:70 αυτων     K *al*
         παντων     ℵ B D E G L Z Θ 090 13 33 *al* lat sy[p,h]
   αυτων παντων     *Byz* A C W Γ Δ 0133 1 *pm*

(Shall we say that the "Byzantine" text has a conflation based on a handful of late MSS on the one hand and the combined "Alexandrian-Western" text-types on the other? It seems more probable that K etc. have simplified the "Byzantine" reading, an easy instance of homoioteleuton. In that event the "Alexandrian-Western" reading is best explained as a separate simplification of the original reading, a bit of parablepsis.)

10. Matt. 27:55 εκει     *Byz* B C *pl* lat
         και     D 56 aur d
     εκει και     F K L Π 33 sy[h,pal]
      κακει     ℵ (sy[p])

(Here we seem to have varied witnesses conflating the "Byzantine-Alexandrian" and "Western" readings.)

11. Mark 1:4 ο βαπτιζων εν τη ερημω     B 33 *pc*
       βαπτιζων εν τη ερημω και     *Byz* A K P W Π 1 13 *pl* f sy[h,pal]
    ο βαπτιζων εν τη ερημω και     ℵ L Δ *pc* bo
   (εν τη ερημω βαπτιζων και)     D Θ *pc* lat sy[p]

(Here we have "Alexandrian" witnesses conflating the "Byzantine" reading and that of Codex B. Although there has been no accretion of new evidence, UBS[3] seems to espouse this obvious conflation whereas UBS[1] did not.)

12. Mark 1:28 ευθυς     *Byz* A D E G H K M U V Y Γ Δ Π Σ Φ Ω 0104 *pm* lat sy[p,h]
      πανταχου     W 579 *pc* b e q
  ευθυς πανταχου     ℵ[c] B C L 0133 13 *pc*
     (omit)     ℵ Θ 1 *al* c ff[2] r[1] sy[s]

(Is this not an obvious "Alexandrian" conflation? Yet the UBS text adopts it without giving any indication that there are other readings.)

13. Mark 1:40 κυριε     C L W Θ *pc* e c ff sy[pal]
        οτι     *Byz* ℵ A *pl* sy[h]
    κυριε οτι     B

(This appears to be a clear conflation on the part of B. Since Hort did not follow B here he presumably tended to the same opinion.)

14. Mark 5:42  εξεστησαν    *Byz* P⁴⁵ A K W Θ Π 0133 1 13 *pl* e syᵖ·ʰ
       εξεστησαν ευθυς ℵ B X L Δ 33 892 *pc* bo
       εζεστησαν παντες D it sa

(If the producers of the "Syrian" text followed a policy of conflation, why did they neglect this fine opportunity? Note that Hort's "late Syrian" reading now has the earliest attestation.)

15. John 4:29  παντα οσα  *Byz* P⁶⁶·⁷⁵ A D L W Γ Δ Θ Λ Π Ψ 086 1 13 *pl* lat syʰ
      παντα   α ℵ B C e a d q syᵖ cop
      παντα οσα α  579

(This is an obvious conflation in one late MS. Note the strong early attestation for the "Byzantine" reading.)

16. John 5:37  εκεινος   μεμαρτυρηκεν P⁷⁵ ℵ B L W 213 *pc* a ffᵃ j syᵖ·ʰ
       αυτος μεμαρτυρηκεν *Byz* P⁶⁶ A Γ Δ Θ Λ Π Ψ 063 1 13 *pl* lat
       εκεινος αυτος μαρτυρει D a b c l q

(This appears to be a case of "Western" conflation. Note that Hort's "late Syrian" reading now has very early attestation.)

17. John 7:39  πνευμα        P⁶⁶ᶜ·⁷⁵ ℵ K N T Θ Π Ψ *pc* bo
       πνευμα αγιον     *Byz* P⁶⁶ L W X Γ Δ Λ 0105 1 13 *pl*
       πνευμα   δεδομενον lat syᶜ·ˢ·ᵖ Eusebius
       πνευμα αγιον δεδομενον B 053 *pc* e q syᵖᵃˡ·ʰ
       (το πνευμα το αγιον επ αυτοις) D d f

(It would appear that B here conflates "Byzantine" and "Western" elements. Since Hort did not follow B here he must have tended toward the same opinion. Note that Hort's "late Syrian" reading now has very early attestation.)

18. John 10:19  σχισμα ουν     D 1241 syˢ
       σχισμα   παλιν P⁽⁴⁵⁾⁷⁵ ℵ B L W X 33 *pc* lat syᵖ sa
       σχισμα ουν παλιν *Byz* P⁶⁶ A Γ Δ Θ Λ Π Ψ 1 13 *pl* syʰ

(A century ago this could have been interpreted as a "Syrian" conflation, but now we can scarcely say that P⁶⁶ conflated P⁷⁵ and D. The possibility must at least be considered that Hort's "late Syrian" reading is in fact the earliest, the original.)

19. John 10:31  εβαστασαν      P⁴⁵ Θ
       εβαστασαν ουν     D 28 1780 *pc* lat syˢ bo
       εβαστασαν   παλιν (P⁷⁵) ℵ B L W 33 *pc* syᵖ
       εβαστασαν ουν παλιν *Byz* P⁶⁶ A X Π Ψ 1 13 565 *pl* f syʰ

(A century ago this could have been interpreted as a "Syrian" conflation, but now we can hardly say that P⁶⁶ conflated B and D. The possibility must be entertained that Hort's "late Syrian" reading is in fact the earliest. All three words end in *nu*, so both [or all three] shorter readings could be the result of homoioteleuton.)

20. John 11:22  αλλα     1780
             και P⁷⁵ ℵ B C X 1 33 *pc* itᵖᵗ
       αλλα και *Byz* P⁴⁵·⁶⁶ ℵ² A C³ D L W Θ Ψ Ω 0250 13 *pl* lat syᵖ·ʰ cop

(It seems obvious that the "Byzantine" reading cannot be a conflation of the "Alexandrian" reading and that of one late MS. 1780 has dropped part of the "Byzantine" reading. I suggest the same explanation for the "Alexandrian" reading. Observe that the "Byzantine" reading now has very early attestation.)

21. John 12:9   οχλος πολυς   *Byz* P$^{66,75}$ A B$^2$ I Q X Θ Ψ 065 1 33 *pl* (cop)
               ο οχλος πολυς   א B L *pc* lat
               οχλος ο πολυς   W 1010
               ο οχλος ο πολυς   P$^{66c}$

(Conflation or confusion? Did P$^{66c}$ conflate B and W? Or should we say that P$^{66c}$ has the original reading that everyone else [including P$^{66*}$!] simplified? Note that Hort's "late Syrian" reading now has the earliest attestation, with a vengeance!)

22. John 14:14   τουτο        P$^{75}$ A B L Ψ 060 33 *al* c vg cop
                  εγω   *Byz* P$^{66}$ א D E G Q X Γ Δ Π *pm* it sy$^{p,h}$
               τουτο εγω   P$^{66c}$

(This is an instructive conflation on the part of P$^{66c}$. Note the early attestation for the "Byzantine" reading.)

23. John 16:4   αυτων μνημονευητε           א$^c$ L 13 *al* lat
                μνημονευητε αυτων      *Byz* K Γ Δ Ψ 054 1 *pm* ff$^2$ sy$^{pal}$
           αυτων μνημονευητε αυτων   A B Θ Π 33 *al* sy$^{p,h}$
                μνημονευητε              א D a sy$^s$ cop

    (This would appear to be a not very felicitous conflation on the part of B, etc.)

24. John 17:23   και γινωσκη     P$^{66}$ א W 1 *pc* lat
                 ινα γινωσκη     B C D L 33 *pc* a e sy$^s$
              και ινα γινωσκη   *Byz* A Θ Ψ 054 13 *pm* f q sy$^{p,h}$

(This could be a "Byzantine" conflation, but the first two readings could just as easily be independent simplifications of the longer reading.)

25. John 18:40   παλιν          P$^{60}$ א B L W X 0109 *pc*
                 παντες   G K N Ψ 1 13 33 *al* it sy$^{p,pal}$ cop
              παλιν παντες   *Byz* (P$^{66}$) A Γ Δ Θ 054 0250 *pm* vg sy$^h$
              παντες παλιν   D

(This could be a "Byzantine" conflation, but it could just as easily be the case that the two shorter readings are independent simplifications of the longer one; homoioarcton perhaps. Is the "Western" reading a conflation or simply a reversal of the word order?)

26. Acts 7:16   του Συχεμ     *Byz* P$^{74}$ D Ψ 049 056 0142 *pm* lat
              εν Συχεμ     א B C *al* cop
             του εν Συχεμ   א$^c$ A E

(This is presumably a conflation of the "Byzantine" and "Alexandrian" readings.)

27. Acts 10:48   του κυριου                    *Byz* H L P 049 056 *pm*
                          Ιησου Χριστου       P⁷⁴ ℵ A B E 33 *al* cop
               του κυριου Ιησου       Lect. *al*
               του κυριου Ιησου Χριστου    D 81 d p

(This would appear to be a "Western" conflation of the "Byzantine" and "Alexandrian" readings.)

28. Acts 14:15   τον θεον    ζωντα     D *pc*
                    θεον τον ζωντα    ℵ
              τον θεον τον ζωντα    *Byz* P⁴⁵ H L P *pm*
                       θεον        ζωντα    P⁷⁴ B C E 33 *al*

(A century ago this might have been interpreted as a "Syrian" conflation, but now we can hardly say that P⁴⁵ conflated Aleph and D. Why not say that Hort's "late Syrian" reading is not only the earliest but also the best? I would say that the "Alexandrian" reading is decidedly inferior in terms of the discourse structure of the text, the sort of thing that would appeal to scribes without native speaker control of Koine Greek.[1])

29. Acts 24:14   τοις           προφηταις    *Byz* ℵᶜ A *pm* syr bo
                 εν τοις προφηταις    B C D *al*
             τοις εν τοις προφηταις    ℵ E

(This seems to be a clear conflation on the part of Aleph.)

30. Acts 25:5   τουτω          *Byz pm*
                  ατοπον    ℵ A B C E 33 *al* lat
             τουτω ατοπον    Ψ 69 614 *al* syr bo

(This would appear to be a conflation of the "Byzantine" and "Alexandrian" readings.)

31. 1 Cor. 7:34   η αγαμος και η παρθενος       P¹⁵ B P *al* cop
                       και η παρθενος η αγαμος    *Byz* D F G K L Ψ *pm* it syr
            η αγαμος και η παρθενος η αγαμος    P⁴⁶ ℵ A 33 *pc*

(Although unquestionably early, this really does appear to be a conflation on the part of P⁴⁶, etc.)

32. Phil. 1:18   πλην         *Byz* D E K L *pm*
                 οτι    B syᵖ
            πλην οτι    P⁴⁶ ℵ A F G P 048 33 *pc* sa

(Modern editors have tended to regard the long reading as original, but now that we know that the "Byzantine" text goes back at least to the second century we should reconsider the possibility that P⁴⁶, etc. have a conflation. In the example above they have demonstrated this ability.)

---

[1] For a complete statement of what I mean by "discourse structure", see my book, *A Framework for Discourse Analysis* (Dallas: Summer Institute of Linguistics and University of Texas at Arlington, 1980).

| | | |
|---|---|---|
| 33. Col. 2:2 | του Θεου και Πατρος και του Χριστου | *Byz* $D^c$ K *pm* Lect |
| | του Θεου και Πατρος του Χριστου | $ℵ^b$ Ψ *pc* $sy^h$ |
| | του Θεου Πατρος και του Χριστου | 0208 1908 $sy^p$ |
| | του Θεου Πατρος του Χριστου | A C $it^{pt}$ $sa^{pt}$ bo |
| | του Θεου Πατρος Χριστου | ℵ 048 |
| | του Θεου Χριστου | $P^{46}$ B (alone of MSS) |
| | του Θεου | $D^b$ H P 436 1881 $sa^{pt}$ |
| | (at least seven further variations) | |

(The editors of the UBS text make the reading of B their first choice, and that of the "Byzantine" text their last choice! They must consider the "Byzantine" reading to be a prime illustration of "conflation", but how did it come about? Did "Syrian editors" borrow the two καις from Ψ and 0208 respectively, or did these drop parts of the longer reading? Was Πατρος borrowed from Aleph, A, C or did these drop still other parts of the original? Presumably the UBS editors feel that H omitted part of B, but B could easily show the result of omission also, a not very difficult case of homoioteleuton [four words end in -ου]. I submit that the reading which best explains the rise of all the others is precisely that of the "Byzantine" text.)

| | | |
|---|---|---|
| 34. Col. 3:17 | Κυριου Ιησου | *Byz* $P^{46}$ B (Ψ) *pl* |
| | Ιησου Χριστου | A C D F G |
| | Κυριου Ιησου Χριστου | ℵ□$D^2$ 365 1175 *pc* |

(Aleph conflates, presumably. Note the early attestation for the "Byzantine" reading.)

| | | |
|---|---|---|
| 35. 1 Thess. 5:27 | τοις αγιοις | 103 1984 1985 |
| | τοις αδελφοις | ℵ B D E F G *pc* d e f g sa |
| | τοις αγιοις αδελφοις | *Byz* ($P^{46}$) $ℵ^c$ A K L P Ψ 33 *pl* it syr bo |

(The "Byzantine" reading can scarcely be a conflation based on 103, so 103 must have a simplification of the "Byzantine" reading. I suggest the same explanation for the "Alexandrian-Western" reading. Both short forms could easily be the result of homoioteleuton [3 x -οις].)

| | | |
|---|---|---|
| 36. Heb 7:22 | και | 920 |
| | κρειττονος | *Byz* $P^{46}$ $ℵ^c$ A $C^c$ D E K L P Ψ *pl* lat syr cop |
| | και κρειττονος | ℵ B C 33 *pc* |

(It is clear that B could not have a conflation based on 920, unless it is the sole survivor of a very early tradition, but neither may we say that $P^{46}$ is simplifying B. Note that here it is the "Alexandrian" text that has the "fuller, smoother" reading.)

| | | |
|---|---|---|
| 37 Rev. 6:1/2 | και ιδε και ιδου | $M^{a,b,ept}$ |
| | και ειδον και ιδου | $M^{c,d,ept}$ (A C) |
| | και ιδε και ειδον και ιδου | ℵ (alone) |

(Here Aleph conflates the readings of two groups of minuscule MSS. It follows that though these MSS are much later in date than Aleph they reflect an earlier form of the text. In 6:3/4 Aleph repeats this reading in a clear case of assimilation. The statement of evidence in examples 37, 38, 39 and 49 is taken from *The Greek New Testament According to the Majority Text* [Thomas Nelson, 1982].)

38. Rev. 6:5    και ιδε            και ιδου    M[a,b]
                και ειδον και ιδου    M[c,d,ept] C (A)
                και ιδε και ειδον και ιδου    ℵ (alone)

(Aleph repeats the conflation.)

38. Rev. 6:7/8    και ιδε            και ιδου    M[a,b,ept]
                  και ειδον και ιδου    M[c,d,ept]
                  και ιδον και ιδου    A (C)
                  και ιδε και ιδον και ιδου    ℵ (alone)

(Aleph repeats the conflation again.)

## Group 1. b) Addition plus simple coupling links, or omission.

40. Matt. 4:3    αυτω ο πειραζων    ειπεν        *Byz* C L P Θ 0233 *pm* k sy[h]
                 ο πειραζων    ειπεν αυτω    ℵ B W 1 13 33 *al* vg sy[p] bo
                 αυτω ο πειραζων και ειπεν αυτω    D it sy[c,s,pal]

(Here we presumably have a "Western" conflation of the "Byzantine" and "Alexandrian" readings.)

41. Matt. 9:18    εις ελθων/εισελθων    *Byz* ℵ[2] C D E K M N S V W X Θ 1 33 *pm* d f
                  προσελθων    ℵ 69 157 *pc* q sy[p]
                  εις προσελθων    ℵ[1] B lat *pc*
                  τις προσελθων    L 13 *al* k
                  τις ελθων    Γ□ *al*

(Codex B appears to have a conflation, an opinion with which the editors of the UBS texts evidently concur.)

42. Matt. 27:41    και πρεσβυτερων                A B L Θ 1 13[pt] 33 *al* it[pt] vg sa
                   και                Φαρισαιων D W *pc* it[pt] sy[s]
                   και πρεσβυτερων και Φαρισαιων *Byz* Δ Φ 13[pt] *pm* sy[p,h] bo Diatessaron

(Here, at last, we seem to have a clear "Byzantine" conflation, albeit dating from the second century. The whole clause in the "Byzantine" text reads like this: *οι αρχιερεις εμπαιξοντες μετα των γραμματεων και πρεσβυτερων και φαρισαιων ελεγον.* It really seems to be a bit too full; so much so that editors trained at Alexandria might well have been tempted to improve the style by shortening it. Might the "Western" reading be the result of parablepsis? In fact, both short forms could easily be the result of homoioteleuton.)

43. Luke 24:53 αινουντες                  D it<sup>pt</sup>

ευλογουντες   P<sup>75</sup> ℵ B C L cop sy<sup>s,pal</sup>

αινουντες και ευλογουντες

*Byz* A C² K W X Δ Θ Π Ψ 063 1 13 *pl* it<sup>pt</sup> vg sy<sup>p,h</sup> Diat.

(This is one of Hort's eight "Syrian conflations". According to Hort's own judgment Codex D has omitted 329 words from the genuine text of the last three chapters of Luke, plus adding 173, substituting 146, and transposing 243. Since the producer of D was on something of an omitting spree in these chapters, it is not unreasonable to suggest that D has simply dropped "and blessing" from the original reading, an easy instance of homoioteleuton. Nor is it hard to imagine that editors trained at Alexandria might reduce the longer reading to the proportions exhibited by the "Alexandrian" text-type. Note that once more the "Byzantine" reading has second century attestation.)

44. Acts 20:28   του κυριου            P<sup>74</sup> A C D E Ψ 33 *al* cop

                   του          θεου   ℵ B 056 0142 *al* syr

               του κυριου και θεου   *Byz* L P 049 *pm*

(Here we have a fine candidate for a "Byzantine" conflation, provided that the opposite interpretation is rejected. The reading of A could easily be a case of homoioteleuton and that of B the result of parablepsis or stylistic revision.)

45. Acts 25:6   πλειους        η δεκα     *Byz* Ψ *pm*

                  οκτω η δεκα   2147 *pc* syr

          πλειους οκτω η δεκα   E *al*

      ου πλειους οκτω η δεκα   (P<sup>74</sup> ℵ) A B C 33 *pc* lat bo

(Is this an "Alexandrian" conflation?)

46. 2 Cor. 11:3 της απλοτητος                *Byz* ℵ<sup>c</sup> H K P Ψ 0121 0243 *pm* vg syr

               της αγνοτητος   five early fathers

    της απλοτητος και της αγνοτητος   P<sup>46</sup> ℵ B G 33 *pc* it cop

    της αγνοτητος και της απλοτητος   D

(It appears that the "Alexandrian" and "Western" texts have separate conflations. From their use of brackets we may conclude that the editors of both the Nestle and UBS editions recognize the possibility.)

47. Eph. 2:5   τοις παραπτωμασιν               *Byz* ℵ A D² *pl* cop

                  ταις αμαρτιας   D (G) lat

      τοις παραπτωμασιν και ταις αμαρτιας   Ψ

   εν τοις παραπτωμασιν και ταις επιθυμιαις   B

(Here we have separate conflations on the part of Ψ and B. Since Hort did not follow B here he must have tended to the same opinion. The editors of the Nestle and UBS editions evidently agree as well.)

48. Col. 1:12   τω καλεσαντι                D G 33 *pc* it sa

            τω           ικανωσαντι   *Byz* P<sup>46,(61)</sup> ℵ A C D<sup>c</sup> E K L P Ψ *pl* syr bo

          τω καλεσαντι και ικανωσαντι   B

(This obvious conflation on the part of Codex B was acknowledged by Hort [p. 240], a judgment with which the editors of the Nestle and UBS editions are in full agreement.)

49. Rev. 17:4

| | | |
|---|---|---|
| της πορνειας αυτης | | $M^{b,c,d,e}$ A |
| της πορνειας | της γης | $M^a$ |
| της πορνειας αυτης και της γης | | ℵ (alone) |

(This would appear to be a clear conflation on the part of Aleph.)

Before going on to examples where the required phenomena for possible conflations are less clear, it will be well to pause and see what instruction may be gained from these clear possible examples. Ignoring probabilities for the moment, I will tabulate the "possible" conflations.

| | Total | Examples |
|---|---|---|
| Western text-type | 4 | 7, 16, 27, 40 |
| Codex D | 3 | 3, 25, 46 |
| Alexandrian text-type | 8 | 11, 12, 23, 31, 32, 36, 45, 46 |
| Codex B | 7 | 1, 6, 13, 17, 41, 47, 48 |
| Codex Aleph | 7 | 3, 29, 34, 37, 38, 39, 49 |
| Byzantine text-type | 13 | 4, 9, 18, 19, 20, 24, 25, 28, 33, 35, 42, 43, 44 |

None of the Western "conflations" has early papyrus support, and I believe there is general agreement among scholars that all seven of the "Western" instances are in fact conflations (or secondary readings). None of the B or Aleph "conflations" has early papyrus support. I believe there is general agreement among scholars that all 14 B and Aleph instances are in fact conflations (or secondary readings). (Since Hort was evidently aware of these conflations in B, it is difficult to understand how he could affirm that to the best of his knowledge there were no "Neutral" conflations.) Three of the "Alexandrian" instances (31, 32, 46) have early papyrus attestation. Modern editors have tended to include all eight "Alexandrian" readings in their texts, although some express doubt about 36 and 46. One cannot help but suspect that they are still wearing Hortian blinders, to use Colwell's phrase.

Six of the "Byzantine" instances (18, 19, 20, 25?, 28, 35?) now have early papyrus attestation (another two are attested by the Diatessaron). It follows that although modern editors continue to reject these readings, it can no longer be argued that they are late. If they are conflations then they happened in the second century. It is significant that in fully 35 of the 49 examples given, the "Byzantine" text is possibly being conflated by other witnesses, not vice versa.

It is evident that all "text-types" have possible conflations and that "Western" and "Alexandrian" witnesses have actual conflations. I would argue that all the "Byzantine" instances are original, but in any case it should be clear that "conflation" may not responsibly be used to argue for a late "Byzantine" text-type.  On the contrary, examples like 8, 14, 16, 17, 21, 22, 31, 32, 36, 37, 42, 43, and 46 might reasonably be used to argue for a rather early "Byzantine" text-type.

## Group 2. a) Complicated by substitution, transposition, moderate internal changes, or omissions.

50. Matt. 7:10   η και       ιχθυν αιτησει   ℵ B C (1) 33 *pc*
               και εαν ιχθυν αιτηση   *Byz* (L W) Θ *al* sy^(p,h)
                   εαν ιχθυν αιτηση   lat sy^c
           η και εαν ιχθυν αιτηση   K^c 13 *al*

(This could be either a "Western" or an "Alexandrian" conflation, but presumably not a "Byzantine".)

51. Matt. 7:18   ποιειν ... ενεγκειν   ℵ (alone of MSS)
                ενεγκειν ... ποιειν   B (alone of MSS)
                ποιειν ... ποιειν   *Byz* ℵ^c C K L W X Z Δ Θ Π 0250 1 13 33 *pl* lat syr cop

(The editors of the UBS editions evidently agree that the "Byzantine" reading here is genuine.)

52. Matt. 8:1    καταβαντι  δε αυτω   *Byz* K L (Δ) *pm* (lat sy^(p,h))
           και καταβαντος    αυτου   Z sy^(c,pal)
              καταβαντος δε αυτου   B C W Θ 33 (lat sy^(p,h)) cop
                 καταβαντι  δε αυτου   ℵ

(If anyone has conflated it would seem to be the "Alexandrians". Aleph certainly has a conflation.)

53. Matt. 9:2   σου αι αμαρτιαι   ℵ B C W Δ 1 33 *pc*
            σοι αι αμαρτιαι   D Δ^c *pc* k
           σοι αι αμαρτιαι σου   *Byz* L Θ 0233^v 13 *pm* lat syr
          σου αι αμαρτιαι σου   M

(Codex M has evidently conflated, but should we say the same of the "Byzantine" text? Or are the "Alexandrian" and "Western" readings independent simplifications?)

54. Matt. 10:3                     Θαδδαιος   ℵ
           και                    Θαδδαιος   B *pc* vg cop
           και Λεββαιος              D 122 d k
           και Λεββαιος ο επικληθεις Θαδδαιος   *Byz* C^2 K L W X Δ Θ Π 1 *pl* syr

(The "Byzantine" reading does not really present the phenomena of a conflation. The reading of Aleph is clearly wrong. The "Western" reading could easily have resulted from homoioteleuton. It is not difficult to imagine that editors trained at Alexandria might prefer a shorter reading.)

55. Matt. 10:13  ει  δε μηγη        D sy$^s$
                εαν δε μη η αξια   *Byz* ℵ B *pl* lat sy$^{p,h}$
                ει  δε μη   αξια    L

(This appears to be a conflation on the part of Codex L.)

56. Matt. 12:4  εφαγεν ους  *Byz* (P$^{70}$) C K L Δ Θ Π 0233 1 33 *pl* vg sy$^h$ cop
                εφαγον ο    B 481
                εφαγεν ο    D W 13 it sy$^{p,(c)}$
                εφαγον ους  ℵ

(Aleph and the "Western" text appear to have separate conflations of the
"Byzantine" reading and that of B. P$^{70}$ has εφαγεν but no pronoun [the papyrus
is broken]—thus the "Byzantine" form of the verb has the earliest attestation.)

57. Mat. 12:46  ετι αυτου λαλουντος    ℵ B 33 *pc* lat
                λαλουντος δε αυτου     D L Z 892 sy$^p$
                ετι δε αυτου λαλουντος *Byz* C W Θ 1 13 *pm* sy$^h$

(Is this a "Byzantine" conflation or are the other two readings independent
simplifications?)

58. Matt. 13:28  οι δε αυτω λεγουσιν       B 157 *pc* cop
                 οι δε δουλοι ειπον αυτω   *Byz* L W Θ 1 13 *pm* vg sy$^h$
                 οι δε δουλοι αυτω λεγουσιν C
                 λεγουσιν ουτω οι δουλοι   D it (sy$^{c,s,p}$)
                 οι δε δουλοι λεγουσιν αυτω ℵ

(Conflation or confusion? Both C and Aleph appear to have conflations, both
based on the "Byzantine" reading plus B and D respectively. Surprisingly, the
UBS text follows Aleph, without comment, while Nestle$^{24}$ follows C. The
reading of B would seem to be a clear error.)

59. Matt. 14:6  γενεσιων δε αγομενων   *Byz* W 0119 0136 13 *pm* ff$^1$ sy$^{h\ mg}$
                γενεσιοις δε γενομενοις ℵ B D L Z *pc* (syr)
                γενεσιοις δε αγομενοις  1 *pc*
                γενεσιων δε γενομενων   C K N Θ *al* (syr)

(Codex C and f$^1$ appear to have separate conflations of the "Byzantine" and
"Alexandrian" readings.)

60. Matt. 14:34  επι την γην   Γεννησαρετ       C N 13 *al* sy$^{pal}$
                 εις την γην   Γεννησαρετ       *Byz* L 1 *pm* lat sy$^{p,(c,s)}$
                 επι την γην εις Γεννησαρετ     ℵ B W Δ 0119 33 *pc* sy$^h$
                 επι την γην εις Γεννησαρ       D 700

(Might this be an "Alexandrian/Western" conflation?)

61. Matt. 15:14  οδηγοι εισιν τυφλοι τυφλων  *Byz* C W X Δ Π 0106 *pm* q
                 οδηγοι εισιν τυφλοι         ℵ cop sy$^c$
                 οδηγοι εισιν        τυφλων  K *pc* sy$^s$
                 τυφλοι εισιν οδηγοι         B D 0237
                 τυφλοι εισιν οδηγοι τυφλων  ℵ$^c$ L Z Θ 1 13 33 *al* lat sy$^{p,h}$

(The "Alexandrian" reading appears to be a conflation of the "Byzantine" and "Western" readings. Codices Aleph and K appear to have separate reductions of the "Byzantine" reading, due to homoioarcton.)

62. Matt. 17:7    προσελθων ...     ηψατο αυτων και ειπεν    *Byz* C L W 1 *pm* sy<sup>h</sup>
                  προσηλθεν ... και αψαμενος αυτων ειπεν    ℵ B *pc*
                  προσελθων ... και αψαμενος αυτων ειπεν    Θ 13 *pc*
                  προσηλθεν ... και ηψατο αυτων και ειπεν    D lat sy<sup>p,pal,(c)</sup>

(The "Western" and "Caesarean" readings appear to be separate conflations of the "Byzantine" and "Alexandrian" readings.)

63. Matt. 19:9
μη επι      πορ. και γαμ. αλλην μοιχαται *Byz* ℵ C<sup>c</sup> K L N (W) Z Δ Θ Π 078 *pm* vg sy<sup>s,p,h</sup>
παρ. λογου πορ. ποιει αυ. μοιχευθηναι    (P<sup>25</sup>) B 1 bo
παρ. λογου πορ. και γαμ. αλλην μοιχαται D 13 33 *pc* it sy<sup>c,pal</sup> sa
μη επι πορ. και γαμ. αλλην ποιει αυ. μοι.  C 1216 *pc*

(The "Western" text and Codex C have independent conflations of the "Byzantine" and "Alexandrian" readings.)

64. Matt. 20:10     ελθοντες δε       *Byz* ℵ L W Z 1 *pm* sy<sup>h</sup> bo
                    και ελθοντες       B C D Θ 085 13 33 *pc* e sy<sup>c,s,p</sup>
                    ελθοντες δε και    N 473 *pc* lat arm

(An assortment of witnesses conflate the "Byzantine" and "Alexandrian" readings.)

65. Matt. 22:13
       αρατε αυτον ποδων κ. χειρων και β. α      D it<sup>pt</sup> sy<sup>c,s</sup>
       δησαντες αυτου ποδας κ. χειρας εκβ. α.    ℵ B L Θ 085 1 (13) *pc* it<sup>pt</sup> vg sy<sup>p</sup> cop
       δησαντες αυτου ποδας κ. χειρας αρατε α. και εκβ.  *Byz* C W 0138 *pm* (M Φ *al*) sy<sup>h</sup>

(Is this really a "Byzantine" conflation? The longest reading is perfectly reasonable as it stands; perhaps a bit too 'full' for editors trained at Alexandria, but just right for a Jew speaking Aramaic. Might the "Western" reading be a Latin revision?)

66. Mark 4:5    και οτι    D W it sy<sup>s</sup>
                οπου    *Byz* ℵ A *pl* vg sy<sup>p,h</sup>
                και οπου   B

(An evident conflation on the part of B.)

67. Mark 7:35    διηνοιχθησαν    *Byz* P<sup>45</sup> A N X Γ Π 0131 13 *pm* lat syr
                 ηνοιγησαν       ℵ B D Δ 0274 1 892
                 ηνοιχθησαν      L
                 διηνοιγησαν     W Θ *pc*

(Has P<sup>45</sup> conflated L and W, or have these managed independent conflations of the "Byzantine" and "Alexandrian" readings? Note that Hort's "late Syrian" reading now has the earliest attestation.)

**68. Mark 9:49**

πας γαρ πυρι αλισθησεται        B L (ℵ W) Δ 0274 1 13 *pc* sy$^s$ sa Diat$^{apt}$
      πασα γαρ θυσια αλι αλισθησεται    D it
πας γαρ πυρι αλισθησεται και πασα θυσια αλι αλισθησεται
                  *Byz* A E K N Π Σ (C X Θ Ψ) *pm* f l q vg sy$^{p,h}$ Diat$^{apt,p}$

(This is another of Hort's "Syrian conflations". But the "Alexandrian" reading could easily be the result of homoioteleuton, and a different bit of parablepsis could have given rise to the "Western" reading. Does not the presence of the article with "salt" at the beginning of vs. 50 suggest that "salt" has already been introduced in the prior context? In any case, the "Byzantine" reading has early attestation and may not be dismissed as "late Syrian".)

**69. Mark 12:17**    και αποκριθεις             W 258 *al*
               ο δε Ιησους    ℵ B C L Δ Ψ 33 *pc* sy$^{(p)}$ cop
     και αποκριθεις ο     Ιησους    *Byz* P$^{45}$ A N X Γ Π Φ 1 13 *pm* sy$^{(s),h}$
        αποκριθεις δε ο Ιησους    D 700 *pc* lat
        αποκριθεις δε            Θ 565

(Who is conflating whom? It seems more likely that *Theta* has simplified the "Western" reading than that the latter builds on the former. But the "Western" reading may well be a conflation of the "Byzantine" and "Alexandrian" readings. It seems clear that P$^{45}$ cannot have conflated W and B, but might these have separate simplifications of the "Byzantine" reading? Note that Hort's "late Syrian" reading now has the earliest attestation.)

**70. Luke 9:57**    και          πορευομενων    P$^{45,75}$ ℵ B C L Θ Ξ 33 *pc* sy$^{c,s,p}$ bo
        εγενετο δε   πορευομενων    *Byz* A W Ψ 1 *pm* lat sy$^h$
        και εγενετο πορευομενων    D 13 a c e r$^1$

    (This would appear to be a "Western" conflation.)

**71. Luke 10:42**    ενος    δε εστιν χρεια
                      *Byz* P$^{45,75}$ A C K P W Γ Δ Θ Λ Π Ψ 13 *pl* lat sy$^{c,p,h}$ sa
    ολιγων δε χρεια εστιν η ενος    B
    ολιγων δε εστιν χρεια η ενος    P$^3$ L C$^2$ 1 33 *pc* sy$^{hmg}$ bo
    ολιγων δε εστιν      η ενος    ℵ

(The MSS usually associated with the "Alexandrian" text-type are rather scattered here. Codex L and company might be said to conflate the "Byzantine" reading and that of B. Note that Hort's "late Syrian" reading now has the earliest attestation, with a vengeance.)

**72. Luke 11:12**    η και      P$^{75}$ ℵ B L 1 13 33 cop
          εαν δε και    D
          η και εαν    *Byz* P$^{45}$ R W X Γ Δ Θ Π Ψ *pl* sy$^h$

(Should we say that "Syrian" editors conflated the "Alexandrian" and "Western" readings, or is Hort's "late Syrian" reading really the original?)

**73. Luke 12:30**    ζητει      D it
          επιζητουσιν    P$^{75}$ ℵ B L X 070 13 33 *pc*
          επιζητει    *Byz* P$^{45}$ A Q W Γ Δ Θ Λ Π Ψ 1 *pl*

(Conflation or confusion? Note that Hort's "late Syrian" reading now has very early attestation.)

74. Luke 13:2 οτι ταυτα ℵ B D L *pc* d e r¹
τα τοιαυτα 69 *pc*
οτι τοιαυτα *Byz* P⁷⁵ A W X Γ Δ Θ Λ Π Ψ 070 1 *pm* lat syr

(Did P⁷⁵ conflate B and 69? Note that Hort's "late Syrian" reading now has the earliest attestation.)

75. John 5:15 ανηγγειλεν *Byz* P⁶⁶,⁷⁵ A B Γ Θ Λ Π Ψ 063 1 *pm* sa (lat sy^h)
ειπεν ℵ C L *pc* e q sy^c,s,p bo
ανηγγειλεν και ειπεν αυτοις W
απηγγειλεν D K U Δ 13 33 *al* (lat sy^h)

(Codex W appears to have a conflation involving the "Byzantine" and "Alexandrian" readings. Note that the "Byzantine" reading, which Hort tentatively rejected in spite of B, now has strong early attestation. The "Western" departure is based on the "Byzantine" reading, presumably the original.)

76. John 6:69 ο αγιος του Θεου P⁷⁵ ℵ B C D L W
ο Χριστος ο υιος του Θεου
*Byz* K Π Ψ 0250 13 (Δ Θ 1 33) *pl* lat syr Diat
ο Χριστος ο αγιος του Θεου P⁶⁶ cop

(An instructive conflation on the part of P⁶⁶.)

77. John 7:41 αλλοι ελεγον *Byz* P⁶⁶* ℵ D W Γ Δ Π Ψ 0105 13 *pm* syr
οι δε ελεγον P⁶⁶c,⁷⁵ B L N T X Θ 33 *al* lat
αλλοι δε ελεγον 1 *pc* e bo

(Is this a "Caesarean" conflation? Note that the corrector of P⁶⁶ has taken a "Byzantine" reading and changed it to an "Alexandrian"—since he did that sort of thing repeatedly it would appear that there were exemplars of each type in the scriptorium, the more so in that he frequently did the opposite as well, i.e. changed an "Alexandrian" reading to a "Byzantine". This in A.D. 200!)

78. John 9:6 επεθηκεν B *pc*
εχρισεν 661
επεχρισεν
*Byz* P⁶⁶,⁷⁵ ℵ A C D K L W Δ Θ Π Ψ 0124 0216 1 13 *pl* lat syr cop

(Presumably no one would wish to suggest that the "Byzantine" reading is a conflation of B and 661, even before the advent of P⁶⁶,⁷⁵! And yet, Hort followed B...)

79. John 9:8 τυφλος ην *Byz* C³ Γ Δ *pm*
προσαιτης ην P⁶⁶,⁷⁵ ℵ B C D *al* lat cop sy^s,p,h
τυφλος ην και προσαιτης 69 *pc* e sy^pal

(An evident conflation on the part of a few MSS.)

80. John 11:44   αυτοις ο Ιησους   *Byz* P⁴⁵,⁶⁶ ℵ A C² D X Γ Δ Θ Λ Π Ψ 0250 1 13 *pl* it
                 αυτοις            157
                      ο Ιησους     700 syˢ
                 ο Ιησους αυτοις   L W
                 Ιησους αυτοις     P⁷⁵ B C cop

(157 and 700 have separate simplifications of the "Byzantine" reading. I suggest the same explanation for the "Alexandrian" reading—the editors of the UBS text evidently agree, whereas Hort did not.)

81. John 13:24
πυθεσθαι τις αν ειη π. ου λεγει          *Byz* P⁶⁶ A (D) K W Γ Δ Λ Π 1 13 *pl* syr cop
                     και λεγει αυτω ειπε τις εστιν π. ου λεγει
                     B C I L X 068 33 *pc*
πυθεσθαι τις αν ειη π. ου ελεγεν και λεγει αυτω ειπε τις εστιν π. ου λεγει   ℵ

(This would appear to be an unusually blatant conflation on the part of Aleph, based on the "Byzantine" and "Alexandrian" readings.)

82. John 13:36   απεκριθη          B C L *pc* lat cop
                 λεγει      αυτω    D
                 απεκριθη αυτω      *Byz* P⁶⁶ ℵ A C³ K W X Γ Δ Θ Λ Π Ψ 1 13 *pl*

(A century ago this mighty have been interpreted as a "Syrian" conflation of the "Alexandrian" and "Western" readings, but now the presence of P⁶⁶ rather encourages the opposite conclusion.)

83. Acts 11:7   ηκουσα δε        *Byz* L P *pm*
                και ηκουσα       D *pc* syˢ
                ηκουσα δε και     ℵ A B E *al* cop

(Might this be an "Alexandrian" conflation?)

84. Acts 23:9   τινες                P⁷⁴ A E 33 *pc* bo
                οι γραμματεις      *Byz pm*□
                τινες των γραμματεων   ℵ B C *al* sa

(Might this be an "Alexandrian" conflation?)

85. Rom. 6:12   αυτη                         P⁴⁶ D E F G d f g m
                ταις επιθυμιαις αυτου        ℵ A B C *al* lat cop
                αυτη εν ταις επιθυμιαις αυτου   *Byz* K L P Ψ *pm*

(Here is another fine candidate for a "Byzantine" conflation, unless the other two readings are independent simplifications. If the "Western" reading were original, however could the "Alexandrian" reading have come into being, and vice versa? But if the "Byzantine" reading is original the other two are easily explained.)

290

86. 1 Cor. 9:21  κερδησω         ανομους      *Byz* ℵ<sup>c</sup> K L Ψ *pl*
                κερδανω τους ανομους           ℵ A B C P 33 *pc*
                κερδησω τους ανομους           P⁴⁶
                κερδανω         ανομους      F G
                τους ανομους κερδησω          D E

(Might this case involve a "Western" conflation, or perhaps two of them? Note that P⁴⁶ supports the "Byzantine" form of the verb—if it has a conflation then the "Byzantine" and "Alexandrian" components already existed in AD 200.)

87. 2 Cor. 7:14  επι  τιτου αληθεια     ℵ B *pc*
                η προς τιτον αληθεια     D E F G P Ψ *pc* lat syr cop
                η επι  τιτου αληθεια     *Byz* P⁴⁶ ℵ<sup>c</sup> C K L 0243 *pl*

(A century ago this might have been interpreted as a "Syrian" conflation, but P⁴⁶ now makes the "Byzantine" reading the earliest and enhances its claim to be the original—a claim with which the editors of the UBS text evidently concur.)

88. 1 Thess. 3:2  και διακονον του Θεου και συνεργον ημων      *Byz* K *pl* syr
                  και διακονον του Θεου                         ℵ A P Ψ *pc* lat cop
                                      και συνεργον              B 1962
                                      και συνεργον του Θεου   D 33 b d e mon
                  διακονον           και συνεργον του Θεου   G f g

(Both "Alexandrian" readings could be the result of homoioarcton [2 x και], or did B simplify the "Western" reading? Codex G evidently has a conflation and Codex D might be said to have one. Is the "Byzantine" reading a conflation, or is it the original with which all the others have tampered in one way or another?)

89. 2 Thess 3:4  και εποιησατε και ποιειτε                      G
                          και ποιειτε και ποιησετε      *Byz* ℵ<sup>c</sup> D<sup>c</sup> Ψ *pl*
                              ποιειτε και ποιησετε      ℵ A *pc*
                              ποιειτε και ποιησετε      D☐
                 και εποιησατε και ποιειτε και ποιησετε   B sa

(This would appear to be a not very elegant conflation on the part of B, which is abandoned by both the Nestle and UBS texts. Codex D appears to have a separate conflation.)

90. Heb 9:10   και δικαιωμασιν
               D² K L 056 075 0142 0150 0151 0209 0220 (532 MSS = 94%)[1] a vg sy<sup>h</sup>
                  δικαιωματα    P⁴⁶ ℵ A I P 0278 (24 MSS = 5%) b sa
               και δικαιωματα   ℵ² B (8 MSS = 1%)
                  δικαιωμα      D (alone)

(An evident conflation on the part of B, building on the "Byzantine" and "Alexandrian" readings. Note that 0220 is III century, giving the "Byzantine" reading overt early attestation.)

---

[1] This statement of evidence is based on the series *Text und Textwert,* ed. K. Aland. It represents an almost complete collation of extant MSS.

# Group 2. b) Substantial differences—conflation dubious.

91. Matt. 10:23   φευγετε εις την αλλην                                    *Byz* C K X Δ Π *pl*
                                                                    φευγετε εις την ετεραν
                                                                              ℵ B W 33 *pc*
                        φευγετε εις την αλλην κ. εκ τ. δ. υ. φευγετε εις την ετεραν
                                                                              Θ (D L 1 13) *pc*

(The "Western" reading here seems to include a conflation of the "Byzantine" and "Alexandrian" readings.)

92. Matt. 27:23   ο δε εφη                     ℵ B Θ 028113 33 *pc* sa
                       λεγει αυτοις ο ηγεμων        D L 1 *pc* lat sy[p] bo
                       ο δε ηγεμων εφη              *Byz* A W 064 0250 *pm* sy[h]

(Conflation or confusion?)

93. Mark 6:33
ε. και προηλθον   αυτους και συνηλθον προς αυτον
                                                              *Byz* P[84v] E G K Π (A N Σ 13) *pm* f (q) sy[h]
ε. και προηλθον   αυτους                                       ℵ B (0187[v]) *pc* aur l vg (cop)
ε. και προσηλθον αυτους                                       L *pc*
ε. και προσηλθον αυτοις                                       Δ Θ
ε.                              και συνηλθον     αυτου         D (28 700) b
ε.                              και   ηλθον       αυτου         565 it Diat[p]
         προς           αυτους και συνηλθον προς αυτον        33

(This is another of Hort's eight "Syrian conflations", but unless one is prepared to argue that the "Byzantine" reading is based on 33 it does not meet the requirements for a conflation and may properly be viewed as the original that all the others have simplified. Hort's discussion of this case had been thought by some to be especially impressive, but I would say that he simply misunderstood the basic meaning of the text. In vs. 34 Jesus came out of the boat, not some secluded spot on land. The folks in Egypt could have had the same difficulty as Hort and produced the "Alexandrian" reading. The "Western" reading [and the "Alexandrian"] could be the result of a bit of parablepsis [homoioarcton—2 x και]. The reading of 33 is evidently secondary, however it came about.)

94. Mark 8:26
μηδε εις την κωμην εισελθης μηδε ειπης τινι εν τη κωμη
                                                              *Byz* A C E K N X Δ Π Σ 33 *pl* sy[p,h] Diat
μηδε εις την κωμην εισελθης                                   ℵ[c] B L 1 *pc* cop sy[s]
μη   εις την κωμην εισελθης                                   ℵ W
υπαγε εις τον οικον σου και μηδενι ειπης εις την κωμην   D d q
υπαγε εις τον οικον σου και εαν εις την κωμην εισελθης μηδενι ειπης μηδε εν τη κωμη
                                                              13 (Θ *pc* lat)

(This is another of Hort's "Syrian conflations", but the "Byzantine" reading does not meet the requirements for a conflation and may reasonably be viewed as the original—the folks in Egypt may have felt that it was redundant, reducing it to the "Alexandrian" reading, although the latter could also be the result of homoioarcton [2 x ΜΗΔΕΕΙ]. The "Western" text rewrites the material, as it often does. The "Caesarean" reading evidently involves a conflation.)

95. Mark 9:38
ος ουκ ακολουθει ημιν και εκωλυσαμεν αυτον οτι ουκ ακολουθει ημιν
*Byz* A E K N Π Σ *pm* sy[h]
ος ουκ ακολουθει ημιν και εκωλυσαμεν αυτον  X (W 1) 13 *pc* lat
ος ουκ ακολουθει μεθ ημων και εκωλουμεν αυτον  D
και εκωλυσαμεν αυτον οτι ουκ ακολουθει ημιν
C *pc* aur f cop
και εκωλουμεν  αυτον οτι ουκ ηκολουθει ημιν
ℵ B Δ Θ 0274 (L Ψ) *pc* sy[s,p,pal] Diat

(Here is yet another of Hort's "Syrian conflations". If this is a "Byzantine" conflation, it is built on the lesser "Western" and "Alexandrian" witnesses, and in that event where did D and B get their readings? Is it not more reasonable to regard the "Byzantine" reading as the original that the others have variously simplified? Nestle[24] seems to reflect essentially this opinion. In fact the "Western" reading could easily have resulted from homoioteleuton or a stylistic deletion of the third clause as being redundant. A glance at Luke 9:49 suggests that the Alexandrians harmonized Mark with Luke.)

96. Luke 9:10  τοπον ερημον πολεως καλουμενης Βηθσαιδαν
*Byz* A C W (1) 13 *pm* sy[(p),h]
τοπον ερημον  ℵ *al* sy[c]
πολιν  καλουμενην Βηθσαιδα
ℵ[c] (P[75]) B L Ξ 33 *pc* (sy[s]) cop
κωμην  λεγουμενην Βηθσαιδα  D
κωμην καλουμενην Βηθσαιδαν εις τοπον ερημον  Θ

(This is still another of Hort's eight "Syrian conflations", but the "Byzantine" reading does not meet the requirements for a conflation and may reasonably be viewed as the original. Aleph omitted and B and D have separate revisions—the idea of "a deserted place belonging to a town" apparently gave them difficulty. *Theta* appears to have conflated elements from all four of the other readings!)

97. Luke 9:34  εκεινους εισελθειν  *Byz* P[45] A D P R W X Γ Δ Θ Λ Π Ψ 1 13 *pl* sa
εισελθειν  P[75] S
εισελθειν αυτους  ℵ B L *pc* bo
αυτους  εισελθειν  C *pc*
εισελθειν εκεινους  *pc*

(Conflation or confusion? Codex C would appear to have a conflation. Note that the "Byzantine" reading now has very early attestation.)

98. Luke 11:54
ενδρευοντες α.ζητουντες θηρευσαι τι εκ του στοματος αυτου ινα κατηγορησωσιν αυτου
*Byz* A C W (Ψ 1) 13 33 *pm* (lat)
ενδρευοντες α.  θηρευσαι τι εκ του στοματος αυτου  P[45v,75] (ℵ) B L *pc* cop
ζητουντες αφορμην τινα λαβειν αυτου ινα ευρωσιν κατηγορησαι αυτου
D (Θ sy[s,c])

293

(This is another of Hort's eight "Syrian conflation", but clearly it does not meet the requirements for a conflation. The solution of this problem is linked to textual choices in verse 53, but I submit that the "Byzantine" reading here is a serious candidate for the original. The loss of the last clause in the Alexandrian MSS could be an easy instance of homoioteleuton, or they could have felt it was redundant, which could also have been the motivation for deleting the second participle. Codex D simply rewrote the material.)

99. Luke 12:18   παντα τα γενηματα μου και τα αγαθα μου
                    *Byz* A Q W Θ Ψ *pm* aur f vg sy[p.h]
     παντα τα γενηματα μου           ℵ D it (sy[s.c])
     παντα τον σιτον     και τα αγαθα μου    P[75c] B L 070 1 (13) *pc* cop

(This is the last of Hort's eight "Syrian conflations". The "Western" reading could easily have arisen through homoioteleuton [2 x AMOY] and the "Alexandrian" reading be the result of a stylistic retouching.)

100. Luke 24:47   αρξαμενον   *Byz* P[75] A F H K M U V W Γ Δ Λ Π 063 1 13 *pm* syr
               αρξαμενοι   ℵ B C L N X 33 *pc* cop
               αρξαμενος   S Θ□Ψ□*pc*
               αρξαμενων   D *pc* lat

(Conflation or confusion? Note that Hort's "late Syrian" reading now has the earliest attestation.)

101. John 2:15   ανετρεψεν     P[66] B W X Θ 0162 *pc*
             κατεστρεψεν   P[59] ℵ 13 *pc*
             ανεστρεψεν   *Byz* P[75] A G K L P Γ Δ Λ Π Ψ 1 *pl*

(Conflation or confusion? Note that Hort's "late Syrian" reading now has very early attestation.)

102. John 11:21   ο αδελφος μου ουκ αν ετεθνηκει   *Byz* E G U Γ Δ Θ Λ Π Ω 13 *pm*
               ο αδελφος μου ουκ αν απεθανεν   P[45,66] K 0250
               ουκ αν απεθανεν ο αδελφος μου   P[75] ℵ B C L W *pc*
               ουκ αν απεθανεν μου ο αδελφος   (Ψ) 1 33 565 *pc*
               ουκ αν ο αδελφος μου απεθανεν   (A) D *pc*

(Conflation or confusion? Note that Hort's "late Syrian" word order now has very early attestation. Might P[45,66] have a conflation, albeit early?)

103. John 11:32   απεθανεν μου ο αδελφος   *Byz* P[45] A E G K S X Γ Λ Π 1 *pl*
               μου απεθανεν ο αδελφος   P[66,75] ℵ B C L W Δ Θ 33 *pc*
               απεθανεν ο αδελφος μου   66 lat
               μου ο αδελφος απεθανεν   D

(Conflation or confusion? Note that Hort's "late Syrian" reading now has very early attestation.)

104. John 13:26   και εμβαψας   *Byz* P[66c] A K W Γ Δ Θ Λ Π Ψ 1 13 *pl* lat syr cop
               βαψας ουν   ℵ B C L X 33 *pc*
               και βαψας   D *pc*

(Is this a "Western" conflation? Note that the "Byzantine" reading now has the earliest attestation.)

105. John 14:5
δυναμεθα την οδον ειδεναι     *Byz* P⁶⁶ A L N Q W X Γ Δ Θ Λ Π Ψ 1 13 *pl* lat syr cop
     την οδον ειδεναι δυναμεθα    ℵ K
     την οδον οιδαμεν          D
   οιδαμεν την οδον          B C a b e

(Is B based on D, or did D conflate B and the rest? Note that the "Byzantine" reading now has the earliest attestation. The editors of the UBS text evidently agree that it is original.)

106. 1 Pet. 5:8    τινα καταπιη           *Byz* P⁷² A 056 (33) *pm* lat syr
               τινα καταπιν    ℵ
               τινα καταπιει    0142 *pc*
                    καταπιειν    B Ψ 0206 1175 *pc*
               τινα καταπιειν    ℵᶜ K L P 049 *al* bo

(Line 5 could be a conflation of 1 and 4. Line 2 is probably a misspelling of 1—H became N—while 3 is also a misspelling of 1. Note that the "Byzantine" reading now has the earliest attestation.)

Although many of the examples in Group 2 scarcely offer the required phenomena for possible conflation, others do, to a greater or lesser extent. I will make some observations and draw some conclusions while recognizing that the evidence is not as clear as in the first section.

Ignoring probabilities for the moment, I will tabulate the "possible" conflations (many of which are entirely improbable).

None of the Western "conflations" has early papyrus support, and I believe there is general agreement among scholars that none of the "Western" instances, except 88, is original, whether or not the mechanism that gave rise to the readings was actually conflation in every case.

None of the Alexandrian "conflations" (including those of B and Aleph) has early papyrus support. I believe that all of B's instances and most of Aleph's are universally rejected (the UBS text follows Aleph in 58). Modern editors continue to adopt the "Alexandrian" instances.

| | Total | Examples |
|---|---|---|
| Western text-type | 15 | 50, 56, 60, 62, 63, 64, 69, 70, 86, 88, 89, 91, 93, 104, 105 |
| Alexandrian text-type | 8 | 50, 52, 60, 61, 71, 83, 84, 110 |
| Codex B | 3 | 66, 89, 90 |
| Codex Aleph | 4 | 52, 56, 58, 81 |
| Byzantine text-type | 24 | |
| with early attestation | 9 | 69, 72, 73, 74, 78, 80, 82, 87, 101 |
| lacking phenomena | 5 | 54, 93, 94, 96, 98 |
| really "possible" | 10 | 51, 53, 57, 65, 68, 85, 88?, 92?, 95, 99 |

Nine of the Byzantine "conflations" have early papyrus attestation (and in only five of the instances do any of the other readings have such support), so they may not be used to argue for a late "Byzantine" text-type. Of the fifteen cases without early papyrus attestation, in only four of them do any others have such support (85, 96, 98, 99). I submit that in at least five instances (I think 88 and 92 should also be included) the "Byzantine" reading does not exhibit the required phenomena for a conflation. Most of these are among Hort's eight "Syrian conflations", so I felt obliged to include them lest I be accused of suppressing unfavorable evidence. With reference to the remaining eight instances that may fairly be described as possible conflations, I believe they are most reasonably explained as being the original readings (see the comments under each one). It is significant that in thirty-two of the examples given in Group 2 the "Byzantine" text is being possibly conflated by other witnesses and in twenty-five examples (not necessarily the same ones) the "Byzantine" reading has early papyrus support—in three further cases some significant feature of the "Byzantine" reading has early papyrus support, and in yet another case support from the Diatessaron (2nd cent.). Of the possible "Byzantine conflations" there is general agreement that 51, 80 and 87 are the original reading.

## Conclusion

The evidence presented in this appendix justifies the following statements:

1) "Western" witnesses have clear, undoubted conflations;
2) "Alexandrian" witnesses have clear, undoubted conflations;
3) many putative conflations build upon "Byzantine" readings;
4) numerous readings that were once thought to be late "Syrian conflations" now have overt early attestation;
5) it follows that Hort's statement and use of "conflation" are erroneous.

It has been customary to refer to the "Byzantine" text as "the later, conflated text,"[1] as if "conflation" were a pervading characteristic of this text. The evidence presented above scarcely supports such a characterization since in fully sixty percent of the examples the "Byzantine" text is being built upon and not vice versa. Reference has already been made to Hutton's *Atlas* (on p. 31) which provides evidence that there are over eight hundred places where the producers of the "Byzantine" text could have conflated "Western" and "Alexandrian" readings (following Hort's hypothesis) but did not.

I trust that the reader will not judge me to be unreasonable if I express the hope that all concerned will loyally concede that the specter of "Syrian conflation" has been laid to rest. Henceforth no one may reasonably or responsibly characterize the "Byzantine" text-type as being "conflate" nor argue therefrom that it must be late.[2]

---

[1] Metzger, *The Text*, p. 136. To my astonishment, D.A.Carson appears to still be of this opinion so recently as 1979. In his critique of the first edition of this book (*The King James Version Debate*, Grand Rapids: Baker, "Appendix") he declares that "textual scholars hold that a primary feature of the Byzantine text-type is its tendency to conflate readings" (p. 110) and speaks of "the Byzantine tradition in its mature conflated form" (p. 112). The reader is now in some position to form his own opinion on this subject.

[2] I am aware that the mechanism at work, especially in the Gospels, was probably harmonization in many/most cases rather than conflation. Since both mechanisms produce secondary readings the basic thrust of this appendix is not altered by a choice between them. I am also aware that I cannot **prove** conflation or harmonization in any instance, but then, of course, neither could Hort, and neither can anyone else.

# APPENDIX E
# Mark 16:9-20 and the Doctrine of Inspiration

For over a hundred years it has been a commonplace of New Testament textual criticism to argue that Mark 16:9-20 was not and could not have been written by Mark (or whoever wrote the rest of the book), that it was a subsequent accretion. However, among those who wish to believe or claim that Mark's Gospel was inspired by the Holy Spirit, that it is God's Word, I am not aware of any who are prepared to believe that it could really have been God's intention to terminate the book with εφοβουντο γαρ (verse 8). The most popular hypothesis seems to be that the Autograph was produced as a codex (not a scroll) and that the sheet (or sheets) containing the original ending was torn off and lost before any copies were made.[1] I wish to examine the implications of the claim that verses 9-20 did not form part of the Autograph and that the original ending has vanished (whatever the explanation offered for such a circumstance).

I am writing from the position of one who believes in the verbal, plenary inspiration of Scripture and am addressing those who believe (or would like to believe) that the Bible is God's Word written—"*all Scripture is God-breathed*" (2 Timothy 3:16).

So, we claim that the Holy Spirit inspired Mark's Gospel. And why would He do something like that? Evidently God wanted subsequent generations to have an official biography of Jesus Christ, a description of His life, death and resurrection whose accuracy was guaranteed and whose content was sufficient for His purpose. (That there are several official biographies written from different perspectives does not obviate the integrity of each one individually.)[2] I find it inconceivable that an official biography, commissioned by God and written subject to His quality control, should omit proofs of the resurrection, should exclude all post-resurrection appearances, should end with the clause *"because they were afraid"*!

But most modern critics assure us that such is the case, that the genuine text ends at verse 8. So where was God all this time? If the critics' assessment is correct we seem to be between a rock and a hard place. Mark's Gospel as it stands is mutilated (if it ends at verse 8), the original ending having disappeared without a trace. But in that event what about God's purpose in commissioning this biography? Are we to say that God was unable to protect the text of Mark or that He just could not be bothered? Either option would be fatal to the claim that Mark's Gospel is *"God-breathed"*.

---

1 See, for example, B.M. Metzger, *A Textual Commentary on the Greek New Testament* (New York: United Bible Societies, 1971), p. 126, fn. 7.

2 I would say that Matthew wrote for a Jewish audience, Mark for a Roman audience, Luke for a Greek audience, and John for everyone.

If God tried but was powerless to prevent the mutilation of Mark in this way, how can we be sure that the book has not been mutilated in other ways and places, or even systematically? For that matter, how can we be sure that other New Testament books have not been mutilated too, or maybe even all of them? Anyway, the degree of mutilation would no longer be an issue because if God was powerless to protect His Word then He would not really be God and it would not make all that much difference what He says. The Bible would lose its authority and consequently its importance.

What about the other option—that God could have protected Mark but chose not to? Of what value would quality control be if it extended only to the writing? If God permitted the original ending of Mark to be lost before any copies were made then the biography was 'published' in a seriously incomplete form, and it becomes decidedly awkward to speak of its 'verbal, plenary' inspiration. If God would permit a mutilation of such magnitude, then what assurance do we have that He would not permit any number of further mutilations? Again, the problem extends to the other New Testament books. Quality control would be gone out the window and we would be left 'whistling in the dark'. If God is not going to protect His text will not the purpose of inspiration be frustrated? 1 Chronicles 16:15 speaks of "the Word which He commanded, for a thousand generations"—there have been fewer than 300 since Adam.

## But, What About All the Variants?

It is a plain fact that the extant manuscripts contain a great many copying mistakes and even deliberate alterations. Since we cannot deny that God permitted this to happen, it remains to ask why and with what implications. First, the why.

Why would God permit mistakes and alterations in the copying process? I have no direct revelation to offer on the subject but I suppose the answer begins with God's purpose in creating the human race. It appears that He desired a type of being that could respond to Him in worship and love, a being that could choose (John 4:23-24). In Hebrews 11:6 we are taught that God demands faith and rewards those who **diligently** seek Him. It would seem that His purpose in creating man entails an element of test. The evidence may not be overwhelming, crushing, inescapable or there would be no adequate 'test'. Thus, God permitted textual variants to test our faith and determination, to test our attitude, to test our willingness to humbly and patiently look for answers (Proverbs 25:2 and Revelation 5:10).

Another aspect of the creation of beings with volition is that both God and man must live with the consequences of the exercise of that volition. If He exerts complete control, we become robots and the whole point of the experiment is lost. Alas, most of man's volition is expressed in rebellion against our Creator. A fair share of that rebellion has been directed against His Word—usually by rejecting it, but sometimes by trying to alter it.

Besides all that, our abilities and capacity to understand are limited. As it says in 2 Corinthians 4:7, we are mere *"earthen vessels"*, clay pots. Even if the Autographs had been engraved on gold tablets and miraculously preserved intact to this hour, who among us could offer a 'perfect' interpretation of that Text? (Anyone working from a translation is dealing with some imperfection before he even starts, because no translation can be perfect—the nature of language does not permit it.) Since our understanding is condemned to be imperfect in any case, is it really necessary to have a perfect Text? If not, is there some point at which the amount of imperfection ceases to be 'tolerable'? Which brings us to the implications. I will begin with some analogies.

Our everyday lives furnish several analogies which illumine this question. All our lives we use measuring devices—rulers, yardsticks, tapes—that vary slightly from each other. We buy many things according to measure without questioning the accuracy of the instrument, even though a precise comparison would reveal discrepancies between instruments. Why? Because the discrepancies are not big enough to concern us and because we know there is an absolute standard to refer to should the need arise. At the Bureau of Standards in Washington, D.C., in a hermetically sealed case, is the absolute, unvarying standard yardstick. How many Americans have ever seen that standard? Very few, comparatively. Yet we are born, live and die without seeing the standard and without feeling any inconvenience. We assume that our rulers are close enough for ordinary practical purposes, as indeed they are, and live happily with them. We know that we can go to Washington if a question arises that warrants the expense.

If someone asks a group of people for the time of day he may well get up to ten different answers, scattered along a ten-minute continuum. We daily live with one or two-minute discrepancies among the several time pieces we may consult and think nothing of it. Two different radio stations in a city often differ from each other by a minute or two, and so on. The system works well enough because there is a recognized standard in Greenwich, England. I have never been there and I suppose few Americans have, but we get along handily just the same. But if there were no standard we would soon be in trouble.

When a legislature draws up a law great care is taken with the precise wording, because once it is published it is law—it becomes a standard, binding upon the people under its jurisdiction. Great care is taken with the standard, but law enforcement officers are not expected to memorize it. All they need is a reasonably accurate understanding of the intent and provisions of the law. When an officer arrests an offender and cites the law he will probably only give the gist of it. No court will countenance a plea by the defendant that the arresting officer did not cite the law verbatim. (Similarly, I doubt that God will countenance an unbeliever's plea that he did not have access to the Law verbatim—it is enough to have the gist.) However, during a trial emphasis is often given to the precise 'letter' of the law and the whole disposition of the case may depend on the interpretation given to that 'letter'.

Alcohol (ethanol) may be found on the shelf at any drugstore, but seldom exceeding 92%; perhaps the pharmacist has a private supply of 96% for special purposes. For ordinary household use 92% is more than adequate—in a pinch a stout 60% rum will burn and may be used to disinfect. It may be that certain scientific experiments require 100% alcohol but it will be hard to come by and quite expensive. As with all manufactured goods, the higher the degree of precision or 'perfection' the more difficult and costly it is to attain. Different purposes require different degrees of precision (in any area), but for most people and most purposes most of the time the degree of precision does not have to be very high. In fact, in the majority of cases a superlative degree of precision would be wasted—the context simply does not allow for its full utilization or appreciation.

So, why has God allowed errors to get into the Text, or why does He permit faulty interpretation? In the first place the whole point of having a human race apparently involves giving us the ability and freedom to sin and take the consequences (both individually and corporately—the larger the group is that participates in a sin, the more serious and far-reaching are the consequences). But in the second place normal and daily use does not require a superlative degree of precision—in any event we have more of God's Truth than we can possibly appropriate. However, it is the availability of a recognized standard that enables us to tolerate minor imperfections, in a given area. We have the treasure in *"earthen vessels"*, but the *"treasure"* must exist!

## But, Are Not the Autographs Lost?

The question of a lost standard remains. Returning to the analogy of measuring devices, what would happen if someone stole the 'inerrant' yardstick from the Bureau of Standards? Well, there would be no inconvenience so long as we did not know about it—we would continue happily as we always have. But if the loss became known then confidence in the individual instruments would be undermined and our business dealings would become complicated by arguments about the standard of measurement (as I have observed in certain places). I believe we have seen this syndrome with reference to the Bible. Until the 19th century there was no question (to speak of) about the standard, and the Bible was accepted as authoritative even though in fact the text they were using was not identical to the Original. But during the past 200 years critics have convinced the majority (in Europe and North America) that the standard is gone, with the resulting spiritual and moral confusion we see on every side.

The problem is largely one of perception. Generations have lived and died happily using their imperfect rulers and yardsticks without suffering any damage or inconvenience—the discrepancies were not big enough to matter. (If someone had convinced them that they had an insuperable problem, however, they would have been damaged—gratuitously.) Similarly, our manuscripts and versions contain discrepancies, most of which are not serious enough to matter for ordinary purposes. However, if someone makes a 'court case' out of some issue then the existence and identity of the relevant standard become crucial.

I submit that the central 'issue' has to do with the authority of Scripture. When the Protestant Reformation appealed to the Scriptures (in the original languages) as the supreme authority, the Roman Catholic Church countered by pointing to the textual variation in the manuscripts and challenging the

Reformation leaders to produce the standard.[1] In the eighteenth and nineteenth centuries destructive critics went beyond the variants to challenge the date, authorship and composition of the individual books of the Bible. I consider that these challenges have been adequately handled by others and return to the problem of textual variation.

How does textual variation affect the authority of Scripture? It depends. Is that authority to be seen as absolute or relative? If we are prepared to settle for a relative authority, the 'Neo-orthodox' position, we can assimilate an admixture of error in the Text. But if we wish to claim absolute authority the standard must be perfect. Scripture derives its authority from divine inspiration, but if any part of the text is not inspired that part lacks authority. Specifically, the errors and alterations introduced by fallible men down through the centuries of copying lack authority. For this reason those who claim that the Bible is inerrant usually limit the claim to the Autographs. But since the Autographs are gone (they were probably worn out from use within the first one hundred years) what good does that do us? It depends.

The analogies already given show that we can coexist with minor discrepancies quite handily without feeling that we have been cheated or deceived. In fact, in most contexts to insist on absolute perfection would be deemed unreasonable, if not intolerable. We accept small discrepancies, but not **big** ones! If we feel that someone is trying to take advantage of us our reaction is prompt. Similarly, we must distinguish between honest copying errors, due to inattention, and deliberate alterations. Further, many alterations appear to be relatively 'harmless', while others are overtly damaging.

In Matthew 13:25 and 39 the Lord Jesus explains that Satan sows tares among wheat—this is true of the Church and it is true of the Biblical text; although the analogy is not perfect, in the latter case the "tares" may be likened to poison mixed with the Bread of Life. To give a few quick examples: the variants in Matthew 1:7 and 10 that introduce Asaph and Amos into Jesus' genealogy are poison; the variant in Matthew 1:18 that ascribes to Christ a "beginning" is poison; the variant in Mark 6:22 that turns Herodias into Herod's daughter is poison; the variant in Luke 3:33 that inserts the fictitious Admin and Arni into Jesus' genealogy is poison (these were probably the result of scribal carelessness, or ignorance, but for modern editors to intrude them into the printed text is irresponsible); the variant in Luke 23:45 that has the sun being eclipsed is poison; the variant in John 1:18 that reads "an only begotten god" is poison; the variant in 1 Corinthians 5:1 that denies the existence of incest among the Gentiles is poison; the omission of Mark 16:9-20 is poison; the use of brackets in printed Scripture (in whatever language) to insinuate to

---

[1] See Theodore P. Letis, "John Owens Versus Brian Walton", *The Majority Text: Essays and Reviews in the Continuing Debate* (Fort Wayne: The Institute for Reformation Biblical Studies, 1987), pp. 145-90. For more on this subject please see Appendix I.

the user that the enclosed material is spurious is poison. By 'poison' I mean violence done to the Biblical text that undermines its credibility.[1]

So where does that leave us? It leaves us with thousands of manuscript copies (of the NT writings) from which we may recover the precise wording of the Autographs, provided we evaluate the evidence on the basis of what the Bible says about itself, about God and His purposes, about man, and about Satan and his ways. To these must be added the declarations of the early Church Fathers and the facts of history that have come down to us. By careful attention to all relevant considerations we can weed out the errors and alterations and affirm with reasonable certainty what must have been the wording of the Autographs. Please see Chapter 7 for my answer.

Since God the Son on earth emphatically declared, *"till heaven and earth pass away not one jot or one tittle will by any means pass from the Law till all is fulfilled"* (Matthew 5:18), I conclude that He would never permit a true reading to disappear from the manuscript tradition. I am well aware that Jesus was presumably referring specifically to the Pentateuch. How then can I apply His statement to the NT? First, jots and tittles refer to **letters**, not concepts or ideas; in fact they are the smallest of letters. Our Lord's words constitute a rather radical declaration about the preservation through time of the precise form of the Sacred Text. The third chapter of 2 Corinthians makes clear that the *"new covenant"* (verse 6) is *"more glorious"* (verse 8) than the old, including the very Decalogue itself ("e*ngraved on stones,"* verse 7). Chapters 7 through 9 of Hebrews demonstrate the general superiority of the new covenant over the old and Jesus Himself both guarantees (7:22) and mediates (8:6) this "better" covenant. I conclude that God's protective interest in the New Testament must be at least as great as His protective interest in the Old. 1 Chronicles 16:15 declares that interest to extend to a thousand generations; in other words, to the end of the world (there have yet to be 300, since Adam).

To be faced with the task of recognizing the genuine reading among two or more variants is one thing; to affirm that something so crucial as the ending of a Gospel has disappeared without a trace is altogether different. If Mark 16:9-20 is not genuine then it would seem that Christ's statement in Matthew 5:18 is in error.

## The Matter of Canonicity

There is a further question—why do we claim that Mark is "Gospel" in the first place? Where did it get its canonicity? Or to put it another way, if God is going to inspire a text for the use of subsequent generations He has to make sure that people recognize it for what it is. If the nature of such a text is not perceived and it is relegated to oblivion, or treated with no more respect than any other bit of literature, then God's purpose is frustrated. So why do we say that Mark's Gospel is "Bible"? Because the Church, in her corporate capacity, has so declared, and she has done so down through the centuries, beginning

---

[1] I have a fuller treatment of the subject of variation in Appendix F.

in the second (at least). (We do not have hard evidence from the first century, but we do from the second and all subsequent centuries.) Of necessity God worked through the Church to achieve both canonicity (the public recognition of its quality) and preservation. (I would say that the superior quality of the inspired writings is intrinsic and can be perceived by a spiritual person in any age, but if the early Church had not recognized them they would not have been copied through the centuries and thus would not have come down to us.)

What has the Church, down through the centuries, said about Mark 16:9-20? With united voice she has declared its canonicity. If she was deceived on this point, how do we know she was not deceived about the rest of the book? However, satanic activity on the fringes produced variant readings that in some cases were quite damaging. The primary evidence is furnished by the continuous text Greek manuscripts.

## The External Evidence

The passage in question is contained in every extant Greek manuscript (about 1,700) except three: codices B (Vaticanus) and ℵ (Sinaiticus) and the twelfth century minuscule 304. It is also contained in all extant lectionaries (compendia of the established Scripture lessons linked to the ecclesiastical calendar). The importance of this lectionary evidence has been explained by J.W. Burgon: "That lessons from the New Testament were publicly read in the assemblies of the faithful according to a definite scheme, and on an established system, at least as early as the fourth century,—has been shown to be a plain historical fact."[1] And again:

> It is found that, from the very first, S. Mark xvi. 9-20 has been everywhere, and by all branches of the Church Catholic, claimed for **two** of the Church's greatest Festivals,—Easter and Ascension. A more weighty or a more significant circumstance can scarcely be imagined. To suppose that a portion of Scripture singled out for such extraordinary honour by the Church universal is a spurious addition to the Gospel, is purely irrational.[2]

Although after a time there came to be prescribed Scripture passages for every day of the year, the practice evidently began with the weekends, and most especially the most important ones. According to Baumstark's Law the lections associated with the great festivals seem to have been the earliest to have been adopted.[3] Since the idea was borrowed from the Jewish

---

[1] *The Last Twelve Verses according to S. Mark,* 1871, p. 207. Reprinted in 1959 by the Sovereign Grace Book Club, but the pagination given refers to the 1871 edition (to find the corresponding place in the 1959 edition add 78 to the page number).

[2] *Ibid.*, p. 210.

[3] W.R. Farmer, *The Last Twelve Verses of Mark* (Cambridge University Press, 1974), p. 35. On pp. 34 and 35 he gives a good summary of the lectionary evidence.

synagogue the practice may well have been generalized during the second century, if not the first.

Before the Church started producing lectionaries as such (as well as after), regular manuscripts were adapted by putting symbols in the margins (or in the text) to indicate the beginning and ending of lections. These included the word τελος "end", either in full or abbreviated. Statements of evidence for omitting verses 9-20 usually mention a number of MSS that have such symbols at the end of verse 8 (and thus at the beginning of verse 9), claiming that they were put there to indicate doubt about the genuineness of the following verses. It happens that not only is Mark 16:9-20 itself one of the most prominent of all lections in the liturgical calendar, but a separate lection ends precisely with verse 8.

Consider what Bruce Metzger writes concerning MS 2386:

> The latter, however, is only an apparent witness for the omission, for although the last page of Mark closes with εφοβουντο γαρ, the next leaf of the manuscript is missing, and following 16:8 is the sign indicating the close of an ecclesiastical lection…a clear implication that the manuscript originally continued with additional material from Mark.[1]

Notice his "clear implication". Is it not obvious? One cannot read beyond the end of a book so there is no point in putting a lection sign there. Which makes one wonder about the intentions of the editors of UBS[3]. In their apparatus, as evidence for the omission of verses 9-20, they include *"(Lect? Lection ends with verse 8)"*—this presumably refers to lection signs in the margins since it cannot mean that the lectionaries do not have verses 9-20. But lection signs in the margin are evidence for, not against! Notice that in discussing the evidence for variant sets within verses 9-20 UBS[3] invariably cites *Byz Lect*, which means that they recognize that the lectionaries contain the passage. In fact, from the circumstance that they also list '/185m' it appears that lectionary 185 is the only one that does not have the verses in the Synaxarion (just in the Menologion).

The Syriac, Latin, Coptic and Gothic versions all massively support the passage. Only the Armenian and Georgian versions (both fifth century) omit it. To be more precise, every Syriac MS (about 1,000?) except one (the Sinaitic, usually dated around 400) contains the passage. Although the Sinaitic is the oldest extant Syriac MS, apparently, it is not representative of the Syriac tradition. B.F. Westcott himself, writing in 1864, assigned the Peshitta to the early second century, in accord with the general opinion of the Scholarly world of the time.[2] The demands of the W-H theory subsequently led them to assign the Peshitta to the fifth century, but Vööbus demonstrates that the Peshitta

---

[1] Metzger, p. 122, fn. 1.

[2] *The Bible in the Church* (London: MacMillan) p. 132 (reprintings in the 1890s still contain the statement).

goes back to at least the mid-fourth century and that it was not the result of an authoritative revision.[1] The Sinaitic is a palimpsest; it was scraped off to make way for some devotional material, which is an eloquent commentary upon the contemporary evaluation of its quality!

Every Latin MS (8,000?) except one (Bobiensis, usually dated about 400) contains the passage. But Bobiensis (k) also seems to be the only witness of any kind to offer us the so-called 'shorter ending' by itself—every other witness that contains the 'shorter ending' also contains the 'longer ending', thereby displaying a conflation (an incredibly stupid one!). Now then, so far as I know everyone recognizes the 'shorter ending' to be an aberration, which means that Bobiensis is aberrant at this point and does not represent the Latin tradition. If the Latin tradition dates to the second century here we have second century support for the 'longer ending'. It appears that the only Coptic witness that omits the passage is one Sahidic MS, although there are a few that exhibit the conflation already mentioned (they are thereby convicted as being aberrant).

The Diatessaron (according to the Arabic, Italian and Old Dutch traditions) and Irenaeus clearly attest the last twelve verses in the second century! As does Hippolytus a few years later. Then come Vincentius, the Gospel of Nicodemus and the Apostolic Constitutions in the third century; Eusebius, Aphraates, Ambrose and Chrysostom in the fourth; followed by Jerome, Augustine, Cyril of Alexandria, Victor of Antioch, etc.

Clement of Alexandria and Origen are usually cited as being against these verses, but it is an argument from silence. Clement's surviving works seem not to refer to the last chapter of Mark, but neither do they refer to the last chapter of Matthew. So?

The main patristic source used to argue against Mark 16:9-20 is Eusebius. It appears that he wrote a defense against four alleged discrepancies between resurrection accounts of the Gospels put forward by a certain "Marinus" (our knowledge is based on a tenth century abridgement of what he presumably wrote, an abridgement that lacks internal consistency). The first alleged discrepancy is between Matthew 28:1 and Mark 16:9. On the face of it "Marinus" is assuming that verse 9 is genuine "Gospel" or there would be no problem, so we may conclude that he understood that to be the position of the Church. That Eusebius takes the time to answer as he does points in the same direction. Further, in answering the second alleged discrepancy Eusebius simply assumes the genuineness of the Marcan account and argues that Matthew's turn of phrase has been misunderstood. However, in answering the first allegation (according to the abridgement) he offers two options: "One might say that the passage is not contained in all the copies of Mark's Gospel...another says that both accounts (Matthew and Mark) are genuine and must be properly understood." With the first option he employs the

---

[1] *Early Versions of the New Testament* (Stockholm: Estonian Theological Society in Exile, 1954), pp. 100-102.

optative mood, appropriate to the genre of hypothetical rhetoric (which means that nothing said by the hypothetical speaker is being vouched for by Eusebius), while with the second he switches to the indicative mood, presumably an indication of what he himself considered to be the correct position—so much so that when he moves on to the second "discrepancy" he does not offer the option of rejecting the passage.

However, the "canons" or "sections" of Eusebius (but not the so-called "sections of Ammonius") may not have included verses 9-20. In some Greek MSS the sectional number "233" is placed in the margin beside verse 8 and is the last such number (in Mark)—which means that section 233 started at verse 8, but since many "sections" contained more than one verse we do not know the extent of this one. But, there is more to the story. Burgon checked out 151 Greek MSS that have "Eusebian sections" marked in the margin and offers the following tabulation of results:

in   3 MSS the last section number is 232, set against v. 6,
in 34 MSS the last section number is 233, set against v. 8,
in 41 MSS the last section number is 234, set against v. 9 (?),
in   4 MSS the last section number is 235, set against v. 10 (?),
in   7 MSS the last section number is 236, set against v. 12 (?),
in 12 MSS the last section number is 237, set against v. 14 (?),
in   3 MSS the last section number is 238, set against v. 15,
in   1 MS   the last section number is 239, set against v. 17,
in 10 MSS the last section number is 240, set against v. 19,
in 36 MSS the last section number is 241, set against v. 20.

Added to this, the following information may be of interest:

the oldest MS that stops with 232 is A of the 5th century,
the oldest MS that stops with 233 is L of the 8th century,
the oldest MS that stops with 234 is Δ of the 9th century,
the oldest MS that stops with 237 is Λ of the 9th century,
the oldest MS that stops with 239 is G of the 9th century,
the oldest MS that stops with 240 is H of the 9th century,
the oldest MS that stops with 241 is C of the 5th century.[1]

For sections 235, 236 and 238, the earliest MS is 10th century or later. So, in three-fourths of these MSS the section numbers overtly go beyond verse 8, and the two oldest ones (A and C) do not aid the case for omission.

Jerome is cited as being against the passage because he put Marinus' questions in a certain "Hebidia's" mouth and used an abridgement of Eusebius' answers in reply. However, Jerome's own evaluation is clear from the fact that he included Mark 16:9-20 in his Latin Vulgate; he also quotes verses 9 and 14 in his writings. Hesychius of Jerusalem (not Severus of Antioch, nor Gregory of Nyssa) reproduces Eusebius in his own words in a treatise about the familiar "problems". However, since he quotes Mark 16:19

---

[1] Burgon, p. 313; for the general discussion see pp. 127-134 and 297-314.

and expressly states that St. Mark wrote the words, his own position is clear. Victor of Antioch repeats Eusebius yet again, and acknowledges that "very many" copies of Mark lack verses 9-20 (it is not clear whether he had verified this to be true or was just quoting Eusebius). Then he affirms that he himself has verified that "very many" contain them, and appeals to "accurate copies" and most especially to "the Palestinian exemplar of Mark which exhibits the Gospel verity" in support of his own contention that the passage is genuine. He even blames the omission on individuals who thought the verses to be spurious.[1]

# Parenthesis—down with forgery!

((Every now and again I am handed a question that starts out by irritating me, but after I calm down I perceive that God is nudging me to clarify a point that needs it. This happened recently with the 'jewel' attributed to Jerome that in his day 'most' or 'almost all' of the Greek manuscripts did not have the last twelve verses of Mark. Since of the 1700 or so Greek MSS known to us that contain the last chapter of Mark only three don't have them (one of them being a falsification at this point), how could a vast majority in the $5^{th}$ century be reduced to a small fraction of one percent later on? In terms of the science of statistical probability, such an inversion is simply impossible. Only a world-wide campaign that was virtually 100% successful could bring about such a switch, and there is not a shred of evidence for such a campaign. Recall that Diocletian's campaign to destroy NT MSS (applied unevenly in different areas) was past history by a century (not to mention Constantine's 'conversion' and the consequences thereof). Kenneth Scott Latourette (*A History of Christianity* [New York: Harper,1953], p. 231) describes Eusebius Hieronimus Sophronius (alias Jerome) as "a gifted and diligent scholar, enormously erudite, a master of languages, a lover of books, wielding a facile, vigorous, and often vitriolic pen" who "was an eloquent advocate of the monastic life". He doubtless had his defects [don't we all], but he was not ridiculously stupid, as he would have had to be to make the statement attributed to him. Our knowledge of the 'jewel' comes from the tenth century [the interval of five centuries does not inspire confidence]; it is almost certainly a forgery (someone 'borrowing' a famous name to give credence to some statement). Since 'sacred cows' don't like to die, a review of some relevant history is in order.

## K. Aland on Egypt

Even that great champion of an Egyptian text, Kurt Aland, recognized that during the early centuries, including the $4^{th}$, Asia Minor (especially the Aegean area) was "the heartland of the Church". (It also became the heartland of the Byzantine Empire and the Orthodox Churches.) The demand for copies of the NT would have a direct bearing on the supply, and on the areas where copies would be concentrated. But on the subject of Egypt, Aland had this to say:

---

[1] For detailed documentation and an exhaustive discussion, see Burgon, pp. 19-31, 38-69, 265-90.

Our knowledge of the church in Egypt begins at the close of the 2$^{nd}$ century with bishop Demetrius who reorganized the dominantly Gnostic Egyptian church by founding new communities, consecrating bishops, and above all by establishing relationships with the other provinces of the church fellowship. Every church needed manuscripts of the New Testament—how was Demetrius to provide them? Even if there were a scriptorium in his own see, he would have to procure "orthodox" exemplars for the scribes. The copies existing in the Gnostic communities could not be used, because they were under suspicion of being corrupt. There is no way of knowing where the bishop turned for scribal exemplars, or for the large number of papyrus manuscripts he could give directly to his communities.[1]

But just a minute, please. In the year of our Lord 200, who in Egypt was still speaking Greek? (For that matter, who among the ordinary people had ever spoken Greek there?) What Greek speaking communities could the worthy Demetrius have been serving? Would the scholars linked to the library in Alexandria be likely to bow to Demetrius? So far as we know, no apostle ever ministered in Egypt, and no Autograph of a New Testament book was held there. The Gnostic dominance probably should not surprise us. But the situation in Alexandria is relevant to the question in hand because of Clement, and especially Origen, who was mentor to Pamphilus, who was mentor to Eusebius of Caesarea.

## Eusebius (Caesarea)

One suspects that the forger who 'borrowed' Jerome actually started out by 'borrowing' Eusebius (Caesarea). He has Eusebius answering a certain 'Marinus' with, "One might say that the passage is not contained in all the copies of Mark's Gospel..." The 'not all' became 'some' or even 'many', here and there. If Eusebius actually wrote such a thing, of which we aren't sure [the interval of six centuries does not inspire confidence here either], how was he qualified to do so? After the Roman destruction in 70 AD, Palestine became a backwater in the flow of the Christian river. The transmission of the true NT Text owes nothing to Caesarea. By the 4$^{th}$ century there would have been thousands, literally, of NT MSS in use around the world, of which Eusebius (d. 339, b. about 265) probably would not have seen more than a dozen (most from Alexandria, not Asia Minor). If Codex B was produced in Alexandria in time for Eusebius to see it, it would indeed permit him to say 'not all' copies; but why would he do so? And why should we pay any attention to him if he did? Here again, who in Palestine was still speaking Greek in the 4$^{th}$ century? What use would Eusebius have for Greek manuscripts? One other point: had Eusebius written such a thing, it would have been after Diocletian's campaign, presumably, but it would still be fresh in his memory and he should have

---

[1] "The Text of the Church?" Kurt Aland, *Trinity Journal*, Vol. 8, N° 2, Fall, 1987, p. 138 [actually sent out in the Spring, 1989].

mentioned it. Emboldened by success, as I suppose, the forger decided to 'up the ante' attributing the same exchange to Jerome, answering a certain 'Hebidia', except that now it is 'most' or 'almost all'.

## Jerome (Bethlehem)

Jerome was born around 342 and died in 420 (or so). During 382-384 he was secretary to Pope Damasus, in Rome, and began work on the Latin Vulgate. Not long after the death of Damasus (384) he moved to Bethlehem, followed a few months later by the wealthy Paula, who helped him build a monastery, and so on. Jerome spent the last 30+ years of his life in Bethlehem, even more of a 'backwater' than Caesarea, and a century after Eusebius. All the negative observations made about Caesarea apply here with added force. Further, who in the Pope's entourage in Rome was speaking Greek in 380 AD? From Rome Jerome moved to Bethlehem. How many actual Greek MSS of the NT would Jerome have seen? Certainly fewer than 1% of the total in use (at that time there would be few Greek MSS in Italy and Palestine—who would use them?). In lists of early Church 'fathers' Jerome is usually listed with those who wrote in Latin, not Greek. The statement attributed to him is patently false, scientifically impossible; and he would have been ridiculously unqualified to make it. Not being stupid or dishonest, he didn't!

## Addendum

After I circulated the above, my Canadian friend, Charles Holm, called my attention to historical research done by Timothy David Barnes that is relevant to the credibility of Jerome (*Tertullian: A Historical and Literary Study*, Oxford: Clarendon Press, 1971). In an appendix dealing specifically with Jerome, there is a section called "Jerome and Eusebius" wherein Barnes offers the following observations (pages 236-238).

> First, Jerome never questions the reliability of Eusebius. Thus he accepts Eusebius' interpretation of what a writer says without asking whether it is correct.

> Secondly, Jerome far surpasses Eusebius in credulity. What was in Eusebius presented as surmise or mere rumour is for Jerome established and indubitable fact.

> Thirdly, Jerome mistranslates and misunderstands.

> Fourthly, Jerome dishonestly conceals both his ignorance and his debt to Eusebius.

Well, well, well, it appears that one should read Jerome with a full salt shaker to hand. Perhaps my closing sentence above should have been: Not being stupid, he didn't! However, I continue to insist that Jerome could not have been so grossly stupid and/or dishonest as to make the ridiculous statement attributed to him. Down with **forgery!**))

Unfortunately, commentaries can still be found that reproduce certain misstatements of yesteryear about "scholia" and "catenae". The "catenae" may not be adduced for the omission, as demonstrated by Burgon (pp. 135-157). As for the "scholia" (critical notes), the situation seems to be something like this: at least 22 MSS simply repeat Victor of Antioch's statement, which includes the affirmation that he himself had verified that "very many" copies, including "accurate" ones and most especially the "true Palestinian exemplar", contained verses 9-20; several have footnotes defending the verses on the basis of "ancient copies at Jerusalem" (attention is directed to the footnote by a "+" or "*" in the text which is repeated before the footnote—much as we do today); two MSS say the passage is missing in "some" copies but present in "many"; four MSS say it is missing in "some" copies while present in "others"; three say it is missing in "many" and present in "many".[1] Now the earliest of these MSS is from the 10th century (most are later), so the copyists were repeating the "scholia" blindly, with no way of knowing if they were true or not. The fact remains that of the extant MSS only three lack the passage.

Codices L, Ψ, 099, 0112 and 579 are sometimes claimed as being against the genuineness of verses 9-20 because they also contain the so-called 'shorter ending'. Metzger's comment (p. 126) is misleading—these five MSS did not "replace" one ending with another, they conflated both. A conflation condemns the MSS that contain it, at that point, but says nothing about the relative merits of the component parts.

We must return to codices B and ℵ, both of the 4th century and both from Egypt (presumably, see Farmer, p. 37), being generally regarded as the two most important MSS of the New Testament (frequently referred to as the "oldest and best"). Their agreement in omitting verses 9-20 has been an important factor in the thinking of those who reject the passage (since they generally regard the "Alexandrian text-type" as superior to all others). However, the evidence is not quite straightforward. Codex B is written in three columns and upon completing a book it normally begins the next book at the top of the next column. But between Mark and Luke there is a completely vacant column, the only such column in the codex. Considering that parchment was expensive (and B is on very fine vellum), the "wasting" of such a space would be quite unusual. Why did the copyist do it?

As for Codex ℵ, the folded sheet containing the end of Mark and beginning of Luke is, quite frankly, a forgery. Tischendorf, who discovered the codex, warned that those four pages appeared to be written by a different hand and with different ink than the rest of the manuscript. However that may be, a careful scrutiny reveals the following: the end of Mark and beginning of Luke occur on page 3 (of the four); pages 1 and 4 contain an average of 17 lines of printed Greek text per column (there are four columns per page), just like the rest of the codex; page 2 contains an average of 15.5 lines of printed text per column (four columns); the first column of page 3 contains only **twelve** lines of

---

[1] Burgon, pp. 116-125, 290-292.

printed text and in this way verse 8 occupies the top of the second column, the rest of which is blank (except for some designs); Luke begins at the top of column 3, which contains 16 lines of printed text while column 4 is back up to 17 lines. On page 2 the forger began to spread the letters, displacing six lines of printed text; in the first column of page 3 he got desperate and displaced **five** lines of printed text, just in one column! In this way he managed to get two lines of verse 8 over onto the second column, avoiding the telltale vacant column (as in B). That second column would accommodate 15 more lines of printed text, which with the other 11 make 26. Verses 9-20 occupy 23.5 such lines, so there is plenty of room for them. It really does seem that there has been foul play, and there would have been no need for it unless the first hand did in fact display the disputed verses. In any event, ℵ as it stands is a forgery and therefore may not legitimately be alleged as evidence against them.

To sum up: every extant Greek MS (about 1,700) except two (B and 304—ℵ is not 'extant' because it is a forgery at this point) contains verses 9-20. Every extant Greek lectionary (about 2,000?) contains them (one of them, 185, doing so only in the Menologion). Every extant Syriac MS (about 1,000?) except one (Sinaitic) contains them. Every extant Latin MS (8,000?) except one (k) contains them. Every extant Coptic MS except one contains them. We have hard evidence for the 'inclusion' from the 2nd century (Irenaeus, Diatessaron?). We have no such hard evidence for the 'exclusion'.

It would appear that sometime during the 3rd century MSS lacking the passage began to be produced in Egypt, probably in Alexandria, of which two (or one) from the fourth century have survived to our day. Although the idea gained some currency in Egypt, it did not take over even there since most Alexandrian witnesses, including the Coptic version, contain the verses. The translators of the Armenian version had studied in Alexandria, and the Georgian version was based on the Armenian, which explains how the idea escaped from Egypt. The rest of the Christian world seems not to have picked up this aberration. As stated at the outset, with united voice, down through the centuries, in all parts of the world (including Egypt), the Church universal has affirmed and insisted that Mark's Gospel goes from 1:1 to 16:20. Since that is so, how can someone who denies the authenticity of Mark 16:9-20 still affirm the Divine Inspiration of Mark 1:1-16:8? Is he not being inconsistent?

# The Internal 'Evidence'?

It should not be necessary to prolong this exercise, but something probably ought to be said about the "internal evidence" that some critics evidently feel to be fatal to the passage. We are told that Mark "never" uses certain words or phrases, which nonetheless occur there; that others which he "always" uses are missing; that the style is "foreign" to Mark; that there are insuperable problems with the discourse structure and the very content; in short, that it is "impossible" that the same person could have penned 1:1-16:8 and 16:9-20. Alas, what to do?

Most of the 'arguments' of this sort that have been advanced reveal a disappointing degree of superficiality in research and ignorance of language.

Such supposed arguments were thoroughly refuted over 100 years ago by J.A. Broadus (*The Baptist Quarterly*, July, 1869, pp. 355-62) and Burgon (pp. 136-90). A more recent (1975) treatment is offered by Farmer (pp. 79-103). I will take up one argument that might seem impressive to the uninitiated reader.

It has been alleged as a sinister circumstance that Jesus is not mentioned by name in verse 9 (or in the following verses).[1] The rules of discourse structure have been violated, so they say. Really? Let's consider Mark's practice elsewhere. Between Mark 9:27 and 39 Jesus is not mentioned by name, although there are two paragraph breaks and one section break in between, plus two changes in location. Jesus is next named in 10:5, five verses after a section break and another change of location. Between Mark 3:7 and 5:6 (75 verses) Jesus is not named even though there are numerous participants and several radical changes in location, scene and content. In each case it is only when another man is introduced in the narrative, creating a potential for ambiguity, that Jesus is again named since a mere pronoun would be ambiguous in reference. In Mark 16 there is only one dead person in focus, precisely the participant who has dominated the whole book, so verse 9 could only refer to Him—there is no ambiguity so a proper name is not necessary. Throughout verses 9-20 no other singular masculine participant is introduced so there is no need to identify Jesus by name. By way of contrast, Mary Magdalene had to be fully identified, because not only is there more than one woman in the account, there is more than one Mary! (The background information, "out of whom He had cast seven demons", is entirely appropriate here, and only here, because this is the first time she is brought into focus—in the prior references she was just part of the group.)

There is one aspect of this situation which has not received sufficient attention that I am aware of. The more strident and caustic a critic becomes in proclaiming the "impossibility" of accepting Mark 16:9-20 as genuine (because of style, vocabulary and discourse features), the more he insults the ancients and undercuts his own position. After all, Irenaeus was a native speaker of Koine Greek (presumably)—why didn't he notice the "impossibility"? How come the native speakers of Koine Greek who lived in Greece and Asia Minor and copied Mark down through the years didn't recognize the "obvious stupidity", the "odious fabrication"? How come? How is it that modern critics who deal with Koine Greek as a dead language, and at a distance of 1800 years, are more competent to judge something like this than the native speakers who were on the scene? Irenaeus knew Polycarp personally, who knew the Apostle John personally, who knew Mark personally. Irenaeus declares that Mark wrote 16:19. Who among us is qualified to say that he was deceived?

It would seem to be obvious that the more preposterous the pericope is affirmed to be, the more difficult it becomes to explain how it imposed itself on the Church universal, beginning in the second century (at least). In fact, if the

---

[1] The true Text has "Jesus" at the beginning of verse 9, as well as at the end of verse 1.

passage contains difficulties this would easily account for its omission in certain quarters. The perceived difficulties would be a more than sufficient stimulus to activate editors and copyists trained in the Alexandrian school of textual criticism. Indeed, in our own day there are not a few who find the content of Mark 16:9-20 to be unpalatable and greet the claim that the passage is spurious with relief.

Hopefully all concerned will agree that the identity of the text of Scripture is to be established on the basis of the evidence, not personal prejudice. I submit that the evidence in this case is perfectly clear and that the overwhelming testimony of the Church down through the centuries should be loyally accepted.

I see a corollary here: not only is Mark 16:9-20 vindicated, but codices B and ℵ stand convicted of containing 'poison'. They also contain the poison (mentioned above) in Matthew 1:7, 1:10 and 1:18, Mark 6:22, Luke 3:33 and 23:45, John 1:18 and 1 Corinthians 5:1. Does this not diminish their credibility as witnesses?

I confess that I am puzzled at the dedication and industry of the opponents of these verses. Why do they go to such lengths and expend so much energy to discredit them? Another curious feature of their work is the frequent misrepresentation of the evidence. For instance, in his advice to translators about how to proceed at the end of verse 8, A. Pope suggests putting the following:

"[Some manuscripts end at this point]
[In some manuscripts the following words are found]
SHORTER ENDING
[In some manuscripts the following words are found after verse 8]
LONGER ENDING"[1]

What interests me here is the lack of semantic precision in the use of the word "some". The first time it means "three". The second time it means "six". The third time it means "about 1,700"! Will the unsuspecting reader of Pope's article not be misled? And if anyone follows Pope's advice will not his readers also be misled?

I wonder sometimes if people really believe what the glorified Jesus said in Revelation 22:19.

---

[1] *Selected Technical Articles Related to Translation*, Oct., 1984, p. 22. Pope should also have mentioned that in the six MSS that have the 'shorter ending' the 'longer ending' is also found (so they are convicted of having an obvious conflation, and therefore of being corrupt).

# APPENDIX F
## What Difference Does it Make?

It has been commonly argued, for at least 200 years,[1] that no matter what Greek text one may use no doctrine will be affected. In my own experience, for over fifty years, when I have raised the question of what is the correct Greek text of the New Testament, regardless of the audience, the usual response has been: "What difference does it make?" The purpose of this article is to answer that question, at least in part.

The eclectic Greek text presently in vogue, N-A[26]/UBS[3] [hereafter NU] represents the type of text upon which most modern versions are based.[2] The KJV and NKJV follow a rather different type of text, a close cousin of the Majority Text.[3] The discrepancy between NU and the Majority Text is around 8% (involving 8% of the words). In a Greek text with 600 pages that represents 48 solid pages' worth of discrepancies! About a fifth of that reflects omissions in the eclectic text, so it is some ten pages shorter than the Majority Text. Even if we grant, for the sake of the argument, that up to half of the differences between the Majority and eclectic texts could be termed 'inconsequential', that leaves some 25 pages' worth of differences that are significant (in varying degrees). In spite of these differences it is usually assumed that no cardinal Christian doctrine is at risk (though some, such as eternal judgment, the ascension and the deity of Jesus, are weakened). **However**, the most basic one of all, the divine inspiration of the text, is indeed under attack.

The eclectic text incorporates errors of fact and contradictions, such that any claim that the New Testament is divinely inspired becomes relative, and the doctrine of inerrancy becomes virtually untenable. If the authority of the New Testament is undermined, all its teachings are likewise affected. For well over

---

[1] John Bengel, a textual critic who died in 1752, has been credited with being the first one to advance this argument.

[2] *Novum Testamentum Graece*, Stuttgart: Deutsche Bibelstiftung, 26th ed., 1979. *The Greek New Testament*, New York: United Bible Societies, 3rd ed., 1975. The text of both these editions is virtually identical, having been elaborated by the same five editors: Kurt Aland, Matthew Black, Carlo Martini, Bruce Metzger and Allen Wikgren. Most modern versions were actually based on the 'old' Nestle text, which differs from the 26th edition in over 700 places. UBS[4] and N-A[27] do not offer changes in the text, just in the apparatus—it follows that the text was determined by the earlier set of five editors, not the present five (Matthew Black and Allen Wikgren were replaced by Barbara Aland [Kurt's wife, now widow] and Johannes Karavidopoulos).

[3] *The Greek New Testament According to the Majority Text*, Nashville: Thomas Nelson Publishers, 2nd ed., 1985. This text was edited by Zane C. Hodges and Arthur L. Farstad. Very similar to this is *The New Testament in the Original Greek: Byzantine Textform 2005*, Southborough, MA: Chilton Book Publishing, 2005. This text was edited by Maurice A Robinson and William G. Pierpont. These differ somewhat from the *Textus Receptus* upon which the KJV and NKJV are based.

a century the credibility of the New Testament text has been eroded, and this credibility crisis has been forced upon the attention of the laity by the modern versions that enclose parts of the text in brackets and have numerous footnotes of a sort that raise doubts about the integrity of the Text.

The consequences of all this are serious and far-reaching for the future of the Church. It seems unreasonable that individuals and organizations that profess to champion a high view of Scripture, that defend verbal plenary inspiration and the inerrancy of the Autographs, should embrace a Greek text that effectively undermines their belief.[1] Since their sincerity is evident, one must conclude that they are uninformed, or have not really looked at the evidence and thought through the implications. So I will now set out some of that evidence and discuss the implications. I wish to emphasize that I am not impugning the personal sincerity or orthodoxy of those who use the eclectic text; I am challenging the presuppositions that lie behind it and calling attention to the 'proof of the pudding'.

In the examples that follow, the reading of the Majority Text is always given first and that of NU second, followed by any others. (Where NU uses brackets, or some modern version follows Nestle[25], that will be clearly explained.) Immediately under each variant is a literal equivalent in English. To each variant is attached a statement of manuscript support taken from my edition of the Greek Text of the New Testament.[2] The set of variants with their respective supporting evidence is followed by a discussion of the implications. First I will present errors of fact and contradictions, then serious anomalies and aberrations.

---

[1] For years it has been commonly stated that no two known Greek manuscripts of the NT are in perfect agreement (however, for Galatians, Ephesians, Philippians, Colossians, 1 & 2 Thessalonians, 1 & 2 Timothy, Titus, Philemon, James, 1 & 2 Peter, 1 & 2 & 3 John and Jude I have in my possession copies of at least two identical manuscripts—not the same two for each book). In consequence, claims of Biblical inerrancy are usually limited to the Autographs (the very original documents actually penned by the human authors), or to the precise wording contained in them. Since no Autograph of the NT exists today (they were probably worn out within a few years through heavy use) we must appeal to the existing copies in any effort to identify the original wording.

The text-critical theory underlying NU presupposes that the original wording was 'lost' during the early centuries and that objective certainty as to the original wording is now an impossibility. A central part of the current debate is the argument that the text in use **today** is not inerrant—this is a recurring theme in *The Proceedings of the Conference on Biblical Inerrancy 1987* (Nashville: Broadman Press, 1987), for example.

This book offers objective evidence in support of the contention that the original wording was **not** 'lost' during the early centuries. I further argue that it is indeed possible to identify with reasonable certainty the original wording, based on objective criteria—today.

[2] This Greek New Testament may be downloaded free from www.walkinhiscommandments.com; the last footnote in Matthew, for example, explains the apparatus and the symbols used.

# Errors of Fact and Contradictions

**Luke 4:44** της Γαλιλαιας—**f**³⁵ A,D (94.7%) CP,HF,RP,TR,OC
[in the synagogues] of Galilee

της Ιουδαιας—P⁷⁵אB,C,Q (4.1%) NU
[in the synagogues] of Judea

των Ιουδαιων—W (0.2%)
αυτων—(0.5%)

Problem: Jesus was in Galilee (and continued there), not in Judea, as the context makes clear.

Discussion: In the parallel passage, Mark 1:35-39, all texts agree that Jesus was in Galilee. Thus NU contradicts itself by reading Judea in Luke 4:44. Bruce Metzger makes clear that the NU editors did this on purpose when he explains that their reading "is obviously the more difficult, and copyists have corrected it...in accord with the parallels in Mt 4.23 and Mk 1.39."[1] Thus the NU editors introduce a contradiction into their text which is also an error of fact. This error in the eclectic text is reproduced by LB, NIV, NASB, NEB, RSV, etc. NRSV adds insult to injury: "So he continued proclaiming the message in the synagogues of Judea."

**Luke 23:45** εσκοτισθη—**f**³⁵ A,D,Q,W (96.8%) CP,HF,RP,TR
[the sun] was darkened

εκλιπουτος—P⁷⁵אC (0.4%) NU
[the sun] being eclipsed

εκλειπουτος—B (0.4%) OC
εσκοτισθευτος—(0.7%)
conflations—(1.2%)

Problem: An eclipse of the sun is impossible during a full moon. Jesus was crucified during the Passover, and the Passover is always at full moon (which is why the date for Easter moves around). NU introduces a scientific error.

Discussion: The Greek verb εκλειπω is quite common and has the basic meaning 'to fail' or 'to end', but when used of the sun or the moon it refers to an eclipse ('eclipse' comes from that Greek root). Indeed, such versions as Moffatt, Twentieth Century, Authentic, Phillips, NEB, New Berkeley, NAB and Jerusalem overtly state that the sun was eclipsed. While versions such as

---

[1] *A Textual Commentary on the Greek New Testament*, New York: United Bible Societies, 1971, pp. 137-38.

NASB, TEV and NIV avoid the word 'eclipse', the normal meaning of the eclectic text that they follow is precisely "the sun being eclipsed."[1]

**Mark 6:22** αυτης της Ηρωδιαδος—**f**<sup>35</sup> A,C,N (96.5%) HF,RP,CP,TR,OC
[the daughter] herself of Herodias

αυτου --- Ηρωδιαδος—ℵB,D (0.4%) NU
his [daughter] Herodias

--- της Ηρωδιαδος—(1.3%)
αυτης --- Ηρωδιαδος—W (0.7%)
αυτου της Ηρωδιαδος—(0.9%)

Problem: NU in Mark 6:22 contradicts NU in Matthew 14:6.

Discussion: Matthew 14:6 states that the girl was the daughter of Herodias (Herodias had been the wife of Philip, King Herod's brother, but was now living with Herod). Here NU makes the girl out to be Herod's own daughter, and calls **her** "Herodias". Metzger defends the choice of the NU Committee with these words: "It is very difficult to decide which reading is the least unsatisfactory" (p. 89)! (Do the NU editors consider that the original reading is lost? If not it must be 'unsatisfactory', but are those editors really competent to make such a judgment? And just what might be so 'unsatisfactory' about the reading of over 98% of the MSS? I suppose because it creates no problem.) The modern versions that usually identify with NU part company with them here, except for NRSV that reads, "his daughter Herodias".

**1 Corinthians 5:1** ονομαζεται—**f**<sup>35</sup> (96.8%) HF,RP,OC,TR,CP
is named

--- —P<sup>46</sup> ℵA,B,C (3.2%) NU

Problem: It was reported that a man had his father's wife, a type of fornication such that not even the Gentiles talked about it. However, the NU text affirms that this type of incest does not even exist among the Gentiles, a plain falsehood. Every conceivable type of sexual perversion has existed throughout human history.

Discussion: Strangely, such evangelical versions as NIV, NASB, Berkeley and LB propagate this error. I find it interesting that versions such as TEV, NEB and Jerusalem, while following the same text, avoid a categorical statement.[2]

---

[1] Arndt and Gingrich (*A Greek-English Lexicon of the New Testament and Other Early Christian Literature*. Chicago: University of Chicago Press, 1957, p. 242), referring to this passage, state: "Of the sun **grow dark**, perh. **be eclipsed**". One suspects that this statement was designed specifically to defend the reading of the eclectic text. We are not surprised to find Metzger dismissing the reading of over 97% of the MSS as "the easier reading" (p. 182).

[2] The UBS apparatus gives no inkling to the user that there is serious variation at this point (but N-A does); in consequence Metzger doesn't mention it either. He would

**Luke 3:33** του Αμιναδαβ,

|   |   | του Αραμ—**f**[35] A(D) [95%] |
|---|---|---|
|   |   | CP,HF,RP,TR, OC |

of Aminadab    of Aram

| του Αμιναδαβ, | του Αδμιν, | του Αρνι—none!! NU |
|---|---|---|
| of Aminadab | of Admin | of Arni |

|   | του Αδμειν, | του Αρνει—B |
|---|---|---|
| του Αδαμ, |   | του Αρνι?—syr[s] |
| του Αδαμ, | του Αδμιν, | του Αρνει—ℵ |
| του Αδαμ, | του Αδμειν, | του Αρνει—cop[sa] |
| του Αδμειν, | του Αδμιν, | του Αρνι—cop[bo] |
| του Αμιναδαβ, | του Αδμιν, | του Αρνει—ℵ[x] |
| του Αμιναδαβ, | του αδμιν, | του Αρηι—φ[13] |
| του Αμιναδαβ, | του Αδμη, | του Αρνι—Ξ |
| του Αμιναδαβ, | του Αδμειν, | του Αρνι—Λ |
| του Αμιναδαβ, | του Αραμ, | του Αρνι—N |

Problem: The fictitious Admin and Arni are intruded into Christ's genealogy.

Discussion: UBS has misrepresented the evidence in their apparatus so as to hide the fact that no Greek MS has the precise text they have printed, a veritable 'patchwork quilt'. In Metzger's presentation of the UBS Committee's reasoning in this case he writes, "the Committee adopted what seems to be the least unsatisfactory form of text" (p. 136). Is this not a good candidate for 'chutzpah' of the year? The UBS editors concoct their own reading and proclaim it "the least unsatisfactory"! And just what might be "unsatisfactory" about the reading of over 95% of the MSS except that it doesn't introduce any difficulties?

There is complete confusion in the Egyptian camp. That confusion must have commenced in the second century, resulting from several easy transcriptional errors, simple copying mistakes. *APAM* to *APNI* is very easy (in the early centuries only upper case letters were used); with a scratchy quill the cross strokes in the A and M could be light, and a subsequent copyist could mistake the left leg of the M as going with the Λ to make N, and the right leg of the M would become I. Very early "Aminadab" was misspelled as "Aminadam", which survives in some 25% of the extant MSS (in the minuscule MSS the *beta* was frequently written like a *mu*, only without the 'tail'). The "Adam" of Aleph, syr[s] and cop[sa] arose through an easy instance of homoioarcton (the eye of a copyist went from the first A in "Aminadam" to the second, dropping "Amin-" and leaving "Adam"). A and Λ are easily confused, especially when written by hand—"Admin" presumably came from "AMINadab/m", though the process

---

probably have told us that the reading of 96.8% of the MSS is "unsatisfactory".

was more complicated. The *'ī* of "Admin" and "Arni" is corrupted to *'eī* in Codex B (a frequent occurrence in that MS—perhaps due to Coptic influence). Codex Aleph conflated the ancestor that produced "Adam" with the one that produced "Admin", etc. The total confusion in Egypt does not surprise us, but how shall we account for the text and apparatus of NU in this instance? And whatever possessed the editors of NASB, NRSV, TEV, LB, Berkeley, etc. to embrace such an egregious error?

**Matthew 19:17** Τι με λεγεις αγαθον ουδεις αγαθος ει μη εις ο Θεος
—f³⁵ C,W (99%) RP,HF,OC,CP,TR
Why do you call me good? No one is good but one, God.

Τι με ερωτας περι του αγαθου εις εστιν ο αγαθος
—א(B,D) (0.9%) NU
Why do you ask me about the good? One is good.

Problem: NU in Matthew 19:17 contradicts NU in Mark 10:18 and Luke 18:19 (wherein all texts agree with the Majority here).

Discussion: Presumably Jesus spoke in Hebrew, but there is no way that whatever He said could legitimately yield the two translations into Greek given above.[1] That the Latin versions offer a conflation suggests that both the other variants must have existed in the second century—indeed, the *Diatessaron* overtly places the Majority reading in the first half of that century. The Church in Egypt during the second century was dominated by Gnosticism. That such a 'nice' Gnostic variant came into being is no surprise, but why do modern editors embrace it? Because it is the "more obscure one" (Metzger, p. 49). This 'obscurity' was so attractive to the NU Committee that they printed another 'patchwork quilt'—taking the young man's question and this first part of the Lord's answer together, the precise text of NU is found only in the **corrector** of Codex B; further, with reference to the main Greek MSS given as supporting the eclectic text here (א,B,D,L,Θ,f¹), the fact is that no two of them precisely agree! (Should they be regarded as reliable witnesses? On what basis?) Most modern versions join NU in this error also.

**Acts 19:16** αυτων—f³⁵ [90%] HF,RP,OC,TR,CP
them

αμφορερων—אA,B,D [5%] NU
both of them

Problem: The sons of Sceva were seven, not two.

Discussion: To argue that 'both' can mean 'all' on the basis of this passage is to beg the question. An appeal to Acts 23:8 is likewise unconvincing. "For

---

[1] In His teaching on general themes the Lord presumably repeated Himself many times, using a variety of expressions and variations on those themes, and the Gospel writers preserve some of that variety. In this case we are dealing with a specific conversation, which presumably was not repeated.

Sadducees say that there is no resurrection—and no angel or spirit; but the Pharisees confess both." 'Angel' and 'spirit' if not intended as synonyms at least belong to a single class, spirit beings. The Pharisees believed in "both"— resurrection and spirit beings. There is no basis here for claiming that "both" can legitimately refer to seven (Acts 19:16).[1] Still, most modern versions do render "both" as "all". NASB actually renders "both of them", making the contradiction overt!

**Matthew 1:7-8** $A\sigma\alpha$—f35 W [98%] RP,HF,OC,CP,TR
Asa

$A\sigma\alpha\phi$—P1vℵ,B,C [2%] NU  (twice)
Asaph

Problem: Asaph does not belong in Jesus' genealogy.

Discussion: Asaph was a Levite, not of the tribe of Judah; he was a psalmist, not a king. It is clear from Metzger's comments that the NU editors understand that their reading refers to the Levite and should not be construed as an alternate spelling of Asa; he overtly calls Asaph an "error" (p. 1). In fact, "Asaph" is probably not a misspelling of "Asa". Not counting Asa and Amon (see v. 10) Codex B misspells 13 names in this chapter, while Codex Aleph misspells 10, which undermines their credibility. However, their misspellings involve dittography, gender change, or a similar sound ($\underline{z}$ for $\underline{s}$, $\underline{d}$ for $\underline{t}$, $\underline{m}$ for $\underline{n}$)—not adding an extraneous consonant, like $\underline{f}$, nor trading dissimilar sounds, like $\underline{s}$ for $\underline{n}$.

In response to Lagrange, who considered "Asaph" to be an ancient scribal error, Metzger writes: "Since, however, the evangelist may have derived material for the genealogy, not from the Old Testament directly, but from subsequent genealogical lists, in which the erroneous spelling occurred, the Committee saw no reason to adopt what appears to be a scribal emendation" (p. 1). Metzger frankly declares that the spelling they have adopted is "erroneous". The NU editors have deliberately imported an error into their text, which is faithfully reproduced by NAB (New American Bible) and NRSV. RSV and NASB offer a footnote to the effect that the Greek reads "Asaph"—it would be less misleading if they said that a tiny fraction of the Greek MSS so read. The case of Amon vs. Amos in verse 10 is analogous to this one. Metzger says that "Amos" is "an error for 'Amon'" (p. 2), and the NU editors have duly placed the error in their text.

---

[1] Arndt and Gingrich's note (p. 47) seems designed to protect the reading of the eclectic text here. Metzger's discussion is interesting: "The difficulty of reconciling [seven] with [both], however, is not so great as to render the text which includes both an impossible text. On the other hand, however, the difficulty is so troublesome that it is hard to explain how [seven] came into the text, and was perpetuated, if it were not original,..." (pp. 471-72). Notice that Metzger assumes the genuineness of "both" and discusses the difficulty that it creates as if it were fact. I would say that his assumption is gratuitous and that the difficulty it creates is an artifact of his presuppositions.

**Matthew 10:10** μηδε ραβδους—f³⁵ C,N,W [95%] RP,HF,CP
neither staves

μηδε ραβδον—א,B,D [5%] OC,TR,NU
neither a staff

Problem: In both Matthew 10:10 and Luke 9:3 NU has "neither a staff," thus contradicting Mark 6:8 where all texts have "only a staff".

Discussion: In Luke and Matthew the Majority text reads "neither staves", which does not contradict Mark—the case of the staves is analogous to that of the tunics; they were to take only one, not several. A superficial reader would probably expect the singular; that some scribe in Egypt should have trouble with "staves" and simplify it to "a staff" comes as no surprise, but why do the NU editors import this error into their text? Almost all modern versions follow NU both here and in Luke 9:3.

**Mark 1:2** εν τοις προφηταις—f³⁵ A,W (96.7%) HF,RP,CP,TR,OC
[as it is written] in the prophets

εν τω Ησαια τω προφητη—אB (1.3%) NU
[as it is written] in Isaiah the prophet

Ησαια τω προφητη—D (1.8%)

Problem: The NU text ascribes extraneous material to Isaiah.

Discussion: The rest of verse 2 is a quote from Malachi 3:1 while verse 3 is from Isaiah 40:3. Once again Metzger uses the 'harder reading' argument, in effect (p. 73), but the eclectic choice is most probably the result of early harmonizing activity. The only other places that Isaiah 40:3 is quoted in the New Testament are Matthew 3:3, Luke 3:4 and John 1:23. The first two are in passages parallel to Mark 1:2 and join it in agreeing with the LXX verbatim. The quote in John differs from the LXX in one word and is also used in connection with John the Baptist. The crucial consideration, for our present purpose, is that Matthew, Luke and John all identify the quote as being from Isaiah (without MS variation). It seems clear that the "Alexandrian-Western" reading in Mark 1:2 is simply an assimilation to the other three Gospels. It should also be noted that the material from Malachi looks more like an allusion than a direct quote. Further, although Malachi is quoted (or alluded to) a number of times in the New Testament, he is never named. Mark's own habits may also be germane to this discussion. Mark quotes Isaiah in 4:12, 11:17 and 12:32 and alludes to him in about ten other places, all without naming his source. The one time he does use Isaiah's name is when quoting Jesus in 7:6. In the face of such clear evidence the 'harder reading' canon cannot justify the forcing of an error into the text of Mark 1:2. Almost all modern versions agree with NU here.

324

**Luke 9:10** [εις τοπον ερημον πολεως καλουμενης Βηθσαιδα(ν)
—f³⁵ (A)C(N)W [98%] CP,HF,RP,TR,OC
into a deserted place belonging to a town called Bethsaida

εις πολιν καλουμενην Βηθσαιδα—(P⁷⁵)B [0.5%] NU
into a town called Bethsaida

εις κωμην legomenhn bhdsaida—D
εις τοπον ερημον—ℵ

Problem: NU has Jesus and company going into Bethsaida, but in verse 12 the disciples say they are in a deserted area; thus a contradiction is introduced. NU here is also at variance with NU in the parallel passages.

Discussion: In Matthew 14:13 all texts have Jesus going to a deserted place, and in verse 15 the disciples say, "the place is deserted…send the crowd away to the towns". In Mark 6:31-32 all texts have Him going to a deserted place, and in verse 35 the disciples say it is a deserted place, etc. So NU not only makes Luke contradict himself, but sets him against Matthew and Mark. The modern versions do not surprise us.

**John 18:24** απεστειλεν—f³⁵ A [90%] CP,HF,RP,OC,TR
[Annas] had sent [Him bound to Caiaphas]

απεστειλεν ουν—B,C,W [9%] NU, some TRs
then [Annas] sent [Him bound to Caiaphas]

απεστειλεν δε—ℵ [1%]

Problem: The NU variant sets up a contradiction within the immediate context. Verse 13 says Jesus was taken first to Annas, but all four Gospels are agreed that Peter's denials and the judging took place in the house of Caiaphas—here in John, verses 15-23 happened there. The NU variant puts verses 15-23 in the house of Annas, making John contradict the other three Gospels.

Discussion: Only John records that Jesus was taken first to Annas; the other three go directly to Caiaphas, so for them the difficulty of changing houses does not arise. After penning verses 15-23, John saw that his readers could get the idea that Jesus was still with Annas, so he wrote verse 24 to avert that misunderstanding. Verse 24 should be translated in parentheses: (Annas had sent Him bound to Caiaphas the high priest).

**John 6:11** τοις μαθηταις οι δε μαθηται—f³⁵ D [97%] CP,HF,RP,OC,TR
to the disciples, and the disciples

---        ---        --- ---        ---        —P⁶⁶,⁷⁵ᵛℵA,B,W [3%] NU

Problem: The NU text contradicts itself. In Matthew 14:19, Mark 6:41 and Luke 9:16, parallel passages, NU agrees with the Majority that Jesus handed the bread to the disciples, who in turn distributed it to the people. Here in John NU omits the disciples and has Jesus Himself distributing the bread to the people.

Discussion: This variant may be explained as an easy transcriptional mistake, a case of homoioarcton, a similar beginning—in this case jumping from one τοις to the next. There is no need to appeal to the 'harder reading' canon. If this were the only instance, it could be explained away, but when added to the others it has a cumulative effect.

I am well aware that the foregoing examples may not strike the reader as being uniformly convincing. However, I submit that there is a cumulative effect. By dint of ingenuity and mental gymnastics it may be possible to appear to circumvent one or another of these examples (including those that follow), but with each added instance the strain on our credulity increases. One or two circumventions may be accepted as possible, but five or six become highly improbable; ten or twelve are scarcely tolerable.

## Serious Anomalies/Aberrations

**John 7:8**  ουπω—f$^{35}$ P$^{66,75}$B,N,T,W [96.5%] CP,HF,RP,OC,TR
not yet

ουκ—אD [3%] NU
not

Problem: Since Jesus did in fact go to the feast (and doubtless knew what He was going to do), the NU text has the effect of ascribing a falsehood to Him.

Discussion: Since the NU editors usually attach the highest value to P$^{75}$ and B, isn't it strange that they reject them in this case? Here is Metzger's explanation: "The reading ["not yet"] was introduced at an early date (it is attested by P$^{66,75}$) in order to alleviate the inconsistency between ver. 8 and ver. 10" (p. 216). So, they rejected P$^{66,75}$ and B (as well as 96.5% of the MSS) because they preferred the "inconsistency". NASB, RSV, NEB and TEV stay with the eclectic text here.

**John 6:47**  εις εμε—f$^{35}$ A,C,D,N (99.5%) CP,HF,RP,OC,TR
[believes] into me

--- --- —P$^{66}$אB,T,W (0.5%) NU
[believes]

Problem: Jesus is making a formal declaration about how one can have eternal life: "Most assuredly I say to you, he who believes into me has everlasting life." By omitting "into me" the NU text opens the door to universalism.

Discussion: Since it is impossible to live without believing in something, everyone believes—the object of the belief is of the essence. The verb 'believe' does occur elsewhere without a stated object (it is supplied by the context), but not in a formal declaration like this. The shorter reading is probably the result of a fairly easy instance of homoioarcton—three short words in a row begin with *E*. And yet Metzger says of the words "in me", "no good reason can be suggested to account for their omission" (p. 214). The editors grade the omission as {A}, against 99.5% of the MSS plus 2nd century attestation! TEV, NASB, NIV, NRSV and Jerusalem reproduce the UBS text precisely.

**Acts 28:13** περιελθοντες—f[35] A,048 [95%] HF,RP,OC,TR,CP
tacking back and forth [we reached Rhegium]

περιελοντες—ℵB [5%] NU
taking away (something) [we reached Rhegium]

Problem: The verb chosen by NU, περιαιρεω, is transitive, and is meaningless here.

Discussion: Metzger's lame explanation is that a majority of the NU Committee took the word to be "a technical nautical term of uncertain meaning" (p. 501)! Why do they choose to disfigure the text on such poor evidence when there is an easy transcriptional explanation? The Greek letters O and Θ are very similar, and being side by side in a word it would be easy to drop one of them out, in this case the *theta*. Most modern versions are actually based on the 'old' Nestle text, which here agrees with the Majority reading. NRSV, however, follows NU, rendering it as "then we weighed anchor".

**Mark 16:9-20** (have)—every extant Greek MS (a. 1,700)
except three; HF,RP,CP,TR,OC[[NU]]

(omit)—ℵ[c],B,304

Problem: A serious aberration is introduced—it is affirmed that Mark's Gospel ends with 16:8.

Discussion: UBS[3] encloses these verses in double brackets, which means they are "regarded as later additions to the text", and they give their decision an {A} grade, "virtually certain". So, the UBS editors assure us that the genuine text of Mark ends with 16:8. But why do critics insist on rejecting this passage? It is contained in every extant Greek MS (about 1,700) except three (really only two, B and 304—Aleph is not properly 'extant' because it is a forgery at this point).[1] Every extant Greek Lectionary (about 2,000?) contains

---

[1] Tischendorf, who discovered Codex Aleph, warned that the folded sheet containing the end of Mark and the beginning of Luke appeared to be written by a different hand and with different ink than the rest of the manuscript. However that may be, a careful scrutiny reveals the following: the end of Mark and beginning of Luke occur on page 3 (of the four); pages 1 and 4 contain an average of 17 lines of printed Greek text per column (there are four columns per page), just like the rest of the codex; page 2 contains an average of 15.5 lines of printed text per column (four columns); the first column of page 3 contains only **twelve** lines of printed text and in this way verse 8 occupies the top of the second column, the rest of which is blank (except for some designs); Luke begins at the top of column 3, which contains 16 lines of printed text while column 4 is back up to 17 lines. On page 2 the forger began to spread out the

them (one of them, 185, doing so only in the Menologion). Every extant Syriac MS except one (Sinaitic) contains them. Every extant Latin MS (8,000?) except one (k) contains them. Every extant Coptic MS except one contains them. We have hard evidence for the 'inclusion' from the II century (Irenaeus and the Diatessaron), and presumably the first half of that century. We have no such hard evidence for the 'exclusion'.

In the face of such massive evidence, why do the critics insist on rejecting this passage? Lamentably, most modern versions also cast doubt upon the authenticity of these verses in one way or another (NRSV is especially objectionable here). As one who believes that the Bible **is** God's Word, I find it to be inconceivable that an official biography of Jesus Christ, commissioned by God and written subject to His quality control, should omit proofs of the resurrection, should exclude all post-resurrection appearances, should end with the clause "because they were afraid"! If the critics' assessment is correct we seem to be between a rock and a hard place. Mark's Gospel as it stands is mutilated (if it ends at v. 8), the original ending having disappeared without a trace. But in that event what about God's purpose in commissioning this biography?

**John 1:18** ο μονογενης υιος—f³⁵ A,C,W (99.6%) (CP)HF,RP,OC,TR
the only begotten Son

-- μονογενης θεος—P⁶⁶ℵB,C (0.3%) NU
an only begotten god

ο μονογενης θεος—P⁷⁵ (0.1%)
the only begotten god

Problem: A serious anomaly is introduced—God, as God, is not begotten.

Discussion: The human body and nature of Jesus Christ was indeed literally begotten in the virgin Mary by the Holy Spirit; God the Son has existed eternally. "An only begotten god" is so deliciously Gnostic that the apparent Egyptian provenance of this reading makes it doubly suspicious. It would also be possible to render the second reading as "only begotten god!", emphasizing the quality, and this has appealed to some who see in it a strong affirmation of Christ's deity. However, if Christ received His 'Godhood' through the begetting process then He cannot be the eternally pre-existing Second Person of the Godhead. Nor is 'only begotten' analogous to 'firstborn', referring to priority of

---

letters, displacing six lines of printed text; in the first column of page 3 he got desperate and displaced **five** lines of printed text, just in one column!

In this way he managed to get two lines of verse 8 over onto the second column, avoiding the telltale vacant column (as in Codex B). That second column would accommodate 15 more lines of printed text, which with the other eleven make 26. Verses 9-20 occupy 23.5 such lines, so there is plenty of room for them. It really does seem that there has been foul play, and there would have been no need for it unless the first hand did in fact display the disputed verses. In any event, Aleph as it stands is a forgery (in this place) and therefore may not legitimately be alleged as evidence against them.

position—that would place the Son above the Father. No matter how one looks at it, the NU reading introduces a serious anomaly, and on the slimmest of evidence.

Presumably μονογενης is intended to mean something more than just μονος, 'only'. In Luke 7:12, even though for reasons of style a translator may put "the **only** son of his mother", we must understand that he is her own offspring—he could not be an adopted son. The same holds for Luke 8:42 and 9:38. In Hebrews 11:17, with reference to the promise and to Sarah, Isaac was indeed Abraham's "only begotten", even though he in fact had other sons with other women. Note that in Genesis 22:12 & 16 God Himself calls Isaac Abraham's "only" son. John uses μονογενης five times, always referring to the Son of God (John 1:14, 18; 3:16, 18; 1 John 4:9). I see nothing in New Testament usage to justify the rendering 'unique'.

That P[75] should have a conflation of the first two readings is curious, but demonstrates that the discrepancy arose in the second century. (Articles modify nouns not adjectives, when in a noun phrase such as we have here, so the article is part of the same variation unit.) Most modern versions avoid a straightforward rendering of the NU reading. NIV offers us "but God the only [Son]"—a bad translation of a bad text. (A subsequent revision has "God the One and Only"—a pious fraud since none of the variants has this meaning.) TEV has "The only One, who is the same as God"—only slightly better. NASB actually renders "the only begotten God"! (the reading of P[75]). Not to be outdone Amplified serves up a conflation, "the only unique Son, the only begotten God". Ho hum!

**John 7:53-8:11** (retain)—**f**[35] D [85%] CP,HF,RP,OC,TR[[NU]]

(omit)—P[66,75]ℵB,N,T,W [15%]

Problem: UBS[3] encloses these verses in double brackets, which means they are "regarded as later additions to the text", and they give their decision an {A} grade, "virtually certain". The omission introduces an aberration.

Discussion: The evidence against the Majority Text is stronger than in any of the previous examples, but assuming that the passage is spurious (for the sake of the argument), how could it ever have intruded here, and to such effect that it is attested by some 85% of the MSS? Let's try to read the larger passage without these verses—we must go from 7:52 to 8:12 directly. Reviewing the context, the chief priests and Pharisees had sent officers to arrest Jesus, to no avail; a 'discussion' ensues; Nicodemus makes a point, to which the Pharisees answer:

(7:52) "Are you also from Galilee? Search and look, for no prophet has arisen out of Galilee."

(8:12) Then Jesus spoke to them again, saying, "I am the light of the world...."

What is the antecedent of "them", and what is the meaning of "again"? By the normal rules of grammar, if 7:53-8:11 is missing then "them" must refer to the

"Pharisees" and "again" means that there has already been at least one prior exchange. But, 7:45 makes clear that Jesus **was not there** with the Pharisees. Thus, NU introduces an aberration. And yet, Metzger claims that the passage "interrupts the sequence of 7.52 and 8.12 ff." (p. 220)! To look for the antecedents of 8:12 in 7:37-39 not only does despite to the syntax but also runs afoul of 8:13—"the Pharisees" respond to Jesus' claim in verse 12, but "the Pharisees" are somewhere else, 7:45-52 (if the pericope is absent).

Metzger also claims that "the style and vocabulary of the pericope differ noticeably from the rest of the Fourth Gospel"—but, wouldn't the native speakers of Greek at that time have been in a better position than modern critics to notice something like that? So how could they allow such an 'extraneous' passage to be forced into the text? I submit that the evident answer is that they did not; it was there all the time. I also protest their use of brackets here. Since the editors clearly regard the passage to be spurious they should be consistent and delete it, as do NEB and Williams. That way the full extent of their error would be open for all to see. NIV, NASB, NRSV, Berkeley and TEV also use brackets to question the legitimacy of this passage.

**1 Timothy 3:16**   θεος—f³⁵ A,Cᵛ [98.5%] RP,HF,OC,TR,CP
God [was manifested in flesh]

ος—ℵ [1%] NU
who [was manifested in flesh]

ο—D
that [was manifested in flesh]

Problem: A grammatical anomaly is introduced. "Great is the mystery of godliness, who was manifested in flesh" is worse in Greek than it is in English. "Mystery" is neuter in gender while "godliness" is feminine, but "who" is masculine!

Discussion: In an effort to explain the "who" it is commonly argued that the second half of verse 16 was a direct quote from a hymn, but where is the evidence for this claim? Without evidence the claim begs the question.[1] That the passage has some poetic qualities says no more than that it has some poetic qualities. "Who" is nonsensical, so most modern versions that follow NU here take evasive action: NEB and NASB have "he who"; Phillips has "the one"; NRSV, Jerusalem, TEV and NIV render "he". Berkeley actually has

---

[1] A pronoun normally requires an antecedent, but quoted material might provide an exception. Thus, 1 Corinthians 2:9 is sometimes offered as an instance: the quote from Isaiah 64:4 begins with a pronoun, without a grammatical antecedent (although "mystery" in verse 7 is presumably the referential antecedent). However, the words from Isaiah are formally introduced as a quotation, "as it is written", whereas the material in 1 Timothy 3:16 is not, so there is no valid analogy. Colossians 1:13 or 1:15 have been suggested as analogies for "who" in 1 Timothy 3:16, even claimed as "hymns", but there is no objective support for the claim. The antecedent of the relative pronoun in Colossians 1:15 is "the son" in verse 13, and the antecedent of the relative pronoun in verse 13 is "the father" in verse 12. Again, there is no valid analogy.

"who"! The Latin reading, "the mystery...that," at least makes sense. The true reading, as attested by 98.5% of the Greek MSS, is "God". In the early MSS "God" was written ΘC (with a cross stroke above the two letters to indicate an abbreviation), "who" was written OC, and "that" was written O. The difference between "God" and "who" is just two cross strokes, and with a scratchy quill those could easily be light (or a copyist could be momentarily distracted and forget to add the cross strokes). The reading "who" can be explained by an easy transcriptional error. The reading "that" would be an obvious solution to a copyist faced with the nonsensical "who". Whatever the intention of the NU editors, their text emasculates this strong statement of the deity of Jesus Christ, besides being a stupidity—what is a 'mystery' about any human male being manifested in flesh? All human beings have bodies.

**2 Peter 3:10** κατακαησεται—**f³⁵** A,048 (93.6%) RP,HF,OC,TR,CP
      [the earth...] will be burned up

      ευρεθησεται—(P⁷²)אB (3.2%) NU
      [the earth...] will be found

Problem: The NU reading is nonsensical; the context is clearly one of judgment.

Discussion: Metzger actually states that their text "seems to be devoid of meaning in the context" (p. 706)! So why did they choose it? Metzger explains that there is "a wide variety of readings, none of which seems to be original"— presumably if "shall be burned up" were the only reading, with unanimous attestation, he would still reject it, but he can scarcely argue that it is meaningless. The NU editors deliberately chose a variant that they believed to be "devoid of meaning in the context". NASB abandons UBS here, giving the Majority reading; NEB and NIV render "will be laid bare"; TEV has "will vanish".

**Jude 15** παντας τους ασεβεις—**f³⁵** A,B,C (97.8%) RP,HF,OC,TR,CP
      [to convict] all the ungodly [among them of all their ungodly deeds]

      πασαν ψυχην—P⁷²א(only one other MS) NU
      to convict] every soul [of all their ungodly deeds]

Problem: NU introduces a serious anomaly.

Discussion: Certain very evil persons have been rather graphically described in verses 4, 8 and 10-13. In verse 14 Jude introduces a prophecy "about these men", the same ones he has been describing, and the quotation continues to the end of verse 15. Verse 16 continues the description of their perversity, but verse 17 draws a clear distinction between them and the believers that Jude is addressing. So, Enoch cannot be referring to "every soul"—the NU reading is clearly wrong. In fact, Nestle²⁵ and UBS² stayed with the Majority, reading "all the ungodly". UBS³ changes to "every soul", without comment! Is this not a curious proceeding? The UBS editors reverse an earlier position, following just three MSS and the Sahidic version, and do not even mention it in their apparatus. This is especially unfortunate, given the serious nature of the change. Most modern versions are with the Majority here, but NRSV has "convict everyone".

**Matthew 5:22**  εικη—**f³⁵** D,W (96.2%) RP,HF,OC,CP,TR
without a cause

--- —P⁶⁴ℵB (1.9%) NU

Problem: The NU omission has the effect of setting up a conflict with passages like Ephesians 4:26 and Psalm 4:4, where we are commanded to be angry, and even with the Lord's own example, Mark 3:5.

Discussion: God hates injustice and will judge it; but He also hates evil and commands us to do likewise, Psalm 97:10. The NU variant has the effect of forbidding anger, which cannot be right. Again, if this were the only instance, it could be explained away, but when added to the others it has a cumulative effect.

**Mark 10:24**  τους πεποιθοτας επι χρημασιν
—**f³⁵** A,C(D)N (99.5%) HF,RP,CP(TR)OC
for those who trust in riches

--- --- --- --- —ℵB (0.4%) NU

πλουσιον—W

Problem: The NU variant has Jesus saying: "How difficult it is to enter the Kingdom of God!" Within the context this is a stupidity, besides having the effect of making Him contradict Himself, since in other places He gives an open invitation: "Come unto me, all you who labor and are heavy laden, and I will give you rest" (Matthew 11:28).

Discussion: Within the context the Majority reading is clearly correct. Taking into account all that Scripture offers on the subject, being rich in itself is not the problem; the problem is precisely one of trust—are you really trusting God, or is it your wealth? Or to put it differently, where is your treasure? Most modern versions follow NU here, and some offer a footnote that says, "some (later) manuscripts add, 'for those who trust in riches'." It is their way of referring to 99.5% of the manuscripts; and the Latin and Syriac versions take the Majority reading back to the 2ⁿᵈ century. Such footnotes are clearly perverse.

There are many further examples, some of which, taken singly, may not seem to be all that alarming. But they have a cumulative effect and **dozens** of them should give the responsible reader pause. Is there a pattern? If so, why? But for now enough has been presented to permit us to turn to the implications.

# Implications

How is all of this to be explained? I believe the answer lies in the area of presuppositions. There has been a curious reluctance on the part of conservative scholars to come to grips with this matter. To assume that the editorial choices of a naturalistic scholar will not be influenced by his theological bias is naive in the extreme.

To be sure, both such scholars and the conservative defenders of the eclectic text will doubtless demur. "Not at all", they would say, "our editorial choices derive from a straightforward application of the generally accepted canons of NT textual criticism" ["generally accepted" by whom, and on what basis—that is, what are the presuppositions behind them?]. And what are those canons? The four main ones seem to be: 1) the reading that best accounts for the rise of the other reading(s) is to be preferred; 2) the harder reading is to be preferred; 3) the shorter reading is to be preferred; 4) the reading that best fits the author's style and purpose is to be preferred. It could be said that the first canon sort of distills the essence of them all, and therefore should be the ruling canon, but in practice it is probably the second that is most rigorously applied. From B.M. Metzger's presentation of the NU Committee's reasoning in the examples given above it appears that over half the time they based their decision on the 'harder reading' canon (for four of them he has no comment because the UBS apparatus does not mention that there is any variation; for two of them he says that all the variants are unsatisfactory!). But, how are we to decide which variant is 'harder'? Will not our own theological bias enter in?

Let's consider an example: in Luke 24:52 the Nestle editions 1-25 omit "they worshipped him" (and in consequence NASB, RSV and NEB do too). UBS[3] retains the words, but with a {D} grade, which shows a "very high degree of doubt". Only one solitary Greek manuscript omits the words, Codex D, supported by part of the Latin witness. In spite of the very slim external evidence for the omission it is argued that it is the 'harder' reading—if the clause were original, what orthodox Christian would even think of removing it? On the other hand, the clause would make a nice pious addition that would immediately become popular, if the original lacked it. However, not only did the Gnostics dominate the Christian church in Egypt in the second century, there were also others around who did not believe that Jesus was God—would they be likely to resist the impulse to delete such a statement? How shall we choose between these two hypotheses? Will it not be on the basis of our presuppositions? Indeed, in discussing this variant set, along with Hort's other "Western non-interpolations", Metzger explains (p. 193) that a minority of the UBS committee argued that "there is discernible in these passages a Christological-theological motivation that accounts for their having been added, while there is no clear reason that accounts for their having been omitted". (Had they never heard of the Gnostics?)

## Why Use Subjective Canons?

It is clear that the four canons mentioned above depend heavily upon the subjective judgment of the critic. But why use such canons? Why not follow the manuscript evidence? It is commonly argued that the surviving MSS are not representative of the textual situation in the early centuries of the Church. The official destruction of MSS by Diocletian (AD 300), and other vagaries of history, are supposed to have decimated the supply of MSS to the point where the transmission was totally distorted—so we can't be sure about anything. (Such an argument not only 'justifies' the eclectic proceeding, it is used to claim its 'necessity'.) But, the effectiveness of the Diocletian campaign was uneven in different regions. Even more to the point are the implications of the Donatist movement which developed right after the Diocletian campaign passed. It was predicated in part on the punishment that was deserved by those who betrayed their MSS to destruction. Evidently some did **not** betray their MSS or there would have been no one to judge the others. Also, those whose commitment to Christ and His Word was such that they withstood the torture would be just the sort who would be most careful about the pedigree of their MSS. So it was probably the purest exemplars that survived, in the main, and from them the main stream of transmission derives.

Since the Byzantine (Majority) textform dominates over 90% of the extant MSS, those who wish to reject it cannot grant the possibility that the transmission of the text was in any sense normal. (If it was then the consensus must reflect the original, especially such a massive consensus.) So it is argued that the 'ballot box' was 'stuffed', that the Byzantine text was imposed by ecclesiastical authority, but only after it was concocted out of other texts in the early IV century. But, there is simply no historical evidence for this idea. Also, numerous studies have demonstrated that the mass of Byzantine MSS are not monolithic; there are many distinct strands or strains of transmission, presumably independent. That at least some of these must go back to the III century (if not earlier) is demonstrated by Codex Aleph in Revelation, in that it conflates some of those strands. Asterius (d. 341) used MSS that were clearly Byzantine—presumably most of his writing was not done on his deathbed, so his MSS would come from the III century. There are further lines of evidence that militate against the eclectic position, not least the very nature of their canons.

"The shorter reading is to be preferred." Why? Because, we are told, scribes had a propensity to add bits and pieces to the text. But that would have to be a deliberate activity. It is demonstrable that accidental loss of place results in omission far more often than addition—about the only way to add accidentally is to copy part of the text twice over, but the copyist would have to be really drowsy not to catch himself at it. So, any time a shorter reading could be the result of parablepsis it should be viewed with suspicion. But even when deliberate, omission should still be more frequent than addition. If there is something in the text that you don't like it draws your attention and you are tempted to do something about it. Also, it requires more imagination and effort to create new material than to delete what is already there (material suggested by a parallel passage could be an exception). Further, it is demonstrable that most scribes were careful and conscientious, avoiding even unintentional mistakes. Those who engaged in deliberate editorial activity were really rather few, but some were flagrant offenders (like Aleph in Revelation).

"The harder reading is to be preferred." Why? The assumption is that a perceived difficulty would motivate an officious copyist to attempt a 'remedy'. Note that any such alteration must be deliberate; so if a 'harder' reading could have come about through accidental omission (e.g.) then this canon should not be used. But in the case of a presumed deliberate alteration, how can we really ascribe degrees of 'hardness'? We don't know who did it, nor why. Due allowance must be made for possible ignorance, officiousness, prejudice and malice. In fact, this canon is unreasonable on the face of it—the more stupid a reading is, whether by accident or design, the stronger is its claim to be 'original' since it will certainly be the 'hardest'. It does not take a prophet to see that this canon is wide open to satanic manipulation, both in the ancient creation of variants and in their contemporary evaluation. But in any case, since it is demonstrable that most copyists did not make deliberate changes, where there is massive agreement among the extant MSS this canon should not even be considered. Indeed, where there is massive agreement among the MSS none of the subjective canons should be used—they are unnecessary and out of place. Of the 6,000+ differences between NU and the Majority Text, the heavy majority of the readings preferred by the NU editors have slender MS attestation.

## The Myth of Neutrality

We need to lay to rest the myth of neutrality and scholarly objectivity. Anyone who has been inside the academic community knows that it is liberally sprinkled with bias, party lines, personal ambition and spite—quite apart from a hatred of the Truth.[1] Neutrality and objectivity should never be assumed, and most especially when dealing with God's Truth—because in this area neither God nor Satan will permit neutrality. In Matthew 12:30 the Lord Jesus said: "He who is not with me is against me, and he who does not gather with me scatters abroad." God declares that neutrality is impossible; you are either for Him or against Him. Jesus claims to be God. Faced with such a claim we have only two options, to accept or to reject. (Agnosticism is really a passive rejection.) The Bible claims to be God's Word. Again our options are but two. It follows that when dealing with the text of Scripture neutrality is impossible. The Bible is clear about satanic interference in the minds of human beings, and most especially when they are considering God's Truth. 2 Corinthians 4:4 states plainly that the god of this age/world blinds the minds of unbelievers when they are confronted with the Gospel. The Lord Jesus said the same thing when He explained the parable of the sower: "When they hear, Satan comes immediately and takes away the word that was sown in their hearts" (Mark 4:15, Luke 8:12).

Furthermore, there is a pervasive satanic influence upon all human culture. 1 John 5:19 states that "the whole world lies in the evil one". The picture is

---

[1] By "the Truth" I mean the fact of an intelligent and moral Creator, Sovereign over all, to whom every created being is accountable. Many scholars will sacrifice the evidence, their own integrity and other people rather than face the Truth.

clearly one of massive influence, if not control—NASB, RSV, NEB and Jerusalem render "in the power of", TEV has "under the rule of", NIV has "under the control of", NKJV has "under the sway of". All human culture is under pervasive satanic influence, including the culture of the academic community. Ephesians 2:2 is even more precise: "in which you once walked according to the course of this world, according to the prince of the power of the air, the spirit who now works in the sons of disobedience." Satan actively works in the mind of anyone who rejects God's authority over him. Materialism has infiltrated the Church in Europe and North America to such an extent that what the Bible says on this subject has been largely ignored. But I submit that for someone who claims to believe God's Word to accept an edition of the Bible prepared on the basis of rationalistic assumptions is really to forget the teaching of that Word.

Interpretation is preeminently a matter of wisdom. A naturalistic textual critic may have a reasonable acquaintance with the relevant evidence, he may have knowledge of the facts, but that by no means implies that he knows what to do with it. If "the fear of the LORD is the **beginning** of wisdom" (Proverbs 9:10), then presumably the unbeliever doesn't have any, at least from God's point of view. Anyone who edits or translates the text of Scripture needs to be in spiritual condition such that he can ask the Holy Spirit to illumine him in his work as well as protect his mind from the enemy.

In Jesus' day there were those who "loved the praise of men more than the praise of God" (John 12:43), and they are with us still. But, the "praise of men" comes at a high price—you must accept their value system, a value system that suffers direct satanic influence. To accept the world's value system is basically an act of treason against King Jesus, a type of idolatry. Those conservative scholars who place a high value on 'academic recognition' on being acknowledged by the 'academic community', etc., need to ask themselves about the presuppositions that lie behind such recognition. Please note that I am not decrying true scholarship—I have three earned graduate degrees myself—but I am challenging conservatives to make sure that their definition of scholarship comes from the Holy Spirit, not from the world, that their search for recognition is godly, not selfish. I rather suspect that were this to happen there would be a dramatic shift in the conservative Christian world with reference to the practice of NT textual criticism and to the identity of the true NT text.

# Conclusion

To sum it up, I return to the opening question: "What difference does it make?" Not only do we have the confusion caused by two rather different competing forms of the Greek text, but one of them (the eclectic text) incorporates errors and contradictions that undermine the doctrine of inspiration and virtually vitiate the doctrine of inerrancy; the other (the Majority Text) does not. The first is based on subjective criteria, applied by naturalistic critics; the second is based on the consensus of the manuscript tradition down through the centuries. Because the conservative evangelical schools and churches have generally embraced the theory (and therefore the presuppositions) that underlies the eclectic text (UBS[3]/N-A[26]),[1] there has been an ongoing hemorrhage or defection within the evangelical camp with reference to the doctrines of Biblical inspiration and inerrancy (especially). The authority of Scripture has been undermined—it no longer commands immediate and unquestioned obedience. As a natural consequence there is a generalized softening of our basic commitment to Christ and His Kingdom. Worse yet, through our missionaries we have been exporting all of this to the emerging churches in the 'third world'. Alas!

So what shall we do, throw up our hands in despair and give up? Indeed no! 'It is better to light one candle than to sit and curse the darkness.' With God's help let us work together to bring about a reversal of this situation. Let us work to undo the damage. We must start by consciously trying to make sure that all our presuppositions, our working assumptions, are consistent with God's Word. When we approach the evidence (Greek MSS, patristic citations, ancient versions) with such presuppositions we will have a credible, even demonstrable, basis for declaring and defending the divine preservation, the inspiration and the inerrancy of the New Testament text. We can again have a compelling basis for total commitment to God and His Word. The present printed Majority Text (whether H-F or R-P) is a close approximation to the original, free from the errors of fact and contradictions discussed above. (All modesty aside, I consider that my Greek Text is even closer.)

---

[1] UBS[4] and N-A[27] have changes in the apparatus, but not the text, so the text is still that of the prior editions.

# APPENDIX G
# 7Q5

The identification of papyrus fragment 5 from Qumran cave 7 with Mark 6:52-53 by Jesuit scholar Jose O'Callaghan in early 1972 produced a flurry of reaction.[1] The implications of such an identification are such that I suppose it was inevitable that much of the reaction should be partisan. But the lack of objectivity and restraint on the part of some scholars can only be construed as bad manners, at best.

O'Callaghan was an experienced papyrologist, a careful scholar, and is entitled to a respectful hearing.

To my mind, the lack of restraint and objectivity in M. Baillet's response borders on the reprehensible.[2] Unfortunately Baillet's article has been widely quoted and seems to have influenced many people, including K. Aland.[3] Having myself done a little work with papyri from the Ptolemaic period (third century B.C.) I should like to comment upon Baillet's response to O'Callaghan's transcription of 7Q5. The fragment contains five lines of text and I will discuss them in order.

Line 1: All that remains is a vestige of the bottom of one letter—that it is the bottom can be seen by measuring the average distance between the other lines. O'Callaghan reconstructs an *epsilon* and puts a dot under it to show that what is left of the ink itself is not sufficient to allow a certain identification of the letter. This is in strict accord with the norm universally followed by papyrologists. Baillet calls it a "gratuitous hypothesis" even though he himself gave *epsilon* as one of four possibilities in the *editio princeps*. In fact, the vestige looks precisely like the bottom extremity of either an *epsilon* or a *sigma*. It is important to note that the identification of the fragment is not based on this letter at all; it does not play a positive role. It could play a negative role if the vestige did not seem to fit the letter required by the reconstruction. But far from being an embarrassment to O'Callaghan's reconstruction, the vestige of ink agrees very nicely with it. Baillet's criticism is entirely unwarranted.

Line 2: Since there is some ink left on the papyrus, O'Callaghan is at perfect liberty to reconstruct an *epsilon* provided he puts a dot under it, as he has. Baillet grants that it is possible. Again, the identification of the fragment is not

---

[1] J. O'Callaghan, "Papiros neotestamentarios en la cueva 7 de Qumran?" *Biblica*, LIII (1972), 91-100. 7Q5 is dated at around 50 A.D.

[2] M. Baillet, "Les manuscrits de la Grotte 7 de Qumran et le N.T." *Biblica*, LIII (1972) 508-516. Baillet was one of the two editors of the *editio princeps* that presented the 7Q fragments to the scholarly world in 1962.

[3] K. Aland, "Neue Neutestamentliche Papyri III," *New Testament Studies*, XX (July, 1974), 358-76.

based on this letter; it is only necessary that the ink traces not be against the identification.

Everybody agrees that the *tau* and *omega* are certain. Following the *omega* O'Callaghan reconstructs a *nu*, which initiative Baillet dignifies with the epithets "absurd" and "impossible" while opining that an *iota* "appears certain". Baillet's rhetoric is disappointing and I begin to doubt his competence as a papyrologist. The most sharply preserved letter on the whole fragment is the *iota* in line 3, and the vertical stroke immediately following the *omega* in line 2 differs substantially from it. What it more nearly resembles is the left-handed vertical stroke of the *nu* or the *eta* in line 4. The horizontal extremity of the following vestige could easily be the bottom extremity of the diagonal stroke of a *nu* (but not the horizontal stroke of an *eta*). In short, O'Callaghan's reconstruction of a *nu* here, with a dot under it of course, is perfectly reasonable.

As for the *eta* that completes line 2 in O'Callaghan's reconstruction, although Baillet prefers an *alpha* he concedes that *eta* is possible, and the *editio princeps* (of which Baillet was co-editor) suggested *eta* as a possibility. O'Callaghan remarks that for him this is the most difficult piece in the puzzle— his response to Baillet's discussion of line 2 is a model of restraint and competence.[1]

A further consideration must be kept in mind. It is a rule of thumb among papyrologists that any proposed reconstruction of a text be accompanied by a translation (or an identification with a known piece of literature)—in other words, it must make sense. Frequently there are so many individual points that are uncertain, taken alone, that there is little point in offering a reconstruction unless a reasonable translation or identification can also be offered—it is the total picture that carries force. O'Callaghan has produced an identification, but Baillet has not.

Line 3: It is generally agreed that the line begins with an *eta* (with a dot under it) followed by a notable space, then the letters KAIT which are quite clear. After the *tau* O'Callaghan reconstructs an *iota*, which Baillet declares to be "impossible". I fail to see how any careful scholar could use the term "impossible" so freely. The letter in question is a close replica of the indubitable *iota* two spaces to the left, so much so that it could reasonably be written without a dot under it. But O'Callaghan does put a dot under it and is therefore above reproach.

Line 4: There is general agreement about this line. It begins with half a letter which is almost certainly a *nu*, followed by a clear *nu* and *eta*, followed by a dubious *sigma*. This is a very important line because of the unusual sequence of letters.

---

[1] O'Callaghan, "Notas sobre 7Q tomadas en el 'Rochefeller Museum' de Jerusalén" *Biblica*, LIII (1972), 519-21.

Line 5: There is general agreement that the first letter is a dubious *theta* and the second an indubitable *eta*. O'Callaghan calls the third letter a clear *sigma* while Baillet prefers to call it an *epsilon*. Just with the naked eye I would call it an obvious *sigma*, but O'Callaghan affirms that seen with a scope what appears to be a short crossbar is in reality two dots; how they got there or what they may signify is not known, but they evidently should not be used to interpret the letter as an *epsilon*.[1]

The last letter is given by O'Callaghan as a possible *alpha*; Baillet rises to new heights, "Mais jamais de la vie un *alpha*,...".[2] The papyrus is too lacerated at this point to tell much from a photograph, but after studying the original with a strong lens O'Callaghan affirms that the left half of an *alpha* is clearly visible, and he invites Baillet to go see for himself.[3]

In sum, I see no reason to take Baillet's criticisms seriously—on the contrary, wherever he says "impossible" we should understand "most likely". It seems to me that O'Callaghan's reconstruction is eminently reasonable, but there are several problems connected with identifying the fragment with Mark 6:52-53.

The fragment presents us with two variations from the wording found in all our printed texts. In line 3 the fragment has an indubitable *tau* where the text has a *delta*. More serious, the identification involves the omission of the words επι την γην between lines 3 and 4. Can anything be said in relief of these problems? Yes. Apparently the difference between a voiced and a voiceless alveolar stop (*delta* and *tau* ) was not obvious to some users of Greek. At any rate, the substitution of one for the other is not infrequent in ancient Greek literature. O'Callaghan offers twenty examples from four biblical papyri of the very change in question.[4] What we have in 7Q5 could easily be just one more instance.

The omission of three words seems more awkward, until it is remembered that it is a characteristic of the earliest N.T. MSS that they are full of eccentricities. I have already discussed this at some length above. I will cite two specific examples.

$P^{66}$ is so full of errors that I suspect it would be nearly impossible to find any five consecutive lines such that if superimposed on a fragment the size of 7Q5 the reconstruction would not present us with singular variants. $P^9$ is similar to 7Q5 in that it also consists of only five lines, albeit with over three times as many letters. It has been identified with 1 John 4:11-12 by everyone. But it badly garbles a word in the first line, misspells a word in the second, omits a word and misspells another in the third and adds a nonsense word in the

---

[1] *Ibid.*, p. 523.

[2] Baillet, p. 511.

[3] O'Callaghan, "Notas", p. 524.

[4] O'Callaghan, "El cambio δ>τ en los papiros biblicos," *Biblica,* LIV (1973), 415-16.

fourth (line 5 is all right). If only the first four or five letters of each line were preserved (instead of twelve or thirteen) I doubt that it would have been identified, or the suggestion of 1 John 4:11-12 accepted.[1]

The point is, our whole experience with early papyri should lead us to expect unique variants in any new one that is discovered—it would be far more surprising to discover one that had no variants. The identification of 7Q5 with Mark 6:52-53 should not be rejected on such grounds.

In spite of the problems, there is evidence in favor of the identification. In the first place, the total effect of the reconstruction is impressive—to match fifteen clear or reasonably clear letters spread over four lines with a stichometry of 23, 20, 21, 21 for the respective lines is all but conclusive. The felicitous way in which the unusual letter sequence NNHC fits into the reconstruction is a favorable argument. The sequence would presumably indicate a form related to the Greek word "generation" or a proper name like "Gennesaret".

Even more striking is the obvious space (two letters' worth—recall that words are run together in early MSS so there are usually no spaces) which occurs precisely at the boundary between verses 52 and 53. Since verse 53 begins a new paragraph the space is appropriate, so much so that to ascribe the occurrence of the space to mere chance seems scarcely credible. The combination of the space at a paragraph break and a felicitous match for NNHC I believe to be compelling. I see no reasonable way to reject O'Callaghan's identification.[2] For further considerations and a discussion of some implications see the series of articles in the June, 1972 issue of *Eternity*.

Once 7Q5 is firmly identified with Mark 6:52-53 then the probability that 7Q4 is to be identified with 1 Tim. 3:16, 4:1,3 and 7Q8 with James 1:23-24 becomes very strong. The remaining fragments are so small that dogmatism is untenable—O'Callaghan's identifications are possible, but cannot be insisted upon. It seems to me that 7Q5, 4, and 8 may be viewed as relevant to the thesis of this book in the following sense. That someone should have such a collection of New Testament writings at such an early date may suggest their early recognition as Scripture and even imply an early notion of a New Testament canon.[3]

---

[1] My discussion of $P^9$ is based on O'Callaghan, "Notas", pp. 528-30.

[2] An international meeting of papyrologists reached the same conclusion. *Christen und Christliches in Qumran?* Bernhard Mayer, ed., Eichstatter Studien n.F. XXXII, Verlag Friedrich Pustet, Regensburg, 1992. More recently a similar meeting assigned $P^{64,67}$ to the first century, so the Qumran fragments begin to have company.

[3] One might even be inclined to join F.F. Bruce in his flight of the imagination (*Eternity*, June, 1972, p. 33, last paragraph). Anything hidden in those caves was presumably placed there before 70 AD, and any manuscript placed there would of necessity have been copied still earlier. Before O'Callaghan's identification, 7Q5 had been dated at around 50 AD. If it is a copy of Mark then the Autograph was written even earlier, and by an eyewitness. Indeed, some 50% of the extant Greek manuscripts, including the best line of transmission, have a colophon stating that Mark was 'published' ten years after the ascension of Christ, 40 AD.

# APPENDIX H
## How Often Did Jesus Say Peter Would Deny Him?

The question can be understood in two different senses, and I wish to explore them both. How often was Peter to deny the Lord, and how often did the Lord warn him? I will consider the second question first. Each Gospel records a warning—the relevant passages are Matthew 26:30-35, Mark 14:26-31, Luke 22:31-34, 39 and John 13:36-38, 18:1. For reasons that will presently become apparent I will start to discuss the passages in reverse order.

## How Many Warnings?

First, John 13:36-38:

> 36 Simon Peter says to Him, "Lord, where are you going?" Jesus answered him, "Where I am going you cannot follow me now, but later you will follow me". 37 Peter says to Him: "Lord, why can't I follow you now? I will lay down my life for your sake!" 38 Jesus answered him: "You will lay down your life for my sake? Most assuredly I say to you, no rooster can crow until you have denied me three times!"[1]

Notice the distinctive context that leads into our Lord's warning. Notice also the emphatic nature of His declaration—by employing a double negative (in the Greek text) He leaves no question but that three denials will take place before the first rooster crows from that moment on. Notice finally where and when this exchange took place. They were in the upper room where they had gathered to observe the Passover. Evidently this conversation between the Lord and Peter came comparatively early in the proceedings, because it was followed by the contents of chapters 14, 15, 16 and 17 before they left the room and went to the garden on the Mount of Olives (18:1).

Second, Luke 22:31-34:

> 31 Then the Lord said, "Simon, Simon, indeed Satan has asked for you (pl) that he may sift you as wheat, 32 but I have prayed for you (sg) that your faith should not fail, and when you have returned to

---

[1] The emphasis here is on the obligatory absence of any cockcrow until Peter has denied [at least] three times. There is no definite article with 'rooster', so it is "a rooster"; the negative is double, therefore emphatic, "absolutely not". If you have lived where there were a number of roosters, you know that one or another can sound off at any time, and some one of them will crow almost on the hour throughout the night, while at dawn they put on a chorus. It was probably somewhere around 9 p.m. when Jesus issued this warning, and Peter's first denial probably happened at least five hours later. For not a single rooster to crow anywhere within earshot during that time required supernatural intervention—which is why I render "no rooster can crow" (if an angel can close lions' mouths [Dan. 6:22], closing roosters' beaks would be a cake walk).

me strengthen your brothers." 33 But he said to Him, "Lord, I am ready to go with you both to prison and to death!" 34 So He said, "I tell you, Peter, no rooster can crow this day before you will deny three times that you know me!"

Notice again the distinctive context that leads into our Lord's warning. It is clearly different from that given in John 13. Notice also that there seems to be an increase in the intensity of their exchange. There is a note of reproach in Peter's speech, and the use of Peter's name gives a stern note to the Lord's response. The addition of "today" (compared to John 13) and the shifting of "thrice" to an emphatic position (in the Greek text—again as compared to John) contribute to the feeling of heightened intensity. Also, now Peter will deny that he even knows Him. Note finally where and when this exchange took place. They were still in the upper room, but this conversation evidently came near the end of the proceedings, because only the contents of verses 35-38 intervened before they left the room and went to the Mount of Olives (22:39). Of course, more may have actually happened than is recorded in 22:35-38, but it seems clear that the warning recorded in Luke is not the same as the one recorded in John, and that the one in John happened first.

I find a comparison of the two warnings in Greek to be impressive and convincing:

John 13:38: "Τὴν ψυχὴν σου ὑπερ εμου θησεις; Αμην, αμην λεγω σοι, ου μη αλεκτωρ φωνηση ἑως οὗ απαρνηση με τρις."

Luke 22:34: "Λεγω σοι, Πετρε, ου μη φωνηση σημερον αλεκτωρ πριν ἡ τρις απαρνηση μη ειδεναι με."

Really, there's no comparison; they are obviously different (even taking into account that they probably spoke Hebrew, so we are looking at a translation). As in John, here again we have a plain affirmation that three denials [at least] will take place before the first rooster crows.

Third, Matthew 26:30-35:

30 And after hymn-singing they went out to the Mount of Olives. 31 Then Jesus says to them, "All of you will be caused to stumble because of me this night, for it is written: 'I will strike the Shepherd and the sheep of the flock will be scattered'. 32 But after I am raised I will go before you to Galilee." 33 Peter answered and said to Him, "Even if everyone *else* is caused to stumble because of you, I will never be caused to stumble!" 34 Jesus said to him, "Assuredly I say to you that this night, before *any* rooster crows, you will deny me three times!" 35 Peter says to Him, "Even if I have to die with you, I will **not** deny you!" All the *other* disciples said the same.

Notice that this exchange took place after they had left the upper room and were on their way to the Garden of Gethsemane. Again the context is distinct from that in Luke or John—here the Lord begins by warning all the disciples.

346

Peter counters by contradicting Him. The Lord's reiterated specific warning to Peter contains no new elements except that now it is "this very night". Peter contradicts again, using a double negative for emphasis—he 'has his back up' and is starting to get impertinent. It seems clear that Matthew records a third warning to Peter, subsequent to those in Luke and John.

Fourth, Mark 14:26-31:

> 26 And after hymn-singing they went out to the Mount of Olives. 27 And Jesus says to them, "All of you will be caused to stumble because of me this night, for it is written: 'I will strike the Shepherd and the sheep will be scattered'. 28 But after I am raised I will go before you to Galilee." 29 But Peter said to Him, "Even if all are caused to stumble, yet I will not be!" 30 And Jesus says to him, "Assuredly I say to you that you, today, even this night, before a rooster crows twice, you will deny me three times!" 31 But he spoke the more vehemently, "If I have to die with you, I will certainly not deny you!" And they all said the same.

The first four verses are virtually identical with the parallel passage in Matthew, so we evidently have the same time and place in both. But now we come to verse 30, the despair of those who defend scriptural inerrancy and the delight of their opponents. Our Lord's statement here differs in several ways from that in Matthew 26:34 but the main problem is the word "twice". What are we to say: Are Matthew 26:34 and Mark 14:30 contradictory accounts of the same warning?

Before settling for that explanation, the precise turn of phrase in Mark 14:30 invites our attention. I believe it will help to see a word for word rendering of what Jesus said. "Assuredly I say to you that you, today, this very night, before twice a rooster crows, thrice you will deny me." The Lord's declaration here seems quite sharp. There is extraordinary emphasis on the second "you". "Twice" is also heavily emphasized. How are we to account for such severity? Peter's effort in verse 29 scarcely seems to merit such a reaction—the reaction recorded in Matthew 26:34 seems much more appropriate. And what shall we say to Mark 14:31? Peter's words here are virtually identical to those in Matthew 26:35 but they are introduced by "but he spoke the more vehemently". Why the vehement reiteration?

I suggest that the solution is to read the following sequence. Matthew 26:30-35[a] then Mark 14:30-31:

> Jesus: "All of you will be caused to stumble because of me this night…"
> Peter: "Though all are caused to stumble because of you, I will never be caused to stumble."
> Jesus: "Assuredly I say to you that this night, before any rooster crows, you will deny me three times."
> Peter: "Even if I have to die with you I will certainly not deny you!"
> Jesus: "Assuredly I say to you that you, today, this very night, before a rooster crows twice, you will deny me three times."

347

Peter, more vehemently: "If I have to die with you, I will certainly not deny you!"

In other words, Mark omitted the exchange recorded in Matthew 26:34-35[a] while Matthew omitted the exchange recorded in Mark 14:30-31[a]. (The editorial comment "and they all said the same" comes at the end of the whole episode.)

On three separate occasions Jesus warned Peter that he would deny Him [at least] three times before a rooster crowed during that night. Peter's responses became increasingly belligerent until after the third warning he even contradicted the Lord with an emphatic double negative (Mat. 26:35). Finally the Lord lost His patience, as it were, and said in effect, "Listen, not only will you deny me three times before a rooster crows once, you will deny me another three times before a rooster crows twice!" For answer Peter repeats his prior statement even more vehemently.

The reader will perceive that in answering the second question I have anticipated the answer to the first one. The Lord warned Peter four times, each Gospel recording a separate instance, and there would be [at least] six denials, three before the first crowing of a rooster (John, Luke, Matthew) and another three before the second (Mark). It remains to enquire whether the several accounts of Peter's denials will countenance this proposal. The relevant passages are Matthew 26:57-75, Mark 14:53-72, Luke 22:54-62 and John 18:15-27.

# How Many Denials?

A cursory reading of these passages suggests that Peter's denials were provoked by eight different challenges—the maid at the outside entrance (John), a maid in the courtyard (Matthew, Mark, Luke), the same maid a second time (Mark), a different maid in the gateway (Matthew), two different men (Luke, John), and the bystanders on two occasions (John and Matthew, Mark). Although it may be possible to combine one pair or another, there is no reasonable way to get the number down to three. But what if there were at least six denials?

To really get the complete picture we need to plot the relevant information on a chart. We need to know who issued the challenge, where, when, just how was it done, what was Peter's reaction, and if a rooster crowed. Because of constraints of space and paper size, I will do a Gospel at a time, beginning with John.[1]

---

[1] A comparison of the contents of the four Gospels reveals that in the main John supplies information not recorded in the other three; he wrote last, with the purpose of supplementing their accounts. Here again, the three denials he describes are all new information, not to be found in the other three.

John 18:15-27:

| | 1st denial | 2nd denial | 3rd denial |
|---|---|---|---|
| Who? | the gatekeeper (f) | servants and operatives | a relative of Malchus |
| Where? | outside gate | by the fire | by the fire (?) |
| When? | at the beginning of the proceedings | a little while after the first one | a little while after the second one (?) |
| How was it done? | she asks: "You aren't one of this man's disciples too, are you?" | they ask: "You aren't one of his disciples too, are you?" | he asks: "Didn't I see you with him in the garden?" |
| What was the reaction? | he says: "I am not!" | he said: "I am not!" | (Peter denied again) |
| Rooster? | (no) | (no) | immediately a rooster crowed |

Luke 22:54-62:

| | 1st denial | 2nd denial | 3rd denial |
|---|---|---|---|
| Who? | a servant girl | a man | another man |
| Where? | by the fire | by the fire (?) | by the fire (?) |
| When? | fairly early on (?) | a little later | about an hour later |
| How was it done? | she looked intently and said: "This man was also with him." | he said: "You also are of them." | he confidently affirmed: "Surely this fellow also was with him, for he is a Galilean." |
| What was the reaction? | he said: "Woman, I do not know him!" | he said: "Man, I am not!" | he said: "Man, I do not know what you are saying!" |
| Rooster? | (no) | (no) | immediately, while he was yet speaking, a rooster crowed. |

Matthew 26:57-75:

|  | 1st denial | 2nd denial | 3rd denial |
|---|---|---|---|
| Who? | a servant girl | another girl | bystanders |
| Where? | by the fire | in the gateway | by the fire (?) |
| When? | fairly early on (?) | a little later | a little later |
| How was it done? | approached him saying "You too were with Jesus the Galilean." | says to the others: "This fellow also was with Jesus the Natsorean." | come up to Peter and say "Really, you too are one of them, because your very accent gives you away!" |
| What was the reaction? | denied before them all: "I don't know what you are saying." | denied with an oath: "I do not know the man!" | began to curse and to swear: "I do not know the man!" |
| Rooster? | (no) | (no) | immediately a rooster crowed |

Mark 14:53-72:

|  | 1st denial | 2nd denial | 3rd denial |
|---|---|---|---|
| Who? | a servant girl | the same girl | bystanders |
| Where? | by the fire | in the fore-court (?) | by the fire (?) |
| When? | fairly early on (?) | a little later | a little later |
| How was it done? | looked at him and said "You also were with Jesus the Nazarene." | says to the bystanders "This is one of them." | say to Peter again: "Surely you are one of them; for you are a Galilean and your speech shows it!" |
| What was the reaction? | denied, saying: "I neither know nor understand what you are saying!" | (he denied again) | he began to curse and to swear: "I do not know this man of whom you speak!" |
| Rooster? | he went out to the fore-court and a rooster crowed | (no) | a rooster crowed a second time |

If you compare all the parameters—who, where, when, how, what—there really is no way to come out with only three denials; even to come out with only six requires some gymnastics (something I attempted to do in an early draft). Let's try to arrange the events in chronological sequence and see what happens.

350

John 18:17 gives us what is clearly the first challenge—as the maid who kept the outside door let Peter in, at John's request, she asked, "You aren't one of this man's disciples too, are you?"[1] Even though John was evidently standing right there, Peter denied, "I am not". He then went in to stand near the fire in the courtyard. The other Gospels have Peter sitting, while John has him standing. Evidently there were quite a few people about—they could not all sit close to the fire. Presumably they would take turns standing near the fire to warm up and then move away a bit to sit down. Thus they, including Peter, would be alternately sitting and standing.

All four Gospels have Peter in the courtyard near the fire (Mat. 26:58 and 69, Mark 14:54 and 66, Luke 22:55, and John 18:18 and 25) and three of them (Matthew, Mark, John) give some account of the council's dealings with Jesus before going on with Peter's denials.[2] We know from Luke 22:61 that Jesus was at a window that looked out on the courtyard, only with His back to it. John is the only one who records that the high priest asked Jesus about His disciples (v. 19)—he is facing Jesus and therefore the open window, and would be speaking loudly enough for everyone in the room to hear clearly, so the people in the courtyard also heard everything he said—then in verse 25 we read, "<u>Therefore</u> they said to him, 'You aren't one of his disciples too, are you?'" I suggest that verse 25 gives us the second challenge and denial. The guards around the fire, presumably prompted by the high priest's questioning Jesus about His disciples, put their question to Peter. He answers them as he did the girl at the gate, "I am not". So far the challengers have only questioned, rather than affirm, but now the tempo quickens.

I take it that the first denials recorded in Matthew (26:69-70), Mark (14:66-68) and Luke (22:56-57) form a single episode. Collating them we may understand the following. A certain serving girl of the high priest came by and saw Peter sitting near the fire. She looked closely at him and said to the others, "This man also was with him" (Luke). She then addressed Peter directly, "You also were with Jesus the Nazarene, of Galilee" (Matthew, Mark). But he denied before them all, saying, "Girl, I don't know him; I neither know nor understand what you're talking about!" He then went out to the fore-court, and a rooster crowed (Mark 14:68). Thus, there were [at least] three denials before the first cockcrow.

---

[1] Everyone there, including the girl, knows that John belongs to Jesus, so her question is perfectly natural, without malice—since John is vouching for Peter, she assumes that Peter must also belong to Jesus. John had heard all the warnings, so when Peter denied at the gate, in his presence, John doubtless kept a close eye on him the whole rest of the night. So we have an eyewitness account. Of course Peter himself would also be an eyewitness, but since he was undergoing satanic interference in his mind, his powers of recollection might be impaired.

[2] It is after midnight and chilly in the courtyard, hence the fire; but there must have been over fifty people in the room where the questioning was going on, and all windows would be open.

I say 'at least' because the third denial in John probably belongs here as well. In 18:26 the verb "to say" is in the present tense, which seems to suggest a brief interval rather than nearly an hour (Luke 22:59); also the challenge is still framed as a question, "Didn't I see you with him in the garden?", rather than a direct accusation, which would fit better toward the beginning than at the end. I see no problem with suggesting that all three of the denials in John were part of the first set and thus he records the first rooster crow. In that event I would understand that there were actually four denials before the first crowing, the three in John plus the first one in the others. Because the rooster crowed "immediately" I imagine that the order would be as follows: the first two in John, in that order, then the first one in the others, and then, as Peter was moving toward the fore-court, the relative of Peter's victim comes alongside and puts his question, so that Peter is at the fore-court when the first rooster crows (Mark 14:68). Actually, I am inclined to suspect that indeed there were four denials before the first cockcrow, which is recorded by both Mark and John (recall that Jesus neither said nor implied that there would be 'only' three).[1]

Now for the next round. In Mark (14:69) the <u>same</u> girl sees Peter again and starts telling the bystanders, "This fellow is one of them". In Matthew (26:71) a different girl sees him and tells the bystanders, "This fellow was with Jesus the Natsorean". In Luke (22:58) a man saw him and said, "You also are one of them". In order to come out with only three denials in the second set, two of these would have to be combined, but as already stated, I am not aware of anything in the Text that rules out the possibility that there could be more than three. It seems to me that there is a progression in Peter's desperation which culminates in his cursing and swearing. On that basis I would consider the instances in Mark and Luke as forming a single episode (if I had to)—the girl speaks, Peter denies, a man backs the girl up and Peter answers, "Man, I am not!" Then the instance in Matthew would be the sixth denial—notice that now Peter adds an oath! Because of the oath I consider that this denial comes after the other two just mentioned; also, Peter has moved out to the gateway. Actually, I am inclined to suspect that there were also four denials before the second cockcrow, so I will start again on that basis.

The girl that provoked the third denial is not about to let Peter get away with that denial. Whether she followed him out to the fore-court, or he moved back toward the fire, I imagine that Mark 14:69 records the fifth denial. If so, Luke 22:58 records the sixth denial, perhaps near the fire. Peter is definitely uncomfortable; he is getting altogether too much unwelcome attention. He moves out to the gateway (perhaps thinking of abandoning the premises)[2] where he is challenged by a different girl (Matthew 26:71); Peter denies with an <u>oath</u> (number seven). Luke (22:59) puts 'about an hour' between denials six

---

[1] The satanic interference in Peter's mind was so effective that not even the rooster's crowing woke him up.

[2] So why didn't Peter just bolt out the gate at that point? I would say that there was supernatural intervention—he simply was not allowed to leave.

and eight, so perhaps Peter was left alone for a bit. However, the 'trial' is over but the bosses are waiting for dawn so they can take Jesus to Pilate. Since the bosses aren't going home, the guards and employees can't either—they are obliged to wait out in the cold, bored stiff—so Peter is now the only show in town.

For the eighth denial three Gospels offer a candidate (Mat. 26:73-74, Mark 14:70-72, Luke 22:59-60). The accounts in Matthew and Mark are very similar and evidently parallel. Since Matthew has the rooster crowing "immediately" and Mark "the second time" this has to be last denial—since by now Peter is cursing and swearing it is fitting that it should be. By that time most of the people on the premises would be aware of Peter and his denials. After listening for a while they closed in, citing his accent. The account in Luke has just one man speaking, but his words are in the same vein. This also has to be the last denial because we are told that the rooster crowed while Peter was still speaking. Evidently a number of people were speaking at once (but not in unison), or in rapid succession, and different writers preserve some of the variety of statement. It would appear that they were ganging up on Peter, because he is driven to curse and to swear. And so we have a second set of four denials, before the second cockcrow. Even then it took a direct look from the Lord (Luke 22:61) to break Satan's spell and bring Peter to a realization of what he had done.

But the question may well be asked, why did each Gospel writer report and speak of only three denials (albeit giving different selections) if there were really six or eight?[1] I suggest that we are looking at a prime example of the grace and sensitivity of God. It would be quite humiliating enough to have denied the Lord three/four times, but to go on to do so another three/four times, even after hearing a rooster crow, would be almost too much to bear. Rather than put the full extent of Peter's ignominy on display the Holy Spirit

---

[1] Some 50% of the Greek manuscripts that contain the Gospels have colophons; these colophons state that Matthew was 'published' 8 years after Christ's ascension, Mark 10 years after, Luke 15 years after and John 32 years after Christ's ascension. (So the four Gospels are arranged in chronological order, not only in our Bibles but in the vast majority of the Greek manuscripts.) "To the Jew first,..."—since Matthew wrote for a Jewish audience, God's priorities dictated that Matthew's should be the first inspired account of our Savior's life on earth to circulate. Then Mark, with Matthew's Gospel open in front of him, and Peter at his elbow, wrote for the Roman mind (since Romans would care nothing for Hebrew Scriptures, Mark removed virtually all reference to fulfilled prophecy). Then Luke, with both Mark and Matthew to hand, wrote the third, for the Greek mind. Then John, with the first three open, wrote to fill in the gaps, preserving important information not provided by the others, for all minds. Now let's consider Peter's denials within that framework. Matthew wrote first, with one cockcrow. Mark says there were really two cockcrows and changes the second denial (1 and 3 are the same in Mark and Matthew). Luke speaks of just one cockcrow, changes the second denial yet again and provides added information (specific) about the third. So just with these three accounts we are up to five denials. John speaks of just one cockcrow but records three new denials, not mentioned by the other three. If these are inspired accounts, then God did it on purpose, and it is up to us to try to figure out why (see my concluding paragraph).

had each writer give only a partial account, enough for the purposes of the record but without flaying Peter unnecessarily. I find it interesting to note that it is Mark who furnishes the necessary clue that there was to be a second set of denials. The opinion is widely held that Peter influenced the composition of this Gospel—this is overtly stated in the introduction to the Gospel found in many manuscripts—and if so he may have insisted on including the hint as to the extent of his humiliation, whereas the others delicately avoided it.

## The Text-critical Problem

Although there are around a hundred textual differences reflected in the printed editions of the Greek Text (in the passages considered), I will confine my remarks here to the set that is especially bothersome in terms of the subject matter of this paper.

There are four places in Mark's account that relate to the two cockcrows: "twice" in 14:30, "and a rooster crowed" in 14:68, "the second time" and "twice" in 14:72. Instances 1, 3 and 4 go together and appear to contradict the account in Matthew, Luke and John. Instance 2 is apparently even worse because according to Mark's account Peter had only denied once when the rooster 'jumped the gun' and crowed before he was supposed to (Jesus had said there would certainly be three denials, as recorded in the other three Gospels). Accordingly, ever since the second century there have been those who tried to 'help' Mark out of his difficulties, tampering with the text.

According to the present state of our knowledge it appears that seven Greek MSS omit "twice" in 14:30 (but they do so in two different ways), nine MSS omit "and a rooster crowed" in 14:68 (but in two ways), five omit "the second time" in 14:72$^a$, and seven omit "twice" in 14:72$^b$ (two others omit the whole clause). The roster of MSS shifts in each case, as does the versional evidence that sides with the omissions. Only three witnesses are thoroughgoing and omit all four: Codex Aleph, cursive 579 and the Old Latin "c" (it$^c$). This is a curious state of affairs. If the purpose of the omissions was to make Mark conform to the other Gospels, only Aleph, 579 and it$^c$ have succeeded. Of the seventeen MSS involved, twelve omit only one of the four; one MS omits two of them; and two MSS omit three (there is some doubt here). Unless someone is prepared to show why Aleph and 579 are to be preferred above every other MS (some 1700 for Mark), and it$^c$ above all the rest of the versional evidence, Latin and otherwise, there is really no reason to take the omissions seriously. However, the eclectic school does take them seriously, even without the requisite demonstration.

It appears that the 'harder reading' canon has come to the aid of the vast majority of the MSS, at least as far as the editors of the 'critical' or eclectic texts presently in vogue are concerned. Instances 1, 3, and 4 are retained in all Nestle and UBS editions (although UBS ascribes "a considerable degree of doubt" to 1 and 3, and "some degree of doubt" to 4—the change in grade here is strange). However, when it comes to instance 2 ("and a rooster crowed") we get some variety: Nestle editions 1 to 25 omit the words; Nestle$^{26}$ and all three UBS editions retain them, but in single brackets (the UBS editors ascribe "a very high degree of doubt" to these words, along with the brackets which themselves signify "dubious textual validity"). Presumably the crucial datum here is that Codex B joins the evidence for omission with instance 2 (but not the others). From W-H through N[25] that was enough to banish the words from the Text. One supposes that it was the "harder reading" canon that restored them to UBS and N[26], if only in brackets. It seems to me that this case affords a clear example of the superficiality that characterizes the work of the eclectic school—to challenge the authenticity of a reading supported by over 99% of the MSS is unreasonable at any time, but to do so in the face of a perfectly obvious motivation for the omission is irresponsible.

The English versions that I have consulted all retain instances 1, 3 and 4, but deal variously with instance 2. AV, LB, NKJV, Phillips and TEV all retain "and a rooster crowed", but LB favors us with a footnote: "This statement is found in only some of the MSS". What might the purpose of such a footnote be? From the use of the word "only" it would appear that the purpose is to raise a doubt in the reader's mind about the reliability of the Text. Why would they want to do that? The use of the word "some" also invites comment: it is their way of referring to some 1700 MSS, against nine! Will the reader not be deceived?

Jerusalem, NASB, NEB, NIV and RSV all omit the clause, but only Jerusalem does so without comment. The footnote in NEB reads, "Some witnesses insert 'and a cock crew'." As in LB, by "some" they mean some 1700 MSS, not to mention massive versional support and almost unanimous lectionary support. Will the reader not be deceived? The footnote in RSV reads, "Other ancient authorities add 'and the cock crowed'." The footnote in NIV reads, "Some early MSS add 'and the rooster crowd'." The footnote in NASB reads, "Later mss. add: 'and a cock crowed'." In order to evaluate such footnotes we would need to know the precise definitions for "ancient", "early" and "later". However, I submit that the uninitiated reader of such footnotes will certainly be misled as to the massive evidence against omission.

The case of the NIV invites special comment. It is the only version that offers a footnote at all four instances. At 14:30 we read, "Some early MSS omit 'twice'." At 14:68 we read, "Some early MSS add 'and the rooster crowed'." At 14:72[a] we read, "Some early MSS omit 'the second time'." At 14:72[b] we read, "Some early MSS omit 'twice'." (The meaning of "some" in the second instance is quite different from that in the other three.) What possible reason could the editors have had for including these footnotes? The immediate effect is to call in question the reliability of the Text at those points. Since the NIV editors held to a high view of Scripture, why would they want to do that? I suppose that it was precisely their concern for the inerrancy of the Text that was at work here. It appears that they did not see any other solution to the seeming discrepancy between Mark and the other Gospels than to imply that Aleph and Old Latin "c" might be right after all. Alas!

The NIV editors are barking up the wrong tree. The worst thing to be done here would be to follow Aleph in deleting all four instances. As already pointed out, the four Gospels record eight different challenges resulting in denials, but no two Gospels have the same selection. So to follow Aleph would force us to try to accommodate eight denials before the first rooster crow, which seems to me to be hopeless. The best thing to be done here is to follow the true Text, which God has graciously caused to be preserved, in this case, in over 99% of the evidence. Peter denied three/four times before the first rooster crow and another set of three/four before the second. The Lord had warned him: "Simon, Simon, indeed Satan has asked for you, that he may sift you as wheat" (Luke 22:31). Peter should have paid attention.

## Implications

One question that arises is this: What about the internal integrity of each account? For instance, in John's account, even if we were to claim that two of the denials occurred before the first rooster crow, while the third denial came after the first and before the second, would this claim do violence to the integrity of John's Gospel? Why would it? Let's review the record. In John 13:38 Jesus said to Peter, "Most assuredly I say to you, a rooster shall not crow till you have denied me three times!" The Lord did not say "only" three times—the emphasis is on the obligatory absence of any rooster crow until Peter has denied three times, at least three times (there is nothing in the Lord's turn of phrase to preclude the possibility that there could be more than three). In the Greek text there is no definite article with "rooster" and there is an emphatic double negative with the verb "to crow"—"a rooster shall not crow!" (These observations also apply in Luke 22:34; in fact, in all four Gospels, in both the predictions and the fulfilments, it is always "a" rooster.)

Turning to John's account of the denials themselves, the first one, at the outside door (18:17), poses no difficulty. The second denial (18:25) likewise poses no difficulty—these two occurred before any rooster crow. But what if the third denial (in John's account, 18:26-27) came after the first crowing?[1] I see no problem, in principle. The Lord made a statement of fact, correctly recorded by John—there had to be three denials before the first rooster crow. This was precisely fulfilled, the Synoptics supplying the third denial. Nothing in John's account precludes the possibility that there should be subsequent crowings. (Anyone who has lived near roosters knows that they start crowing off and on anytime after midnight and at daybreak put on a concert—it seems obvious to me that the first two crowings were overtly controlled by God so as to match Christ's predictions.) In 18:27, after the third denial recorded by John, we read, "and immediately a rooster crowed". John does not say that it was the first crowing. Someone without access to the other Gospels would naturally assume that John records the first rooster crow, and that the three denials he gives are the whole story—but nothing in John's statement demands that interpretation; it simply arises from incomplete information. The other three present several added denials that are clearly distinct. The several Evangelists provide distinct sets of details, much like the pieces of a puzzle,

---

[1] As the reader knows, I believe the third denial in John comes before the first cock crow, but I am covering this possibility for the sake of those who may prefer to have it in the second set.

that must be fitted together to get the whole picture. The several accounts are complementary, not contradictory.

But how about the internal integrity of Mark's account? He is the only one who mentions the second rooster crow, as such, and in fact his account is tied to it. Jesus said, "before a rooster crows twice you will deny me three times," and Mark records three denials before the second rooster crow. Again, Jesus did not say "only" three times, the emphasis is on "you" and "twice". The other Gospels are needed to get the full picture, but Mark's account is entirely self consistent.

And how about Luke? In the warning the emphasis is on the obligatory absence of a rooster crow until Peter has denied three times—at least three times (Jesus did not say "only" three times). After describing three of the denials Luke writes, "and immediately, while he was still speaking, a rooster crowed". "A" rooster—he does not say it was the first. Then Luke has Peter remembering that Jesus said, "Before a rooster crows you will deny me three times". Presumably Peter remembered every detail of all the warnings, but Luke (and each of the other Evangelists) gives only a partial description—in fact, Luke has him recalling the warning recorded by Matthew, not the one he himself gave. A reader having only Luke's account may assume that he told the whole story, but it is an unwarranted assumption. Luke's account is internally consistent yet the precise turn of phrase is such that it does not preclude my proposal.

So what about Matthew? Virtually everything said about Luke above can be repeated here. He has Peter remembering the warning he himself recorded. Again it is "a" rooster. Matthew's account is internally consistent yet the turn of phrase will accommodate my proposal without being violated. All of which brings us back to the question: Why does each Gospel speak of three denials, rather than six, eight or whatever? I don't know; we aren't told. My best guess is that God chose to draw a veil over the full extent of Peter's ignominy (and perhaps to test our disposition when faced with the unexplained). But it remains a plain fact that each Gospel offers a different assortment of challenges and denials, giving a total of at least eight denials.

Another question that I have heard concerns the validity of attempting an exercise such as this at all. I believe that God deliberately brings difficulties into our lives (Job in the ash heap, Abraham on Moriah, Moses herding sheep, Joseph in prison, Daniel with the lions, and on, and on), and puts puzzles in the world, to test our disposition and fiber, and to cause us to grow. "It is the glory of God to conceal a matter, but the glory of kings is to search out a matter" (Proverbs 25:2). [Even if you aren't a king, you get the point.] The case of John the baptizer in prison comes closer to home. He is frustrated, maybe disillusioned; he did his job but his expectations aren't being realized. So he sends two disciples to ask Jesus for an explanation. In effect Jesus answers, "Check the evidence; do your homework", and closes with, "And blessed is he who is not offended because of me" (Matthew 11:6). When faced with the difficult or unexplained we must be careful not to rebel. It is much better to obey the command recorded in 1 Peter 3:15. "Sanctify the Lord God in your hearts, and always be ready to give a defense to everyone who asks you a reason for the hope that is in you,...." Since opponents of a Text with objective authority have used the accounts of Peter's denials as an argument against any idea of inerrancy, I consider that a defense of that inerrancy is in order.

# APPENDIX I
# Is NT Textual Criticism a Science?

Have you ever heard or read (or said) the phrase, 'the science of NT textual criticism'? How about the phrase, 'textual critic'? So what does a critic do? He criticizes. What does he criticize? In this case it is the text of the NT in Greek. But just what is he criticizing? A literary critic looks at things like style and choice of vocabulary; a commentator tries to decide what was the meaning intended by the author of the text. So what does a textual critic do? He attempts to reconstruct the original wording of a text—notice that he is assuming that the original wording is 'lost', in the sense that no one knows for sure what it is, or was. (Notice also that this places the critic above the text, to which I will return.) Textual criticism only exists for texts whose original wording is deemed to be 'lost'. No one does textual criticism on today's newspaper, or last week's news magazine. No one even does textual criticism on the 1611 King James Version, since we still have printed copies thereof. Any and all arguments surrounding the KJV come under other headings; they are not textual criticism.

Anyone familiar with the terrain knows that for the last 150 years (at least) the academic world has been dominated by the notion that the original wording of the NT text is in fact 'lost'. Just to illustrate, some 65 years ago Robert M. Grant wrote, "it is generally recognized that the original text of the Bible cannot be recovered".[1] For a number of further references echoing that sentiment please see page 3 at the beginning. Before attempting to rebut that fiction [canard?], as I believe, I will sketch a bit of relevant history.

## A Bit of Relevant History

The discipline as we know it is basically a 'child' of Western Europe and its colonies; the Eastern Orthodox Churches have generally not been involved. (They have always known that the true Text lies within the Byzantine tradition.) In the year 1500 the Christianity of Western Europe was dominated by the Roman Catholic Church, whose pope claimed the exclusive right to interpret Scripture. That Scripture was the Latin Vulgate, which the laity was not allowed to read. Martin Luther's 95 theses were posted in 1517. Was it mere chance that the first printed Greek Text of the NT was published the year before? As the Protestant Reformation advanced, it was declared that the authority of Scripture exceeded that of the pope, and that every believer had the right to read and interpret the Scriptures. The authority of the Latin Vulgate was also challenged, since the NT was written in Greek. Of course the Vatican library held many Greek MSS, no two of which were identical (at least in the

---

[1] R.M. Grant, "The Bible of Theophilus of Antioch", *Journal of Biblical Literature*, LXVI (1947), 173. Notice the pessimism, it 'cannot be recovered'. In that event, the critics are wasting their time, and ours. Surely, because we would have no way of knowing whether or not they have found it.

Gospels), so the Roman Church challenged the authenticity of the Greek Text. In short, the Roman Church forced the Reformation to come to grips with textual variation among the Greek MSS. But they didn't know how to go about it, because this was a new field of study and they simply were not in possession of a sufficient proportion of the relevant evidence.[1] (They probably didn't even know that the Mt. Athos peninsula with its twenty monasteries existed.)

In 1500 the Roman Catholic Establishment was corrupt, morally bankrupt, and discredited among thinking people. The Age of Reason and humanism were coming to the fore. More and more people were deciding that they could do better without the god of the Roman Establishment. The new imagined freedom from supernatural supervision was intoxicating, and many had no interest in accepting the authority of Scripture ('sola Scriptura'). Further, it would be naive in the extreme to exclude the supernatural from consideration, and not allow for satanic activity behind the scenes—Ephesians 2:2.[2] 'Sons of the disobedience' joined the attack against Scripture. The so-called 'higher criticism' denied divine inspiration altogether. Others used the textual variation to argue that in any case the original wording was 'lost', there being no objective way to determine what it may have been (that is, they could not perceive such a way at that time).

The uncritical assumption that 'oldest equals best' was an important factor and became increasingly so as earlier uncials came to light. Both Codex Vaticanus and Codex Bezae were available early on, and they have thousands of disagreements, just in the Gospels (in Acts, Bezae is wild almost beyond belief). **If** 'oldest equals best', and the oldest MSS are in constant and massive disagreement between/among themselves, then the recovery of a lost text becomes hopeless. Did you get that? **Hopeless, totally hopeless!** However, I

---

[1] Family 35, being by far the largest and most cohesive group of MSS, was poorly represented in the libraries of Western Europe. For that matter, very few MSS of whatever text-type had been sufficiently collated to allow for any tracing of the transmissional history.

[2] Strictly speaking the Text has "according to the Aeon of this world, according to the ruler of the domain of the air"—the phrases are parallel, so 'Aeon' and 'ruler' have the same referent, a specific person or being. This spirit is presently at work (present tense) in 'the sons of the disobedience'. 'Sons' of something are characterized by that something, and the something in this case is 'the' disobedience (the Text has the definite article)—a continuation of the original rebellion against the Sovereign of the universe. Anyone in rebellion against the Creator is under satanic influence, direct or indirect (in most cases a demon acts as Satan's agent, when something more than the influence of the surrounding culture is required—almost all human cultures have ingredients of satanic provenance; this includes the academic culture [the academic requirement that one demonstrate 'acquaintance with the literature' obliges one to waste time on all that Satan's servants have written—consider 1 Corinthians 3:18-20]). Anyone in rebellion against the Creator will also have strongholds of Satan in his mind. Since Satan is the 'father' of lies (John 8:44), anytime you embrace a lie you invite him into your mind—this applies to any of his sophistries (2 Corinthians 10:5) currently in vogue, such as materialism, humanism, relativism, Marxism, Freudianism, Hortianism, etc.

have argued that 'oldest equals <u>worst</u>', and that changes the picture, radically.[1]

Since everyone is influenced (not necessarily controlled) by his milieu, this was true of the Reformers. In part (at least) the Reformation was a 'child' of the Renaissance, with its emphasis on reason. Recall that on trial Luther said he could only recant if convinced by Scripture <u>and reason</u>. So far so good, but many did not want Scripture, and that left only reason. Further, since reason cannot explain or deal with the supernatural, those who emphasize reason are generally unfriendly toward the supernatural. [To this day the so-called historic or traditional Protestant denominations have trouble dealing with the supernatural.]

Before Adolf Deissmann published his *Light from the Ancient East* (1910), (being a translation of *Licht vom Osten*, 1908), wherein he demonstrated that Koiné Greek was the *lingua franca* in Jesus' day, there even being a published grammar explaining its rules, only classical Greek was taught in the universities. But the NT is written in Koiné. Before Deissmann's benchmark work, there were two positions on the NT Greek: 1) it was a debased form of classical Greek, or 2) it was a 'Holy Ghost' Greek, invented for the NT. The second option was held mainly by pietists; the academic world preferred the first, which raised the natural question: if God were going to inspire a NT, why wouldn't He do it in 'decent' Greek?

---

[1] The benchmark work on this subject is Herman C. Hoskier's *Codex B and its Allies* (2 vols.; London: Bernard Quaritch, 1914). The first volume (some 500 pages) contains a detailed and careful discussion of hundreds of obvious errors in Codex B; the second (some 400 pages) contains the same for Codex Aleph. He affirms that in the Gospels alone these two MSS differ well over 3,000 times, which number does not include minor errors such as spelling (II, 1). Well now, simple logic demands that one or the other has to be wrong those 3,000+ times; they can't both be right, quite apart from the times when they are <u>both</u> wrong. **No amount of subjective preference can obscure the fact that they are poor copies, objectively so.**

John William Burgon personally collated what in his day were 'the five old uncials' (א,A,B,C,D). Throughout his works he repeatedly calls attention to the *concordia discors*, the prevailing confusion and disagreement, which the early uncials display between themselves. Luke 11:2-4 offers one example.

"The five Old Uncials" (אABCD) falsify the Lord's Prayer as given by St. Luke in no less than forty-five words. But so little do they agree among themselves, that they throw themselves into six different combinations in their departures from the Traditional Text; and yet they are never able to agree among themselves as to one single various reading: while only once are more than two of them observed to stand together, and their grand point of union is no less than an omission of the article. Such is their eccentric tendency, that in respect of thirty-two out of the whole forty-five words they bear in turn solitary evidence. (*The Traditional Text of the Holy Gospels Vindicated and Established*. Arranged, completed, and edited by Edward Miller. London: George Bell and Sons, 1896, p. 84.)

Yes indeed, <u>oldest equals worst</u>. For more on this subject, please see pages 81-85, above.

All of this placed the defenders of an inspired Greek Bible on the defensive, with the very real problem of deciding where best to set up their defense perimeter. Given the prevailing ignorance concerning the relevant evidence, their best choice appeared to be an appeal to Divine Providence. God providentially chose the TR, so that was the text to be used (the 'traditional' text).[1]

To all appearances Satan was winning the day, but he still had a problem: the main Protestant versions (in German, English, Spanish, etc.) were all based on the *Textus Receptus*, as were doctrinal statements and 'prayer books'. Enter F.J.A. Hort, a quintessential 'son of the disobedience'. Hort did not believe in the divine inspiration of the Bible, nor in the divinity of Jesus Christ. Since he embraced the Darwinian theory as soon as it appeared, he presumably did not believe in God.[2] His theory of NT textual criticism, published in 1881,[3] was based squarely on the presuppositions that the NT was not inspired, that no special care was afforded it in the early decades, and that in consequence the original wording was lost—lost beyond recovery, at least by objective means. His theory swept the academic world and continues to dominate the discipline to this day.[4]

Moreover, Hort claimed that as a result of his work only a thousandth part of the NT text could be considered to be in doubt, and this was joyfully received by the rank and file, since it seemed to provide assurance about the reliability

---

[1] Please note that I am not criticizing Burgon and others; they did what they could, given the information available to them. They knew that the Hortian theory and resultant Greek text could not be right.

[2] For documentation of all this, and a good deal more besides, in Hort's own words, please see the biography written by his son. A.F. Hort, *Life and Letters of Fenton John Anthony Hort* (2 vols.; London: Macmillan and Co. Ltd., 1896). The son made heavy use of the father's plentiful correspondence, whom he admired. (In those days a two volume 'Life', as opposed to a one volume 'Biography', was a posthumous status symbol.) Many of my readers were taught, as was I, that one must not question/judge someone else's motives. But wait just a minute; where did such an idea come from? It certainly did not come from God, who expects the spiritual person to evaluate everything (1 Corinthians 2:15). Since there are only two spiritual kingdoms in this world (Matthew 12:30, Luke 11:23), then the idea comes from the other side. By eliminating motive, one also eliminates presupposition, which is something that God would never do, since presupposition governs interpretation (Matthew 22:29, Mark 12:24). Which is why we should always expect a true scholar to state his presuppositions. I have repeatedly stated mine, but here they are again: 1) The Sovereign Creator of the universe exists; 2) He delivered a written revelation to the human race; 3) He has preserved that revelation intact to this day.

[3] B.F. Westcott and F.J.A. Hort, *The New Testament in the Original Greek* (2 Vols.; London: Macmillan and Co., 1881). The second volume explains the theory, and is generally understood to be Hort's work.

[4] For a thorough discussion of that theory, please see chapters 3 and 4 above.

of that text—however, of course, that claim applied only to the W-H text (probably the worst published NT in existence, to this day). [1]

# The Nature of a Scientific Exercise

So much for my sketch of history. I will now return to the question in the title. To begin, I observe and insist that in any scientific exercise a rigorous distinction must be made between evidence, interpretation, and presupposition. It is dishonest to represent one's presuppositions as being part of the evidence (opinion is not evidence). So, if NT textual criticism is to be a 'science', presuppositions must be excluded. But if we exclude the presupposition that the original wording is 'lost', then textual criticism ceases to exist; and how can you have a 'science' of something that doesn't exist? Science is one thing; theory is another. A theory is based on presupposition, of necessity, so it is legitimate to speak of a Hortian <u>theory</u> of textual criticism, since he considered the original wording to be lost. My own theory does not include textual criticism, since I consider that the original wording is <u>not</u> lost. I defend a theory of the divine preservation of the NT Text. [2]

**By now it should be evident to the reader that the question of a 'lost' original is the crux, the central issue in any attempt to identify the original wording of the NT.** So to that issue I now turn. To be fair, I need to recognize two definitions of 'lost': 1) lost beyond recovery, at least by objective means; 2) lost from view, in the sense that the available evidence has not been sufficiently studied to permit an empirical choice between/among competing variants. I consider that this book provides more than enough evidence to demonstrate that the first definition is false. The Hortian theory and all derivatives thereof, such as eclecticism (of whatever type), is not science, and may not honestly be called science. The second definition allows for scientific procedure. I suggest and recommend that we start using the term 'manuscriptology', rather than 'textual criticism'—manuscriptology refers to the study of the MSS, and is neutral as to presupposition. Any scientific exercise should begin with the evidence; so what is the evidence?

The primary evidence is furnished by the continuous text manuscripts (Greek) of the NT. The evidence furnished by the lectionaries is secondary. The evidence furnished by ancient versions and patristic citations is tertiary. Genuine historical evidence (to the extent that this can be determined) is ancillary. Where the primary evidence is unequivocal, the remaining types

---

[1] I would say that their text is mistaken with reference to 10% of the words—the Greek NT has roughly 140,000 words, so the    W-H text is mistaken with reference to 14,000 of them. I would say that the so-called 'critical' text currently in vogue is 'only' off with reference to some 12,000, an improvement (small though it be). And just by the way, how wise is it to use a NT prepared by a servant of Satan?

[2] I consider myself to be a textual scholar, not critic. The Text is above me, not the opposite. In eclecticism the critic is above the text, is above the evidence; instead of faithfully following the evidence, he makes the evidence follow him. The MSS are reduced to the role of 'supplier of readings'.

should not come into play. For example, at any given point in the four Gospels there will be around 1,700 extant continuous text MSS, representing all lines of transmission and all locales.[1] Where they all agree, there can be no legitimate doubt as to the original wording. But what if an early Papyrus comes to light with a variant, does that change the picture? The very fact of being early suggests that it is bad; why wasn't it used and worn out?

We have probably all heard/read the canard, 'manuscripts are to be weighed, not counted'. The basic meaning of the verb 'to weigh' refers to an objective procedure; it is done with physically verifiable weights. But do the followers of Hort (who are the main ones who keep repeating it) 'weigh' manuscripts using objective criteria? They do not, which is why I call it a 'canard'. That said, however, I submit for the consideration of all concerned that it is indeed possible to weigh MSS using objective criteria. I will here draw on my treatment of the subject on pages 97-99 above.

Just how are MSS to be weighed? And who might be competent to do the weighing? As the reader is by now well aware, Hort and most subsequent scholars have done their 'weighing' on the basis of so-called 'internal evidence'—the two standard criteria are, 'choose the reading which fits the context' and 'choose the reading which explains the origin of the other reading'.

One problem with this has been well stated by E.C. Colwell. "As a matter of fact these two standard criteria for the appraisal of the internal evidence of readings can easily cancel each other out and leave the scholar free to choose in terms of his own prejudgments."[2] Further, "the more lore the scholar knows, the easier it is for him to produce a reasonable defense of both readings…"[3] The whole process is so subjective that it makes a mockery of the word 'weigh'. The basic meaning of the term involves an evaluation made by an objective instrument. If we wish our weighing of MSS to have objective validity, we must find an objective procedure.

How do we evaluate the credibility of a witness in real life? We watch how he acts, listen to what he says and how he says it, and listen to the opinion of his neighbors and associates. If we can demonstrate that a witness is a habitual liar or that his critical faculties are impaired then we receive his testimony with skepticism. It is quite possible to evaluate MSS in a similar way, to a considerable extent, and it is hard to understand why scholars have generally neglected to do so.

---

[1] Of course we know that there are many MSS not yet 'extant', not yet identified and catalogued, so the number can only go up.

[2] Colwell, "External Evidence and New Testament Criticism", *Studies in the History and Text of the New Testament*, eds. B.L. Daniels and M.J. Suggs (Salt Lake City: University of Utah Press, 1967), p. 3.

[3] *Ibid.*, p. 4.

Please refer back to the evidence given in the discussion of the oldest MSS (pages 81-85).[1] Can we objectively 'weigh' $P^{66}$ as a witness? (It is the oldest one of any size.) Well, in the space of John's Gospel (not complete) it has over 900 clear, indubitable errors—as a witness to the identity of the text of John it has misled us over 900 times. Is $P^{66}$ a credible witness? I would argue that

---

[1] $P^{75}$ is placed close to $P^{66}$ in date. Though not as bad as $P^{66}$, it is scarcely a good copy. Colwell found $P^{75}$ to have about 145 itacisms plus 257 other singular readings, 25 percent of which are nonsensical (E.C. Colwell, "Scribal Habits in Early Papyri: A Study in the Corruption of the Text", *The Bible in Modern Scholarship*, ed. J.P. Hyatt [New York: Abingdon Press, 1965], pp. 374-76). Although Colwell gives the scribe of $P^{75}$ credit for having tried to produce a good copy, $P^{75}$ looks good only by comparison with $P^{66}$. (If you were asked to write out the Gospel of John by hand, would you make over 400 mistakes? Try it and see!) It should be kept in mind that the figures offered by Colwell deal only with errors which are the exclusive property of the respective MSS. They doubtless contain many other errors which happen to be found in some other witness(es) as well. In other words, they are actually worse even than Colwell's figures indicate.

$P^{45}$, though a little later in date, will be considered next because it is the third member in Colwell's study. He found $P^{45}$ to have approximately 90 itacisms plus 275 other singular readings, 10 percent of which are nonsensical (*Ibid.*). However $P^{45}$ is shorter than $P^{66}$ ($P^{75}$ is longer) and so is not comparatively so much better as the figures might suggest at first glance. Colwell comments upon $P^{45}$ as follows:

Another way of saying this is that when the scribe of $P^{45}$ creates a singular reading, it almost always makes sense; when the scribes of $P^{66}$ and $P^{75}$ create singular readings, they frequently do not make sense and are obvious errors. Thus $P^{45}$ must be given credit for a much greater density of intentional changes than the other two (*Ibid.*, p. 376).

As an editor the scribe of $P^{45}$ wielded a sharp axe. The most striking aspect of his style is its conciseness. The dispensable word is dispensed with. He omits adverbs, adjectives, nouns, participles, verbs, personal pronouns—without any compensating habit of addition. He frequently omits phrases and clauses. He prefers the simple to the compound word. In short, he favors brevity. He shortens the text in at least fifty places in **singular readings alone**. But he does **not** drop syllables or letters. His shortened text is readable (*Ibid.*, p. 383).

$P^{46}$ is thought by some to be as early as $P^{66}$. Zuntz's study of this manuscript is well-known. "In spite of its neat appearance (it was written by a professional scribe and corrected—but very imperfectly—by an expert), $P^{46}$ is by no means a good manuscript. The scribe committed very many blunders.... My impression is that he was liable to fits of exhaustion" (Gunther Zuntz, *The Text of the Epistles* [London: Oxford University Press, 1953], p.18).

It should be remarked in passing that Codex B is noted for its 'neat appearance' also, but it should not be assumed that therefore it must be a good copy. Even Hort conceded that the scribe of B "reached by no means a high standard of accuracy" (Westcott and Hort, p. 233). Aleph is acknowledged on every side to be worse than B in every way. Zuntz says further: " $P^{46}$ abounds with scribal blunders, omissions, and also additions" (*Op.Cit.*, p. 212).

the scribe who wrote the papyrus did his work very badly. Of his innumerable faults, only a fraction (less than one in ten) have been corrected and even that fraction—as often happens in manuscripts—grows smaller and smaller towards the end of the book. Whole pages have been left without any correction, however greatly they were in need of it (*Ibid.*, p. 252).

neither of the scribes of P[66] and P[75] knew Greek; should we not say that as witnesses they were impaired?[1]

Recall from Colwell's study that the scribe of P[45] evidently made numerous **deliberate** changes in the text—should we not say that he was morally impaired? In any case, he has repeatedly misinformed us. Shall we still trust him? Similarly, it has been demonstrated that Aleph and B have over 3,000 mistakes between them, just in the Gospels. Aleph is clearly worse than B, but probably not twice as bad—at least 1,000 of those mistakes are B's. Do Aleph and B fit your notion of a good witness?[2] Again I say: oldest equals worst!

We really need to understand that age guarantees nothing about quality. Each witness must be evaluated on its own, quite apart from age. Further, and perhaps more to the point, we need to know how a given MS relates to others. Once a MS has been empirically identified as belonging to a family (line of transmission), then it is no longer an independent witness to the original—it is a witness to the family archetype. As Colwell so well put it, "the crucial question for early as for late witnesses is still, 'WHERE DO THEY FIT INTO A PLAUSIBLE RECONSTRUCTION OF THE HISTORY OF THE MANUSCRIPT TRADITION?'"[3]

Lamentably, the Hortian theory, allied to the fiction that 'oldest equals best', has had a soporific effect upon the discipline such that comparatively few MSS have been fully collated, and in consequence few families have been empirically defined. A rough idea based on spot checking is not adequate; there is too much mixture.

## The Transmission of the Text

Going back to the 1,700 extant MSS for any given point in the Gospels, it should be evident that a variant in a single MS, of whatever age, is irrelevant—it is a false witness to its family archetype, at that point, nothing more. If a number of MSS share a variant, but do not belong to the same family, then they made the mistake independently and are false witnesses to their respective family archetypes—there is no dependency. Where a group of MSS

---

[1] The fact that the transcriber of P[75] copied letter by letter and that of P[66] syllable by syllable (Colwell, "Scribal Habits", p. 380) suggests strongly that neither one knew Greek. When transcribing in a language you know you copy phrase by phrase, or at the very least word by word. P[66] has so many nonsensical readings that the transcriber could not have known the meaning of the text. Anyone who has ever tried to transcribe a text of any length by hand (not typewriter) in a language he does not understand will know that it is a taxing and dreary task. Purity of transmission is not to be expected under such circumstances.

[2] If you copied the four Gospels by hand, do you think you could manage to make a thousand mistakes? Try it and see!

[3] Colwell, "Hort Redivivus: A Plea and a Program", *Studies in Methodology in Textual Criticism of the New Testament*, E.C. Colwell (Leiden: E.J. Brill, 1969), p. 157. [Emphasis in the original.]

evidently reflect correctly the archetypal form of their family, then we are dealing with a family (not the individual MSS). Families need to be evaluated just as we evaluate individual MSS. <u>It is possible to assign a credibility quotient to a family, based on objective criteria</u>. But of course any and all families must first be empirically identified and defined, and such identification depends upon the full collation of MSS.

Although the discipline has (so far) neglected to do its homework (collating MSS), still a massive majority of MSS should be convincing. For example, if a variant enjoys 99% attestation from the primary witnesses, this means that it totally dominates any genealogical 'tree', because it dominated the global transmission of the text. The INTF *Text und Textwert* series, practitioners of the Claremont profile method, H.C. Hoskier, von Soden, Burgon, Scrivener—in short, anyone who has collated any number of MSS—have all demonstrated that the Byzantine bulk of MSS is by no means monolithic. There are any number of streams and rivulets. (Recall that Wisse posited 34 groups within the Byzantine bulk, with 70 subgroups.) It is clear that there was no 'stuffing the ballot box'; there was no 'papal' decree; there was no recension imposed by ecclesiastical authority. In short, the transmission was predominantly normal.

> Under normal circumstances the older a text is than its rivals, the greater are its chances to survive in a plurality or a majority of the texts extant at any subsequent period. But the **oldest** text of all is the autograph. Thus it ought to be taken for granted that, barring some radical dislocation in the history of transmission, a majority of texts will be far more likely to represent correctly the character of the original than a small minority of texts. This is especially true when the ratio is an overwhelming 8:2. Under any reasonably normal transmissional conditions, it would be…quite impossible for a later text-form to secure so one-sided a preponderance of extant witnesses.[1]

I insist that the transmission of the NT Text was in fact predominantly normal, based on historical evidence. Chapter 5 above lists and discusses that evidence (which please see). But here is a thumbnail sketch:

1) The authors of the NT books believed they were writing Scripture;
2) The Apostles recognized that their colleagues were writing Scripture;
3) The 'Church Fathers' of the I and II centuries regarded the NT writings as Scripture;
4) The NT writings were used along with the OT by the Christian congregations from very early on;
5) The early Christians were concerned about the purity of the NT Text.

---

[1] Z.C. Hodges, "A Defense of the Majority Text" (unpublished course notes, Dallas Theological Seminary, 1975), p. 4. Appendix C above shows that the mathematical science of statistical probability gives ample support to Hodges' statement. It is statistically impossible for a late comer to dominate the transmission.

6) What regions started out with the Autographs? Aegean area (18-24), Rome (2-7), Palestine  (0-3), Egypt (0).
7) Where was the Church strongest during the II and III centuries? Asia Minor and the Aegean area.
8) Where was Greek used most and longest? Aegean area and Asia Minor.
9) What are the implications of Diocletian's campaign and the Donatist movement?

I submit that the evidence is clear to the effect that the transmission was in fact predominantly normal. I again borrow from pages 70-71 above.

Now then, what sort of a picture may we expect to find in the surviving witnesses, given the understanding that the history of the transmission of the New Testament Text was predominantly normal? We may expect a broad spectrum of copies, showing minor differences due to copying mistakes but all reflecting one common tradition. The simultaneous existence of abnormal transmission in the earliest centuries would result in a sprinkling of copies, helter-skelter, outside of that main stream. The picture would look something like the following figure.

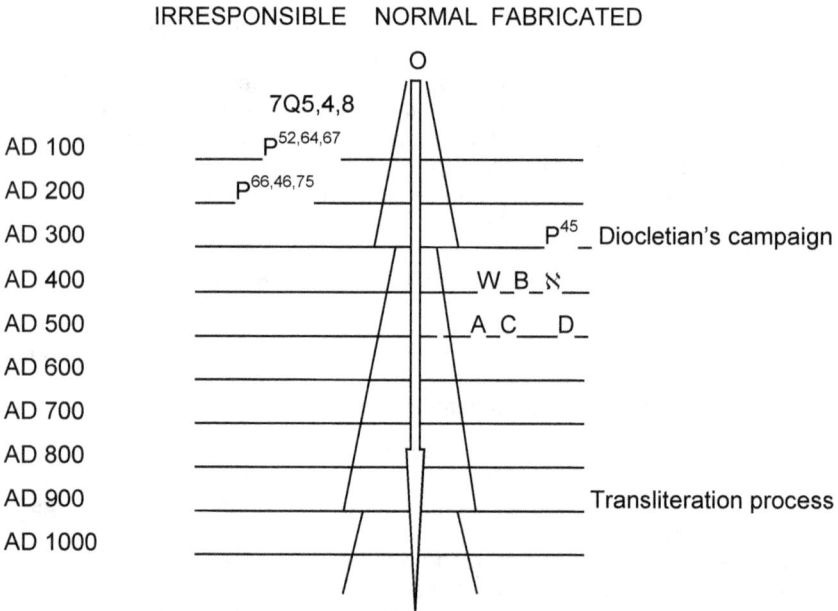

The MSS within the cones represent the 'normal' transmission. To the left I have plotted some possible representatives of what we might style the 'irresponsible' transmission of the text—the copyists produced poor copies through incompetence or carelessness but did not make deliberate changes. To the right I have plotted some possible representatives of what we might style the 'fabricated' transmission of the text—the scribes made deliberate changes in the text (for whatever reasons), producing fabricated copies, not true copies. I am well aware that the MSS plotted on the figure above contain both careless and deliberate errors, in different proportions (7Q5,4,8 and P$^{52,64,67}$ are too fragmentary to permit the classification of their errors as deliberate rather than careless), so that any classification such as I attempt here must be relative and gives a distorted picture. Still, I venture to insist that ignorance, carelessness, officiousness and malice all left their mark upon the transmission of the New Testament text, and we must take account of them in any attempt to reconstruct the history of that transmission.

As the figure suggests, I argue that Diocletian's campaign had a purifying effect upon the stream of transmission. In order to withstand torture rather than give up your MS(S), you would have to be a truly committed believer, the sort of person who would want good copies of the Scriptures. Thus it was probably the more contaminated MSS that were destroyed, in the main, leaving the purer MSS to replenish the earth (please see the section "Imperial repression of the N.T." in Chapter 6). The arrow within the cones represents Family 35 (see Chapter 7).

Another consideration suggests itself—if, as reported, the Diocletian campaign was most fierce and effective in the Byzantine area, the numerical advantage of the 'Byzantine' text-type over the 'Western' and 'Alexandrian' would have been reduced, giving the latter a chance to forge ahead. But it did not happen. The Church, in the main, refused to propagate those forms of the Greek text. Codices B, א, D, etc., have no 'children'. Since it is impossible to produce an archetypal form for either the 'Western' or the 'Alexandrian' text-types, so-called, based on manuscript evidence, do they even exist?

# The 'Crux' of a 'Lost' Original

Returning to the 'crux', is/was the original wording lost? I answer with an emphatic, "**No**". It certainly exists within the Byzantine bulk, but what do we do if there is confusion within that bulk? (To insist that it must be one of the existing variants is better than nothing, I suppose, but I, at least, want to identify the original wording.) To my mind, any time at least 90% of the primary witnesses agree, there can be no reasonable question; it is statistically impossible that a non-original reading could score that high.[1] Any time a reading garners an attestation of at least 80%, its probability is very high. But for perhaps 2% of the words in the NT the attestation falls below 80% (a disproportionate number being in the Apocalypse), and at this point we need to shift our attention from MSS to families.[2] I have already mentioned assigning a credibility quotient to each family, based on objective criteria, and this needs to be done. Unfortunately, there is a great deal of 'homework' waiting to be done

---

1 See Appendix C above.

2 Once all MSS have been collated and have been empirically assigned to families, then we can confine our attention to those families, from the start (as I have done in the Apocalypse).

in this area (so far as I know, only Family 35 has an empirically defined profile),**1** but enough work has been done to allow for some rough ideas.

We are indebted to the *Institut für Neutestamentliche Textforschung* for their *Text und Textwert* series. A careful look at their collations indicates that there probably is no $K^x$, anywhere (and remember Wisse). Take, for example, the *TuT* volumes on John's Gospel, chapters 1-10. They examined a total of 1,763 MSS (for 153 variant sets) and included the results in the two volumes. Pages 54 - 90 (volume 1) contain "Groupings according to degrees of agreement" "agreeing more often with each other than with the majority text". Only one group symbol is used, $K^r$—the first representative of the family, MS 18, heads a group of about 120 MSS, but all subsequent representatives have only a $K^r$ (that I call $f^{35}$). Following $K^r$, there are 22 groups with between 52 and 25 MSS, and all but four of them are really $K^r$ / $f^{35}$, and the same holds for a number of smaller groups, so their $K^r$ should probably be over 200 (I would say that Family 35 in the Gospels has over 250 representatives, but their ranking here is based on only 153 variant sets, in half of John).

Consider the largest group apart from $K^r$: 2103. Of its 52 members, 15 show only a 95% agreement with MS 2103. If those 52 MSS are ever collated throughout the Gospels, it is entirely predictable that the 'group' will shrink considerably; it may even disappear.

Some years ago now, Maurice Robinson did a complete collation of 1,389 MSS that contain the P.A.,**2** and I had William Pierpont's photocopy of those collations in my possession for two months, spending most of that time studying those collations. As I did so, it became obvious to me that von Soden 'regularized' his data, arbitrarily 'creating' the alleged archetypal form for his

---

**1** So far as I know, neither $f^1$ nor $f^{13}$ exists outside of the Gospels, but even there, has anyone ever produced an empirically defined profile for either one? Consider the following statement by Metzger:

It should be observed that, in accord with the theory that members of $f^1$ and $f^{13}$ were subject to progressive accommodation to the later Byzantine text, scholars have established the text of these families by adopting readings of family witnesses that differ from the Textus Receptus. Therefore the citation of the siglum $f^1$ and $f^{13}$ may, in any given instance, signify a minority of manuscripts (or even only one) that belong to the family. (*A Textual Commentary on the Greek New Testament* [companion to UBS$^3$], p. xii.)

Would it be unreasonable to say that such a proceeding is unfair to the reader? Does it not mislead the user of the apparatus? At least as used by the UBS editions, those sigla do not represent empirically defined profiles.

**2** 240 MSS omit the PA, 64 of which are based on Theophylact's commentary. Fourteen others have lacunae, but are not witnesses for total omission. A few others certainly contain the passage but the microfilm is illegible. So, 1389 + 240 + 14 + 7(?) = about 1650 MSS checked by Robinson. That does not include Lectionaries, of which he also checked a fair number. (These are microfilms held by the *Institut* in Münster. We now know that there are many more extant MSS, and probably even more that are not yet 'extant'.) Unfortunately, so far as I know, Robinson has yet to publish his collations, thus making them available to the public at large.

first four families, $\mathbf{M}^{1,2,3,4}$ —if they exist at all, they are rather fluid. His $\mathbf{M}^{5\&6}$ do exist, having distinct profiles for the purpose of showing that they are different, but they are a bit 'squishy', with enough internal confusion to make the choice of the archetypal form to be arbitrary. In fact, I suspect that they will have to be subdivided. In contrast to the above, his $\mathbf{M}^7$ (that I call Family 35) has a solid, unambiguous profile—the archetypal form is demonstrable, empirically determined.

As for the Apocalypse, of the nine groups that Hoskier identified, only his Complutensian (that I call Family 35) is homogenous. Of the others, the main ones all have sub-divisions, that will require their own profile.

I will borrow from pages 130-32 above. Given my presuppositions, I consider that I have good reason for declaring the divine preservation of the precise original wording of the complete New Testament Text, to this day. That wording is reproduced in my edition of the Greek NT, available from www.walkinhiscommandments.com. BUT PLEASE NOTE: whether or not the archetype of $f^{35}$ is the Autograph (as I claim), the fact remains that the MSS collated for this study reflect an incredibly careful transmission of their source, and this throughout the middle ages. My presuppositions include: God exists; He inspired the Biblical Text; He promised to preserve it for a thousand generations (1 Chronicles 16:15); so He must have an active, ongoing interest in that preservation [there have been fewer than 300 generations since Adam, so He has a ways to go!]. **If He was preserving the original wording in some line of transmission other than $f^{35}$, would that transmission be any less careful than what I have demonstrated for $f^{35}$?** I think not. So any line of transmission characterized by internal confusion is disqualified—this includes **all** the other lines of transmission that I have seen so far!1

On the basis of the evidence so far available I affirm the following:

1) The original wording was never 'lost', and its transmission down through the years was basically normal, being recognized as inspired material from the beginning.

2) That normal process resulted in lines of transmission.

3) To delineate such lines, MSS must be grouped empirically on the basis of a shared mosaic of readings.

4) Such groups or families must be evaluated for independence and credibility.

5) The largest clearly defined group is Family 35.

6) Family 35 is demonstrably independent of all other lines of transmission throughout the NT.

7) Family 35 is demonstrably ancient, dating to the 3$^{rd}$ century, at least.

---

**1** Things like $\mathbf{M}^6$ and $\mathbf{M}^5$ in John 7:53-8:11 come to mind.

8) Family 35 representatives come from all over the Mediterranean area; the geographical distribution is all but total.

9) Family 35 is not a recension, was not created at some point subsequent to the Autographs.

10) Family 35 is an objectively/empirically defined entity throughout the NT; it has a demonstrable, diagnostic profile from Matthew 1:1 to Revelation 22:21.

11) The archetypal form of Family 35 is demonstrable—it has been demonstrated (see Appendix B).

12) The Original Text is the ultimate archetype; any candidate must also be an archetype—a real, honest to goodness, objectively verifiable archetype; there is only one—Family 35.**1**

13) God's concern for the preservation of the Biblical Text is evident: I take it that passages such as 1 Chronicles 16:15, Psalm 119:89, Isaiah 40:8, Matthew 5:18, Luke 16:17 and 21:33, John 10:35 and 16:12-13, 1 Peter 1:23-25 and Luke 4:4 may reasonably be taken to imply a promise that the Scriptures (to the tittle) will be preserved for man's use (we are to live "by *every* word of God"), and to the end of the world ("for a thousand generations"), but no intimation is given as to just how God proposed to do it. We must deduce the answer from what He has indeed done—we discover that He **did**!

14) This concern is reflected in Family 35; it is characterized by incredibly careful transmission (in contrast to other lines). [I have a perfect copy of the Family 35 archetypal text for most NT books (22); I have copies made from a perfect exemplar (presumed) for another four (4); as I continue to collate MSS I hope to add the last one (Acts), but even for it the archetypal form is demonstrable.]

15) If God was preserving the original wording in some line of transmission other than Family 35, would that line be any less careful? I think not. So any line of transmission characterized by internal confusion is disqualified—this includes **all** the other lines of transmission that I have seen so far.

16) I affirm that God used Family 35 to preserve the precise original wording of the New Testament Text; it is reproduced in my edition of the Greek Text. (And God used mainly the Eastern Orthodox Churches to preserve the NT Text down through the centuries—they have always used a Text that was an adequate representation of the Original, for all practical purposes.)

---

**1** If you want to be a candidate for the best lawyer in your city, you must be a lawyer, or the best carpenter, or oncologist, or whatever. If there is only one candidate for mayor in your town, who gets elected?

I claim to have demonstrated the superiority of Family 35 based on size, independence, age, distribution, profile and care. I challenge any and all to do the same for any other line of transmission!

Honesty used to be part of the definition of a true scholar. Anyone who wishes to be one should absolutely stop representing his presuppositions as being part of the evidence. Since the original was never lost, there is no legitimate textual criticism of the NT, and therefore no science of such. Since NT textual criticism (as practiced by the academic community during the past 130 years) depends on a false presupposition, it cannot be a science. Those who reject the primary evidence can, and probably will, continue to propound a theory of textual criticism. I suppose they have a right to their theory, but I cannot wish them well.

# REFERENCES

Aland, Barbara, Mink, Gerd, and Wachtel, Klaus (eds.). *Novum Testamentum Graecum, Editio Critica Maior.* Stuttgart: Deutsche Bibelgesellschaft, 1997.

Aland, Kurt. "The Greek New Testament: its Present and Future Editions," *Journal of Biblical Literature,* LXXXVII (1968).

_____. "Neue Neutestamentliche Papyri III." *New Testament Studies,* XX (July, 1974).

_____. "The Present Position of New Testament Textual Criticism," *Studia Evangelica,* ed. F. L. Cross and others. Berlin: Akademie – Verlag, 1959. Pp. 717-31.

_____. "The Significance of the Papyri for Progress in New Testament Research," *The Bible in Modern Scholarship,* ed. J. P. Hyatt. New York: Abingdon Press, 1965. Pp. 325-46.

_____. *Synopsis Quattuor Evangeliorum.* Stuttgart: Wurttembergeshe Bibelanstalt, 1964.

_____. "The Text of the Church?", *Trinity Journal,* (1987) 8NS:131-144.

Aland, Kurt (ed.). Kurzgefasste Liste der Griechischen Handschriften des Neuen Testaments. Berlin: Walter de Gruyter, 1994.

Aland, Kurt (ed.). Text und Textwert der Griechischen Handschriften des Neuen Testaments. Berlin: Walter de Gruyter, 1993.

Aland, Kurt and Aland, Barbara. *The Text of the New Testament.* Grand Rapids: Eerdmans, 1987.

Aland, Kurt, Black, Matthew, Metzger, Bruce M., and Wikgren, Allen (eds.). *The Greek New Testament,* New York: American Bible Society, 1966.

Aland, Kurt, Black, Matthew, Martini, Carlo M., Metzger, Bruce M., and Wikgren, Allen (eds.). *The Greek New Testament,* 3rd ed. New York: United Bible Societies, 1975.

Anderson, H. and Barclay, W. (eds.). *The New Testament in Historical and Contemporary Perspective.* Oxford: Basil Blackwell, 1965.

Aune, D. E. (ed.). Studies in New Testament and Early Christian Literature. Leiden: E.J. Brill, 1972.

Barry, G. D. *The Inspiration and Authority of Holy Scripture.* New York: The Macmillan Company, 1919.

Bartlett, J. V. *The New Testament in the Apostolic Fathers.* Oxford: Clarendon Press, 1905.

Birdsall, J. N. *The Bodmer Papyrus of the Gospel of John.* London: Tyndale Press, 1960.

_____. "The Text of the Gospels in Photius," *Journal of Theological Studies,* VII (1956).

Birdsall, J. N. and Thomson, R. W. (eds.). *Biblical and Patristic Studies in Memory of Robert Pierce Casey.* New York: Herder, 1963.

Black, Matthew. *An Aramaic Approach to the Gospels and Acts.* Oxford: Oxford University Press, 1946.

Burgon, John William. *The Causes of the Corruption of the Traditional Text of the Holy Gospels.* Arranged, completed, and edited by Edward Miller. London: George Bell and Sons, 1896.

_____. *The Last Twelve Verses of the Gospel According to S. Mark.* Ann Arbor, Michigan: The Sovereign Grace Book Club, 1959.

_____. *The Revision Revised.* London: John Murray, 1883.

_____. *The Traditional Text of the Holy Gospels Vindicated and Established.* Arranged, completed, and edited by Edward Miller. London: George Bell and Sons, 1896.

Burkitt, Francis C. *Evangelion da-Mepharreshe.* 2 vols. Cambridge: Cambridge University Press, 1904.

Buttrick, George A. and others (eds.). *The Interpreter's Dictionary of the Bible.* 4 vols. New York: Abingdon Press, 1962.

Carson, D. A. *The King James Version Debate.* Grand Rapids: Baker Book House, 1979.

Clark, K. W. "The Effect of Recent Textual Criticism upon New Testament Studies," *The Background of the New Testament and its Eschatology,* ed. W. D. Davies and D. Daube. Cambridge: The Cambridge University Press, 1956. Pp. 27-51.

_____. "The Manuscripts of the Greek New Testament," *New Testament Manuscript Studies,* ed. M. M. Parvis and A. P. Wikgren. Chicago: The University of Chicago Press, 1950. Pp. 1-24.

_____. "The Theological Relevance of Textual Variation in Current Criticism of the Greek New Testament," *Journal of Biblical Literature,* LXXXV (1966).

_____. "Today's Problems with the Critical Text of the New Testament," *Transitions in Biblical Scholarship,* ed. J. C. R. Rylaarsdam. Chicago: The University of Chicago Press, 1968.

Colwell, Ernest Cadman. "Biblical Criticism: Lower and Higher," *Journal of Biblical Literature,* LXVII (1948), 1-12.

_____. "The Complex Character of the Late Byzantine Text of the Gospels," *Journal of Biblical Literature,* LIV (1935), 211-21.

_____. "External Evidence and New Testament Criticism," *Studies in the History and Text of the New Testament,* ed. B. L. Daniels and M. J. Suggs. Salt Lake City: University of Utah Press, 1967.

_____. "Genealogical Method: Its Achievements and its Limitations," *Journal of Biblical Literature,* LXVI (1947), 109-33.

_____. "The Greek New Testament with a Limited Critical Apparatus: its Nature and Uses," *Studies in New Testament and Early Christian Literature,* ed. D. E. Aune. Leiden: E. J. Brill, 1972.

_____. "Hort Redivivus: A Plea and a Program," *Studies in Methodology in Textual Criticism of the New Testament,* E. C. Colwell. Leiden: E. J. Brill, 1969.

_____. "The Origin of Texttypes of New Testament Manuscripts," *Early Christian Origins,* ed. Allen Wikgren. Chicago: Quadrangle Books, 1961. Pp. 128-38.

_____. "Scribal Habits in Early Papyri: A Study in the Corruption of the Text," *The Bible in Modern Scholarship,* ed. J. P. Hyatt. New York: Abingdon Press, 1965. Pp. 370-89.

_____. "The Significance of Grouping of New Testament Manuscripts," *New Testament Studies,* IV (1957-1958), 73-92.

_____. Studies in Methodology in Textual Criticism of the New Testament. Leiden: E. J. Brill, 1969.

_____. *What is the Best New Testament?* Chicago: The University of Chicago Press, 1952.

Colwell, Ernest Cadman and Riddle, Donald W. (eds.). Studies in the Lectionary Text of the Greek New Testament: Volume I, Prolegomena to the Study of the Lectionary Text of the Gospels. Chicago: The University of Chicago Press, 1933.

Colwell, E. C. and Tune, E. W. "The Quantitative Relationships between MS Text-Types," *Biblical and Patristic Studies in Memory of Robert Pierce Casey,* ed. J. N. Birdsall and R. W. Thomson. Freiberg: Herder, 1963.

Colwell, E. C. *et al.* "The International Greek New Testament Project: a Status Report," *Journal of Biblical Literature,* LXXXVII (1968).

Conybeare, F. C. *History of New Testament Criticism.* London: Watts & Co., 1910.

Cross, F. L. and others (eds.). *Studia Evangelica.* Berlin: Akademie—Verlag, 1959.

Dain, A. *Les Manuscrits.* Paris, 1949.

Daniels, B. L. and Suggs, M. J. (eds.). Studies in the History and Text of the New Testament in Honor of Kenneth Willis Clark, Ph.D. (Studies and Documents, 29). Salt Lake City: University of Utah Press, 1967.

Davies, W. D. and Daube, D. (eds.). *The Background of the New Testament and its Eschatology.* Cambridge: The Cambridge University Press, 1956.

Downey, Glanville. A History of Antioch in Syria, from Seleucus to the Arab Conquest. Princeton: University Press, 1961.

Ehrman, Bart D. "New Testament Textual Criticism: Search for Method." M.Div. thesis, Princeton Theological Seminary, 1981.

Elliott, J. K. The Greek Text of the Epistles to Timothy and Titus. (Studies and Documents, 36). Salt Lake City: University of Utah Press, 1968.

Epp, E. J. "The Claremont Profile Method for Grouping New Testament Minuscule Manuscripts," *Studies in the History and Text of the New Testament in Honor of Kenneth Willis Clark, Ph. D. (Studies and Documents,* 29), ed. B. L. Daniels and M. J. Suggs. Salt Lake City: University of Utah Press, 1967.

_____. "The Twentieth Century Interlude in New Testament Textual Criticism," *Journal of Biblical Literature,* XCIII (1974).

Farmer, W. R. *The Last Twelve Verses of Mark.* Cambridge: Cambridge University Press, 1974.

Fee, G. D. "A Critique of W. N. Pickering's *The Identity of the New Testament Text:* A Review Article," *The Westminster Theological Journal,* XLI (Spring, 1979).

_____. "Modern Text Criticism and the Synoptic Problem," *J. J. Griesbach: Synoptic and Text-Critical Studies 1776-1976,* ed. B. Orchard and T. R. W. Longstaff. Cambridge: University Press, 1978.

_____. Papyrus Bodmer II (P$^{66}$): Its Textual Relationships and Scribal Characteristics. Salt Lake City: University of Utah Press, 1968.

_____. "Rigorous or Reasoned Eclecticism—Which?" *Studies in New Testament Language and Text,* ed. J. K. Elliott. Leiden: E. J. Brill, 1976.

Geerlings, J. *Family E and its Allies in Mark.* Salt Lake City: University of Utah Press, 1967.

Geerlings, Jacob and New, Silva. "Chrysostom's Text of the Gospel of Mark," *Harvard Theological Review, XXIV (1931), 122-42.*

Goulburn, Edward M. *Life of Dean Burgon.* 2 vols. London: John Murray, 1892.

Grant, F. C. "The Citation of Greek Manuscript Evidence in an Apparatus Criticus," *New Testament Manuscript Studies,* ed. M. M. Parvis and A. P. Wikgren. Chicago: The University of Chicago Press, 1950. Pp. 81-94.

Grant, Robert M. "The Bible of Theophilus of Antioch," *Journal of Biblical Literature*, LXVI (1947), 173-96.

_____. A Historical Introduction to the New Testament. New York: Harper and Row, 1963.

Greenlee, J. H. *The Gospel Text of Cyril of Jerusalem.* Copenhagen: Ejnar Munksgaard, 1955.

_____. *Introduction to New Testament Textual Criticism.* Grand Rapids: Wm. B. Eerdmans Publishing Co., 1964.

_____. "Some Examples of Scholarly 'Agreement in Error'," *Journal of Biblical Literature,* LXXVII (1958), 363-64.

Harris, J. Rendel. *A Study of the Codex Bezae.* London: S. J. Clay and Sons, 1891.

Harrison, Everett F. *Introduction to the New Testament.* Grand Rapids: Wm. B. Eerdmans Publishing Co., 1964.

Hemphill, S. *A History of the Revised Version.* London: Elliot Stock, 1906.

Hills, E. F. "Harmonizations in the Caesarean Text of Mark," *Journal of Biblical Literature,* LXVI (1947), 135-52.

_____. *The King James Version Defended!* Des Moines, Iowa: The Christian Reseasrch Press, 1956.

Hodges, Zane Clark. "A Defense of the Majority Text." Unpublished course notes, Dallas Theological Seminary, 1975.

_____. "The Ecclesiastical Text of Revelation—Does it Exist?" *Bibliotheca Sacra,* CXVIII (1961), 113-22.

_____. "The Greek Text of the King James Version," *Bibliotheca Sacra,* CXXV (October-December, 1968).

Hodges, Zane C. and Farstad, Arthur F. (eds.). *The Greek New Testament according to the Majority Text.* Nashville: Thomas Nelson, 1982.

Horne, T. H. An Introduction to the Critical Study and Knowledge of the Holy Scriptures, 4th American ed. 4 vols. Philadelphia: E. Little, 1831.

Hort, Arthur Fenton. *Life and Letters of Fenton John Anthony Hort.* 2 vols. London: Macmillan and Co., Ltd., 1896.

Hoskier, Herman C. *Codex B and its Allies.* 2 vols. London: Bernard Quaritch, Ltd., 1914.

_____. *Concerning the Text of the Apocalypse.* 2 vols. London: Bernard Quaritch, Ltd., 1929.

_____. A Full Account and Collation of the Greek Cursive Codex Evangelium 604. London: David Nutt, 1890.

_____. "A Study of the Chester-Beatty Codex of the Pauline Epistles," *The Journal of Theological Studies,* XXXVIII (1937), 149-63.

Hutton, Edward Ardson. *An Atlas of Textual Criticism.* London: The Cambridge University Press, 1911.

Hyatt, J. Philip (ed.). *The Bible in Modern Scholarship.* New York: Abingdon Press, 1965.

International Greek New Testament Project. *The New Testament in Greek: The Gospel According to St. Luke, Vol. 1.* Oxford: Clarendon Press, 1984.

Kenyon, Frederick G. *Handbook to the Textual Criticism of the New Testament,* 2nd ed. Grand Rapids: Wm. B. Eerdmans Publishing Co., 1951.

_____. Recent Developments in the Textual Criticism of the Greek Bible. London: Oxford University Press, 1933.

Kilpatrick, G. D. "Atticism and the Text of the Greek New Testament," *Neutestamentliche Aufsatze.* Regensburg: Verlag Friedrich Pustet, 1963.

_____. "The Greek New Testament Text of Today and the *Textus Receptus,*" *The New Testament in Historical and Contemporary Perspective,* ed. H. Anderson and W. Barclay. Oxford: Basil Blackwell, 1965.

_____. "The Transmission of the New Testament and its Reliability," *The Bible Translator,* IX (1958), 127-36.

Klijn, A. F. J. A Survey of the Researches into the Western Text of the Gospels and Acts; part two 1949-1969. Leiden: E. J. Brill, 1969.

Lake, Kirsopp. *The Text of the New Testament,* 6th ed. Revised by Silva New. London: Rivingtons, 1959.

Lake, Kirsopp, Blake, R. P., and New, Silva. "The Caesarean Text of the Gospel of Mark," *Harvard Theological Review,* XXI (1928), 207-404.

Lake, Kirsopp and Lake, Silva. *Family 13 (The Ferrar Group) (Studies and Documents 11).* Salt Lake City: University of Utah press, 1965.

Letis, Theodore P. "John Owens Versus Brian Walton," *The Majority Text: Essays and Reviews in the Continuing Debate.* Fort Wayne: The Institute for Reformation Biblical Studies, 1987.

Metzger, Bruce Manning. *Chapters in the History of New Testament Textual Criticism.* Vol. IV of *New Testament Tools and Studies,* ed. B. M. Metzger. Grand Rapids: Wm. B. Eerdmans Publishing Co., 1963.

_____. *The Early Versions of the New Testament.* Oxford: Clarendon Press, 1977.

_____. "The Evidence of the Versions for the Text of the N.T.," *New Testament Manuscript Studies,* ed. M. M. Parvis and A. P. Wikgren. Chicago: The University of Chicago Press, 1950. Pp. 25-68.

_____. "Explicit References in the Works of Origen to Variant Readings in N. T. MSS.," *Biblical and Patristic Studies in Memory of Robert Pierce Casey,* ed. J. N. Birdsall and R. W. Thomson. New York: Herder, 1963. Pp. 78-95.

_____. *Historical and Literary Studies.* Vol. VIII of *New Testament Tools and Studies,* ed. B. M. Metzger. Grand Rapids: Wm. B. Eerdmans, 1968.

_____. "Patristic Evidence and the Textual Criticism of the New Testament," *New Testament Studies,* XVIII (1972).

_____. "St. Jerome's Explicit References to Variant Readings in Manuscripts of the New Testament," *Text and Interpretation: Studies in the New Testament Presented to Matthew Black,* ed. Best and McL. Wilson. Cambridge: University Press, 1979.

_____. *The Text of the New Testament.* London: Oxford University Press, 1964.

_____. A Textual Commentary on the Greek New Testament. London: United Bible Societies, 1971.

Miller, Edward. *A Guide to the Textual Criticism of the New Testament.* London: George Bell and Sons, 1886.

Nestle, Erwin and Aland, Kurt. *Novum Testamentum Graece.* 24th ed. Stuttgart: Privilegierte Wurttembergische Biblelanstalt, 1960.

*New International Version of the New Testament.* Grand Rapids: Zondervan Bible Publishers, 1973.

Oliver, H. H. "Present Trends in the Textual Criticism of the New Testament," *The Journal of Bible and Religion,* XXX (1962), 308-20.

Oxford Society of Historical Research, *The New Testament in the Apostolic Fathers.* Oxford: Clarendon Press, 1905.

Parvis, Merrill M. "The Nature and Task of New Testament Textual Criticism," *The Journal of Religion,* XXXII (1952), 165-74.

_____. "The Need for a New *Apparatus Criticus* to the Greek New Testament," *Journal of Biblical Literature,* LXV (1946), 353-69.

_____. "Text, NT.," *The Interpreter's Dictionary of the Bible.* 4 vols. New York: Abingdon Press, 1962. Pp. 594-614.

Parvis, Merrill M. and Wikgren, A. P. (eds.). *New Testament Manuscript Studies.* Chicago: The University of Chicago press, 1950.

Pickering, W. N. *A Framework for Discourse Analysis.* Dallas: Summer Institute of Linguistics and University of Texas at Arlington, 1980.

_____. "'Queen Anne...and all that: a Response," *Journal of the Evangelical Theological Society,* XXI (June, 1978), 165-67.

*Revised Standard Version.* London: Thomas Nelson and Sons Ltd., 1952.

Richardson, C. C. (ed.). *Early Christian Fathers.* Philadelphia: The Westminster Press, 1953.

Riddle, Donald W. "Fifty Years of New Testament Scholarship," *The Journal of Bible and Religion,* X (1942), 136-40, 183.

Rist, Martin. "Pseudepigraphy and the Early Christians," *Studies in New Testament and Early Christian Literature,* ed. D. E. Aune. Leiden: E. J. Brill, 1972.

Roberts, A. and Donaldson, J. (eds.). *The Ante-Nicene Fathers.* Grand Rapids: Wm. B. Eerdmans Publishing Co., 1956.

Roberts, Colin H. *Manuscript, Society and Belief in Early Christian Egypt.* London: Oxford University Press, 1979.

Robinson, Maurice A. "Preliminary Observations regarding the *Pericope Adulterae* based upon Fresh Collations of nearly all Continuous-Text Manuscripts and over One Hundred Lectionaries." Presented at Evangelical Theological Society, Nov., 1998.

Robinson, Maurice A. "Two Passages in Mark: A Critical Test for the Byzantine Priority Hypothesis." Presented at Evangelical Theological Society, Nov., 1994.

Robinson, Maurice A. and Pierpont, William G. (eds.). *The New Testament in the Original Greek according to the Byzantine/Majority Textform.* Roswell, GA: Original Word Publishers, 1991.

Rylaarsdam, J. C. R. (ed.). *Transitions in Biblical Scholarship.* Chicago: The University of Chicago Press, 1968.

Salmon, George. Some Thoughts on the Textual Criticism of the New Testament. London: n.p. 1897.

Schopp, Ludwig (ed.). *The Apostolic Fathers.* New York: Cima Publishing Co., Inc., 1947.

Scrivener, F. H. A. *A Plain Introduction to the Criticism of the New Testament,* 4th ed. Edited by E. Miller. 2 vols. London: George Bell and Sons, 1894.

_____. (ed). The New Testament in the Original Greek, together with the Variations Adopted in the Revised Version. Cambridge: Cambridge University Press, 1880.

Soden, Hermann F. von. *Die Schriften des Neuen Testaments.* 2 vols. Göttingen: Vandenhoeck und Ruprecht, 1911.

Streeter, Burnett H. *The Four Gospels: A Study of Origins.* London: Macmillan and Co., 1930.

Sturz, H. A. The Byzantine Text-Type and New Testament Textual Criticism. Nashville: Thomas Nelson, 1984.

Suggs, M. J. "The Use of Patristic Evidence in the Search for a Primitive New Testament Text," *New Testament Studies,* IV (1957-1958), 139-47.

Swanson, R. J. The Horizontal Line Synopsis of the Gospels, Greek Edition, volume I. The Gospel of Matthew. Dillsboro, NC: Western North Carolina Press, 1982.

Tasker, R. V. G. (ed.). *The Greek New Testament.* Oxford: Oxford University Press, 1964.

_____. "Introduction to the Manuscripts of the New Testament," *Harvard Theological Review,* XLI (1948), 71-81.

Taylor, R. A. "Queen Anne Resurrected? A Review Article," *Journal of the Evangelical Theological Society,* XX (December, 1977), 377-81.

Taylor, Vincent. *The Text of the New Testament.* New York: St. Martin's Press Inc., 1961.

Tenney, M. C. *New Testament Survey.* Grand Rapids: Eerdmans, 1961.

Thiessen, Henry C. *Introduction to the New Testament.* Grand Rapids, Michigan: Wm. B. Eerdmans Publishing Co., 1955.

Tischendorf, Constantinus. *Novum Testamentum Graece*, 8th ed. 2 vols. Lipsiae: Giesecke and Devrient, 1869-72.

Turner, C. H. "Historical Introduction to the Textual Criticism of the New Testament," *Journal of Theological Studies,* (Jan. 1910).

Vaganay, Leo. *An Introduction to the Textual Criticism of the New Testament.* Translated by B. V. Miller. London: Sands and Co., Ltd., 1937.

Van Bruggen, Jakob. *The Ancient Text of the New Testament.* Winnipeg: Premier, 1976.

_____. *The Future of the Bible.* Nashville: Thomas Nelson, 1978.

Vööbus, Arthur. *Early Versions of the New Testament.* Stockholm: Estonian Theological Society in Exile, 1954.

Walters, P. *The Text of the Septuagint. Its Corruptions and their Emendation*, ed. D. W. Gooding. Cambridge: University Press, 1973.

Wasserman, Tommy. *The Epistle of Jude: Its Text and Transmission.* Stockholm: Almqvist & Wiksell International, 2006.

Westcott, Brooke Foss. *The Bible in the Church.* London: MacMillan, 1890.

Westcott, Brooke Foss and Hort, Fenton John Anthony. *The New Testament in the Original Greek.* 2 vols. London: Macmillan and Co. Ltd., 1881.

Wikgren, Allen. "Chicago Studies in the Greek Lectionary of the New Testament," *Biblical and Patristic Studies in Memory of Robert Pierce Casey*, ed. J. N. Birdsall and R. W. Thomson. New York: Herder, 1963. Pp. 96-121.

_____. (ed). *Early Christian Origins.* Chicago: Quadrangle Books, 1961.

Williams, Charles S. C. Alterations to the Text of the Synoptic Gospels and Acts. Oxford: Basil Blackwell, 1951.

Wisse, Frederik. The Profile Method for Classifying and Evaluating Manuscript Evidence. Grand Rapids: Eerdmans, 1982.

Wisselink, W. F. *Assimilation as a Criterion for the Establishment of the Text*. 4 vols. Kampen: Uitgeversmaatschappij J. H. Kok, 1989.

Zuntz, Gunther. "The Byzantine Text in New Testament Criticism," *Journal of Theological Studies,* XLIII (1942), 25-30.

_____. *The Text of the Epistles.* London: Oxford University Press, 1953.

www.ingramcontent.com/pod-product-compliance
Lightning Source LLC
Chambersburg PA
CBHW060835110426
R18122100001BA/R181221PG42736CBX00039BA/51